Geographies of Development

An Introduction to Development Studies

Fourth Edition

Robert Potter, Tony Binns, Jennifer A. Elliott, Etienne Nel and David W. Smith

Routledge
Taylor & Francis Group

LONDON AND NEW YORK

Fourth edition published 2018
by Routledge
2 Park Square, Milton Park, Abingdon, Oxon, OX14 4RN

and by Routledge
711 Third Avenue, New York, NY 10017

Routledge is an imprint of the Taylor & Francis Group, an informa business

© 2018 Robert Potter, Tony Binns, Jennifer A. Elliott, Etienne Nel and
David W. Smith

First edition published by Pearson Education Limited 1999
Third edition published by Routledge 2008

British Library Cataloguing-in-Publication Data
A catalogue record for this book is available from the British Library

Library of Congress Cataloging-in-Publication Data
Names: Potter, Robert B., author.
Title: Geographies of development : an introduction to development
    studies / Robert Potter, [and four others].
Description: Fourth edition. | Abingdon, Oxon ; New York, NY :
    Routledge, 2018. | Includes bibliographical references and index.
Identifiers: LCCN 2017023637| ISBN 9781138794290
    (hardback : alk. paper) | ISBN 9781138794306 (pbk. : alk. paper) |
    ISBN 9781315759319 (ebook)
Subjects: LCSH: Economic development. | Economic geography. | Human
    geography.
Classification: LCC HD82 .G387 2018 | DDC 338.9—dc23
LC record available at https://lccn.loc.gov/2017023637

ISBN: 978-1-138-79429-0 (hbk)
ISBN: 978-1-138-79430-6 (pbk)
ISBN: 978-1-315-75931-9 (ebk)

Typeset in Minion
by Swales & Willis Ltd, Exeter, Devon, UK

Printed and bound in Great Britain
by Bell and Bain Ltd, Glasgow

Visit the eResources: https://www.routledge.com/9781138794306

This book is dedicated to

Rob Potter

An inspirational colleague and a great friend

(1950–2014)

Contents

Plates

Figures

Tables

Preface to the fourth edition

From its first publication in 1999, the intention of *Geographies of Development* was to provide an up-to-date and innovative approach to teaching and learning in the broad interdisciplinary fields of development geography and development studies. From the outset, we were keen to get away from the sector-by-sector approach that had been so typical of earlier texts, together often with a distinctly regional orientation. As with the earlier editions, this fourth edition uses a threefold structure, broadly dealing respectively with: (i) conceptualising development, (ii) development in practice and (iii) spaces of development.

We have, of course, been delighted that the three previous editions have all been welcomed in both critical and commercial terms, and that the general tenor of the comments we have received has been very positive, whether in the form of written reviews or general comments and reactions received from those who are using the book. It seems therefore that, as intended, *Geographies of Development* has generally been well received as an innovative and comprehensive text for undergraduates, as well as for some taught postgraduates, who are studying development in a variety of fields, not just geography.

As well as those reviews appearing in journals, running up to the fourth edition, the publishers commissioned a number of detailed reviews of the third edition. We should like to thank those involved in this process for their constructive and generally highly positive responses, as these greatly helped us in shaping this fourth edition. In embarking on this fourth edition of *Geographies of Development*, once again we did not feel that the structure of the book needed to be changed in any significant fashion. Inevitably, it was clear that the text should be improved by means of general and specific updates and revisions, and this is what we have done. In fact, quite substantial revisions have been made to the material in light of the significantly changed global context since the previous edition. And this time round, the publishers were enthusiastic about upgrading the overall presentation of the book.

In the third edition the publishers were keen that as authors we should make every effort to provide more entry points into the text. We responded to this by increasing the number of sections and subsections throughout the book, and we have maintained this strategy in the fourth edition.

In order to further aid the reader in accessing the text, short statements concerning the aims and content are provided right at the start of each chapter and these are then fleshed out by means of more detailed bullet-point summaries. In addition, a listing of key points is provided at the end of each chapter.

Further, in this fourth edition, a new 'hierarchy' of boxed materials has been introduced to support the text. Thus, the substantive boxed *Case studies* presented in the earlier editions are still to be found, and we have included *Key idea* and *Key thinker* boxes where these are likely to inform and further assist the reader. This Edition also includes *Critical reflections*, which seek to engage the reader with key issues and debating points. It is our intention that groups in a classroom or tutorial setting can use these just as easily as the individual reader.

The biggest change in putting together this fourth edition has been in the composition of the writing team. Since the first edition was launched in 1999, we have unfortunately lost two good friends and co-authors. David Smith sadly died in December 1999, and then in April 2014 we lost Rob Potter. David made an important intellectual input to the first edition, whilst Rob was the 'driving force' behind the whole project through the first, second and third editions. In light of their valuable contributions, we had no hesitation in retaining David's and Rob's names on the cover of the fourth edition. The successful completion of the fourth edition is due in no small measure to Etienne Nel, who kindly agreed to join Jennifer and Tony at a crucial stage in the project.

As with the earlier editions, we look forward to receiving the reactions of students, lecturers and general readers who use this fourth edition, in the form of reviews, the passing of comments as mentioned previously and, of course, as is more likely these days, via e-mail messages sent to us in our respective institutions. All of these will help us to shape the next edition of *Geographies of Development*.

Finally we are extremely grateful to Andrew Mould at Routledge, who from the outset showed genuine and sustained enthusiasm for the Fourth Edition to be produced in a timely fashion. No publisher could have shown more interest in the project or provided more support: thank you Andrew from us all. A little further into the process, Egle Zigaite helped substantially in all manner of ways and we extend our warm thanks to her for this support. Chris Garden deserves special mention for the drawing or redrawing the majority of the Figures. His cartographic skill is clearly reflected in the excellent standard of the diagrams.

Tony Binns, Jenny Elliott and Etienne Nel
August 2016

Introduction

The fourth edition of *Geographies of Development* aims to build on the contribution made by the previous three editions in providing a comprehensive introductory textbook for students, primarily those taking courses in the field of development geography and the interdisciplinary area of development studies. The feedback on all previous editions has shown that, although the text is mainly directed at the second-year undergraduate market, given the global importance of the subject matter, the book is just as appropriate for first-year students taking broader courses, along with those reading for more specialist options in the final year of their degree programmes. Indeed, we are directly aware that the book is also recommended as a key text on a number of taught Masters programmes.

At the outset, the distinctive aim of *Geographies of Development* was to move away from what had at that time become the traditional structure of geography and development textbooks, which all too frequently started with definitions of the 'Third World' and colonialism, and then proceeded to consider, step by step, topics such as population and demography, agriculture and rural landscapes, mining, manufacturing, transport, urbanisation, development planning and so on. Having provided detailed accounts on such topics, many texts unfortunately terminated at that juncture, but those that endeavoured to provide a broader picture generally went on to present a selection of country- or region-based case studies.

In *Geographies of Development*, we have endeavoured to break this mould of development-oriented textbooks in a manner that reflects the rapidly changing concerns about development itself. In this sense, its *raison d'être* is to provide a text for learning and teaching about development in the early twenty-first century. As such, the structure of this fourth edition remains broadly the same as the first three editions, with a division into three relatively equal parts, dealing respectively with conceptualising development (Part I), development in practice (Part II) and the spaces of development (Part III). This structure is shown diagrammatically in the figure.

Part I (Chapters 1, 2, 3 and 4) provides a detailed overview of the concepts, ideas and ideologies that have underpinned writings about the nature of development, as well as pragmatic attempts to promote development in the global arena. It also addresses how 'development' has been conceptualised and measured, and gives detailed consideration to important topics such as the histories, meanings and strategies of development, the emergence of the 'Third World' (the term commonly used before 'Global South' became the more accepted descriptor of the developing world), the nature of imperialism and colonialism and its various stages of mercantile, industrial and late colonialism, together with key concepts such as the new international division of labour and the new international

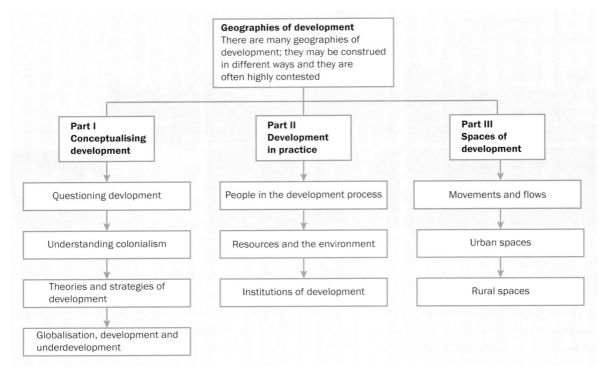

Figure 0.1 Book structure

economic order. Part I also provides thorough reviews of relevant and related topics such as modernity, enlighten-ment thinking, the relevance of postmodernity, anti-developmentalism, global shifts and time–space convergence. Updated sections emphasise important topics such as anti-development, global poverty and inequalities, the neo-liberalisation of development, gender-related issues, the digital divide, global shifts, the legacies of colonialism, post-colonialism, decolonisation, participatory and 'bottom-up' development strategies, and progress from the Millennium Development Goals (MDGs) to the Sustainable Development Goals (SDGs).

As with the other parts of the book, these early chapters exemplify the title and the overarching theme of the volume. Part I makes it clear that ideas concerning development have been many and varied, and have been highly contested through time. Thus, definitions of, and approaches to, development have varied from place to place, from time to time, from country to country, region to region, and group to group within the general populace. It is essen-tially this plural nature of development that *Geographies of Development* seeks both to examine and exemplify. Furthermore, this part of the book demonstrates that current global processes are not leading to the homogenisa-tion of the world's regions. Far from it, the evidence shows all too clearly that contemporary global processes are leading to increasing differences between places and regions and rising social inequality within and between coun-tries, and thus to the generation of progressively more unequal patterns of development and change, and associated social, economic and environmental conflict. This is evidenced in a range of dimensions including the continuing 'digital divide', the selective benefits of the MDGs, the differential effects of the Global Financial Crisis, the varying effects of climate change impacts, and the playing out of political tensions, particularly in the Middle East. Hence, the emphasis is on multiple geographies of development.

Part II (Chapters 5, 6 and 7) covers what may be regarded as the basic components of the development equation – people, environments, resources, institutions and communities – together with the increasingly complex and multifaceted interconnections that exist between them. New sections have been included on the effects of the HIV/

AIDS pandemic, gender, the position of children in conflict situations and the effects of ageing populations on development processes. In considering resources and environment, this edition gives further attention to issues of resource scarcity and global environmental changes, including climate change, but also to concerns that Planetary Boundaries may have been crossed and the 'services' provided by ecosystems for human well-being irreversibly degraded. Greater attention is given to the equity and justice challenges of moving to lower carbon and more sustainable development paths in future. The inclusion of a chapter specifically dealing with institutions in the development process serves to exemplify the utility of the overall approach adopted in *Geographies of Development*. The organisations considered extend from the agents of global governance – the United Nations, World Bank, International Monetary Fund and World Trade Organisation – via the country level, involving the role of the state, but also transnational business, through to civil society, community participation and the empowerment of the individual, embracing non-governmental and community-based organisations. This account serves to stress the plurality of decision makers and the complexity of alliances between and amongst them that are shaping contemporary geographies of development, just as the detailed expositions on population, resources, environment and development exemplify the diversity of opinion that exists on how wealth and well-being should be created and distributed, including in ways that respect the environmental limits of the Earth and the future rights of people and non-human species.

Part III (Chapters 8, 9 and 10) focuses on what development means in relation to particular places and people. This is achieved by consideration of the flows and movements that occur between geographically separate locales, and in terms of the distinctive issues raised by development and change in both urban and rural spaces. Once again, notwithstanding the difference in focus, the theme is the diversity and complexities of the movements and flows of people, finance and technologies, along with the diverse realities of transport and communications and spatially diverse outcomes. Pressing topics of current significance, such as patterns of international development assistance, energy security, pro-poor tourism, world trade and responses to the Global Financial Crisis, the recent internationalisation of land markets, the persistent challenges of poverty and women's empowerment, receive detailed attention in this part of *Geographies of Development*. The nature and scale of urbanisation in countries of the Global South, evolving urban systems and the incidence of unequal development, the need for urban and regional planning, the salience of basic needs and human rights, and the quest for sustainable cities in relation to the 'brown agenda', are prominent topics reviewed in relation to urban spaces and development imperatives. Consideration of the importance of urban–rural relations is an additional feature. Rural spaces are analysed with particular reference to diverse rural livelihood systems (particularly the importance of flexibility in coping with and adapting to social, economic and environmental change) and the examination of the multiple meanings and outcomes of approaches to rural development, such as land reform, the 'green' and 'gene' revolutions in agriculture, and the challenges of managing forests to deliver both global environmental benefits and local livelihood objectives. Forming the last major part of the book, these chapters draw heavily on earlier accounts presented in Parts I and II, and they make frequent reference to the realities of globalisation, urban bias, rights to resources, industrialisation and sustainable development, as well as other topics.

The thematic structure and orientation of *Geographies of Development* means that important contemporary development issues are considered such as civil society, NGOs, anti-development, neo-liberalism, governance, resilience, globalisation, gender mainstreaming, structural adjustment, poverty reduction programmes, climate change, sustainable development, human rights, empowerment and participatory democracy. These issues are not dealt with in standalone chapters, but rather are treated as appropriate at various points in the text, and sometimes from a variety of different perspectives. This approach reflects the complexity of these issues in the context of multiple geographies of development. A case in point is the relationship between tourism and development, which brings both benefits and costs to host countries. This is first identified in Part I in considering processes of globalisation. International tourism then reappears when Chapter 8 in Part III considers global movements and flows, and in Chapter 10 as a factor in the widespread purchases of land in the Global South, so-called 'land grabbing'.

Geographies of Development focuses on the processes that are leading to change, whether for better or worse. In this sense, the book follows Brookfield's (1975) simple and straightforward definition of development as change, whether positive or negative. Thus, although the primary remit of the book is the Global South, the focus of the book is very much on development as change, regardless of where or how it is occurring. As in previous editions, every effort has been made in the fourth edition of *Geographies of Development* to elucidate clear and cogent examples of the issues under discussion, in the form of diagrams, maps, tables, photographs, boxed materials and critical reflections. Many new illustrations are included in this edition, and updated boxed case studies and examples are presented throughout the chapters. These seek either to extend definitions of basic concepts, or to provide detailed illustrations of the generic topics under consideration, or to promote critical reflection and discussion. In Part I of *Geographies of Development*, the nature and definition of terms such as 'Third World', 'developing countries', 'less-developed countries' and the 'Global South' are the subject of detailed discussion. In this fourth edition, whilst we recognise that none of these terms are perfect, we have decided to use the 'Global South' throughout the book. Some might suggest that in the contemporary context the term 'poor countries' is a more indicative and more useful one, reflecting the need to implement progressive and effective poverty reduction strategies.

As authors we have embarked on this fourth edition with the firm belief that teaching, learning and researching about places and communities other than the ones in which we live, and of which we have direct experience, are demanding, but vitally important tasks (Unwin and Potter, 1992). The amount of media attention given to development issues in poor countries seems to have declined steadily in recent years. John Vidal (2002) cited the results of a survey carried out by the Third World and Environment Broadcasting Trust (3WE), funded by Oxfam, Christian Aid, Comic Relief and other charities. The survey provided a detailed analysis of programming on British television during 2001, revealing that only four programmes dealing with the politics of developing countries were shown during that year. Further, in 2001 three of the five major channels broadcast no programmes at all in this category. Not only was it found that the serious international documentary is virtually dead, but when the developing world was depicted on television it was usually in the context of travel programmes, or in providing 'exotic' backgrounds for holiday 'challenges', reality television and 'docusoaps' featuring celebrities (Vidal, 2002).

We believe that the post-war development of geography as a discipline has, for most of its history pivoted too strongly around a UK/Europe/North America 'core' focus, leading to a relative neglect of the 'study of distant places', and also the existence of little empathy among the broad academic community for the relatively few colleagues who have directed their research activities towards an investigation of patterns and processes in the Global South. Such issues have been the subject of a lively debate in the pages of academic geography journals such as *Area* (R.B. Potter, 2001a, 2002a; A. Smith, 2002). These notions are now being challenged by the rise of new powers in the Global South, globalisation of the economy and the nature and effects of global crises.

We would advocate a reshaped vision of geography, in which both theories and empirical studies travel in all directions, recognising the porosity of boundaries in this era of increasing transnationality and globalisation. Furthermore, it seems important that geography and geographers should show greater responsibility to distant 'others' at a time when increasing interdependence is occurring alongside progressively greater inequality between the world's 'haves' and the 'have-nots' (D.W. Smith, 1994). It is the ultimate aim of *Geographies of Development* to assist students and teachers alike in structuring their observations and discussions of the multiple meanings of development in this increasingly complex and interdependent contemporary world.

Further reading

Vidal, J. (2002) Britons grow dull on trivia as TV ignores developing world. *Guardian Weekly*, 18 July. Accessed 28 July 2016. https://www.theguardian.com/GWeekly/Letter_From/0,,757276,00.html.

PART I

Conceptualising development: changing meanings of development

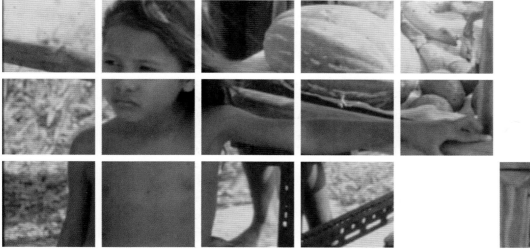

Chapter 1
Questioning development

Having outlined the overall aims and the structure of *Geographies of Development* in the Introduction, the present chapter provides a background context for understanding the evolving nature, changing conceptualisation and meaning of development and the degree to which contextual change has shaped its focus. This account provides an overarching context for the chapters that make up the rest of this book on development studies. This initial chapter is about the ways in which actors in the development process think about development: how they seek to define it, determine its components and conceptualise its purpose. It is also about understanding fundamental critiques of development, or so-called 'post-development' and 'anti-development'. Factors influencing current conceptualisations of development are explored, as is the globalisation of the development agenda through the Millennium Development Goals and, more recently, the Sustainable Development Goals. In the second half of the chapter, the spatial expression of development in the form of the Third World, Developing World, Global South and Poor Countries is considered in the light of current patterns and processes of development. More specifically the chapter:

➤ Overviews how development has been, and can be defined and conceptualised for academic and policy-related purposes;

➤ Explores how development has been measured, from quantitative counts of relative wealth per person such as Gross Domestic Product/Gross National Product/Gross National Income (GDP/GNP), to the Human Development Index (HDI) and the qualitative conception of development as 'freedom' and human rights;

➤ Overviews how development has been defined over time and how its application has evolved as a result of theoretical advances and applied considerations;

➤ Seeks to make readers aware of recent critiques of development, such as those presented by anti-development and post-development;

➤ Stresses that while general indicators show that the developing world has witnessed substantial socio-economic improvements as a whole since the 1970s, during that same period the world has become progressively more unequal;

➤ Introduces the Millennium Development Goals (MDG) as an agreed set of global

(continued)

(continued)

development targets adopted in 2000, and reviews the degree to which they had obtained their objectives by 2015;

➤ Overviews the focus of the Sustainable Development Goals introduced in 2015;

➤ Reviews and assesses the genesis and nature of spatial categorisations of development such as the 'Third World', 'Developing Countries', the 'Global South' and 'Poor Countries';

➤ Finishes by linking geography and development through a concern with what we may refer to as 'distant others' – people who live far away from us.

Introduction: from 'underdevelopment' and 'development' to 'post-development'

The application and pursuit of the concept of 'development' has been one of the defining features of the modern world. While the concept of development is used in various fields to detail processes of change – such as in the disciplines of psychology and education – in geography, economics and the work of international organisations it relates to efforts to bring about changes which impact on the well-being of countries and their inhabitants. The type of changes required, their focus and the strategies needed to achieve them are the subject of debate and underlie the evolving and often contested nature of development which we overview in this chapter.

This chapter first looks at the ways in which the term 'development' has been defined and characterised. This proceeds from the simple consideration of the general use of the word 'development' in everyday life. Following on from this, the major focus of the chapter is on a detailed overview of the multifarious approaches that have been adopted, over time, to implement changing conceptualisations of what development is. This section considers the changing interpretations of how development has been understood, measured and applied since the Second World War. The role played by broader political and economic processes also helps to shape the discussion.

A closely related argument is that such development initiatives have not worked effectively in the past, and indeed (by definition) the view that the types of development attempted could never ultimately be successful, is considered. This line of argument is referred to as 'anti-development', 'post-development', or 'beyond development', and is associated with what has been referred to as the 'impasse in development studies' (Schuurman, 2008; Power, 2003). In addition, we need to acknowledge that 'development' is not an apolitical or neutral process. It has been influenced by key global concerns and economic shifts since the Second World War, including, amongst others, the Cold War, the rise of neo-liberalism as the dominant economic discourse in the world, the 2008 Global Financial Crisis and, more recently, incipient signs of post-neo-liberalism.

As part of this discussion, efforts to improve conditions in developing countries are considered, specifically in respect of what were known as the International Development Targets or, more commonly now, the Sustainable Development Goals (which superseded the Millennium Development Goals in 2016).

The current state of the gap existing between the poorer and richer nations of the world is also examined in this chapter, with emphasis being placed on whether conditions are improving or worsening, that is 'converging' (getting more similar) or 'diverging' (getting more varied), at the international scale.

In the latter part of the chapter, spatial aspects of development and development initiatives are considered in detail. Such an approach involves interrogating the utility of terms such as the 'Third World', 'Developing World', 'Global South', 'Poor Countries' and the like. Globally speaking, to which spaces do these sorts of terms apply? Are they helpful labels? Which terms have the widest currency at the present time?

The chapter finishes with a brief discussion of the changing relationships between geography and development. It is the express aim of this chapter to set out a number of major themes that will have pertinence at many points in the rest of the book.

The meanings of the word 'development'

The *Concise Oxford Dictionary of Current English* defines the word 'development' as '[g]radual unfolding,

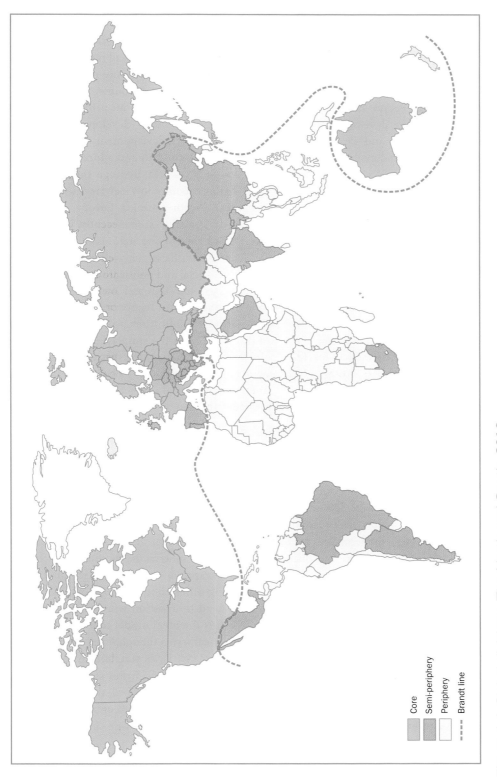

Figure 1.1 Global divisions: The North and South, 2010

Source: Adapted from Willy Brandt, *North-South: A Program for Survival*, figure 'Models on the 1980s: North and South; core, periphery and semi-periphery', © 1980 The Independent Bureau on International Development Issues, by permission of the MIT Press and also from *North-South: A Programme for Survival*, Pan, (Brandt, W. 1980). Copyright © W. Brandt, 1980, by permission of Pan Macmillan.

Core
Semi-periphery
Periphery
Brandt line

fuller working out; growth; evolution . . . ; well-grown state, stage of advancement; product; more elaborate form . . . ; Development area, one suffering from or liable to severe unemployment'.

As this dictionary definition suggests all too clearly, 'development' is a word that is almost ubiquitous within the English language. People talk about the 'development of the child' and the 'development of the self'. Many firms have 'research and development' divisions, in which the creation and evolution of new products, from sports trainers and car exhausts to laptop computers and mobile phones, is the specific focus of attention.

Turning to the level of the state, 'physical development (land use) plans' are produced; so too are 'national economic development plans', dealing with the economy as a whole. These sorts of plans are expressly designed to guide the process of development and change in the sense of unfolding and working out how things should be in the future. In this sense, development has a close connection with planning. Planning itself may be defined as foreseeing and guiding change (Hall, 1982; Potter, 1985; Pugh and Potter, 2003).

In the arena of development policy, development processes are influenced by development planning, and most plans are in turn shaped by the prevailing development theories that ultimately reflect the way in which development is perceived; in other words, by what we may refer to as the ideology of development. Prevailing ideologies, such as belief in state determined leadership – called Keynesiasm (after the economic theorist Keynes whose ideas were implemented after the Great Depression in the 1930s), and neo-liberalism (which is defined later, but broadly refers to support for and reliance on market forces as opposed to state control), have shaped how development is understood and the associated strategies and mechanisms deemed necessary to achieve it.

However, the development process is affected by many factors other than ideologies (Tordoff, 1992), although ideologies often condition state and institutional reactions to these. The precise nature of development theories, development strategies and development ideologies forms the subject of the review of development theories and strategies that is provided in Chapter 3.

Applied development in terms of efforts to bring about changes in physical and human conditions (e.g. building roads and improving education provisions, etc.) is undertaken in all countries, however, in terms of the focus of this book, our primary focus is on the application of the term 'development' at the global scale. At this level, development is conceived of as an approach to respond to and address one of the main divisions of the world, between the so-called 'developed nations' commonly referred to as the 'Global North' (i.e. North America, Europe, Japan, Australia and New Zealand, sometimes referred to as the 'West') and 'developing nations' often referred to as the 'Global South', which is manifest in a range of economic, social and political scores (see Figure 1.1.). In this sense development is frequently understood to involve stages of advancement and evolution, as in the dictionary definition provided at the beginning of this section. At the simplest level, countries of the North are seen as assisting the countries of the South by means of development aid, in an effort to reduce unemployment and other indicators of 'underdevelopment'. In recognising this argument, and whilst not denying the value of improvements in health, education, transport, etc., we must however be conscious of the fact that such an approach has traditionally privileged conceptions of 'development' held by the North and assumed that their interventions are appropriate and even desirable in the rest of the world. Such a view marginalises the scope for internal development, or for South–South development, where countries in the South, such as China and Brazil, are playing increasingly important roles in assisting other countries to 'develop'. In addition, we also need to question whether the experience of the North is the ideal model to follow.

In practical terms though, what exactly is meant by *development*? (See Critical reflection on development). Further, do individuals, firms, states and global institutions understand the word 'development' to mean much the same thing, or are our perceptions shaped by our own background, culture, beliefs and economic understanding?

Critical reflection

The nature of development

In considering the ethics of development, Gasper (2004), citing Thomas (2001), recognises a number of different usages of the word 'development' in the development studies literature. These are worth noting here as they effectively expand upon the simple dictionary definition of 'development' given at the outset of this section:

1. Development as fundamental or structural change – for example, an increase in income;
2. Development as intervention and action, aimed at improvement, regardless of whether betterment is, in fact, actually achieved;
3. Development as improvement, with good as the outcome;
4. Development as the platform for improvement – encompassing changes that will facilitate development in the future.

These sub-definitions start to make us think that development may not always lead to an overall improvement, but only a partial one. For example, income per head may go up, but inequality might increase rapidly at the same time. And if when incomes increase more people can afford cars, and more large cars, then road congestion, increased journey times, parking problems and pollution are likely to follow soon after.

Critical reflection

It is quite often observed that those with higher incomes may not always be the most contented when asked to evaluate their level of satisfaction with different aspects of their lives. Why might this be the case – cannot money help to buy happiness? Looking at points 1–4 above, what other factors might be involved, and what other things may people be looking for in their lives? And can the same sorts of arguments be scaled up and applied at the level of nations? Are the richest countries likely to be those within which the population is, on average, the most satisfied? Are you aware of data that support or refute any such broad association between income levels and social satisfactions?

Significantly, Sen (2000) (see below) argues that development is much more than just material or physical change, and we also need to acknowledge that a range of other factors need to be addressed if 'development' is to be achieved. Can you list some additional considerations? Sen's thinking builds on earlier discussion by Seers (1972) (also discussed below), who argued that development is not just about improving incomes and wealth, but also involves qualitative improvements in social aspects such as health and education.

It is important to recognise that, over time, understanding what 'development' is has changed. Initially, it was conceived of purely in terms of material advances (higher incomes and salaries), the benefits of which, it was argued, would 'trickle down' to the gain of all in society. Later, when this form of development clearly led to selective benefits, Seers (1972) argued that social factors – such as health and education – were also part of development and needed specific support. Sen (2000) took the argument to a new level when he argued that 'freedom' and empowerment were equally important to attain.

Despite the increasingly sophisticated understanding of what development is, its application has often been fraught with difficulties. Table 1.1 lists some 'good' and 'bad' outcomes that are frequently associated with the process of development. On the plus side is the idea that development brings economic growth and national progress, and should involve other positive outcomes such as the provision of basic daily needs (food, clothing, housing, basic education and health care), better forms of governance and a move towards patterns of growth that are more sustainable in the long term.

In respect of the negative consequences of development, the occurrence and often the persistence of inequalities between rich and poor regions, countries and groups of people is often referred to, along with the

Table 1.1 Alternative interpretations of development

Good	Bad
Development brings economic growth	Development is a dependent and a subordinating process which
Development brings overall national progress	privileges a 'western'/'Northern' perspective
	Development is a process creating and widening spatial inequalities
Development brings modernisation along Western lines	Development undermines local cultures and values
Development improves the provision of basic needs	Development perpetuates poverty and poor working and living conditions
Development can help create sustainable growth	Development is often environmentally unsustainable
Development brings improved governance	Development infringes human rights and undermines democracy

Source: adapted from Rigg (1997).

perpetuation of relative poverty. Another line of criticism suggests that so-called development is associated with the dependency of poor countries on richer nations, and the maintenance of forms of economic, social, political and cultural subordination.

For the most part in this chapter, and indeed in the book as a whole, the concept and practice of development are discussed in relation to the experiences of what is frequently referred to as the Global South, or what traditionally have been known as the 'developing countries' or 'poor countries'. But it should be borne in mind that development relates to all parts of the world at every level, from the individual to the global. Thus, development relates just as much to poor areas in cities, and relatively poor regions in rich nations (see Potter, 2000, 2001b). Growing inequality and deprivation in the nations of the North also make development in those countries a matter of concern. In fact, the 2015 Sustainable Development Goals, which are discussed below, recognise that development needs to be pursued in all countries, not just in the South. Growing socio-economic inequalities within the countries of the North emphasise the need to consider the wider application of development.

Despite this, the understanding and application of development has become most often linked with the so-called South, often still referred to as the 'Third World', which itself is a value-laden term, the emergence of which was closely associated with the evolution of the concept of development in the political context of the second half of the twentieth century. The second part of this chapter will examine the emergence, use and persistence of what some now regard as an outmoded terminology, and will associate this with thinking about development itself.

In conclusion, the working definition of development assumed by this text at the outset is that initially provided by Brookfield (1975), namely that development is change, either for the better or for the worse. Specifically in this text it is assumed that progressive and effective development represents change that is intended to lead to the betterment of people and places around the globe and to enhance the common good (Potter et al., 2012).

Thinking about development

Understanding development over time: the Enlightenment, modernity, neo-colonialism, trusteeship and post-World War Two thinking

Most people writing about both development and what has come to be referred to recently as 'post-' or 'antidevelopment' (Andrews and Bawa, 2014; Escobar, 1995; Power, 2003; Preston, 1996; Sachs, 1992; Sidaway, 2007) situate the origins of the modern process of development in the late 1940s. More precisely, they link the *modern era of development* to a speech made by President Truman in 1949, in which he employed the term 'underdeveloped areas' to describe what was soon to be known as the *Third World* (and later the Global South). Truman also set out what he saw as the duty of the West (later called the North) to bring 'development' to such relatively underdeveloped countries. In doing this, the USA was challenging the old European Empires about their continued pursuit of colonialism as much as advocating a strategy which privileged western achievements, technology, values and concepts of ideal 'progress' as something all nations should pursue.

If *colonialism* is defined as the direct political control and administration of an overseas territory by a foreign state, then effectively Truman was establishing a *new colonial*, or *neo-colonial* role for the USA within the newly independent countries that were emerging from the process of decolonisation. He was encouraging the so-called 'underdeveloped nations' to recognise their condition and to turn to the USA for long-term assistance.

This introduced the concept of 'modernism' or 'modernisation' into the development lexicon, which may be defined as the belief that development is all about transforming 'traditional' countries into *modern, westernised nations* i.e. that 'successful development' implies the pursuit and attainment of technology, values and systems characteristic of the 'modern' western countries. Viewed in this light, it is undoubtedly true that the genesis of much modern(ist) development theory and practice lay in the period between 1945 and 1955.

For many Western governments, particularly former colonial powers, such views represented a continuation of the late colonial mission to develop colonial peoples within the concept of *trusteeship* (Cowen and Shenton, 1995; Chapter 2).

Trusteeship can be defined as the holding of property on behalf of another person or group, with the belief that the latter will be better able to look after it themselves at some time in the future. There was little recognition that many traditional societies might in fact have been content with the ways of life they already led. Indeed, development strategists often tried to persuade them otherwise. Thus Rigg (1997: 33) cites the American advisers to the Thai government of the 1950s as trying to prevent the monks from preaching the virtues of contentedness, which was seen as retarding modernisation.

Many other writers, however, recognise that the origins of modern development lay in an earlier period. Specifically, it was closely linked with the rise of rationalism and humanism in the eighteenth and nineteenth centuries, respectively. During this period, the simple definition of development as 'change' became transformed into what was seen as a more directed and logical form of evolution.

Collectively, the period when these changes took place is known as the 'Enlightenment'. The Enlightenment generally refers to a period of European intellectual history that continued through most of the eighteenth century (Power, 2002).

In broad terms, Enlightenment thinking stressed the belief that science and rational thinking could progress human groups from 'barbarism' to 'civilisation'. It was the period during which it came to be increasingly believed that by applying rational, scientific thought to the world, change would become more ordered, more predictable and more valuable.

The new approach challenged the power of the clergy and largely represented the rise of a secular (that is a non-religious) intelligentsia. Hall and Gieben (1992) list a number of threads which made up Enlightenment thinking: the primacy of reason/rationalism; the belief in empiricism (gaining knowledge through observation); the concept of universal science and reason; the idea of orderly progress; the championing of new freedoms; the ethic of secularism; and the notion that all human beings are essentially the same (cited in Power, 2008).

Those people and cultures who could not adapt to such views came to be thought of as 'traditional' and 'backward'. As an example of this, the Australian Aborigines were denied any rights to the land they occupied by the invading British in 1788 because they did not organise and farm it in a systematic, rational way, that is in what was construed as a 'Western' manner.

It was in this fashion, and at this juncture, that the whole idea of development became directly associated with Western values and ideologies. Thus, Power (2002: 67) notes that the 'emergence of an idea of "the West" was also important to the Enlightenment . . . it was a very European affair which put Europe and European intellectuals at the very pinnacle of human achievement'. Thus, development was seen as being directly linked to Western religion, science, rationality and principles of justice. This theme is explored in Chapters 3 and 4.

In the nineteenth century, Darwinism began to associate development with evolution; that is, a change towards something more appropriate for future survival (Esteva, 1992). When combined with the rationality of Enlightenment thinking, the result became a narrower, but what many saw as the 'correct' way of development, one based on Western social theory and science.

During the Industrial Revolution, this thinking became heavily economic in nature. But by the late nineteenth century a clear distinction seems to have emerged between the notion of 'progress', which was held to be typified by the unregulated chaos of pure capitalist industrialisation, and 'development', which was representative of Christian order, modernisation and responsibility (Cowen and Shenton, 1996; Preston, 1996).

It is this latter notion of development that, as Chapter 2 discusses, began to permeate the colonial mission from the 1920s onwards, firmly equating development in these lands with an ordered progress towards a set of standards laid down by the West; or as Esteva views it, 'robbing people of different cultures of the opportunity to define the terms of their social life' (Esteva, 1992: 9).

Little recognition was given to the fact that 'traditional' societies had always been responsive to new and more productive types of development. Indeed, had they not done so they would not have survived, as ample evidence about the value of traditional farming strategies adapted to harsh environments has shown in India and Kenya. Furthermore, the continued economic exploitation of the colonies made it virtually impossible for such development towards Western standards and values to be achieved, as societies and economies were structured not to be independent entities, but rather as suppliers of produce for the colonial powers. In this sense, enforced 'underdevelopment' (i.e. the failure to attain a state of economic and social independence) was the result of colonial exploitation, an argument that is considered in several of the following chapters of this text, but especially in Chapter 3, in relation to what is known as 'dependency theory' and was written about by Rodney (1982) in his book: *How Europe Underdeveloped Africa*.

Development as economic growth and the limitations of this approach: 1950s–1970s

Chapter 3 discusses in detail the theories and strategies by means of which development was, for much of its conceptual history, portrayed as a materialist process of change, i.e. the pursuit of economic growth. It was only widely appreciated from the 1970s that development involved dimensions other than just growing the economy. This present section overviews 'authoritative intervention', based on defined beliefs in the role that economic growth would play, based on the perceived understanding of what had transformed or developed the USA. It was only from the 1970s, that the limitations of this approach were appreciated and responded to.

President Truman, in his speech of 1949, noted how the underdeveloped world's poverty is 'a handicap and threat both to them and more prosperous areas . . . greater production is the key to prosperity and peace. And the key to greater production is a wider and more vigorous application of modern scientific and technical knowledge' (Porter, 1995: 78).

Enlightenment values were thus combined with nineteenth-century humanism to justify the new trusteeship of the neo-colonial mission, a mission that was to be accomplished by 'authoritative intervention', primarily through the provision of advice and aid programmes (Preston, 1996). Such thinking underlay the approach which the Western nations adopted to the rest of the world in the colonial and the postcolonial eras, which accorded pre-eminence to the ideology, values and technology of the West. Salient aspects of this approach are summarised in Figure 1.2. Clearly, this 'modern notion of development' (Corbridge, 1995: 1) had long and well-established antecedents. Figure 1.2 sees the origins of growth theory and authoritative intervention in the three strands of Keynesianism (i.e. the pre-1970s belief in the role that the state should play in national development), the rise of the political agenda of the USA (i.e. to assert its international role, advance capitalism and oppose Russia and China), along with nationalist developmentalism (i.e. the aspiring goals of newly independent countries).

These forces were then articulated via economic growth models, planning systems and aid mechanisms, giving rise to the ultimate goal of replicating the historical experience of the North in the South. It is, therefore, perhaps not too surprising that, in its earliest manifestation in the 1950s, development became synonymous with economic growth. Growth theory and models of growth, based largely on the experience of the USA, were developed and pursued, with the support of international aid and imported planning systems, backed up by the support of global institutions, such as the World Bank, in an effort to achieve 'growth'.

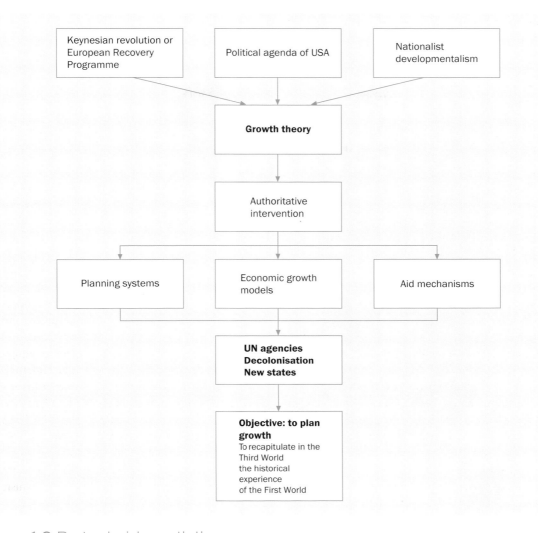

Figure 1.2 Post-colonial growth theory
Source: Adapted from Preston (1996)

It is also important to point out that this American led approach was also pursued at the time of the Cold War, when the USA and its allies were anxious to ensure that nations in the rest of the world pursed 'Western' ideals and did not align themselves with socialism and communism which Russia and China were advocating as alternatives. The net result was that development support and aid were often conflated with the formation of military alliances to bolster the different power groups.

One of the principal writers supporting this approach, Arthur Lewis, was uncompromising in his interpretation of the modernising mission: 'it should be noted that our subject matter is growth, and not distribution' (Esteva, 1992: 12). In other words, increasing incomes and material wealth were seen as being of far more importance than making sure that such income was fairly or equitably spread within society.

During the second half of the twentieth century, therefore, debates about development were dominated by economists. This is not to say that other aspects of development have not contributed, often crucially, to the debate. This is particularly true of sociologists and geographers in respect of the social and spatial unevenness of development, but the dominant influence in both theory and practice has been economics.

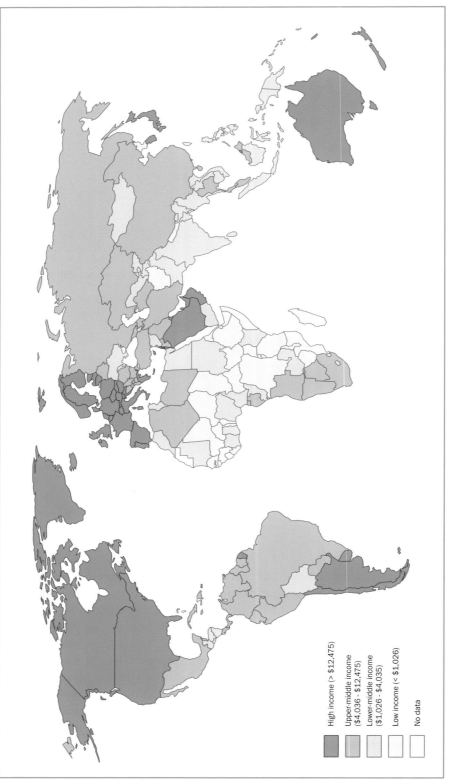

Figure 1.3 Global unevenness: Gross National Income per capita, 2010

Source: adapted from http://data.worldbank.org/data-catalog/GNI-per-capita-Atlas-and-PPP-table

Class levels: http://blogs.worldbank.org/opendata/category/tags/news

High income (> $12,475)

Upper-middle income
($4,036 - $12,475)

Lower-middle income
($1,026 - $4,035)

Low income (< $1,026)

No data

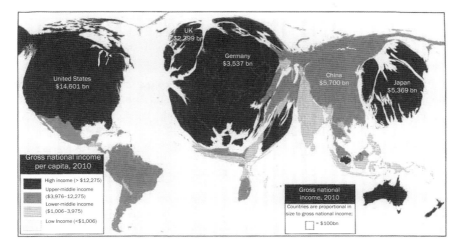

Figure 1.4 Variation in market size: Gross National Income, 2010
Source: Dicken, 2015.

The prominence and influence of development economics in the 1950s and 1960s have had clear repercussions on other terminologies related to development, most notably the way in which underdeveloped countries were identified and described, a point which is elaborated in the second half of this chapter.

The earliest, and for many, still the most convenient way of quantifying underdevelopment and development has been through the level of *Gross National Product* (GNP) per capita pertaining to a nation or territory i.e. the total wealth (from goods and services) produced in a country from internal and external sources in a year, usually measured in US Dollars. *Gross Domestic Product* (GDP), is also used, and is similar to GNP, but focuses on internally generated wealth in a country. Similarly, *Gross National Income* (GNI) is an aggregate of GDP plus incomes earned by foreign residents (Todaro and Smith, 2011). When divided by the total national population, per person or per capita scores of GNP, GDP and GNI facilitate comparison between countries. As Michael Watts (1996) has noted, these figures are still a principal way in which the poverty of the South and the failure of development are blandly laid out in the statistical sections of World Bank and United Nations development reports. Figure 1.3 uses recent data to depict standardised wealth-based indicators of development, showing variations in GNI per capita across the world. It also shows the income bands which the World Bank employs to divide the world into four distinctive regions and these in turn determine

international aid assistance. The clear dominance of the North, in GNI terms, is evident from this map. Figure 1.4 depicts the same information, but through the use of a cartogram which scales the size of countries, not according to their true physical size, but rather in terms of the information being depicted, in this case, relative differentials in the size of the GNI. This Figure shows the dominance of key European countries, Japan and the USA in terms of total GNI (rather than per capita data) and the poor performance of much of the South in relative terms. While economically based measures of development are instructive, and reflect very real wealth and income gaps between countries, they cannot tell us about inequalities within countries, nor can they tell us about other measures such as educational and health levels and relative levels of freedom. These constraints in understanding the true nature of development, encouraged theorists, from the 1970s, to consider whether there were more inclusive ways of defining development.

Measuring development and global differences: from economic measures to Human Development Indices – 1960s–2000s

The real problem with GNP per capita and related measures is that it gives no indication of the distribution of national wealth between different groups within the population and of other developmental considerations such as health and education.

Nevertheless, as Seers (1972: 34) pointed out, to argue that GNP per capita is a totally inappropriate measure of a nation's development is to weaken the significance of the growing GNP per capita gap between rich and poor nations, a gap which is dealt with extensively later in this chapter.

In other words, the serious criticisms that one can make of development statistics do not deny them some use in the analysis of the development process, particularly its unevenness. Seers himself, with his egalitarian leaning, suggested the use of three criteria to measure comparative development: poverty, unemployment and inequality. He accepted that the statistical difficulties involved in doing so were considerable, but argued that they produced data that were no less reliable than GNP per capita, and were a far better reflection of the distribution of the benefits of growth. Although Seers considered them to be economic criteria, they clearly include social dimensions; indeed, Seers suggested social surrogates for their measurement.

The 1970s and 1980s were conspicuous for the appearance of a whole series of social indicators of development, such as those relating to health, education and nutrition, which were produced either as tables attached to major annual reviews, for example, the annual *World Development Report* (produced by the World Bank), or less frequently as maps that accompanied attempts to identify the developing world per se.

Eventually these social indicators were broadened still further to incorporate measures of gender inequality, environmental quality and political and human rights. As with all statistical measures, these data are open to a variety of criticisms, some technical, some interpretational. For example, how does one measure human rights when cultural interpretations are not consistent (Drakakis-Smith, 1997)?

Moreover, by the late 1980s a plethora of economic, social and other indicators were being produced on an annual basis. These were not always consistent with one another and could be manipulated to show that some 'development' had occurred almost anywhere.

The consequence was, not surprisingly, that as indicators multiplied so there emerged a renewed enthusiasm for the single composite measure. Such measures did not always produce results that matched the GNP-based categories of development that have graced the pages of the *World Bank Development Report* for so long.

In Richard Estes' (1984) Index of Social Progress, the USA was ranked well below countries such as Cuba, Colombia and Romania. As usual, one can always prove a point with statistics. Other measures were even more complex in an effort to be all-embracing.

Tata and Schultz (1988) constructed a human welfare index from ten variables using factor analysis. The final scores, however, were more or less arbitrarily divided into three sets, producing a table and map little different from those of the three worlds (First, Second and Third World) in vogue at that time.

However, almost inevitably, single measures, usually in conjunction with multiple tables of individual indicators, remain popular as easily digestible summaries of world development trends. One of the most widely used is the *Human Development Index* introduced and developed by the United Nations. In the words of the 2001 Human Development Report, the 'HDI measures the overall achievements in a country in three basic dimensions of human development – longevity, knowledge and a decent standard of living' (UNDP, 2001: 14). Thus, the HDI is measured by life expectancy, educational attainment (adult literacy and combined primary, secondary and tertiary enrolment), plus adjusted income per capita in purchasing power parity (PPP) US dollars.

The manner in which the basic index is calculated is shown in Figure 1.5. The three basic dimensions are translated into a series of indicators, and these are summed to give a single Human Development Index. This summary measure has come to be used in a wide variety of contexts. For example, the Government of Barbados has used the HDI in a number of promotional contexts, basically to show that Barbados is 'the most highly developed of developing nations'; indeed, one Barbadian administration went so far as to announce that its express aim was to make Barbados a 'First World' nation within the foreseeable future (Potter, 2000).

It needs to be stressed that HDI is a summary statistic, and not a comprehensive measure of development. As such, over the years since its introduction, various methodological refinements have been tried by the United Nations. Such refinements include Human Poverty Indexes 1 and 2, the Gender-related Development Index

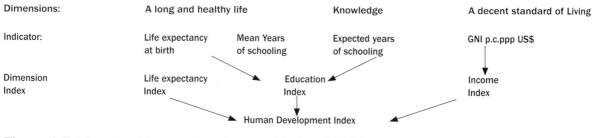

Figure 1.5 How the Human Development Index (HDI) is calculated
Source: adapted from UNDP, 2015.

and the Gender Empowerment Measure. These are all variations on the basic Human Development Index. In each instance, additional variables are brought in to reflect the revised index. For example, for the Human Poverty Index 2, a measure of social exclusion is included in the calculation, measured by the long-term unemployment rate. For the gender-related index variables such as female life expectancy, literacy and estimated earnings are factored into the calculation of the HDI. More recently, the HDI has been redefined to reflect the reality of significant measures of inequality within societies i.e. not all people share the benefits of development equally, hence the inequality adjusted HDI measures average human development after inequality is taken into account (UNDP, 2015).

In respect of the HDI of those nations classified as being characterised by high human development, the majority are countries in the North or 'developed countries', such as the USA, Canada, Sweden, Japan, Switzerland, United Kingdom and New Zealand. But a number of those recording high scores are nations from the Global South, such as Hong Kong, Singapore, the Republic of Korea, Barbados, Chile, the Bahamas and the United Arab Emirates. Medium-level human development nations include Trinidad and Tobago, Venezuela, Romania, Peru, Sri Lanka, Jamaica, China, Egypt and Namibia. Low HDI scores are returned by Pakistan, Haiti, Tanzania, Senegal, Guinea, Rwanda, Niger, Sierra Leone and Burundi. Figure 1.6 is a map showing how countries around the world compare in terms of HDI scores. It is significant that scores achieved in the countries of the North, generally stand in contrast to the scores achieved in the South. Figure 1.7 is a graph which indicates, at a global level, the degree to which there have been apparent advances in development if gauged in terms of changes in the three key variables measured

by the HDI index. While the fall in number of people in the lower bands, and the rise in the higher bands is very significant and a clear indicator of development progress, we need to be aware of the reality that these scores do not reflect income and gender inequality, which is considered below.

This difference between the North and the South is further reflected in Tables 1.2 and 1.3. These Tables are extracted from the *United Nations Development Report* (2015) and use the United Nations regional classifications for the countries of the world. Table 1.2 shows the differing scores for the different world regions and the global average. It also shows the Inequality Adjusted Index and the Gender Inequality Index. While it is significant that HDI levels have improved in all regions of the world, often significantly, whilst the poor performance of the South and Sub Saharan Africa in particular, relative to the North, is especially apparent, particularly when the inequality and gender indices are factored in. In this Table the Organization of Economic Cooperation and Development (OECD) partially parallels the North. While HDI may not be a perfect measure of development attainment, the scores partially reflect the outcomes of 60 to 70 years of development progress. While Latin America and the Caribbean score better than much of the rest of the South, and have achieved clear 'development' advances, particularly when compared with South Asia and Sub Saharan Africa, this region's inequality and gender scores remain cause for concern. Table 1.3 compares the HDI ranking of the three top scoring and the three lowest scoring countries in the world with the world average. The Table also includes the three composite indices from which the HDI score is calculated. The three top scoring countries are all in the North and the three at the bottom are all in Africa. Life expectancy differs by 20 or more years

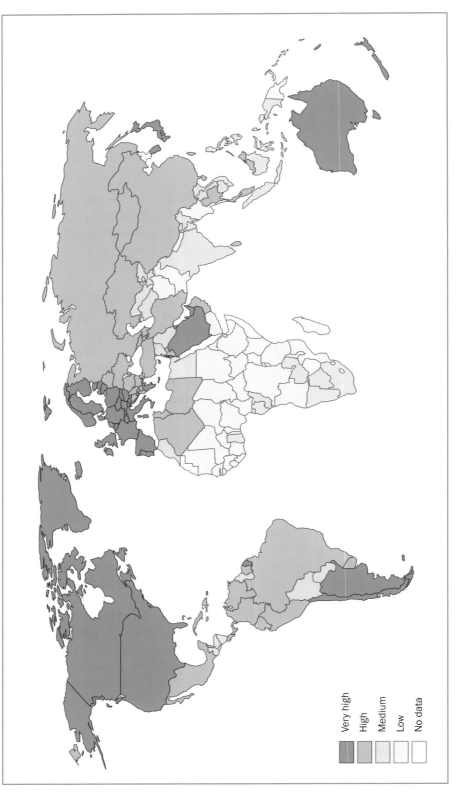

Figure 1.6 Global differences in Human Development Index (HDI) scores, 2014

Source: adapted from http://hdr.undp.org/en/composite/HDI.

Very high

High

Medium

Low

No data

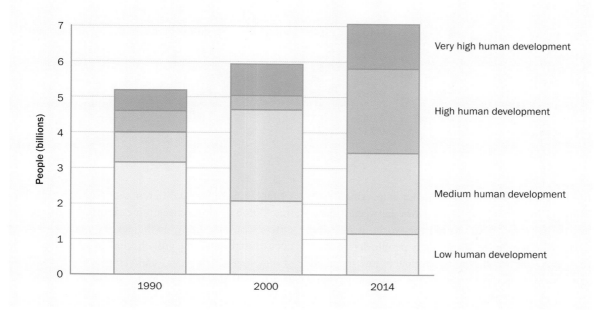

Figure 1.7 Changing Human Development Index scores, 1990–2014
Source: adapted from UNDP, 2015.

between the two clusters, while average years schooling differs by a factor of three and income up to more than a 100-fold difference in the case of the CAR (Central African Republic). These stark differences both validate the urgency of development but also raise questions about why such gaps have persisted for so long.

When we seek to understand global differences and the progress made within countries, in addition to using economic measures such as GNP, GDP and GNI and composite indices such as HDI, a range of other measures also exist which summarise the situation within

countries and allow for international comparisons. Table 1.4 indicates GDP scores at the national and per capita (pc) levels in each of the major regions, and it also considers key labour scores i.e. labour force participation rates (the proportion of those able to work who are employed or who are looking for work – a figure which excludes those not looking for work), unemployment scores and youth unemployment. The significant per capita GDP contrasts, while being an unreliable measure of development, do reflect on the limited capacity of governments and peoples in the poorer regions to

Table 1.2 Human Development Index

Region	1990	2000	2010	2014	Inequality Adjusted HDI 2014	Gender Inequality Index 2014
World	0.597	0.641	0.697	0.711	0.711	0.449
OECD	0.785	0.834	0.872	0.880	0.763	0.231
Least Developed	0.348	0.399	0.484	0.502	0.347	0.566
Developing Countries	0.513	0.568	0.642	0.660	0.490	0.478
East Asia & Pacific	0.516	0.593	0.686	0.710	0.572	0.328
Latin America and Caribbean	0.625	0.684	0.734	0.748	0.570	0.415
South Asia	0.437	0.503	0.586	0.607	0.433	0.536
Sub Saharan Africa	0.400	0.422	0.499	0.518	0.345	0.575

Source: UNDP (2015) Human Development Report

Table 1.3 International comparison based on HDI ranking 2014

Country	HDI Rank	HDI	Life Expectancy	Mean Years Schooling	GNI per capita $
Norway	1	0.944	81.6	12.6	64992
Australia	2	0.935	82.4	13	42261
Switzerland	3	0.930	83	12.8	56431
Eritrea	186	0.391	63.7	3.9	1130
Central African Rep.	187	0.350	50.7	4.2	581
Niger	188	0.348	61.4	1.5	908
World Average	–	0.711	71.5	7.9	14301

Source: UNDP (2015) Human Development Report

fund social improvements, provide for employment, etc. Further, while there are similarities between labour force participation rates around the world, it must be remembered that in the South many people derive their livelihoods from what is often marginal or low-incomed employment in the informal sector and state welfare benefits seldom exist.

Table 1.5 employs a different set of indicators to illustrate global differences. It examines population differences, including growth rates. If population growth rates exceed economic growth, challenges exist in terms of the provision of services and employment. The Table also reflects dependency ratios for under-14-year-olds and over-65-year-olds, i.e. the higher the score the more

Table 1.4 Global differences: economic and employment indicators

Region	GDP 2013 $billions	GDP pc 2013 $	Labour Force Participation rate %	Unemployment Total %	Unemployment Youth 15–24 %
World	97104	13964	63.5	6.1	15.1
OECD	46521	36923	59.7	8.2	16.5
Least Developed	1770	2122	74	6.3	10.3
Developing Countries	49539	8696	64.3	5.6	14.6
East Asia & Pacific	20776	10779	71.1	3.3	18.5
Latin America and Caribbean	7911	13877	66.4	6.2	13.7
South Asia	9305	5324	55.6	4.2	10.9
Sub Saharan Africa	2997	3339	70.9	11.9	13.5

Source: UNDP (2015) Human Development Report

Table 1.5 Global differences: population indicators

Region	Population 2014 millions	Population 2030 millions	Average growth rate %	Dependency Ratio 0–14	Dependency Ratio 65+	Total Fertility Rate	Child Malnutrition %
World	7243	8424	1.1	39.6	12.5	2.5	29.7
OECD	1272	1366	0.6	27.8	24.7	1.8	–
Least Developed	919	1287	2.3	69.1	6.2	4.2	40.5
Developing Countries	5962	7091	1.3	42.7	9.6	2.7	31
East Asia & Pacific	2051	2211	0.8	29.5	11.8	1.9	18.1
Latin America and Caribbean	618	711	1.1	39.4	11.4	2.2	13.9
South Asia	1771	2085	1.3	44.2	8.1	2.6	45.1
Sub Saharan Africa	911	1348	2.7	78.9	5.8	5.1	37.2

Source: UNDP (2015) Human Development Report

the dependents which people in the working bracket (15–64 years) have to support, which may dilute individual prospects for improvement. Child malnutrition rates reflect the preceding considerations, and the harsh economic and environmental conditions in which many of the world's poor are forced to live.

As is evident from the above discussion, a range of development indicators are available to both determine global differences and to justify support and response. Despite the value of such measures, as Esteva (1992) notes, human development is thus translated into a linear process indicated by measuring levels of deprivation, or how far countries depart from the Western ideal. Moreover, if one chooses other similar variables in the same categories, quite different overall indices can be obtained. Despite their limitations, we cannot dispose of development indicators too readily, for above all they indicate trends over time and even the anti-development critics (defined shortly below) use collated statistics of this nature in order to consolidate their starting point that 'development' has been a myth. Indeed, Ronald Horvath (1988) has conceded that, in endeavouring to measure development, he was 'measuring a metaphor'.

The notion of development as economic growth has broadened over the years to incorporate social indicators and political freedoms, such as by Seers (1972). This has, more recently, been explored by Amartya Sen (2000) in his book *Development as Freedom*. The approach outlined by Sen is summarised in the Key thinker box.

In addition to defining how we understand and measure development, there is the need to also factor in other contextual considerations which impact on global well-being and future prospects. Given the vulnerable position which humankind finds itself in as a result of climate change, resource depletion and rapid population growth there is a crucial need to ensure 'sustainable' development, i.e. development which meets current needs but does not impact on the survival prospects of future generations. Efforts at climate change mitigation need to go hand in hand with efforts to ensure human survival and well-being and development needs to better appreciate and articulate interventions and outcomes which address these considerations (see Chapter 6).

Critical reflection

The material examined in the above sections has illustrated the changing range of variables used to measured development. It has also shown the nature and scale of differences between key regions in the world. Examine Tables 1.2–1.5 and reflect on:

➤ What are the causes of these global differences and why do they persist?

➤ Why is the youth unemployment rate higher than the total unemployment rate (i.e. for all age groups)?

➤ What differences will having rapid population growth have on development prospects?

Critiques of development and the search for alternative conceptualisations of development: 1960s–2000s

Criticism of development as conceptualised and practised in the ways described above has been continuous since the 1960s, and has clearly influenced theory and strategy, as will be discussed in Chapter 3. Even the narrow focus on economic growth for several decades by the agents of development (international bodies and governments) failed to produce a convergence in income between countries and within countries. Far from it, there is evidence that inequality between and within countries has increased substantially (Griffin, 1980; Potter, 2008a).

This is referred to as the 'convergence debate', and we will return to it in detail later in the chapter. Trickle-down economics had not worked and the call came for a more diversified and broader interpretation of development (Dwyer, 1977).

Explanations were sought and offered for the failure of the *modernisation* project (Brookfield, 1978) and new strategies were devised. But in most of this discussion, development as a linear and universal process was seldom questioned or addressed (see the Rostow Model discussed in Chapter 3). What was debated was the variable and erratic nature of development, and explanations were sought in relation to both its chronological and spatial unevenness. It was only later that more sustained and theoretically grounded critiques emerged which started to question the fundamental bases of development.

Key thinker

Amartya Sen and *Development as Freedom*

Plate 1.1 Amartya Sen
(*photo*: Getty Images/AFP)

The Nobel Laureate Amartya Sen published a book in 2000 under the title *Development as Freedom*. Sen was awarded the Nobel Memorial Prize for Economic Science in 1998. Over the years he has written widely on many aspects of development economics, including poverty, famine, capabilities, inequality, democracy and issues of public policy in developing economies.

Sen (2000) argues that development consists of the removal of various types of 'unfreedoms' that leave people with little choice and little opportunity for exercising their reasoned agency (or self-choice). One of the vital points is that one human freedom tends to promote freedoms of other kinds: 'There are very many different interconnections between distinct instrumental freedoms' (Sen, 2000: 43).

For example, Sen argues that there is strong evidence that economic and political freedoms help reinforce one another. But in a less contested manner,

it can be argued that social opportunities in the fields of health care and education, which generally require public action, complement individual opportunities for economic and political participation. Such linkages emphasise the intrinsic importance of human freedoms.

Sen's emphasis is on substantive freedoms. It makes little sense to celebrate the freedom to pollute, torture or employ child labourers (Corbridge, 2002a). Sen's focus is very much upon 'instrumental freedoms', that is those which allow us to live lives free from starvation, undernourishment, escapable morbidity, premature mortality, illiteracy and innumeracy. Being able to enjoy political participation and free speech are further vital freedoms. How much more difficult is it likely to be if people cannot read?

It is clear that this list maps out political freedoms, such as the right to vote, but also relates to the existence of economic opportunities, social facilities, transparency within society (trust and openness), as well as a measure of protective security.

A particular issue that Sen deals with is gender discrimination. As noted by Corbridge (2002a), Sen writes movingly in *Development as Freedom* about this key issue. Sen interprets this in terms of women not enjoying the same substantive freedoms as men. They suffer from unfair food sharing and health care within households, and have little voice.

It is clear that in Sen's work the differences that matter the most are those that define us as individual human beings. Centrally, Sen's approach serves to emphasise that development needs to be measured by means other than GDP. The approach celebrates individual freedom.

Key thinker (continued)

On the other hand, using instances, mainly drawn from China and India, Corbridge (2002a) argues that some examples that Sen uses suggest that the curtailment of individual freedoms can have beneficial impacts on the poor, or on a certain, prescribed social grouping. And there are further points: individual freedoms may be enhanced by social mobilisations, some of which may be anything but liberal and democratic. These do not invalidate Sen's argument, but they do limit the agency of individual freedoms.

Critical reflection

What are the relative freedoms that you most enjoy day to day and in what areas of your life and do you consider that you experience 'unfreedoms', or a relative lack of freedom? Dependent on where you live in the world, how do you feel these compare with somebody living in another part of the world? Thinking about the freedoms you most enjoy, do you feel that some of them might be bought at the expense of someone else's freedoms?

Eurocentricity, unequal economic relations and development outcomes; the 'development impasse' and the search for new approaches to development

For some critics the answer as to why development was not addressing its objectives was straightforward; it was, and still is, the Eurocentricity (European orientation) of economic development theories that distorted patterns and processes of development, especially through their pseudoscientific rationale (Table 1.6).

Mehmet (1995), in particular, has been virulent in his criticism:

> As a logical system, Western economics is a closed system . . . in which assumptions are substituted for reality, and gender, environment and the Third World are all equally dismissed as irrelevant . . . [However], mainstream economics is neither value free nor tolerant of non-western cultures.

Of course, Eurocentrism is a criticism that can be levied at more than mainstream development economics and its associated modernisation strategy (Hettne, 1995; McGee, 1995). Indeed, as Chapter 3 indicates, almost all of the major strategies for development have been Eurocentric in origin and in bias, from modernisation through to neo-Marxism to the neo-liberal 'counterrevolution' of the 1980s.

Table 1.6 Eurocentricity: some principal points of criticism

Denigration of other people and places
Ideological biases
Lack of sensitivity to cultural variation
Setting of ethical norms
Stereotyping of other people and places
Tendency towards deterministic formulations
Tendency towards empiricism in analysis
Tendency towards male orientation (sexism)
Tendency towards reductionism
Tendency towards the building of grand theories
Underlying tones of racial superiority
Unilinearity
Universalism

Moreover, it can be argued that most approaches tend to equate 'development' with capitalism (Harriss and Harriss, 1979). Certainly, all are universalist in their assumptions that development is a big issue that needs to be understood through grand theories, or so-called 'metanarratives'.

It is not surprising that such arrogant approaches began to be criticised. After all, these were approaches in which the developed nations devised the parameters of development, set the objectives and shaped the strategies applied in the rest of the world.

Over and above criticism of eurocentric bias in development is the stark reality of unequal power and economic relations between the North and South. The 'power' which the North exerts over the South economically and dependence on western corporates has ensured a capital and resource transfer from the South to the North. As evidence from global capital flows indicates (see Chapter 8) and, despite the provision of critically important aid, more wealth flows from the South to the North and not the other way around. Not only was this 'westernised' development not working for most of the South countries, but the North itself was continuing to be the 'beneficiary' of the distorted development that it produced, which was an extension of colonialism (Bond, 2006; Collier, 2008). A recent estimate is that, in the case of Africa, the continent receives US $132 billion in loans, foreign investment and development aid per annum (aid accounts for some $30 billion), but the continent exports $192 billion in debt repayments, profit repatriation and as a result of tax evasion (nearly six times the value of aid received). The perception that aid is helping African countries 'has facilitated a perverse reality in which the UK and other wealthy governments celebrate their generosity whilst simultaneously assisting their companies to drain Africa's resources' (Anderson, 2014).

While many gains have been made in the South in terms of improving health and education levels, and the probable reduction in absolute poverty, it is also apparent, that, in relative terms global inequality is growing. Since 1960, which marked the start of the major 'push' to promote development, and was called the first *United Nations Development Decade*, disparities of global wealth distribution doubled, so that by the mid-1990s the wealthiest quintile of the world's population controlled 83 per cent of global income, compared to less than 2 per cent for the lowest quintile (UNDP, 1996). At a global level, by 2015, this gap had grown, and it is now the case that of the world's wealth, $65 trillion is held by just 1% of the world's population. This amount is 65 times the wealth held by the poorest 50% of the world's population (IMF, 2015).

However, despite these growing disparities and the extensive criticism that began to appear, we must also recognise the fact that some societies were able to absorb selectively from this imposed development to their own advantage. The Asian industrialising societies, for example, provided ample evidence of this. The rapid economic growth of countries such as Singapore, Taiwan and South Korea are cases in point, albeit they often enjoyed selected support from the North during the Cold War.

Two principal sets of voices began to be heard in the widespread criticism of the general situation. The first was characterised by a stance that recommended greater input into defining development and its problems from those most affected by it – 'development from below', as Stöhr and Taylor (1981) expressed it, or 'putting the last first', as Robert Chambers (1983) termed it. This is often seen as having given rise to distinctly alternative and populist approaches to development and change. These are fully aired in Chapter 3.

The second set of critical views exhibited similar values, but its supporters were not prepared to work within what they regarded as an unfair and heavily manipulated dialogue of development in which the West, through the medium of international development agencies and 'national governments', assigns to itself the ability to speak and write with authority about development (Corbridge, 1995: 9). This group has become known, therefore, for its 'anti-development' stance; perhaps a somewhat misleading description, as we will see later.

Some of the values of this group cut across the opinions of what might be termed 'postmodern development' with its rejection of metatheory (large-scale, all-embracing theories, e.g. modernisation) and its embracing of meso- or micro-approaches to development problems, which would include gender and environmental issues (see Chapter 4 and 6). Stated simply, postmodern development is development that rejects the tenets of modernity and the Enlightenment.

Both of these approaches can be interpreted as emerging as responses to what came to be referred to as the 'impasse in development studies' (see Booth, 1985; Schuurman, 1993; 2008). Seen as affecting development studies from the mid-1980s, the impasse was attributed to the failure of development itself, along with a growing postmodern critique of the social sciences and the rise of globalisation. The impasse was a reflection of the failure of development theory and practice to effectively address development backlogs and significantly improve well-being for all.

The neo-liberalisation of development

The development impasse did not imply that applied interventions ceased, rather that from the 1980s, there has been a greater reliance on market forces in terms of the widespread adoption of neo-liberal practice by the global development institutions, such as the World Bank and the International Monetary Fund and most governments, which advocated a reduction in the role of the state and support for market forces. The outcomes of these shifts are considered further in Part III.

The ability of the global development bodies to require these changes came about as a result of historical circumstances, not least the reality that many western states, notably the USA and UK largely abandoned the notion of state economic control – known as Keynesianism – in favour of market based or neo-liberal policies as advocated by the Monetarist economists. In parallel nations of the South, in an effort to modernise, significant international debts were incurred and were often unable to be repaid following the dual blows of the global economic crises of the 1970s and the hike in fuel prices. Hence, in the 1980s many nations in the South defaulted on their loan repayments and were obliged to accept 'Structural Adjustment Packages' imposed by the International Monetary Fund and the World Bank, which delayed loan repayments and granted new loans on condition that countries scaled back the role that their states played, opened their economies to trade and market forces, and devalued their currencies. The net effect was a period of economic stagnation and job losses in much of the South. In Africa, the 1980s was known as the 'lost decade' which saw many earlier development advances being lost.

Increasingly 'development', once again based on western conceptualisation, was seen as promoting international investment and trade, creating 'market-friendly' conditions to support local entrepreneurs and assuming that the private sector would be able to play a central role in addressing key challenges such as providing housing and services through privatisation and investment choices (Desai and Potter, 2014).

Following some very tough years, many governments did become more efficient in their operations and, while there were some improvements in aspects of social provision, job and wealth creation in the South since then, these achievements have not lived up to the ideal of neo-liberalism to spread the benefits of 'growth'. Rather there has been an aggravation of disparities, entrenching dependence of the South on the North (Bond, 2006).

In respect of the latter, what was regarded as the lessening importance of the role of the state was increasingly seen as cutting right across existing theories and conceptualisations of development and change. The effective failure of modernisation and state-led or 'top-down', development led many development theorists to argue that new ways of thinking about development were needed if the lives of ordinary citizens were to be improved. At this juncture, the alternative/populist reactions and the post- and anti-development schools are now reviewed.

Alternative and populist approaches to development; 'bottom-up' development and the role of NGOs

Alternative, or 'other' forms of development to those espoused by the modernisation discourse, which were much discussed in the 1990s, are not necessarily recent phenomena. Indeed, principles of locally driven development and community self-reliance espoused earlier by the Indian activist Mahatma Gandhi (see Key thinker box), had influenced development practice and thinking in many communities since the 1940s.

Even in the 1960s there were reactions against the idea that development could be narrowly defined in modernisation terms and superimposed upon a variety of situations across the South. More locally oriented views began to emerge; for example, the Dag Hammarskjöld Foundation's concept of 'another development', was one that was more human centred (see also Chapter 3) and which gained traction in the 1990s. This thinking was later bolstered by the argument of Hettne (1995) about 'alternate development' and the need to actively seek out and support processes which could be more empowering and effective than what had been pursued to date.

From the 1960s, arguments about the need for micro-level, human focused (or people-centred) development started to emerge. These approaches were soon co-opted into official development policies, underpinning the 'basic needs' strategies of the 1970s, which fragmented the monolithic targets for development into what were seen as more locally and socially oriented goals. This occurred when the World Bank sought to promote 'basic needs' i.e. micro-level interventions too, for example, to enhance mass water provision, and provide health care and education, often through low-cost and low technology interventions, while persisting with mainstream modernisation thinking.

Unfortunately, these worthy objectives relating to shelter, education or health not only competed with one another for funding, but were also compromised by the same universalist approaches that had compromised earlier development strategies.

Key thinker

Mahatma Gandhi

Plate 1.2 Mahatma Gandhi
(*photo*: Alamy Images/Dionodia Images)

For many, the Indian activist Mahatma Gandhi has come to symbolise the call for peaceful principles of locally driven development and change. Born in western India in 1869, and having studied law in England, Gandhi lived in South Africa for over 20 years. He opposed the 'pass laws' which restricted peoples' movements on the basis of their race and all forms of racial discrimination (see Singh, 2006).

The time that Gandhi spent in South Africa greatly influenced his views, and on returning to India in 1914 he became a leading figure in the rise of the Indian nationalist and development movements. In his writings he referred to what we would today call the process of development as 'progress' (Singh, 2006). Above all, Gandhi proposed a philosophy of non-violent agitation, with the intention of creating mass awareness and cultural unity.

Linked to this, Gandhi stressed that every human has the right to feed, clothe and house themselves. To this end, villages should become self-sufficient, on a local, 'bottom-up' basis. It was maintained that the locus of power should firmly reside with the village or neighbourhood, and the aim should be an equitable distribution of resources. Gandhi was a great advocate of the development of small-scale rural-based industries.

Regrettably, in 1948 while he was conducting a prayer meeting in Delhi, Gandhi was shot dead by a fanatic (Singh, 2006). But by then Gandhi had become the doyen of rural-based, bottom-up development, based on principles of peaceful action and socio-economic change.

By the 1980s, the concept of locally-oriented, endogenous development was firmly established and was given a considerable boost by the work of Stöhr and Taylor (1981) and Robert Chambers (1983), as noted above, with their 'development from below' and 'bottom-up development' (as opposed to the 'top down' precepts of modernisation), and belief in participatory or community-based development philosophy, designed to address the needs of the poorest in appropriate ways (see Plate 1.3).

Although initially discussed with reference to peasants and rural development in general, the philosophy

of community participation has been widely adopted as an approach to development that is people oriented (Friedmann, 1992). But, as Munslow and Ekoko (1995) have suggested, empowerment of the poor has been stronger on rhetoric than in reality. Nevertheless, facilitating 'people's participation' now has a place on the agenda of the major development institutions, as witnessed by the extensive review of participation and democracy which was provided by the UN (1993).

A major facilitator in this process of empowering the poor through participation in the development process have been non-governmental organisations (NGOs) (for the discussion of the role of NGOs see also Chapter 7).

The blanket term 'NGO' covers a wide variety of aid, charitable, faith-based and community-based organisations (CBOs). The largest have operating budgets greater than those of some developing countries, whereas the smallest struggle on with little official encouragement or funding, blending almost imperceptibly with social movements (Desai and Potter, 2014).

The role of NGOs has been scrutinised intensively over recent years, with some seeking to promote linkages away from purely local, community-level projects. In these circumstances, NGOs become involved with more comprehensive larger-scale planning projects, building stronger bridges with the state (Korten, 1990a, 1990b).

Plate 1.3 Rural hawker and child in Guyana: ultimately development is about improving the life chances of people
(*photo*: Rob Potter)

Others, however, see NGOs, particularly the larger, Northern NGOs, as extensions of the state, helping to maintain existing power relations and legitimising the existing political system (Botes, 1996). Indeed, within the changes that have accompanied structural adjustment programmes (that is economic recovery programmes imposed by international agencies), NGOs may be seen as facilitators in the process of the privatisation of welfare functions, freeing the state from its social obligations within the development arena.

Many other criticisms have been levelled at NGOs and the role of outsiders in community participation; most of them have been lucidly summarised by Botes (1996). These cover the paternalistic actions of development experts who see their role as transferring knowledge to those 'who know less', disempowering them in the process; selective participation of local partners, often bypassing the less articulate or visible groups; favouring 'hard' issues, such as technological matters, over the more difficult and time-consuming 'soft' issues, such as decision-making procedures or community involvement; promoting 'gate-keeping' by local elites; and, particularly important, accentuating product at the expense of process.

Development from below *can* be qualitatively different from conventional development as envisaged by modernisationists, but this process must be realistic rather than romantic in its praxis. Societies, even at the local scale, can be heterogeneous, divided and fractious; and 'grassroots development', through keen to encourage participatory development, must take this into account. Of course, neo-liberal development strategists would argue that their recommendations and seek to encourage the empowerment of individuals through greater freedom of choice within an open market economy.

This approach is criticised by Munslow and Ekoko (1995: 175) as the 'fallacy of empowerment' and the 'mirage of power to the people'. In reality, they argue, 'participatory democracy is really about a transfer of power and resources, [if] not to people directly, [then] to NGOs and other representatives at grassroots level'. This is a theme taken up by another group of developmental thinkers, the post and anti-developmentalists.

Sustainable development

From the 1980s growing global concerns over the long term future of the planet and how we manage it has become a key element in development thinking. Concerns over resource exploitation, depletion and irreparable damage, coupled with growing concerns over the possible impacts of climate change have come to influence how we view and manage the planet's finite resources (see further discussion on this issue in Chapters 3 and 6).

Key in this regard was the work of the Brundtland Commission in 1987, as part of the 'World Commission on Environment and Development: Our Common Future' which drew attention to the need for 'sustainable development' of the planet's resources, i.e. development which meets present needs, but does not compromise future generations' ability to meet their own needs. The concept of 'sustainable development' as a key developmental goal was endorsed by the 'Rio Conference' in 1992, the UN Conference on Environment and Development and encapsulated in the ensuing 'Earth Charter'.

While it would be fair to say that increasing environmental concerns do influence planetary management and development thinking and that there has been global progress, for example, in terms of control of the release of pollutants and gases, much more needs to be done to prevent the loss of forests, wildlife, soils and rivers to name but a few key aspects. The Earth simply does not have the resources to allow for the unbridled pursuit of economic growth at the scale which many countries in the North have pursued it and 'green' issues must increasingly shape our thinking (Williams et al., 2014; Elliott, 2013).

Towards a new understanding of development

It is necessary to stress that ideas about what development is now understood as being, and how it may be achieved have changed significantly since the 1940s. As revealed in this account so far, up to the late 1970s development was almost universally seen as being concerned with increasing incomes and overall national levels of economic growth (Figure 1.8). In the main, so-called 'modernisation' was seen as the vehicle by means of which this improvement would occur. Reflecting the times, this could be directly

monitored and assessed in quantitative terms – measured in US dollars, or the volume of goods, numbers of cars and so on.

However, the 2000/2001 *Human Development Report* (UNDP, 2001) of the United Nations stated that 'human development is about much more than the rise or fall of national incomes' (UNDP, 2001: 9). The passage goes on to note that, 'development should be about creating an environment in which people can develop their full potential in order that they should be enabled to lead productive and creative lives, in accord with their needs and interests'. Thus, development is now seen as being more about 'expanding the choices people have to lead lives that they value' (UNDP, 2001: 9).

Such a perspective promotes the idea that development involves the building of human capabilities. Some of the arguments which follow from this are summarised in Figure 1.8 and reflect the arguments of Sen (2000) and the adoption of the Human Development Index (as discussed above). The most basic of human capabilities are to lead long and healthy lives, to be knowledgeable, to have access to the resources which are needed to achieve a decent standard of living and to be able to participate in the life of the community. Approached in this light, the promotion of human well-being can be regarded as the ultimate purpose or end-purpose of development, so that development shares a common vision with the enhancement of human rights.

The *Human Development Report* concludes its argument on the definition of development by equating it directly with the promotion of human freedom: 'The goal is human freedom . . . People must be free to exercise their choices and to participate in decision-making that affects their lives' (UNDP, 2001: 9).

Again, several of the strands concerning the nature and definition of development are summarised in Figure 1.8. These approaches stress the qualitative dimensions of the development equation, whereas considerations of income and GDP place emphasis on quantitative aspects. Ultimately development, however it is understood and applied, must be multi-faceted in its conceptualisation, focus and implementation, and should engage with as many of the aspects depicted in Figure 1.8 as is possible.

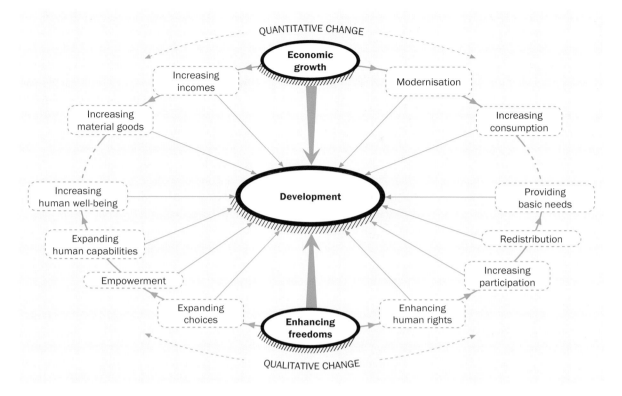

Figure 1.8 Development as economic growth and development as enhancing freedoms

Anti-development, post-development and beyond development

There is considerable overlap between populist interpretations of development and the anti-developmentalists who have emerged in recent years to challenge the notion of development as a whole.

However, as Corbridge (1995) argues, there are long antecedents to anti-(Western) developmentalism stretching back to the nineteenth century. Anti-development is sometimes also referred to as 'post-development' and 'beyond development' (Andrews and Bawa, 2014; Blaikie, 2000; Corbridge, 1997; Desai and Potter, 2014; Nederveen Pieterse, 2000; Parfitt, 2002; Schuurman, 2000, 2008; Sidaway, 2007, 2008; Simon, 2007).

It is also claimed that the failures of neo-Marxism 'to provide practical assistance to those on the front lines of development' (Watts and McCarthy, 1997: 79) have turned disillusioned radicals towards anti-developmentalism (Booth, 1993). Thus, Nederveen Pieterse (2000: 175) comments that 'along with "anti-development" and "beyond development", post-development is a radical reaction to the dilemmas of development', and an effort not just to oppose development as a western construct, but also to seek new ways of addressing community needs, which are generally seen as being anchored in the capacity and resources of the community (Escobar, 1995).

In essence, the ideas surrounding anti-developmentalism are not new, since they are essentially based on the failures of modernisation. Thus, anti-developmentalism is based on the criticism that development is a Western construction in which the economic, social and political parameters of development are set by the West and are imposed on other countries in a neo-colonial mission to normalise and develop them in the image of the West.

In Pieterse's (2000: 175) words, 'Development is rejected because it is the "new religion" of the west'. In this way, the local values and potentialities of 'traditional' communities are largely ignored.

There is much of the 'globalisation steamroller' argument of the anti-developmentalists, particularly in their assumption that the universalism of contemporary development discourse is obliterating the local, that is contested by the reassertion of the 'local' on the global development stage (see Chapter 4).

The central thread holding anti-developmentalist ideas together is that the discourse or language of development has been constructed by the West, and that this promotes a specific kind of intervention 'that links forms of knowledge about the Third World (the South) with the deployment of terms of power and intervention, resulting in the mapping and production of Third World societies' (Escobar, 1995: 212).

Escobar argues that development has 'created abnormalities' such as poverty, underdevelopment, backwardness, landlessness, and has proceeded to address them through a normalisation programme that denies value or initiative to local cultures.

There are, in these arguments, many similarities to Said's perspectives on orientalism, similarities that are both implicit and explicit in the views of the anti-development school of thought, which sees both the 'problems' of the South and their 'solutions' as the creations of Western (Northern) development discourse and practice (see Chapter 2). Of course, there is a recognition that these situations are not static, but change according to contemporary power structures.

However, a consistent factor within the anti-developmental discourse is the negative role of the state in the South in facilitating the 'Westernisation' of the so-called 'development mission'. It follows, therefore, that the restructuring of development must come from below. Here the anti-developmentalists in general, and Escobar (1995) in particular, place enormous emphasis not just on grassroots participation, but more specifically on new social movements as the medium of change, which he argues can lay a basis for situationally and community relevant appropriate change.

The nature of these new social movements is allegedly quite different, not only from the class-based group of 'social movements' in the nineteenth century (Preston, 1996). Escobar dismisses these as 'pursuing goals that look like conventional development objectives (chiefly, the satisfaction of basic needs)' (Escobar, 1995: 219).

In contrast, the new social movements upon which Escobar pins so many of his hopes are anti-developmental, promoting egalitarian, democratic and participatory politics within which they seek autonomy through the use and pursuit of everyday knowledge. He points to the example of autonomous community groups in Latin America as examples of the way forward.

Indeed, some observers have gone even further, and claim that the new social movements 'transcend any narrow materialist concerns' (Preston, 1996: 305–6). Escobar warns that such movements must be wary of being subverted into the developmentalist mission through compromised projects such as 'women and development', or 'grassroots development'.

Not surprisingly, anti-developmentalism in these terms has been subject to some stinging criticism, particularly by Watts and McCarthy (1997), who point out that Escobar is guilty of considerable reductionism in his critique of development, painting a picture very much resembling the dependency theories of the 1970s, in which a monolithic capitalism, particularly in the guise of the World Bank, monopolises development within a largely complacent South.

As Rigg (1997) observes, Escobar is very selective in his evidence, with little discussion of those Asia-Pacific countries that might contradict his polemic. Corbridge (1995) also argues that Escobar ignores the many positive changes that Western-shaped development has brought about in terms of improved health, education and the like, no matter how uneven this has been.

Some maintain that Escobar attributes to people in the South his own mistrust of development, a view they may not share. Indeed, some would argue that the intellectual tradition in many Asian universities is to support the state and its policies rather than to criticise them (Rigg, 1997).

The assumptions of anti-developmentalism, while legitimately critiquing the weaknesses and contradictions of mainstream development, cannot realistically be said to provide a significant and viable alternative. This is particularly in the absence of significant evidence that the new social movements have gone beyond voicing valid dissatisfaction against the prevailing system, and effected real change or an alternative to development. In many ways they generally seem to exist only at the micro-level and are difficult to replicate. Indeed, as many observers have noted, the poor of the South simply get on with the business of survival, and holding views on development is a luxury of the privileged.

It can be argued that many poor people in the South are inherently conservative and resent imposed or introduced change of any kind, despite the fact that they are often very innovative and adaptive in their own coping mechanisms and survival strategies.

Corbridge (1995) suggests that anti-developmentalism romanticises and universalises the lifestyles of indigenous peoples. Do the actions of the poor and vulnerable really constitute a resistance to development, or are they simply seeking to manipulate development to improve their access to basic resources and to justice?

Certainly, the anti-developmentalists have reinforced our sense of the local in the face of what appears to be an overwhelming process of globalisation. Indeed, the alleged retreat of the state and return to democracy that have occurred in some parts of the world, have opened up new spaces in which social movements can seize the initiative.

Yet, as Watts and McCarthy (1997: 84) note, 'a central weakness of the social movements-as-alternative approach is precisely that greater claims are made for the movements than the movements themselves seem to offer'. Moreover, what is wrong with social movements having modest, self-centred aims which focus on basic needs if they result in improvements in the quality of life for a group?

Despite the weaknesses of their strategies, the anti-development movement *has* brought about a re-emphasis of the importance of the 'local' in the development process, as well as the important skills and values that exist at this level. It also reminds us what can be achieved at the local level in the face of the 'global steamroller', although few such successes are free of modernist goals or external influences. It has also encouraged a valid critique of the shortcomings and bias of eurocentric and 'top-down' development and of the need to be more objective in the determination of future policy actions and interventions.

The postmodernist stance

Of all the recent changes within developmental thinking, perhaps the most successful and least heralded has been the shift away from large-scale theory to meso-conceptualisations that focus on specific issues or dimensions of development in an attempt not merely to separate out a slice of development for scrutiny, but to see how it relates to the development process as a whole and to local situations. A good illustration of this might be the fusion of gender and shelter debates that has made a strong impact on theory and policy in the 1990s and early 2000s (Chant, 1996; Desai and Potter, 2014).

Some might claim that this illustrates the influence of postmodernism in development studies (Corbridge, 1992), involving a liberation of thought, a recognition of a local 'otherness' and support for small-scale development drawing on local resources, skills and opportunities. However, one could argue that such approaches have been part of development geography for some time, reflecting its empirical traditions. As McGee (1997) points out, the accumulated experiences (histories) of empirical studies are invaluable in bringing out a sense of the local within the development process.

On the other hand, postmodernism has also been interpreted as merely 'the cultural logic of late capitalism, effectively representing the new conservatism . . . preoccupied with commodification, commercialisation and cheap commercial developments' (Potter and Dann, 1994: 99). Under this latter formulation, most of the new meso- and micro-narratives of development thinking have little in common with postmodernism.

Indeed, the rise of post-development is seen as a part of the rise of 'postmodernism' or 'post-structuralism' (see Parfitt, 2002; Simon, 1998). Thus, postmodern theory would deny that if history is examined, a process of progression to 'higher' levels of civilisation can be identified. Rather, postmodernism sees history as a contingent succession of events, so that it is difficult to think in terms of goals – including development goals (Parfitt, 2002).

Following this brief introduction to the links between postmodernism and development, the topic will be pursued in further detail in Chapters 3 and 4.

The focus on poverty

Despite the increasingly sophisticated understanding of what constitutes development and how can it be achieved, and the critique advanced by the anti- and post-development theorists, a very strong anti-poverty discourse emerged in the 1990s. Driven by concern about widespread famine in the 1980s and the recognition that more than a billion people were surviving in a state of desperate poverty (Collier, 2008), strenuous efforts to better understand the response to poverty were initiated.

A focus emerged amongst the global development institutions, on trying to raise the number of people living above the threshold of $1 per day (later raised to $1.25 per day), which was deemed to be global level below which a person was deemed to be living in extreme poverty. The validity of using such a low figure can be debated, relative to the real costs of human existence, the reality of different living costs in different parts of the world and the fact that a money-focused score does not consider other issues such as health, education and employment. Despite this addressing global poverty became a rallying cry for many of the world's countries and, significantly, the United Nations and the World Bank, which, through the Millennium Development Goals introduced in 2000, effectively set in place a new development agenda focused on addressing poverty (Desai and Potter, 2014).

While the morality of a focus on poverty cannot be questioned, issues can, however, be raised about whether a focus on basic welfare, is likely to bring about a change in global power relations and the persistence of fundamental inequalities. Since 2000 the global development discourse clearly shifted from one previously conditioned by precepts of modernisation and achieving basic needs towards a narrower focus on addressing poverty, albeit within the context of the prevailing neo-liberal economic order. From the 1990s, aid extended to many countries in the South became conditional on their drafting and implementing a Poverty Reduction Strategy Paper, which was largely geared to address poverty concerns within the context of market reform (Williams et al., 2014).

Despite the nature of the debate, there is evidence which suggests that global poverty rates are indeed falling – although as we will see this has been contested. Figure 1.9 clearly shows these trends, which show that, with the key exception of Sub-Saharan Africa, global poverty rates are falling.

As time advanced and attention has focused on the true nature of poverty, what drives it and what keeps people in poverty, more sophisticated analyses of poverty have emerged. The Multidimensional Poverty Index (MPI) is one such score which goes beyond purely income measures to consider factors such as access to water and food. According to this score, while the UN (2015a) estimates that there were over 800 million living in extreme poverty using purely economic scores, according to the UNDP (2015) the figure is in fact 1.5 billion. It is estimated that in the worst affected countries (most of them in Africa) over half the population live in multi-dimensional poverty. The score for Ethiopia is 88.2%, 50.9% for Nigeria and 49.5% for Bangladesh (UNDP, 2015).

While having a poverty focus is a logical course of action, we clearly need to ensure that we have a holistic understanding of what poverty is and how to address it. In addition, we need to be wary of over-reliance on income scores alone as indicators of poverty.

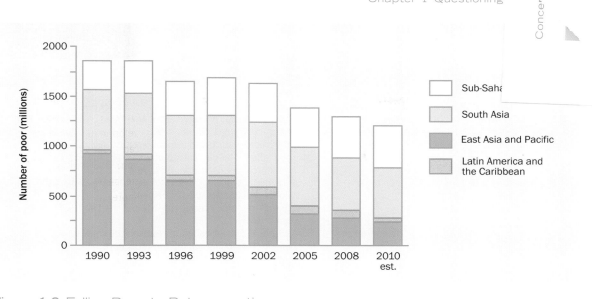

Figure 1.9 Falling Poverty Rates over time
Source: adapted from Dicken, 2015 (based on World Bank, World Development Indicators, 2013).

The Millennium Development Goals (MDGs) and the Sustainable Development Goals (SDGs)

As noted above, since the 1990s a focus on addressing poverty has come to dominate the development discourse, particularly as it is articulated and implemented by global development bodies (Mawdsley et al., 2014). On 18 September 2000, following a protracted negotiation and planning process, 190 world leaders agreed at the United Nations to commit to achieving a set of internationally determined development targets. Known as the Millennium Summit, the UN endorsed the following eight Millennium Development Goals (MDGs) to be achieved by 2015 to:

1 Eradicate Extreme Poverty and Hunger
2 Achieve Universal Primary Education
3 Promote Gender Equality and Empower Women
4 Reduce Child Mortality
5 Improve Maternal Health
6 Combat HIV/AIDS, Malaria and other Diseases
7 Ensure Environmental Sustainability
8 Develop a Global Partnership for Development (UN, 2015b).

The goals each had a set of indicators attached to them (48 in total), e.g. under Goal 6 one of the indicators was to reduce the prevalence of deaths associated with tuberculosis, and many were quantifiable targets, e.g. under goal one to halve the portion of the world suffering from hunger.

The launching of the MDGs was of dramatic significance in terms of global development thinking. The formulation of the MDGs has made addressing development backlogs, and poverty in particular, a global focus of attention. The securing of international support through the UN, most world governments and the international development financing institutions was clearly a significant achievement. Critics of the process, however, point to the reality that the MDGs did not challenge the status quo in terms of the global dominance of capitalism and the unequal economic and power relations in the world, and in a sense, the MDGs maintained the prevailing system (Hickel, 2016).

Key challenges concerning the pursuit of the MDGs related to how they were to be funded. While international donors pledged significant resources, few countries fully delivered on their promises. By 2008, half way through the implementation of the 15-year programme, it was apparent that while progress was being made, achievements were patchy, and many parts of the world, Africa in particular, were lagging,

Table 1.7 The MDG scorecard, 2000–2015

MDG Goal	Key Achievements by 2015
MDG 1 – To eradicate extreme poverty and hunger (and reduce the number of people living in extreme poverty by 50% i.e. under $1.25 per day)	Poverty target achieved: people living in extreme poverty fell by 50% (1.9bn to 836mn). Target of halving undernourishment not achieved.
MDG 2 – To achieve universal primary education	Not achieved but primary school enrolment, has reached 91% from 83% in 2000.
MDG 3 – To promote gender equality and empower women	Two-thirds of countries have achieved gender parity in education. The percentage of women in the non-agricultural workforce has risen from 35% to 41%.
MDG 4 – To reduce child mortality	Child mortality has halved in 25 years but the target of a two-thirds reduction was not attained.
MDG 5 – To improve maternal health	Maternal mortality has fallen 45% but the two-thirds target was not attained.
MDG 6 – To combat HIV/AIDS, malaria and other diseases	AIDS has not been halted or reversed, but new infections have fallen 40%. Malaria infection rates have fallen by 37% and the mortality rate by 58%.
MDG 7 – To ensure environmental sustainability	2.6 bn have gained access to improved drinking water – the target was achieved (but 663mn still do not have access). The release of ozone depleting substances has nearly been eliminated. 2.1bn have gained access to improved sanitation.
MDG 8 – Develop a global partnership for development	ODA (Overseas Development Assistance) from richest nations increased 66% and reached new high of $135bn, but this is less than was initially proposed.

Source: The Guardian, 2015a; UN, 2015b

while significant advances were being made in parts of Asia (Rigg, 2008).

In 2015, when the MDG programme ended, it was apparent that although significant progress had been made, not all the goals had been realised (see Table 1.7). The UN did, however, proclaim that extreme poverty globally had been reduced by 50%, and that one billion people had been lifted out of poverty – with absolute numbers falling from 1.9 billion to 836 million (News 24, 2015; UN, 2015b). This was clearly a very significant achievement which should not be underestimated. Critics, however, have raised concerns about relying on a money-metric measure of poverty and not questioning the relative value of using $1.25 as an indicator compared with the other ways in which poverty exists – e.g. access health, food etc. An additional concern is the fact that, by back-dating the starting date of the MDGs to 1990, the significant socio-economic progress which China made in the 1990s, could be factored in as an achievement (before the MDGs were actually agreed) (Pogge, n.d.; Hickel, 2014, 2016). It is significant to note that, despite the UN's claim, they also acknowledged that Africa and South Asia were experiencing significant challenges in trying to meet the goals (News 24, 2015).

It is apparent that the MDGs, though not fully meeting all of their targets, have impacted significantly on the lives of hundreds of millions of people, and the focus of the MDGs has helped to address some of the core socio-economic needs of the world's poorest people. That said, the MDGs have not striven to promote national development in the modernisation sense, and it would be difficult to argue that the status of the majority of the countries in the South has altered significantly in terms of their global role and place. We also need to be conscious of the stark differences related to where the most gains have been made, compared with where far less progress has come about. Figure 1.10 below indicates global differences in the reduction of extreme poverty. While all regions have improved, it is apparent that Africa has lagged while significant progress has been made in parts of Asia. Unfortunately, the implication is the perpetuation of uneven economic development in the world.

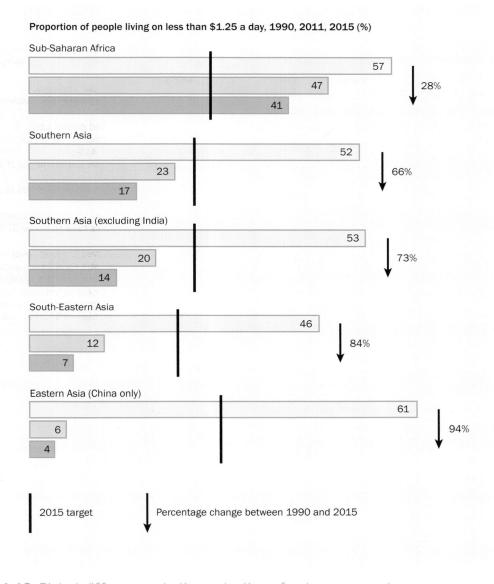

Proportion of people living on less than $1.25 a day, 1990, 2011, 2015 (%)

Sub-Saharan Africa
57
47
41
28%

Southern Asia
52
23
17
66%

Southern Asia (excluding India)
53
20
14
73%

South-Eastern Asia
46
12
7
84%

Eastern Asia (China only)
61
6
4
94%

2015 target   Percentage change between 1990 and 2015

Figure 1.10 Global differences in the reduction of extreme poverty
Source: adapted from UN, 2015b.

Worryingly, when all the Goals are considered, according to Chonghaile (2014), despite not insignificant economic growth in the corresponding time period, only four of the 39 lesser developed countries outside South and SE Asia were on track to meet the goals in 2014, namely Ethiopia, Malawi, Rwanda and Uganda. According to the 'States of Fragility Report' of 2015 (OECD, 2015b), many countries will not be able to eradicate poverty if concentrated efforts to address their fragility are not made now. Fragile countries are states with low incomes and weak state structures. According to the report these trends point to a growing concentration of absolute poverty in fragile countries. Today, the 50 fragile countries and economies monitored by the OECD are home to 43% of people living on less than $1.25 a day; by 2030, the concentration could be 62% of the world's poor in those countries. The report also points out that a serious flaw with the MDGs was the reality that they did not directly address governance, conflict and fragility.

In Fukuda-Parr's (2012) critique of the MDGs, the argument is raised that while they succeeded in making the issue of addressing global poverty an urgent international priority, their narrow focus diverted attention away from broader developmental concerns, not least concerns about equity, empowerment and the impacts of globalisation, liberalisation and privatisation on poor countries. Concerns are also raised that the MDGs conflated development and addressing poverty and they were more of a development 'narrative' than a strategy.

In September 2015, the eight MDGs were formally replaced with the 17 SDGs, the Sustainable Development Goals (set to start from January 2016). In terms of the declaration at the United Nations in New York, world leaders pledged to 'leave no one behind' and to eliminate poverty and inequity, globally by 2030 (Good, 2015). The SDGs are detailed below:

1 End poverty in all forms everywhere. (Eradicate extreme poverty and halve portion in poverty in all its dimensions.)
2 End hunger, achieve food security and improved nutrition and promote sustainable agriculture.
3 Ensure healthy lives and promote well-being for all ages.
4 Ensure inclusive and equitable quality education and promote lifelong learning opportunities for all.
5 Achieve gender equality and empower all women and girls.
6 Ensure availability and sustainable management of water and sanitation for all.
7 Ensure access to affordable, reliable, sustainable and modern energy for all.
8 Promote sustained, inclusive and sustainable economic growth, full and productive employment and decent work for all.
9 Build resilient infrastructure, promote inclusive and sustainable industrialisation and foster innovation.
10 Reduce inequality within and among countries.
11 Make cities and human settlements inclusive, safe, resilient and sustainable.
12 Ensure sustainable consumption and production patterns.
13 Take urgent action to combat climate change and its impacts.
14 Conserve and sustainably use the oceans, seas and marine resources for sustainable development.
15 Protect, restore and promote sustainable use of terrestrial ecosystems. Sustainably manage forest, combat desertification, and halt and reverse land degradation and halt biodiversity loss.
16 Promote peaceful and inclusive societies for sustainable development, provide access to justice for all and build effective, accountable and inclusive institutions at all levels.
17 Strengthen the means of implementation and revitalise the global partnership for sustainable development. (UN, 2015c)

The 17 SDGs and the associated 169 targets will strongly influence the global development agenda from 2016–2030. The SDGs are extremely significant in that their aspirations are more comprehensive than the MDGs, they are anchored in the key consideration of sustainable development and *de facto* they have made 'development' a global concern and not just one affecting the South (Scoones, 2015).

While the SDGs are clearly significant and will shape international understanding and critiques of development theory and practice for the next two decades, they have been questioned. Critiques have argued that the SDGs do not address fundamental differences in the global order, they fail to address issues of human rights adequately, and there are far too many goals and targets for the majority of the world's countries to effectively implement and monitor and the sheer costs of applying them will be prohibitive (Good, 2015; Pogge and Sengupta, 2015). According to *The Economist* (28 March 2015), they will cost $2–3 trillion p.a. to implement, which is equivalent to 15% of global savings and 4% of world GDP (at present the North gives less than 0.7% of its GDP as aid).

Despite these concerns, we need to monitor the application of the SDGs with interest and hope that they do have a meaningful impact on the quality of lives of billions of people.

Progress in development from the 1970s to the 2010s: the unequal world persists

An examination of the information contained in Figures 1.3, 1.4, 1.6 and 1.7 and Tables 1.2 to 1.5 and 1.7 is illuminating regarding the outcomes of applied development. Averaged scores such as income and HDI suggest that slow advances have been made in a wide range of development indices and there is certainly evidence from across the South that over the last 50 years life expectancy and education levels have increased, health care has improved and incomes have gradually risen. This is also suggested by the slow rise in HDI scores since 1990 and in the findings detailed in reports of the United Nations, with respect to the achievement of the MDG interventions (UN, 2015b).

Despite this, as shown in the above-mentioned Tables, staggering differences remain between the countries of the North and South (see Table 1.3 which vividly shows differences in HDI scores between the North and the South; and Tables 1.4 and 1.5 which indicate that, after decades of interventions, many core differences persist between the North and the South).

Hence while development advances have been recorded within countries in the South, the relative global development gap is growing. The income ratios between the North and South have risen consistently since 1820 (see Table 1.8), which raises serious questions about the effectiveness of development interventions and the morality of the growing trend of global inequality which prevails.

Sadly, the 'unequal world' persists, as development advances remain sluggish, tend to privilege the few and not the many, and inequalities between and within countries remain and are growing. This reality should not, however, prevent the continual quest for new and better ways to improve the human condition globally.

From a theoretical perspective, interpretations differ as to where we have reached at this juncture in time with addressing development disparities. While the UN, as we have seen above, argues that significant progress has been made in achieving poverty relief and development targets, other authors question what has actually been achieved. Writers such as Hickel (2016) and Pogge (n.d.) have questioned the reliability of the statistics on which these assertions are based, and the reality that the original goals set for the MDGs were diluted and back-dated to allow for socio-economic developments in China to be factored into the goals. As a result, they question whether any real changes have been made in terms of addressing extreme poverty and nutritional deficiencies in the poorest parts of the world.

For Hickel (2016), claims of development success further entrench the current global system and persistent inequalities. Meanwhile Pogge and Sengupta (2014) argue the need to reform the global development institutions and address the trade and economic barriers which restrict the potential of the South.

For Andrews and Bawa (2014), the concept of development has become vague and imprecise and needs to be reformulated. They argue that:

> development's survival depends to a large extent on how the paradigms (including theories, approaches and methodologies) is able to adapt and reinvent itself to the changing times . . . being more open to alternatives that are context-specific and more in tune with the socio-cultural dynamics of the people development targets.
>
> (Andrews and Bawa, 2014: 933)

Table 1.8 Income ratios between the richest and poorest countries, 1820–2013

Year	Income of richest 20% divided by the income of the poorest 20%
1820	3:1
1913	11:1
1960	30:1
1970	32:1
1980	45:1
1990	59:1
2000	70:1
2013	80:1

Source: Fik, 2000; Hickel, 2014; Seitz, 2000; UNDP, 1998

New determinants of development in the early 21st century

As our review has clearly indicated, 'development' is not a static concept, its interpretation and application have evolved significantly over time, being influenced by global forces, applied outcomes and theoretical advances. The early beliefs in modernisation and the pursuit of the western model have all been abandoned in the face of patent failure, the need for more situationally relevant interventions and the reality of the development impasse and neo-liberalisation of development.

We recognise that development is not constant, but rather is continually evolving, and it is apparent that a range of evolving global issues will impact on development and how it is conceptualised and applied.

One of the most significant of these forces is the rise of key countries in the South, as global role players and supporters of South–South development assistance and aid. The role of the BRICS countries (Brazil, Russia, India, China and South Africa) (which are discussed in greater depth in Chapter 8) as new development actors and new leaders in the global economy has been the subject of considerable research (Chen, 2014). The formation of the BRICS Development Bank, though still in its infancy, could herald a gradual realignment in global politics and the pursuit and support of the 'developmental state' model in preference to the western neo-liberal one (Chin, 2014). The 'development state' is one in which a government takes more directed action over the management of the economy and development than is the case in the neo-liberal state (see also Chapter 7).

The key role which the state plays in many of the BRICS and SE Asian countries is a clear point of difference from the western model and is an approach which has long merited the interest and attention of many countries in the South, which have come to question the impact that neo-liberalism has had on their economies. The exploration and pursuit of the concept of a more interventionist or 'developmental state' in Latin America and South Africa marks an active effort to respond to the failures of neo-liberalism and previous development intervention, but empowering states to play a greater role in development process. The institution of mass state welfare in countries such as Brazil and Argentina,

and the role that the South African state is seeking to play in its economy, may well herald new insights into alternate ways to strive for development (Grugel and Riggirozzi, 2012).

Challenges imposed by neo-liberalism, particularly with respect to the causes and consequences of the 2008 Global Financial Crisis, have encouraged new debates about a future 'post-neo-liberalism'. This is reflected at one level in the rise of popular resistance, as expressed in opposition to capitalism and growing inequality, as evidenced by growing popular protest and movements such as the Occupy Movement and the Arab Spring (see below). At another level, particularly in Latin America, in countries such as Bolivia, Ecuador and Argentina, left-wing victories have encouraged thinking about 'neo-developmentalism', linked to the notion of the development state. There has been a reaction to what is deemed as excessive marketisation, leading to the formation of pacts between states, labour and business and the state playing a stronger role in the economy, in poverty alleviation, the management of exports and the enhancement of citizenship rights (Felix, 2012). Some regard this as a new social contract in Latin America within the confines of the market economy. Dependent on how successful these initiatives are, as with BRICS, new actors may well transform how development is perceived and mark a break from the traditional western model.

Other key factors which are shaping the development discourse include the defined impact which climate change is already having and will continue to have in the world. Rising sea-levels in the Pacific, growing flood risks in Bangladesh and looming food shortages in Africa are some of the more immediate concerns. These considerations will shape funding priorities and human well-being (Desai and Potter, 2014).

A term which is gaining significant attention in the social sciences is 'resilience'. Borrowed from the natural sciences, where it is used to examine the capacity of natural systems to return to their original state after shocks are experienced, its use is becoming more widespread in the social sciences. In terms of development in particular, it plays a role in helping to provide an understanding of how societies respond to crises and their capacity to change and adapt. The concept will probably have increasing value in the study of conflict and post-conflict scenarios and as a response mechanism to natural disasters which are likely to become more frequent with global warming (Radcliffe, 2015).

A worrying trend is the 'development fatigue' which seems to characterise many countries in the North. Hickel (2014) and other critics note that many in the North see the South as a 'bottomless' pit, with limited progress achieved causing a loss of popular interest in the plight of 'distant others' in the South. Some countries such as Finland has cut their aid budgets, while hardly any countries in the North have met the commitments that they made in the early 1990s to increase aid. The result, according to Hickel (2014) have been efforts by agencies such as Oxfam and the Bill and Melinda Gates Foundation to try and re-popularise development through stressing partnerships, self-reliance and identification between donors and potential recipients of aid.

To a certain degree 'development fatigue' can be linked to the 2008 Global Financial Crisis which impacted on all countries in the North. In many countries in the North financial austerity has reduced aid budgets and global commitments, while in the South reduced manufacturing output and sales have negatively impacted on employment, government resources and local development capacity (Dicken, 2015).

One of the more demonstrable changes in the nature of democratic and social processes has been the increasing role which social movements are playing in the world. Given the reality that millions of people feel cut-off from the benefits of growth, as a result of globalisation, skewed development and growing inequality, it is unsurprising that there has been significant growth in popular protests globally. The widespread protests associated with the Arab Spring risings throughout the Middle East and North Africa and the Occupy Movement protests of 2011 symbolise both the sense of disenfranchisement felt by millions of people and the degree to which people are demanding a 'better' and more equitable world, politically, economically and socially (Williams et al., 2014). Popular movements including global alliances of the peasantry such as *Via Campesina,* and national groups such as the Homeless Peoples' Movement in South Africa are indicative of rising frustration and popular mobilisation. While the actions of such groups are often ignored by ruling elites, increasingly local political protests do influence considerations such as the payments for water services in Peru and student fees in South Africa.

Reviewing development

So, what are we left with after all this discussion of the nature of development? For the anti-developmentalists, development has become 'an amoeba-like concept, shapeless but ineradicable [which] spreads everywhere because it connotes the best of intentions [creating] a common ground in which right and left, elites and grass-roots fight their battles' (Sachs, 1992: 4). To some critical commentators, the anti-development alternative of 'cosmopolitan localism' based on regeneration, unilateral self-restraint and a dialogue of civilisations unfortunately seems no more than a utopia for New Age travellers.

Despite its eighteenth- and nineteenth-century origins, 'development has never been a scientific concept, it has always been ideology' (Friedmann, 1992: v) – quite simply, development is always political. Thus, development can mean all things to all people; poor squatters are highly likely to have a completely different view of what constitutes change for the better in their lifestyle as opposed to a senior politician or national planner, a theme elaborated in Chapter 3.

This is clearly evident in discussions of the so-called 'brown agenda', in which Satterthwaite (1997) and others have pointed out that many of the concerns of the international agencies and national planners with global warming and ozone layers reflect a 'Northern' agenda that is far away from the clean water needed by most squatter households. As Hettne (1995: 2) notes, 'there can be no fixed and final definition of development, only suggestions of what development should imply in particular contexts'.

The debates over the definition of what development is and how people think about it are not simply academic, although for some this is the limit of their interest. Thoughts and views about the development condition underlie policy formulation and subsequent implementation and impact on the lives of billions of people.

Development is an historical process of change which occurs over a very long period but it can be, and usually is, manipulated by human agency. It is often forgotten that culture (particularly religion) can play an important role in characterising national and local development strategies. Many of the industrialising states in Asia claim to have followed an 'Asian way' to development, although this in itself has been criticised for its reductionism and selectivity (Rigg, 1997). It is the nature of these manipulations and the associated goals that will be discussed in Chapter 3.

However, what we have now established is that development is not unidirectional, nor is it without fault, neither have its proponents achieved all their stated goals since development was first attempted at the international level in the 1940s. Improvement in the human condition has many different dimensions and the speed of change may vary enormously for any individual or community. While fair and balanced development may be a desirable goal, for most of the world's population it is far from being attainable (Friedmann, 1992). It is to the characterisation of this proportion of the world's population that this chapter now turns.

Spatialising development: the Third World/Developing World/ Global South/Poor Countries

The terms that have most commonly been employed to refer to spatial contrasts in types of development, different levels of development and different patterns of development are examined in this section, along with other terms that have come to be employed alongside it, or instead of it.

Specifically, the evolution of the term *Third World* will be traced, along with its proponents, its critics and the alternatives they have posed, such as the *Global South* (which is now the most widely accepted term, and the one preferred in this text), the *Developing World* and *Poor Nations* (Dodds, 2008).

Almost inevitably there will be a degree of overlap with the first half of this chapter, since in many ways we are examining the public lexicon concerning the more theoretical issues which were discussed previously. Indeed, the wider currency that the terms *development* and *underdevelopment* allegedly experienced as a result of President Truman's inaugural address of 1949 (Esteva, 1992; Sachs, 1992) was to a certain extent clarified by the new 'three world' terminology that was also emerging at the same time.

Thus, the First World was promoting 'western' development, the Second World (i.e. the socialist world) was

opposing it, and the Third World was the express object of the exercise. In the rigidities and absurdities of Cold War politics from the 1950s this seemed to make good sense to at least some. However, over the years the association between the notion of three worlds and the development process has changed considerably. It will be useful to examine this association within a broad chronological framework.

The emergence of the 'Third World' in the 1950s and 1960s

As with *development*, the antecedents of the term 'Third World' go back beyond 1949, although not much further. Moreover, in contrast to the current largely economic interpretation of the Third World (Milner-Smith and Potter, 1995), particularly in terms of poverty, the origins of the term were political, largely centring around the search for a 'third force' or 'third way' as an alternative to the Communist–Fascist extremes that dominated Europe in the 1930s.

In the Cold War politics of the immediate post-war years, this notion of a third way was revived initially by the French Left, which was seeking a non-aligned path between Moscow and Washington (Pletsch, 1981; Wolfe-Phillips, 1987; Worsley, 1979).

It is this concept of non-alignment that was seized upon by the newly independent states in the 1950s, led in particular by India, Yugoslavia and Egypt, and culminating in the first major conference of non-aligned nations held in Bandung in Indonesia in 1955. Indeed, at one point 'Bandungia' appeared to be a possibility for their collective title. Friedmann (1992: iii) claims that as a result of this meeting 'the Third World was an invention of the non-western world', in spirit if not etymologically.

The sociologist Peter Worsley (1964) played a major role in the popularisation of the term Third World, principally via his book under this title. For Worsley the term was essentially political, labelling a group of nations with a colonial heritage from which they had recently escaped, and to which they had no desire to return within the ambit of new forms of colonialism, or 'neo-colonialism'.

Nation building was therefore at the heart of the project, and it is no coincidence that the loudest voices came from those states with the most charismatic leaders.

For India, Yugoslavia and Egypt, therefore, read Nehru, Tito and Nasser.

But the emerging Third World in the 1950s was not quite the same as it is today; many countries had still to gain their independence and Latin American countries were not present in Bandung. Moreover, both the Bandung group and Worsley's Third World 'excluded the communist countries' (Worsley, 1964: ix).

Nevertheless, for a while in the 1950s and 1960s, this Afro-Asian bloc did attempt to pursue a middle way in international relations. In economic terms, however, it was a different story. Almost all newly independent states lacked the capital to sustain their inherited colonial economies, let alone expand or diversify, remaining reliant on Western markets and investors. Most remained trapped in the production of one or two primary commodities, often for their former colonial masters, the prices of which were steadily falling in real terms, and they were unable to expand or improve infrastructure and their human resources.

Once Worsley had identified the common political origins of the Third World in anti-colonialism and non-alignment, he cemented this collectively through the assertion that its current bond was poverty (Plate 1.4). The same feature had also been noted by Keith Buchanan (1964) in the first substantial geographical contribution to the debate. Buchanan's diagrammatic representation of the

Third World, shown here as Figure 1.11, bears a close resemblance to that of the Brandt Commission 20 years later, but makes somewhat more geographical sense.

In particular, Buchanan's diagram is helpful in showing the population size of countries. Hence, the overwhelming contribution of the populations of China and India within the Third World is one of the most prominent features of the map.

The 1960s witnessed a major shift in interest on the part of several social science disciplines towards the nature of development and underdevelopment, prompted largely by the failure of modernisation strategies to bring predicted growth to what was increasingly becoming called the Third World.

It is important to note, however, that in the 'West', much of this economic debate was predicated on deeper political concerns: the fear that widespread and persistent poverty would lead to insurrection and a further round of Communist coups. In Asia, the puppet regimes of South Vietnam and South Korea were looking somewhat shaky, whereas the continuing strength of Castro's revolution in Cuba raised fears of a Caribbean domino effect and the spread of communism.

The principal concern, particularly among development economists, was to find out what had gone wrong and where the problems were located. In geography this

Plate 1.4 People making a living by a variety of means, Old Delhi
(*photo*: Rob Potter)

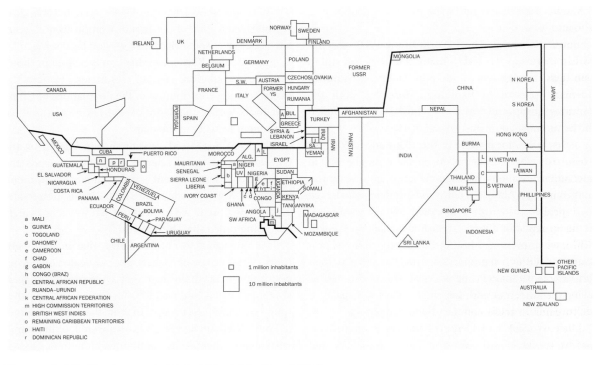

Figure 1.11 Buchanan's Third World in the 1950s
Source: Adapted from Buchanan (1964)

was the era of the 'quantitative revolution' with its focus on the search for scientific and objective truth derived from the careful analysis of statistical data. From both disciplines there arose a series of measurements designed to rank Third World nations in terms of needs with the usual signifier being Gross National Product (GNP) per capita (see earlier discussion).

Within some of the individual states, 'modernisation surfaces' were drawn which indicated spatially uneven development by means of depicting the presence (or absence) of multiple indices of development 'attributes' (schools, hospitals, roads, street lighting, etc.), most of which closely mirrored the spatial imprint of colonialism itself (Gould, 1970; Soja, 1968).

Despite the largely uninformative nature of these academic developments, the term *Third World* was by this stage in widespread use, even by its constituent states in forums such as the United Nations (Wolfe-Phillips, 1987). Conceptually, therefore, by this juncture, the world was firmly divided into three clusters, namely the West, the Communist bloc and the Third World, but the terms being used were etymologically inconsistent.

The first is an abstract geographical term (west of where?), the second is a political epithet, and the last is numerical – hardly an example of consistent logic, but one which had by the 1970s obtained a significant measure of popular acceptance.

The 1970s: critiques of the concept of the Third World

By the early 1970s, the rather loose combination of political and economic features that constituted the Third World had already come in for criticism. The French Socialist Debray (1974: 35) argued that it was a term imposed from without rather than within, although more developing nations were beginning to use it.

Anti-developmentalists consider the 1970s to be a critical point in the development process, a time when the Third World was beginning to recognise its own underdevelopment and adopting Western evaluations of its own condition.

Many other critics, however, also felt the term was derogatory since it implied that developing countries occupied a third place in the hierarchy of the three worlds (Merriam, 1988). An even more valid criticism was that users of the term had still failed to situate the socialist developing states in the three-world terminology.

The main cause of the doubts that emerged during the 1970s was related to the growing political and economic fragmentation of the Third World as it 'postmodernised' from a 'meta-region' into a plethora of sub-groupings.

Ironically, perhaps the biggest impetus to the breakup of the group of 77 non-aligned nations came from within, when the Organization of Petroleum Exporting Countries (OPEC) nations raised the price of their oil massively in 1973–74, with a second wave in 1979 following the fundamentalist revolution in Iran. Associated wealth gains in these countries, lying primarily in the Middle East and North Africa, created, on certain development scores, significant differences between OPEC countries as the rest of the Third World.

Initially conceived as a political weapon against the West for its support of Israel, the price rise had a much greater effect on the non-oil-producing countries of the developing world, many of which were following oil-led industrial and transport development programmes. The result was a widening income gap between different developing countries.

This was further reinforced by the New International Division of Labour (NIDL) in the 1970s, in which capital investment via multinational corporations and financial institutions poured out of Europe and North America in search of industrial investment opportunities in developing countries. The NIDL refers to the situation from the 1970s when, in an effort to reduce production costs, particularly after the oil price hikes, rising wage demands in the West and improvements in global transport and reduced trade barriers, a significant proportion of world industrial production came to be sourced from the countries of the developing world and SE Asia in particular.

Most of this overseas investment was highly selective, and 'cheap labour' alone was not sufficient to attract investment: good infrastructure, an educated and adaptable workforce, local investment funds, docile trade unions were also important factors.

The outcome, of course, was that investment focused on a handful of developing countries (specifically, SE Asian states such as Taiwan, South Korea and Hong Kong, plus Mexico and Brazil) where GNP per capita began to rise rapidly, further stretching relative economic and social contrasts within the Third World. This relative 'global shift' is the subject of detailed attention in Chapter 4.

The widening differences began to exercise academic minds. Journals such as *Area* and *Third World Quarterly* published articles about the merits and demerits of the term 'Third World' as a descriptive concept (Auty, 1979; Mountjoy, 1976; O'Connor, 1976; Worsley, 1979).

The debate soon spread to some of the 'serious' journals of the popular press, where various ways of regrouping the developed and developing countries were suggested. For example, *Newsweek* identified four worlds; the Third World comprised those developing countries with significant economic potential and the Fourth World consisted of the 'hardship cases'.

Not to be outdone, *Time* magazine subsequently put forward a five-world classification in which the Third World contained those states with important natural resources, the Fourth World were the newly industrialising countries (NICs) and the Fifth World comprised what were clearly regarded as the 'basket cases'.

Many academics joined in this semantic debate. Goldthorpe (in Worsley, 1979) produced a list of nine worlds; at the lower end of which came 'the better-off poor', 'the middling poor', 'the poor' and 'the poorest' – indefinable refinements of poverty that were of little conceptual value and even less comfort to those under such scrutiny. To cause even greater confusion, the term 'Fourth World' was also coming into general use to describe underdeveloped regions within developed nations, particularly where this referred to the exploitation of indigenous peoples, as in the cases of the Canadian Inuit or Australian Aborigines (see the special edition of *Antipode* 13(1) in 1981).

The changes were reflected to a certain extent in the classification system employed by the World Bank in its annual Development Reports. In the early 1980s, the developed countries were classified by their dominant mode of industrial production. Thus, the socialist states of Eastern Europe and the former Soviet Union were politically identified as 'centrally planned'. The non-oil-exporting developing countries were divided on the basis of wealth into low- and middle-income states.

Subsequently, following the apparently worldwide demise of socialism, the classification has regressed to an entirely income-based one. After 30 years of constant criticism, GNP per capita still ruled as a development indicator with the World Bank.

The 1980s: the 'lost decade' for development in the Third World and the emergence of the 'Global South'

Despite the regression at the World Bank to an economically based stratification of the Third World, the 1980s in general saw considerable widening of the scores on a range of indicators used for classifying the various nations of the developing world, and soon they were being amalgamated into composite indices of well-being or quality of life as previously reviewed in this chapter. However, such indices did little to address the debate on the concept of the Third World per se.

Nevertheless, during the 1980s a growing critique of the term began to emerge from the new right-wing development strategists, who argued that the Third World is merely the result of Western guilt about colonialism, a guilt which is exploited by the developing countries through the politics of aid.

Economist Lord Bauer (1975: 87), one of the leading exponents of this view, expressed it like this: 'The Third World [is] the collection of countries whose governments, with the odd exception, demand and receive foreign aid from the West . . . the Third World is the creation of foreign aid; without foreign aid there is no Third World.'

In the eyes of the New Right, virtually all developing countries were tainted with socialism and their groupings have invariably been anti-Western and therefore anti-capitalist, a view which has effectively been taken to task by John Toye (1987). Ironically, many Marxists also found it difficult to accept the term 'Third World' because they regarded the majority of its constituent countries as underdeveloped capitalist states and fundamentally linked to advanced capitalism.

Thus, in the eyes of Marxists, there were only two worlds, those of capitalism and Marxian socialism, with Marxian socialism being subordinate to capitalism. There was little agreement among Marxists as to what constituted the socialist Third World.

The notion of two worlds perhaps represented the most concerted challenge to the three-world viewpoint and, indeed, most of the semantic alternatives that we currently use are structured around this dichotomy, namely rich and poor, developed and underdeveloped (or less developed), North and South. Indeed, this perspective leads to dualism, a concept which is reviewed in Chapter 3.

The notion of a two-world division received a significant boost in the 1980s following the works of the Brandt Commission (1980). Chancellor Brandt, of what was then West Germany, chaired the work of the Independent Commission for International Development Issues. The widely publicised report which resulted from their work, sought ways to reduce economic disparities between the rich 'North' and the developing 'South'. In the report the world was divided into two parts – the North and the South using the 'Brandt line' which was an economic measure based on GNP per capita to separate the wealthy from the less wealthy countries (see Figure 1.1).

Despite the economic origins of the term, the incongruent reality that Australia and New Zealand, which lie in the southern half of the world are included in the 'North', and several high income countries in Asia are excluded which make the distinction flawed, the distinction enjoys considerable acceptance. More correctly referred to as the 'Global North' and 'Global South', these terms are now widely used to help us appreciate the core economic, welfare and development differences in the world (Singer, 1980; Potter and Lloyd-Evans, 2008).

Some critics have claimed that this two-fold division is spatial reductionism of the worst kind, apparently undertaken specifically to divide the world into a wealthy, developed top half and a poor, underdeveloped bottom half – North and South, 'them' and 'us' – although the terms did no more than rename pre-existing spatial concepts (see Figure 1.1).

Despite its acceptance as a descriptive tool, one problem with the North–South division of the Brandt Report was that it lacked explanatory power and compares unfavourably with another dichotomous model that also became popular in the 1980s. This is the core and periphery model (Wallerstein, 1979). The Brandt line does not allow for, or explain, the immense variety that exists both in the core and periphery, nor does it incorporate change over time, whether growth or decline.

In order to accommodate this, a semi-periphery was introduced; this is a category of countries allegedly incorporating features of both the periphery and the core. The core, semi-periphery and periphery classification of the world is also shown in Figure 1.1. The outcome is referred to as the 'world systems approach' (for a summary see Klak, 2008), which is fully reviewed in Chapter 3.

Effectively, the semi-periphery gives us another division of the world into three sections, but although apparently based on very different principles from those identified earlier, the various components are still bound together by the overarching operations of capitalism. The detailed and accurate map of core, semi-periphery and periphery after the 1990s, following the break-up of the former Soviet Union, clearly looks quite different over much of Central Asia and Eastern Europe (Klak, 2008).

As the 1980s wore on, however, the old Truman goal of development based on the Western capitalist model began to fade. The finishing line had in any case been moving away from most in the South faster than they were moving towards it.

The unified social and economic objectives of the second *United Nations Development Decade* (the 1970s) began to look limp in the face of worsening world recession and a harder attitude towards a set of nations that were now being looked upon as a drag on world development through their incessant demand for aid and their growing debt defaulting.

The dualism of North and South thus took on a much harsher complexion as the World Bank, the IMF and the regional banks began to impose what are referred to as 'structural adjustment programmes' (SAPs) on the Third World. SAPs are economic austerity packages that were made conditional on countries wanting financial loans and aid. Such programmes are examined in greater detail in Chapters 3 and 7, and were imposed on countries in the South which had defaulted on their loans to Western Banks in the 1980s (see also Simon, 2008). Similarly to the situation in Greece and other Mediterranean countries after the more recent Global Financial Crisis (GFC), the IMF delayed debt repayments and gave loans conditional on countries following economic austerity programmes.

Universalism and convergence?

The growing confusion over whether the world should be divided into two or three components, both in conceptual and policy terms, was further accentuated in the 1980s by a feeling among some commentators that the original universalism of the United Nations had somehow been lost and that we should return to thinking of the world as a single entity.

Allan Merriam (1988) notes that views on the unity of humanity are long established, and he cites the seventeenth-century Czech educator Comenius, who stated that 'we are all citizens of one world, we are all of the same blood . . . let us have but one end in view, the welfare of humanity'. Such sentiments have featured frequently in the speeches of some Third World leaders, such as Indira Gandhi and Julius Nyerere, although often as rhetoric rather than reality.

Much of this growth in one-worldism was sustained by a belief that development in the Third World is characterised by a *convergence* along those paths experienced by the West towards the current lifestyles and political–economic structure of developed countries (Armstrong and McGee, 1985; Potter, 1990, 2008a).

For many, the thought of such convergence is alarming, since pursuit of the same economic ends by the same means will simply lead to a faster use of the Earth's finite resources and will only exacerbate its environmental problems. However, many of these concerns spring from self-interest in that ultimately it is the Western way of life that may be threatened. The people of the Third World are therefore being asked to make sacrifices 'for the greater good of humankind', sacrifices that those in the West have never made.

Sachs (1992) sees the convergence theories of the ecologists as yet another example of universalism, perpetuating the single goal, single strategy of the Truman doctrine and denying any role or opportunity for diversity. He claims that the 'one world or no world' warnings of environmental scientists suggest that preservation of our fragile global ecosystem demands that everyone has a responsible and specific role to play. 'Can one imagine a more powerful motive for forcing the world into line than that of saving the planet?' he asks (Sachs, 1992: 103).

Under such a view, as the Third World poor have been conveniently found to be the worst offenders in resource destruction, so their re-education could usefully be combined with scaled-down poverty reduction programmes through 'sustainable development'. The West can now give less aid and still feel good about it! However, perhaps the basic premise of this concern is unfounded. There may be convergence towards the Western model, but this is very selective and uneven – an issue which is fully addressed in Chapter 4.

Moreover, even the high-flyers among the NICs still have a long way to go to match the levels of economic and social well-being attained in the West. Although attention in recent years has focused on these growing contrasts within the South itself, it has also masked the more important fact that global contrasts too are continuing to widen.

In particular, there has been much concern that a large number of countries, particularly in Africa, have not only failed to exhibit any significant signs of development, saddled as they now are with spiralling debts and occupying a dependent position in the global economy.

In this context, convergence theory could be seen as a myth. Indeed, it is arrogant to assume that the process of economic and cultural transfer is one-way. The West has not merely exported capitalism to the developing world, capitalism itself was built up from resources transferred to the West from those same countries.

Similarly, acculturation is not simply the spread of Gucci and McDonald's around the world. In almost every developed country, clothes, music and cuisine, together with many other aspects of day-to-day living, are permeated with influences from Asia, Africa, Latin America and the Caribbean, such as bamboo furniture, curries and reggae music.

The Third World/Global South since the 1990s

The extension of the world recession into the 1990s and the 2008 Global Financial Crisis (GFC) meant that fragmentation of interests has continued, and weaker communities at both the local and the global levels have faced increasing difficulties.

One response to this was the emergence of regional economic blocs in the image of the European Union, such as NAFTA (North Atlantic Free Trade Agreement) and APEC (Asia-Pacific Economic Cooperation), and various regional trading agreements in Africa and Latin America, all of which were designed to protect their member states and which sometimes cut across the traditional boundaries of the three worlds.

Of course, the three-world conceptualisation suffered an even greater blow from the effective demise of the Second World with the break-up of the Soviet Empire after the fall of the Berlin Wall in 1989 and the, admittedly uneven, democratisation and capitalisation of Eastern Europe.

If the Second World no longer exists, can there be a Third World? In this etymological sense, there is little justification for retaining the term, particularly since the early commonality of non-alignment and poverty has also long been fragmented.

Many commentators in the 1990s, particularly those who form part of the anti-development school, suggested that it is time for the term Third World to be abandoned. Sachs (1992: 3) forcefully, stated that, 'the scrapyard of history now awaits the category "Third World" to be dumped'. Corbridge (1986: 112) too joined 'with others in questioning the current validity of the term the Third World'. Friedmann (1992) also rejected the term in favour of a focus on people rather than places, preferring to identify and build policy around the disempowered. And yet, despite such strong condemnation, the term persists in common usage, even by some of those who have criticised its overall validity.

Critical reflection

Different worlds – different words?

How do you view the term 'Third World' – do you use it? If not, when you are talking about poorer countries within the world context, how do you refer to such nations? As we have seen, people use a very wide array of terms, including 'Developing Countries', 'Less Economically Developed Countries' ('LEDCs'), 'Underdeveloped Countries', the 'Global South', 'Poor Countries', 'Former Colonies', etc.

What do you regard as the merits and limitations of each of these descriptors? Might it be better to always refer to broad continental divisions, thereby suggesting that African, Asian, Latin American and Caribbean countries should be seen as possessing their own distinct characteristics, and that these outweigh any broad commonality?

Despite the variations in the nature of the Third World that we have noted in this section, most people in most developing countries continue to live in grinding poverty with little real chance of escape. This is the unity that binds the diversity of the casual labourer in India, the squatter resident in Soweto or the street hawker in Lima. All are victims of the unequal distribution of resources that the world exhibits.

Moreover, this unity is not merely one of pattern or distribution, but of fundamental processes that are linked to the past, present and probable future roles of these states within the world economy, as exploited suppliers of resources – human as well as physical. It is these countries that have faced structural adjustment programmes, and now are the focus of poverty reduction strategies. It is among these countries that the debt crisis and massive levels of poverty and preventable death loom large.

Further, it still holds true that there is a unity provided by colonisation, decolonisation and antipathy, but a lack of resistance to imperialism (socialist as well as capitalist), something noted by Mao Tse Tung, Peter Worsley and John Toye. The same sort of view gives rise to the argument that 'the Third World is **SIC**', that is it is the outcome of the forces of **S**lavery, **I**mperialism and **C**olonialism.

Given the persistence of inequality in the world – between countries with high and low levels of human development and the redundant nature of the concept of the Third World, a more realistic, but still flawed, concept to employ is that of the 'Global South', the origins of which were explained above, to distinguish countries in Latin America, the Caribbean, Africa, the Middle East, Asia and the Pacific, which in general terms score lower on a range of developmental, welfare and economic indices than the countries which were identified as being the 'Global North'. While acknowledging the above-mentioned challenges with the concept outlined above, and the reality that some countries, such as Singapore, are ill-placed to be considered as part of the South, this dual classification of North and South has merit in helping avoid the econometric classification of the World Bank and still allows us, within reason, to identify the parts of the world

Plate 1.5 Rebuilding efforts in Kathmandu following the 2015 earthquake
(*photo*: Lola Odessey Waters)

which are the focus of development attention. This book, while acknowledging the shortcomings of the terms North and South, employs them as the most appropriate terms currently available.

No matter what abstract conceptualisations are used to structure development debates – three worlds, two worlds, the South, nation states, cities or whatever – we must not forget that we are discussing human beings and their livelihoods. Their welfare and how to improve it must be the focus for our debates, rather than the sterile question of what label is politically correct. In addition, there is vulnerability to natural disasters (see Plate 1.5) which we always need to be conscious of because of the impact these have on populations and the need to incorporate disaster responses into development planning.

Rich and poor worlds: relative poverty and inequalities at the global scale

The salience of inequalities and relative poverty

Descriptive phrases and terms such as the 'Third World' are just that: they are descriptors of ongoing dynamic processes of change. Viewed in this light, it is unrealistic to expect any one term to describe the global pattern of development over time.

This book focuses attention on the processes of development and underdevelopment, wherever they occur, be it in the former colonial world, poor regions in former colonial powers, in what has in the past been referred to as the Third World, or the Global South today.

But at the same time, as recognised above, some commentators emphasise that the real commonality between the countries that we study is their relative poverty. They are the countries that are generally poorer than other nations. It is worth recalling Worsley's (1979) identification of the commonalities of Third World countries in terms of their historic colonial domination, non-alignment and poverty. But per capita income

levels, literacy levels and educational enrolment still represent major dimensions in the United Nations Human Development Index.

Indeed, the argument that inequalities within society are more important than the overall average level of income or wealth is a telling one. It can be argued that the gap between the rich worlds and the poor worlds is most significant in determining the kind of world in which we live. Indeed, it has been argued that one of the greatest development challenges currently facing the world, as a whole, has been growing socio-economic inequality both within and between countries. Following the GFC, the support which countries in the North generally provided to shore up their financial and banking systems, was often at the expense of support for low income earners, manufacturing workers and those on the margins of the housing market, particularly in the USA. The OECD (2014) has noted, that in almost all countries in the North social inequalities have grown significantly, with an escalation in the fortunes of the wealthy and a squeeze on the middle class. The IMF has noted the growing gap between countries and within the South. In China, the wealthiest 1% now control 30% of the country's wealth, and as identified earlier, half of the world's wealth is now held by just 1% of the world's population (IMF, 2015).

While there is evidence to suggest that extreme poverty is falling around the world, the gap between the rich and the poor countries is clearly growing, as Table 1.8 has vividly shown. According to the United Nations, the number of people living in extreme poverty (less than $1.25 per day) has fallen from 36% of the world's population in 1990 to 15% in 2011 (UN, 2015a). While such advances are to be welcomed, many of those people, whose income has crossed the questionable score of $1.25 still live below $2.50 per day and remain in 'relative poverty'. Hence we need to be cautious about how we 'measure' development, and whether slight increases in average income scores indicate widespread income improvements, or perhaps only marginal change and, perhaps worse still, whether the gains of the few have in fact weighted up the averages.

Once more we are reaching the same general conclusions regarding the current nature and disposition of global development patterns as we did in the last major section on trends from 1970. While progress is being made in certain regions, and in particular respects, there remains an enormous amount to do if gross inequalities are to be meaningfully reduced.

Development and anti-development are extremely important concepts, for they exist in a global context where differences in wealth, opportunity and choice appear to be widening (diverging) at their extremes, rather than narrowing (converging). Thus, while some poorer nations are showing enhanced incomes in relation to the rich nations of the West, the majority are continuing to fall yet further behind.

The politico-strategic salience of this widening gap seems likely to increase in the future. Talking in the aftermath of the events of 11 September 2001, Bill Clinton (in *The Richard Dimbleby Lecture*, 2001) argued that 'we in the wealthy countries have to spread the benefits of the twenty-first century world and reduce the risks so we can make more partners and fewer terrorists in the future' (Clinton, 2001: 2).

In the same speech, Clinton attributed the events of 11 September to increased liberalisation and globalisation: 'we have built a world where we tore down barriers, collapsed distances and spread information. And the UK and America have benefited richly' (Clinton, 2001: 2) (see also Potter, 2003).

But, in addressing what he regards as the burdens of the twenty-first century, Clinton observed that over half the world's people are excluded from the benefits of the new global economy, and he cogently asks, 'what kind of economy leaves half the people behind?' (Clinton, 2001: 3).

Concluding issues: geography and development

Terry McGee (1997) has drawn attention to some of the implications of the shifts into postmodern development, particularly those that emphasise globalisation as 'a variable geometry of production or consumption, labour, capital management and information – a geometry that denies the specific meaning of place outside its position in a network whose shape changes relentlessly' (Castells, in McGee, 1997: 8).

For some time since Alvin Toffler's *Future Shock* (1970), commentators have been arguing for the 'end of geography'. Toffler himself based his arguments on increased flows of people, goods and information that serve to dissolve difference and distinctions. Apart from geographical differences still being very evident in the world (Chapter 4), Toffler also ignored the fact that linkages and flows between places are largely the province of the geographer. Similarly, Richard O'Brien (1991) also claimed an end to geography on the basis that location matters much less for economic development than it has done in the past.

Although the recent development of technologies does 'challenge conventional notions of distance, boundaries and movement . . . geography matters . . . because global relations construct unevenness in their wake *and* operate through the pattern of uneven development laid down' (Allen and Hamnett, 1995: 235). It is, however, important that we recognise that these unequal relations have been in existence for many decades, and as global inequalities have grown, as shown in Table 1.8 (and Plate 1.5), it is increasingly difficult for countries in the South to escape from the situation of dependence into which they are locked (Hickel, 2015).

Thus, the choice for new investment is often conditioned by the facilities and resources that are already in a region, thus perpetuating inequalities. Not surprisingly, therefore, many would argue (Massey and Jess, 1995) that place is more fundamental than ever, since the realities of development within the South are represented by an unevenness and by a constantly shifting fusion and conflict between the global and local, usually filtered through national or regional agency. Our review of current development patterns and global inequalities in the last section has shown as much.

Thus, it is appropriate to emphasise in this opening chapter that the relationships between the realities of development and geography remain very strong. If development is regarded as the improvement of lives and opportunities, then the challenge is generally about improving the situation for billions across large swathes of the globe.

Indeed, Potter (1993a, 2001a, 2002a) has argued that questions of development have been generally neglected in the academic discipline of geography, in the sense of faraway places and peoples receiving a surprisingly small share of the attention of academic geographers, relative to their salience in the world at large.

In general, a disproportionate amount of attention is focused on the European and North American realms. Potter (2001a) argues that an increasing responsibility to what may be described as 'distant geographies' is urgently required. This concept is an embellishment of the more general 'responsibility to distant others' or 'distant strangers' (see Smith, 1994, 2008).

The issue of our responsibility to distant others basically asks how likely we are to be beneficient to people who are worse off than ourselves, but who live far away. Beneficence is the process of 'active kindness', and may be distinguished from benevolence, which involves charitable feelings and the desire to do good (Smith, 2002).

The central question posed, therefore, is 'how spatially extensive beneficence can be justified by moral argument, given what might appear to be the natural human tendency to favour our nearest and dearest over more needy strangers farther away' (Smith, 2000: 132).

In many ways, this moral issue is at the heart of the complex relations that exist between contemporary geography and development. The rapidly ongoing processes of globalisation make this pressure much more intense than in the past (see Chapter 4 on this). For greater responsibility to be shown to the global poor in particular, a greater commitment to the mobilisation of resources at the international level is required (Smith, 2000). Thus, the issue underpins giving to charitable foundations and the provision of aid at the global level.

It is true that at one level the processes of globalisation are creating super-regions, such as the European Union, NAFTA and APEC, all with varying degrees of cohesion, together with their global and regional mega-cities, such as Paris, London or Tokyo.

But at other levels and in other localities in the interstices of the global network, neglect, ignorance and even resistance combine to produce patterns of development that are strongly geared to place and history, and which must be studied as such in order for development to be fully understood (Chapter 4).

What constitutes the heart of this approach is that geographical investigation is rooted in an empiricism that focuses on the interaction of society and environment, on networks and flows of people and goods, on uneven and unequal development and, most important in these contexts, on the nature of local places.

All of these factors, according to McGee (1997), place development geography firmly in the humanist tradition. What needs to happen now is for the local not only to become the object of the exercise, but also the medium, with local input into the development process itself. Only in this way will our preconceived ideologies or images of development be changed (Massey, 1995).

As this chapter has shown what is conceptualised as constituting 'development', and how it is measured and applied, has evolved significantly over time and, no doubt, will continue to do so into the future. It is apparent that development, as it was originally conceived was never fully realised, and while there clearly has been progress in a range of key socio-economic scores globally, much of the South has yet to fully realise its human and economic potential. This is a reality made all the more difficult by the prevailing economic system in the world and the role which much of the South plays within that system.

Key points

> Development is a frequently used word in all sorts of contexts. In the arena of socio-economic change, it implies efforts to improve the lives of people around the world.

> Early ideas on development stemmed from the Enlightenment period and were then allied with concepts of westernisation and modernity and neo-classical economic thinking in the post-1947 period. Over time, our understanding of what development is has evolved to reflect theoretical advances and applied challenges.

> Early on, development was measured with respect to quantitative economic indicators, principally Gross National Product (GNP) and Gross Domestic Product (GDP). Increasingly now, the Human Development Index (HDI) stresses a wider set of dimensions and commentators talk about development in more qualitative terms, including 'development as freedom'.

Key points (continued)

- Since the 1990s, alternative and populist stances and sustainability concerns have represented a re-conceptualisation of the meaning of development.
- The concept of the Third World has its origins in the global geopolitics of the post-Second World War period. Many other terms, such as Developing Countries, Underdeveloped Countries, Less Economically Developed Countries, Poor Nations and the Global South are now used.
- Statistics show that overall the world as a whole is showing signs of development and improving conditions – and this is taken as the evidence of continued development by those who believe in the so-called 'development mission'.
- However, data show all too clearly that global inequalities have continued to widen considerably over the past 40–50 years. It is circumstances such as this that are cited by anti-developmentalists.
- The Millennium Development Goals 2000–2015 represented a global agenda to address development issues. But progress since 2000 emphasises that much remains to be done and much is expected of the Sustainable Development Goals.

Further reading

Black, R. and White, H. (2004) *Targeting Development: Critical Perspectives on the Millennium Development Goals.* London and New York: Routledge. Provides an overview of issues relating to the Millennium Development Goals.

Collier, P. (2008) *The Bottom Billion.* Oxford: Oxford University Press. An insightful study of the very real development challenges faced by millions of people in the world.

Department for International Development (2000) *Eliminating World Poverty: Making Globalisation Work for the Poor.* Cmnd 5006. London: The Stationery Office. Worth reading as a strong template for the argument that globalisation is the way forward in delivering countries from poverty.

Desai, V. and Potter, R.B. (eds) (2014) *The Companion to Development Studies,* 3rd edn. London and New York: Routledge. An accessible source that brings together short, 2,000-word summaries of important facets of the interdisciplinary field of development studies.

Escobar, A. (1995) *Encountering Development.* Princeton, NJ: Princeton University Press. A well-cited critical review of the development mission.

Gasper, D. (2004) *The Ethics of Development.* Edinburgh: Edinburgh University Press. An interesting overview of ethical aspects of development theory and practice.

Greig, A., Hulme, D. and Turner, M. (2007) *Challenging Global Inequality: Development Theory and Practice in the 21st Century.* Basingstoke: Palgrave Macmillan. Stresses global poverty and inequality in reviewing contemporary development theory and practice.

Kothari, U. (ed) (2005) *A Radical History of Development Studies: Individuals, Institutions and Ideologies.* Cape Town: David Phillip; London and New York: Zed Books. An interesting set of specially commissioned chapters that consider the nature and development of development studies.

Simon, D. (ed) (2005) *Fifty Key Thinkers on Development.* London and New York: Routledge. A useful source which brings together short essays on those who are deemed to have had a noticeable impact on studies of development.

Williams, G., Meth, P. and Willis, K. (2014) *Geographies of Developing Areas.* London: Routledge. A very readable overview on what development is and the key processes which influence it.

Websites

www.un.org/millenniumgoals/
A useful site which provided access to salient documents like the Millennium Development Goals Report 2015.

http://www.un.org/sustainabledevelopment/
This site contains information overviewing the SDGs, their targets and related initiatives.

www.undp.org

Site of the United Nations Development Programme (UNDP) giving direct access to the United Nations Human Development Reports.

www.dfid.gov.uk

The website of the Department for International Development (DFID) of the UK Government. Provides details of, and access to, DFID publications.

www.eldis.org

Described as the gateway to development information, providing access by subject area and country, plus news, etc.

Discussion topics

➤ Examine the argument that development should be about reducing 'unfreedoms' rather than promoting economic development.

➤ Elaborate the view that measures of relative development must include non-economic variables.

➤ Assess the current applicability of the assertion that the 'Third World' exists whatever we choose to call it.

➤ Have the MDGs succeeded? What hope for success are there for the SDGs?

➤ To what extent is it helpful to think in terms of poor countries rather than developing nations?

Chapter 2
Understanding colonialism

This chapter examines the development and demise of colonialism and its impacts in the Global South. After considering definitions of colonialism and imperialism, the issue of post-colonialism is critically reviewed. With reference to case study material, three phases of colonialism are then discussed: mercantile colonialism, industrial colonialism and late colonialism. This is followed by an examination of the process of decolonisation and a consideration of some of the most significant legacies of colonialism.

This chapter:

➤ Examines different perceptions of colonialism and imperialism;
➤ Reviews the debate about post-colonialism and the effects of colonisation on local people;
➤ Considers the key features of the three phases of colonialism;
➤ Examines the increasing pressure for independence and the process of decolonisation;
➤ Assesses some of the beneficial and detrimental aspects of colonialism;
➤ Evaluates the concepts of a New International Division of Labour and a New International Economic Order.

Introduction: colonialism and imperialism

The literature on colonialism is as plentiful, and at times as opaque, as the literature on development. There is an unfortunate tendency to equate colonialism with the expansion of capitalism in the nineteenth and twentieth centuries, implying that it primarily comprises an economic process. Clearly, there is an essential, and at times overwhelming, economic impetus to colonialism, but to construct a framework of analysis based on such a simple equation would be unhelpful. Colonialism is essentially a political process, and the establishment of colonies long pre-dates the genesis and subsequent globalisation of modern European capitalism. Right through this period, colonies were acquired for motives other than the economic imperative for material resources, labour or markets. As in Roman times, otherwise barren or unpromising territory was annexed for strategic reasons: to protect the periphery of pre-existing colonies, to control important military routes or simply to prevent the expansion of rival European powers. Although some of these lands eventually proved to have some economic value, the original motivation was often quite different.

Much of the development literature conceptualises the global expansion of capitalism as imperialism rather than colonialism, although even here there is a debate about when this process began (see Key idea, Colonialism and imperialism). For some neo-Marxists, imperialism begins with the division of Africa at the Treaty of Berlin in 1885, reinforced by the assertion that the term *imperialism* was first coined in the nineteenth century by Napoleon III. Most, however, believe that imperialism began in the late fifteenth and early sixteenth centuries with the rise to prominence of the European nation state, although the commercial underpinning to the feudal system had also stimulated some colonialism before this period (Blaut, 1993).

At some point in the eighteenth or nineteenth century, depending on whom you read, development itself becomes an identifiable process in its own right, underpinning and fusing with imperialism and the expansion of capitalism (Dixon and Heffernan, 1991) (see Chapter 1). Throughout this period, colonies continued to be founded for a variety of complex motives and in many different forms. The particular nature of colonialism varied not only with the motives, but also with contemporary political economies and cultures of both the metropolitan power and colonised territory (Box 2.1). Indeed, in recent years there has been a tendency to define colonialism as much by the means it employed as by the impetus behind it. Thus 'colonialism is often defined as a system of government which seeks to defend an unequal system of commodity exchange' (Corbridge, 1993a: 177), whereas Said (1979, 1993) maintains that colonialism existed in order to impose the superiority of the European way of life on that of the Oriental, a colonisation of minds and bodies as much as of space and economies and 'much harder to transcend or throw off' (Corbridge, 1993a: 178).

Key idea

Colonialism and imperialism

Colonialism and imperialism are not interchangeable ideas, although they overlap considerably. Anthony King (1976: 324), in the index of his seminal text on colonial urbanisation, states simply, 'see colonialism' under the entry for imperialism. Consequently, his definition of colonialism is only partial: 'the establishment and maintenance for an extended time, of rule over an alien people that is separate and subordinate to the ruling power'. The concept of one state establishing political control over another is a recurring theme in definitions of colonialism, for example, 'the policy or practice of acquiring political control over another country, occupying it with settlers, and exploiting it economically' (*Concise Oxford Dictionary*, 1999: 282).

Blauner (quoted in Wolpe, 1975: 231) is more comprehensive than King in his approach, defining colonialism as, 'the establishment of domination of a geographically extended political unit, most often inhabited by people of a different race and culture, where this domination is political and economic and the colony exists subordinated to and dependent on the mother country'. However, once again the specific mode of domination and exploitation is left unidentified and, as with so many analyses of colonialism, the focus is on internal processes at the expense of outward linkages.

A useful working definition of imperialism is, 'a policy of extending a country's power and influence through colonization, use of military force, or other means' (*Concise Oxford Dictionary*, 1999: 711). But there are some serious inconsistencies in the various uses of the term 'imperialism'. One of the most obvious is that the term is employed in two distinct ways: 'a technical sense – to define the latest stage in the evolution of capitalism – and a colloquial sense – to describe the relationships between metropolitan countries and underdeveloped countries' (Bell, 1980: 49). These need not be incompatible, although difficulties of reconciliation between the two approaches have certainly led to contradictions in the chronology of imperialism. Marxist (Leninist) analysts believe that this monopoly stage of capitalism only began around the start of the twentieth century, at least that is what Bell (1980) argues. Barratt-Brown (1974), on the other hand, has extended consideration of imperialism to roughly the last 400 years.

Key idea (continued)

Barratt-Brown's chronology is preferable, largely because it permits a broader definition of imperialism to be used, referring to 'both formal colonies and privileged positions in markets, protected sources of materials and extended opportunities for profitable employment of labour'

(Barratt-Brown, 1974: 22). This permits us to examine the way in which the expansion of imperialism affected, and was affected by, the parallel colonisation process in the Americas, Asia and Africa from the early sixteenth century to the decolonisation phases of the 1950s and 1960s.

BOX 2.1

Politics, society and trade in pre-colonial sub-Saharan Africa

Before the arrival of European traders from the sixteenth century onwards, there were many substantial and sophisticated communities throughout Asia, Africa and Latin America. Although we must recognise the achievements of these societies, given the distorted picture communicated by early European trader-colonists (Blaut, 1993), we must not romanticise 'traditional' societies. Many such societies were not repositories of simple communism and were probably challenging environments for most of their inhabitants, with a substantial slave trade in which indigenous chiefs willingly participated. Slavery was widespread before the contact with Europeans. As Hopkins observes in West Africa, 'Slaves were employed as domestic servants, they acted as carriers, they maintained oases and cut rock salt from the desert, they laboured to build towns, construct roads and clear paths, they were drafted as front line troops, and they were common in all types of agricultural work' (Hopkins, 1973: 24). Change was sometimes for the better. In sub-Saharan Africa, the 'traditional' indigenous crops, sorghum and millet, were nutritionally inferior to the manioc (cassava) and maize introduced from the Americas by European traders. According to Iliffe, 'In moist savanna regions maize produces nearly twice as many calories per hectare as millet and 50 per cent more than sorghum. Cassava produces 150 per cent more calories than maize and is less vulnerable to drought' (Iliffe, 1995: 138).

Organisationally, many societies in the immediate pre-European period were (semi-) subsistent, but this did not preclude trade or the emergence of large, powerful states. At various times in pre-colonial West Africa a series of empires and kingdoms existed, for example, Ghana, Mali, Songhai in the savanna–Sahel region, and Ashanti, Oyo and Benin in the forest region. Much of the power and wealth of these states was based on a flourishing north–south trade in commodities such as gold, ivory and kola nuts from the forest region, salt from the Sahara, and manufactured goods from Europe and north Africa. Busy trade routes developed across the Sahara, linking the north African coast and Europe with sub-Saharan Africa. Certain West African towns grew rapidly as a result of this profitable commerce, most notably Djenné (now in Mali), founded in the ninth century, Gao (Mali) and Kano (Nigeria), all dating from the late tenth century, and Zaria (Nigeria) and Timbuctu (Mali) founded in the eleventh century. Timbuctu became an important religious and educational centre with the first university in West Africa, while Kano, now in northern Nigeria, had some 75,000 inhabitants by the sixteenth century (Binns, 1994a).

Essentially, these societies were structured on two levels. At the local level was a patriarchal agrarian community, where land was allocated and used on a more or less equitable basis and in which the redistribution of surplus took place on a social rather than a market basis. Reciprocity and obligation brought status. At the elite level, status was inherited

▶

or was enhanced by wealth accumulated by raids, confiscation or conquest outside the community. Trade in valuable items such as gold or salt was dominated by a small group of elites. Pre-European, pre-capitalist societies were therefore ravaged by constant wars, fought on behalf of the elites in order to control the production or trade of valuable items or to control people. Before the arrival of European capitalism, life was not comfortable for most Africans. Unfortunately, it did not change for the better with the arrival of the market economy and the ensuing revaluation of commodities.

Perceptions of the non-European world

This myriad of possibilities does not mean to say that some common ground cannot be discerned or that broad phases of colonial development cannot be identified. Indeed, in order to make some sense of the colonial discourse, we need a framework within which we can address it, identify its principal processes and set out the legacies that persist within current society, in both the Global North and South. Preston (1996: 140) has identified several dimensions to what he terms 'the process of absorption and reconstruction of other peoples' (Figure 2.1). However, he does not elaborate on the links between parallel processes and suggests a rather simplistic sequence of ways in which Europeans represented the non-European world: first as exotic cultural equals, then as representatives of innocence and noble savagery during the Age of Enlightenment, subsequently as the 'uncivilised savages' of the nineteenth century who had to be controlled, then improved and eventually guided to independence. Although this sequence is not untrue, it suggests a set of ideologies that were uniform over space and through time. The reality was, of course, very different, particularly over the long period from the early sixteenth to the early nineteenth century. The Enlightenment, as we noted in Chapter 1, is a period in which the concept of development and the role of the 'enlightened' within this was crystallised. The romantic notion of the 'noble savage' was applied rather sparingly during this period and was very much influenced by the nature of the non-European society encountered. Even Cook on the same journey around the Pacific could both admire the Polynesians and despise Australian Aborigines according to a particular set of British values.

'Waves' of colonialism

The chronological sequence suggested by Preston, despite its oversimplicity, presents an approach that has been used by many other analysts of colonialism, especially by world system advocates such as Wallerstein (1979). Taylor (1985), in particular, has set out very clearly a sequence of waves or phases in which imperialism and colonialism combine to produce a series of long and short waves or cycles of development. The long waves coincide with major economic systems: feudalism, mercantilism and industrial capitalism. The shorter waves, often termed 'Kondratieff waves' after their founder, are said to fit into the long waves in roughly 50-year cycles. All the waves are characterised by phases of growth and stagnation; during the stagnation phases economic restructuring occurs in order to re-establish economic strength. Such restructuring can involve one or more of a variety of actions, from the development of new technologies, through social change to new sources of raw materials or cheap labour. It is alleged that the acquisition of colonies formed part of this restructuring process by giving access to materials, food and labour. The long waves of mercantilism and industrial colonialism can be seen, therefore, to coincide with the rise and fall of major cycles of colonialism (Figure 2.2).

Despite its rigidity, the chronological sequences of world system theory do present a useful framework from which to examine phases of colonial–imperial development and within which the legitimating ideologies, material base and machineries of control and order may be examined. However, as many writers have noted (Kabbani, 1986; Said, 1993), the narratives from which we draw our material to interpret or read colonialism are themselves subject to deeply embedded

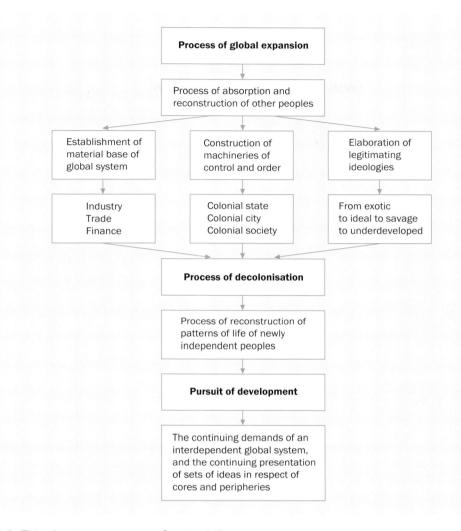

Figure 2.1 Principal processes of colonialism
Source: Adapted from Preston (1996)

prejudices that have found expression in both development thinking and development practice, albeit varying
through time (Key idea, Post-colonialism). In similar
fashion, we need to be cognisant of the fact that the
power exercised within colonialism is not homogeneous; it is often diffuse, fragmented, local and, above
all, highly personalised.

In this account, *colonialism* is used to refer to the
period from the beginning of the sixteenth century
onwards in which economic and political motivations
fused together to give spatial expression to the accelerating globalisation of capitalism. The phases of

colonialism identified in Figure 2.3 were common to
most parts of the non-European world, but the
chronology, rationale and reactions involved varied
enormously. In Clapham's (1985: 13) words, there
were 'the Americas, both rich and easy to control;
Asia, rich but difficult to control; and Africa, for the
most part poor and so scarcely worth controlling'.
Latin America and sub-Saharan Africa therefore
experienced more intensive plundering activities than
either Asia or North America, but during very different historical periods (Figure 2.4). Indeed, most of
both North and South America passed through these

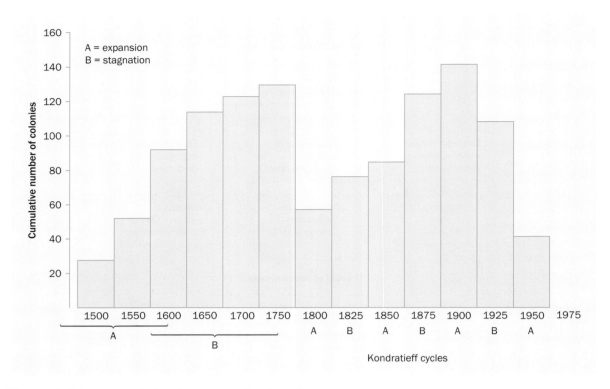

Figure 2.2 Long and short waves of colonialism
Source: adapted from *Political Geography*, Taylor, P., Pearson Education Ltd © 1985

phases into independence, and in the case of South America into neo-colonialism, before the intensive phase of the colonial project began in Asia or Africa. In most of sub-Saharan Africa, formal colonies were a relatively short-lived political process, lasting only around 80 years from the 1880s to the 1960s, although exploitation was present before and after this period. The phases identified here are therefore indicative rather than definitive of the major changes that occurred in the expansion of colonial capital.

Key idea

Post-colonialism

As Balagangadhara and Keppens suggest, 'Like all massive and significant social processes (revolutions, fascism, war, etc.), colonisation too is complex. It involved not only the colonizing of land and resources, subjugating peoples and their traditions, but also the colonizing of their experience and imagination' (Balagangadhara and Keppens, 2009: 60). In the last three decades there has been much debate across the humanities and social sciences about the nature of colonialism and the perceptions of both the colonisers and those who have been colonised. Much of the debate has surrounded what are referred to as 'post-colonial' perspectives or 'post-colonialism', which is concerned with the effects of the process of colonisation on cultures and societies. These terms are confusing and contested, since in one sense they refer to the post-colonial period, which was 'after' the period of decolonisation and the winning of independence, but in another sense, since the 1980s, they have been more widely used to refer to the political, linguistic and cultural experience of societies that were former

Key idea (continued)

European colonies (Ashcroft et al., 1998). McEwan suggests five possible meanings of post-colonialism, as 'after-colonialism', as a 'condition', as a 'metaphysical, ethical and political theory', as a 'literary theory', and as 'anti-colonialism, critiquing all forms of colonial power' (McEwan, 2009: 17). Writers on post-colonialism, who adopt a broadly anti-colonial standpoint, critique the popular discourses relating to the period of European colonialism, which they argue are 'unconsciously ethnocentric, rooted in European cultures and reflective of a dominant Western worldview' (McEwan, 2002: 127).

Post-colonial studies attempt to dissect the many attributes of the colonial experience, '(revealing) the historical and geographical diversity of colonialism and the need to ground such critiques in material and specific contexts' (Blunt and Wills, 2000: 170). Importantly, post-colonial studies attempt to appreciate the viewpoints and empathise with those who were marginalised and oppressed.

It has been suggested that Mahatma Gandhi, in playing such a key role in winning independence for India in 1947, has 'a valid claim to be called the Father of the Postcolonial World', but Trivedi argues that post-colonial studies actually give very little attention to Gandhi, 'in stark contrast with the place that Gandhi occupies in the histories of India' (Trivedi, 2011: 522).

'Subaltern' studies

The Subaltern Studies Group (SSG) or Subaltern Studies Collective (SSC) of scholars emerged in India in the 1980s and were concerned with providing new perspectives on the history and colonial experience of India and South Asia. Ranajit Guha's book *Elementary Aspects of Peasant Insurgency in Colonial India*, (Guha, 1983) was considered to be a classic, and inspired others to join the Group. Gayatri Spivak, a US-based Indian literary critic and a key figure in post-colonial studies, later published an influential essay titled 'Can the subaltern speak?' Spivak refers to marginalised and oppressed people as 'subalterns', 'men and women among the illiterate peasantry, the

tribals, the lowest strata of the urban subproletariat' (Spivak, 1993), for example, lower caste Indian women under British colonial rule. 'Subaltern' is a military term relating to lower ranking officers in the British army, below the rank of captain (McEwan, 2009). Spivak argues that histories of the colonial period, and accounts of the modern world, are usually written by powerful people, invariably men, and the voices of the 'subalterns' are rarely heard or even wilfully ignored. Spivak has played a key role in the SSG in gathering together a group of Indian historians who aim to write critical histories of South Asia, 'which followed the traditions neither of imperialist histories of conquest, nor of nationalist histories that charted a singular and linear development of nationalist consciousness. Subaltern histories have focused on the lives, agency and resistance of those people who had been silenced and erased from both imperialist and nationalist accounts of the past' (Blunt and Wills, 2000: 190). As Ranajit Guha comments, 'The historiography of Indian nationalism has for a long time been dominated by elitism – colonialist elitism and bourgeois-nationalist elitism . . . sharing the prejudice that the making of the Indian nation was exclusively or predominantly an elite achievement' (Guha, 1982: 1).

Edward Said: East and West

Born into a wealthy Palestinian family in Jerusalem, the literary critic Edward Said subsequently moved to the USA where he became Professor of English and Comparative Literature at Columbia University, New York. Probably his most well-known book is *Orientalism*, first published in 1978, and which is 'commonly regarded as the catalyst and reference point for postcolonialism' (Gandhi, 1998: 64). Said's book, which examines how the West imagined the East (the Orient), has a strong cultural focus and is concerned with understandings and images. He argues that, 'to speak of Orientalism therefore is to speak mainly, although not exclusively, of a British and French cultural enterprise, a project whose dimensions take in . . . disparate realms' (Said, 1978: 4). Said

▶

Key idea (continued)

shows how Western ideas about the world as a whole are still informed by ideas that were widespread during the colonial period, and he considers how visual and textual representations can shape knowledge about a place, and condition behaviour in relation to that place. Said believes that the West was able to manage the East as colonial, dependent territory because 'orientals' were seen as being in need of Western guidance and guardianship. As he says,

Neither imperialism nor colonialism is a simple act of accumulation and acquisition. Both are supported and perhaps even impelled by impressive ideological formations which include notions that certain territories and people require and beseech domination, as well as forms of knowledge affiliated with that domination.

(Said, 1993: 8)

Said is concerned with the views of both the coloniser and the colonised, and how dichotomies developed and were perpetuated, for example, if the East was static then the West was dynamic; if the East was savage, then the West was civilised; if the East was despotic, then the West was enlightened. Summing up the significance of Said's contribution, McEwan comments, 'The importance of Said's discussion of Orientalism lies in its exposure of the subtle and persistent Eurocentric prejudice against Arab-Islamic peoples and their culture, and of the links between false images in western culture and its colonial and imperial ambitions' (McEwan, 2009: 63).

Homi Bhabha: hybridity, mimicry and ambivalence

Another writer, Homi Bhabha, in his influential book, *The Location of Culture* (1994), is concerned with the place of colonised people in these discourses. His work is complex, but in essence he deals with three concepts: hybridity, mimicry and ambivalence.

➤ Hybridity is concerned with the fact that Europeans who took their culture with them to the colonies had their beliefs, values and practices affected by the culture of the indigenous people who they

encountered and vice versa. The end product of the cultural encounter, Bhabha suggests, is neither a fixed and pure European identity, nor a pre-existing Asian, African or Latin American identity.

➤ Linked to hybridity is the practice of mimicry, where the British and the Indians, Africans and others, adopted aspects of each other's cultures. For example, the colonial encounter between the Indians and the English led to influential Indians emulating the British upper classes with their European clothing, Christianity, private education and sports such as cricket and polo, while Britons acquired a desire to eat Indian food, to build extravagant Indian-style homes, such as Brighton's Royal Pavilion (Plate 2.1), and terms such as bazaar, bungalow, jungle and jodhpur became part of the English vocabulary.

➤ Ambivalence is reflected in the way that colonial discourse was grounded in an innate assumption of European control and superiority, while at the same time resting on somewhat insecure foundations and anxiety. In relation to individual colonisers there was disgust about the savagery and backwardness of those being colonised, while at the same time a desire to be more like the colonised and to have sex with them (Bhabha, 1994).

As Blunt and Wills suggest,

Rather than represent the colonized subject as simply either complicit or opposed to the colonizer, Bhabha suggests the coexistence of complicity and resistance. The hegemonic authority of colonial power is made uncertain and unstable because the ambivalent relationships between colonizers and colonized are complex and contradictory.

(Blunt and Wills, 2000: 187)

Post-colonial geographies

During the 1990s, much interest developed in so-called 'post-colonial geographies'. As Livingstone has suggested, 'Geography was the science of imperialism par excellence' . . . [because] exploration, topographic and social survey,

Key idea (continued)

cartographic representation, and regional inventory . . . were entirely suited to the colonial project' (Livingstone, 1993: 160, 170). From its foundation in 1830, the Royal Geographical Society played an important role in shedding light on the 'dark continent' by supporting and reporting on major expeditions to Africa (Plate 2.2). As Binns comments, '[this] fascination with distant and different peoples and environments, together with a burning desire to expand the British Empire and develop world trade (often under the guise of eradicating slavery and spreading the gospel), were the driving forces behind many expeditions' (Binns, 1995a: 310). A strong justification for enhancing the position of geographical education in schools in the late nineteenth century was to educate young people about the Empire. As a leading geographer of the time, Halford Mackinder, wrote, 'We should aim at educating the citizens of the many parts of the British Empire to sympathize with one another and to understand Imperial problems by teaching geography visually, not only from the point of view of the Homeland, but also of the Empire' (Mackinder, 1911–12: 86, quoted in Binns, 1995a). In 1906, the journal *The Geographical Teacher*, aimed at informing school teachers about new developments in geography, contained a fascinating, yet somewhat arrogant and jingoistic, report on recent impressions of northern Nigeria by Louis La Chard.

Perhaps in no part of our world-wide Empire has that indefatigable energy and cheerful indifference to depressing circumstances, so characteristic of the Anglo-Saxon race, been better displayed than in the various colonies and protectorates which form our West African possessions. In the very face of disease and death the white pioneer has marched forward and has built, almost in defiance of nature herself, a firm and comparatively healthy basis for the construction of the western cornerstone of our Empire in the Dark Continent.
(La Chard, 1906: 191, quoted in Binns, 1995a)

Plate 2.1 Brighton Royal Pavilion
Source: Tony Binns

Key idea (continued)

More recently there has been a call for 'critical, contextual histories of geography that examine the culture of imperialism' (Driver, 1992). Meanwhile, there is also concern from geographers and others that perspectives and writing about the colonial experience have been strongly gendered, 'embodied in exclusively masculine terms of virility and bravery' (Blunt and Wills, 2000: 196), with little attention given to the voices of women. Those women who did travel overseas encountered what today might be regarded as sexist and patronising advice in early travel books about the importance of the appearance and behaviour of the traveller herself (Blunt, 1994). As Driver suggests, 'contemporary writings on geography were infused with assumptions about gender, as well as empire' (Driver, 1992: 28).

Post-colonialism has undoubtedly been an important and thought-provoking perspective on the colonial experience, not least because 'It demonstrates how the production of Western knowledge forms is inseparable from the exercise of Western power. It also attempts to loosen the power of Western knowledge

TENTS

FOR THE COLONIES.

Fitted with VERANDAH, BATHROOM, &c.

As used by most eminent Travellers, and supplied to H.M. Government for East, West, Central, and South Africa, &c.

SPECIAL TENTS FOR EXPLORERS & MOUNTAINEERING

COMPLETE EQUIPMENT.

CAMP FURNITURE WITH LATEST IMPROVEMENTS. AIR AND WATERTIGHT TRUNKS. UNIFORMS AND CLOTHING OF ALL KINDS.

Plate 2.2 Tents for the colonies
Source: Allen (1979).

Key idea (continued)

and reassert the value of alternative experiences and ways of knowing' (McEwan, 2002: 130). The works of Bhabha, Said and Spivak are complex and not always easy to follow. Some would criticise their lack of clarity and their need to explain the relevance of their ideas to current grassroots situations of poverty and inequality by drawing upon empirical evidence. As Dirlik comments, 'Contemporary postcolonial criticism, whatever its virtues, is also an elite affair, an expression of cultural conflict and contention within a global elite; former colonials who are integrated into the system no longer have any interest in criticism of the system of which they are part, but rather assert their new-found power through varieties of cultural nationalism' (Dirlik, 2002: 439).

Meanwhile, Marxists would argue that post-colonialism has too strong a focus on culture at the expense of class, while others would even question the appropriateness of the term 'post-colonial' when the world continues to experience other forms of colonialism.

Phases of colonialism

Mercantile colonialism

The predominant features of this first phase of colonialism were commerce and trade, although in the earliest stages of contact in sixteenth century Latin America it was plunder and conquest which motivated the conquistadors. Within North America and the Caribbean, trade and commerce were underpinned by production within the plantation system using slave labour (see Chapter 3).

In Africa, and more especially Asia, the initial contact was structured much more around commodity exchange. In this early period, the impact of mercantile colonialism was determined by a variety of factors, including the type of European involvement, the nature of the commodities sought by the Europeans and the strength, culture and organisation of the non-European state.

The plantation system and slave labour

The plantation system and the massive demand for slave labour had a very significant impact on economy and society in Africa and the Americas from the late sixteenth and seventeenth centuries. The plantation system originated in the offshore islands of West Africa during the fifteenth and sixteenth centuries. It was from the Canary Islands that the Spanish took the system to the Caribbean, and from the Cape Verde Islands and the island of São Tomé in the Gulf of Guinea that the Portuguese introduced it into Brazil.

During the seventeenth century, intense competition between the Dutch, English and French in the Caribbean region, and the growing popularity of sugar in Europe, led to a massive demand for labour to work the plantations, resulting in the development of the slave trade between West Africa and the Americas. A decree issued by Louis XIV of France in 1670 read, 'There is nothing which contributes more to the development of the colonies and the cultivation of their soil than the laborious toil of the Negroes'. Whereas before 1600, an estimated 900,000 slaves had been taken from West Africa to the Americas, in the seventeenth century this trade, initially led by the Dutch, increased to 2.75 million, and in the eighteenth and nineteenth centuries rose further to a massive 7 million and 4 million, respectively (Oliver and Fage, 1966).

The most important sugar producers in the eighteenth century were Jamaica, a British possession, and St Domingo, which belonged to France. It was estimated that by 1688, Jamaica alone needed an annual input of 10,000 slaves. Many slaves did not survive the crossing from West Africa. It has been estimated that between 1630 and 1803 the average Dutch voyage killed 14.8 per cent of the slaves, mainly from diseases such as smallpox, dysentery and scurvy (Iliffe, 1995).

The organisation of the slave trade was entrusted by the British to the Company of Royal Adventurers in 1663, which was replaced in 1672 by the Royal African Company. The monopoly of the French slave trade was at first assigned to the French West India Company in 1664 and then transferred in 1673 to the Senegal

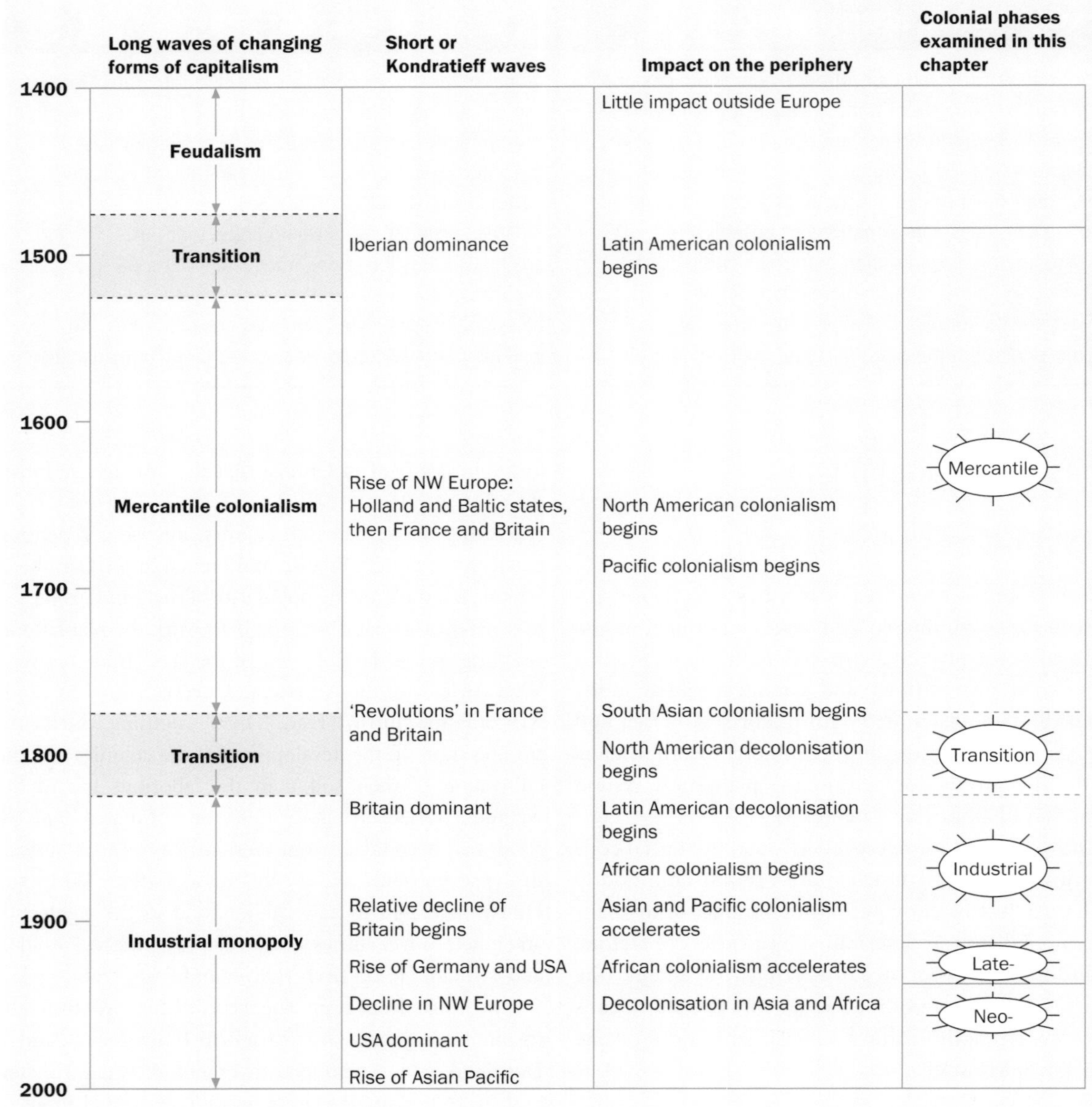

Long waves of changing forms of capitalism	Short or Kondratieff waves	Impact on the periphery	Colonial phases examined in this chapter
1400		Little impact outside Europe	
Feudalism			
1500 **Transition**	Iberian dominance	Latin American colonialism begins	
1600			Mercantile
Mercantile colonialism	Rise of NW Europe: Holland and Baltic states, then France and Britain	North American colonialism begins	
1700		Pacific colonialism begins	
	'Revolutions' in France and Britain	South Asian colonialism begins	
1800 **Transition**		North American decolonisation begins	Transition
	Britain dominant	Latin American decolonisation begins	
		African colonialism begins	Industrial
1900	Relative decline of Britain begins	Asian and Pacific colonialism accelerates	
Industrial monopoly	Rise of Germany and USA	African colonialism accelerates	Late-
	Decline in NW Europe	Decolonisation in Asia and Africa	Neo-
	USA dominant		
2000	Rise of Asian Pacific		

Figure 2.3 Phases of colonialism and imperialism

Source: adapted from *Political Geography*, Taylor, P., Pearson Education Ltd © 1985, and Bernstein (1992a)

Company. Meanwhile, the Dutch West India Company had the monopoly of the Dutch slave trade from its foundation in 1621. Crops such as coffee, cotton, indigo and tobacco were grown on the plantations, but sugar was overwhelmingly the most important export.

The so-called 'triangular trade' linked West Africa with the Caribbean and the cities of western Europe. The cities of Liverpool and Nantes, for example, benefited tremendously from their involvement in the shipment of slaves from West Africa to the Americas, and the movement of sugar and other commodities across the Atlantic to Europe. By 1750, ships from Liverpool were carrying over half the slaves transported in English vessels, and the Liverpool slavers had acquired a reputation for ruthless efficiency

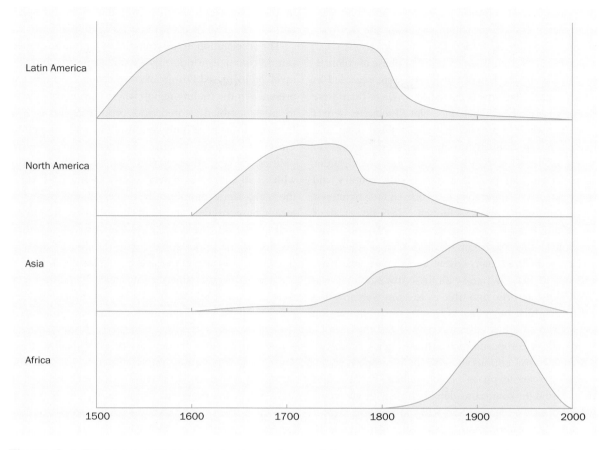

Figure 2.4 Regional colonialism: a chronology of the rise and fall in the numbers of colonies
Source: adapted from Lowder, 1986

compared with their rivals in cities such as Bristol (Hopkins, 1973). There is much debate among historians concerning the total number of slaves transported from West Africa during the entire period of the Atlantic slave trade, but a figure somewhere between 8 million and 10.5 million seems appropriate, thus representing one of the greatest migrations of all time (Hopkins, 1973).

The intensification of trading links

The organisation of the non-European state varied enormously and European traders found themselves in contact with societies whose ways of life were in material, administrative and spiritual terms often far superior to their own. China, for example, thought little of the European goods brought in trade, and in 1793 Emperor Chen Lung condescendingly informed George III's emissary Earl Macartney that,

> Our celestial empire possesses all things in prolific abundance and lacks no product within its borders. There is therefore no need to import the manufactures of outside barbarians. . . . But as tea, silk and porcelain . . . are absolute necessities to European nations, and yourselves, we have permitted . . . your wants [to] be supplied and your country [to] participate in our beneficence.

For many years up to this date, European traders were forced to exchange their goods for silks and porcelain only at intermediary ports in Southeast Asia, such as Macao. Here the Europeans were regarded as just one more commercial community and were allocated their own quarter in the flourishing port alongside the Arab, Javanese and Chinese traders (McGee, 1967).

Preston (1996) summarises this first phase of colonialism as one in which non-Europeans were regarded as cultural equals, but this occurred only where there were trading goods to be competed for. Not all societies were at their peak when Europeans first encountered them, and the French were distinctly unimpressed by the Angkorian empire of the Khmers, whose 'hydraulic' or irrigation-based society had peaked in the twelfth century and whose extensive temple complexes offered little of interest to the European market. Although inherently precious commodities, such as gold or silver, attracted early Europeans, other exotic commodities such as silk, spices or sugar soon lured many adventurers to particular parts of the world. Initially, trade with these 'distant others' was a high-risk enterprise into which vast sums were invested and from which huge profits were realised. To varying degrees, these trading adventurers were accompanied by other kinds of Europeans, such as missionaries, emissaries or even scientists, curious about the non-European world.

The mercantile phase of colonialism in Asia and Africa lasted for some considerable time without extensive European settlement and with no uniform sign of the dominant–subordinate relationship which was to come later. In Africa,

For centuries Europeans knew the coastline of Africa but not the interior. Climate, tropical diseases, Islam and resistant Africans deterred exploration. There was also a lack of interest, partly because trade at the coast was adequate and partly because there was little spirit of curiosity.

(Griffiths, 1995: 30)

But this was to change in the late eighteenth century. In the Americas, the situation was quite different, with intensification of trade in the seventeenth and eighteenth centuries accompanied by much more extensive settlement from Iberia, France and Britain. Moreover, in North America and the Caribbean, the colonisers were heavily involved in the production process, something which did not occur in Asia and Africa until much later. However, as trade with these two continents grew in both volume and value, so it became more organised in its structure, usually within the context of a trading company. In Asia, it was the Dutch that began this trend

in the seventeenth century, and the other European nations soon had their own East India companies too.

The acceleration in the scale and organisation of mercantile colonialism not only expanded profits, but also involved increased European commitment to a physical presence in the trading region where commodities were to be assembled, stored and protected (Plate 2.3). In order to acquire both commodities and protection, Europeans involved themselves increasingly in local politics, making alliances and inciting conflicts, all of which had enormous repercussions. In much of Africa the slave trade dramatically increased the power of locally based traders and indigenous chiefs often living well away from the coastal area, intensifying conflicts because of the rewards that could be achieved through the sale of prisoners into slavery.

Although at this time the Europeans had only a relatively small physical presence in much of the non-European world outside the Americas, this varied enormously. Re-victualling posts were, however, established across the globe as part of a vital network for supporting exploration and commerce. For example, European settlement in South Africa was initiated in 1652, when the powerful Dutch East India Company ordered that a supply station for passing ships be established by a group of Company employees in the sheltered harbour of what is now Cape Town. In that year, Jan van Riebeeck, the commander of the outpost, organised the setting up of facilities for growing fresh fruits and vegetables in the so-called 'Company Gardens', while relations were developed with the local Khoikhoi people to supply cattle for meat in exchange for European products (Lester et al., 2000; Plate 2.4).

But even with limited European settlement, change had occurred on an extensive scale by the end of the eighteenth century. The extended trading networks had increasingly drawn many parts and peoples of the non-European world into the capitalist system. European goods, particularly weaponry, European values and ideas, religious and secular, had penetrated most regions. Even where direct impact was still relatively limited, change occurred; for example, in Thailand (formerly Siam), where the present Chakri dynasty was established in the mid-eighteenth century through a series of reformist, modernising monarchs who sought to resist the Europeans by becoming more like them. For the great mass of peasants in Asia or

Plate 2.3 Macao: remnants of Portuguese presence during the mercantile colonial period (*photo*: David Smith)

Africa, however, life seemed to continue as it had for thousands of years, but their activities, whether subsistence or market-oriented, had over the long mercantile colonial period been subtly linked to a fledgling world economy, the core of which lay in Europe.

The transition to industrial colonialism

The mercantile colonial period merged into the era of industrial colonialism in a highly differentiated transition period. In North America, the USA had decolonised itself with the declaration of independence in 1776 and was preparing to become an enthusiastic and powerful metropolitan power in its own right. In Latin America and the Caribbean, colonial production and trade were beginning to be challenged from within. In Asia, the East India companies were going bankrupt, as their shift into commodity production, in order to ensure quantity and quality of supplies, had escalated their costs of administration and protection. In Europe itself, political revolutions and continental-scale war consumed state resources and attracted the

Plate 2.4 Cape Dutch style home in Graaff-Reinet, South Africa
(*photo*: Tony Binns)

individual adventurers who had underpinned much of the mercantile colonialism. But, above all, Europe offered new and lucrative profits for the reinvestment of accumulated merchant capital in its accelerating industrial transformation. Even so, the nineteenth century witnessed the establishment of colonial concessions related to trade and commerce, in parallel with the broader changes wrought by state-structured colonialism. Thus, the trading islands of Penang (1786), Singapore (1819) and Hong Kong (1841) were acquired, respectively, by Francis Light, Thomas Stamford Raffles and Charles Elliot on behalf of the crown rather than their companies, as were the 'Treaty Ports' in China (Guangzhou, Xiamen, Fuzhou, Ningbo and Shanghai) following the Treaty of Nanking signed by Britain and China in 1842.

But if mercantile colonialism had begun to fade, its impact was already fuelling the Industrial Revolution and the renewed burst of colonialism that began in the nineteenth century. The fortunes that had been made from plunder, from commodity trade and, particularly, from the triangular trade between West Africa, the Caribbean and Europe, were underpinning the accelerating industrial age. As Blaut (1993) argues, the point is not just that profits had been made, but that they were in the hands of a new breed of entrepreneur rather than the old elite. The mercantile colonial period not only created new money, but it was accompanied by a social

and political revolution, the combination of which gave Britain and other European powers a strong platform from which to launch into a more spatially extended and economically intensive form of colonialism. In short, by the late eighteenth and early nineteenth century, 'capitalism arose as a world-scale process: as a world system. Capitalism became concentrated in Europe because colonialism gave Europeans the power both to develop their own society and to prevent development from occurring elsewhere' (Blaut, 1993: 206).

Industrial colonialism

Certain changes characterised the colonialism of the nineteenth and twentieth centuries. The first was related to the dynamics of capitalism itself. Although commerce and trade still made money for the merchants of Liverpool, Bristol and London, the manufacturers themselves were eager to find methods of expanding production, or at least stabilising costs and extending their profits. Two obvious ways were to seek expanded and/or cheaper sources of raw materials and to find new markets overseas. A further development was to expand the production of cheap food overseas, thus lowering the costs of labour production in Europe by keeping wages down. Although markets took a while to develop, all of these and more were made available in the restructured colonies of the nineteenth century. These colonies were established and organised by the state rather than the company, although business and the state worked together through their representatives to transform production, consumption and cultures. The key to this process was territorial acquisition. Before 1870, annexation and occupation tended to follow resource exploitation, whereas after 1870 they tended to precede it.

Although the needs of capitalism may have been the driving force behind the industrial colonialism of the nineteenth century, the rationale for the colonial project itself was provided by a consolidation of the ideology of justifiable intervention and occupation of what had become either 'uncivilised savages' or traditional groups, whose history was ignored and whose societies and activities were seen as either static or disintegrating (Box 2.2).

Science, reason and, above all, organisation for most nineteenth-century thinkers elevated Europeans to their 'superior' position and placed them above the brutality and poverty of the peoples in their occupied lands. For Porter (1995) there were 'master metaphors' provided by physics (stability, equilibrium) and biology (constituent parts functioning for the whole) that shaped the ideologies of both colonialism and development. These gave rise to a modernist theme, a universal process of change which is clear and predetermined (Porter, 1995). Sympathetic motives could therefore be written into this process underpinned by a parent–child metaphor (Manzo, 1995), often expressed vividly by the image of the 'mother country' and her fledgling colonies.

BOX 2.2

The scramble for Africa

Although colonialism expanded rapidly throughout the nineteenth century, the speed of Africa's partition was new. The 'scramble for Africa' usually refers to the 30-year period between 1884 and 1914 when most of Africa was partitioned among the European powers. The key event in this period was when German Chancellor, Otto von Bismarck, called the European powers to Berlin in 1884 to draw up rules to regulate the partition of Africa. The General Act of the Conference of Berlin was signed in February 1885, which was concerned with 'the development of trade and civilization in Africa; the free navigation of the Rivers Congo, Niger, etc; the suppression of the slave trade by sea and land; the occupation of territory on the African coasts' (Griffiths, 1995: 38). However, even before the Berlin Conference, some of the continent had already passed under the control of the imperial powers, through various treaties with African leaders. One of the key factors motivating the conference was undoubtedly the speed of developments in South Africa, where diamonds were discovered in 1868 just across the Cape Colony's northern border in Griqualand West, and in the following year rich reserves were found in Kimberley. Britain annexed the tribal territory to prevent costly warfare generated by settler land-grabbing and security concerns on the Cape's borders. Then, in the year of the Berlin Conference, 1884, vast quantities of gold were discovered on the Witwatersrand, leading to the rapid expansion of mining activities and the mushrooming of the city of Johannesburg. European, and particularly British, investment in South African mining was massive, and between 1887 and 1898 gold production increased in value from £80,000 to £16 million, representing one-quarter of the world total (Lester et al., 2000).

We can summarise the processes, both within Africa and outside, which gave rise to the scramble for territory. Some of these processes were chronologically or spatially specific.

External processes

1. During the 1870s, between the first and second industrial revolutions (i.e. the shift from coal and iron to oil, electricity and steel), Europe and North America went through a deep recession. As rates of profit fell, European firms began to seek new

▶

BOX 2.2 (continued)

material sources, new markets and new investment opportunities on an extensive scale, partly to forestall other European rivals.

2. The last quarter of the nineteenth century saw the newly united countries of Italy and Germany using colonialism to sidestep internal tensions. As Africa was at the time the largest uncolonised area, it became the focus of a national scramble for territory and prestige, with France seeking compensation for its defeat (1871) by Germany within Europe. In this process, governments were supported by a popular imperialism created and sustained by a jingoistic media boom in newspapers, journals and books.

3. These processes were facilitated by a technological revolution, particularly in transport, where steamships, railways and telegraphic links accelerated both decision-making and physical

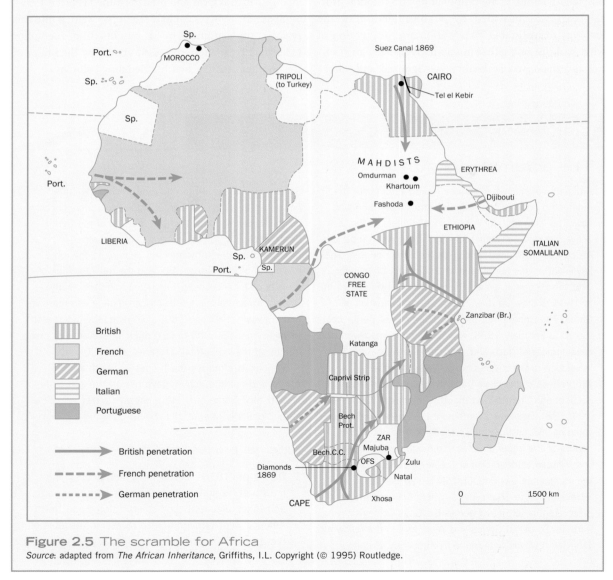

Figure 2.5 The scramble for Africa
Source: adapted from *The African Inheritance*, Griffiths, I.L. Copyright (© 1995) Routledge.

BOX 2.2 (continued)

advances into Africa. New armaments, such as machine-guns, facilitated this process by smaller and smaller European forces.

4. Once acquired, many colonies were also seen as healthy places for the surplus European population that technological advances in medicine and hygiene were beginning to produce. The Kenyan highlands, for example, had a pleasant climate and proved to be a particularly attractive place for white settlers (mainly British), accessing the area by the railway that was constructed (1895–1901) from Mombasa on the coast, through Nairobi to Lake Victoria. The settlers eventually took some 18 per cent of the colony's best agricultural land. Further south in Southern Rhodesia (now Zimbabwe), white settlers 'seized one-sixth of its land during the 1890s, mostly on the central highveld and including almost the entire Ndebele Kingdom, together with most of its cattle' (Iliffe, 1995: 205). In North Africa, by 1914, Europeans (mainly French) owned 920,000 hectares of land in Tunisia, and had also settled in large numbers in Algeria and Morocco. There was also considerable expansion of white settlement in South Africa during the nineteenth and early twentieth centuries.

Internal processes

1. The acceleration and intensification of European capitalism brought about a breakdown of existing relationships between traders and African societies, goading many of the African societies into reaction and providing excuses for further European invasion.

2. Sub-imperialism occurred when European settlement became extensive and decision making was wrested from the metropolitan centre by ambitious local individuals or groups, forcing retrospective recognition of highly personalised adventurism. Cecil Rhodes provided the most blatant example of such actions, a visionary British entrepreneur who amassed great wealth from mining and business deals, and dreamed of a 10,000 km railway from the Cape to Cairo to be built, with imperial as well as commercial considerations, across territories coloured red on the map (Griffiths, 1995) (see Key thinker, Cecil Rhodes; Plate 2.5).

3. Some African groups facilitated and accelerated the colonial process by 'inviting' Europeans to 'collaborate' against other groups. Often, however, such invitations were manufactured. Taken individually, no single reason explains the sudden scramble for Africa, but the conjuncture of many factors in the 1870s and 1880s gave rise to a spiral of European ambition and nationalism that, once started, proved difficult to stop.

The drive for profit and prestige

We should be careful not to overemphasise the power of ideology and discourse within this process; colonialism had at its heart the economic drive for profit. Every Sir Alfred Milner (Governor of the Cape Colony) had his Cecil Rhodes whispering or bellowing into his ear about the returns to investment that would follow annexation and control of yet another piece of territory occupied by traditional people not using it to its full potential. As the explorer David Livingstone wrote to Sir Roderick Murchison, President of the Royal Geographical Society, in 1855, justifying the funding of future expeditions, 'The future of the African continent will be of great importance to England in the way of producing the raw materials of her manufactures as well as an extensive market for the articles of her industry' (quoted in Pachai, 1973: 30). To be sure, there was also prestige for the 'mother country', annexation would be one in the eye for other European rivals and would promote pastures new for grazing missionaries of the true church; but the underlying impetus was usually greed.

Key thinker

Cecil Rhodes (1853–1902)

Cecil Rhodes was born the fifth son of a vicar in Bishop's Stortford, Hertfordshire, England in 1853. He first visited South Africa in 1870, where his older brother, Herbert, had a cotton farm in Natal. In 1871 Rhodes left the colony to go west to Kimberley where diamonds had been discovered. He returned to study at Oxford in 1873, but his studies were repeatedly interrupted by frequent visits to South Africa. In 1880 he launched the De Beers Mining Company, and by 1888 he had secured a monopoly of the Kimberley diamond production and had amassed an enormous personal fortune. In 1888 he tricked Lobengula, king of the Ndebele of Matabeleland into an agreement by which Rhodes secured important mining concessions in Matabeleland and Mashonaland. He exploited these concessions through his British South Africa Company, which was given a charter by the British Government in 1889, and soon established complete control of the territory.

From 1877 until his death in 1902 Rhodes represented the constituency of Barkly West in the Cape House of Assembly and was Prime Minister of the Cape Colony from 1890 until 1896. Rhodes has been accused of being racist, and during his time as Prime Minister he introduced legislation to push black people from their lands and to restrict the franchise to literate persons, thus reducing the African vote.

Rhodes played a key role in British imperial policies in southern Africa. He was deeply committed to the expansion of the British Empire and yearned for a railway from the Cape to Cairo constructed entirely on land belonging to Britain, and coloured red on the map. In his will, he said of the British, 'I contend that we are the finest race in the world and that the more of the world we inhabit the better it is for the human race'. Through close collaboration with agents of the British Government in South Africa, his imperial ambitions and capital investment progressed simultaneously. By 1894, the British South Africa Company controlled an area of 1.1 million sq km between Lake Tanganyika in the north and the Limpopo River on South Africa's northern border. The following year, the name of this territory was changed from 'Zambesia' to 'Rhodesia', which later became Northern and Southern Rhodesia and after independence, respectively, Zambia and Zimbabwe.

Rhodes died near Cape Town in 1902 and was buried at World's View in the Matobo Hills near Bulawayo in present-day Zimbabwe (then Rhodesia). He left over £6 million and at the time was one of the richest men in the world. His will provided for the establishment of the Rhodes Scholarships, to enable students from territories under British rule, formerly under British rule, or from Germany, to study at Oxford University. More than 80 scholarships are now awarded annually to both men and women from the former British colonies, the USA and Germany.

Plate 2.5 Cecil Rhodes
(*Photo*: Alamy Images/Popperfoto)

Strengthening control over the colonies

Whatever their nature, ideologies need to be translated into action, and for colonialism this was through the elaboration and enablement of, first, its material base, i.e. production, trade and finance; and, second, the establishment of the administrative machinery of control and order. There is no necessary sequence in this process, annexation and the provision of administrative structures could follow economic interests, as in the Transvaal (South Africa), or could precede them, as in the French occupation of Indo-China. There was, however, clearly an expanded role for the state vis-à-vis the trading company in the administrative system.

In contrast to the mercantile period, the main medium of exploitation was not the trading concessions, although they continued to be squeezed out of 'independent' states, but rather the acquisition of land on which to organise the mechanics of production. The colonial state then established the infrastructure of legal, transport, administrative and police systems through which the pursuit of wealth and order could be controlled. It is no coincidence that Sir Harry Johnston (Box 2.3), in his address to the Royal Geographical Society in 1895, following a tour of duty as Commissioner in British Central Africa (now Malawi), attributed the transformation of Mlanje District to the fact that the natives 'above all, are trained to respect and to value settled and civilised government' (Crush, 1995a: 2).

But if the colonial state was an administrative state, it was usually a productive state too, since it was regarded as right and proper for the metropolitan state, metropolitan companies and metropolitan individuals to secure a profitable return on their investment. Ensuring such a return from colonising Africa was for some a daunting challenge. As Lord Lugard, Governor-General of Nigeria (1914–1919) admitted,

Neither the Foreign Office nor the Colonial Office had any experience of Central African conditions and administration, when, at the close of the nineteenth century, the summons for effective occupation compelled this country to administer the hinterlands of the West African colonies, and to assume control of vast areas on the Nile, the Niger, the Zambezi, and the great lakes in the heart of Africa.

(Lugard, 1965: 607)

The production of export commodities

The spatial expression of economic exploitation was experienced for the most part in the rural areas in which the export commodities were produced. This varied substantially according to the nature of the commodity, local customs and the metropolitan power involved. In some areas agricultural restructuring occurred through the creation of large-scale plantations, whereas in others local producers were encouraged to amalgamate their holdings. Both processes resulted in widespread landlessness, creating labour pools for the new commercial holdings. Lonsdale and Berman (1979) report how the Kenyan landscape was transformed by the colonisers:

In the 1880s the inland areas of Kenya comprised a web of subsistence economies which exploited complementary ecological niches suited either to predominantly pastoral or predominantly agricultural forms of production. Between cattlemen and cultivators there was a symbiotic exchange of commodities and intermittent adjustment of populations . . . Three decades later the economic and political structures of the region had been subject to profound transformation, under the sway of a state apparatus linking them to the capitalist world economy. Maasailand was now the core of the White Highlands.

(Lonsdale and Berman, 1979: 494–5)

Others were shifted into agricultural or mining industries by new taxes that often forced farmers to migrate into wage labour to meet these demands, often ruining prosperous and well-organised indigenous systems. In many parts of Africa, poll taxes and hut taxes were introduced and, 'tax evasion was brutally discouraged and could lead to harsh punishment and forced labour' (Binns, 1994a: 10). Where local labour proved to be 'inadequate' for commercial agriculture, workers were often imported from elsewhere in the country (as in Vietnam, where the French shifted workers from north to south), or from overseas (as in Malaya, where the British brought in workers from India). However, labour also moved 'voluntarily', recruited through family or kinship systems (e.g. from south China to the Malayan tin mines).

The new agricultural systems often meant that, over large areas, the range of crops produced was narrowed to those commodities required by metropolitan industries, such as cocoa, coffee, cotton, groundnuts, palm oil, rubber, sisal, sugar and tea. Colonies thus became associated with the production of one or two items, being forced to import whatever else was needed; 'Economically, colonialism programmed [African] countries to consume what they do not produce and to produce what they do not consume' (Binns, 1994a: 5). Needless to say, metropolitan firms were in control of both directions of trade. Although some of these commodities were new introductions to the colonies, such as rubber or coffee in various Southeast Asian countries, more traditional crops continued to play an important role, for example, coconuts and groundnuts. Local food crops too became an important export crop. Siamese rice, for example, was exported to many other Asian countries, largely through British firms, where it helped lower the cost of labour reproduction, particularly in the cities (Dixon, 1998).

BOX 2.3

The nineteenth-century logic of colonialism

The discourse of colonialism which first justified and then ratified colonial intervention is well expressed by Jonathan Crush (1995b) in his edited book *Power of Development*, where he caricatures the transformation of Mlanje District in British Central Africa (now Malawi) through the eyes of Sir Harry Johnston, its Commissioner (Crush, 1995a: 1–2). Johnston's first description is of Mlanje in 1895 before colonialism extends its benign hand to that unfortunate land:

> In the Mlanje District there was practically chaos . . . the few European planters were menaced in their lives and property, and the only mission station had to be abandoned . . . throughout all this country there was absolutely no security for life and property for natives, and not over-much for the Europeans . . . Everything had got to be commenced.

This picture of scorned opportunities was blamed on disinterested local tribes and evil-minded slave traders and was contrasted by Sir Harry Johnston with the scene after just three years of British rule as a placid paradise where:

> The natives who pass along are clothed in white calico . . . A bell is ringing to call the children to the mission school. A planter gallops past on horseback . . . long rows of native carriers pass in Indian file, carrying

loads of European goods. You will see a post office, a court of justice, and possibly a prison, the occupants of which, however, will be out mending roads under the superintendence of some very businesslike policeman of their own colour . . . The most interesting feature in the neighbourhood of these settlements at the present time is the coffee plantation, which, to a great extent, is the cause and support of our prosperity.

(Crush, 1995a: 1–2)

The influential colonial statesman Lord Frederick Lugard had an interesting perspective on the objectives of colonialism. He asserted that there was a need to fulfil what he called a 'Dual Mandate' delivering mutual benefits for coloniser and colonised. In his book of the same title, he argued:

> Let it be admitted at the outset that European brains, capital and energy have not been, and never will be, expended in developing the resources of Africa from motives of pure philanthropy; that Europe is in Africa for the mutual benefit of her own industrial classes, and of the native races in their progress to a higher plane; that the benefit can be made reciprocal, and that it is the aim and desire of civilized administration to fulfil this dual mandate.

(Lugard, 1965: 617)

Expanding markets

As a result of the drastic economic, social and demographic changes of industrial colonialism, the last quarter of the nineteenth century also witnessed the acceleration of market potential for Western manufactured products. Indeed, in Pacific Asia it was the purchasing power of the Chinese and Japanese markets that was as important as access to their products in encouraging the Western powers in their almost frantic attempts to gain trading concessions. In the colonies themselves, the initial markets for Western goods were confined to wealthy expatriate and indigenous elites. But the quality and price of these goods and the demonstration effect of purchases by the wealthy soon resulted in imported commodities dominating the expenditure pattern of all social groups, even those in rural subsistence, thus further destroying the indigenous artisan economy and increasing dependency on the West.

Particularly poignant in these circumstances was the re-export of cheap food to the growing markets among the urban and rural poor. Their diet of flour, sugar and tea often had colonial origins, but was processed (and value-added) in Europe, thus facilitating a double exploitation of the colonial poor: first, through their labour in growing the crops, and then through their subsequent purchase of it at exorbitant prices.

Critical reflection

Why was manufacturing industry discouraged in the colonies?

In many areas in the colonies, where indigenous manufacturing posed a real threat to imported manufactured goods from Europe, local industries were quickly suppressed, as in the Indian textile towns (Blaut, 1993). The corollary of this situation is that manufacturing was relatively limited during the industrial colonial phase. Any manufacturing that existed was largely concerned with the preliminary processing of primary products, such as rice milling or tin smelting. Most of the more sophisticated processing, and the creation of profits, occurred within the booming industrial areas of the metropolitan country. This is the era during which the big dockside manufacturing plants for tobacco and sugar proliferated in Liverpool, Glasgow and London.

With reference to specific examples, consider the nature of manufacturing industry today in former colonies. To what extent is this still dominated by the preliminary processing of primary products which was a feature of the industrial colonialism phase?

It would not be correct to assume that colonial cities were simply points of control and administration. Although few were centres of production, commercial activity, ranging from the manufacture of small consumer goods to the retailing of imported products, was very extensive. Much of this activity was in the hands of non-Europeans. This is not the same as saying that they were the prerogative of local entrepreneurs, because almost all of the colonial powers in East Africa and in Pacific Asia, other than the Japanese, made a point of encouraging or permitting immigrant groups, usually Chinese or Indian, to infiltrate and monopolise local commerce. In this way, a convenient demographic, cultural and economic buffer was placed between the colonised and the colonialists. Discontent on the part of indigenous populations with the cost of living was therefore often directed against those who were immediately available, rather than those who were ultimately responsible.

The period from 1850 to 1920 saw a massive restructuring of urban systems (Drakakis-Smith, 1991). Colonial production may have been based in the countryside, but colonial political and economic control was firmly centred on the city. Usually, just one or two centres were selected for development, giving rise to the urban primacy which still characterises many countries of the South today (see Chapters 3 and 9). In some cases, completely new cities were built, such as Kaduna in Northern Nigeria, which served as the colonial administrative capital of the region. Within these cities, despite the numerical dominance of the indigenous populations, most of the land space was given over to European activities. Spacious residential and working areas were paralleled by extensive military cantonments, all physically separated from the usually cramped, crowded indigenous city by railway lines, parks or gardens. Little face-to-face contact took place between the colonisers and the colonised, except within a dominant–subordinate relationship. It was a situation that seemed as though it would go on forever, but the First World War intervened and widespread changes ensued. Within a generation, the political world order of 1914 was totally undermined and the sun began to set rapidly over the colonial empires.

Late colonialism

A fundamental change occurred in the ethos of colonialism after 1920. Put simply, the 'heroic' age of creating empires gave way to a more prosaic phase of imperial governance. The key to this change was the concept of 'trusteeship', which had permeated the formation of the League of Nations, and which elevated to a high priority the well-being and development of colonial peoples (see Chapter 1). In practice, this did not necessarily mean indigenous colonial peoples. Indeed, prevailing anthropological theory conveniently explained that such progress was impossible for 'backward' and 'traditional' societies which did not hold in proper esteem social values such as democracy or the business ethic. Not until after 1945 did metropolitan governments seriously consider fairer representation for indigenous interests, but this was too little, too late.

Styles of colonial rule varied (Box 2.4), but between the wars, colonial government was dominated by bureaucrats, both in metropolitan capitals and overseas, striving on behalf of the colonies, with little appreciation either of indigenous aspirations or of the changing world economy in which they were situated. The world wars and the intervening depression severely disrupted colonial economies, with investment from Europe being limited and commodity prices falling steadily. Much of the capital sustaining growth in this inter-war period was American, or, in Asia, from the overseas Chinese community. Thus, in the Dutch East Indies, 80 per cent of all domestic trade was controlled by Nanyang Chinese, whereas the largest rubber plantation was owned by a US tyre company. The declining profitability of commodity exports helped to cause a shift in the nature of government investment during this period, with increasing amounts of capital being invested in infrastructure – roads, utilities or railways.

BOX 2.4

Styles of colonialism in Africa

The European powers had different ideas about colonialism and the way their African colonies should be ruled. The general philosophy was to establish and maintain a level of order, if necessary with swift military imposition, and to do this as cheaply as possible, while at the same time generating as much funding as possible from taxes and exports to support the metropolitan power.

British policy was to adopt a pragmatic and decentralised approach to governing its African colonies. The strategy of 'Indirect Rule', introduced by Lord Frederick Lugard into Northern Nigeria, 'became the accepted ideal of British colonial administration' (Fage, 1995: 394), with the colonial administrators working through traditional local leaders. Britain feared the problems which might follow the possible demise of indigenous cultures, and so maintained traditional institutions and African rulers, wherever possible working through these leaders who were delegated with the difficult task of keeping order over the mass of the people. If necessary, military forces were used to defeat ruling emirs without destroying their administrations. Although the sort of strong indigenous institutions that existed in Northern Nigeria were not necessarily replicated elsewhere in Africa, the policy of

Indirect Rule was nevertheless widely introduced – for example in 1925 in the former German colony of Tanganyika, which came under British control following the First World War. Subsequently, in the 1930s, Indirect Rule was also introduced into Nyasaland (Malawi) and Northern Rhodesia (Zambia), and then into Basutoland (Lesotho), Bechuanaland (Botswana) and Swaziland. As Iliffe comments,

> The policy's conservative thrust was strong. In Sudan, for example, the Egyptian and Sudanese elites initially employed for their anti-Mahdist sympathies were abandoned after 1924 when an army mutiny revealed the first glimpses of Sudanese nationalism. Instead, the British adopted 'Indirect Rule' and rehabilitated 'tribal chiefs' in a policy described by the governor as 'making the Sudan safe for autocracy'.
>
> (Iliffe, 1995: 201)

Although Indirect Rule was not adopted in Southern Rhodesia (Zimbabwe) and Kenya, where the white settlers felt it restricted labour supply and made the local chiefs too powerful, other colonial powers sometimes used similar policies in administering their territories.

BOX 2.4 (continued)

The French approach to managing its colonial territories was very different from the British. 'Whereas British colonialism was designed to create Africans with British characteristics, French policy was designed to create black Frenchmen' (Binns, 1994a: 9). The French regarded their colonies as part of France, 'Overseas France', with the aim of assimilating the colonies and their people into France and the French way of life. In fact, the process of assimilation was a driving force in the French colonial design. But to acquire full French citizenship was a lengthy procedure, requiring 'education in French schools, performing military service and a minimum of civilian French employment, and agreeing to be monogamous and to foreswear traditional or Islamic law and custom' (Fage, 1995: 411). By 1939, only 80,000 of the 15 million Africans in French West Africa had actually gained full citizenship. The vast majority of those inhabitants of the colonies that did not achieve this distinction could only be 'associated' with France. White settlement was common in Francophone colonies, particularly in the countries bordering the Mediterranean (notably, Algeria, Morocco and Tunisia), but there were also quite sizeable white minorities in Dakar (Senegal) and in the plantation areas of Cameroon, Guinea, Ivory Coast and Madagascar.

The French established a centralised, bureaucratic, authoritarian and hierarchical state, and there was little attempt to work through traditional institutions or leaders as in the British territories. Early French administration in West Africa was preoccupied more with military than with commercial motivation. In 1904, France's eight West African colonies were amalgamated into a single federation with its capital in Dakar (Senegal), where the Governor-General was based, taking his directives from the Colonial Ministry in Paris, and himself disseminating policy through a hierarchy of governors in each colony, and down to their provincial commissioners and *commandants de cercle*, the officers in charge of each district.

Belgium controlled the vast territory known initially as the Congo Independent State from the establishment of its boundaries after the Treaty of

Berlin in 1885, and later from 1908 it became the Belgian Congo (now Democratic Republic of Congo, formerly Zaire). The Congo Free State was initially a personal possession of King Leopold, who seized the territory when others in his country were apparently showing little interest in colonisation. Despite arguing that he was involved in humanitarian and philanthropic activities, Leopold ruled in a dictatorial manner and decreed that all land in Congo apart from villages and surrounding cultivated areas belonged to him as Head of State. There were strict controls on what produce Africans could buy and sell, and inhabitants were heavily taxed. Leopold established several concessionary trading companies with exclusive trading rights over defined areas and he took a 50 per cent stake in each. The so-called 'Congo System', which heavily exploited both people and resources, 'attracted much contemporary criticism and opprobrium, largely because of the way in which the private companies, backed by the "official army" of the state, brutally abused and exploited Africans' (Griffiths, 1995: 53). Joseph Conrad's book *Heart of Darkness* (1899) further provoked widespread condemnation of the atrocities carried out in Congo. This criticism, much of it directed at the King himself, eventually led to the renaming of the colony as 'Belgian Congo' from 1908, when it formally became a colony of Belgium. However, the exploitative Congo System persisted and there was considerable international surprise when at the Treaty of Versailles in 1919, Belgium was given the trust territory of Ruanda-Urundi (formerly German, and now Rwanda and Burundi) under League of Nations mandate.

Portugal was the other major colonial power in Africa, and as early as 1482 had established fortified trading posts on the west coast from Senegal to the Gold Coast. Despite its longstanding contacts with Africa, Portugal was less successful than Britain and France in gaining territory during the competitive 'scramble'. By the early twentieth century, Portugal controlled the small West African territory of Portuguese Guinea (now Guinea-Bissau), and the two much larger colonies of Angola and Mozambique.

▶

BOX 2.4 (continued)

Like the French, Portugal adopted a policy of assimilation, with all territories being regarded as part of the Portuguese Union. Substantial numbers of white settlers moved to the Portuguese colonies, as in the French territories. According to Rodney, the Portuguese colonial regime had an appalling record of slavery-like practice in its African colonies;

One peculiar characteristic of Portuguese colonialism was the provision of forced labour, not only for its own citizens, but also for capitalists outside the boundaries of Portuguese colonies. Angolans and Mozambicans were exported to the South African mines to work for subsistence, while the capitalists in South Africa paid the Portuguese government a certain sum for each labourer supplied.

(Rodney, 1972: 167)

There is an ongoing debate among historians and others about the relative merits and problems of 'direct' compared with 'indirect' colonial rule. A study undertaken by Lange (2004) of 33 former British colonies, found that post-colonial levels of development were generally greater in those countries where direct rule was practised. In relation to indirect rule, Lange concluded that, 'dispersed forms of domination hinder state governance when they create extremely powerful local intermediaries and limit state infrastructural power' (Lange, 2004: 917).

During the economic recession of the 1920s, official metropolitan and colonial ties grew closer. Thus, by 1930 some 44 per cent of British trade was with the empire. This was reinforced by demographic changes, with increasing numbers migrating away from the European recession to the perceived opportunities of the colonies, often encouraged enthusiastically by their governments. Although most British migrants went to the settler colonies, such as Canada or Australia, most Dutch and French migrants moved to already heavily populated colonies and were forced into a variety of urban occupations rather than farming as in earlier decades. Many unqualified migrants took up relatively low paid work in retail or office locations.

The effect of this growing European presence was complex. For the small, educated indigenous group, it made personal advancement even more difficult, sending many off to Europe for further education and to sharpen their political and organisational skills. The huge peasant population, however, suffering dreadfully from the recession, were not organised enough to threaten more than the local representatives of the system. But the growing urban indigenous population posed more of a problem – not an overtly political problem in the late colonial period, rather one associated more with social issues.

The inter-war years

For the majority of European colonists, the inter-war years seemed like 'a golden age', despite the economic vicissitudes. Even those with more modest incomes had status and privilege relative to the indigenous population, which compensated somewhat. This was the era from which most contemporary images of colonialism are drawn in the media, particularly in the cinema, for example in the film *Out of Africa* (1985). The attractive way of life was facilitated by the shift in the balance of administrative power from the metropolitan centre to the colonies, certainly in the British Empire, so that salaries, privileges and jobs overseas remained secure and rewarding, despite the economic situation at home. This shift in power also enabled the administrators to more or less ignore trusteeship as far as indigenous populations were concerned, favouring the colonial settlers in numerous ways.

Urban planning became a distorted version of European concepts, so the garden city movement in Africa and Asia was largely used to segregate European and indigenous populations further by swathes of greenery, particularly recreational areas such as golf courses and racecourses. Despite the health risks, burgeoning indigenous populations were often crammed into crumbling 'old quarters'. In 1911 in Delhi, on the eve of the emergence of the new imperial capital, the old Mughal city of Shahjahanabad contained almost a quarter of a million people in its 2.5 square miles (King, 1976).

The Second World War destroyed the myth of European invincibility, particularly in Asia as a result of Japanese victories, although ironically the eventual success of the European allies owed not a little to the colonial or imperial forces that served under the metropolitan flag and to the resources that the colonies continued to supply. Indeed, it has been estimated that some 200,000 Africans fought alongside the British and the French during the war, and, as Fage comments,

Since the direct or indirect result of their endeavours had been to free lands like Ethiopia, Burma, India and even France from foreign rule . . . these men . . . were naturally inclined to ask why this benefit should be withheld from them. All these people, the ex-soldiers especially, looked for a better life now that the war was over.

(Fage, 1995: 476)

Post-war decolonisation and independence

In the post-war period the movement towards decolonisation gathered momentum. There were several reasons why this occurred.

First, France and Britain were exhausted after the Second World War, their economies were weak and they were dependent on the USA for financial support. Two new superpowers had emerged, the USA and former USSR, both of them committed to the end of overt colonialism. In fact, decolonisation was strongly encouraged by the USA, partly because it wished to extend its own sphere of economic influence through a kind of informal imperialism, which might be more appropriately termed either 'global capitalism' or 'neocolonialism'. With regard to the former USSR, Kwame Nkrumah, the first leader of independent Ghana (formerly Gold Coast), apparently commented, 'Had it not been for Russia, the African liberation movement would have suffered the most brutal persecution' (Nkrumah, quoted in Iliffe, 1995: 246).

A second motivation for decolonisation came from the Africans and Indians who had received a Western education, and who used their skills of oratory and writing to campaign and mobilise the masses. The Indian Congress Movement, founded as early as 1885, was led by such men, who initially campaigned for more respect and greater elected representation from the British rulers. From 1917, however, the party waged a battle of varied tactics, including periods of intense nationalist agitation, with Gandhi playing a pre-eminent role. The Congress was able steadily to raise the financial and moral price which the British would have to pay if they wished to remain in power. In 1947 India won its independence and Congress helped to form the interim government, in power until 1951, when Jawaharlal Nehru as Prime Minister then assumed the Congress presidency. The independence of India had a very significant impact on nationalist movements in other colonies across the world.

Further momentum was given to the decolonisation process by the signing of the Atlantic Charter during the Second World War, the tone and sentiments of which were taken up later in the UN Charter. Indeed, the UN set timetables for independence in Libya (1951) and Somalia (1960), and also decreed the federation of Italy's former colony, Eritrea, with Ethiopia, while the former USSR supported full independence for Eritrea.

Finally, the increasing mobility of European and US capital also facilitated the decolonisation process, since with the incorporation of the colonies into the global capitalist economy, Western companies could continue to move capital and other resources into and out of these territories irrespective of whether or not they actually governed them. It was suggested that independent governments would continue to permit such transactions, not least because their governing elites would require access to outside capital and technology.

Not all the metropolitan powers responded to the call for decolonisation and to the call of the colonial peoples for independence. Britain found it easier than most to withdraw because of its less formal and more decentralised administrative systems, although there were one or two places such as Southern Rhodesia where settler resistance saw the colonial sun set rather more slowly than elsewhere. Indeed, Southern Rhodesia did not become independent Zimbabwe until 1980, over 20 years after Ghana had been the first British colony in Africa to be given self-rule after the Second World War (1957), following the earlier granting of independence to South Africa (1910) and Egypt (1922). In Kenya, the Mau Mau uprising took place during the 1950s, in which predominantly dispossessed Kikuyu protested over the alienation of land for European settler farms.

The raiding of settler farms and indiscriminate killings proved to be a threat to stability and British troops were needed to brutally restore control. This eventually led to the colonial government putting pressure on the white settlers to accept a movement towards independence in 1963, when Jomo Kenyatta, who had been detained during the uprising, was elected the first president.

For France and the Netherlands, however, decolonisation was an altogether more complex and bloody affair, with settlers resentful of being abandoned and unwilling to return to a war-ravaged Europe putting up fierce resistance. Brutal decolonisation wars resulted in Algeria, the East Indies and Indo-China. In North Africa, both Morocco and Tunisia gained independence from France in 1956, whereas in Algeria young militants started a guerrilla war in 1954. In the next eight years, over half a million French troops virtually defeated the *Front de Libération Nationale* within Algeria, but it was kept alive in neighbouring Morocco and Tunisia. President de Gaulle was forced to agree to Algerian independence in 1962, and there followed an exodus of some 85 per cent of the European settlers. Portugal abandoned its African colonies abruptly in 1975 following the *coup d'état* in Portugal in 1974. Colonial administrators were withdrawn quickly with very little time to hand over the trappings of power and bureaucracy to the local people. Portuguese businessmen, industrial managers and technicians also departed. Portugal had been struggling against liberation wars in both Angola and Mozambique, and after the departure of the colonial power both countries disintegrated into many years of civil war, which at various times was fuelled by the intervention of other countries.

Eventually, however, independence came to all except a few small territories, though their development paths were strongly affected, not only by the neo-colonial forces that quickly moved into the political and economic vacuum, but also by the considerable legacies that colonisation had bequeathed to these nascent states.

Legacies of colonialism

Colonialism has undoubtedly had a lasting impact on many countries, as we will see in later chapters. As Dirlik observes, 'Colonialism, however oppressive and unjust in its practices, also created cultural bonds between the coloniser and the colonised, which have shaped irrevocably the cultural identities of both and which survive decolonisation' (Dirlik, 2002: 445). Politically, the national units that emerged between the 1940s and 1970s essentially comprised the territorial divisions of the colonial era and often had limited correlation with environmental geographies, pre-colonial structures or with contemporary cultural and ethnic patterns. As Clapham (1985: 20) has remarked, 'There is still no more striking, even shocking, reminder of the impact of colonialism in Africa than to cross an entirely artificial frontier and witness the instant change of language . . . that results'. Moving from Zambia (English) to Angola (Portuguese) illustrates this comment very vividly.

The Malay world of Southeast Asia was divided between three countries, Malaysia, Indonesia and the Philippines, in accordance with the territorial spread of the British, Dutch and Spanish-American empires. Even non-Malay areas were incorporated into these territories if they had been part of the colonial territory. Thus Indonesia has held on to Melanesian Irian Jaya, despite the cultural and ethnic contradictions, and is attempting to flood the area with Javanese migrants as part of its accumulation process.

There is a lively and ongoing debate among historians, political scientists and others as to whether colonialism was beneficial or detrimental to the economies and societies of those countries that were colonised. In the second decade of the twenty-first century, it is a fact that many African countries and former colonies are probably worse off now than they were at independence in the 1960s. Some historians would argue that colonialism was too varied and, in some instances, too brief to judge whether it has left a beneficial or detrimental legacy. Certainly, the local textures of colonialism were immensely complex, but as a component of a broader, changing global process, there were immense overall repercussions.

Two much-quoted and contrasting viewpoints are provided by Peter Bauer (1976) and Walter Rodney (1972). Bauer in his influential book *Dissent on Development* asserts:

It is untrue to say that colonial status is incompatible with material progress, and that its removal is a necessary condition of economic development. Some of the richest countries were colonies in their earlier history, notably the United States, Canada,

Australia and New Zealand; and these countries were already prosperous while they were still colonies. Nor has colonial status precluded the material advance, from extremely primitive conditions, of the African and Asian territories which became colonies in the nineteenth century. Many of these territories made rapid economic progress between the second half of the nineteenth century, when they became colonies, and the middle of the twentieth century, when most of them became independent.

(Bauer, 1976: 148)

In his important and thought-provoking text *How Europe Underdeveloped Africa*, Walter Rodney (1972) takes a very different view from Bauer on the merits and problems of colonialism:

The colonisation of Africa lasted for just over seventy years in most parts of the continent. This is an extremely short period within the context of universal historical development. Yet, it was precisely in those years that in other parts of the world the rate of change was greater than ever before . . . The decisiveness of the short period of colonialism and its negative consequences for Africa spring mainly from the fact that Africa lost power. Power is the ultimate determinant in human society, being basic to the relations within any group and between groups. It implies the ability to defend one's interests and if necessary to impose one's will by any means available.

(Rodney, 1972: 224)

Bauer and Rodney, among many others, provide what might seem to be credible, or at least seriously debatable perspectives. The debate will undoubtedly go on, but some of the legacies of the colonial era will now be considered to inform and illuminate the different perspectives in the debate.

Demographic effects of colonialism

The demographic legacy of colonialism was considerable and manifested in many different ways. The effects of colonialism on standards of health and nutrition have been investigated by a number of researchers (see for example, Moradi, 2008). During the late colonial period the rate of indigenous population growth began to accelerate, partly due to transfers of medical technology, improvements in health care and hygiene and wider food security. Not that they were provided on either a widespread or enthusiastic basis by the colonial authorities, but improvements did occur and fertility did rise to the extent that the newly independent nations inherited an accelerating population growth.

Most colonial powers adopted a top-down hierarchical model for health care provision in their colonies, with an emphasis on curative rather than preventative medicine. In this model, patients were referred to successively higher levels which, in theory at least, possess greater skills and technical resources. In practice, the highest level in the hierarchy, the specialist and/or teaching hospital, was invariably located in large urban centres and in some cases only in the capital cities.

Such a health care system inevitably led to greater expenditure and better provision in the cities, while the poorer and remoter rural areas had (if any) only basic provision. Indeed, much rural health care was, and still is, provided by missionary bodies and non-governmental organisations (Phillips, 1990). Many people in both rural areas and cities depended on traditional medicine, which was (and indeed still is) widely available and usually less expensive than Western medicine.

In the 1970s, Ghana, for example, had only one teaching hospital, in Accra, the capital city, eight regional hospitals and 32 district hospitals. Although only 18 per cent of the population was concentrated in towns larger than 20,000 persons, over 66 per cent of the country's doctors were based in such towns. Furthermore, in terms of expenditure on health, a specialist teaching hospital benefiting only 1 per cent of the population received 40 per cent of the national health budget, whereas primary health care, serving some 90 per cent of the population, was allocated only 15 per cent of total health spending. Such inequalities were also found in India, where large cities and port towns were given priority, 'Local populations were cut off from modern medicine, but ironically, indigenous systems were often discouraged and certainly neglected' (Phillips, 1990: 114).

Former colonies have had to come to terms with these 'alien' medical systems since independence but, in reality, relatively few countries have been able to restructure their health care delivery systems. A much-quoted exception to this is Tanzania, where under the country's first president, Julius Nyerere, there was a stated commitment to redressing the inherited colonial imbalance of health expenditure and provision, and extending the provision of health care to rural areas through trained community health workers, as in the Chinese 'barefoot doctor' model (see Chapter 5).

Much research was done by the colonial powers into the causes of ill health in tropical regions, for example, the incidence and prevention of diseases transmitted by mosquitoes and tsetse flies. Medical research stations were established, such as the British Medical Research Council's hospital at Fajara in The Gambia, while other research stations were concerned with improving the health of livestock.

Colonial governments also introduced emergency programmes when epidemics occurred. For example, when the plague came to Bombay in 1896, the health authorities began to disinfect houses to kill the plague-carrying fleas that infested rats in the city.

A further demographic effect of colonialism was the mixing of populations that occurred as a result of labour movements, whether forced, contracted or voluntary. Add to this the multiple ethnic groups that were already in the artificial colonial states which became independent territories, and the consequence has been an ethnic melting pot that has simmered and bubbled almost everywhere during the post-colonial period, at best considerably hampering the development process, at worst resulting in appalling acts of expulsion or genocide, such as the expulsion by President Idi Amin of 80,000 Asians from Uganda from 1972.

Education

Some would argue that, along with health, the provision of formal education systems was another benefit gained from the colonial experience. In many colonies a respectable group of educated indigenous people emerged who spoke the colonial language and absorbed themselves in the alien culture. As Gould comments,

> The respectful, educated professional or civil servant of the British colonies, as personified by E.M. Forster's Dr Aziz in *A Passage to India*, or a figure of fun like Joyce Cary's *Mister Johnson* in Nigeria, aspired to the colonial cultural values, and provided an implicit model for others.
>
> (Gould, 1993: 13)

The French and British adopted different approaches to colonial education. In their African colonies, whereas the British made an effort to train local teachers and deliver some aspects of the school curriculum in the vernacular languages, many teachers in French Africa actually came from France and teaching was delivered in French. Grier comments that in the French colonies, 'Very few Africans received the benefits of a colonial education, and those that did were isolated and alienated from their original cultures' (Grier, 1999: 319). By the late 1960s, Grier asserts, 'Up to 95% of the population in France's former Black African territories were illiterate' (Grier, 1999: 319)

However, in Francophone countries, as in former British colonies, there were groups of educated indigenes, for example, Léopold Senghor (who became the first president of Senegal) and Aimé Césaire of Martinique. They published poetry and essays in the 1930s which celebrated 'négritude' (blackness), in which they reaffirmed African culture by writing in impressively fluent French. Césaire's poetic account *Return to my Native Land* tells of a journey back to Martinique after years of schooling in France, in which he presents a critique of colonial rule, whilst also giving beautiful images of blackness and the survival of African traditions. Both Senghor and Césaire showed equally close attachments to African tradition and to metropolitan French culture.

As part of the administrative machinery of colonialism, the colonisers required a small, educated local workforce. As Rodney comments,

> In practice, it was not necessary to educate the masses because only a minority of the . . . population entered the colonial economy in such a way that their performance could be enhanced by education. Indeed, the French concentrated on selecting a small minority, who would be thoroughly subjected to French cultural imperialism.
>
> (Rodney, 1972: 257)

The missionaries were also keen to promote reading and writing so that indigenous people could read the Bible. In Muslim areas, the Koranic schools played an important role before the establishment of the Western-style school system and continued alongside their newer counterpart. Like the colonial health systems, the education systems were generally centralised, hierarchical and bureaucratic (Watson, 1982). There was a strong emphasis on achieving academic excellence, and syllabuses and assessment methods were frequently transported with little, if any, modification from the metropolitan country to the colonies.

In terms of educational provision, universities, where they existed, were usually located in the large cities, notably the capitals, and they received a disproportionately large amount of funding. In West Africa, for example, provision for higher education was very limited. In fact, in 1951 the whole of predominantly Muslim Northern Nigeria had only a single graduate – a Christian (Iliffe, 1995). Rodney reports that, 'In 1874, when Fourah Bay College (Freetown, Sierra Leone) sought and obtained affiliation with Durham University, *The Times* newspaper declared that Durham should next affiliate with the London Zoo' (Rodney, 1972: 141).

Meanwhile, rural education facilities were rudimentary and concentrated on very little more than 'the three Rs'. In some colonies the provision of secondary and higher education was negligible, as in the Belgian Congo, where although in the early 1950s a higher proportion of the population (one in 12) was attending primary school than almost anywhere else in tropical Africa, the provision of secondary education for the African population was virtually non-existent, with only one secondary school for every 870 primary schools. At the same time, the ratio of secondary schools to primary schools was 1:25 in French West Africa, and 1:70 in both Gold Coast (Ghana) and Nigeria.

Transport

In material terms, too, the legacies of colonialism have been substantial, particularly in the form of transport and communications links. The basic road and rail networks of many contemporary states owe their origins to the colonial era. Unfortunately, most of these lines of communication reflected the economic needs of the colonial powers and do not necessarily coincide with the contemporary needs of independent states. In West Africa, for example, there was little connectivity in road, rail and air links between Anglophone and Francophone countries. Meanwhile in Southern Rhodesia (now Zimbabwe), the principal road and rail links connected the main areas of European settlement and economic

activity on the highveld, and exited through what was British South Africa.

Transport and communication links were, in a way, subordinate to the urbanisation process which, as we have seen, was either established for the first time, or completely restructured during the colonial period to favour one or two major ports that functioned as crucial connecting points between the colonial and global economies. Many instances of exaggerated urban primacy in the contemporary world have their origins in the colonial economy (see also Chapter 9). Within these cities, too, there is often a considerable physical legacy of colonial triumphalism in architectural form, planning layout and infrastructure provision (Plates 2.4 and 2.6; King, 1990).

Administrative, legal and judicial systems

Colonial cities were points of administration, rather than production, and some would argue that the most useful legacy of colonialism is the administrative, legal and judicial systems that were established by the metropolitan powers. There is certainly some truth in this as far as orderly and efficient administration was concerned. But the elitism inherent within these systems still continues in their successors, particularly the use of European languages in the highest echelons of the state.

In Hong Kong, the colonial experience ended as recently as 1 July 1997. By the 1980s, Hong Kong's civil service had developed a relatively high degree of autonomy and institutional integrity and had taken effective measures to prevent other groups and institutions from challenging its authority. In 1958, financial and budgetary autonomy was granted to Hong Kong by the UK (Burns, 1999).

For most of the colonial era, the colonial government banned political parties and a mainly appointed legislature was kept weak and largely ineffective, being answerable only to the Governor. The bureaucracy in colonial Hong Kong managed to remain neutral in relation to business and political interests, and government positions were denied to party activists. However, certain colonial practices undermined morale in the civil service, for example, hiring expatriates to do jobs that could easily be done by local people.

Plate 2.6 Grand French colonial architecture in Dakar, Senegal
(*photo*: Tony Binns)

Earlier in the colonial period many of Hong Kong's administrative officers had middle class origins and were recruited from Oxford and Cambridge. Although there was a move towards employing local staff from 1984, even as late as 1997 some 23 per cent of the top 1130 positions in the civil service directorate were held by expatriates (Burns, 1999). The fact that all government business was conducted in English rather than Chinese (Cantonese) also added to both inefficiency and criticism. Only in 1974 did the government adopt both English and Chinese as official languages, though publication of laws in both languages did not occur until 1989.

The common law legal system defined the relationship between state and society and between the state and its employees, and all civil servants held office 'at the pleasure of the Crown'. Elsewhere, former colonies have attempted to modernise their legal systems (e.g. Senegal and Madagascar), but in many countries present-day legal systems still bear a strong resemblance to those inherited from the former colonial power. Fairness was rarely a characteristic of colonial administrative and legal systems, and here again some unfortunate legacies have persisted. Thus Singapore, like many other countries, retained and uses legislation on detention without trial. In similar fashion, building regulations and standards retained from the colonial period have long prevented more effective

housing policies being pursued within contemporary cities of the Global South.

The relationships between different styles of colonial governance structures and subsequent levels of political stability and instability in the post-colonial period have also been examined. Blanton et al. (2001) have shown how the French colonial strategy of centralisation and assimilation in Africa led to the development of a ranked system of ethnic stratification, whereas in British colonies ethnic minorities had a greater opportunity to engage in political action in what was 'an unranked system of ethnic stratification' (Blanton et al., 2001: 489). It is suggested that post-colonial ethnic conflict has been a greater problem in Anglophone African countries because 'the unranked nature of Anglophone polities – a direct result of their colonial legacy – provides the mobilization structures that facilitate violent collective action' (Blanton et al., 2001: 488).

Economic activities

What underpinned almost all these consequences of colonialism were its economic activities and here the direct legacy has also been substantial. For example, with the development of the cocoa industry in the early twentieth century, Ghana (then Gold Coast) experienced an economic boom, such that Moradi concludes that 'Ghana achieved a remarkable rate of development at the beginning of the twentieth century' (Moradi, 2008: 1117). However, the narrowing of production into one or two commodities persisted in the great majority of countries. This posed enormous problems for those countries, the great majority of which watched commodity prices continue to fall and failed to diversify their economies. And the spatial concentration of these activities continues to cause problems of regional inequality and imbalance, often reinforced by post-colonial urbanisation trends. As Blaine Harden (1993) cynically sums up the African colonial experience,

> Africans were not asked whether they wanted to be guinea pigs. They were bullied into it. Europeans overwhelmed the continent in the last quarter of the nineteenth century, looking for loot. They carved it up into weirdly shaped money-making colonies, many of them landlocked, all of them administered from the top down. The colonies bore little or no relation to existing geographical or tribal boundaries. Total conquest took all of about twenty-five years. Then, after sixty years or so – the shortest introduction to so-called civilization that any so-called primitive people have ever had – the Europeans turned their authoritarian creation over to the Africans.
>
> (Harden, 1993: 16–17)

For some 25 years after the end of the Second World War the economies of the newly independent states of Asia and Africa remained virtually unchanged under the development strategies of neo-classical advisers such as Lewis or Rostow (see Chapter 3). These economies were still reliant on the export of a narrow range of primary commodities, possibly with some diversification into import substitution industries. For the most part, these economies were still controlled from the outside through the medium of tied aid or the activities of trans-national corporations (TNCs) (see Chapters 7 and 8). Although metropolitan powers continued to be linked in this way with their former colonies, new international players were equally dominant, particularly the USA.

Neo-colonialism

Some would argue that colonialism has given way to 'neo-colonialism', in which powerful states such as the USA, the former USSR, Japan, China, India and,

collectively, the member states of the European Union, exercise economic and political control over the economies and societies of the underdeveloped world. Although the colonies might have gained their independence, their economic and political systems are still controlled from outside, notably through aid, trade and political relationships. It might be suggested, for example, that the Lomé Conventions, linking the EU and some 60 African, Caribbean and Pacific states, are a new form of colonialism, or 'neo-colonialism', in laying down guidelines for aid, trade and investment agreements. Similarly, since the 1980s, the structural adjustment programmes of the World Bank and International Monetary Fund have imposed liberal economic policies and a wide range of conditions on the poor countries that have sought financial help (see Chapters 3 and 7).

New International Division of Labour (NIDL)

From the 1970s, there occurred a more sustained and substantial outflow of investment funds from Europe and North America as industrial profits began to decline in those areas. The various reasons for this are often related to the rising costs of labour and environmental protection. New financial systems, and the windfall profits from the OPEC oil price rise, facilitated the investment of money overseas in new manufacturing plants in the Global South. The usual term to describe this post-colonial phenomenon is the New International Division of Labour (NIDL), in which the low-cost labour-intensive parts of the manufacturing process are siphoned off to the Global South where costs are lower. A detailed critique of this fragmentation of the production process and the role played by TNCs can be found later in Chapter 4. However, at this point, and as a link to Chapter 4, it might be useful to examine the concept of NIDL as it has become almost synonymous with the post-colonial period.

NIDL is perhaps the third international division of labour:

➤ The first comprised the production and extraction of primary commodities in the colonies and their manufacture in the metropolitan countries.

➤ The second involved the shift of some industry into the newly independent countries under import substitution policies.

➤ The third began to expand in the 1970s, and involves the fragmentation of the manufacturing process and the shift of a large proportion of this to the Global South, largely through the medium of TNCs.

It is important to realise that all three international divisions of labour are currently in operation. In particular, large amounts of TNC investment continue to sustain primary resource production in countries such as Papua New Guinea, almost all of which is exported to advanced capitalist economies.

The latest international division of labour came about through a conjuncture of changes: reduced profitability in Europe and USA, largely through increased production costs, cheap production costs in the Global South, encouragement given to urban-industrial growth in the South by international development agencies, facilitating developments in communications technology and the parallel increasing mobility and flexibility of financial services. The result was new levels of extraction of surplus value created by super-exploitation of poor country labour, which accrues few skills and with limited backward linkages into the local economy (see Chapter 3).

The problem with NIDL is that it over-emphasises the inevitability of this exploitation and fails to credit peripheral social formations with any autonomy to manipulate foreign investment to maximise local advantage. The concept is also undermined in its global applicability by the fact that NIDL was initially very selective, with just six countries, usually identified as the four Asian tigers (Hong Kong, Singapore, South Korea, Taiwan), together with Mexico and Brazil, receiving the majority of TNC investment, largely because TNCs rely on more than just cheap labour for efficient and profitable production.

It can be argued that the range of countries which are industrialising through the medium of foreign investment is widening. In particular, analysts point to the rapid rise of countries such as Malaysia, Thailand and Indonesia. But these countries receive much, if not most, of their investment from within the Asia-Pacific region, notably from the four Asian tigers which used NIDL to retain surplus value and generate regional investment.

It is clear in this context that national governments have not been overwhelmed or displaced by Western TNCs, but act in concert with indigenous equivalents to promote joint interests overseas. What has emerged, therefore, is a regional division of labour (RDL) operating both within and in conflict with NIDL. Nascent RDLs exist in other areas of the Global South too, such as the Middle East or South Asia, or even southern Africa, but the extended world recession of the 1980s and 1990s slowed their emergence considerably.

New International Economic Order (NIEO)

Often confused with NIDL, largely because it first surfaced at about the same time, was the New International Economic Order (NIEO). This concept mainly derived from the United Nations and was underpinned by a mounting concern with the failure of modernisation strategies (Chapter 3) to achieve much for most people in poor countries.

Mounting poverty, growing national debts and the pessimistic environmental predictions of the Club of Rome all resulted in the declaration by the UN in 1994 of its intention to establish an NIEO, although we must also be aware of the self-interest of Western nations threatened by recession, oil price hikes and inflation. The five principal areas of concern identified were trade reform, monetary reforms, debt relief, technology transfer and regional cooperation.

In fact, very little was achieved for the lasting benefit of the developing nations, not least because of their growing diversity of interests (Chapter 1), and eventually the NIEO became suffused into the structural adjustment programmes of the New Right (Chapter 3). In effect, the NIEO became a justification for TNC investment in the Global South in the name of development, and as such was a factor in the internationalisation of the division of labour which paralleled it.

Conclusion

Colonialism has undoubtedly done much to shape the world in which we live today. The configuration and character of particular countries was in many cases determined by the European powers dividing territory and drawing boundaries at some distance from the colonies.

In the post-independence phase, many former colonies have retained the language, education, legal and health systems of their colonial masters, whilst trading networks and communications links often bear strong similarity to those of the colonial period. The process, experience and legacies of colonialism remain highly controversial and hotly contested issues. The extent to which the European powers benefited from exploitation of their colonies, and whether particular African, Asian and Latin American countries would actually have been better off today without a colonial history, are just two elements of the ongoing debate.

Key points

- The particular nature of colonialism varied according to the motives and also with the political economies and cultures of both the metropolitan power and the colonised territory.

- Post-colonialism has provided an important perspective on the colonial experience in demonstrating how the production of Western knowledge is inseparable from the exercise of Western power.

- Commerce and trade dominated the first phase of colonialism – mercantile colonialism. Trading companies were heavily involved in both production and trade during this phase. The plantation system and slave labour were key features of this phase.

- The second phase of colonialism – industrial colonialism – involved the expansion of overseas markets for European manufactured goods and the overseas production of raw materials and food for European countries. Colonies were increasingly established and organised by the state rather than by trading companies, although business and state often worked together.

- During the phase of late colonialism, the two world wars and the intervening depression severely disrupted colonial economies, with a reduction in investment from Europe and falling commodity prices. The period was characterised by increasing European migration to the colonies, and by a shift in the balance of administrative power from the metropolitan centres to the colonies. The post-Second World War period saw a move towards decolonisation and the granting of independence to colonial states.

- There is an ongoing debate about whether colonialism was on balance beneficial or detrimental to the economies and societies of those countries that were colonised.

Further reading

Blunt, A. and McEwan, C. (eds) (2002) *Postcolonial Geographies*. London: Continuum.
A valuable collection of papers which help to de-mystify the concept of post-colonialism.

Blunt, A. and Wills, J. (2000) *Dissident Geographies*. London: Prentice Hall.
This book contains some useful ideas on post-colonial studies.

Crush, J. (ed) (1995) *The Power of Development*. London: Routledge.
A much-cited text which examines a variety of perspectives on the concept of 'development', written by some leading scholars in the field.

Duncan, J.S., Johnson, N.C. and Schein, R.H. (eds) (2004) *A Companion to Cultural Geography*. Oxford: Blackwell.
A very useful reference book on issues relating to cultural geography.

Griffiths, I.L. (1995) *The African Inheritance*. London: Routledge.
An excellent text on the colonisation and decolonisation of Africa.

McEwan, C. (2002) Postcolonialism, in Desai, V. and Potter, R.B. (eds), *The Companion to Development Studies*. London: Arnold, 127–31.
A particularly clear and concise introductory essay on post-colonialism.

McEwan, C. (2009) *Postcolonialism and Development*. London: Routledge.
A key text on post-colonialism

McLeod, J. (2000) *Beginning Postcolonialism*. Manchester: Manchester University Press.
A helpful text which explores the concept of post-colonialism.

Rodney, W. (1972) *How Europe Underdeveloped Africa*. Washington, DC: Howard University Press.
A classic and thought-provoking text which examines how, in the views of the author, Africa suffered as a result of European colonisation.

Said, E. (1978) *Orientalism*. New York: Pantheon Books.

A seminal book, which has played an influential role in understanding relationships between colonisers and colonised.

Sartre, J.P. (1964, 2001) *Colonialism and Neo-colonialism*. English translation (2001). London: Routledge.
An important text from a key French thinker on colonialism.

Williams, P. and Chrisman, L. (eds) (1993) *Colonial Discourse and Postcolonial Theory*. London: Prentice Hall.
A collection of essays examining colonisation, colonial perceptions and post-colonialism.

Websites

http://pulsemedia.org/2009/03/25/edward-said-culture-and-imperialism/
Speech by Edward Said on 'Culture and Imperialism', given at York University, Toronto, 10 February, 1993. An interesting speech from a leading thinker and the author of the influential book, *Orientalism*, first published in 1978.

http://www.mkgandhi.org/
Useful wide-ranging website on Mahatma Gandhi, who played a key role in the drive for independence in India, which in turn had a significant impact on the wider decolonisation process.

Discussion topics

➤ Select a country that was colonised and examine what you believe are the positive and negative legacies of colonialism.

➤ Identify some of the key elements in writings on post-colonialism and suggest how these have enhanced understanding of the colonial experience.

➤ Examine the ideological and practical differences between the phases of mercantile, industrial and late colonialism.

Chapter 3
Theories and strategies of development

This chapter introduces readers to the main theories of development that have been advanced over time, and indicates how these have been put into practice. By the end of the chapter, readers should be aware of the most important characteristics of different theories and strategies of development. At the outset, the terms 'theory', 'strategy', 'ideology' and 'paradigm' are defined in respect of the field of development studies.

Throughout the chapter, it is emphasised that thinking about development tends to be evolutionary rather than revolutionary, so that new ideas and approaches often come into existence without the eradication of older ones, which often continue to exist and are applied in parallel. Amongst other reasons this is because different approaches to development have been pursued in different parts of the world, often as a result of unique political processes, which in turn emphasises the contested nature of development. The chapter:

➤ Considers the nature and role of theories, strategies and ideologies in the field of development studies.

➤ Reviews classical and neo-classical approaches to development theory, these approaches being based on traditional economic theory. Such approaches represent 'top-down' development. The more recent impact of neo-liberalism on development is also considered.

➤ Considers the findings of historical– empirical approaches to the understanding of development – that is, learning from what has actually happened in the past in various regions.

➤ Overviews radical and Marxist-inspired theories, especially the dependency school.

➤ Stresses the diversity of alternative approaches to development, including an array of 'bottom-up' formulations.

➤ Reviews alternate perspectives on development and how livelihoods are understood, including the Sustainable Livelihoods Framework and the notion of 'diverse economies'.

➤ Links the conditions of modernity and postmodernity to development theory.

Introduction

Since the mid-twentieth century, a major feature of development practice and theory has been a series of fundamental changes in thinking about the process of development and indeed what constitutes development itself. This search for new conceptualisations of development has been mirrored by changes in development practice in the field. It is important to note that the theories discussed in this chapter have influenced the practice of the agencies which have applied development, which is discussed in Chapter 7.

There has been much debate and controversy about what development is, which parallels changing views as to its definition, and the strategies by means of which it may be pursued. Chapter 1 exemplified this in respect of the recent debates about the value of the concept of development itself, in terms of anti-development and post-development. This was also demonstrated by the variety of approaches to development that have been adopted, ranging from development as economic growth, to development as promoting human rights and freedoms.

The period since the 1950s has seen the promotion and application of many varied geographies of development and there is much vitality in the field. Such diversity is demonstrated by the number and variety of major books and other items published on 'development' over the decades (see, for example, Apter, 1987; Brohman, 1996; Clark, 2006; Corbridge, 1986; Cowen and Shenton, 1996; Crush, 1995b; Desai and Potter, 2014; Escobar, 1995; Greig et al., 2007; Hettne, 1995; Hopper, 2012; Kothari, 2005; Leys, 1996; Mehmet, 1999; O'Tuathail, 1994; Panayiotopoulos and Capps, 2001; Power, 2003; Preston, 1987, 1996; Rapley, 1996; Schuurman, 1993; Sen, 2000; Simon, 2006; Slater, 1992a, 1992b, 1993; Streeten, 1995; Thirlwall, 1999 and Williams et al., 2014).

The purpose of this chapter is to provide an introduction to the different approaches to development that have been proposed and followed, principally since around 1940, both in theory and in practice. As noted above, these different approaches reflect the changing paradigms of development that were outlined in Chapter 1. Many of these paths to development will be further elaborated on in Parts II and III of this text.

In many ways the information detailed here is an historical account of how, primarily since the 1940s, development theory and thinking have evolved and this is presented here to document what was, and often still is considered as the key thinking underlying development theory and practice. While some of the material presented enjoys less credence than it once did, it is reviewed here to illustrate what the core foci of development thinking have been over time. It should be noted that the theories outlined in the four sections below, which constitute the bulk of the thesis, often exist and are still subscribed to in parallel, by different schools of thought.

A major theme in the present account will be to illustrate that ideas about development have long been highly controversial and contested. This is because thinking about development paths and states is essentially political. This argument is further highlighted in the conclusion to the chapter, which briefly sets out some of the relationships between development theory and the societal conditions of modernity and post-modernity. The linked contention that development theory and development studies have currently reached an impasse or deadlock is also considered as part of this account, an argument that draws on the positions of anti- and post-development introduced in Chapter 1.

Theories, strategies and ideologies of development

Introductory definitions

The view provided of development thinking in this chapter is very wide and eclectic. Accordingly, a broad definition of paths to development is also adopted at the outset. To use Hettne's (1995) nomenclature, the chapter reviews selected aspects of development theories, development strategies and development ideologies. Before doing so, these three basic terms must be defined:

1 *Development theories* may be regarded as sets of apparently logical propositions which purport to explain how development has occurred in the past, and/or should occur in the future. Development theories can either be normative, when they generalise about what should be the case in an ideal world, or positive in the sense of dealing with what has actually been the case. The arena of development theory is primarily, although by no means exclusively, to be encountered in the academic literature.

2 On the other hand, *development strategies* can be defined as the practical paths to development that may be pursued by international agencies, states around the world, non-government organisations and community-based organisations, in an effort to stimulate change within particular nations, regions and continents.

3 Different development agendas will reflect different goals and objectives. These goals will reflect social, economic, political, cultural, ethical, moral and even religious influences. Thus, what may be referred to as different *development ideologies* may be recognised. Chapter 1 stressed how, both in theory and in practice, early perspectives on development were almost exclusively concerned with promoting economic growth. Subsequently, however, the predominant ideology within the academic literature changed to emphasise political, social, ethnic, cultural, ecological and other dimensions of the wider process of development and change. Sometimes the term *paradigm* is used to refer to broad sets of ideas about development (see Key idea box).

A sensible approach is to follow Hettne (1995) and to employ the idea of *development thinking* in the body of this chapter. The expression 'development thinking' may be used as a catch-all phrase indicating the sum total of ideas about development, including pertinent aspects of development theory, strategy and ideology. Thus, the present chapter takes a very broad remit in presenting an overview of development strategies.

Key idea

What is a paradigm?

Paradigms are generally defined as supra-models — that is, broad sets of ideas that come to dominate particular groups of scholars and/or particular disciplines. Once accepted, these form the agreed or consensus view of the discipline or scholarly group, and are generally defended until the evidence is so overwhelming that they have to be replaced by a new paradigm or supra-model. In the context of development, major theories of how economies have developed and how best economies should be developed, can be regarded as giving rise to paradigms. It is the evolution and nature of these paradigms in the field of development studies that forms the focus of this chapter.

The contested nature of development thinking

Development thinking has evolved through many sharp twists and turns during the twentieth century. Thus the various theories that have been produced have not commanded attention in a strictly sequential temporal manner. In other words, as a new set of ideas about development has come into favour, earlier theories and strategies have not been totally discarded and replaced. Rather, theories and strategies have tended to stack up upon one another, coexisting in what can sometimes be described as a very convoluted manner. Thus, in discussing development theory, Hettne (1995: 64) has drawn attention to the 'tendency of social science paradigms to accumulate rather than fade away'.

This characteristic of development thinking as a distinct field of enquiry can be considered in more detail, using Thomas Kuhn's ideas on the structure of scientific revolutions (Figure 3.1). Kuhn (1962) argued that scientific disciplines are dominated at particular points in time by communities of researchers and their associated methods and foci, and they define the subjects and the issues deemed to be of importance within them.

Kuhn referred to these as 'invisible colleges', and he noted that they serve to define and perpetuate research which confirms the validity of the existing paradigm; he called this 'normal science'. Kuhn noted that a fundamental change occurs only when the number of observations and questions confronting the status quo of normal science becomes too large to be dealt with by means of small changes. However, if the proposed changes are major, and a new paradigm is adopted, a scientific revolution can be said to have occurred, linked to a period of so-called extraordinary research.

In this model, therefore, scientific disciplines basically advance by means of revolutions in which the prevailing normal science is replaced by 'extraordinary 'science, and ultimately a new form of 'normal' science develops.

In dealing with social scientific discourses, it is perhaps inevitable that the field of development theory is characterised by evolutionary rather than revolutionary change. Evidence of the persistence of ideas in some quarters, years after they have been discarded elsewhere, is a reality in the world.

Given that development thinking is not just about the theoretical interpretation of facts, but rather about values, aspirations, social goals, and ultimately, that which is moral and ethical, it is understandable that change in development theory leads to the parallel evolution of ideas, rather than revolution. Hence conflict, debate, contention and positionality are all inherent in the discussion of development strategies and associated plural and diverse geographies of development.

There are many ways to categorise development thinking through time. Broadly speaking, it is suggested here that four major approaches to the examination of development theory can be recognised, and these are shown in Figure 3.2. This categorisation follows the framework originally suggested by Potter and Lloyd-Evans (1998). The four approaches are:

1 the classical–traditional approach;
2 the historical–empirical approach;
3 the radical–political economy–dependency approach; and

4 alternative and bottom-up approaches (including themes of anti-development, diverse economies and sustainable livelihoods).

Following the argument presented in the last section, each of these approaches may be regarded as expressing a particular ideological standpoint, and can also be identified by virtue of having occupied the centre stage of the development debate at particular points in time.

However, each approach still retains currency in certain quarters. Hence, in the realm of development theory and academic writing, left-wing views may well be more popular than classical–traditional and neo-classical formulations. But in the area of practical development strategies, the period since the 1980s has seen the implementation of neoliberal interpretation of classical theory, stressing the liberalisation of trade, along with public sector cutbacks, as a part of structural adjustment programmes (SAPs), aimed at reducing the involvement of the state in the economy and promoting the free market.

The account which follows uses these four divisions to overview the leading theories, strategies and ideologies that have been used to explain and promote the development process. It is important to note that the four broad approaches detailed below exist, or have existed in parallel, and that the material listed in the next four sections does not necessarily follow chronologically from one section to the next. Hence neo-liberalism, which is an extension of earlier 'classical–traditional' approaches, exists in parallel with the pursuit of alternate or bottom-up approaches.

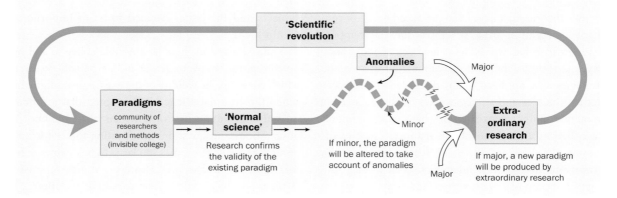

Figure 3.1 Scientific revolutions: picturing Kuhn's model of their structure

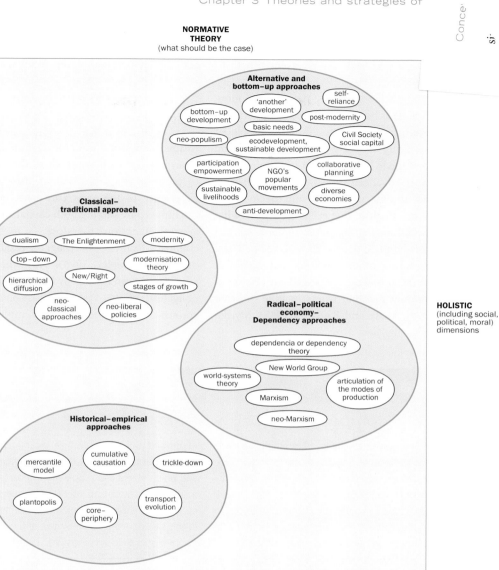

NORMATIVE THEORY
(what should be the case)

ECONOMIC
(focus on economic dimensions alone)

HOLISTIC
(including social, political, moral) dimensions

POSITIVE THEORY
(what has been the case)

Figure 3.2 Development theory: a framework for this chapter

Classical–traditional approaches: early views from the 'developed' world (North)

Introduction

The traditional approach to the study of development derives from classical and neo-classical economics and has generally dominated policy thinking at the global scale. Classical economic theory, dating from before 1914, was strongly based on the writings of Adam Smith (1723–1790) and David Ricardo (1772–1823). Both Smith and Ricardo equated economic development with the growth of world trade and the law of comparative advantage (Sapsford, 2008) (see Key idea box). Neo-classical theories, those having generally been produced ce 1945 (although some date back to the 1870s), take an essentially similar worldview, stressing the importance of liberating world trade as the essential path to growth and development.

Traditional approaches generally regard developing countries (the South) as being characterised by a dualistic structure. Hettne (1995) notes the strong role of dichotomous thinking in early anthropology, where comparisons were made between what were referred to as 'backward' and 'advanced' societies, the 'barbarian' and the 'civilised', and the 'traditional' and the 'modern'.

The fundamental dualism that exists is between what is seen as a traditional, indigenous, underdeveloped sector on the one hand, and a modern, developed and Westernised one on the other. It follows that the global development problem is seen as a scaled-up version of this basic dichotomy. Seminal works include those of Hirschman (1958), Meier and Baldwin (1957), Myrdal

(1957), Perloff and Wingo (1961), Perroux (1950) and Schultz (1953), who all sought to understand and address the identified developmental differences.

The basic framework: the contribution of A.O. Hirschman

In this framework, underdevelopment was understood as an initial state beyond which the West has managed to progress (Rapley, 1996). It also envisages that the experience of the West can assist other countries in catching-up by sharing both capital and know-how. The avowed intention, therefore, is to bring developing countries to the modern age of capitalism and liberal democracy (Rapley, 1996). This concept parallels the argument raised in 1949 by President Truman about the obligation of the West to assist the underdeveloped countries to copy the western example (see Chapter 1).

Key idea

The law of comparative cost advantage

The bases of the economic principles of international trade were formulated by the economist Adam Smith in his book *The Wealth of Nations*, which was published in 1776. Smith argued that it made sense for particular regions and nations to produce those commodities for which they possessed the greatest comparative advantage. In this manner, at least in theory, global production can be maximised. Subsequently, by engaging in trade, countries can obtain the goods that they do not themselves produce, and which others can supply more cheaply. The arguments advanced by Smith and later Ricardo suggested the economic efficiency of 'open' or 'liberal' trade policies, and in this sense were the forerunners of the arguments in favour of globalisation (Sapsford, 2008).

The general economic development model of the American economist A.O. Hirschman forms a convenient starting point for discussion of the traditional approach. Hirschman (1958), in *The Strategy of Economic Development*, advanced a notably optimistic view in presenting the neo-classical position (Hansen, 1981). Specifically, Hirschman argued that polarisation should be viewed as an inevitable characteristic of the early stages of economic development. This represents the direct advocacy of a basically unbalanced economic growth strategy, whereby investment is concentrated in a few key sectors of the economy. It is envisaged that the growth of these sectors will create demand for the other sectors of the economy, so that a chain of disequilibria will lead to growth, what has commonly been called the 'spread of growth'. The corollary of sectorally unbalanced growth is geographically uneven development, and Hirschman specifically cited Perroux's (1955) idea of the natural growth pole as an ideal intervention to pursue. Perroux argued that governments should focus and encourage public and private sector investment on particular centres from which growth would diffuse to their hinterlands.

The forces of concentration were collectively referred to by Hirschman as 'polarisation'. The crucial argument, however, was that eventually development in the core will lead to the 'trickling down' of growth-inducing tendencies to backward regions. These trickle-down effects were seen by Hirschman as an inevitable and spontaneous process.

Thus, the clear policy implication of Hirschman's thesis was that governments should not intervene to reduce inequalities, for at some juncture in the future the search for profits will promote the spontaneous spin-off of growth-inducing industries to backward regions. Hirschman's approach is therefore set in the traditional liberal model of letting the market decide. The process whereby spatial polarisation gives way to spatial dispersion out from the core to the backward regions (later called the periphery) has subsequently come to be referred to as the point of 'polarisation reversal' (Richardson, 1977, 1980).

The doctrine of unequal growth

The full significance of these ideas concerning polarised development extends far beyond their use as a basis for understanding the historical processes of urban-industrial change, for in the 1950s and 1960s they came to represent an explicit framework for regional development policy (Friedmann and Weaver, 1979). Hence the doctrine of unequal growth gained both positive and normative currency in the first post-war decade, and the path to growth was actively pursued via urban-based industrial growth interventions. The policies of non-intervention, enhancing natural growth centres, and creating new induced sub-cores became the order of the day. As Friedmann and Weaver (1979: 93) observe, the 'argument boiled down to this: inequality was efficient for growth, equality was inefficient', so that, 'given these assumptions about economic growth, the expansion of manufacturing was regarded as the major propulsive force'. The result, for many years, was the belief that expanding manufacturing industry was a key way in which to achieve national development, with the outcome that many countries offered incentives to manufacturing firms to establish in identified growth centres.

The elaboration of modernisation theory

Hirschman's ideas can be seen as part of a wider modernisation theory, which was in vogue during the 1950s and 1960s. The paradigm was grounded on the view that the gaps in development which exist between the developed and developing countries can gradually be overcome on an imitative basis. The emphasis was placed on a simple dichotomy between development and underdevelopment. Thereby, developing countries would inexorably come to resemble developed countries, and 'in practice, modernization was thus very much the same as Westernization' (Hettne, 1995: 52).

The modernisation thesis was largely developed in the field of political science, but was taken up from an essentially spatial viewpoint by a group of geographers in the late 1960s (Gould, 1970; Riddell, 1970; Soja, 1968, 1974), although sociologists also spent some considerable time working along these lines.

In such works, sets of indices which, were held to reflect modernisation, were mapped and/or subjected to multivariate statistical analysis to reveal the 'modernisation surface' of a country. For example, using such an approach, Gould (1970) examined what he regarded as the modernisation surface of Tanzania (Box 3.1).

One of the classic papers written in this mould was by Leinbach (1972), who investigated the modernisation surface in Malaya (now Malaysia) between 1895 and 1969, using indicators such as the number of hospitals and schools per head of the population, together with the incidence of postal and telegraph facilities and road and rail densities. This modernisation approach served to emphasise that core urban areas of Malaya and the transport corridors running between them were the focus of dynamic change (Leinbach, 1972). In 1895, early growth was almost exclusively related to the west coast, specifically centering on Kuala Lumpur, with a clear inland island around Ipoh. By 1955, the so-called modernisation surface had penetrated to the east of the nation along two 'corridors' (Figure 3.3). In many parts of the world an endeavour was made, from the 1950s, to determine the modernisation surfaces and to promote modernisation through support for growth centres and manufacturing industries.

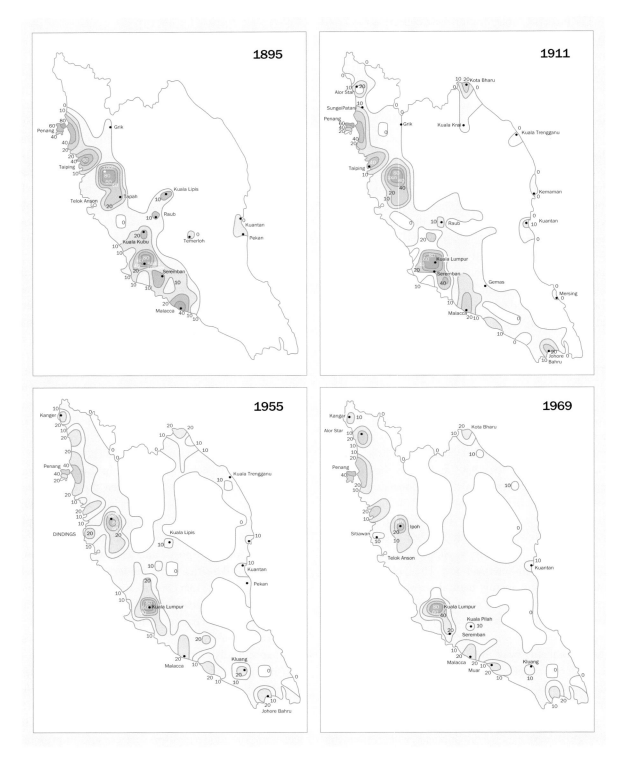

Figure 3.3 The modernisation surface for Malaya, 1895–1969
Source: Adapted from Leinbach (1972)

BOX 3.1

Modernisation and development in Tanzania

Tanzania became independent in 1961 after a British and German colonial history (Hoyle, 1979). The area was occupied by Germans in the 1880s, and after the First World War it became British-administered Tanganyika. Like many former colonies, the population was very concentrated along the narrow coastal region (see Figure 3.4). The other major urban nodes such as Morogoro, Iringa and Mbeya formed a corridor running in a south-westerly direction from Dar-es-Salaam on the Indian Ocean coast.

During the era when modernisation thinking was in vogue, 'islands' of development linked by major transport lines were recognised by geographers such as Gould (1969, 1970), Hoyle (1979) and Safier (1969). Traditionally, the settlement pattern had comprised dispersed villages, although strong urban concentration around Dar-es-Salaam occurred during the colonial period, with Hoyle (1979) referring to it as an 'hypertropic cityport' (O'Connor, 1983).

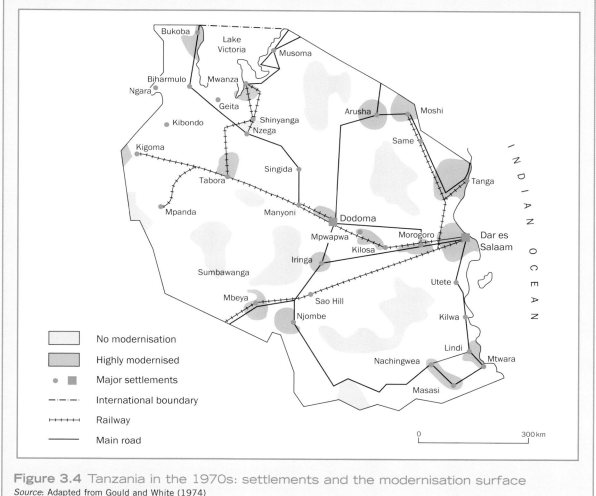

Figure 3.4 Tanzania in the 1970s: settlements and the modernisation surface
Source: Adapted from Gould and White (1974)

BOX 3.1 (continued)

Lundqvist (1981) identified four main phases of development planning in Tanzania between 1961 and 1980. The period from 1961 to 1966 was indeed seen as the legacy of the colonial era, during which such planning as was carried out, was sectoral rather than regional in scope, as a result of which infrastructure remained concentrated in the principal towns and urban–rural disparities were maintained. Thus, one could talk about a highly polarised 'modernised–non-modernised' development surface which largely reflected colonial penetration.

However, subsequently, development in Tanzania has been far more complex than this simplistic overview implies. Thus, the principal policy efforts to reduce urban–rural differences can be identified as giving rise to the second and most important development phase, lasting from 1967 to 1972, and witnessing the emergence of a strong commitment to rural-based development, linked to strong principles of traditional African socialism, championed by President Julius Nyrere of Tanzania.

These policies were based on the Arusha Declaration of 1967, which attacked privilege and sought to place strong emphasis on the principles of equality, cooperation, self-reliance and nationalism. Such ideas were put into practice in the second five-year plan, 1969–1974. The major policy imperative was *ujamaa* villagisation, which was regarded as the expression of 'modern traditionalism', i.e. a twentieth-century version of traditional African village life. The word *ujamaa* is Swahili for familyhood. The intention was to concentrate scattered rural populations and, by this process of villagisation, to provide the services required for viable settlements. Reducing rural-to-urban migration was a major goal, along with lessening the dependence on major cities such as Dar-es-Salaam. *Ujamaa* villages were envisaged as cooperative

ventures by means of which initiative and self-reliance would be fostered, along socialist lines. In addition, efforts were also made to spread urban development away from Dar-es-Salaam towards nine selected regional growth centres. In overall terms, President Nyerere regarded these policies as a distinct move away from a slavish imitation of Western-style planning and development, based on uncritical 'modernisation'.

Despite having received much praise from certain quarters, the policies adopted in Tanzania have been viewed with considerable scepticism by others, especially those from a committed Marxist perspective. During the third phase, from 1973 to 1986, enforced movement to development villages occurred. Furthermore, by the fourth stage, starting in 1978, industry and urban development were once again being upgraded at the expense of *ujamaa* villages and rural progress. Thus, the fourth five-year plan, 1982/83 to 1985/86, gave priority to industrial development, and by this juncture the *ujamaa* concept appeared to have all but fallen from the consciousness of both planners and politicians alike.

Critical reflection

The word 'modernisation' is frequently used in the media and by politicians. For example, the former Prime Minister of the UK, Tony Blair, frequently talked about 'modernisation'. For a limited period, keep a note of all instances that you encounter the word – in written accounts or via broadcasts. In such references, what is it being suggested needs to be modernised? Are there clear implications as to the essential nature of modernising processes? How often is the term used in relation to processes in the Global South as opposed to the Global North?

Empirical and conceptual elaborations of modernisation theory

The process involved in the Malaysian case (Figure 3.3) is shown as an ideal-typical sequence in the four boxed diagrams depicted in the lower two-thirds of Figure 3.5. In the

lower figure, T1 to T4 refer to successive time-periods. The figure essentially represents the diffusion downwards of 'development' from the largest to the smallest settlement spatially, as shown schematically at the top of Figure 3.5. Thus, from a critical perspective, Friedmann and Weaver (1979: 120) argued that the approach only succeeded in 'mapping the penetration of neo-colonial capitalism'.

The hallmark of this work was that it posited that modernisation is basically a temporal–spatial process. In such a vision, underdevelopment is seen as something which can be overcome, principally by the spatial diffusion of modernity. A number of studies argued that growth occurs within the settlement system from the largest urban places to the smallest in a basically hierarchical sequence.

This is shown in the upper part of Figure 3.5. Foremost among the proponents of such a view was Hudson (1989), who applied the ideas of Hagerstrand (1953), concerning spatial diffusion, to the settlement or central place system, which is seen as existing in all countries and which was seen as having the potential to facilitate the 'diffusion' of modernisation and development. Hudson argued that, first, innovations can travel through the settlement system by a process of contagious spread, where there is a neighbourhood or regional effect of clustered growth. This was close to Schumpeter's (1911) general economic theory, in which he argued that the essence of development is the volume of innovations. Opportunities tend to occur in waves which surge after an initial innovation.

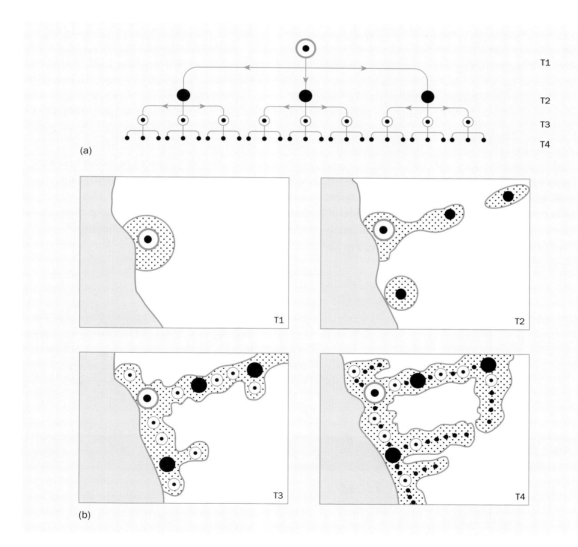

Figure 3.5 The spread of modernisation: hypothetical examples (a) down through the settlement system from the largest places to the smallest places and (b) over the national territory

Thus, Schumpeter argued that development tends to be 'jerky' and to appear in 'swarms', forming natural, spontaneous growth poles.

Second, Hudson noted that diffusion can occur downwards through the settlement system in a progressive manner, the point of introduction being the largest city. Pedersen (1970) argued the case for a strictly hierarchical process of innovation diffusion, an assertion which seemed to be borne out by some historical–empirical studies carried out in advanced capitalist societies such as the USA (Borchert, 1967) and England and Wales (Robson, 1973). Pedersen drew a very important distinction between domestic and entrepreneurial innovations; entrepreneurial innovations were the instrument of urban growth, not domestic innovations. In another frequently cited paper of the time, Berry (1972) also argued strongly in favour of a hierarchical diffusion process of growth-inducing innovations; this was seen as the result of the sequential market-searching procedures of firms, along with imitation effects.

But, notably, Berry's analysis was based on the diffusion of domestic, as opposed to entrepreneurial innovations, e.g. of television receivers. In other words, it dealt with what was happening to consumption rather than production. Furthermore, the critique of modernisation has to accept that even larger firms are currently coming to dominate the world capitalist system, a major development that is detailed in Chapter 4.

The 'top-down' paradigm of development and the 'Western world view'

All of these approaches, involving unequal and uneven growth, modernisation, urban industrialisation, the diffusion of innovations and hierarchic patterns of change and growth poles may be grouped together and regarded as constituting the 'top-down' paradigm of development (Stöhr and Taylor, 1981). Such approaches were generally determined by governments, foreign powers etc. i.e. from the 'top' and advocated the establishment of strong urban-industrial nodes as the basis of self-sustained growth, and is premised on the occurrence of strong trickle-down effects, by means of which, through time, it was believed that modernisation will inexorably be spread from urban to rural areas (Figures 3.3 and 3.5). This gives rise to the concept of the planned growth pole. Case study 3.1 presents the case of Singapore, where industrial development has formed an important component of development since independence in 1965.

As with modernism, all such approaches 'had a great appeal to a wider public (Western) due to the paternalistic attitude toward non-European cultures' (Hettne, 1995: 64). These approaches, together with modernisation, reflected the desire of the USA to order the post-War world, and were used to substantiate the logic of 'authoritative intervention', as noted in Chapter 1 (Preston, 1996). As Mehmet (1999: 1) stated, 'a Western worldview is the distinctive feature of the mainstream theories of economic development, old and new'. This world view has been predominantly 'bipolar', stressing a strict belief in Western rationality, science and technology.

Rostow's Stage Model of Economic Growth

Such models, including Rostow's (1960) classic *The Stages of Economic Growth*, see urban-industrial nodes as engines of growth and development. Rostow's work can be seen as the pre-eminent theory of modernisation to appear in the early 1960s (Preston, 1996). Rostow's position was avowedly right-wing politically (see Key thinker box).

Key thinker

The contribution of Walt Rostow

Walt Whitman Rostow's (1916–2003) classic work *The Stages of Economic Growth* carried the subtitle *A Non-Communist Manifesto*, bearing testimony to its highly political orientation during the time of the Cold War and the pursuit of competing ideologies designed to draw the countries of the South into either the 'capitalist' or 'socialist' camps. Rostow was fiercely anti-communist.

Key thinker (continued)

Plate 3.1 Walt Rostow
Source: Getty Images/Time & Life Pictures

The book, which was published in 1960 at the height of the Cold War, offered the prospect of automatic or almost formulaic growth, suggesting that by following a few simple rules the capitalist Western model could be emulated in any developing country. As Menzel (2006) notes, Rostow was fully aware that his development theory could be employed as an instrument in East–West relations, stressing the Washington path to development. As the same author notes, Rostow's theory was a very simple formulation, which was presented and recommended with 'missionary-zeal'.

Following a series of academic and governmental posts, when John Kennedy became President of the United States, Rostow became a full-time staff member of the US government and was successful in promoting development policy as US foreign policy. After the assassination of President Kennedy, Rostow continued to work under the new President Lyndon B. Johnson, and did so up until Richard Nixon became President. Above all else, Rostow's work shows the strongly political nature of development theory.

Case study 3.1

Industrialisation and development: the case of Singapore

Singapore is frequently held up as a nation which has created a strong 'Third World' economy in a relatively short period. Yet when Singapore became an independent republic in 1965 the prospects for growth did not seem much better than for many newly emerging nations. As noted by Drakakis-Smith (2000), Singapore is a very clean and green city which has led by example with respect to its environmental policies. But, as the same author notes, in social terms there has been a price to pay for this continued growth.

Singapore is a good example of a state that has grown by early industrialisation. The programme which was embarked upon in 1968 focused on both light industrialisation and some forms of heavy industry, such as oil refining, iron and steel, ship building and repairing. Thus, the contribution of manufacturing to GDP grew from 11.9 per cent in 1960, the average figure for developing nations, to 29.1 per cent in 1980. By 1995, this figure had increased to over one-quarter of GDP, standing at 26.5 per cent. The Government of Singapore was one of the first in Asia to realise the limitations of growth via low technology industrial development. Accordingly, throughout the 1980s, it sought to transform the economy by focusing on high-tech, high-value-added industries. It was fully intended that this 'second industrial revolution' would transform Singapore into the 'Switzerland' of Asia. Singapore's major trading partners are now the USA, Malaysia, Hong Kong, Japan and the European Union. The city-state has also become an important centre for financial services, with 149

Case study 3.1 (continued)

commercial banks and 79 merchant banks in 2000 (Whitaker's, 1999).

The World Bank frequently holds Singapore up as a model of what can be achieved by free market policies and industrial development, but several analysts have noted that there are local factors and that these are unlikely to be repeated elsewhere, and the strong role played by the state does not fully accord with current Western market policies. For instance, Drakakis-Smith (2000) argues that Singapore's success has been strongly predicated on its people, and the degree of human resource management has been intensive and ultimately authoritarian. Specifically, as in many states in the region, there have been very tough controls on labour unions, with the general introduction of factory unions rather than occupational unions. Many argue that this has also served to reduce social class solidarity. Japanese-style company loyalty has been the desired outcome. In addition, since the 1960s there has been strict state population control, both in respect of migration and also directed education programmes, with children being allocated to 'hand' and 'brain' streams at an early stage of their education. Drakakis-Smith (2000) also notes that ethnic disparities in wealth are prominent in Singapore, with Malays forming the most disadvantaged group, but within a general societal context where middle-class consumerism dominates.

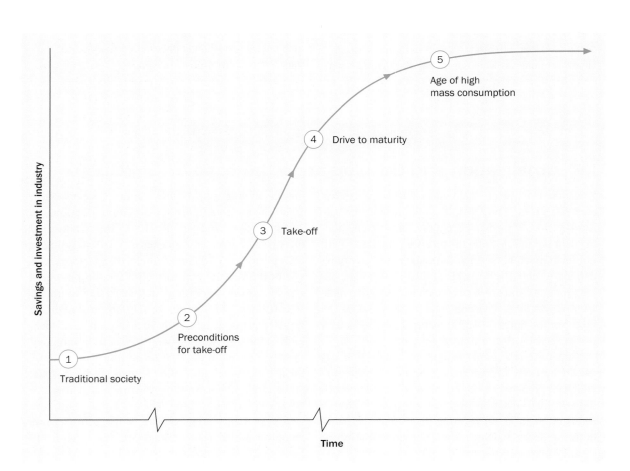

Figure 3.6 Rostow's five-stage model of development

Rostow envisaged that there were five stages through which all countries have to pass in the development process: the traditional society, preconditions to the take-off phase, take-off, the drive to maturity, and the age of mass consumption, as depicted in Figure 3.6. Rostow's stage model encapsulates faith in the capitalist system, as expressed by the subtitle of the work: a non-communist manifesto for economic growth. For Rostow, the critical point of take-off can occur where the net investment and savings as a ratio to national income grows from 5 to 10 per cent, thereby facilitating industrialisation.

Although Rostow's framework can, in many respects, be regarded as a derivation of Keynesian economics, based on the principle of state-led growth which prevailed in many parts of the world after the Great Depression and until the 1970s, its real significance lies in the simple fact that it seemed to offer every country an equal chance to develop (Preston, 1996). In particular, the 'take-off' period was calibrated as requiring 20 or so years to achieve, long enough to be conceivable, but short enough not to seem unattainable. The importance of the Rostowian framework was that it purported to explain the advantages of the Western development model. Further, in the words of Preston (1996: 178), the 'theory of modernisation follows on from growth theory, but is heavily influenced by the desire of the USA to combat the influence of the USSR in the Third World'.

In order to achieve 'take-off' and develop, the central argument was that developing nations needed to industrialise. The various approaches that could be followed in pursuing this aim are reviewed in Chapter 4, and include import substitute industrialisation (ISI), industrialisation by invitation (I by I), as well as 'big-push' industrial programmes (i.e. the provision of state direction and incentives).

For a number of reasons, it was the industrialisation by invitation model that received the most attention. One reason for this was the influential work of Arthur Lewis (1950, 1955), an economist from the West Indies, who was working at the University of Manchester at the time. Lewis set out the foundations of modernisation theory when he maintained that the juxtaposition of a backward traditional sector with an advanced modern sector meant that an 'unlimited supply of labour' existed for development. This duality means that industry can expand rapidly if industrialisation is financed by foreign capital according to his argument. This led to the so-called policy of 'industrialisation by invitation' (Plates 3.2 and 3.3). The metaphor of a snowball was used, arguing that once the process started to move it would develop its own self-sustaining momentum, like a snowball rolling downhill. This is, of course, an essentially similar argument to that of Walt Rostow.

The evaluation of modernisation and top-down approaches

Indeed, all such formulations place absolute faith in the existence of a linear and rational path to development, based on Western positivism and science, and the possibility that all nations can follow this in an unconstrained manner. All such thinking was directly related to the 'enlightenment' (see Power, 2002). Modernism was very much an urban focused phenomenon from 1850 onwards (Harvey, 1989). What is often referred to as 'universal' or 'high' modernism became hegemonic after 1945. Thus, the top-down approach was strongly associated with the 1950s, through to the early 1970s.

Taken together, many writers refer to these theories as representing 'Eurocentric development thinking', i.e. development theories and models rooted in Western European history and experience (see Chapter 1) (Hettne, 1995; Mehmet, 1999; Slater, 1992a, 1992b). Through such approaches, during the 1950s and 1960s development was seen as a strengthening of the material base of society, principally by means of industrialisation and urban development. Inevitably, the history of the first industrial state was taken as the model which should be followed, not only by the rest of Europe, but ultimately by the rest of the world, for 'it is quite natural that the original recipe for development given by the developed countries should emanate from their own experiences and prejudices' (Hettne, 1995: 37). It is notable that all the early theories of development were authored by men, and that virtually all of them were of Anglo-European origin.

It would be wrong, however, to give the impression that the focus on top-down, urban-industrial growth, linked to the quest for modernisation, was associated with a single and unified path. Four more or less distinct development strategies making up the early Western tradition can be identified (Hettne, 1995):

Plate 3.2 Part of an industrial estate in Bridgetown, Barbados
(*photo*: Rob Potter)

Plate 3.3 US-owned baseball factory in Port au Prince, Haiti
(*photo*: Sean Sprague, Panos Pictures)

1 *The liberal model*, the strategy implicitly discussed through much of the above account, stresses the importance of the free market and largely accepts the norm based on English development experience during the Industrial Revolution. In the 1980s and 1990s such views gained fresh currency in the form of the requirements that countries on the South were obliged to follow, when structural adjustment programmes (SAPs) were enforced by the International Monetary Fund (IMF), United States Agency for International Development (USAID) and the World Bank as the condition of loans given for so-called 'economic restructuring'. However, there have been major outcries against the impact of SAPs,

principally in respect of the harm that they do to the poor, and especially to women and children (see Chapter 7). This is fully exemplified by the Oxfam campaign that likened SAPs to medicines which need to be withdrawn from the marketplace, due to their risk to the health of vulnerable groups (see Figure 3.7). Noticeably, by 2000 all reference to SAPs had been expunged from the World Bank website (Simon, 2008). More positive sounding programmes focusing on poverty reduction strategies (PRSs) are now the order of the day. There seems little doubt that anti-capitalist demonstrations since Seattle in 1999 have also been influential in this regard. In these recent developments the battle between the left and the right, and its outcome in outpourings of rhetoric and labelling can be witnessed within the liberal and neo-liberal paths. Neo-liberal policies will receive further attention in several sections later in this book; meanwhile its essential nature is reviewed in the Key idea box.

2 *Keynesianism* departs from the liberal tradition by virtue of arguing that the free-market system does not self-regulate effectively and efficiently, thereby necessitating the intervention of the state in order to promote growth in capitalist systems. J.M. Keynes argued, at the time of the Great Depression in the 1930s, that state intervention to manage an economy and create employments was essential, particularly during periods of economic stress. Since the 1930s, Keynesianism has been a prominent development ideology in the industrialised capitalist world, especially in countries with a social democratic tendency (Hettne, 1995).

3 *State capitalist strategies* refer to an early phase of industrial development in continental Europe, principally Tsarist Russia and Germany. The approach advocated the development of enforced industrialisation based primarily on agrarian economies in order to promote nationalism and for reasons pertaining to national security.

4 *The former Soviet model* represents a radical state-oriented strategy inspired by Stalin's five-year mandatory economic development plans. The approach regarded modernisation as the goal, to be achieved by means of the transfer of resources from agriculture to industry. The agricultural sector was collectivised, and heavy industry was given the highest priority. The state completely replaced the market mechanism.

Key idea

Neo-liberalism

Liberalism, as the belief in free markets and the abolition of government intervention in the economy, dates back to the work of the English economist Adam Smith in his book *Wealth of Nations* (1776). In contrast to the view of Smith, during the Great Economic Depression of the 1930s the renowned British economist John Maynard Keynes argued that governments needed to be involved in creating employment in order to steer economies out of recession. However, with the rise of what is referred to as the 'New Right' in the 1980s, there was a return to calls for a strongly market-driven approach, which is referred to as *Neo-liberalism*, that is new forms of liberal free-market policy.

Influenced by the writings of economists such as Hayek and Milton Friedmann the chief proponents of the approach in the 1980s were the politicians Ronald Reagan, President of the USA, and Margaret Thatcher, the Prime Minister of the United Kingdom. Their new political project argued that the state should be progressively removed from the economy, with this ideology frequently being referred to as 'the rolling back of the state', and that measures should be taken to deregulate the economy. Since then, the tenets of neo-liberalism have become the policy orthodoxy of international development agencies such as the World Bank and the International Monetary Fund (Power, 2003).

As a critique, Conway and Heynen (2006) argue, citing Bourdieu (1998), that neo-liberalism is more than a belief in free trade. They suggest that the neoliberal doctrine is based on what they refer to as the structured violence of unemployment, job insecurity and the threatened layoff from work – in

▶

Key idea (continued)

other words, that neo-liberalism is a coercive economic system. It is a short step to the argument that the system stresses the supremacy of economic entrepreneurs over the subordination of nation states, and that it has exacerbated national and global inequalities and the global divide reviewed in Chapter 1. The same authors argue that neo-liberalism is serving to hit the South once more, just as slavery and colonialism did in the past. Neo-liberalism is giving rise to accumulation and self-interest over communal obligations and social obligations to neighbours and the wider community.

Critical reflection

How do you respond to these arguments? Thinking of a sector of the economy, be it manufacturing, agriculture, education, health or indeed any other, outline the major changes that you know have occurred to it over the past say 25 or so years. How many of these fundamental shifts can be seen as the direct outcome of neo-liberal policies? In the case of many nations, the university sector, is an interesting example to consider from this perspective, as there have been many changes experienced in terms of issues such as student fees.

The common denominator linking these four approaches is an unswerving faith in the efficacy of urban-based industrial growth (Plate 3.4), although some approaches in the early modernisation phase also emphasised resource-based development strategies. Notwithstanding the variations noted above, Hettne (1995) comments on the fact that, through time, the role of the state has generally been central to Western development strategies. This was certainly true of the Keynesian, state-capitalist and Soviet models.

Neo-liberalism as the new economic orthodoxy

Despite the above processes, in recent decades we have seen the dismantling of the welfare state and the reduced role of government in the pursuit of neo-liberalism. Arguing that the modern 'welfare state' together with trades unions and state bureaucracies have destroyed the market system, Friedmann (1962) and others opposed Keynesianism and promoted the ideas of the 'New Right' or neo-liberalism.

In this way, the New Right neo-liberal theorists have been seen as having given rise to a counter-revolution (i.e. against state control), celebrating the unrestrained power of the unregulated free market, arguing both for its economic efficiency and its role in liberating the social choices of the individual. There can be little doubt that the general pro-market position of the New Right has served to inform the policies of the World Bank, the IMF and the United States government since the 1980s.

Thus, as detailed in many of the chapters of this book, but particularly Chapter 7, the World Bank and the IMF have pressed for economic liberalisation, the elimination of market imperfections and market-inhibiting social institutions, plus the redefinition of planning regulations in countries in the South. Some sections of the New Right have even gone so far as to argue that the 'Third World only exists as a figment of the guilty imaginations of First World scholars and politicians' (Preston, 1996: 260).

In Britain, neo-liberalism was witnessed in the form of Thatcher's popular capitalism in the 1980s, and in America in the guise of Reaganism. Both Reagan and Thatcher saw the extension of the market into new fields such as hospitals, schools, universities and other public sector establishments, often in the form of performance-related league tables and ratings and privatisation schemes.

On the global scale, the 1980s also saw 'liberalisation' being advocated in the South, especially by the monetarist school (a group of neo-liberal authors seeking reduced government intervention in favour of market forces), which advanced an extreme *laissez-faire* (free market) approach, as in the so-called 'global Reaganomics'. Using the example of the newly industrialising countries (NICs), particularly those of S.E. Asia, countries were advised to liberalise their economies, encourage entrepreneurship and to seek comparative cost advantage, i.e. to focus on where their economic strengths lay. From the 1980s, monetarism has become

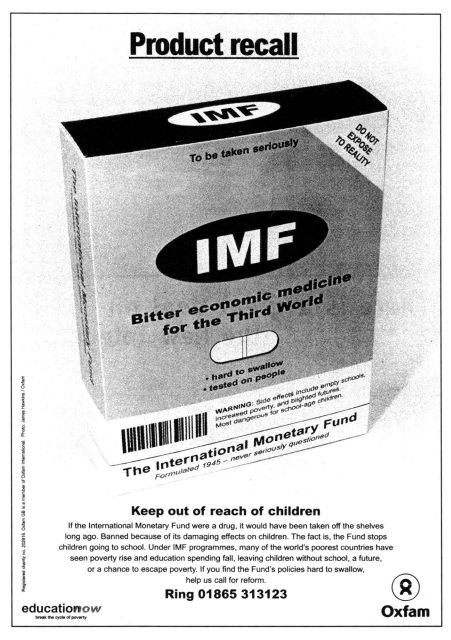

Figure 3.7 Oxfam's campaign against IMF policies including SAPs
photo: James Hawkins/Oxfam

the firm policy of the World Bank and the International Monetary Fund, and was applied in much of the South through the requirements imposed by these institutions in return for granting new loans (in terms of Structural Adjustment Programmes). Globally, neoliberalism, despite its failings, has become the dominant economic system in the world. Policies of free trade, privatisation, reduced social welfare systems, and encouragement of the market have become hallmarks of most countries and certainly underlie the strategies advocated by the major international development agencies. In 2008 some economists felt that the Global

Plate 3.4 Urban-based modernisation: the CBD of Johannesburg, South Africa
(*photo*: Tony Binns)

Financial Crisis (GFC) might witness a return of state intervention. While it is true that some governments in the North did intervene in their economies, the measure was short-term and they soon reverted to following neo-liberal policies.

However, Preston (1996: 260), among others, has argued that 'the schedule of reforms inaugurated by the New Right have not generally proved to be successful'. It is also true to say that the rhetorically important attempt to annex the development experiences of Pacific Asia to the position of the New Right has been widely ridiculed by development specialists. One of the reasons for this is the 'Krugman thesis' developed by the prominent American economist Paul Krugman. This argues that the so-called miracles of Asian development can largely be attributed to once-in-a-lifetime changes which, having once been enacted, cannot by definition be repeated. This has included massive increases in female participation in the labour force (Watters and McGee, 1997; see also Case study 3.1). Others have pointed to the lack of unionisation, poor working conditions and authoritarian government as factors promoting high productivity, but in ways which are not acceptable elsewhere (see also Case study 3.1).

A further example is to be found in the case of the Caribbean, where the World Bank was keen to point to the low wage levels and high productivity of the Asian tiger economies as a model to follow. Local Caribbean economists and policy makers respond by saying that the policies which underlie Asian development are just not feasible in the Caribbean context. This dialogue can be followed in the World Bank publication edited by Wen and Sengupta (1991).

Historical approaches: empirical perspectives on change and development

The nature of historical approaches

Another way in which scholars and practitioners can seek to generalise about development is by empirical or real-world observations through time. By definition, this approach will give rise to descriptive–positive models of development (see Figure 3.2), and some feel these frameworks have a key role to play in the discussion of development, specifically for grounding theory in the historical realities of developing nations. Although such approaches deal primarily with the colonial and pre-independence periods, it can be argued that they may still afford invaluable insights regarding contemporary patterns and processes of development and change.

Gunnar Myrdal and cumulative causation

In contrast to Hirschman, the Swedish economist, Gunnar Myrdal (1957), although writing at much the same time, took a noticeably more pessimistic view, maintaining that capitalist development is inevitably marked by deepening regional and personal income and welfare inequalities. Myrdal followed the arguments of the 'vicious circle of poverty' in presenting his theory of 'cumulative causation'. Thereby, it was argued that once differential growth has occurred, internal and external economies of scale will serve to perpetuate the pattern.

Such a situation is the outcome of the 'backwash' effect, whereby population migrations, trade and capital movements all come to focus on the key growth points of the economy (and not spread or diffuse as the modernisation theorists had argued). Increasing demand, associated with multiplier effects, and the existence of social facilities also serve to enhance the core region. Although 'spread' effects will undoubtedly occur, principally via the increased market for the agricultural products and raw materials of the periphery, Myrdal concluded that, given unrestrained free-market forces, these spread effects would in no way match the backwash effects. Myrdal's thesis leads to the advocacy of strong state policy in order to counteract what is seen as the normal tendency of the capitalist system to foster increasing regional inequalities.

Core–periphery and the work of John Friedmann

The view that, without intervention, development is likely to become increasingly polarised in transitional societies, was taken up and developed by a number of scholars towards the end of the 1960s and the beginning of the 1970s. As such, they ran counter to the conventional wisdom of the time.

These works were based mainly on empirical studies which encompassed an historical dimension.

Undoubtedly, the best-known example is provided by American planner John Friedmann's (1966) core–periphery model. From a purely theoretical perspective, Friedmann's central contention was that 'where economic growth is sustained over long time periods, its incidence works toward a progressive integration of the space economy' (Friedmann, 1966: 35) which would eventually occur after an extended period of polarisation. This process is made clear in the much-reproduced four-stage ideal-typical sequence of development shown here in Figure 3.8.

The first stage, independent local centres with no hierarchy, represents the pre-colonial stage and is associated with a series of isolated self-sufficient local economies. There is no surplus production to be concentrated in space, and an even and essentially stable pattern of settlement and socio-economic development is the result.

In the second stage, there is a single strong centre, and it is posited that as the result of some form of 'external disruption' – a euphemism for colonialism – the former stability is replaced by dynamic change. Growth is envisaged to occur rapidly in one main region and urban primacy is the spatial outcome. What may be referred to as 'social surplus product' is strongly concentrated – essentially this is a concentrated surplus of production over need. The centre (C) feeds on the rest of the nation, and the extensive periphery (P) is drained. Advantage tends to accrue to a small elite of urban consumers, who are located at the centre. However, Friedmann regarded this stage as inherently unstable.

The outcome of this instability is the development of a single national centre with strong peripheral sub-centres. Over time, the simple centre–periphery pattern is progressively transformed to a multi-nuclear one. Sub-cores develop (SC1, SC2), leaving a series of intermetropolitan peripheries (P1 to P4). This is the graphical representation of the point of polarisation reversal when development starts to be concentrated in parts of the former periphery, albeit on a highly concentrated basis.

The fourth and final stage, which sees the development of a functionally interdependent system of cities, was described by Friedmann as 'organised complexity', and is one where progressive national integration continues, eventually witnessing the total absorption of the intermetropolitan peripheries. A smooth progression of cities by size and a smooth process of national development are envisaged as the outcomes.

An evaluation of core–periphery models and frameworks

The first two stages of the core–periphery model describe the history of the majority of developing countries. Indeed, it is often not appreciated that, in the first stage, the line along which the small independent communities are drawn represents the coastline. The occurrence of uneven growth and urban concentration in the early stages of growth is seen as being the direct outcome of exogenic forces. Thus, Friedmann commented that the core–periphery relationship is essentially a colonial one, his work having been based on the history of regional development in Venezuela.

The principal idea behind the centre–periphery framework is that, early on, factors of production will be displaced from the periphery to the centre, where

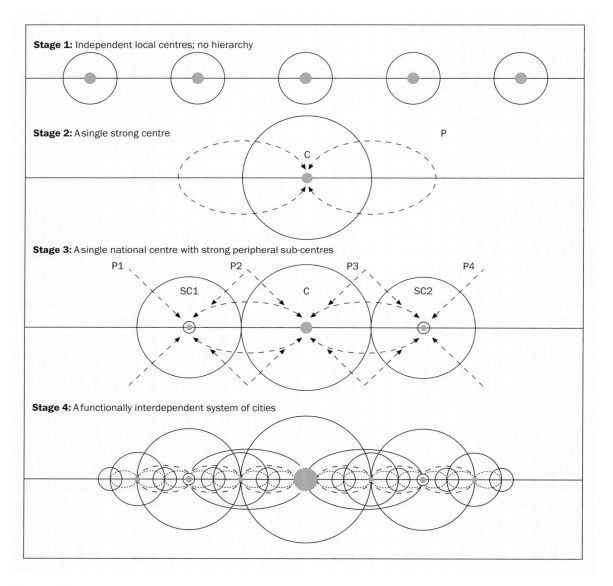

Stage 1: Independent local centres; no hierarchy

Stage 2: A single strong centre

P

C

Stage 3: A single national centre with strong peripheral sub-centres

P1 P2 P3 P4

SC1 C SC2

Stage 4: A functionally interdependent system of cities

Figure 3.8 An overview of Friedmann's core–periphery model

Source: Adapted from Friedmann (1966). © 1966 Massachusetts Institute of Technology, by permission of the MIT Press

economic productivity and earnings are higher. Thus, at an early stage of development nothing succeeds like success. However, the crucial change is the transition between the second and third stages, where the system tends towards equilibrium and equalisation. Friedmann's model is one which suggests that, in theory, economic development will ultimately lead to the convergence of regional incomes and welfare differentials.

But at the very same time as he was presenting the simplified model as a template, Friedmann observed that, in reality, there was evidence of persistent disequilibrium. Thus, in a statement which appeared right alongside the model, Friedmann (1966: 14) observed that there was 'a major difficulty with the equilibrium model: historical evidence does not support it'. Despite this damning caveat, many authors have represented the model as a statement of invariant truth, ignoring Friedmann's warning that 'disequilibrium is built into transitional societies from the start' (Friedmann, 1966: 14).

Effectively, Friedmann was maintaining that, without state intervention, the transition from the second stage to the third stage will not occur in developing societies; in this respect he was in agreement with Myrdal's prescription that development will become ever more concentrated in space, with polarisation always tending to exceed the so-called trickle-down effect.

The mercantile model and spatially uneven development

Writing just a few years after the appearance of Friedmann's much-cited model, an American geographer Jay E. Vance (1970) noted that it was with the development of mercantile societies (i.e. where trade is a key economic driver) from the fifteenth century onwards that settlement systems started to evolve along more complex lines. The model draws on European experience.

According to Vance, the main development impulse came with colonialism, but continued economic growth required greater access to land resources. Frequently, this requirement was initially met by local colonial expansion via trading expeditions. By the seventeenth and eighteenth centuries, however, this need was increasingly fulfilled by distant colonialism, the transoceanic version of local colonialism. The implications of

these historical developments have been well summarised by Vance (1970: 148):

> The vigorous mercantile entrepreneur of the seventeenth and eighteenth centuries had to turn outward from Europe because the long history of parochial trade and the confining honeycomb of Christaller cells that had grown up with feudalism left little scope there for his activity. With overseas development, for the first time the merchant faced an un-organised land wherein the designs he established furnished the geography of wholesale-trade location. By contrast, in a central-place situation (such as that affecting much of Europe and the Orient), to introduce wholesale trade meant to conform to a settlement pattern that was premercantile.

During the period of mercantilism (see also Chapter 2), ports came to dominate the evolving urban systems of both the colony and the colonial power. In the colony, once established, ports acted as gateways to the interior lands.

Subsequently, evolutionary changes occurred that first saw increasing spatial concentration at certain nodes, then lateral interconnection of the coastal gateways and the establishment of new inland regions for expansion. The settlement pattern of the homeland also underwent considerable change, for social surplus product flowed into the capital city and the principal ports, thus serving to strengthen considerably their position in the urban system.

These historical facets of trade articulation led Vance (1970) to suggest what amounted to an entirely new model of colonial settlement evolution; one that was firmly based on history. This is referred to as the 'mercantile model', and its main features are summarised in Figure 3.9. The model is illustrated in five stages. In each of these, the colony is shown on the left of the figure, and the colonial power on the right:

1 The first stage represents the initial search phase of mercantilism, involving the quest for economic information on the part of the prospective colonising power.

2 The second stage sees the testing of productivity and the periodic harvesting of staples such as fish, furs and timber. However, no permanent settlement is established in the colony.

3 At the third stage, the planting of settlers who produce staples and who consume the manufactures of the home country occurs. The settlement system of the colony is established via a point of attachment. The developing symbiotic relationship between the colony and the colonial power is witnessed by a sharp reduction in the effective distance separating them. The major port in the homeland becomes pre-eminent.

4 The fourth stage is characterised by the introduction of internal trade and manufacture in the colony. At this juncture, penetration occurs inland from the major gateways in the colony, based on staple production. There is rapid growth of manufacturing in the homeland to supply the overseas and home markets. Ports continue to increase in significance.

5 The fifth and final stage sees the establishment of a mercantile settlement pattern and central-place infilling occurs within the colony; there emerges a central place settlement system with a mercantile overlay in the homeland.

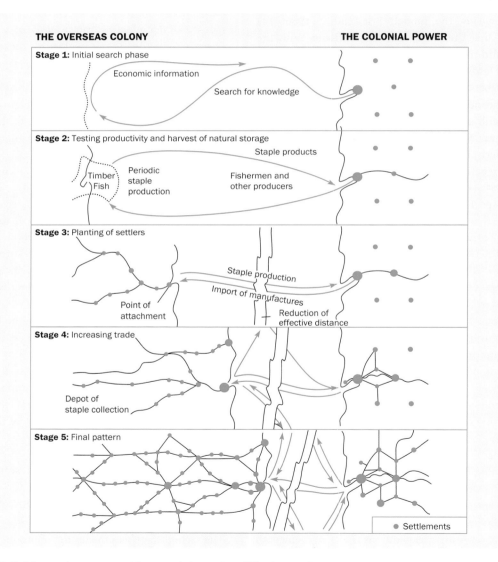

Figure 3.9 Vance's mercantile model: a simplified version
Source: Adapted from Potter (1992a).

The mercantile model stresses the historical–evolutionary viewpoint in examining the development of national patterns of development and change. The framework offers what Vance sees as an alternative and more realistic picture of settlement structure, based on the fact that in the seventeenth and eighteenth centuries mercantile entrepreneurs turned outwards from Europe. Hence the source of change is external to developing countries. In contrast, the development of settlement patterns and systems of central places in the developed world was based on endogenic principles of local demand, thereby rendering what was essentially a closed settlement system (Christaller, 1933; Lösch, 1940).

The hallmark of the mercantile model is the remarkable linearity of settlement patterns, first along coasts, especially in colonies, and then along the routes that developed between the coastal points of attachment and the staple-producing interiors.

These two alignments are also given direct expression in Taaffe et al.'s (1963) model of transport development in less developed countries, as shown in Figure 3.10a. The model was based on the transport histories of West African nations such as Nigeria and Ghana, plus Brazil, Malaya and East Africa. Hoyle's (1993) application of the framework to East Africa is shown in Figure 3.10b.

Figure 3.11 deals specifically with the example of Brazil, showing the foundation of the earliest towns. The early ports along the Atlantic coast were small and served thinly settled hinterlands. The evolving plantation economy later focused on sugar mills and gave rise to small inland settlements. The concentration of the first 12 colonial towns of Brazil on the seaboard is very apparent from Figure 3.11.

Plantopolis and uneven development

In plantation based economies such as those of the Caribbean, a local historical variant of the mercantile settlement system is provided by the plantopolis model. A simplified representation of this is shown in Figure 3.12. The first two stages are based on Rojas (1989), and the graphical depiction of the sequence and its extension to the modern era have been effected by Potter (1995a, 2000):

1 In the first stage, plantopolis, the plantations formed self-contained bases for the settlement pattern, such that only one main town was required for trade, service and political control functions.

2 Following emancipation of the country, the second stage, small, marginal farming communities – clustered around the plantations, practising subsistence agriculture and supplying labour to the plantations – added a third layer to the settlement system. The distribution of these communities would vary according to physical and agricultural conditions.

3 Figure 3.12 suggests that, in the Caribbean, the modern era has witnessed the extension of this highly polarised pattern of development; this is the third stage. The emphasis is placed on extension, for this may not, in all cases, amount to intensification per se. This has come about largely as the result of industrialisation and tourism being taken as the new twin paths to development. Augelli and West (1976: 120) commented on what they regarded as the disproportionate concentration of wealth, power and social status in the chief urban centres of the West Indies. As shown in Figure 3.12, such spatial inequality is sustained by strong symbiotic flows between town and country. This theme is picked up in detail in Chapter 9, in respect of the nature of rural–urban interrelations in developing countries.

An evaluation of the mercantile and plantopolis frameworks

The virtues of the mercantile and plantopolis models are many. Principally, they serve to stress that the evolution of most developing countries amounts to a highly dependent form of development. Certainly, we are reminded that the high degree of urban primacy (the focus of urban development in one primary centre), and the coastal orientation of settlement fabrics in Africa, Asia, South America and the Caribbean, are all the direct product of colonialism, not accidental happenings or aberrant cases: hence the comment that modernisation surfaces essentially chart colonial and neo-colonial penetration.

According to these models, ports and other urban settlements became the focus of economic activity and of the social and economic surplus that accrued. The concept of surplus product, defined as an excess of

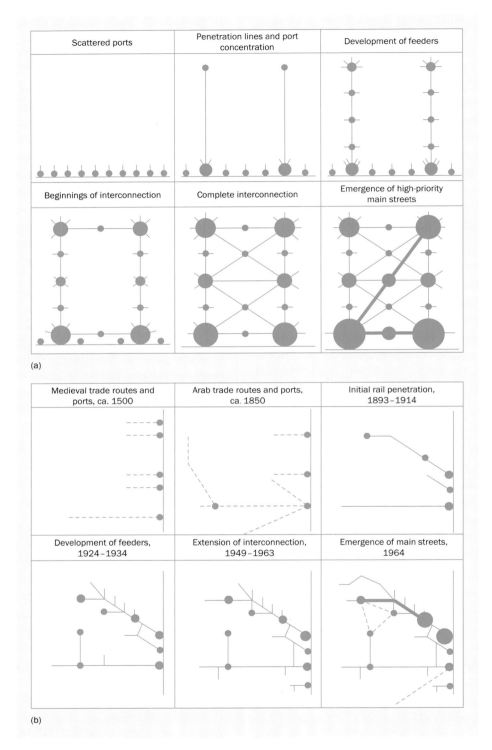

Figure 3.10 The Taaffe, Morrill and Gould model of transport development and its application to East Africa
Source: adapted from Hoyle (1993)

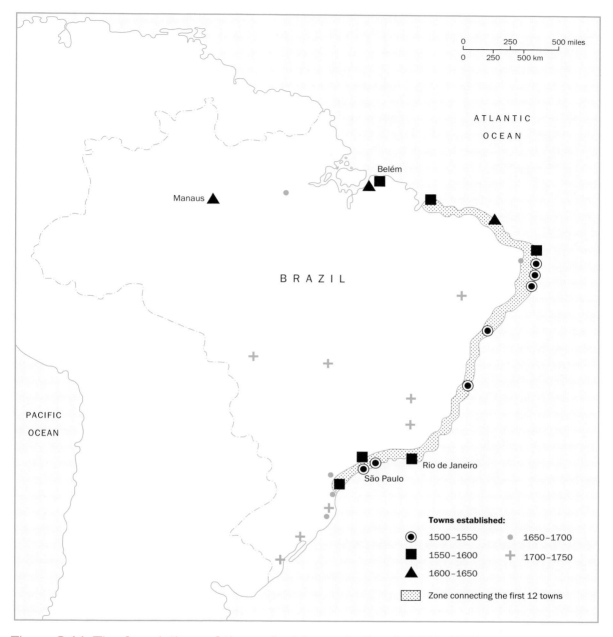

Figure 3.11 The foundations of the earliest towns in Brazil, 1500–1750
Source: From *Latin America and the Caribbean: A Systematic and Regional Survey*, (Blouet, B.W. and Blouet, O.M.), © 2002 John Wiley & Sons Inc. Reprinted with permission of John Wiley & Sons, Inc.

production over need or consumption, is developed more fully in the next major section, which deals with radical approaches to development. A similar, but somewhat less overriding spatial concentration also applies to the colonial power. Hence a pattern of spatially unequal or polarised growth emerged as the norm due to the strengthening of this symbiotic relationship between colony and colonial power.

The overall suggestion is that, due to the requirements of the international economy, far greater levels of inequality and spatial concentration are produced than may be socially and morally desirable.

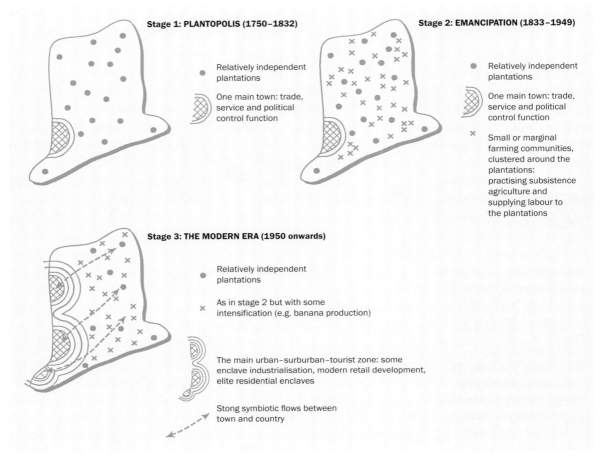

Figure 3.12 The plantopolis model and its extension to the modern era
Source: Adapted from Potter (1995a).

Radical dependency approaches: the South answers back?

Introduction: an indigenous approach?

A major advance in theory formation came with what some refer to as the indigenisation of development thinking; that is, the production of ideas purporting to emanate from, or which at least relate to, the sorts of conditions that are encountered in the South, rather than ideas emanating from European experience. As Slater (1992a, 1992b) has averred, the core can learn from the periphery – and it needs to learn.

The empirically derived mercantile and plantopolis models reviewed in the last section can be regarded as graphical depictions of the outcome of the interdependent development of the world since the 1400s. The *dependencia*, or dependency school, specifically took up this theme as a rebuttal of the modernisation paradigm. Although some consider that dependency theory developed as a voice from the South, others have maintained that its most cogent formulation represents Eurocentric development thinking by virtue of the origins of its leading author, a German-born economist, Andre Gunder Frank. Or, put another way, as Clarke (2002) states, although in the English-speaking world dependency theory focused on the work of Frank, the main body of contributions was Latin American and Caribbean in origin (Marshall, 2002).

However, before we look in more detail at the origins of dependency theory in the South, we should first consider the reasons why radical approaches started to be adopted in the academic literature at this juncture.

Preston (1996), in a useful overview, notes that before the 1960s little attention was paid to the Marxian tradition of social theorising (see Key idea box on Marxism). The intellectual and political revival of interest in Marx at the end of the 1960s was brought about by a number of different factors, as shown in Figure 3.13. This was partly to do with America's military involvement in Vietnam, the collapse of consensus politics due to the civil rights movement, as well as the moribund nature of academic social science (Preston, 1996). In Europe, the trend was also reflected in reactions to the Vietnam war and the perceived need for university reform. What is referred to as the 'New Left' emerged as a broad progressive movement, which linked to the struggles of anti-colonial movements in the South (Figure 3.13).

Key idea

Marxism

The terms 'Marxism' or 'Marxist' can be applied to sets of ideas or practices that are based on the writings of Karl Marx (1818–1883) and Friedrich Engels (1820–1895). Marx was a German-born political scientist and revolutionary, who together with Engels published the *Communist Manifesto* in 1848, an early statement on their general principles. Their writings were strongly class-based, stressing the struggles of the working classes and the need to replace the capitalist system if the lot of ordinary people was to be improved.

Marx and Engels regarded all history as the history of class struggles. An essential view was that control over the forces of production is critical, giving rise to a two-fold class division. On the one side are the owners of the means of production (land and capital), and on the other there are the workers, who only have their labour to sell. Workers have to toil long hours and the value of what they produce is far higher than what they are paid. Thus, an economic surplus is accrued by the owners of capital and land and the economy exploits labour. The early forms of surplus were created by merchants i.e. 'primitive accumulation', acquired by 'raiding' non-capitalist societies for commodities such as gold and silver. Later the surplus represented the value expropriated from workers. In the views of Marx and Engels, due to the inhumane nature of capitalism and its inherent contradictions, in time the system would ultimately fail and be replaced by socialism, which they regarded as a more just system.

Paul Baran and the critical role of the economic surplus

Paul Baran, reflecting the general mood of the time, turned to a radical perspective in respect of development theory, promulgating a clear neo-Marxist approach (Baran, 1973; Baran and Sweezy, 1968). The principal idea was that economic surplus is created by the inherent working of the capitalist system. It is clear that Baran was defining a surplus as an excess of production over the needs of consumption, and which therefore exists as a material quantity of goods. The concept of social surplus product is discussed in the next Key idea box.

The basic point is that once surplus production is redistributed within society, it effectively becomes a surplus of time and energy (Potter and Lloyd-Evans, 1998). Those who do not have to produce their own means of subsistence are freed for other activities. Part of the surplus can be redistributed to parasitic groups (i.e. groups which depend on the produce of others), and part can be used for conspicuous consumption or for state monumentalism – in other words it can be concentrated both in space and among different groups. It can be argued that this surplus redistribution has characterised the mercantile period onward, and has witnessed surplus value being expropriated from the South.

Baran's Marxist framework also envisaged that during the colonial period advanced nations entered into special partnerships with powerful elite groups in less

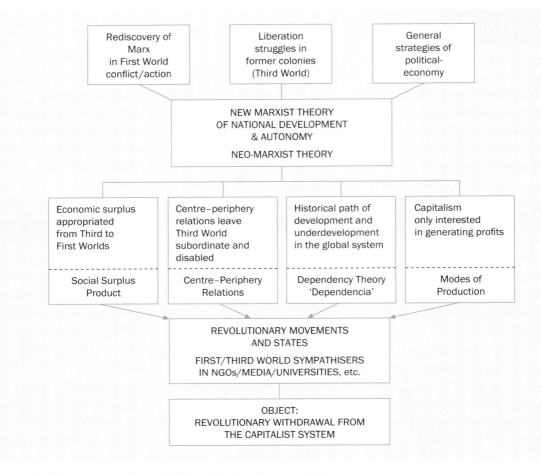

Figure 3.13 An overview of Marxist development theory
Source: Adapted from Preston (1996).

developed and pre-capitalist countries. By such means, surplus was extracted and appropriated by elite groups. Thus, for countries in the South, Baran saw the key to development as disengagement from the deforming impact of the world capitalist economy, as capitalism creates, and then diverts, much of the economic surplus into wasteful and sometimes immoral consumption (Baran, 1973).

Key idea

Social surplus product

The idea of a surplus can be looked at as a social surplus product – that is, a surplus of production over societal need. This first occurred when human groups were able to produce more food than they needed on a daily basis. This meant that some members of society could be released from the need to produce their own food and could take on other roles in society, such as religious, military and political leadership. In other words, the food surplus became a surplus of time and energy within society, and it is this that can be referred to as social surplus product. This surplus can be concentrated in space, and distributed highly

Key idea (continued)

unequally among the members of society, or it can be spread more equitably, spatially and socially. It is thus central to the development process.

Critical reflection
It is an interesting exercise to think about the different places and contexts in which social surpluses can be witnessed – from monumental buildings, regional variations in house prices, art collections, to conspicuous personal displays of wealth. Make a list of regions, places, organisations and buildings where signs of the accumulation of social surplus value have been accrued and can be witnessed.

The contribution of dependency theory

These types of arguments were perhaps most cogently promulgated by the dependency school, the origins of which can be traced back to the 1960s (see Figure 3.13). Full-blown dependency theory became a global force in the 1970s. It had its origins in the writings of Latin American and Caribbean radical scholars known as structuralists, because they focused on the unseen structures that may be held to mould and shape society (Clarke, 2002; Conway and Heynen, 2002; Girvan, 1973; Marshall, 2002).

The approach was the outcome of the convergence of pure Marxist ideas on Latin American and Caribbean writings about underdevelopment. Essentially, through this process, the Eurocentric ideas of Marxism became more relevant to the Latin American context. Marx and Engels had seen capitalism as initially destructive of non-capitalist social forms (Preston, 1996). Prebisch (1950) and Furtado (1964, 1965, 1969), who wrote about Argentina and Brazil respectively, are the best-known Latin American structuralists. Raul Prebisch stressed the importance of economic relations in linking industrialised and Latin American less developed countries, and observed that these were primarily prescribed in the form of centre–periphery relations (see Figure 3.13). Furtado (1969) argued that present-day Latin American socio-economic structures were the result of the manner of incorporation into the world capitalist system, an argument which is close to the dependency line of reasoning. Later writers included Dos Santos (1970, 1977) and Cardoso (1976) (see Key thinker box on Cardoso).

As noted by Hettne (1995), opinions differ as to whether the parallel Caribbean or 'New World' school of dependency should be seen as an autonomous form. It is salient to note that the whole history of the Caribbean is one of dependency, and this issue was central to the so-called 'New World Group', which first met in Georgetown, Guyana, in 1992, in order to discuss Caribbean development issues. Key names include George Beckford (1972), Norman Girvan (1973) and Clive Thomas (1989).

The development of the Caribbean-based New World Group has been charted in some detail by Marshall (2002). The founders of the group aspired to identify indigenous paths for the region's development. They were convinced that the twin strands of modernisation and industrialisation were not suited to the region. They were particularly resistant to Arthur Lewis' (1955) call for industrialisation by invitation. Beckford (1972) then added a strong case that the historic plantation slave economy had led to underdevelopment in the region and the evolution of what he termed 'persistent poverty'.

The contribution of A.G. Frank

The dependency approach is strongly associated with the work of Andre Gunder Frank (see Key thinker box). Frank's key ideas were outlined in an article published in 1966, 'The development of underdevelopment', as well as in the book *Capitalism and Underdevelopment in Latin America*, in 1967. Although a scholar of European origin working in the USA, Frank had researched in Mexico, Chile and Brazil.

Key thinker

From radical Latin American structuralist to President – Fernando Cardoso

Plate 3.5 Fernando Cardoso
Source: PA Photos

Fernando Henrique Cardoso (Plate 3.5) offers a fascinating case of an academic interested in development who later became a political figure on the world stage, thereby exemplifying afresh the close relation between politics and development thinking. Cardoso was born in Rio de Janeiro, Brazil, in 1931 and trained as a sociologist. He made a major theoretical contribution with his study of *Dependency and Development in Latin America* (1969). Cardoso regarded dependency as neither stable nor permanent, and he rejected any simple link between dependency and underdevelopment (see Sanchez-Rodrigues, 2006). In the 1970s Cardoso became actively involved in the pro-democracy movement in Brazil and from there he moved into politics, becoming a member of the Brazilian Social Democrat Party in 1982. He was made Foreign Minister in 1992/93, and in 1995 he was elected as President of Brazil. He served two terms of office, with his presidency extending through to 2003. Some argue that, when in power, he abandoned the Marxist roots he showed as a structuralist, and that he served the neo-liberal interests of multinational business elites (Sanchez-Rodrigues, 2006).

Key thinker

Andre Gunder Frank

Plate 3.6 Andre Gunder Frank
Source: with kind permission from Andre Gunder Frank

Andre Gunder Frank (1929–2005) (Plate 3.6) was born in Germany, but his family fled to Switzerland during the ascendancy of Adolf Hitler, and then in 1941 moved to the United States. Frank undertook a PhD at the University of Chicago, where in 1957 he received his doctorate for a thesis on agriculture in the Ukraine. After working in a number of American universities, Frank moved to South America, and at one point was Professor of Sociology and Economics at the University of Chile.

During this period he underwent a rapid and thorough radical conversion (Brookfield, 1975). The time he spent in Chile is seen as the foundation of his work on dependency theory. His seminal ideas were

Key thinker (continued)

summarised in the phrase 'the development of underdevelopment'. The large body of books and papers written by Frank were directly shaped by the ideas of Marx, especially the concept of accumulation on a global scale (Watts, 2006). Throughout his career Frank moved from post to post and from country to country. Watts (2006: 90) has argued that Andre Frank was 'at once too radical, too ornery and too unconventional for most universities on both sides of the Atlantic'.

Frank (1967) maintained that development and under-development are opposite sides of the same coin, and that both are the necessary outcome and manifestation of the contradictions of the capitalist system of development.

The thesis presented by Frank was devastatingly simple. It was argued that the condition of developing countries is not the outcome of inertia, misfortune, chance, climatic conditions or whatever, but rather a reflection of the manner of their incorporation into the global capitalist system. Viewed in this manner, so-called underdevelopment, and associated dualism, are not a negative or void, but the direct outcome and reciprocal of development elsewhere (Figure 3.14). The only real alternative for such nations was to weaken the grip of the global system by means of establishing trade barriers, controls on transnational corporations and the formation of regional trading areas, along with the encouragement of local or indigenous production and development (see Plate 3.7).

The phrase 'the development of underdevelopment' (Frank, 1966) has come to be employed as a shorthand description of the Frankian approach, which, as noted previously, has a strong graphical tie-in with the mercantile and plantopolis models. Quite simply, if the development of large tracts of the Earth's surface has depended upon metropolitan cores, or 'metropoles', then the development of cities has also depended principally upon the articulation of capital and the accumulation of surplus value (Figure 3.15).

The process has operated internationally and internally within countries. Viewed in this light, so-called backwardness results from integration at the bottom of the hierarchy of dependence, not a failure to integrate within the global economy. Indeed Frank argued that the more 'satellites' are associated with the metropoles, the more they are held back, and not the other way around. In this connection, Frank specifically cited the instances of north-east Brazil and the West Indies as regions of close contact with the core, but where processes of internal transformation had been rendered impossible due to such close contact.

Conway and Heynen (2008) note how Frank presents Brazil as the clearest case of national and regional underdevelopment. He argued that the expansion of capitalism beginning in the sixteenth century sequentially incorporated urban cores and their extensive hinterlands into the global economy as exporting nodes. Cities such as Rio de Janeiro, São Paulo and Paraná figured most prominently in this expansion. Frank (1967) argued that this process witnessed the apparent development of these nodes, but in the long run led to the underdevelopment of the wider region.

As shown by the example of Brazil, dependency theory represents a holistic view because it describes a chain of dependent relations which has grown since the establishment of capitalism as the dominant world system, so its expansion is regarded as coterminous with colonialism and underdevelopment.

The chain of exploitative relations witnesses the extraction and transmission of surplus value via a process of unequal exchange, extending from the peasant, through the market town, regional centre, national capital, to the international metropole, as shown in Figure 3.15. The terms of trade have always worked in favour of the next higher level in the chain, so that social surplus value becomes progressively concentrated (Castells, 1977; Harvey, 1973).

By such means, dependency theorists argue that the dominant capitalist powers, such as England and then the USA, encouraged the transformation of political and economic structures in order to serve their own interests. According to this view, colonial territories were organised to produce primary products at minimal cost, while simultaneously becoming an increasing market for industrial products. Inexorably, social surplus value was siphoned off from poor to rich regions, and from the developing to the developed world.

Figure 3.14 Dependent relations according to the *New Internationalist*
Source: Cartoon by Paul Fitzgerald

The critique of dependency and the rise of world systems theory

The chief criticism of dependency theory is that it is economistic, seeing all as the outcome of a form of economic determinism, conforming with what Armstrong and McGee (1985: 38–9) have described as the 'impersonal, even mechanical analysis of structuralism'.

Furthermore, the theory only appears to deal with class structure and other factors internal to a given nation, insofar as they are the outcome of the fundamental economic processes described. Another point of contention is how dependency theory suggests that

countries can only advance their lot by delinking from the global economy, whereas the capitalist world system is busily becoming more global and interdependent. For all these reasons, dependency theory has largely been out of fashion in the North since the 1980s (Preston, 1996). But again we should stress that in radical quarters such ideas and ways of thinking have never gone out of fashion. It continues to play a role as a critique of more conventional approaches to development.

Wallerstein (1974, 1980) attempted to get around some of the criticisms of basic dependency theory, including the internal–external agency debate, by stressing the existence of a somewhat more complex and finely divided 'world system' (Taylor, 1986). The essential

Plate 3.7 'Organisation for Rural Development' poster advocating more domestic production and fewer imports in St Vincent
(*photo*: Rob Potter)

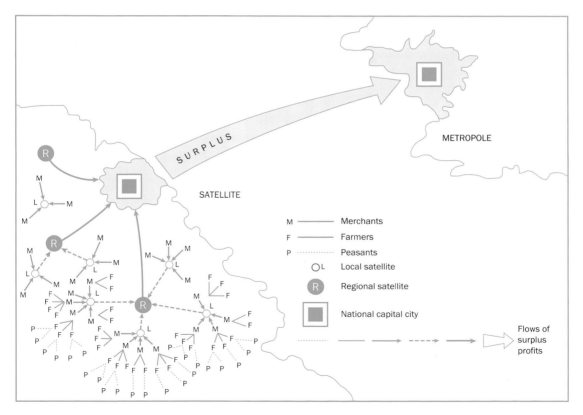

Figure 3.15 Dependency theory: a graphical depiction
Source: adapted from Potter (1992a).

point is that Wallerstein distinguishes not only between the core nations, which became the leading industrial producers, and the peripheral states, which were maintained as agricultural providers, but also identifies the semi-peripheries (see also Klak, 2008).

It is argued that the semi-peripheries play a key role, for these intermediate states are strongly ambitious in competing for core status by increasing their importance as industrial producers relative to their standing as agricultural suppliers. For the semi-peripheral capitalist nations, read the NICs (Newly Industrialising Countries) of SE Asia and Latin America. Within the world system since the sixteenth century there have been cyclical periods of expansion, contraction, crisis and change. Hence it is envisaged that the fate of a particular nation is not entirely externally driven, but also depends on the internal manner in which external forces have been responded to and accommodated.

Dependency theory: final comments

Frank's ideas are seen by many as being near to the orthodox Marxist view that the advanced capitalist world both exploited and kept the South underdeveloped (Rodney, 1982). Although many would undoubtedly refute this view as extreme, it may be argued that elements of the analysis, even if in a world-systems form, are likely to provide food for thought for those interpreting patterns of development.

As Hettne (1995) notes, dependency theory stressed that the biggest obstacles to development are not a lack of capital or entrepreneurial skill, but are to be found in the international division of labour. As already observed, certainly the graphical representation of pure dependency theory exhibits parallels with the spatial outcomes of the core–periphery, mercantile and plantopolis models of settlement development and structure (see Figure 3.15).

Articulation theory

One final element of radical development theory stressing exploitation is the so-called theory of the articulation of the modes of production. The basic argument is that the capitalist mode of production exists alongside (and is articulated with) non-capitalist and pre-capitalist modes of production. The capitalist system replaces the non-capitalist system where profits are to be accrued in so doing. However, the pre-capitalist form is left intact wherever profits are unlikely to be made, and it is therefore advantageous to leave things the way they are.

A frequently cited example is low-income housing, where the poor are left to provide their own folk or vernacular homes, whereas the formal sector provides for the middle and upper classes (Burgess, 1990, 1992; Drakakis-Smith, 1981; McGee, 1979; Potter, 1992b, 1994; Potter and Conway, 1997).

A macro-spatial, but more specific, example of the modes of production approach was provided by the operation of apartheid in South Africa prior to 1994. In this, the so-called 'homelands' preserved the traditional mode of production in order to conserve black labour, which was then allowed to commute to 'White South Africa'.

Hence, according to this radical perspective, dualism is a product of the contradictions of the capitalist system, not some form of aberration. Similarly, according to this view, underdevelopment can be described as a stalemate in the process of articulation. In other words, underdevelopment continues where there is no direct interest in the capitalist system in transforming the existing situation. Case study 3.2 discusses the position of Aborigines in Australia, using the modes of production framework of analysis as an example.

Case study 3.2

Aborigines, development and modes of production

As noted by Drakakis-Smith (1983), Australia has experienced many different facets of colonialism. For much of the last 200 years it was a direct colony of Britain and was exploited as such for its mineral wealth and agricultural produce. However, throughout its history as a 'white' nation state, whether colony or independent, Australia has harboured its own internal process of exploitation – that of its of exploitation – that of its indigenous

Case study 3.2 (continued)

Aboriginal population by whites. There can be little doubt that Aborigines do in fact comprise a subordinate, deprived and exploited group within Australian society.

Close investigation reveals how government measures have effectively institutionalised Aboriginal dependency in an unequal relationship which brings benefits principally to the white middle classes. Before the initial settlement by the British in 1788, Aborigines lived in what Meillassoux (1972, 1978) has termed a natural economy where land is the subject rather than the object of labour. The technology was simple but effective, with human energy alone being employed to tap the environmental resources through systems of hunting and collecting. Although life was primarily organised around the collection and consumption of subsistence food, a considerable amount of time was given over to ritual and ceremonial activities and to the production of consumer durables in the form of hunting weapons, tools and items with religious significance.

The mode of distribution was based on sharing the hunted and gathered food, and was therefore strongly related to the mode of production. One of the most important features of the pre-capitalist Aboriginal economy was an intense involvement with the land, both in physical and spiritual terms, with a strong emphasis on the spiritual. The small numbers, simple lifestyle and apparent lack of political organisation among the Aborigines convinced the British that there was no need for negotiation or treaties with such a 'primitive' people. Accordingly, all land was declared to be Crown land from the outset, so no compensation was paid to the Aborigines and no pre-existing rights were recognised. This legalistic appropriation of the land itself has been a fundamental factor in the subsequent exploitation of the Aboriginal people in Australia. Simply on the grounds that the indigenous population appeared to be disorganised and primitive, the British removed at one administrative stroke both the economic and spiritual basis of Aboriginal society.

For several decades after these developments, Aborigines appeared to be unimportant within the Australian colonial economy. In the first instance, labour was provided by assigned convicts, and later by larger landowners buying out many of the initial smallholders. By the 1830s, however, the rapid development of sheep farming to supply wool for export had led to the encouragement of large-scale labour migration from Britain.

But this rapid expansion of pastoral farming in the second half of the nineteenth century brought Aborigines once more into direct contact with the vanguard of white settlement. Hitherto, they had been virtually ignored – despised, left destitute and were decimated by starvation and disease. By the mid-nineteenth century pastoral settlement was beginning to push into the central and northern regions of the country, where conditions were harsher and Aborigines more numerous. Thus, Aboriginal labour was for the first time becoming a necessity on those properties where sheer size and harsh climate led to a sharp reduction in the enthusiasm of recruited white labour to move north.

Thus, Aboriginal labour, either as station hands or as domestic workers, was extensively used from the 1880s onwards. Bands and families were encouraged to stay on the land after its appropriation, where they received payment in kind for work undertaken on the station. Labour relations were at best paternalistic, but more often than not the property owners or managers had little interest in the reproduction of Aboriginal labour, considering the supply to be limitless and the individuals unworthy of detailed attention. Living conditions and diet were often totally inadequate and populations were decimated. As the value of the Aboriginal labour began to be more appreciated, so the Australian government began to establish a series of expanded reserves and settlements.

Australia has changed markedly since 1945. Although it still makes a notable contribution to the production process, the Aboriginal community is now more important as a consumer group for the goods and services of an extensive tertiary system operated almost entirely by whites. In effect, this comprises a third stage in the institutionalisation of Aborigines within a dependency framework, following the appropriation of their land and labour power.

In the contemporary situation in Aboriginal Australia, therefore, the dominant capitalist mode of production conserved the Aboriginal pre-capitalist mode of production largely for its role as a consumer of goods and services. The class position and economic prosperity of the white population is largely dependent on this relationship.

e, bottom-up and ory approaches: ...ves on 'another' ...development

Introduction

The somewhat inelegant and uninformative expression *another development* has been used to denote the suggested watershed in thinking which characterised the period since the mid-1970s (Brohman, 1996; Hettne, 1995).

The concept was born at the Seventh Special Session of the United Nations General Assembly and the allied publication by the Dag Hammarskjöld Foundation of *What Now?* The session stressed the need for self-reliance to be seen as central to the development process, and for the emphasis to be placed on endogenous (internal) rather than exogenous (external) forces of change (see also Chapter 1).

It also came to be increasingly suggested that development should meet the basic needs of the people (see Chapter 1). At the same time, development needed to be ecologically sensitive and to stress more forcefully the principles of public participation (Potter, 1985).

Thus, from the mid-1970s a growing critique of top-down policies, especially growth-pole policy, argued that such approaches had merely replaced concentration at one point in space with 'concentrated deconcentration' at a limited number of new localities. In other words, the status quo had been maintained, even if the pattern had changed.

However, assertions that there is only one linear path to development and that development is the same thing as economic growth also came to be seriously challenged, at least in some quarters. Liberal and radical commentators suggested that top-down approaches to development were acting as the servants of transnational capital (Friedmann and Weaver, 1979). In a similar vein, other commentators argued that what had been achieved in the past was economic growth without development, but with increasing poverty (Hettne, 1995).

It is very important to recognise that issues of gender, as discussed in multiple chapters in this book, have strongly influenced alternative development theory, particularly in terms of topics such as diverse economies and livelihoods. To try and understand development without understanding the key roles played by gender issues and gender politics would be a significant oversight. Gender issues have now often become central in processes of participatory planning and development.

The territorial bases of development

In their book *Territory and Function*, John Friedmann and Clyde Weaver (1979) presented the important argument that development theory and practice up to that point had been dominated by purely functional concerns relating to economic efficiency and modernity, with all too little consideration being accorded to the needs of particular territories, and to the territorial (indigenous) bases of development and change.

Since the mid 1970s, a major new paradigm came to the fore, which involved stronger emphasis being placed on rural-based strategies of development. As a whole, this approach is described as 'development from below'. Other terms used to describe the paradigm include 'agropolitan development', 'grassroots development' and 'urban-based rural development'. In the context of wider societal change, such developments can be related to the rise of what is called 'neo-populism'.

Neo-populism involves attempts to recreate and re-establish the local community as a form of protection against the rise of the industrial system (Hettne, 1995: 117). The territorial manifestation of neo-populism has been the rise of the green ideology as a global concern, allied to green politics.

Basic needs and development

The provision of basic needs became a major focus during the early 1970s. The idea of basic needs originated with a group of Latin American theorists, and was officially launched at the International Labour Organization's World Employment Conference, which was held in 1976. Preston (1996) argues that the pessimistic view of the Club of Rome's Limits to Growth (Chapters 5 and 6), was the motivating force behind basic needs strategies.

The approach stressed the importance of creating employment over and above the creation of economic growth. This was because the economic growth that had occurred in the South seemed to have gone hand in hand with increases in relative poverty. Development, it appeared, was failing to improve conditions for the poorest and weakest sectors of society.

The argument ran that what was needed was redistribution of wealth to be effected alongside growth. During this period, the basic needs approach was accepted and adopted by a range of international agencies, not only the International Labour Organization (ILO), but also the United Nations Environmental Programme (UNEP) and the World Bank. However, it has to be recognised that many basic needs approaches used the aegis of the poor to support cheap basic needs programmes in place of greater state commitment to poverty alleviation. This is probably why the World Bank became such a rapid convert to the approach. In these circumstances it has to be acknowledged that the practical implementation of basic needs had little to do with socialist principles per se.

The principal idea is that basic needs, such as food, education, water supply, clothing and housing, must be met as a clear first priority within particular territories. In the purest form, it is argued that this can only be achieved by nations becoming more reliant on local resources, the communalisation of productive wealth, and closing up to outside forces of change. This aspect of development theory is known as selective regional and territorial closure.

Development from below or bottom-up development

In basic terms, therefore, it is argued that countries in the South should try to reduce their involvement in processes of unequal exchange. The only way round the problem is to increase self-sufficiency and self-reliance. It is envisaged that the economy can later be diversified and non-agricultural activities introduced. It was argued that, in these circumstances, urban locations are no longer likely to be mandatory, and city development can in this sense be based on agriculture. Thus, Friedmann and Weaver (1979: 200) comment that 'large cities will lose their present overwhelming advantage'.

Clearly, such approaches are inspired by, if not entirely based on, socialist principles. Classic examples of the enactment of bottom-up paths to development have been China, Cuba, Grenada, Jamaica and Tanzania under the *ujaama* policies inspired by African socialism. As Hettne (1995) notes, self-sufficiency has frequently been perceived as a threat to the influence of superpowers, as in the case of tiny Grenada (Brierley, 1985a, 1985b, 1989; Potter, 1993a, 1993b; Potter and Welch, 1996). This example is discussed in some detail in Case study 3.3.

Case study 3.3

Paths to development: the case of Grenada

The experience of Grenada in the eastern Caribbean is useful in demonstrating that alternative paths to development do not have to be revolutionary in the Marxist political sense (Potter and Lloyd-Evans, 1998).

In March 1979, Maurice Bishop, a UK-trained lawyer, overthrew what was regarded as the dictatorial and corrupt regime of Eric Gairy. Maurice Bishop led the New Jewel Movement (NJM), the principal theme of which was anti-Gairyism allied with anti-imperialism. The movement also expressed its strong commitment to genuine independence and self-reliance for the people of Grenada (Brierley,

1985a, 1985b; Ferguson, 1990; Hudson, 1989, 1991; Kirton, 1988; Potter, 1993a, 1993b).

On the eve of the revolution, Grenada suffered from a chronic trade deficit, strong reliance on aid and remittances from nationals based overseas, dependence on food imports and very substantial areas of idle agricultural land. After the overthrow of Gairy, the NJM formed the People's Revolutionary Government (PRG), the movement taking a basic human needs approach as the core of its development philosophy. The PRG stated its intention of preventing the prices of food, clothing and other basic items

▶

Case study 3.3 (continued)

from rocketing, along with its wish to see Grenada depart from its traditional role as an exporter of cheap produce. The government also set up the National Cooperative Development Agency in 1980, the express aim of which was to engage unemployed groups in villages in the process of 'marrying idle hands with idle lands'.

Between 1981 and 1982, two agro-industry plants were completed, one producing coffee and spices, the other juices and jams. A strong emphasis was placed on encouraging the population to value locally grown produce together with local forms of cuisine, although the scale of this task was clearly not appreciated by those concerned (Potter and Welch, 1996). The PRG also pledged itself to the provision of free medicines, dental care and education. Finally, it was an avowed intention of the People's Revolutionary Government to promote what Bishop referred to as the 'New Tourism', a term which is now widely employed in the literature. 'New Tourism' meant the introduction of what the party regarded as sociologically relevant forms of holidaymaking, especially those which emphasised the culture and history of the nation, and which would be based on local foods, cuisine, handicrafts and furniture-making (Patullo, 1996). Such forms of tourist development, it was argued, should replace extant forms based on overseas interests and the exploitation of the local environment and socio-cultural history.

The salient point is that, throughout the period, 80 per cent of the economy of Grenada remained in the hands of the private sector, and a trisectoral strategy of development that encompassed private, public and cooperative parts of the economy was the declared aim of the PRG. In this sense, the so-called Grenadian Revolution was nothing of the sort. The economy of Grenada grew quite substantially from 1979 to 1983, at rates of between 2.1 and 5.5 per cent per annum. During the period, the value of Grenada's imported foodstuffs fell from 33 to 27.5 per cent. Even the World Bank commented favourably on the state of the Grenadian economy during the period from 1979 (Brierley, 1985a).

For many it was a matter of great regret that Maurice Bishop was assassinated in October 1983, and the island invaded by US military forces, because this saw the end of the four-year experiment in alternative development set up in this small Commonwealth nation (Brierley, 1985a). This deprived other small dependent Third World states of the fully worked-through lessons of grassroots development that Grenada seemed to be in the process of providing.

Critical reflection

Grenada provides a good example of how a small island nation can endeavour to localise and indigenise development. Most countries are, of course, far larger than Grenada and have more extensive resource bases. Think of the wider strategies that nations can employ in a number of different economic sectors in order to promote bottom-up development. How easy is it to implement such approaches in the global economy of the present day?

Walter Stöhr (1981) provides an informative overview of development from below. In particular, his account stresses that there is no single recipe for such strategies, as there is for development from above. Development from below needs to be closely related to specific socio-cultural, historical and institutional conditions. Simply stated, development should be based on territorial units and citizens should endeavour to mobilise their indigenous natural and human resources. More particularly, the approach is based on the use of indigenous resources, self-reliance and appropriate technology, plus a range of other possible factors, many of which are shown in Table 3.1.

It is noticeable that bottom-up strategies are varied, with alternative paths to development being stressed. They share the characteristic of arguing that development and change should not be concentrated at each higher level of the social and settlement systems, but should focus on the needs of the lower echelons of these respective orders. It is this characteristic which gives rise to the term *bottom-up* development, for such strategies are in fact often enacted by strong state control and direction from the political 'centre'.

Table 3.1 Stöhr's criteria for the enactment of 'development from below'

Broad access to land
A territorially organised structure for equitable communal decision making
Granting greater self-determination to rural areas
Selecting regionally appropriate technology
Giving priority to projects which serve basic needs
Introduction of national price policies
External resources used only where peripheral ones are inadequate
The development of productive activities exceeding regional demands
Restructuring urban and transport systems to include all internal regions
Improvement of rural-to-urban and village communications
Egalitarian societal structures and collective consciousness

Source: Based on Stöhr (1981)

Grassroots development and indigenous knowledge

Important within the context of bottom-up development is the growing recognition of the need to recognise, respect and, where appropriate, support community-based grassroots development. Communities, often in rural areas in the South, frequently rely on their 'indigenous technical knowledge', particularly with respect to issues such as land management, farming and resource use. Such approaches often have lower levels of environmental impact and are more sustainable than introduced methods of farming and resource use. The practice of intercropping, or the growing of multiple crops on the same piece of land to allow for staggered harvesting and natural fertilisation, as opposed to the more costly and environmentally stressful practice of mono-cropping, is a particular case in point, which is widespread in Asia and Africa (Wlliams et al., 2014). The concept of grassroots development in further explored in Chapters 9 and 10, with respect to urban and rural development.

Grassroots development also involves a host of community-based and NGO supported initiatives. These often involve having a singular, locally relevant focus, such as making school uniforms in a community, or the bulk-buying of food etc., which though small-scale in its focus, can make a substantive difference in the lives of the poor and disadvantaged.

In order to better understand, and where appropriate, support grass-roots endeavours, a suite of bottom-up and community sensitive research approaches have been developed. Broadly referred to as 'participatory research', these approaches seek to learn from communities rather than impose western knowledge. Initially developed by Robert Chambers, these approaches privilege learning from local perceptions and traditional skills and only advocate 'action research' where value can be gained by a community through a degree of external support. Such approaches are regarded as empowering and less disruptive, particularly in rural communities (Chambers, 1983) (these ideas are discussed more fully below and in Chapter 10).

Environment and development

Another major development since the 1970s has been the emergence of concerns about environmental consciousness in the arena of development thinking, particularly in light of environmental damage wrought to date (see Plate 3.8). Central to this evolving concern was the Brundtland Commission on Environment and Development which reported in 1987 (WCED, 1987) (see Chapter 1). Even more important was the Earth Summit held in Rio de Janiero in the summer of 1992. This United Nations Conference on Environment and Development (UNCED) brought together some 180 nations. It was at this stage that principles of environmental sustainability became a political issue in the development debate (Pelling, 2002). This interest continued in the Rio+10 (years) conference, the World Conference on Sustainable Development held in Johannesburg, South Africa in 2002 and the Rio+20 summit in 2012.

Growing concerns about long-term resource depletion, environmental damage and climate change have become more prominent in current development planning, with 'green' issues starting to influence energy choice and resource management. Equally important, and stemming from the work of the Brundtland Commission, has been the embedding of the principle of 'sustainable development' (see below) into many development programmes, particularly those initiated at the local level where environmental concerns are often more pressing and immediate (Hopper, 2012). The United Nations role in supporting sustainable development is further examined in Chapter 7.

Plate 3.8 Environmental costs of development: Anshan, China
(*photo*: Tony Binns)

Ecodevelopment becomes sustainable development

'Ecodevelopment', now known as 'sustainable development', has become one of the leading development paradigms since the 1990s, stressing the need to preserve the natural biological systems that underpin life and the global economy (Redclift, 1987; Elliott, 2013). These approaches are fully explored in Chapter 6.

Sustainability constitutes the ecological dimension of territorialism discussed previously (Hettne, 1995). Territory, it is argued, should be considered before function, and developing countries should not look to developed nations for the template on which to base their development. Rather, they should look towards their own ecology and culture (see Case study 3.3).

In this context, too, it is recognised that development does not have a universal meaning. Strongly allied to this, the need for emancipatory views on women and development, and ethnicity and development have started to receive the attention that they deserve, not least in the guise of ecofeminism.

It is in this sense that sustainable development means more than preserving natural biological systems. There is the assumption of implicit fairness or justice within sustainable development, so the poor and disadvantaged are not forced to degrade or pollute their environments in order to be able to survive on a day-to-day basis. In Chapter 6 current framings of sustainable development with respect to considerations of equity and justice are examined.

The much-quoted definition of sustainable development was provided by the Brundtland Commission as development 'that meets the needs of the present without compromising the ability of future generations to meet their own needs' (WCED, 1987: 43). This is a far cry from the unilinear, Eurocentric functional perspectives advanced during the 1960s and 1970s, and demonstrates the wide-ranging changes that have occurred in development theory, development policies and geographies of development over the past 40 years.

However, as noted at the outset of this chapter, the promotion of sustainable development is occurring in a context where neo-liberal economic policies remain dominant, and many would stress the potential incompatibility of these two forces of change at their extremes – as is witnessed in the current debates about cheap air flights and global warming.

Climate change has ratcheted up the significance of these considerations. For example, the emergence of eco-tourism, community-based tourism, alternate tourism and sustainable tourism are initiatives to support tourism activities, which often have defined developmental impacts in the South. These tourism endeavours are based on principles of sustainability, minimising impact and often working directly with host communities. These initiatives are being pursued in contrast to mass tourism which is often regarded as exploitative and both environmentally and culturally harmful (Desai and Potter, 2014).

Alternative development: a summary

Brohman (1996) provides a useful summary of what he sees as the main elements of alternative development strategies:

➤ A move towards direct redistributive mechanisms specifically targeting the poor.
➤ A focus on local small-scale projects, often linked to urban or rural community-based development programmes.
➤ An emphasis on basic needs and human resource development.
➤ A refocusing away from growth-oriented definitions of development, towards more broadly based human-oriented frameworks.
➤ A concern for local and community participation in the design and implementation of projects.
➤ An emphasis on self-reliance, reducing outside dependency and promoting sustainability.

New forms of governance: civil society, social capital and participatory development

The account thus far has considered the provision of basic needs, and the promotion of redistribution and self-reliance, and these can certainly be seen as some of the basic characteristics of alternative development, both in terms of its origins and its early practice. But alternative development has now also come to be associated with new and wider conceptualisations of planning and development.

The main distinguishing feature here is the fostering of participatory development, associated with more equitable principles of growth. Given the long hegemony of so-called 'top-down', Western, rational planning and development, increasing the involvement of people in their own development is seen by many as imperative. Chambers (1983) suggested that it was time for the 'last to be put first', i.e. to focus on the people at the bottom, the 'recipients' of development (see also Mohan, 2002).

In this context, participation means much more than involvement or mere consultation (Conyers, 1982; Potter, 1985). While these calls seem eminently reasonable, how is this to be achieved, and who exactly is to participate? Clearly, not everybody can participate in all decisions all of the time. Indeed, it has to be recognised that it is a democratic right not to participate.

These changes have become involved with wider issues, suggesting the need for the evolution of new forms of governance. In turn, the account on governance is closely associated with newer concepts, 'civil society' and 'social capital'. As the state has progressively withdrawn from specific areas during the neo-liberal era, so organisations, such as NGOs, community and voluntary organisations, have become more and more important. This is referred to as the rise of 'civil society' (Edwards, 2001a; Fukuyama, 2001). Civil society may be regarded as forming a so-called 'third sector', in addition to the traditional two of the state and the marketplace.

Non-governmental organisations (NGOs) form a vital part of civil society, along with other types of civil associations. These have come to play an increasingly important role in local and community-based initiatives in the Global South (Desai, 2014; Mercer, 2002).

One of the principal merits of NGOs is seen as their extreme sensitivity to local conditions and their dedication to the tasks at hand (Brohman, 1996). NGOs are also often linked to wider forms of global citizen action in the form of popular movements in the fields of health, education, welfare and employment. Further, much of the work of NGOs has involved poverty reduction measures. On the negative side, there is a strong argument that NGOs have been used to fill the vacuum left by the rolling back of the state as part of structural adjustment programmes and neo-liberalism, and they have occasionally been seen as 'agents' of foreign states (see Chapter 1).

The rise of civil society is also based on greater recognition of the importance of social capital (Bebbington, 1999; Fukuyama, 2001). The expression 'social capital' first emerged in the early 1990s, and has quickly become a key term used by international agencies, governments and NGOs.

An American academic, Robert Putnam (1993), who studied community linkages in southern Italy and the USA, is often mentioned as the key figure in the field. However, many difficulties surround both the definition of, and attempts to measure, social capital. One commonly employed definition sees social capital as comprising the informal norms that promote cooperation between two or more individuals. These norms also lead to cooperation and the pursuit of mutual benefit in groups and organisations. The idea that promoting development is about increasing the stock of social capital within a given societal context is one that has come to be articulated by a number of academics since the 1990s. Perhaps the most realistic perspective is to see an awareness of social capital as critical to understanding, fostering and guiding development (Fukuyama, 2001).

But it would be naive to see 'social capital' as a miracle cure for development problems wherever they occur. In any given territorial context, social capital is likely to be the product of a wide range of factors, including shared historical experiences, local cultural norms, traditions and religion. Thus, it is hard to suggest ways in which the ties which bind people together can easily be created or manufactured as a part of developing different areas.

Further, it has to be recognised that social capital can have as many negative connotations as positive ones. As a simple example, the ties which serve to bond together members of a criminal fraternity also, simultaneously, serve to exclude non-members, who are among those likely to be exploited. In this manner, we are left with a similar argument to that encountered in relation to wider civil society; namely, that the concept can be employed to 'paper over the cracks' left by the withdrawal of the state under World Bank and IMF neo-liberal economic packages. Thus, while some may see social capital as a key concept in promoting participatory development, it must be recognised that it can also meet many of the needs of the neo-liberal right. In Chapter 7 governance and civil society receive further attention.

A changing paradigm is also discernible in the field of planning, where since the late 1990s, there has been a clear move away from expert-based and top-down systems. The argument runs that all too often planning and

development in the past have been directly associated with 'outside' experts being brought in to solve problems (see, for example, Potter and Pugh, 2001; Pugh and Potter, 2000).

It is increasingly being argued that all stakeholders relating to particular issues need to be brought into the framework as part of a 'good governance' agenda (see Chapter 7). Indeed, the World Bank itself has increasingly adopted this stance in its public pronouncements.

An early representation of such an argument in the field of development was Chambers (1983; see also 1997). Chambers drew attention to the Eurocentric and other biases which have customarily pervaded development and urged the use of participatory rural appraisal (PRA) to counter such tendencies. PRA rejects written means of investigation because of potential literacy issues. Rather, it is argued that in exploring local community development issues, visual and oral techniques should be employed. Thus, PRA advocates the use of oral histories, mapping exercises, and the ranking of preferences to explore community-based issues. The aim is to articulate and listen to a wider set of local voices as part of community planning and development.

Fundamentally, it must be recognised that all meaningful participation in planning and development practice is about changing existing power relations in the arena of decision making. Thus, changing the ways in which planning and development are carried out involves the empowerment of new groups of stakeholders. More recently, this move towards 'people power' or 'citizen control' (Nelson and Wright, 1995) has given rise to what are referred to as 'collaborative approaches' to planning.

In collaborative planning, the accent is placed on developing collaboration among the various stakeholders, in respect of both policy development and delivery. The approach has been explored in the European context by Healey (1997, 1998, 1999) and Tewdwr-Jones and Allmendinger (1998). Essentially, it is recognised that reactive institutional frameworks need to be fostered which will allow a wide range of stakeholders to be involved in decision making, and not just trained experts, professionals and elites. It is a prime requirement of the 'communicative turn' that the many different forms of local knowledge that exist are taken into account.

All such approaches basically involve consensus-building in decision making. The approach is sometimes also referred to as 'communicative planning', as it is in part based on Habermas' concept of communicative rationality. It also incorporates Foucault's ideas concerning the centrality of power in all social spheres.

Debate continues concerning exactly how practical such ideas are in reality, and whether consensus can ever be established in areas where fragmentation and conflict seem to be built into the system. However, collaborative and communicative planning must be seen as new perspectives in development thinking, which may have a direct bearing on development theories and strategies.

All such approaches, involving greater participation and empowerment, reflect a movement towards considering development at the local scale, but such approaches are not without their potential problems. Thus, Mohan and Stokke (2000) argue that the focus on the local carries the danger that the power relations and inequalities that underlie development issues and problems may be lost sight of. The authors argue that a stronger emphasis must be placed on the politics of the local if such 'dangers of localism' are to be avoided. Purcell and Brown (2005) have argued that there is no inherent reason why decision making at the local level should necessarily be more efficient or just. Scale, they argue, is a backdrop to good decision making.

Anti-development/Post-development

The concepts of anti- and post-development were explored in-depth in Chapter 1. From a theoretical perspective the insight which they provide has been invaluable in helping us to question the meaning, definition and focus of what development is, and to recognise the risks of imposing a construct either from the North on the South. The approach has also helped to focus attention on the many failures of externally driven development and the need to pursue approaches which are more socially and contextually relevant (Andrews and Bawa, 2014; Sidaway, 2008).

While being strong on the critique, the offering of an alternative has been relatively underplayed. However, as argued in Chapter 1, authors such as Escobar (1995) have placed considerable faith in the potential and role which local social movements can play as alternate forms of 'development'. While, as critiques of these approaches note, evidence on the ground is limited, this line of thinking shares parallels with the basic tenets of grassroots development and bottom-up development. These approaches all focus on local responses and coping strategies to deal with how, what are often, marginalised communities seek to negotiate a role and place for themselves in what is often an unsupportive macro-environment. It is indeed evident that social movements in both the North and the South are becoming more pro-active, but whether in themselves they can be transformative movements is open to question.

The informal sector and diverse economies

From the 1970s considerable attention was devoted to the role and place of the informal sector in applied, local development. Research drew attention to the fact that a significant proportion of transactions, purchases, sales and service provision, both legal and illegal, took place outside of the 'modern' western or formal sector economy. Activities ranging from backyard mechanics, to producers of craft goods, informal care systems, theft and hawking to name a few, were cited as evidence of a large and significant 'informal sector' which is often regarded as being larger than the formal sector, given the skills and income barriers which deny entry of most residents in the South to the limited available formal sector opportunities (Potter and Lloyd-Evans, 1998).

With the support of the International Labour Organization, support for micro-entrepreneurs has become a standard intervention in many countries. Support has included the provision of training, micro-loans and basic workspace. While clearly assisting with what are often survivalist enterprises, there is little evidence that workers in the informal sector ever attain the resources and skills to join the formal sector.

Thinking about the operation of 'alternate' economies to the mainstream has been taken significantly further by the work of Gibson-Graham (2008, 2014). Drawing on a feminist critique she has argued that the world, in economic terms, is composed of 'diverse economies' with a significant proportion of the activities, critical to the lives of people in the North and the South, taking outside of capitalist markets and wage labour. These include activities such as gift giving, voluntary activities, care, barter, fair trade, co-operatives and family-based activities. This reasoning led to the drawing

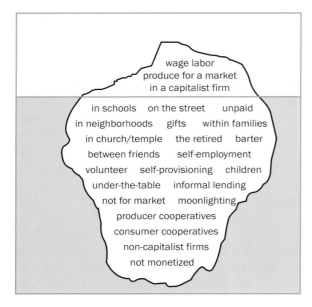

Figure 3.16 The Iceberg Model
Source: adapted from Byrne in Gibson-Graham, 2006.

the 'diverse economy'. The Figure shows how, in terms of enterprise, labour, property, transactions and finance, three parallel and interwoven systems exist, namely the capitalist (i.e. the formal sector), the alternative, but legally recognised activities, e.g. not for profit organisations, and the non-capitalist. Analyses such as this provide a more holistic appreciation of the operation of economies and societies in the North and the South, and the complex interlinkages which exists within them. By better appreciating the operation of such interconnections, future development has the potential to be more socially relevant and appropriate.

The Sustainable Livelihoods Framework

The Sustainable Livelihoods Framework is discussed in detail in Chapter 10. However, in the context of reviewing key theoretical constructs over time, it is important to acknowledge its contribution as an alternative approach. Similar to Gibson-Graham (2008), the approach is anchored in the notion that a diverse range of considerations and assets – human and natural – impact on our livelihoods. In addition, we are influenced by forces beyond our control which creates vulnerabilities and risks. Advancing from the appreciation of how livelihoods are constructed, the Sustainable Livelihoods Framework model was developed to better understand life and survival and the factors which impact on it, particularly in rural areas (Scoones, 2009). By implication, the model also provides a degree of insight into potential development interventions and support.

of the 'iceberg' model (see Figure 3.16) which uses the analogy of an iceberg to suggest that a vast range of often poorly appreciated activities take place within society which are seldom immediately obvious when we try and understand economies. From a development perspective, this line of reasoning provides a new lens to better appreciate how societies operate and survive, and it also has the potential to shape development thinking to become more appreciative of what is needed and how to react to needs.

Gibson-Graham's (2014) analysis has been extended over time and Table 3.2 indicates her understanding of

Enterprise	Labour	Property	Transactions	Finance
Capitalist	Wage	Private	Market	Mainstream Market
Alternative Enterprise e.g. state owned / non-profit	Alternative Paid e.g. self-employed / cooperative	Alternative private e.g. state owned / customary	Alternative Market e.g. Fair Trade / Barter / Community supported	Alternative Market e.g. loan sharks / co-op banks / state banks
Non-Capitalist e.g. co-ops / community enterprise	Unpaid e.g. housework / family care / volunteer / slave labour	Open Access e.g. air / water / ocean	Non-Market e.g. sharing / gifts / hunting / theft	Non-Market e.g. sweat equity / family lending / donations

Table 3.2 Diverse economies

Source: adapted from Gibson-Graham, 2014.

Development theory, modernity and postmodernity

A postmodern age?

Abandoning the evolutionary and deterministic modernisation paradigm associated historically with the enlightenment era of the eighteenth century opens up several postmodern options for future development, and some of them have been reviewed in the previous section on bottom-up, alternative and participatory conceptualisations of development.

These trends in development thinking can be linked with the idea that, globally speaking, we are entering a postmodern age, associated with the rise of a knowledge-based post-industrial economy. It is also associated with greater plurality and hybridity. This theme is briefly addressed here, and receives more explicit attention in relation to globalisation trends and development in the next chapter. Some aspects of postmodernity in relation to development ideologies have already been outlined in Chapter 1.

Postmodernism as twenty-first century development

In simple terms, postmodernity involves moving away from an era dominated by notions of modernisation and modernity (Plate 3.9a,b and Figure 3.17). It is therefore intimately associated with development theory and practice. It involves the rejection of modernism and a return to pre-modern and vernacular forms, as well as the creation of distinctly new post-modern forms (Harvey, 1989; Soja, 1989; Urry, 1990). It can be seen as a reaction against the functionalism and austerity of the modern period in favour of a heterogeneity of styles, drawing on the past and on contemporary mass culture (Plate 3.10).

As argued earlier in this chapter, there is much in the idea that the whole ethos of the modern period privileged the metropolitan over the provinces, the developed over the developing worlds, North America over the Pacific Rim, the professional expert over the general populace, and men over women (see Figure 3.18).

In contrast, the postmodern perspective potentially involves a diversity of approaches, which may serve to

Plate 3.9a Modern Hong Kong
(*photo*: Jennifer Elliott)

Plate 3.9b Modern high-rise apartments in Havana, Cuba
(*photo*: Rob Potter)

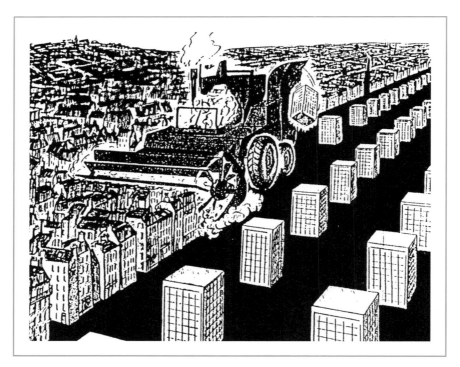

Figure 3.17 Modernism destroying the urban fabric
Source: Cartoon by J.F. Batellier

Plate 3.10 Resonances of postmodernity in a tourist setting: tourists and members of a traditional 'Tuk' band in Barbados
(*photo*: Rob Potter)

empower 'other' alternative voices and cultures (Figure 3.18). A strong emphasis on bottom-up, non-hierarchical growth strategies, which endeavour to get away from the international sameness, depthlessness and ahistoricism of the modern epoch, can be seen as part and parcel of the postmodern world (Figure 3.18 and Table 3.3). The accent can potentially be placed on growth in smaller places, rather than bigger, and in the periphery rather than the core.

Postmodernism as late capitalism? And thinking ahead

However, although postmodernism may in certain respects be seen in this optimistic manner, as a liberating force associated with small-scale non-hierarchical development and participatory change, there is another distinctive facet to the trend of postmodernism.

This is very much like the arguments presented in the last section regarding the different ways in which civil society, social capital, NGOs and collaborative planning can all be regarded as serving the imperatives

Table 3.3 Some polar differences between modernism and postmodernism that have relevance to development

Modernism	Postmodernism
Form	Antiform
Conjunctive, closed	Disjunctive, open
Purpose	Play
Design	Chance
Hierarchy	Anarchy
Finished work	Performance, happening
Synthesis	Antithesis
Centring	Dispersal
Root, depth	Rhizome, surface
Interpretation, reading	Against interpretation, misreading
Narrative	Antinarrative
Master code	Idiolect
Determinancy	Indeterminancy
Transcendence	Immanence

Source: adapted from Harvey (1989).

of both the political right and the left. As well as the rejection of the modern and a hankering for the premodern, there is the establishment of 'after the modern'. This is frequently interpreted as 'consumerist postmodernism', involving the celebration of commercialism, commercial vulgarity, the glorification of consumption and the related expression of the self (Cooke, 1990). These processes Northern perceptions of the world and in turn the North's perception of what development should be about.

As will be explored in Chapter 4, these are trends which are of interest in relation to what is happening in parts of the South, an example being the promotion of international tourism as a major plank of development, shaping how the South is perceived and 'used' by the North (Plate 3.10; see also Chapter 4) (Jones et al., 1993).

Such a condition is related to a conflation of trends in which aspects of art and life, high and low culture are

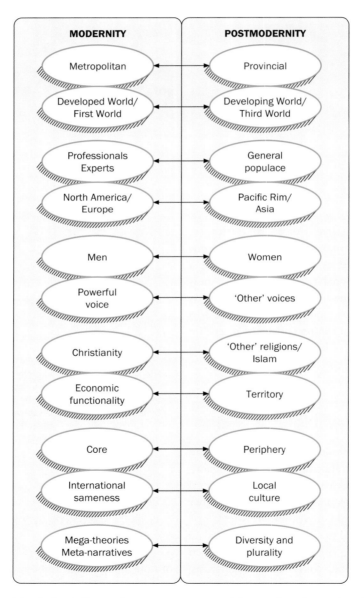

Figure 3.18 A graphical depiction of some common ideas about modernity and postmodernity

fused together, or 'pastiched'. Images, signs, hoarding and advertisements are potentially more important than 'reality'. Mass communications lead to mass image creation (Massey, 1991; Robins, 1989, 1995).

History and heritage may be rewritten and reinterpreted in order to meet the needs of international business and consumerism. This may all lead to further external control, exploitation and neo-colonialism. Many of these features can be interpreted in terms of the overconsumptive lifestyles which were offered to members of the upper white-collar strata of society in the Reagan–Thatcher era, and more recently in response to the 2008 GFC where financial and banking systems were 'bailed out' by states. Several of these themes will be further explored in the next chapter.

In this regard, rather than being seen as a freeing and enabling force, postmodernism may alternatively be interpreted as essentially the logical outcome of late capitalism (Cuthbert, 1995; Dann and Potter, 1994; Harvey, 1989; Jameson, 1984; Kaarsholm, 1995; Potter and Dann, 1994, 1996; Sidaway, 1990). Sardar (1998) argues that with its roots in colonialism and modernity, postmodernity, in fact, operates to marginalise the realities of the non-Western world further.

The role of TNCs in the promotion of tourism in the Caribbean may be seen as another instance where advertising and promotion campaigns may be interpreted as being aimed directly at increasing both the environmental and social carrying capacities of the nation. Such developments have interesting implications in contexts where nations themselves are still endeavouring to modernise (Austin-Broos, 1995; Masselos, 1995; Potter and Dann, 1994; Thomas, 1991). This theme is picked up and developed in Chapter 4.

The development of postmodern trends that influence developing societies, in particular via the activities of transnational corporations and tourists, is of further interest in the new world order following the collapse of the communist world in 1989. We are certainly entering a noticeably less certain, less monolithic and unidirectional world. Hence the already wide diversity of development strategies and thinking and the many varied geographies of development, seems likely to get more complicated, rather than less, over the coming years.

For example, some authorities are now talking of the 'tripolarity' of development, with the Americas, Europe and Pacific Asia each presenting a particular version of industrial capitalism (Preston, 1996). The recent problems being faced by Asian economies and the 2008 GFC are further signs of increasing global volatility and dynamism. The events of 11 September 2001 confirm only too cogently the validity of such a view.

This perspective is reflected in what has been called the 'impasse in development studies' (Booth, 1985; Corbridge, 1986; Preston, 1985; Schuurman, 1993, 2008; Slater, 1992a). The world has become a much more complex place since the collapse of communism in

Plate 3.11 Images of development ideology in Cuba: 'Revolution Yes!'
(*photo*: Rob Potter)

1989, making the division into the First, Second and Third Worlds much more questionable, or perhaps even meaningless, as discussed in Chapter 1 (Plate 3.11).

Hettne (1995) argued that the rise of neo-conservatism in the global political realm, and monodisciplinary trends in the academic world have both presented development thinking with fundamental challenges. Some have pointed to what they regard as an impasse in theorising development itself, although this seems unduly pessimistic given the range of ideas considered in this chapter. Hettne (1995) also referred to the failure of development in practice as contributing to self-criticism, pessimism and 'development fatigue', especially in relation to the ultimate relevance of Western-developed research and ideas.

Notwithstanding these justifiable concerns, it is axiomatic that 'development', defined as change for the better (Brookfield, 1975), will proceed in each and every corner of the globe. This being the case, there continues to be a need for the generation and discussion of realistic, although challenging and often conflicting, sets of ideas concerning the process of development, as well as the conditions and responses that are to be encountered on the ground in developing countries themselves.

Key points

> Development theories and strategies have been many and varied, with new approaches generally being added alongside existing ones.
> Multiple development strategies and approaches exist in parallel, even though one, such as neo-liberalism, currently appears to be dominant.
> Classical and neo-classical economic approaches generally stress the need for unrestrained, polarised growth and of letting the market decide for itself.
> Neo-liberalism as a generic development paradigm stems from the New Right and emphasises what is seen as the continuing need for market liberalisation and for the economy to be market- and performance-driven.
> Historical models give a normative impression of the degree to which in the past, since mercantilism and colonialism, development has been highly uneven and spatially polarised.
> Alternative approaches have a focus on bottom-up development and show sensitivity to issues of gender, the environment and the diverse economies which people live in.
> Both dependency (radical) approaches and alternative/another development can be seen as direct critiques of modernisation theory. Thus the economic growth paradigm of the 1950s was challenged by socialist and environmentally oriented paradigms in the 1960s and 1970s respectively.
> Development thinking reflects political views – views on how economies should work and how societies should be structured. Postmodernity is leading to less dominant approaches to development.

Further reading

Cowan, M.P. and Shenton, R.W. (1996) *Doctrines of Development*. London: Routledge.
A comprehensive text dealing with principles of development.

Desai, V. and Potter, R.B. (eds) (2014) *The Companion to Development Studies*, 2nd edn. Part 2: Theories and strategies of development, London: Routledge.
Contains a range of short essays covering the most important aspects of development theories and strategies.

Greig, A., Hulme, D. and Turner, M. (2007) *Challenging Global Inequality: Development Theory and Practice in the 21st Century*. Basingstoke: Palgrave Macmillan.
Stresses global poverty and inequality in reviewing contemporary development theory and practice.

Hettne, B. (1995) *Development Theory and the Three Worlds*, 2nd edn. London: Longman.
Although produced in the mid-1990s, this book still affords a very clear introduction to the principal paradigms of development.

Preston, P.W. (1996) *Development Theory: An Introduction*. Oxford: Blackwell.
Another book dealing with the theory and practice of development.

Simon, D. (ed) (2006) *Fifty Key Thinkers on Development*. London: Routledge.
A useful source which brings together short essays on those who are deemed to have had a noticeable impact on studies of development.

Thornton, P. (2014) *The Great Economists*. Harlow: Pearson.
This book view overviews the ideas of the key economic theorists over time in a series of 10 essays.

Williams, G., Meth, P. and Willis, K. (2014) *Geographies of Developing Areas*. London: Routledge.
A very readable overview on what development is and the key processes which influence it.

Websites

www.iedconline.org
The website of the International Economic Development Council based in Washington DC. IEDC is a non-profit membership organisation dedicated to assisting 'economic developers' to do their job more effectively. With over 4,500 members worldwide, IEDC offers support for professional development, advisory and legal services and regular conferences on development topics.

www.ids.ac.uk
The Institute of Development Studies (IDS) at the University of Sussex (Brighton, UK) offers an extensive website giving access to the online catalogue of the IDS Library, with good holdings on development strategies and ideologies.

www.eldis.org
This is a reporting scheme, reflecting a selection of the 'latest and best' UK-based development research, based at the Institute of Development Studies at the University of Sussex.

Discussion topics

➤ Assess the extent to which 'modern' development theories have been discredited by the rise of so-called 'alternative' and 'postmodern' approaches.

➤ Examine the extent to which Vance's mercantile model can be seen as a graphical representation of classical dependency theory.

➤ 'Old development theories never die. In fact, they don't even seem to fade away!' Discuss.

➤ For one developing nation, outline and assess the national development strategies employed since 1947.

Chapter 4
Globalisation, development and underdevelopment

The term 'globalisation' has increasingly come to be associated with the era in which we live and reflects the degree to which our lives and the societies in which we live are influenced by processes and trends which are global as opposed to national in origin. This chapter seeks to explore the implications of globalisation for the process of development. On the one hand, there is the essentially neo-liberal argument that for development to occur there has to be globalisation – to allow countries to buy and sell goods and to buy into new forms of technology, cultural change and the like from anywhere in the world. At the other extreme are those who are far less happy with the outcomes of contemporary processes of globalisation, who argue that the process is 'distorting' patterns of development and creating ever-increasing global inequalities and reinforcing 'uneven geographical development'. At the extreme, globalisation has been branded as neo-modernisation, a renewed twenty-first century faith in the notion that modernisation will progressively develop the world in a benign, efficient and positive manner. At their extremes, these two arguments are associated with pro-globalisers/ultra neo-liberals on the one hand, and anti-globalisers on the other. This chapter:

➤ Explores the links between globalisation and development, looking at arguments about both the negative and positive aspects of the relations between the two;
➤ Examines the realities of a shrinking world as an increasingly unequal world and the persistence of 'unequal geographical development';
➤ Presents an updated picture of the global digital divide showing just how unequal the world is in terms of communications;
➤ Reviews economic aspects of globalisation, especially what is referred to as 'global shift' in the manufacturing sector and the emergence of what are referred to as 'global production networks';
➤ Defines and explores the realities of the joint processes of global convergence and global divergence as key systems leading to homogeneity in patterns of consumption for those who can afford it, and heterogeneity in respect of production and ownership;
➤ Reviews aspects of cultural globalisation;
➤ Considers political aspects of globalisation;
➤ Overviews protests against the current forms that globalisation is assuming in the form of the anti-globalisation and anti-capitalism movements, including urban social movements.

Defining globalisation

Just as the first pictures of the whole earth from outer space made us aware of the interdependence and ecological fragility of the planet, so the events of 11 September 2001, the 2008 Global Financial Crisis (GFC) and the more recent downturn in the Chinese economy have served to show just how globalised and socio-politically and economically fragile the world is today, certainly in respect to major events and strategic upheavals.

Over the last 40 years or so, one of the major trends has been that the world in which we live is being seen as ever more global in character and orientation. This trend has been witnessed in increasing actual and potential interactions between different parts of the globe. People are increasingly thinking in terms of an 'era of global change' and a 'globalising world', and claiming that we live in a 'global village'. While communication and technological advances, and greater levels of global interaction through the investment decisions of the large corporations, undoubtedly have advanced global 'development' in financial terms, the impact of such growth is distributed unevenly across the Earth. In the South, being included and excluded from globalisation processes can be a major catalyst or hindrance to development, but even for well-integrated places this form of development comes with associated costs.

Such global change is intimately connected with a battery of developments which define our age, including e-mail, the internet, social media and the digital world in general, along with older technologies which are still acting as agents of diffusion and change, including the telephone, fax, television, DVD recorders and wide-bodied jets. The spread of global brands, international media, air connectivity, the work of global bodies such as the UN, and dissemination of fashions and music have all accelerated these processes. Critical in this process is the emergence in manufacturing of what is known as 'global production networks' (GPNs) which source inputs globally, manufacture in different parts of the world and sell their products internationally relying on low trade barriers, reducing transport costs and integrated operations, production and sales as a result of integrated logistics and digital technology (Coe and Yeung, 2015).

Schech and Haggis (2000: 58) define globalisation as the intensification of global interconnectedness, a process that they see as associated with the spread of capitalism as a production and market system. In an essentially similar manner, Kiely (1999a: 3) suggests that 'globalisation refers to a world in which societies, cultures, politics and economies have, in some sense, come closer together'. The same author goes on to note, however, that globalisation involves substantially more than interconnectedness. The process also involves the intensification of worldwide social relations, serving to link events in widely geographically separated places (see Schuurman, 2001; Murray, 2006; Conway and Heynen, 2006; Dicken, 2015). Dicken (2015: 1) argues that this is part of 'an inevitable and inexorable process of increasing geographical spread and increasing functional integration between economic activities'.

Contemporary globalisation is also associated with changing experiences of time and place and with the development of new communications technologies and the rise of what has been referred to as the 'information society' (Castells, 1996). Governments in their turn frequently stress that globalisation involves enhancing the free movement of goods, services, capital, information and, in some instances, people across national boundaries. The process of globalisation is, therefore, inescapably plugged into the neo-liberal world order that was discussed in the previous chapter, which benefits countries and places within them on a differential basis, running the risk of creating and even reinforcing what Harvey (2015: 146) refers to as 'uneven geographical development'. Within this context the poorest nations run the risk of being 'integrated' into a world system, but in a precarious and marginalised position as a result of unequal power, trading and financial arrangements (Bond, 2006; Collier, 2008). Within this context it is interesting to observe the emergence of global protest against the dominant capitalist system, as expressed in the annual demonstrations at meetings of the world's main economic leaders in Davos in Switzerland, the rapid spread of the 'Occupy' movement protests in 2011 and emerging moves to link social movements internationally.

In addition, on occasion, globalisation is directly equated with a distinctly post-modern world within which states and boundaries are becoming less powerful agents of change.

Yet, there remains much controversy about the likely developmental consequences of the diverse strands which make up globalisation (Murray, 2006; Conway and Heynen, 2006). Thus, the major theme of this chapter is that these global tendencies are highly uneven, both spatially (between places and regions), and socially (between peoples and groups). The impacts of globalisation vary from region to region, and group to group, in ways that are clearly contributing to the further development of diverse and plural geographies of development at the beginning of the twenty-first century. The overall diversity and plurality of these processes is contingent upon globalising tendencies and the risk of creating or reinforcing 'uneven geographical development' (Harvey, 2015) which is a major theme in this chapter. An issue that we touch on several times in this chapter is that, however we define it, globalisation has, in fact, been around in different forms for many centuries. However, it is a frequently heard assertion that over the last 40 years or so the rate of globalisation and its intensity have both increased dramatically – and it is the developmental connotations of this claim that form a focus of this chapter.

Globalisation and development: 'for and against'/'solution or problem'?

Introduction

There are at least three distinct aspects to the current processes of global change that we are witnessing.

First, the world is effectively 'shrinking' in terms of the distances that can be covered in a given period of time, due to faster and more efficient transport, although this process works more for the affluent 'jet-set' than for everyone else. Rapid improvements in digital technology have led to the integration of financial and production activity, and have facilitated constant global networking from the activities of stock exchanges to personal contacts.

Second, better communications, such as cable and satellite television, mean that many – though by no means all of us – hear about what is happening elsewhere in the world more swiftly than we ever did before. The global web now has far more connections than it

had in the past (Knox et al., 2014), and those who have ready access to the technology have much more up-to-date information at their disposal.

Third, the ascendancy of global corporations and global marketing activities is resulting in the availability of many standardised and globalised products (Dicken, 2015) and global media throughout the world, again for those who can afford them. In addition, not only do we live in a world of near ubiquitous Big Macs, Coca-Cola, Levi jeans, Starbucks, Amazon, eBay, Facebook and Google, but we are also witnessing the emergence of global financial markets and the integration of global financial systems and stock exchanges. The rapid and profound effects felt around the world of the near collapse in 2008 of elements of the western banking system in the so-called 'Global Financial Crisis' are profoundly illustrative of both the reality of global integration, but more importantly of our global vulnerability to crises often outside our national borders, over which we have minimal control. This is associated with a dramatic acceleration in the speed of financial flows and transactions, with money now moving in purely electronic form, so that it takes only fractions of a second to send sums from one part of the world to another.

Strands of globalisation: economic, cultural and political

Following this argument, Allen (1995) has recognised three broad strands to globalisation: the economic, the cultural and the political.

First, in respect to economic globalisation, distance has become less important to economic activities, and large corporations frequently subcontract to branch plants in far distant regions, effectively operating within a 'borderless' world through their 'global production networks' (Coe and Yeung, 2015).

Secondly, the stereotype of cultural globalisation suggests that as Western forms of consumption and lifestyles spread across the globe, there is an increasing convergence of cultural styles on a global norm, with that norm being codified and defined by the global capitalist system. Figure 4.1a takes a look at this apparent tendency towards global homogenisation.

Thirdly, as already noted, in the arena of political globalisation, internationalisation is regarded as leading

"We've got a wide variety of destinations"

(a)

(b)

Figure 4.1 Contrasting views of globalisation as:

(a) the homogenisation of the whole world – or at least its cities
Source: Private Eye (2000)

(b) the conflagration of the South by the North
Source: David Simonds, Copyright Guardian News & Media Ltd 1999

to the erosion of the former role and powers of the nation state. The role of the EU, UN, World Bank and WTO are indicative of these trends, as are regional economic agreements which foster free-trade and economic integration and harmonisation.

Globalisation and development/ underdevelopment: a contentious issue

Following the overview of development theories and strategies presented in Chapters 1 and 3, the present account focuses on the question of what development means in a contemporary context that is dominated by processes of globalisation and global change.

One of the important questions to be addressed is whether contemporary globalisation is in fact a new

process in any sense of the term. Is there any sense in which globalisation means that the entire world is becoming more uniform? Is there any chance that it means that the world will become progressively more equal over time? If not, is it the case that such a process of accelerated homogenisation will come about in the forseeable future? This accords with the view of' 'pro-globablisers' and the proponents of the benefits of neo-liberalism, who argue that globalisation, while having its flaws, will bring the greatest benefit to the greatest number of people globally through freer trade and integration of economic activity (see Dicken, 2015).

Or does the available evidence point to increasing inequalities between the Global North and the Global South as a result of current global change? This less than positive view of globalisation is depicted in the cartoon reproduced in Figure 4.1b. In short, does globalisation mean that change and development will 'trickle down', and that this will occur with more speed than in the past, or will it be associated with increasing polarisation? This standpoint resonates with the arguments of Harvey, who argues that 'uneven geographical development is not a mere sidebar to how capitalism works, but fundamental to its reproduction' (Harvey, 2011: 213). Geographical differences – such as natural resources or socially constructed endowments, are 'magnified and consolidated not eroded by free market competition' (Harvey, 2006: 98). Cumulative causation ensures enhanced growth of the richer areas and decline of the poorer and 'capital accumulation creates not only spaces, but different forms of spatiality' (Harvey, 2006: 77). Territorial competition is key in capital accumulation and in the disparate structures which emerge. Uneven development is thus seen as a product of the development of capitalism and is critical to its operation.

These are just a few of the basic, but highly contentious issues that will be addressed in this, the fourth and concluding chapter of Part I.

In other words, globalisation has to be seen as a highly contentious issue involving the current operation of the neo-liberal world order. This has clearly been witnessed in the '*anti-globalisation protests*' that have occurred outside major international financial gatherings since 1999, and most profoundly with the 2011 Occupy Movement protests in many cities around the world. These anti-capitalist and anti-globalisation protests are more fully considered later in this chapter. On the other hand, many governments and world financial organisations such as the World Bank, International Monetary Fund and World Trade Organization (WTO) have repeatedly stated the positive case they see for the role of globalisation in enhancing the overall process of global development.

Thus, as already intimated, two generalised views concerning the relationships between globalisation and development have emerged over the last decade, and these are outlined below.

Globalisation as development

The first view is the familiar claim that, to all intents and purposes, places around the world are fast becoming, if not exactly the same, then certainly very similar (see Figure 4.1a). This view essentially dates from the 1960s' belief in the process of modernisation (see Chapters 1

and 3). Such a perspective tacitly accepts that the world will become progressively more 'Westernised', or, more accurately, 'Americanised' (Massey and Jess, 1995).

The approach stresses the likelihood of social and cultural homogenisation, with key American traits of consumption being exemplified by the 'coca-colonisation' or 'coca-colaisation', and the Hollywoodisation or Miamisation of the Global South, replete with McDonald's golden arches. Thus, Westernisation is seen as a natural and desirable reflection of the globalised spread of development. Globalisation is seen by those subscribing to modernisation theory as the outward flow of Western know-how, capital and culture to the rest of the world. It is in this connection that 'globalization studies can be seen as one step on from modernization' (Schech and Haggis, 2000: 57).

This is very much the view of globalisation within the United Kingdom Government's White Paper on International Development presented at the start of the twenty-first century under the title *Eliminating World Poverty: Making Globalisation Work for the Poor* (Department for International Development, 2000a). In the words of Clare Short, the then Secretary of State for International Development, contained in the foreword:

> This second White Paper analyses the nature of globalisation. It sets out an agenda for managing the process in a way that could ensure that the new wealth, technology and knowledge being generated brings sustainable benefits to the one in five of humanity who live in extreme poverty.
>
> (Department for International Development, 2000a: 7)

It is also noted in the White Paper how 'encouragingly, in recent years we have seen the beginnings of a serious political debate about the equitable management of globalisation' and that 'making globalisation work more effectively for the world's poor is a moral imperative' (Department for International Development, 2000a: 14).

In overall terms, the White Paper is clear in its claim that, managed carefully, globalisation will bring specific benefits to the world's poor: 'The UK Government believes that, if well managed, the benefits of globalisation for poor countries can substantially outweigh the costs, especially in the long term' (Department for International Development, 2000a: 19).

Globalisation and marginalisation

However, even the White Paper is aware of the counter-argument, noting of globalisation in respect of developing societies that, 'managed badly . . . it could lead to their further marginalisation and impoverishment' (Department for International Development, 2000a: 15). The UK Government goes on within the same account to set out the beginnings of the anti-globalisation argument that the process is little more than one of neo-modernisation:

> For some, globalisation is inextricably linked with the neo-liberal economic policies of the 1980s and the early 1990s. For them, globalisation is synonymous with unleashing market forces, minimising the role of the state and letting inequality rip. They denounce the increasingly open and integrated global economy as an additional more potent source of global exploitation, poverty and inequality.
>
> (Department for International Development, 2000a: 15)

This cautious perspective regards globalisation as akin to the spread of advanced capitalism. Rather than suggesting that the net outcome is a more equal and more homogeneous world, the stance emphasises the reverse view, that globalisation is resulting in greater flexibility, permeability, openness, hybridity, plurality and difference, both between places and between cultures (Harvey 2006, 2015; Massey, 1991; Massey and Jess, 1995; Potter, 1993b, 1997; Robins, 1995). Following on from this perspective, far from leading to a uniform world, globalisation is viewed as being closely connected with the process of uneven development, and the perpetuation and exacerbation of spatial inequalities (Harvey, 2015).

This view of globalisation argues that, by such processes, localities are being renewed afresh. This is particularly so in respect of economic change, where production, ownership and economic processes are highly place- and space-specific and these processes may not necessarily favour countries, places and people in the Global South who often exist and operate in a 'dominance-dependence' relationship with the corporations and institutions of the Global North. The relatively recent economic ascendancy of countries such as Brazil, China, India and South Korea challenges the notion of uniformity in the South and has led to a scenario in which they in turn have developed their own economic linkages in the South which may in turn favour their own corporate and national goals.

Even in regard to cultural change, it may be argued that, although the hallmarks of Western tastes, consumption and lifestyles, such as Coca-Cola, Disney, McDonald's and Hollywood are available to all, such worldwide cultural icons are reinterpreted locally, and take on different meanings in different places (Cochrane, 1995). Further, it is obviously the case that access to them varies sharply by virtue of income and social standing. This view sees fragmentation and localisation as key correlates of globalisation and postmodernity.

A further major point substantiates this view. Evidence shows that globalisation is anything but a new process – it has been operating for hundreds of years. The process of globalisation can be seen as having started with the age of discovery (Allen, 1995; Hall, 1995). This argument has been clearly summarised by Stuart Hall (1995: 189):

> Symbolically, the voyage of Columbus to the New World, which inaugurated the great process of European expansion, occurred in the same year as the expulsion of Islam from the Spanish shores and the forced conversion of Spanish Jews in 1492. This . . . [is] as convenient a date as any with which to mark the beginnings of modernity, the birth of merchant capitalism as a global force, and the decisive events in the early stages of globalization.

This perspective usefully highlights how globalisation has always been intimately connected with power differentials and changes in culture. Early globalisation was associated with the conquest of indigenous populations, great rivalries between the major European powers in carving up colonial territories, and the eventual establishment of the slave trade, as detailed in Chapter 2. While ancient empires such as that of Rome were early forms of international integration, the later emergence of European trading empires, such as those of France, Britain, Belgium, Spain, Holland and Portugal led to the creation of what was termed an 'international division of labour' in which colonies supplied labour and raw materials to the European powers through a process of subservience.

Thus, globalisation has always been associated with increasing differences between peoples and places, rather than with evenness and uniformity. Further globalisation has been a gradual, as well as a partial and uneven process, which has spread heterogeneously across the globe.

This overarching theme is addressed in the contemporary context in this chapter, first in relation to economic aspects of globalisation, and then in relation to cultural change. First however, we turn to examine the overarching conceptualisation of a shrinking world as one of the fundamental cornerstones of contemporary globalisation.

Global transformations: a shrinking world or a more unequal world?

A shrinking world?

Whatever the respective arguments for and against globalisation as an agent of development, both critics and proponents point to the major changes that have occurred in the fields of transport and communications as technological advances have brought places closer together.

Thus, over the past 40 years there has been much talk about the world becoming a 'global village', and the associated 'compression' or 'annihilation' of space by time, in the context of what is referred to as the 'shrinking world'.

The phrase 'annihilation of space by time' is commonly attributed to Karl Marx (Leyshon, 1995: 23). Leyshon (1995) credits Marshall McLuhan (1962) with the first use of the expression 'global village', noting that the world was becoming compressed and electronically contracted, so that 'the global is no more than a village'. McLuhan went on to observe that due to the evolving electronic media, humans were beginning to participate in village-like encounters, but at a global scale, thereby cogently anticipating the development of electronic mail and the internet (see Chapter 8).

The main aspects of this change were outlined at the start of the present chapter. First, the world has effectively become a 'smaller' place than it was 50 years ago, in terms of the time it takes to travel around it as a result of a process known as 'time-space compression', according to which the time to cross physical distance reduces

with new transport and technological advances. This process of time-space compression, through which improvements in transport technologies have effectively changed the relationship between places vis-à-vis one another within the settlement system, was first described by Janelle (1969). To give a national example, in 1779 it took four days or 5,760 minutes to travel the 330 miles that separate Edinburgh from London. By the 1960s the time taken to travel between them had effectively been reduced to less than 180 minutes by plane, so the two places had been 'converging' at the rate of approximately 30 miles per year.

Digital technologies have meant that global links can now be instantaneous and space has effectively disappeared as a barrier to communication in this regard (Knox et al., 2014). At the global level, this is illustrated by the much-reproduced representation of the world shown in Figure 4.2. In the period between 1500 and 1840 the best average speed of horse-drawn coaches and sailing ships was about 10 miles per hour. In 1830, the first railway was opened between Liverpool and Manchester, and the first telegraph system was patented.

By 1900 a global telegraph system was in place, based on submarine cables, giving rise to the world's first global communications system. By the end of the period 1850–1940 steam trains averaged 65 miles per hour and steamships around 36 miles per hour. But, as shown by Figure 4.2, the real change came after 1950, with propeller-driven aircraft travelling at 300–400 miles per hour. After the 1960s commercial jet aircraft took speeds into the 500–700 miles per hour range. As a result of these progressive changes, the Earth, in relative terms, has effectively been shrunk to a fraction of its effective size over some 500 years ago (Figure 4.2 and Plate 4.1).

From the 1960s, there was an exponential increase in the number of scheduled international flights globally. At the national level, large-scale highway construction proceeded in North America and Europe in association with rapidly increasing levels of car ownership. Between 1950 and 1960, domestic television was disseminated, followed by the exploration of space and the launch of communication satellites (Leyshon, 1995).

At the beginning of the 1970s, Janelle (1973) referred to the '30-minute world', this being the time it would take for an intercontinental missile to travel from its launch site to its target on the other side of the world, and, hypothetically, lead to planetary annihilation.

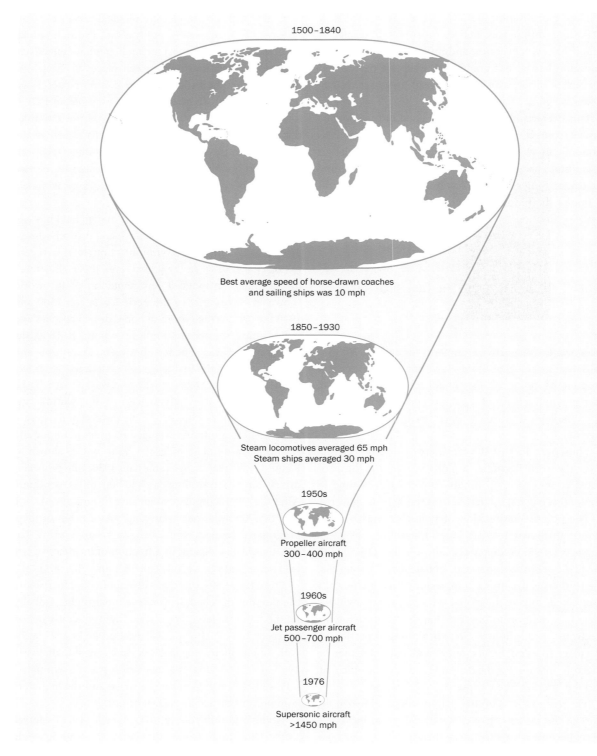

Figure 4.2 The shrinking world
Source: adapted from McHale, J. (1969) *The Future of the Future*. New York: George Braziller.

Plate 4.1 A380 Airbus 'double-decker' aircraft
(*photo*: Jennifer Elliott)

Of course, the world is also shrinking in another sense, in that many of us are potentially increasingly aware of what is happening in other far-distant places, without the need to move from our home localities. This is now achieved via the mass media, social media and the instruments of the digital age which facilitate real time visual and audio communication around the world. As Leyshon (1995: 14) notes, it is 'in the area of news and current affairs that television's ability to shrink space is best illustrated', as was all too clearly first demonstrated by the coverage of the Gulf War by cable news early in 1991.

But cable news depends on relatively sophisticated and expensive technologies, so the relatively rich have also tended to become the information-rich (Leyshon, 1995), and a 'digital divide' separates them from the residents of poor countries in terms of costs and technology, a point to which we shall return at several junctures in this chapter. There are other development-related implications to this set of changing circumstances in that they invite a redefinition of our ethical and moral responsibilities in relation to people who live far away from us in the North or South dependent on your place of residence.

Such 'responsibility to distant others' (Corbridge, 1993b; Potter, 1993a; A. Smith, 2002; D.W. Smith, 1994)

is not unrelated to the observation that the global mass media frequently tend only to refer to the Global South when reporting natural disasters, social disturbances, poverty, mass starvation and other crises and mishaps. Some writers, especially those concerned with Africa, have observed how this is leading to the notion that Africa is literally 'bad news', gradually desensitising the relatively wealthy from the real daily plight of Africans (Harrison and Palmer, 1986; Milner-Smith and Potter, 1995). This is turn exacerbates the risk of 'development fatigue' referred to in Chapter 1, in which the North becomes blasé to the seemingly never improving plight of the South. Such an opinion leads to the implication that parts of the Global South are literally viewed as a disaster zone, and this serves to emphasise its status as something quite separate, representing the global 'Other'. However, as we noted in Chapter 1, the real geography of the Global South is far more complex.

A shrinking world, but an increasingly differentiated one

It is all too easy to conclude that, as the world shrinks, all parts of the 'global village' share in the benefits of global development. However, this leads to a vital argument, namely that the places in the South that derive the largest share from development are generally those that are already the most well connected in the global network, such as SE Asia, Mexico and Brazil. Places which are marginal to it, or which are hardly on the network altogether, such as many countries in Africa, are by definition massively disadvantaged. This is a fundamental point, and pursuing it at the sub-global level makes a very telling point about the differential

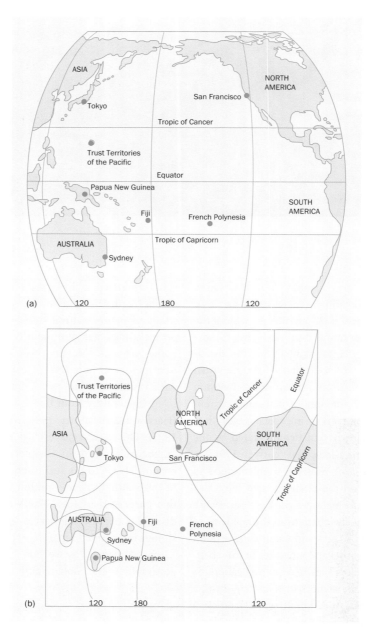

Figure 4.3 Time–space convergence and divergence: (a) the conventional projection of the Pacific; (b) time–space map of the Pacific based on travel times by scheduled airline in 1975

Source: adapted from Haggett, P. (1990) *The Geographer's Art*. Oxford: Blackwell.

impacts of developmental and economic interventions and investments globally. As well as relative distances being reduced by the process of global development, distances to other places can *increase* in *relative terms* within the overall context of a shrinking world, particularly between marginal countries. This is illustrated by the complexities of air travel in West and North Africa where flying between two countries in that region can often involve having to transit London or Paris.

Figure 4.3 gives a specific and very telling example of this. The maps show the Pacific Basin. Figure 4.3a shows the conventional cartographic projection, whereas Figure 4.3b has been redrawn according to travel times between places by scheduled airline. The figure is adapted from Haggett (1990b) and Leyshon (1995). At first sight, North America has 'moved' closer to Asia, and Australia has 'drifted' north towards Asia. If we look in a little more detail, we find that places like Tokyo, San Francisco and Sydney have indeed 'moved' closer to one another.

But if we look at Figure 4.3b more carefully, it is evident that some places have in fact become more 'distant' from each another. Thus, South America has 'trailed behind' North America in its 'convergence on' Asia. Specific places seem to have 'moved' quite substantially relative to one another. In particular, it is noticeable that poorer and less frequent air transport links mean that Papua New Guinea appears to have moved to the south of Australia, away from Asia, and many islands in the Pacific appear to have moved north, apparently now existing outside the Pacific Basin altogether. This clear example of the differential realities of overall time–space convergence shows that the process is far from homogeneous. In fact, it is sufficiently heterogeneous to produce instances of what may be called relative time–space divergence.

The idea that globalised improvements in transport and communications are leading to the intensification of the functional importance of certain places or nodes is confirmed if we look at world airline networks even as early as the 1990s. Figure 4.4 shows the density of air traffic movements in the world. While the figure clearly shows high levels of global connectivity, the higher levels of connectivity between and within regions in the Global North is abundantly clear.

Tables 4.1 and 4.2 indicate where the busiest airports in the world are, first in terms of aircraft movements in 2014 (Table 4.1) and then passenger numbers in 2014 (Table 4.2). While the historical dominance of air travel centred on key Northern cities – particularly in the USA, UK and Japan is apparent, the relatively recent rise to prominence of air traffic in selected Southern countries, namely China, Dubai and Indonesia is clear. While this does show global integration, ultimately certain countries are better connected than others in an uneven world system. The peripheral status of Africa and South America is apparent from these Tables and from Figure 4.4. In 2011 the busiest 100 airports in

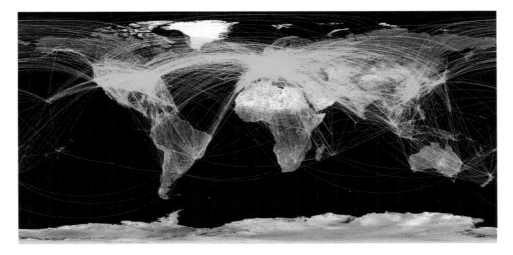

Figure 4.4 Global air traffic flows
Source: **Openflights.org**. https://openflights.org/data.html#route **(accessed 20 January 2016)**

Table 4.1 Busiest airports by flight movement, 2014

Rank	Airport	Location	Total Flights
1	O'Hare	Chicago	881 933
2	Hartsfield	Atlanta	868 359
3	Dallas / Fort Worth		679 820
4	Los Angeles		646 706
5	Beijing		581 773
6	Denver		565 525
7	Charlotte		545 178
8	McCarran	Las Vegas	522 399
9	George Bush	Houston	508 935
10	Heathrow	London	472 817
11	Charles de Gaulle	Paris	471 318
12	Frankfurt		469 026

Source: Airports Council International (2014). Accessed 23 December 2015. http://www.theguardian.com/news/datablog/2012/may/04/world-top-100-airports

Table 4.2 Busiest airports by passenger numbers, 2014

Rank	Airport	Location	Total Passengers
1	Hartsfield	Atlanta	97,178,899
2	Beijing		86,130,390
3	Heathrow	London	73,408,442
4	Haneda	Tokyo	72,826,862
5	Los Angeles		70,665,472
6	Dubai		70,475,636
7	O'Hare	Chicago	70,015,746
8	Charles de Gaulle	Paris	63,80,796
9	Dallas-Fort Worth		63,523,489
10	Hong Kong		63,148,379
11	Frankfurt		59,566,132
12	Soekarno-Hatta	Indonesia	57,005,406

Source: based on Airports Council International (2010)

the world processed 3.2 billion people including 998 million in Europe and 989 millon in North America.

A final, but important example of the concentrated nature of global transport, is provided through an examination of the global shipping network. The pattern reveals once again the three-centred structure of the world economy, with the highest volume flows occurring between Western Europe, North America and SE Asia. This sharp polarisation reflects the evolution of the network of specialised cargo traffic which links the key ports of the world and plays a critical role in the operation of 'global production networks' and the global economy more broadly. Once again, the unevenness of connectivity is evident.

Finally, a commonly experienced feature associated with the phenomenon of time–space compression, as noted by Harvey (1989), is that the capitalist system demands efficiency and this leads to the economic logic of reducing barriers to movement and communications over space, as time costs money. This leads to the progressive acceleration in the pace of life that seems to be universally experienced in the 'modern' world, and which seems to affect countries whether in the North or the South, although perhaps in contrasting and locally specific ways. For those who are part of the network, communication with far-distant others can be a daily reality for hours at a time.

The next section looks at current examples of this in the field of information flows, and essentially comparable conclusions are reached concerning global trends and uneven processes and patterns of development.

Globalisation and the information society: the digital divide and an unequal world, and efforts to close the divide

Another major trend over the past 25 or so years has been the increased information exchange between people and organisations located in different parts of the world. Where once letters, telegraphs and the occasional telephone call were the principal means of communication, now social media, mobile telephone calls, text messages and e-mail are dominant in the business world, and increasingly outside it, in education, commerce, entertainment, leisure and social life. The ability to move information and data quickly and cheaply has been greatly facilitated by the rapid expansion of the internet and the mobile telephone networks and the corresponding fall in set up and operational costs. We have already noted how some refer to the coming of the 'information society'. Figure 4.5 indicates the rapid growth of mobile phone and internet access globally since 1995. Since its inception in the early 1970s, the growth of mobile telephone adoption means that there were 6 billion subscribers in 2014 significantly up from 1.5 billion subscribers in 2006, and more than five times the number of landlines in existence. Significantly, more than 80% of new mobile subscriptions are from the South (Dicken, 2015). It has been observed that in many parts of Africa, mobile phone technology has led to technological 'leapfrogging', with many countries now having high rates of mobile phone access, despite never having developed extensive land-line connections. It is estimated that in Africa in 2013, 36% of the population (311 million) were mobile phone subscribers and this figure could rise to 49% (504 million users) in 2020 (UNDP, 2015).

The internet is seen by some as an optimistic possibility for global change and development with 1.13 billion people having access to it in 2007 (World Internet Usage Statistics, 2007). By 2014 usage had risen to 2.9 billion (UNDP, 2015). Similarly, many argue that new techniques in information processing offer poor nations new opportunities (Department for International Development, 2000a). Table 4.3 shows total use and annual rates of growth globally for a range of key digital technologies.

Some commentators have pointed to what they see as the internet's potential for democratising development. Others have even referred to it as allowing nations to 'leapfrog a stage of development', in what sounds like a direct reference to the Rostowian framework (Chapter 3). While the uptake of mobile phones is significant, there is a lag in terms of the ability to adopt more complex and expensive internet based systems, particularly in the poorer and infrastructurally weak parts of the South. As a result, caution needs to be exercised in respect of optimism about of the uptake and spread of such new technologies. Equally important are weaker economies and education systems which are often unable to adequately prepare people for full participation in the internet age. For example, even the previously referred to UK Government White Paper in 2000 noted that at that point in time more than one-half the population of Africa had never used a telephone, and that fewer than one in 1,000 Africans had access to the internet at that time

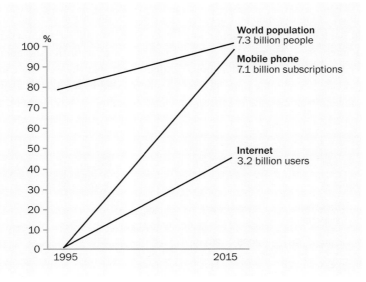

Figure 4.5 Mobile phone and internet uptake, 1995–2015
Source: adapted from UNDP, 2015.

Table 4.3 Digital use and growth rates, 2015

Category	Number of users (billions) and %	New device users (millions), 2014–15	Growth of new users (%)
World population	7.357	177	2.5
Internet users	3.175 43%	225	7.6
Social media	2.206 30%	176	8.7
Mobile phone	3.734 51%	124	3.4

Source: http://wearesocial.net/blog/s015/08/global-statshot-august-2015/. Accessed 16 December 2015.

(Department for International Development, 2000a). Indeed, by 2007 this figure had only increased to around 3.6 per cent. Others have warned that the internet may well serve to Westernise the Global South, so that 'e-imperialism' will be the outcome rather than any simplistic and comfortable notion of 'e-democracy'.

In terms of what is known as the 'digital divide', in 2005 only 7.7% of the population of the South had access to the internet but this had risen to 24.4% in 2011, but was still low compared with 70% in the North. While the scores have since risen in both regions, a clear gap still persists in access and use rates as shown in Table 4.4. It is, however, important to note that within the South, Asia and to a lesser degree South America, are achieving faster rates of internet access than other parts of the South, and Africa in particular. By 2012, some 1 billion of the nearly 3 billion internet users in the world were in Asia (Dicken, 2015).

The massive global inequality in access to telephones, for example, is exemplified in Figures 4.6a and b, based on data from the World Bank (2015c). The graphs show mobile telephone and internet access per 100 of the population up to 2013 for a range of world regions. Once again, the digital divide between the high income (North) and low income countries (South) is apparent.

Figure 4.7 is a cartogram which vividly depicts the nature of what is referred to as the global 'digital divide'. In this map the size of countries has been scaled to reflect the number of internet users. The percentage variations in the number of internet users is shown in Table 4.5. It should be borne in mind that many parts of Africa and elsewhere lack access to electricity, which is a major barrier to participation in the digital world.

On a positive note, many of the countries in the South are now starting to participate in the digital world more fully, which does go some way to ensuring the benefits of this aspect of globalisation are being accessed. In India, one of the leading nations in the South, the number of internet users has risen significantly from 137 million in 2012 to 354 million in 2015 (Internet and Mobile Association of India, 2015).

Despite the relative ease with which computers can be linked through the internet, undue optimism regarding the role of the internet in the Global South would be misplaced. Even the pro-globalisation White Paper of the UK Government acknowledges that 'there is a real risk that poor countries and poor people will be marginalised, and that the existing educational divide will be compounded by a growing digital divide' (Department for International Development, 2000a: 40).

Table 4.4 Telephone and internet subscriptions by type

Subscriptions per 100 habitants

	Land line phones		Cell-phone subscriptions		Internet users	
	2005	2011	2005	2011	2005	2011
North	58	42	55	120	37	70
South	12	12	11	78	5	25

Source: Dicken, 2015

Table 4.5 Internet users (by %) by region, 2015

Africa	26%
N America	88%
S America	58%
E Asia	51%
SE Asia	33%
S Asia	19%

Source: http://www.mobileindustryreview.com/2015/ (accessed 16 December 2015)

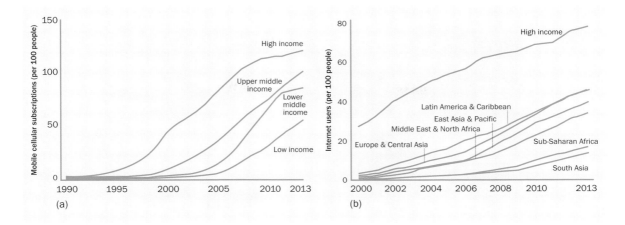

Figure 4.6 Global access by region to (a) Mobile phones and (b) The internet
Source: World Bank, 2015c.

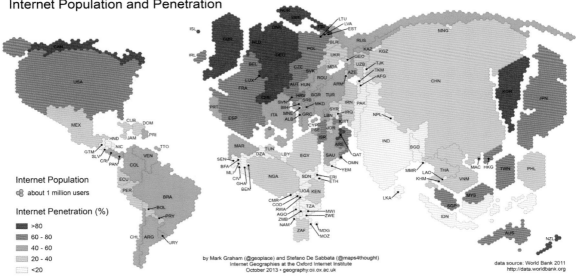

Figure 4.7 The digital divide
Source: Dicken, 2015

Others have referred to the massively unequal global distribution of communications. Quite simply, without telephones and computers, areas of the South cannot race ahead as an outcome of the existence of technologies such as those associated with the internet and e-mail. A key limitation, aside from cost and weak technological capacity in many parts of the South, is the basic reality that most of the South is poorly linked to the key backbone of the global internet, namely the network of submarine fiber optic cables which link the world (Figure 4.8). Instead, they have differing levels of access and bandwidth which will in turn impact on the capacity of the internet to serve as a key tool of business and communication. Figure 4.8 shows the world's submarine cable system.

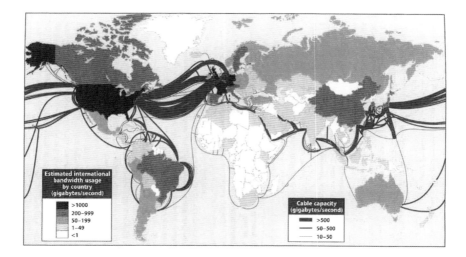

Figure 4.8 The world's submarine cable system
Source: Dicken, 2015

As noted previously, a large proportion of business communications is now made through the internet, and information is available on a huge array of topics via the World Wide Web. For those with access to the technology, personal communication via e-mail has become the preferred form of daily communication. For those people and places with limited access and smaller bandwidth, the digital divide will persist impacting on the potential scale of personal and economic spinoffs and interactions.

In the near future, the greatest growth in internet usage will occur in Asia, which already has the largest total number of users. In 2012, North America and Europe accounted for some 70% of all registered domain names (Dicken, 2015), and the reality is that the growth of the internet and its controlling systems is reflecting already well-connected places.

Critical reflection

Global interconnectivity, social media and the internet

If you will be using the internet, e-mail, social media, chat-rooms or social networking sites during the coming week, keep a list of the people you are in communication with, and the sites you have visited. Where in the world are these various contacts and sites based? You could classify and count them by continent, or broadly by the 'North' and 'South' categorisation. What does the list say about your own global interconnectedness? Does the outcome of this reflection accord with the patterns outlined in this section of the book?

Thus, just like improvements in transport technologies, improvements in communications are tending to emphasise global and regional differences in the first instance, and privileging certain areas, namely those with the greatest involvement in global production systems. Notwithstanding the claims of governments, much has to be done if these aspects of globalisation are to improve conditions for the poor and moderately poor in the Global South.

However, the situation is changing quickly, and mobile phones especially can act as powerful agents of change, particularly in the more marginalised parts of the South. It is undoubtedly the case that mobile phones and the internet can help those who are in marginal locations to do their shopping, communicate with family, establish and run businesses or, indeed, gain education by distance learning programmes (Unwin and de Bastion, 2008).

For instance, Urbach (2007), in the context of Botswana, notes how mobile phones can reduce communication costs, increase labour mobility and afford enhanced access to banking facilities and information on market prices. Although only 20 per cent of the population have access to mains electricity, enterprising village entrepreneurs offer recharging services using car batteries. The growing use of mobile phone technology by village farmers in Africa to access market information and arrange sales is a significant advance in local empowerment. Equally significant is the recent growth in the development of mobile phone applications or 'apps' in Africa and Kenya in particular. The growth of phone-banking and cash transfer systems such as MPESA has revolutionised individual financial access in a continent were formal banking systems and capacity is limited (Williams et al., 2014). This system promotes savings and financial transfers from migrant workers to their families. In respect to learning and education, the UK Government's Imfundio Programme sought to use information technology to improve primary education in Africa (Department for International Development, 2000a). However, despite the role which mobile phone systems can play, the evidence suggests that without stronger and more all-embracing intervention, the digital divide is likely to exacerbate further the differences between the world's haves and have-nots although there is huge potential where the infrastructure can be provided.

Economic aspects of globalisation: industrialisation, TNCs, world/ global cities and global shifts

Industrialisation

As explored in Chapter 3, the pursuit of industrial development as a matter of policy came to affect the newly independent, formerly colonial territories in the 1960s. It was almost inevitable that in seeking to progress during the post-colonial era, newly independent

countries would associate development with industrialisation and, by implication, the broader concept of modernisation. This was hardly surprising given that the conventional wisdoms of development economics stressed so cogently this very connection (Potter and Lloyd-Evans, 1998; Chapter 3).

For many Third World countries, decolonisation afforded political independence and promoted the desire for economic autonomy to go with it. In the words of Friedmann and Weaver (1979: 91), such nations:

> took it for granted that western industrialised countries were already developed, and that the cure for 'underdevelopment' was, accordingly, to become as much as possible like them.

This section explores the role which industrialisation has played in the processes of global production and development.

Import substitution industrialisation (ISI)

In the immediate post-independence phase, the trend towards industrialisation in the Global South was closely associated with the policy of import substitution industrialisation (ISI). This represented an obvious means of increasing self-sufficiency, as such nations had traditionally imported most of their manufactured goods requirements in return for their exports of primary products such as minerals, sugar, bananas, coffee, tea and cotton. Such developments were encouraged by national governments, which pursued Keynesian-based economic thinking favouring high levels of state intervention in national economies.

During the era of import substitution industrialisation, key industrial sectors for development were those which were relatively simple and where a substantial home market already existed, for example: food, drink, tobacco, clothing and textile production (Plate 4.2).

While many countries of the South have followed this path towards import substitution industrialisation, as Dickenson et al observed in 1996, few countries outside of SE Asia have managed to progress much beyond it and develop robust industrial structures with the capacity to export significant volumes of product

Plate 4.2 Import substitution industrialisation in Burkina Faso: the Brakina brewery
(*photo*: Panos)

internationally. Significant exceptions are to be found in Asia. In Taiwan and South Korea between 1953 and 1960 the ISI policy was put into practice, focusing on textiles, toys, footwear, agricultural goods and the like. During this era, manufacturing output increased by 11.7 per cent per annum. Only after the 1960s did countries develop export-oriented manufacturing, and after 1980 the focus was on technologically advanced, high-value added manufacturing, so as to stay ahead in the industrialisation stakes (Knox et al., 2014).

However, for most countries in the Global South, with limited exceptions, such as in parts of Asia, Brazil and South Africa, the expansion of heavy industries such as steel, chemicals and petrochemicals, along the lines of the former Soviet model, has not been possible. Such a policy – which might seem attractive when following Rostow's (1960) linear model of development (Chapter 3) – requires investment and a level of population and effective demand not normally present in much of the Global South.

Furthermore, the product competition from developed nations, along with capital and infrastructural shortages, and problems of uncertain investment, limited technological transfer and requirements for capital rather than labour intensity, also militate against such heavy industrial development. An exception, however, is provided by India, which has achieved a high level of industrial self-sufficiency since 1945 (Johnson, 1983) and is now the eleventh largest industrial producer in the world (Dicken, 2015).

Export orientated industrialisation (EOI) and industrialisation by invitation (I by I)

From the 1960s onwards a number of countries of the Global South embarked upon policies of 'light industrialisation' by means of making available fiscal incentives to draw in export focused foreign companies (Potter and Lloyd-Evans, 1998; Chapter 3). This policy of so-called 'industrialisation by invitation' was strongly recommended by the Caribbean-born economist Sir Arthur Lewis (1950, 1955). Reviewed in Chapter 3, industrialisation by invitation involved the establishment of branch plants by overseas firms, with the products being exported back to industrialised countries. EOI has played a critical role in global integration and the fostering of global production networks helping to make the world more economically integrated (Dicken, 2015). This became more evident from the 1970s when deindustrialisation in many countries in the North created production opportunities in the South. The establishment of dedicated trade and manufacturing zones, often called SEZs (Special Economic Zones) has helped propel many Southern countries from a reliance on primary production activities to a position in which their economies become more robust and diversified.

The approach became closely associated with the setting up of variants of SEZs, and the most common zones types are free-trade zones (FTZs) and export-processing zones (EPZs). FTZs are typically an area located in or near to a major port, in which trade is unrestricted and free of all duties (Plate 4.3). The EPZ is normally associated with the provision of buildings and services, and amounts to a specialised industrial estate. Firms locating in EPZs frequently pay no duties or taxes whatsoever, and may well be exempt from labour and other aspects of government legislation. The approach is often known as enclave industrialisation. FTZs and EPZs had their historical roots in the Free Ports of the Hanseatic League in late Medieval Europe. After World War II, the establishment of free trade and manufacturing zones in Ireland and Puerto Rico re-established the concept. Since then there has been rapid growth, throughout the world of a range of special zones, variously referred to as FTZs, EPZs, Industrial Development Zones (IDZs), Special Economic Zones (SEZs) and *maquiladora*. Zones differ in the degree to which their focus is on trade, usually duty free and manufacturing – often undertaken in the context of low or zero tax, and the operation of unique legal systems where national laws often don't apply (Farole, 2011). Table 4.6 lists the most common variants of SEZs.

Table 4.6 Types of Special Economic Zones

Type	Development Objective	Example
Free Trade Zone	Support trade	Colon, Panama
Export Processing Zone	Support exports	Karachi, Pakistan
Free Port	Integrated development	Aqaba, Jordan
Enterprise Zone	Urban revitalisation	Chicago
Single factory EPZ	Support exports	Mauritius

Source: adapted from Knox et al., 2014.

According to Hewitt et al. (1992), the first EPZ established in the South was at Kandla in India in 1965, and this was quickly followed by further such developments in Taiwan, the Philippines, the Dominican Republic and on the United States–Mexico border.

In the case of Mexico during the 1960s, legislation was enacted permitting foreign, especially American companies, to establish 'sister plants', called *maquiladoras*, within 19 kilometres of the US border, for the duty-free assembly of products destined for re-export (Figure 4.9). By the early 1990s, more than 2000 such assembly and manufacturing plants had been established, producing electronic products, textiles, furniture, leather goods, toys and automotive parts. In aggregate, the plants generated direct employment for over half a million Mexican workers (Dicken, 2015; Getis et al., 1994).

Returning to the global context, by 1971 nine countries had established EPZs, and this increased to 25 by 1975 and 52 by 1985 (Farole, 2011). In that year, it was estimated that there were a total of 173 EPZs around the world, which together employed 1.8 million workers. By 2011 this had risen to 600 EPZs, and when one adds in other types of zones such as FTZs and SEZs, the total had risen to 3,500 operating in 130 countries. China, whose global economic penetration was greatly assisted by the establishment of SEZs, had over 200 zones in 2011, established as a direct result of its 'open door' policy from the 1970s. India has declared several hundred zones, but many are not operational, and many others have been associated with controversy as a result of the displacement of resident population and poor working

Plate 4.3 The Shanghai Free Trade Zone
photo: Getty

conditions which prevail in them (Farole, 2011). China's main SEZs are shown on Figure 4.10. Note their coastal location, which facilitates global sourcing of raw materials and other inputs and the export of products.

Frequently, programmes of industrial development have been strongly urban-based, as in the case of Barbados from the 1960s, where ten industrial estates were established, all within the existing urban system (Clayton and Potter, 1996). Recently, data processing and the informatics industry have become very important on one of the central Bridgetown industrial estates.

However, such schemes are not without their very real challenges, and the International Labour Organization has branded EPZs 'vehicles of globalisation', arguing that

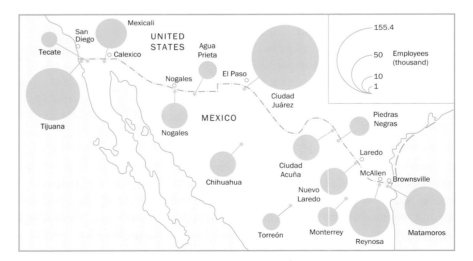

Figure 4.9 The principal *maquiladora* centres on the United States–Mexico border
Source: Adapted from Dicken (1998)

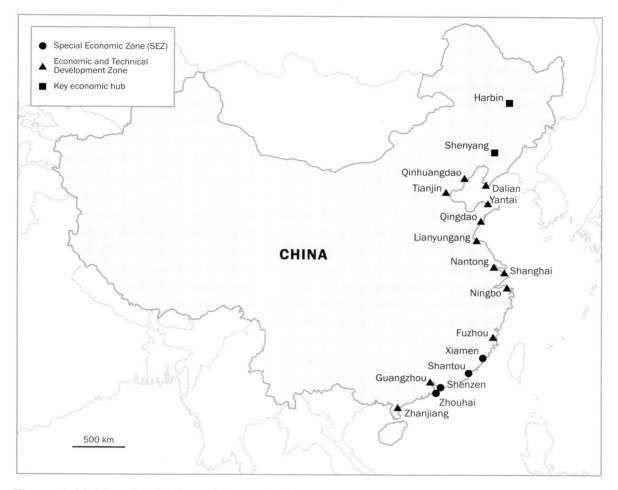

Figure 4.10 The distribution of the main Special Economic Zones in China
Source: adapted from http://www.lib.utexas.edu/maps/middle_east_and_asia/china_econ96.jpg. Accessed 18 August 2016.

few have meaningful links with domestic economies, and that most involve large numbers of low-waged, low-skilled workers. While the macro-benefits of trade, employment and economic diversification are self-evident, as is the degree to which these processes have accelerated global integration, zones have often been directly associated with a range of negative aspects. These include the payment of low wages, worker exploitation, especially of young female labourers, the loss of potential taxation revenue to host countries, and ultimately the potential subservience of Southern countries to corporate demands from the North, which has the potential to reinforce uneven geographical development. Other challenges include the accusation that firms often relocate to zones in another country when available incentives

expire, and the fact that there are often low levels of upskilling of workers and technology transfer to the host country.

Global shift and the emergence of global production networks

Through pursuing EOI, certain countries in the South have increased their overall level of industrialisation and, by implication, the size of their economies and their role in the world economy. From 1938 to 1950, the South experienced a 3.5 per cent growth rate of manufacturing per annum, and from 1950 to 1970 this annual rate increased to 6.6 per cent (Dickenson et al., 1996). By 2015 this figure stood at 5.2% per annum for these countries, compared to a world average of 2.5%, while that of the traditional industrial leaders (North America, Europe and Japan) was only 0.7% (UNIDO, 2015).

Critical within the globalisation of manufacturing production has been the falling net costs of global transport, which occurred through the introduction of much larger, more fuel efficient ships and planes and associated improvements in logistics systems associated with containerisation (see Figure 4.11 which shows falling transport and communications costs over time). Equally important are differential wage rates across the world, which, in an era of global sourcing, encourages corporations to place or relocate labour-intensive manufacturing activities in low wage countries. Figure 4.12 illustrates how hourly wage rates vary across a range of countries.

While the growth rates of manufacturing activity in the South are impressive, it is important to note that growth has been spatially selective, with SE Asia and China experiencing the most rapid growth, while in many other parts of the South such growth has not kept pace with the rate of urbanisation, leading many countries to face significant employment challenges (see Chapter 9). Furthermore, industrial growth has been characterised by several features. The first has been its highly unequal global distribution, and in the post-war period this has been associated with major changes in the global distribution of industrial production. These changes have been in selected areas in particular countries, such as Mexico, Brazil and much of SE Asia. These changes are referred to as giving rise to a 'global shift' in patterns of manufacturing and the parallel emergence and rising significance of global production networks (Coe and Yeung, 2015; Dicken, 2015). The latter concept refers to 'organizationally fragmented and spatially diverse production networks (which) constitute a new form of economic structure that increasingly drives the complex global economy and its uneven development' (Coe and Yeung, 2015: 1). According to this process, corporations deliberately choose to make different parts of a finished product in scattered parts of the world, dependent on where particular parts can be made most cost-effectively, but also where the appropriate skills and resources exist to ensure that necessary quality standards are met. Final assembly then takes place at a single point followed by global sales and distribution of the product. An example is the Boeing 787 'Dreamliner' aircraft, the parts of which are made in 11 different

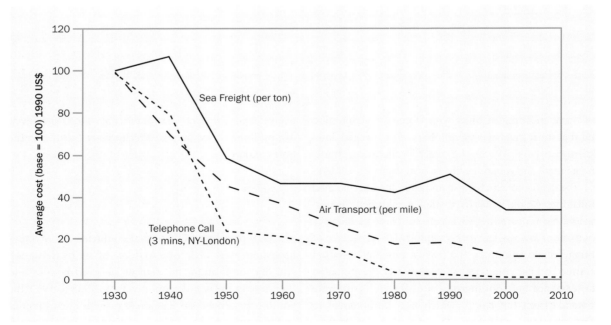

Figure 4.11 Reductions in transport and communications costs over time
Source: adapted from Knox et al., 2014

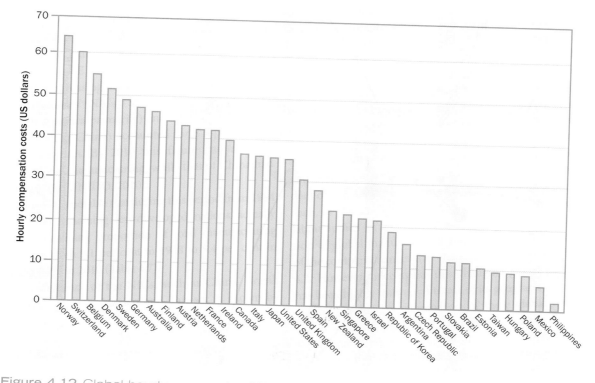

Figure 4.12 Global hourly wage rate differentials between selected countries
Source: adapted from Dicken, 2015.

countries, with final assembly taking place in the USA (Knox et al., 2014). Figure 4.13 shows the production network for the iPhone 5 smartphone. Parts or raw materials are sourced from 16 different places globally. The production system, which is typical of many high-tech production networks, clearly shows the key role played by SE Asia and N America and the relatively marginalised role of much of the South, beyond that of the supply of raw materials.

This system forms the backbone of many core industries – cars, aircraft, computers and IT. Fragmented production processes and global value chains have become critical to the operation of the world's manufacturing economy. Historically, while raw materials were sourced in one part of the world, all elements of production tended to then take place in a single location. A classic example would be the motor car industry in Detroit from the 1930s, with most components being produced in the city. This stands in stark contrast to the globally connected production systems which now

characterise the motor-car industry. This has, in many industries, laid the basis for what is called an 'interconnected world of production', which is assisted by flexible production systems, the search for low cost production centres and vertical specialisation. From a development perspective, regional strategic coupling with global production networks is a defined strategic choice which translates into national support for innovation hubs, global cities, assembly platforms, logistics hubs and SEZs (Coe and Yeung, 2015).

This process is illustrated in Table 4.7, which deals with the period from 1948 to 2010. Britain, Western European countries and then America dominated the core–periphery pattern of manufacturing production for over 300 years. But from 1948 the traditional industrial nations, such as the USA, the United Kingdom, Germany and France, along with other countries in the North, all showed reductions in their percentage share of world industrial production.

This went hand in hand with rising industrial production in Japan, which by 1985 had increased its share

Figure 4.14 Global distribution of manufacturing production, 2013

Source: calculated from http://wdi.worldbank.org/table/4.2

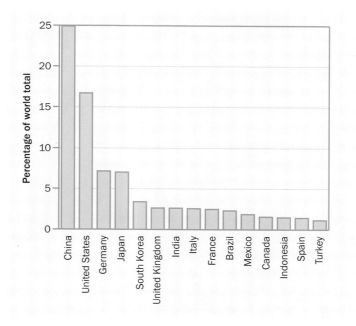

Figure 4.15 The world's leading manufacturing nations (% of world total Manufacturing Value Added)
Source: adapted from Dicken, 2015

Table 4.8 Changing geography of manufacturing employment 1980–2010 in key manufacturing regions (in millions of people)

Region /Country	1980	2010	% Change
USA/Canada	21.4	15.8	−26
Japan	12.1	10,4	−13.2
Western Europe	28.2	23.8	−15.6
South Asia	60.5	63.1	+4
SE and East Asia	68.6	126.7	+84.7
Latin America	8.7	22.5	+158

Source: Knox et al., 2014

15 countries. Just seven East Asian countries – Hong Kong, China, Singapore, Korea, Thailand, Malaysia and Taiwan – account for 50 per cent of all FDI received in the South, this level of concentration having increased from 33 per cent in 1990 (Dicken, 1993).

In comparison, other less developed countries remain more poorly integrated into the global economic system. The story is once again of 'concentrated deconcentration' within the globalised economic system.

World trade, finance and services

Fundamental to the globalisation of manufacturing and globalisation more generally has been the key role played by significant growth in overall levels of world trade and associated global financial flows. As the world becomes more interdependent and reliant on the globalisation of production, trade has grown faster than manufacturing output. This is a reflection of two processes: first, the degree to which global production now involves the movement of semi-produced items to further processing facilities around the world, and secondly, the degree to which we, as consumers, both desire and are able to purchase goods from around the world. In the second half of the twentieth century world merchandise trade increase 20-fold while production increased six-fold (Dicken, 2015). Trading patterns, however, reinforce the economic dominance of the leading economies, which in turn enhances their connectivity and continued growth, particularly as bulk supply tends to reduce costs. While this brings about certain efficiencies, it also marginalises the less connected parts of the

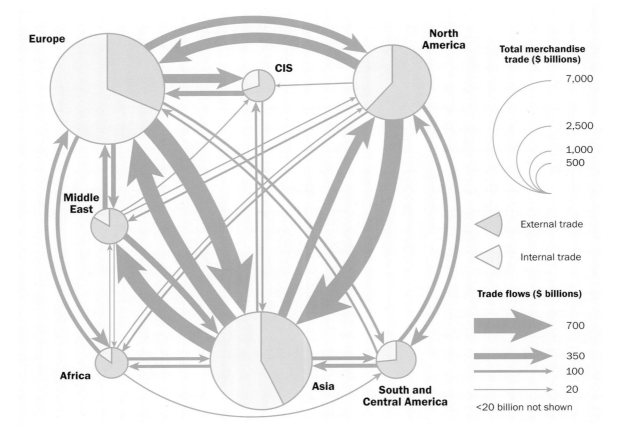

Figure 4.16 Network of world trade by region
Source: adapted from Dicken, 2015

planet, as is shown in Figure 4.16, in which the trading dominance of Asia, Europe and North America is apparent, while other world regions clearly play a far more minor role.

In value terms, far more important than the value of movement of goods are global financial transactions, including foreign exchange dealings, investments – both in banking/financial/stock exchange systems, and in fixed property/manufacturing and migrant labour remittances. It was estimated that in 2010 the daily global foreign exchange turnover was US $3,874 billion, with daily volumes of trade now exceeding 25% of the US annual GDP. Added to this are migrant labour remittances which in 2011 exceeded US $372 billion, a figure larger than the value of aid received by countries of the Global South (Knox et al., 2014).

International financial flows are closely connected with the concept of FDI (Foreign Direct Investment),

which usually involves private or corporate investment in another country, typically to set up operations there or take a controlling share in an already existing operation. The scale of FDI has accelerated dramatically since World War II and is critical to the operation of transnational corporations (see below). FDI clearly favours what are perceived as the lucrative market opportunities of Asia, as shown in Figure 4.17. While Europe and North America are clearly also important FDI destinations, Africa is largely side-lined by these processes. The total value of FDI in 2014 was estimated at $1.2 trillion, with just over half going to a select group of leading manufacturing countries in the South, the NICs (UNCTAD, 2015). This is re-emphasised by what is shown in the map (Figure 4.18) of inward and outward investment (i.e. the source and recipient countries). At present 22% of all investment is sourced from the USA, some 7% from the UK and

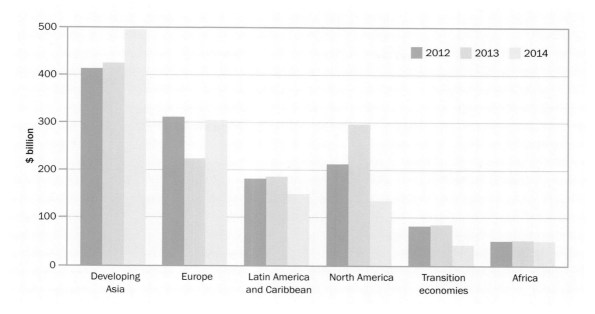

Figure 4.17 FDI inflows by region
Source: adapted from UNCTAD, 2015.

6% from Germany, while the role of NICs and China as investors is slowly increasing.

Of critical importance in the operation of the global economy is the role of the international service industry. Within almost all countries in the North the service industry is now the biggest sector both in terms of employment and value added, far exceeding in size and value the primary sector (mining, agriculture, forestry and fishing) and the secondary sector (manufacturing). The service sector is a very diverse sector, comprising activities ranging from education, to law, government operations, banking, finance, transport, trade, maintenance, leisure and tourism, retail and personal services, such as hairdressing, etc.

At a global level, international banking and investment services, the provision of legal service, employment recruitment, advertising, logistics and transport, tourism and retail have increased dramatically in size and scale as banks, retail chains and airlines, etc. seek new market shares globally. These processes create local employment, boost corporate profits and reinforce the dominance of key corporates. On the negative side, patterns of growth are selective, favouring the most lucrative investment and operating destinations and marginalising places perceived to be

dangerous or less profitable. Figure 4.19 shows where the key global service providers are based, and Figure 4.20 shows the percentage of activity in each of the major countries in the world. These Figures re-emphasise the degree to which North America, Europe and parts of Asia dominate yet another key economic activity both to meet their own internal and also the global demand for such services.

Transnational corporations (TNCs)/MNCs

A further characteristic feature of post-1945 industrial change has been the rise in prominence of transnational corporations (TNCs) (sometimes called MNC or Multi-National Corporations), which now represent the most important single force creating and shaping global changes in production systems (Dicken, 2015). TNCs are the key source of FDI and they use Global Production Networks to operate and make a profit globally. Global adherence to neo-liberalism and support for EOI and SEZs in the South has aided in their growing significance, such that many of the world's largest TNCs now have turnovers which are bigger than some individual countries in the world. Dicken (2015) notes the remarkable

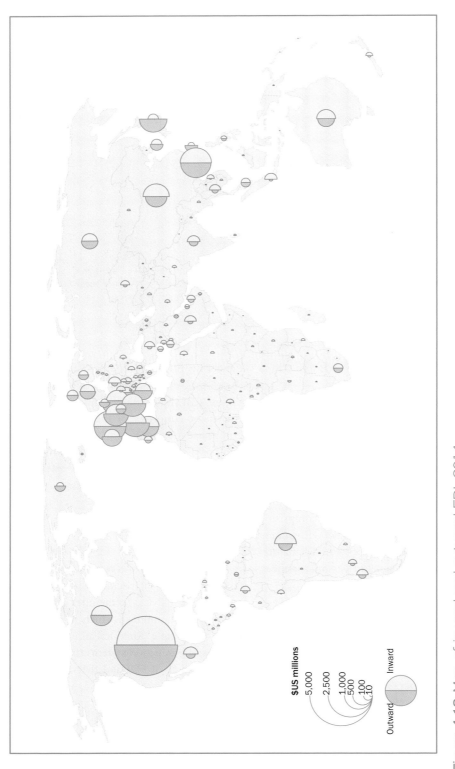

Figure 4.18 Map of inward and outward FDI, 2014

Source: adapted from UNCTAD. http://unctadstat.unctad.org.

Figure 4.19 Global service production, 2014

$US billions

10,000

5,000

1,000
500
100

Source: Calculated from http://wdi.worldbank.org/table/4.2.

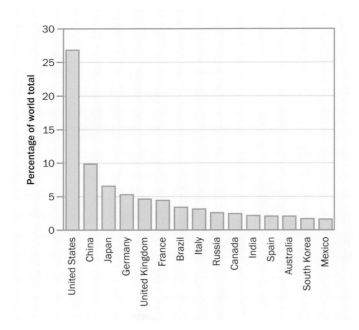

Figure 4.20 The major service providing nations
Source: adapted from Dicken, 2015.

statistic that 51 of the 100 largest economies in the world are in fact corporations, and, for example, the turnover of General Motors is more than the size of the economy of Denmark, while sales of each of the biggest five TNCs in the world – General Motors, Wal-Mart, Exxon Mobil, Ford and DaimlerChrysler all exceeded the GDPs of 182 countries. Box 4.2 presents the example of a particular manufacturing process

BOX 4.2

Globalisation and the production of athletic footwear

The footwear industry is labour-intensive, but it is also highly dynamic. In a paper published in 1993, Barff and Austen show how sales tripled in the USA over the preceding ten-year period. And they also show the industry's volatility, measured in spatial and geographical terms. In 1989, US market leader Nike Inc. had about 2 per cent of its shoes made by Chinese-based subcontractors. Just four years later, in 1993, almost 25 per cent of Nike athletic shoes came from Chinese factories (Barff and Austen, 1993).

Although characterised by such dynamism, the majority of athletic footwear production continues to occur in Southeast Asia. The three US companies which account between them for over 60 per cent of

sales in the USA have the vast majority of their production based there. However, the details of this pattern are quite volatile, and many producers of athletic footwear have developed a complex set of long- and short-term subcontracting agreements with other firms that change from year to year as a result of factory improvements, market fluctuations and technological change (Donaghue and Barff, 1990).

On the other hand, several athletic footwear firms still manufacture in the USA. In particular, the cheapest sport shoes continue to be produced in the USA, whereas the more complex, expensive models tend to be manufactured in Asia. Barff and Austen (1993) show that, in order to understand this complex

BOX 4.2 (continued)

global geography, one must move beyond the basic consideration of international labour-cost differentials.

By means of case studies, the authors demonstrate that domestic production involves very different labour processes from those of production based in other countries. As in many sectors of the economy, domestic producers gain advantage by carrying smaller inventories via faster lead times. However, the best explanation for the globalised pattern of differential production centres is the nature of shoes themselves. The athletic shoes produced in the USA tend to have far fewer stitches in them than those manufactured elsewhere, and this minimises the most expensive component of the production process. Furthermore, the authors explain how tariffs on athletic shoes massively discriminate against imported shoes of a particular construction.

This example of global-scale production therefore demonstrates how processes of globalisation are based on subtle aspects of differentiation between world regions, and suggests that new forms of economic localisation may well be the outcome.

Critical reflection

Make a list of where in the world the goods you use regularly and the food you buy day to day are produced. Are there particular kinds of goods and services that are associated with particular world regions? What are the implications of transporting manufactured goods so far around the world to reach you? What are the benefits and what are the costs? Think who gets the benefits – and who gets the costs.

The establishment of TNCs can be traced back to before the nineteenth century, having their origins in early trading companies such as the Hudson Bay Company and the British East Indies Company. To begin with they focused on accessing agricultural, mining and extractive activities for sale primarily in Europe, but in the period since 1950 they have become increasingly associated with manufacturing and EOI in particular (Jenkins, 1987, 1992; Dicken, 2015).

By 2009 there were an estimated 82,000 'parent' TNCs operating in the world, controlling the operations of some 810,000 affiliated local companies. TNCs now account for at least two-thirds of global trade in goods and services. It is important to note that at least one-third of all trade is now intra-firm trade, as a result of the operation of the GPNs which TNCs largely control (Dicken, 2015). The 100 largest TNCs employ some 15 million workers, while the total number of workers in the affiliated companies of all the TNCs is in the order of 90 million. The total manufacturing output, referred to as 'value added', of the TNCs in 2015 was an estimated US $7.9 trillion (UNCTAD, 2015).

The largest TNCs are headquartered in a handful of countries, namely the USA, Japan and in Europe. The location of TNCs based in the Global South is very

limited geographically, and focuses on Southeast Asia, South Africa, Mexico and parts of South America. Only South Africa stands out within Africa as a whole. The pattern is a very concentrated and uneven one. This is evidenced from data depicted in Figure 4.21 and Table 4.9, which indicate both the home base and the size of the assets of first, the world's 20 largest TNCs, and secondly, (in Table 4.9) the largest non-financial TNCs in the South. Evident from Figure 4.21 is the sheer size of the largest firms in terms of their asset base with many having close to US $300 billion of assets, with General Electric being nearly double the size of the next largest TNC. It is noteworthy that all of the largest TNCs are based either in the USA or Japan, or a Western European country. That said, as Figure 4.21 shows, most of the asset base of these firms is not in the home country which is indicative of their international reach. It is important to note that since 2000 there has been a shift within this leading core group, since in that year six of the largest firms were based in the US, this has since fallen to three as a range of European companies have risen in significance. The product focus of these firms is distinctive with oil, cars, communication and manufactured products clearly being the lead sectors. The first part of Table 4.9 shows more recent data on the 20 largest

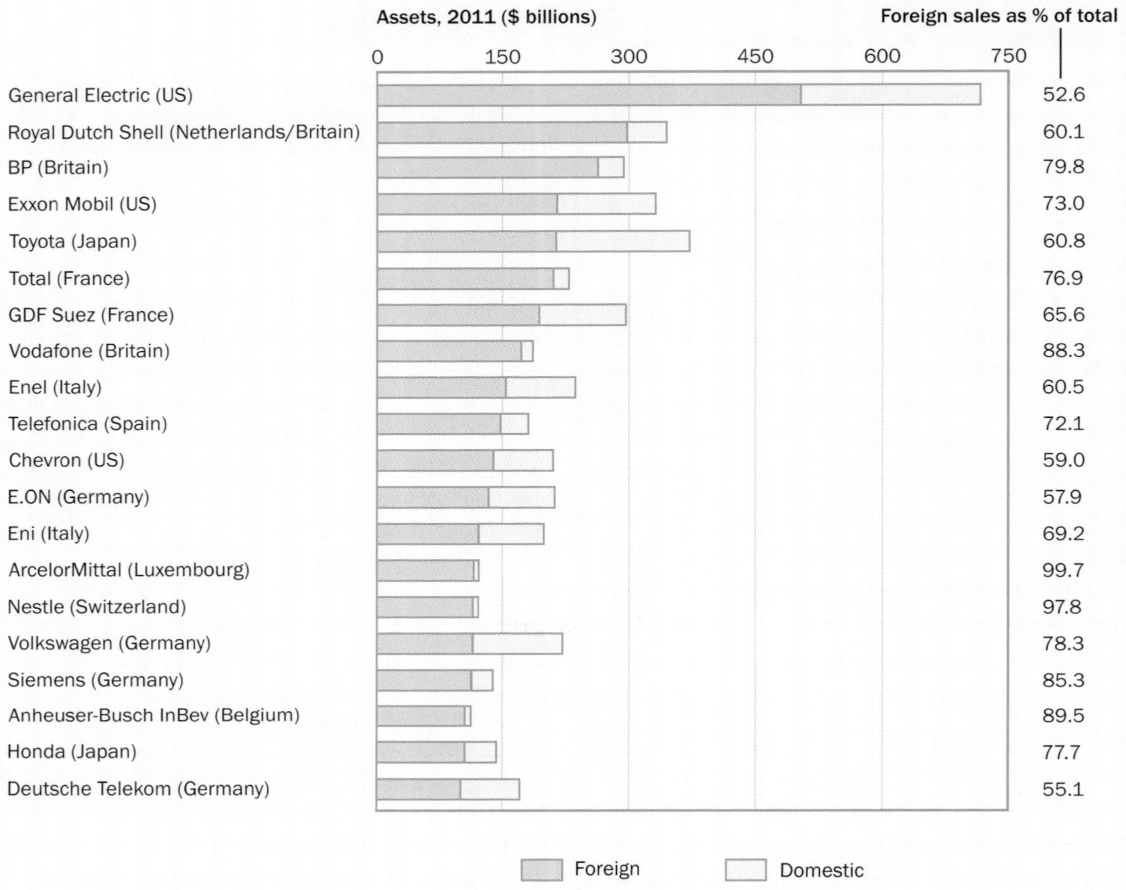

Figure 4.21 The world's largest TNCs, 2010
Source: adapted from http://www.economist.com/blogs/graphicdetail/2012/07/focus-1. Accessed 18 August 2016.

TNCs, and it is important to note the sheer size of their workforce which numbers hundreds of thousands of people, making them larger than the number of government employees in many countries. The German Volkswagen company for example has a staggering 573,800 employees, with the majority working in affiliated companies around the world. The second part of the Table shows the eight largest non-financial TNCs in the South. It is important to note that these are the only TNCs from the South to be included in the list of the 100 biggest TNCs globally according to assets. Distinctive features in this part of the Table include their relatively low ranking in the Global 100 TNC listings, the fact that China (including Hong Kong), unsurprisingly

dominates the list, their relatively small asset size compared to that of the 20 largest TNCs in the world and the fact that all eight TNCs are NIC/BRICS countries, once again emphasizing the skewed nature of production in the South.

The spatial bias in terms of the location of the headquarters of global corporates is re-emphasised when we examine the service sector and finance and banking in particular. Table 4.10 shows the world's 10 largest financial TNCs, showing the degree to which the European banking and financial system is able to exert a controlling hand over the operation of world finances. Nine of the 10 biggest financial TNCs are based in Europe, with three in France and one in the USA.

Table 4.9 The world's 20 largest non-financial TNCs and the top 8 TNCs in the South, 2014: ranked according to assets

Rank	Corporation	Home economy	Industry c	Assets US $mn	Sales US $mn	Employment Foreign	Total
1	General Electric Co	United States	Electrical & electronic equipment	656560	142937	135000	307000
2	Royal Dutch Shell plc	United Kingdom	Petroleum expl./ref./distr.	357512	451235	67000	92000
3	Toyota Motor Corporation	Japan	Motor vehicles	403088	256381	137000	333498
4	Exxon Mobil Coporation	United States	Petroleum expl./ref./distr.	346808	390247	45216	75000
5	Total SA	France	Petroleum expl./ref./distr.	238870	227901	65602	98799
6	BP plc	United Kingdom	Petroleum expl./ref./distr.	305690	379136	64300	83900
7	Vodafone Group Plc	United Kingdom	Telecommunications	202763	69276	83422	91272
8	Volkswagen Group	Germany	Motor vehicles	446555	261560	317800	572800
9	Chevron Corporation	United States	Petroleum expl./ref./distr.	253753	211664	32600	64600
10	Eni SpA	Italy	Petroleum expl./ref./distr.	190125	152313	56509	83887
11	Enel SpA	Italy	Electricity, gas and water	226006	106924	37125	71394
12	Glencore Xstrata PLC	Switzerland	Mining & quarrying	154932	232694	180527	190000
13	Anheuser-Busch InBev NV	Belgium	Food, beverages and tobacco	141666	43195	144887	154587
14	EDF SA	France	Utilities (Electricity, gas and water)	353574	100364	28975	158467
15	Nestlé SA	Switzerland	Food, beverages and tobacco	129969	99669	322996	333000
16	E. ON AG	Germany	Utilities (Electricity, gas and water)	179988	162573	49809	62239
17	GDF Suez	France	Utilities (Electricity, gas and water)	219759	118561	73000	147199
18	Deutsche Telekom AG	Germany	Telecommunications	162671	79835	111953	228596
19	Apple Computer Inc	United States	Electrical & electronic equipment	207000	170910	50322	84400
20	Honda Motor Co Ltd	Japan	Motor vehicles	151965	118176	120985	190338
	The Largest TNCs in the South (2014)						
27	Hutchison Whampoa Limited	Hong Kong, China	Diversified	105169	33035	215265	260000
36	CITIC Group	China	Diversified	565884	55487	25285	125215
41	Hon Hai Precision Industries	Taiwan Province	Electrical & electronic equipment	77089	133362	810993	1290000
62	Petronas - Petroliam Nasiona	Malaysia	Petroleum expl./ref./distr.	163275	94543	5244	46145
66	Vale SA	Brazil	Mining & quarrying	124289	47130	15894	83286
67	Samsung Electronics Co., Ltd	Korea, Republic	Electrical & electronic equipment	203671	209727	149298	240000
73	China Ocean Shipping (Group)	China	Transport and storage	56126	29101	4400	130000
98	China National Offshore Oil	China	Petroleum expl./ref./distr.	129834	83537	3387	102562

Source: UNCTAD, 2014 World Investment Repo unctad.org/Sections/dite_dir/docs/WIR2014/WIR14

Table 4.10 The world's largest financial TNCs, 2011

Rank	Corporation	Home Country
1	Alliannz	Germany
2	Citigroup	USA
3	BNP Paribas	France
4	UBS	Switzerland
5	HSBC	UK
6	Assicurazioni GS	Italy
7	Société Générale	France
8	Deutsche Bank	Germany
9	UniCredit spa	Italy
10	AXA SA	France

Source: adapted from Knox et al., 2014.

Table 4.11 A comparison of the world's largest TNCs and six middle-ranking economies, 2010

Company / Country	Revenue / GDP (US$bn)
Norway	414
Wal-Mart Stores	408
South Africa	364
Greece	305
Exxon-Mobile	285
Chevron	164
Romania	162
General Electric	157
Peru	154
Bank of America	150
Philips	140
Ukraine	138
AT&T	123
Ford	118

Source: adapted from Global Policy Forum/Forbes, 2010.

Out of the top 20, with the exception of one in Japan and two the USA, all of the rest are based in Western Europe, with the UK, France, Germany and Switzerland being the evident leaders. In parallel, in service industries such as legal firms and advertising, which are equally significant in terms of the smooth operation of our globally connected economic system, similar patterns of control are discernible.

As noted at the start of this section, many of the world's largest corporates are in fact larger than the economies of some of the smaller nation states, which indicates both the degree to which TNCs have become key role players in the global economy, and relative change in the position of the nation-state in a global era. Table 4.11 is included for comparative purposes and shows how, in 2010, in terms of turnover the then 12 largest TNCs compared with the GDP of six middle-sized economies in the world. Note that the ranking of the TNCs differs from that in Figure 4.19, owing to the different year in which the comparison is based, and the fact that in Figure 4.19 assets are ranked while in Table 4.11 turnover is the measurement criterion employed.

Given the sheer size of TNCs, their investment and production decisions have a significant influence over the operation of national economies, particularly those of smaller countries in the South. It follows from this that the decision to base production in one nation rather than another will have considerable impact on the geography of uneven development and change, especially when it is remembered that many TNCs have

annual turnovers that greatly exceed the gross national products of some smaller nations.

An additional key feature of TNCs is the indirect nature of their operations, through a reliance on affiliated companies with which they form direct relationships as part of the solidifying of GPNs and the extension of service-related activities. For example, in 2011 the UK headquartered HSBC banking corporation worked with 816 affiliated overseas companies (Knox et al., 2014). A manufacturing company like Ford was operating through 270 affiliates internationally by 2010. Most of these affiliates were, however, in a select group of countries in the North and South: Canada, countries in Western Europe, India, Brazil, Mexico, China, Argentina and Venezuela. The result is the emergence of what have often become distinctive supply chains (GPNs) between corporate headquarters and production, assembly, research, marketing and administrative facilities scattered around the world. The Toyota car manufacturing company serves as an example of a complex GPN. In 2015, Toyota was operating through 53 companies in 28 countries and selling its products in 170 countries. Thirty-five of the 53 companies actually assembled cars, in addition to making components which were redistributed through the production network, with the balance of the companies making a range of components for exports to other Toyota affiliates (Toyota, 2015). Figure 4.22 shows the

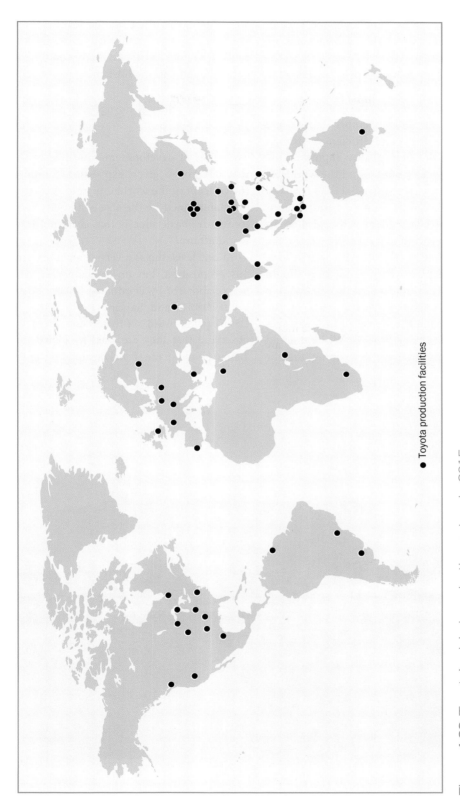

Figure 4.22 Toyota's global production network, 2015

Source: adapted from https://www.toyota-europe.com/world-of-toyota/this-is-toyota/toyota-in-the-world. Accessed 18 August 2016.

● Toyota production facilities

distribution of Toyota's global production network in 2015. The fact that only six of the 53 companies are located in South America or Africa once again shows the degree to which global production systems are biased in their operations.

The supply chains set up between globally dispersed manufacturing and assembly plants are selected to maximise profit and efficiency, through deliberately seeking the best quality inputs at the most cost-effective prices from around the world. By working with affiliates, the financial liability and commitment of TNCs can be reduced with the onus of dealing with local labour demands and government requirements devolved to local affiliates, leaving the parent company free to relocate with relative ease to another more compliant national setting should operating conditions not be deemed to be ideal in a particular location. Labour-intensive parts of the production processes tend to be based in low-wages economies as a result of this process. While it could be argued that such countries are 'developing', the low

wages paid, the often limited technology transfer to the host country and ultimately, the subservient relationships which exist, cast doubts on the nature of the actual benefits to the host country.

The world or global city concept

The types of developments outlined in the last section have been given expression to and reinforced the concept of the world city or global city. Although not determined by the size of the city in population terms, the basic idea is that certain cities dominate world affairs.

At one level, this is a very straightforward and obvious proposition, but its contemporary relevance has been elaborated by Friedmann (1986), Friedmann and Wulff (1982) and Sassen (1991, 2002). Friedmann (1986) put forward six hypotheses about world cities, observing that they are used by global capitalism as 'basing points' in the spatial organisation and articulation

Plate 4.4 A world city – Cape Town
(*photo*: Tony Binns)

of production and markets, and that they act as centres for capital accumulation (see also Potter, 2008b).

Friedmann also suggested that the growth of world cities involves social costs which in fiscal terms the state finds hard to meet. World cities have large populations, but more important, they have large and/or complex manufacturing bases, sophisticated finance and service complexes, and they act as transport and communication hubs, and the locations for corporate headquarters, involving TNCs and NGOs (Simon, 1992a, 1993; see also Friedmann, 1995; Knox and Taylor, 1995; Potter, 2008).

The principal world cities, such as New York, Paris, London, Frankfurt and Milan, are located in the developed world. But Singapore, Hong Kong, Bangkok, Taipei, Manila, Shanghai, Seoul, Osaka, Mexico City, Rio de Janeiro, Buenos Aires and Cape Town (Plate 4.4) have all been recognised as part of an emerging network of world cities (Friedmann, 1995).

This emergence is given spatial expression in Figure 4.23. In short, world cities may be seen as points of articulation in a TNC-dominated capitalist global system. But data show that world cities exhibit a very centric (or centred) structure, with major world cities such as London at the core (Taylor, 1985).

The concept of global or world cities has been criticised for focusing academic and global attention on an elite group of cities in the North, and largely marginalising developments in hundreds of smaller cities around the world which do not host large corporations or have international airports. Robinson (2006) in her book *Ordinary Cities* presents a very clear argument on the need to see all cities as playing a role in the global system, and to recognise that what is happening in them is an equally valid focus of attention if we are trying to understand how the world operates.

Despite this, the implication of the economic dominance of a core set of elite cities is that uneven development is likely to be perpetuated to the disadvantage much of the South, and that the paths to development pursued by their cities and countries in the twenty-first century will be infinitely more difficult to pursue than those which the cities and countries of the North followed earlier. This is because of the entrenched nature of global control, which was recognised by Wallerstein (1980) in his 'World Systems Theory', which relates closely to the map depicted in Figure 4.23, which

Wallerstein saw as entrenching a hierarchical system of dependence and difference globally.

Quite simply, the world is highly centred. This argument has been reviewed in the case of poor countries by Lasuen (1973). He started from the premise that, in the modern world, large cities are the principal adopters of innovations, so that natural or spontaneous growth poles become ever more associated with the upper levels of the urban system. Lasuen also observed that the spatial spread of innovation is generally likely to be slower in the Global South, due to the frequent existence of single plant industries, the generally poorer levels of infrastructural provision and sometimes the lack of political will.

Thus, countries in the South facing spatial inequalities have two policy alternatives. The first is to allow the major urban centres to adopt innovations first. The second option is to attempt to hold and delay the adoption of further innovations at the top of the national urban system, until the filtering down of previous growth-inducing changes has run its course.

This may sound somewhat theoretical, but these options represent the two major practical strategies that can be pursued by states. The first option will result in increasing economic dualism but classical and neo-classical economists and neo-liberalisers would argue there is a chance of a higher overall rate of economic growth. On the other hand, the second option will lead to increasing regional equity, but potentially lower rates of national growth. Most countries of the Global South have adopted policies close to the first option of unrestrained innovation adoption, seeking to maximise growth rather than equity. This theme is re-examined in Chapter 9.

The account presented in this section has shown that industrialisation in the South has been far from characterised by uniformity and homogeneity. In fact, it has been associated with global shifts, non-hierarchic adoption sequences and the growth of global or world cities.

In short, globalisation is leading to increasing differences between regions and places, for example giving rise to centres, peripheries and semi-peripheries at the broadest scale, as noted in Chapter 3 from a theoretical viewpoint. In reality, however, global patterns of differentiation and localisation are much more complex than this in the contemporary context. This chapter now turns to consider this argument in further detail.

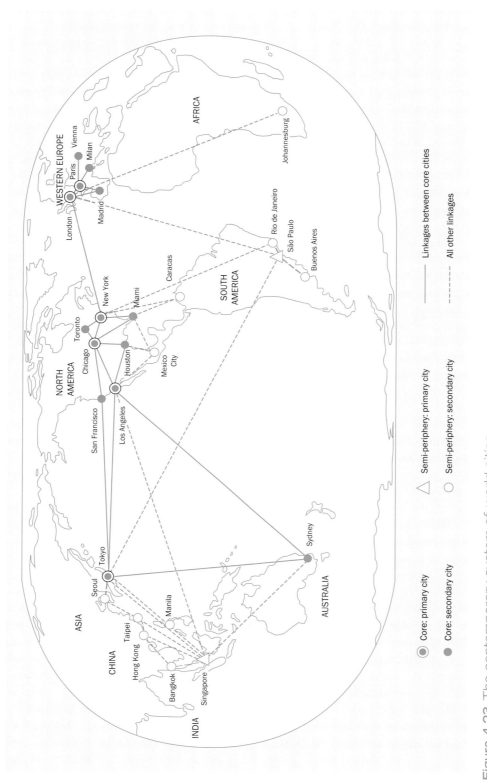

Figure 4.23 The contemporary system of world cities

Source: Adapted from Friedmann, J. (1986) The world city hypothesis. *Development and Change*, 17, Wiley-Blackwell Publishing Ltd.

Economic change and global divergence

The preceding discussion leads to a major conceptual-isation of what is happening in the contemporary world as a result of the acceleration of processes of globalisation, increasing connectivity and the opera-tion of TNCs, and what this means for growth and change in the South.

The basic argument is that the uneven development that has characterised much of the South during the mercantile and early capitalist periods has been intensi-fied post-1945 as a result of the operation of what may be called the dual processes of global convergence and global divergence, terms which originate in the work of Armstrong and McGee (1985; see also Potter, 2008). Together, these processes may be seen as characterising the outcome of processes underlying globalisation. In this section, divergence is the focus of attention. We turn to convergence in the next major section.

Divergence relates to the sphere of production and the observation that places which make up the world system are becoming increasingly differentiated, i.e. diverse and heterogeneous, as discussed in the first part of this chapter. Such differentiation, particularly in production, and the commodity supply terms lead to both specialisation, which may enhance income, and can also lead to vulnerability to price fluctuations and the decisions made in global cities and corporate headquarters. Starting from the observation that the 1970s witnessed a number of fundamental shifts in the global economic system, not least the slowdown of the major capitalist economies and rapidly escalating oil prices, Armstrong and McGee (1985) stressed that such changes had a notable effect on the dispersion of labour-intensive manufacturing industries to a few selected low-labour cost locations, and the increasing control of trade and investment by TNCs. It is this trend which has witnessed the establishment of Fordist production line systems in the NICs, whereas smaller scale, more specialised and responsive, or so-called 'flexible systems' of both production and accumulation have become more typical of advanced industrial nations. The North has tended to retain high-tech industries, such as aero-space, bio-tech, pharmaceuti-cals, luxury products and R & D intensive production and has, in recent years, started to experience a degree of reindustrialisation as a result of specialist market needs and rising labour costs in China.

In the South, since the 1970s, productive capacity has been channeled into a limited number of countries and metropolitan centres, or particular resource cen-tres such as mining regions, like the Zambian Copperbelt or zones of high agricultural productivity. The increasing global division of labour and the enhanced salience of TNCs are leading to greater het-erogeneity or divergence between and within nations with respect to their patterns of production, capital accumulation and ownership.

Thus, divergence leads to differentiation in the South between the industrialising export economies of China (including Hong Kong), Taiwan and South Korea, along with the larger internally directed industrialised coun-tries, such as Mexico, raw material exporting nations, like Nigeria, and low-income agricultural exporters, such as Bangladesh, and so on.

As argued in the previous section, in the contempo-rary world such changes are highly likely to be non-hierarchic, in the sense that they are focusing development on specific localities and settlements. Armstrong and McGee (1985: 41) state that, 'Cities are . . . the crucial elements in accumulation at all levels . . . and the *locus operandi* for transnationals, local oligopoly capital and the modernising state'. It is these features that gave rise to the title of their book, which characterised cities as 'theatres of accumulation' or 'global palladiums'.

Global convergence: perspectives on cultural globalisation

Other commentators point to what initially appears to be the reverse trend: the increasing similarity which seems to characterise world patterns of change and development (Figure 4.24).

There are at least two major respects in which a pat-tern of what may be called 'global convergence' is occurring. This is, first, in the sense of the emerging global class links. Most obvious are the growing 'global middle class' – i.e. a core of middle class, educated and highly mobile professionals in all countries, albeit to varying degrees and scales, who have become key agents

Figure 4.24 Globalisation and Third World societies: Rip Kirby airs the stereotypical argument
Source: Yaffa Advertising and King Features

in the neo-liberal world through their pursuit of middle class values and aspirations, which often link them with the middle class in other countries, and this in turn distances them from the poor majorities in their own countries. In parallel, more marginalised people are also linking globally through social and protest movements (discussed below). Secondly, a convergence can be noted in the sphere of consumer preferences and habits. Of particular importance is the so-called 'demonstration effect', involving the rapid assimilation of North American and European tastes and consumption patterns in the South (McElroy and Albuquerque, 1986).

The influence of the mass media, in particular television, social media, newspapers, magazines and various forms of associated advertising, is likely to be especially critical in this respect. The televising and internet streaming of North American soap operas,

where technology allows this, may well lead to a mismatch between extant lifestyles and aspirations (Miller, 1992, 1994; Potter, 2000, 2008a; Potter and Dann, 1996), although there is equally the chance that such events will be reinterpreted and reconstituted from a local perspective. This argument is developed in Case study 4.1. Within this context, the role of global media broadcast networks such as CNN, Al Jazeera and BBC, in terms of news coverage and a range of commercial and music satellite channels, has the power to influence values but also shape public perceptions of events and news coverage, particularly through the subjective interpretation of events conveyed by media presenters based in particular countries. The privileging of knowledge from the North in the global media runs the risk of marginalising equally important events in the South through a process of cultural imperialism.

Case study 4.1

Global mass media, metropolitanisation and cultural change

British anthropologist Daniel Miller examined the popularity of soap operas produced in metropolitan regions of developed countries in a study published in 1992. This phenomenon can be seen as part of the evolution of 'global forms'. Such global forms have received a good deal of attention in relation to shifts in global production, but less has been written concerning the parallel process in global mass consumption.

Miller was researching on households and culture in Trinidad in the Caribbean, but he observed that 'for an hour a day, fieldwork proved impossible since no-one would speak to me, and I was reduced to watching people watching a soap opera'. The author goes on to note that much of the relevant research has been carried out on the pioneer coloniser of this type of television programme, *Dallas*. However, the programme that was

Case study 4.1 (continued)

receiving so much attention in Trinidad was *The Young and the Restless*. This has been produced since 1973, and has always had a strong emphasis on sexual relations and associated social breakdown.

It is noted that many people went to extreme lengths to watch the programme. Those with low income, e.g. a large squatter community, were found to be the most resourceful in gaining access to the programme. Although most householders had neither domestic electricity nor water, many homes had televisions connected to car batteries so they could watch the show. The car batteries were recharged for a small fee per week by those residents who had electricity.

Although the programme has little to do with the environmental context of Trinidad, Miller notes that it was regarded as realistic in portraying key structural problems of Trinidadian society and culture. In particular, in fashion- and style-conscious Trinidad, local audiences identified with the clothing worn by the characters. Thus, a retailer observed: 'What is fashion in Trinidad today? *The Young and the Restless* is fashion in Trinidad today.' The programme was also seen to match with the local sense of truth, as revealed by exposure and scandal.

The author concludes that 'Trinidad was never, and will never be, the primary producer of the images and goods from which it constructs its own culture', and 'Trinidad is largely the recipient of global discourses for which the concept of spatial origin is becoming increasingly inappropriate', however different they may be in terms of the physical environment. But Miller also stresses it would be wrong to assume that such developments mean an end to Trinidadian culture, which has always been derived from here, there and everywhere – Africa, India, France, Jamaica, USA and UK among others.

Source: Miller (1992)

Critical reflection

How do you respond to this example? To what extent do you feel that television programmes can promote new realities? For example, it has been common for people to blame rising violence in society on the incidence of violence on TV. How much can TV promote the demand for new goods and services, new lifestyles and, indeed, new forms of development? What about the sorts of houses that people live in and their lifestyles as depicted on TV – do these have implications for development, do you feel? Or is it more the case that TV reflects reality in one place and is then re-interpreted to suit local circumstances? This is worth thinking about – and perhaps discussing as a group if you are in a classroom situation.

Other aspects of the wider trend of convergence involve changes in dietary preferences, and the rise of the 'industrial palate', whereby an increasing proportion of food is consumed by non-producers (Drakakis-Smith, 1990; MacLeod and McGee, 1990).

Developing cities in the South may be seen as the prime channels for introduction of such emulatory and imitative lifestyles, which are sustained by imports from overseas, along with the internal activities of transnational corporations and their branch plants. These in turn are frequently related to collective consumption, indebtedness and increasing social inequalities. These changes towards homogenisation are ones that are particularly true of very large cities.

Such a view sees globalisation as a profoundly unsettling process both for cultures and the identity of individuals, and it suggests that established traditions are dislocated by the invasion of foreign influences and images from global cultural industries.

The implication is that such influences are pernicious and are extremely difficult to reject or contain (Hall, 1995). Following this line of argument, Hall (1995: 176) has observed that the view is expressed that 'global consumerism, though limited by its uneven geography of power (Massey, 1991), spreads the same thin cultural film over everything – Big Macs, Coca-Cola and Nike trainers everywhere' (Plate 4.5).

However, once again the suggestion of homogeneity looks fragile when subjected to closer scrutiny. The impact of standardised merchandising is likely to be highly uneven, especially when viewed in terms of social class.

Plate 4.5 McDonald's in Nanjing Road, Shanghai
(*photo*: Getty images)

It stands to reason that it is only the urban elite and the urban upper income groups who are most able to adopt and sustain the 'goods' provided by standardised merchandising – health care facilities, mass media and communications technologies, improvements in transport and the like.

It may be conjectured that the lower income groups within society disproportionately receive the 'bads' – for example, formula baby milk and tobacco products. Thus, once again, forces of globalisation may be seen to etch out wider differences on the ground. This heterogenising effect is true within urban areas too, with the residential subdivisions of the rich contrasting with those extensive areas that are inhabited predominantly by squatters and low-income residents of the city.

The capitalist system must inevitably be recognised as having a vested interest in globalising the expectations of consumption and tastes. This, of course, can be related directly to the theme of the articulation of the modes of production under capitalism, as outlined in Chapter 3.

Global convergence and divergence: patterns of hierarchic and non-hierarchic change – a summary

Introduction

A direct and important outcome of the above discussion is a strong argument that the form of contemporary development which is to be found in particular areas of the South is the local manifestation and juxtaposition of the two seemingly contradictory processes of convergence and divergence at the global scale.

In terms of examples, Armstrong and McGee (1985) look at the ways in which these trends are played out in Ecuador, Hong Kong and Malaysia. Potter (1993c, 1995a, 2000) has examined how well the framework fits the Caribbean, where it has been argued that tourism has a direct effect on the trends of convergence and divergence. This is another way of saying, via changes in production and consumption, that globalisation is not leading to uniformity, but to heterogeneity and differences between places.

This is also reflected in contexts where the South is represented in the North as in connections with music, fashions and the like. Thus, it is necessary to acknowledge that the 'flow' is not one way, and although the North to South flow is dominant, it can be argued that the nature of the South to North flow is of increasing salience. Examples are found in Asian influences in high-street fashion, music and food, and in many other arenas. The spread of international cuisine, particularly from Asia is a particular case in point, as is the attraction of Eastern religions and philosophies to people from the North.

Consumption and convergence

We are now ready to reconcile a number of closely linked arguments. It can be argued that it is the key traits of Northern consumption and demand that are potentially being spread in a hierarchical manner within the global system, from the metropolitan centres of the core world cities to the regional primate cities of the peripheries and semi-peripheries, and subsequently down and through the global capitalist system. But the actual impact of these trends will be highly specific to localities, and be influenced by age, class, gender, religion, etc. It is interesting to observe that the innovations cited by Berry (1961; 1972) and others in the 1960s and 1970s as having spread sequentially from the top to the bottom of the urban system of America were all consumption-oriented – for example, the diffusion of television receivers and stations. But the spread is one of potential, and many real differences are evolving.

Production and divergence

In contrast, aspects of production and ownership are becoming more unevenly spread; they are becoming concentrated into specific locations, or what may be referred to as 'spatial nodes'. This process involves strong cumulative feedback loops. Hence, considerable stability is likely to be maintained at selected points within the global system, frequently the largest world cities, production facilities and tourism centres. In other words, key entrepreneurial innovations are likely to be strongly concentrated in space, and are not likely to be spread through the urban system. This argument has parallels with the view that sees dependency theory as

the diffusion of underdevelopment rather than development, as outlined in Chapter 3.

A graphical summary

The key elements of the argument presented above are summarised in Figure 4.25. On the one hand, the culture and values of the West are potentially being diffused on a global scale. By such means, patterns of consumption are spread through time (T1, T2, T3, etc.), and there is an evolving tendency for convergence on what may be described as the 'global norms of consumption'. The figure recognises that such consumption aspects of global change are primarily expressed hierarchically, and are essentially top-down in nature.

In contrast, cities appear to be accumulating and centralising the ownership of capital, and this process is closely associated with differences in productive capabilities.

The tendency towards divergence is expressed in a sporadic manner, which stresses unique activities in area and by region (A1, A2, A3). TNCs and associated industrialisation are the most important agents involved in this process. This goes a long way towards explaining the plural and sometimes contradictory nature of the postmodern world system.

Cities and urban systems have to be studied as important functioning parts of the world economy. In such a role, cities act as agents of both concentration and spread, at one and the same time. Similarly, it is far too simplistic to ask whether cities spread change in a hierarchical or non-hierarchical manner, for in fact they are doing both simultaneously. In this regard, it is tempting to argue that the breaking down of rigid hierarchical systems at a global level is very much part of the postmodern world. What we can certainly conclude is that globalisation has much to do with new and perpetuated forms of uneven development.

Political aspects of globalisation: the anti-globalisation and anti-capitalist movements

Introduction: communities and the state

The principal theme of this chapter has been that it is a gross oversimplification to think in terms of enhanced

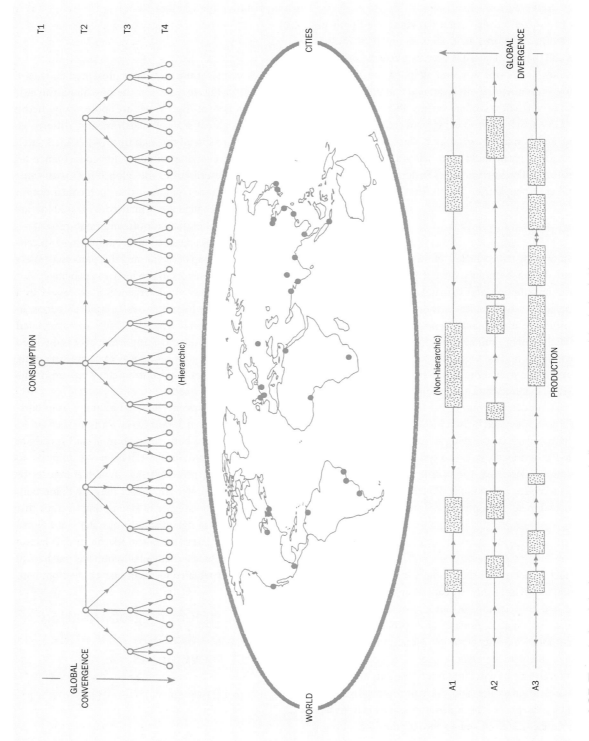

Figure 4.25 Trends in global convergence and divergence: a graphical depiction
Source: adapted from Potter, 1997.

globalisation and the unfolding of the neo-liberal world order as giving rise to a more equal and uniform world. As evidence presented to Chapter 1 showed, the wealth ratio between rich and poor countries in 1830 was 1:3, but by 2015 it was estimated to be 1:80.

In virtually every instance, spread at one scale or in one arena seems to have been matched by polarisation at another. At one level the selective privileging of which countries, regions, cities and individuals are privileged or marginalised by global and national production systems reinforces class and social differences. Marginalisation within societies and growing opposition to homogenising tendencies from the North is encouraging growing dissatisfaction from grassroots groups and communities in all countries. This can be expressed in actions ranging from support for 'transition towns' movements, with their focus on trying to ensure sustainable living, to alignment with global peasant movement such as 'via campesina'.

A frequently cited view is that globalisation is witnessing the erosion of the former role and power of the nation state. This view emanates from the fact that certain large TNCs have annual turnovers that are substantially larger than the GDPs of small nations of the South (see above).

It also relates to the transnational movement of capital and the ascendancy of uncensored forms of global communication, such as the World Wide Web. Thus, in reviewing the changing role of the state in the field of development, Batley (2002) has noted that, while for the first quarter of the twentieth century states held clear authority within their borders, the period since 1975 has seen the evolution of a more porous nation state, with fewer directly performed functions, and more partnerships with other actors. Indeed, the notion of public–private partnerships has become one of the common concepts of our time and which neo-liberalism actively encourages.

The anti-globalisation and anti-capitalist movements

The foregoing observations are also reflected in what may be described as the 'anti-globalisation movement', which since the 1990s has mounted resistance to what is seen as the negative consequences of globalisation.

In fact, the anti-globalisation movement refers to a very broad array of interest, lobby and protest groups, many of which have taken direct action at major capitalist summits and meetings throughout the world (Murray, 2006), most notably at annual meetings of world leaders and the business elite such as the WTO (World Trade Organization) discussions, G8 meetings (the heads of the 'leading' countries) and meetings of the World Economic Forum. The first major expression of mass opposition to the global system was the 'Battle of Seattle' from 29 November to 2 December 1999, when the WTO held its major conference in Seattle. This became the focus for some of the largest protests seen in the USA since the Vietnam War, involving some 600,000 protesters (Madeley, 2000; Murray, 2006).

The anti-globalisation movement can be seen as part of a wider anti-capitalist movement against what are regarded as the excesses of neo-liberalism. A wide group of environmentalists, anarchists, feminists, consumers, unionists, workers and peasant farmers are brought together by the movement. The 'Occupy' movement protests in many cities of the world against the capitalist system in 2011 were a particularly profound expression of popular dissatisfaction and rejection of the neo-liberal system which has privileged business elites – the 1% as alluded to in the common discourse, at the expense of the 99% – the workers around the world. While it would be difficult to assert that the protests brought about change, they nonetheless expressed the reality that large numbers of people globally were dissatisfied with the global neo-liberal system, and we are likely to see a resurgence of such activity as future capitalist expansion variously privileges select groups at the expense of others (Williams et al., 2014). It is interesting that such protest movements exist in both the North and South and, while holding often differing and even competing agendas, such as environmental protection, opposing cheap imports and land sales, to trying to preserve industrial jobs, they do represent a degree of popular dissatisfaction with the prevailing economic order and its global operations and ramifications.

A particular target of protest is the WTO, which is responsible for formulating the rules that govern the conduct of world trade. Its predecessor was known as the General Agreement on Tariffs and Trade (GATT) (see Chapters 8 and 10). The philosophy of the WTO is almost wholly based on free trade. Indeed, the WTO has been staunch in arguing that wider issues, such as those pertaining to labour conditions and labour rights, health and safety issues at work and environmental pollution and degradation, cannot be allowed to stand in the way of large TNCs trading freely and efficiently. Its efforts at various negotiating rounds of proposed new global trade deals to lower trade restrictions globally and protect intellectual property rights have met with popular protests and increasing dissatisfaction from Southern countries aggrieved by the way in which they tend to be worse off from a Northern-dominated trade system. A classic point of dispute is Northern government subsidies to their farmers, which make the farm produce from the South uncompetitive, which should, strictly speaking, not be permissible in terms of global trade, particularly since subsidies to manufacturing from the South would contravene WTO regulations by comparison. This critique merits attention in Chapters 7 and 8.

At the regional level, current negotiations over the Trans-Pacific Partnership agreement and the Transatlantic Trade and Investment Partnership have been particularly controversial, as they are regarded by opposition movements as a way to legally enshrine the rights of Northern corporates to protect and advance their interests in other sovereign states. The counter-argument is that enhanced trade will benefit all signatories.

Madeley (2000) cited Walden Bello, Co-Director of the NGO 'Focus on Global South' in explaining why the WTO arouses so much protest:

> I think it's because it's seen as standing for the subordination of so many aspects of human existence to trade, as an organization that represents primarily the interests of transnational corporations, and, from the South, as an organization with a very anti-development philosophy.

Some commentaries, particularly those in newspapers, have suggested that as a result of these types of protests, views on globalisation have started to show a change since the turn of the millennium. Thus, Elliott (2000: 27) suggests that:

> globalisation is no longer viewed as a force of nature . . . but something that can and must be shaped by human endeavour and integrity. It has been recognised that there are inherent problems in a system where capital calls all the shots . . . while labour is voiceless.

The clarion call is that globalisation must be more people-friendly, and must build core labour standards, with the Global North being as responsible for this as the Global South. Elliott (2001) emphasises that the then British Chancellor Gordon Brown's statement in November 2001, that, if managed badly, globalisation will lead to 'wider inequality, deeper division and a dangerous era of distrust and rising tension'.

The linking of globalisation, inequalities, division and danger in the post-11 September 2001 world is highly salient. On the one hand, a few writers have pronounced the anti-capitalist/anti-globalisation movements to be in tatters in the aftermath of the terrorist attacks on the Twin Towers of the World Trade Center in New York. On the other hand, one of the movement's leaders, Naomi Klein (2001: 31), has warned that the 'debate about what kind of globalisation we want is not "so yesterday"; it has never been more urgent'. Such a stance argues the need for new forms of multilateralism/internationalism, occupying the space between what Klein (2001) refers to as 'McWorld and Jihad'. The mass protest in multiple countries associated with the 'Occupy' movement in 2011 are indicative that a strong undercurrent of resistance persists.

As we saw in Chapter 3, in the scholarly world the same kind of argument is being presented in calls for the increasing localisation and territorialisation of development. This is often linked to the concept of neo-populism and the operation of selected regional closure (Chapter 3).

In the political domain, it is increasingly allied to the call for the relocalisation of production and reductions in 'food miles' (see also Chapter 7 on resources and development). This has been strongly advocated in respect of food production by the British Green Party (see Lucas, 2001a, 2001b). Lucas argues that the ever more international nature of the food trade is serving to increase greenhouse gases and leading to global warming. She also argues that it forces down food and animal welfare standards, and contributes to disasters such as Foot and Mouth Disease.

A global solution to global problems? Tobin-type taxes

Critics of globalisation argue that it is characteristic of the extreme pro-globalists that while they argue for global free trade, they are often noticeably less global in their outlook on other important issues. For example, such commentators are frequently far less keen on the unrestricted movement of labour across borders. There is a major area where this argument seems to fit: and this is in relation to the proposal for globally based taxes in order to fight world poverty and underdevelopment.

Some people argue that what is urgently needed is strong forms of global redistribution. In 1972, James Tobin (see Key thinker box), Professor of Economics at Yale University, suggested what he saw as the need for the global taxation of financial speculation. Tobin once commented that the initial idea 'sank like a rock'. But in 1978 he formalised his proposal, and in 1981 he was awarded the Nobel Laureate for Economics for his work on global taxation.

Key thinker

James Tobin and Tobin-type taxes on speculation

Plate 4.6 Professor James Tobin, Economist
(*photo*: Getty Images/AFP)

Born in 1918, and educated in economics at Harvard University from 1935, James Tobin had a long interest in financial markets and investment decision-making extending back to the 1960s (Simon, 2006). It was in this context that Tobin suggested the need for global currency speculation to be taxed. Tobin referred to this as potential 'sand in the wheels' of international financial markets, which would serve to reduce their overall volatility. At first this suggestion was ignored both by professional economists and policy makers, who were generally against any market interference (Simon, 2006).

Initially at least, Tobin himself seemed to regard the funds raised by such taxation as a mere by-product. But even at 0.1 per cent, around half the rate initially suggested by Tobin, between US $50 and US $300 billion would be raised annually, a sum broadly equal to existing levels of development assistance.

In the late 1990s, the NGOs War on Want and Oxfam, as well as the governments of Canada, France and Belgium, moved to support the introduction of Tobin-type taxes. Anti-globalists also find it relatively easy to align with Tobin taxes as there is a strong

▶

Key thinker (continued)

argument that they would serve to dampen down aspects of financial globalisation.

Tobin formally retired in 1988 and died in 2004 aged 84 years. As Simon (2006) points out, as a key thinker he was also associated with the suggestion that development needs to be defined and assessed in terms of human welfare rather than by measures of GNP and income per head alone. Thus, in the 1970s, James Tobin proposed what he referred to as a Measure of Economic Welfare (MEW). This can be regarded as a forerunner of the United Nations' Human Development Index (HDI), which we reviewed in Chapter 1, and serves to confirm James Tobin as a key thinker in the field of global development.

Over US $3 trillion is traded daily on foreign exchange markets. It is believed that only 5 per cent of this sum is actually necessary to finance global trade. The remainder effectively amounts to speculative trading, that is making profits from changes in currency rates. Tobin-type taxes would involve a levy of around 0.20 to 0.25 per cent on such global financial activities. This would presently yield US $250 billion per annum. This is over five times the total amount that is given in aid around the world. Although formidable issues would have to be faced in collecting and allocating such monies, it is generally argued that revenues should be collected by national central banks and then deposited with a United Nations body, such as the United Nations Development Programme (UNDP), or United Nations Educational, Scientific and Cultural Organization (UNESCO) (see also Chapter 7).

The US $250 billion that could be raised each year only makes sense when we consider it alongside what might actually be achieved with such tranches of money. For example, it has long been estimated that as little as US $8 billion per year would be enough to establish universal primary education on a global basis. Meanwhile, UNDP has calculated that US $80 billion is needed to eliminate the worst forms of global poverty. Further, the Jubilee 2000 campaign argued that US $160 billion per annum would be the cost of wiping out the Global South's unpayable debts (see Chapter 8).

But there is another reason for the introduction of global Tobin taxes, over and above poverty alleviation. A major consideration is that it would also serve to promote greater financial stability by damping down financial markets, rather than the extreme volatility which seems to have characterised them over the years (Rigg, 2002).

At the start of the 2000s, the British NGO War on Want ran a very strong and extensive campaign supporting the introduction of a Tobin-style tax. At the same time, the Canadian Parliament voted two-to-one in favour of introducing such a tax, which was staunchly advocated in the mid-1990s by the French President Francois Mitterand, shortly before his death.

However, it appears that, in general, those very politicians who espouse globalisation are those who dismiss out of hand a globalised tax to tackle world poverty. Thus, in 1995, the then Managing Director of the International Monetary Fund, Michel Casessus, is reported as having commented that 'financing an attack on poverty should be left to governments'.

Notably, the possibility of global taxation is not even mentioned in the UK Government's White Paper in dealing with globalisation and poverty reduction. In the words of L. Elliott (2001: 15): 'It is politics that is the killer . . . the political will for a Tobin tax is absent in the places which matter: Washington, London, Tokyo, Frankfurt'.

More recent concerns have focused on the morality of corporations which operate globally and which, through the questionable system of tax avoidance known as 'transfer pricing', incur profits and losses as a result of trade of goods internationally between branches of the same corporate and its affiliates, leading to losses or low profits being declared in many countries, while significant profits are declared in tax havens such as Caribbean. Similarly, the ability of TNCs to avoid taxation in countries with weak monitoring structures, and their setting of establishment conditions favourable to themselves in countries desperate for investment, is regarded as blatant exploitation of weak national systems which perpetuates poverty and corporate greed.

Concluding comments: globalisation and unequal development

Throughout this chapter it has been argued that the notion of a basic sameness in respect of global culture is clearly a distortion and a gross oversimplification. Clearly, we live in a more globalised world, in which TNCs are, increasingly, coming to dominate world patterns of consumption and production. But there are many reasons why it is wrong to regard the outcome as increasing uniformity.

First, strong resistance is sometimes shown by local and national cultures, especially to the influences of North America. The idea of a single global culture is clearly misplaced. As an example, the opening of McDonald's was fiercely contested for some time in Barbados, despite its status as a leading tourist destination for North Americans and Europeans. When those in power relented, the fast-food chain only lasted six months, largely because Bajans prefer eating chicken to red meat. This is a simple and direct example illustrating that local customs and tastes can run directly across, and indeed against, apparently hegemonic global trends. The regionally based fast food outlet Cheffette/Barbeque Barn is strongly based on chicken meals, and is very popular – but does also serve beef burgers.

Second, rather than serving to erode local differences, global culture often works alongside them; and sometimes it even works via them. Particular groups within society may be targeted for the sale of certain products. In this manner, local differences may be explored and exploited wherever possible (Robins, 1995).

Furthermore, increasingly within the global economy cultural products are being assembled from all over the world, and are being turned into commodities for an emerging cosmopolitan marketplace. This is particularly true of fashion, music and tourism (Crang, 2000). Thus, from reggae to soca to African indigenous music, Asian politics and menus, and in respect of Rastafarianism, the flow is not a one-way movement, and Southern products are being promoted and sold in Northern marketplaces. Thus, globalisation has brought the possibility of the colony 'invading' the colonial power, and the periphery taking on and 'winning against' the centre (Robins, 1995). Hence, in the new globalising system we are encountering many incidences of what, viewed historically, is a reverse or counter flow. Again, such conflations can be interpreted as typical of the postmodern condition.

There is also the important argument that increasing globalisation and time–space compression in the end make us value more strongly than hitherto the notion of place as secure and stable. Thus, it can be posited that globalisation may well serve to engender localisation. This is sometimes described rather inelegantly as 'glocalisation', where there are multiple global–local relations through which locality becomes more salient than hitherto within the world system.

Furthermore, we have witnessed all too clearly that culture has always been characterised by hybridisation, difference, rupture and clashes, so it is possible to argue that nothing very new, strange or different is currently happening. Western European nation states may be seen as masters of modernity, whereas hybridised forms of culture are characterising the postmodern world. This, of course, reflects the fact that culture can never be seen as settled, finalised, complete and internally coherent (Hall, 1995).

It has to be appreciated that cultures (systems of shared meanings), products and lifestyles will inevitably spread, and sometimes contract, in a highly heterogeneous manner. But aspects of production and ownership are far from evenly spread, due to the process of divergence and differentiation reviewed in this chapter.

Finally, the economic competition between places is now intense, given that major corporations can select between them, and this is leading to the possibility of ever-sharper differences between areas, regions and places. Thus, trade liberalisation has brought a wave of anti-globalisation protests.

For all these reasons, we can conclude that uneven and unequal development are still characteristic of the global capitalist system. Globalisation is not all-encompassing and there is much that remains uneven about global relationships and global processes. All of these aspects of dynamic change are strongly skewed towards the developed North (Allen, 1995). The world may effectively be getting smaller, but the majority of its population do not share in the benefits of globalisation, which many (but not all) residents of the North have enjoyed, with some interruptions, for the last 50 years – growing incomes, improving social conditions and access to globally sources goods, often from low-waged producing countries through TNC networks.

In considering development, it has to be recognised that places in the globalising world system are not linked together in a uniform way. They are interrelated in very unequal ways, and such basic inequality would seem to be poised to increase rather than decrease in the near future. Competition between places for global capital is making the world more uneven and differentiated, reflecting the trends of global divergence (Armstrong and McGee, 1985; Cochrane, 1995; Potter, 1993c, 2000) and uneven geographical development (Harvey, 2006, 2015). In the words of Cochrane (1995: 276), 'Globalisation and localisation are not the polar opposites which one might expect them to be', because 'globalisation is underpinned by the realities of uneven development' (277). One might even go further and say that uneven development is actively being promoted by contemporary processes of globalisation.

Key points

> The single word 'globalisation' seems to summarise our contemporary age, even though, in reality, globalisation has been a feature of the world economy and development patterns since the 1400s.
> The precise relationships that are envisaged to exist between globalisation and processes of development are central to thinking about planning and change.
> Some analysts, especially neo-liberals, see globalisation as the mechanism that will spread growth in the twenty-first century, so that neo-liberalism can be regarded as akin to neo-modernisation.
> The world is effectively getting smaller for those who have the resources to travel and use the most up-to-date communications technologies.
> But when diverse aspects of globalisation are viewed – be it digital technology, transport, manufacturing, cultural globalisation – while certain spread effects are recognisable, at a higher resolution the outcome appears to be a sharper polarisation – between both places and people.
> TNCs and the role of FDI are critical in the operation of the global economy, and manufacturing relies increasingly on the emergence of GPNs (Global Production Networks). World/global cities are key basing points for the control of the global economy and their operation tends to enhance the economic control of the North.
> The framework of global convergence and divergence suggests that while patterns of consumption are promoting greater homogenisation for those who can afford it, global patterns of production are creating greater diversity and differentiation among world regions.
> The anti-globalisation and anti-capitalism movements argue forcefully that the effects of globalisation urgently need to be controlled, and in some respects, curtailed.
> The benefits and costs and the inclusionary and exclusionary effects of globalisation are differentially experienced across the world, reinforcing patterns and processes of 'unequal geographical development'.

Further reading

Bond, P. (2006) *Looting Africa*. London: Zed Books.
A critical review of the impact on neo-liberalism on Africa

Coe, N.M. and Yeung, H.W-C. (2015) Global Production Networks: Theorizing Economic Development in an Interconnected World. Oxford: Oxford University Press.
A detailed explanation of key economic processes linking manufacturing globally.

Collier, P. (2008) *The Bottom Billion*. Oxford: Oxford University Press.
A critical examination of the impact of globalisation and related processes on the world's poorest.

Conway, D. and Heynen, N. (2006) Globalization's Contradictions: Geographies of Discipline, Destruction and Transformation. London and New York: Routledge.
A critical overview of globalisation and neo-liberalism.

Department for International Development (2000) *Eliminating World Poverty: Making Globalisation Work for the Poor*, Cmnd 5066. London: The Stationery Office.
Worth reading as a strong template for the argument that globalisation is the way forward in delivering countries from poverty.

Desai, V. and Potter, R.B. (2014) *The Companion to Development Studies*, 3rd edn. London: Routledge.
An accessible source book that brings together over 100

key essays dealing with all aspects of the field of development studies.

Dicken, P. (2015) Global Shift: Mapping the Changing Contours of the World Economy, 7th edn. London: Sage.
A must read for those concerned with the realities of economic globalisation.

Harvey, D. (2006) Spaces of Global Capitalism: Towards a Theory of Uneven Geographical Development. London: Verso.
This book, and the next two, critically examine the operation of capitalism and its spatial and economic contradictions.

Harvey, D. (2011) The Enigma of Capital and Crises of Capitalism. London: Profile Books.

Harvey, D. (2015) Seventeen Contradictions and the End of Capitalism. London: Profile Books.

Knox, P., Agnew, J. and McCarthy, L. (2014) The Geography of the World Economy, 6th edn. London: Routledge.
A detailed overview of the evolving world economy.

Murray, W.E. (2006) Geographies of Globalization. London and New York: Routledge.
An overview of globalisation processes for the undergraduate student market.

Schenk, S. and Haggis, J. (2000) Culture and Development: A Critical Introduction. Oxford: Blackwell.
Endeavours to fill a gap by focusing attention specifically on cultural aspects of the development process.

Schuurman, F. (2001) Globalization and Development Studies: Challenges for the 21st Century. London: Sage.
A good collection of readings dealing with globalisation.

UNCTAD (United Nations Conference on Trade and Development) (2014) World Investment Report. Geneva: UNCTAD.

UNCTAD (United Nations Conference on Trade and Development) (2015) World Investment Report. Geneva: UNCTAD.
The UNCTAD reports detail the nature and scale of global trade, FDI and TNC activity.

UNDP (United Nations Development Report) (2015) Human Development Report. New York: United Nations.
An annual report which details key human development issues, barriers and opportunities.

Websites

www.dfid.gov.uk
As noted at the end of Chapter 1, the DFID site gives direct access to a range of development items, including those on globalisation and related topics.

www.eldis.org
The site aims to share the best in development policy, practice and research.

www.waronwant.org
The site contains details concerning War on Want's 'It's time for Tobin' campaign.

www.internetworldstats.com
Provides updated figures on internet usage levels.

www.unctad.org
Provides access to data on FDI, trade and TNCs

www.undp.org
Provides access to the annual Human Development Report.

www.unido.org
Provide details on global manufacturing trends.

www.worldbank.org
Provides access to a range of statistical sources, policy reports and annual World Development Report and the key statistical source: World Development Indicators.

Discussion topics

➤ Consider the statement that contemporary globalisation is bringing forth new forms of localisation.

➤ Assess the view that while the world may be shrinking, it is also becoming noticeably more unequal.

➤ 'Globalisation dates back over 500 years.' What do you see as the development implications of this statement?

➤ Explain the basis of Tobin-type taxes and consider their potential for changing the face of international development.

➤ What drives the anti-globalisation movement? Is it sustainable?

➤ What are the ethical implications of the operation of TNCs and the WTO in the poorer parts of the South?

PART II

Development in practice: components of development

Chapter 5
People in the development process

This chapter focuses on various aspects concerning people in the development process. Following consideration of issues such as population growth and distribution, we move on to examine a number of important factors which affect the quality of life for individuals, households and communities – notably health, education and human rights. It is suggested that if meaningful development is to be achieved in the world's poorest countries, these issues need to receive high priority both nationally and internationally.

This chapter:

➤ Examines the relationship between population growth and key resources needed for human survival;

➤ Considers the rate of world population growth and distribution;
➤ Explains the key elements of the demographic transition model;
➤ Examines why some countries have pursued anti-natalist population policies, whilst others adopt pro-natalist policies;
➤ Considers the changing structure of national populations in different parts of the world and the particular roles of children and older people;
➤ Reviews some of the key health issues facing people in poor countries;
➤ Examines different policies towards the provision of education and human rights.

Introduction: putting people at the centre of development

People are, or certainly should be, absolutely central to the development process and an essential element in all development strategies. But all too often in the past the needs of people have been ignored and there has been a failure to consider the possible implications of development policies on individuals, households and communities. As we have seen in Part I, there are many different and often conflicting views as to the meanings of development, and the most appropriate strategies to be followed at different points in time and space. However, for one influential development economist, Dudley Seers, development was unequivocally about improving the quality of people's livelihoods, and he argued that the reduction of three key variables – poverty, unemployment and inequality – should be central to the development process. As Seers observed: 'The questions to ask about a country's development are therefore: What has been happening to poverty? What has been happening to unemployment? What has been happening to inequality? If all three of these have become less severe, then beyond doubt this has been a period of development for the country concerned' (1969).

Seers also emphasised the need for the true fulfilment of human potential and improvements in the quality of life. In a later paper entitled 'The new meaning of development', written after the oil crisis of the 1970s, he suggested that 'self-reliance' should be another important goal of development plans (Seers, 1979; see also Chapter 3). In order to reduce poverty, unemployment and inequality, Seers and others have argued that development strategies must fulfil basic human needs such as nutrition, water and sanitation, health and education. It is also important to recognise that these basic needs are inextricably linked, and policies must adopt a holistic approach towards improving human welfare. Too often in the past development strategies have been driven by economic goals, whereas fulfilling basic needs has received less priority, commonly assuming that economic growth will somehow 'trickle down' spontaneously to the most marginal elements of society and space, as reviewed in Chapter 3. In fact, the Global South is littered with so-called development projects which, far from empowering people, supplying their basic needs and raising living standards, have instead produced greater inequality, poverty and unemployment.

A further problem with many development strategies is that 'people' and 'communities' have all too frequently been perceived by developers as being homogeneous and passive, rather than as diverse and dynamic entities. The peculiar needs, knowledge and skills of different individuals and groups within communities have often been ignored in favour of a broad and less sensitive approach. As a result, although development projects might have benefited certain sections of the population, other elements have lost out. For example, in The Gambia, West Africa, where rice is a woman's crop and women possess the detailed knowledge and understanding of its production and processing, a series of overseas-funded irrigated rice development projects in the 1960s and 1970s achieved poor results precisely because women's considerable expertise was ignored by the development teams. As Dey comments, 'By failing to take into account the complexities of the existing farming system and concentrating on men to the exclusion of women, the irrigated rice projects have lost in the technical sense that valuable available female expertise' (1981: 122). It is essential, therefore, that future development strategies are built upon a detailed understanding of the individuals or communities which are the target of such policies, rather than being based upon the assumption that people and societies are homogeneous.

This chapter will investigate the diversity of people and their role as a key resource in the development process. First, a number of important demographic features will be considered, and this will be followed by an evaluation of some broad issues affecting the quality of life.

Population and resources: a demographic time bomb?

The question of the rate of population growth and its relationship to the availability of food and vital natural resources has exercised the minds of many scholars for centuries. Although some commentators see population growth as the 'big issue' in world development, painting a 'gloom and doom' scenario of population growth outstripping food supply, others are much less pessimistic and view population growth more as an 'engine of development' playing an important role in the development process.

A frequently cited starting point in the population and resources debate is Thomas Malthus' *An Essay on the Principle of Population*, published in 1798. Malthus described a highly pessimistic scenario of population growing more rapidly than food supply, and he advocated the need for 'preventative' and 'positive' checks on population growth. He further argued that the tension between population and resources was a fundamental cause of misery for much of humanity (Crook, 1997). More recently, Paul Ehrlich in his book *The Population Bomb* (1968) has commented:

> Americans are beginning to realize that the undeveloped countries of the world face an inevitable population–food crisis. Each year food production in undeveloped countries falls a bit further behind burgeoning population growth, and people go to bed a little bit hungrier. While there are temporary or local reversals of this trend, it now seems inevitable that it will continue to its logical conclusion: mass starvation.
>
> (Ehrlich, 1968: 17)

The Club of Rome's *Project on the Predicament of Mankind* in the early 1970s further echoed Malthus' and Ehrlich's warnings, suggesting that

> demographic pressure in the world has already attained such a high level, and is moreover so unequally distributed, that this alone must compel mankind to seek a state of equilibrium on our planet. Underpopulated areas still exist, but, considering the world as a whole, the critical point in population growth is approaching, if it has not already been reached.
>
> (Meadows et al., 1972: 191)

Key thinker

Thomas Robert Malthus (1766–1834)

Plate 5.1 Thomas Malthus
Source: Getty Images/Hulton Archive

Thomas Malthus was born in 1766 into a prosperous family near Dorking, Surrey, England. He was educated at home until 1784, and then went to Jesus College, Cambridge. Nine years later, after gaining Bachelor's and Master's degrees, he was elected a fellow of Jesus College. He took holy orders in 1797 and took charge of a small parish in Surrey. In 1798, he published the first edition of his most famous work, *An Essay on the Principle of Population as It Affects the Future Improvement of Society, with Remarks on the Speculations of Mr. Godwin,*

M. Condorcet, and Other Writers. Essay received much attention and was subsequently enlarged upon in a total of six editions, the last being published in 1816. The 1803 edition introduced the concept of a preventive check on population growth through what he called 'moral restraint'.

In 1805, Malthus became a professor of modern history and political economy at the East India Company's college at Haileybury (Hertfordshire), a position he kept until he died of heart disease in 1834. Malthus argued that the main aim of his research was to promote the happiness of mankind by identifying the real possibilities of progress. In 1819, he was elected a Fellow of the Royal Society, and in 1821 joined the Political Economy Club, whose members included influential writers such as political theorists David Ricardo and James Mill.

Despite generating a longstanding interest in the relationship between population and resources, Malthus and his followers greatly exaggerated the 'population question', and failed to anticipate the effects of the agricultural revolution (c. 1750–1850), which led to a significant increase in food production in Western Europe, and the later influence of contraceptives, which led to a decline in the fertility rate.

An alternative and much more positive perspective on the relationship between people, environment and resources was provided by economist Ester Boserup in her important book *The Conditions of Agricultural Growth* (Boserup, 1965, 1993). Boserup presented a convincing argument to show that population growth and increasing population density can in fact be key factors in generating innovation and intensification in traditional food production systems. She suggested that, provided the rate of population growth is not too rapid, populations will over time adapt their environment and cultivation strategies such that increased yields can be obtained without any significant degradation of the resource base. This viewpoint has gained greater popularity in recent years, as detailed empirical research has revealed the considerable capacity of indigenous peoples to raise the productivity of their farming systems in the face of increasing population numbers (Tiffen et al., 1994). The continuing credibility of Boserup's thesis is indicated by the re-publication of her book, with a foreword by Robert Chambers, himself a key figure in development research. Chambers comments:

> The Boserupian thesis will continue to stimulate argument and inspire research on the links between population change, agricultural technology, and now sustainability. It has stood the test of time: it is repeatedly referred to by those who have read this book and by many who have not.
>
> (Boserup, 1993: 8)

Key idea

Who is right, Malthus or Boserup?

The debate concerning the relationships between people and environmental resources goes on and on. There are many instances in reports during the colonial period where European colonial officials made scathing remarks about indigenous farming practices in Latin America, Africa and Asia. It was often assumed that environmental management strategies developed in Europe and North America were far superior to traditional methods in tropical countries of the Global South. But in the last 30 years or so, research has revealed that farmers have a remarkably good understanding of environmental resources and are capable of managing the environment so that it becomes more productive and can satisfy the needs of growing populations. Flights of terraced fields and intricate irrigation systems in places as diverse as south-west China, the Peruvian Andes and the High Atlas mountains of Morocco, testify to the ability and endeavours of people living in poor communities who have spent many hours adapting the environment to suit their needs in a perfectly sustainable way. On the contrary, many former colonies are littered with failed development schemes, where the technology which was introduced by European 'experts' proved to be totally inappropriate and machinery now lies idle and decaying. The ill-fated East African Groundnut Scheme in the 1950s, in what is now Tanzania, is a case in point, where, following the collapse of this ambitious project, the local Wagogo pastoralists rather ironically referred to the scheme as 'The white man's madness'. Had the British 'developers' undertaken detailed climate and soil analysis, and interacted with the Wagogo to discover more about local environmental characteristics, it is likely that many of the pitfalls might have been avoided (Binns, 1994a). Ester Boserup's emphasis on understanding how communities manage their local environmental resources seems a sensible way forward in formulating rural development strategies.

The relationship between population and resources also featured strongly in the Brundtland Report of 1987 (WCED, 1987), and at the United Nations Conference on Environment and Development (the so-called Earth Summit), held in Rio de Janeiro, Brazil, in June 1992 (see Chapter 3). This much-publicised event, attended by many world leaders and non-governmental organisations, was concerned with key global resources and a number of major environmental issues, such as global warming and climatic change (see Chapter 6). It was at Rio, and in subsequent publications, that the concept of sustainable development was popularised (see Chapters 3 and 7). The essence of sustainable development is the need to achieve an equilibrium between the world's basic resources and their continuing exploitation by a growing world population, so as not to jeopardise these resources for future generations. Agenda 21, the comprehensive programme of action adopted by governments at the Earth Summit, continually emphasises the links between environment, population and development (UN, 1993).

Ten years after the Rio summit, the World Summit on Sustainable Development was held in Johannesburg, South Africa, in August/September 2002, reputedly the largest conference ever held. Despite the much-publicised non-attendance of President George W. Bush of the world's wealthiest and most powerful nation (the USA), the Summit provided an opportunity to strengthen global commitments on sustainable development, as well as taking stock of progress towards the 2015 Millennium Development Goals (Earth Summit, 2002). In June 2012, in Rio de Janeiro (Brazil), 45,000 delegates and 130 heads of state and government gathered for the Rio+20 conference, but notable absences were President Barack Obama (USA), Chancellor Angela Merkel (Germany) and Prime Minister David Cameron (UK), who claimed they were too busy dealing with the European financial crisis.

The many different viewpoints expressed in the long-running debate on the dynamic relations between population and resources themselves constitute distinctive 'geographies of development'.

Where do the world's people live?

At three minutes after midnight on 12 October 1999 Fatima Nevic gave birth in Sarajevo to a boy who was symbolically heralded by the media as the world's six billionth person. By February 2015 the world's population reached 7.3 billion, and the United Nations Population Division estimated that in 2025 the figure would be 8.1 billion (UN, 2013a). But these people are by no means distributed evenly across the Earth's surface and population density varies widely (Figure 5.1). With the massive populations of China and India, these two countries account for over a third of the world's total population, and some 60% of the world's people live in the Asian region (UN, 2013a). India joined China on 15 August 1999 as the only other nation on Earth with a billion people, and, on present projections, India's population could actually overtake China's by 2030 (UN, 2013a).

Apart from some small and densely settled island states such as Barbados (with 665 persons per square kilometre), the Maldives (1,053) and Malta (1,300), and small enclaves such as Singapore (7,814), the most densely settled countries are to be found in Asia and Europe. India, with its massive population of 1,087 million, has a density of 426 persons per square kilometre, whereas Japan has 349, South Korea 518 and Bangladesh a staggering 1,218. Although European population densities nowhere reach the magnitude of Bangladesh, discounting densely settled small enclaves such as Monaco (19,033), Europe does have some relatively high population densities, such as the United Kingdom with 267 persons per square kilometre, Belgium with 371 and the Netherlands with 500.

With the exception of the polar wastes of Greenland and Antarctica, the world's most sparsely settled areas include Australia and Canada, with respectively, only three and four persons per square kilometre, and large parts of Africa. In fact, Africa is still the world's least densely settled continent, with the desert states of Mauritania and Libya having only four persons per square kilometre. In southern Africa, Botswana and Namibia have, respectively, four and three persons per square kilometre. There are, however, certain countries in Africa with unusually high densities of population, notably the tiny countries of Rwanda and Burundi in central Africa, with densities of 490 and 408 persons per square kilometre, whereas Nigeria, the continent's most populous country with over 178 million people, has a density of 196 per square kilometre (UN, 2013a).

Counting the people

A word of caution is warranted concerning the reliability of national, and therefore regional and global, population statistics. Censuses, which even in some

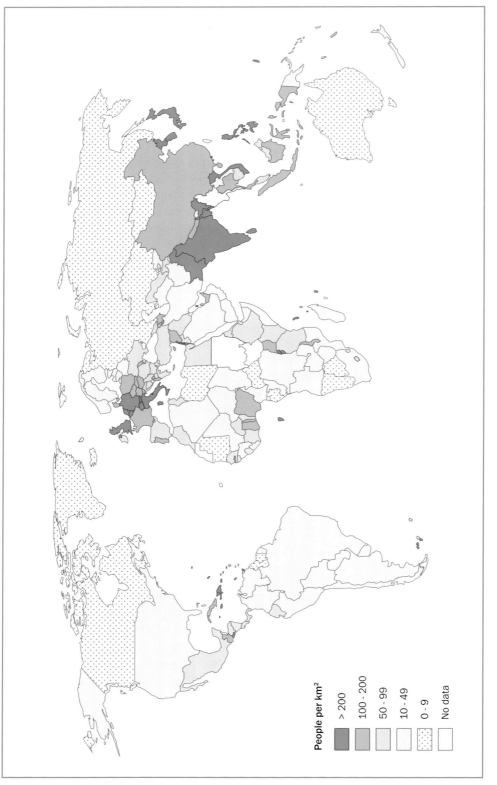

People per km²

- > 200
- 100 - 200
- 50 - 99
- 10 - 49
- 0 - 9
- No data

Figure 5.1 World population density 2014

Source: adapted from United Nations Statistics (2014).

richer countries are not always reliable, are also costly, time-consuming and require considerable expertise to administer and analyse. Consequently, some poor countries, and/or those which are politically unstable, have often been unable to conduct regular censuses, so the available data are frequently old and unreliable. Furthermore, national planning has been hampered by the lack of reliable and up-to-date figures.

Nigeria, for example, undisputedly Africa's most populous country, had its first census for almost 30 years in November 1991. The previous census with any reliability (though this was questioned) was held in 1963, after which there were three further attempts to hold censuses, on each occasion failing because regional leaders submitted exaggerated head counts in an effort to show that their people were more numerous and thus entitled to 'a bigger share of the national cake'.

The Nigerian federal government made great efforts to conduct a successful census in 1991, with three years of careful preparation, an investment of some £75 million and enlisting the help of half a million enumerators, including women who worked in Muslim areas. Estimates before 1991 had put Nigeria's population at well over 100 million, and so many Nigerians seemed genuinely shocked when the 1991 census revealed a total population of only 88.5 million! Fifteen years later, the results of the March 2006 census suggested that Nigeria's total population had increased to 140 million. More recently, the World Bank estimated Nigeria's population to be 178 million in 2014 (World Bank, 2015c).

Population change

For most of human history population growth, averaged over long periods, has remained near zero. In fact, the modern expansion of the world's population only started in the eighteenth century with the slow decline of the death rate in Europe and North America. Population growth then accelerated steadily in the twentieth century and has been particularly rapid in the in the Global South since 1950 (Table 5.1).

Merrick (1986) points out that more people have been added to the world since 1950 than in all of human history before the middle of the twentieth century – a sobering thought. Bongaarts (1995: 8) comments:

> The acceleration in growth is well demonstrated by the shortening of the time intervals needed to add successive billions to the world population. The first billion was reached early in the nineteenth century, the second billion took 120 years, the third 33 years, the fourth 14 years and the fifth (between 1974 and 1987) just 13 years.

If projections prove to be accurate, the next three billion will be added at an even faster pace, each taking just over a decade, to reach eight billion by 2024 (Bongaarts, 1995: 8). Such projections suggest that it is likely the world's population could reach around 10.8 billion in 2100.

Where and how these people will live in the future is of much interest and concern for development, since they will be by no means evenly distributed across the globe. The World Conference on Population and Development, held in Cairo in September 1994, had the aim of drawing up a 20-year programme (up to 2015) to combat overpopulation in the world, but reached deadlock on a number of issues, most notably the question of decriminalising abortion, a move which is rejected by the religious authorities of both the Catholic Church and Islam.

Table 5.1 World population growth, 1900–2100							
	Population (billions)			% increase	Estimated population (billions)		% increase
	1900	1950	1990	1950–1990	2025	2100	1990–2100
South	1.07	1.68	4.08	143	7.07	10.20	150
North	0.56	0.84	1.21	44	1.40	1.50	24
World	1.63	2.52	5.30	110	8.47	11.70	121

Source: From Bongaarts (1995). Adapted and reproduced with permission from the International Food Policy Research Institute.

The United Nations Population Division estimate that the total world population in 2050 will be 9.5 billion, of which no less than 8.2 billion (86 per cent) would be in the Global South (UN, 2013a).

The phenomenal growth of population in the South is revealed in Table 5.1, which shows that, whereas population in the North increased by 44 per cent between 1950 and 1990, the countries of the South experienced a massive growth rate of 143 per cent in the same period. Projected growth rates for the period 1990–2100 indicate a significant decline in the rate of population growth for countries of the North (24 per cent) compared with the earlier period, but there is a marked acceleration in growth in the South to 150 per cent. These countries have growth rates more than four times higher than countries in the North, and the sizes of their populations are also generally much larger than those in the North. Such growth is going to place even greater pressure on resources, which in many poor countries are already stretched. According to the World Bank, in 2013 Bangladesh was ranked 168 out of 213 in the world in terms of per capita Gross National Income (GNI) (US $3,190), and in 2009 it had a total population of 162.0 million, with an average population density of no less than 1,142 people per square kilometre (World Bank, 2013a).

Projecting the size of national and global populations is fraught with difficulty, since it is affected by such unpredictable events as natural disasters, wars and medical advances. For example, the production and wide availability of an effective and cheap vaccine to combat malaria, which affects nearly 50 per cent of the world's population and kills over half a million people every year (WHO, 2013), could have a massive impact on reducing death rates, which in turn would affect population growth rates nationally and globally. The introduction of government policies designed to increase or reduce population, will also affect growth rates, as in China, where its one-child policy had a marked effect on national population growth rates (Plate 5.2; Box 5.1).

A further issue which makes the future prediction of the size and growth of population in specific countries particularly difficult is the question of population redistribution. The movement of people within countries, perhaps from rural to urban areas, and between countries as voluntary migrants, or maybe as refugees escaping from drought or civil war, has had a significant impact on population dynamics in certain countries and regions. Chapter 8 explores this in more detail within the context of movements and flows of both people and commodities.

Plate 5.2 'One-child' poster, Guangzhou, south-eastern China
(*photo*: Tony Binns)

BOX 5.1

China's one-child population policy

The population of the world's most populous country, China, passed the 1 billion mark in 1981 and by 2000 it had reached 1,261 million. However, with an estimated average annual growth rate of 0.5 per cent between 2010 and 2014, this represents a considerable slowing down of population growth, from the 1.8 per cent per annum experienced between 1960 and 1993, and is well below the 2.2 per cent average growth rate for all countries of the South over the same period (World Bank, 2002a). This significant decline in China's population growth rate is due to the implementation of a rigid birth control policy.

In 2014 the World Bank predicted that China's population would reach well over 1.4 billion by 2025 but, with steadily declining population growth rates, the 2050 population would be under 1.4 billion.

raising the age at which a person could get married; it went from 18 to 23 for women and from 20 to 25 for men. Additionally, the county government made great efforts to spread birth control information, and to provide free services for contraception. When contraceptive methods failed, induced abortions became more common (Endicott, 1988). Reducing the fertility rate became a key priority and the slogan 'one is not too few, two will do and three are too many for you' was publicised nationally. Communities were encouraged to recommend which women should be able to have a baby and the practice of 'giving birth in turn' became widespread.

In 1980, as those born during the baby boom of 1963 were approaching the age of marriage and childbearing, the policy of one child per family was officially adopted by the National People's Congress

China: population size

1950	2005	2015	2025	2050
554,760	1,315,844	1,392,980	1,441,426	1,392,307

China: average annual rate of population change (%)

1995–2000	2000–2005	2010–2015	2020–2025	2045–2050
0.88	0.65	0.56	0.24	−0.35

Source: World Bank, 2015c

Following a marked decline in China's population during the late 1950s and 1960s, due to loss of life from disasters such as typhoons and flooding and the severe famines which followed, the country then experienced a 'baby boom' from 1963. The government increasingly questioned the value of a rapidly growing population in relation to resources under increasing pressure, and during the 1970s various attempts were made to encourage both family planning and delaying marriage. For example, in Shifang County of Sichuan Province, the local authorities responded in 1971 by

and was incorporated into the country's new 1982 Constitution (Jowett, 1990: 117). The State Council deemed it 'necessary to launch a crash programme over the coming twenty or thirty years, calling on each couple, except those in minority nationality areas, to have a single child . . . Our aim is to strive to limit the population to a maximum of 1200 million by the end of the century' (quoted in Jowett, 1990: 117). A number of relaxations to the policy were permitted, particularly where the first child was a girl, also

▶

BOX 5.1 (continued)

among minority peoples living mainly in western China, and in the rural areas of certain provinces. It is probably in the urban areas where the policy has been most strictly enforced (Leeming, 1993: 61). To enforce the one-child policy, a system of economic rewards and penalties was introduced, such as parents being offered a 5–10 per cent salary bonus for limiting their families to one child and a 10 per cent salary deduction for those who produced more than two children (Jowett, 1990: 119). In 1988, Mrs Lui, Director of Number 2 Neighbourhood Committee, Hua Long Chao Sub-district in the Sichuan city of Chongqing, commented that the main job of the neighbourhood committee is to 'educate the people to realise the importance of the one-child family' (Binns, personal communication, 1988). Permits to have children were given annually to about 100 women in the neighbourhood, with priority being given to older women. The local factory, where most neighbourhood dwellers worked, evidently played a key role in awarding points to female workers, points that affected their relative position in the queue to receive a permit. Strong sanctions were imposed if a woman became pregnant without a permit, and the committee would notify the government authorities and the factory. An abortion was usually required, a fine imposed, wage increases frozen and a permit to become pregnant again would be further delayed.

China's total fertility rate fell from 6.66 in 1968, to 2.32 in 1987, and in urban areas decreased from 3.2 in 1970 to 1.3 in 1987. However, despite slowing down the population growth rate, the one-child policy has had widespread social implications. The policy fundamentally conflicts with traditional Chinese family values, in which children are seen as a source of happiness and fulfilment, as well as guaranteeing the continuation of the family line. The policy has undoubtedly been unpopular, but much as they would like another child, many women accepted official arguments that they must go without. The policy also led to even greater prestige being given to the birth of a son, particularly in the rural areas where there are no state pensions. Much concern has been expressed in China about the long-term social effects of the creation of a generation of pampered

'little emperors' with no sisters and cousins. Furthermore, the under-registration of female births, abandonment or neglect of girl babies, prenatal sex testing followed by selective abortion, and instances of female infanticide were frequently reported in the Chinese press in the 1980s. In 2000, the sex ratio at birth was 117 boys for every 100 girls, with the imbalance even greater in rural areas. The Chinese government attempted to reduce the cultural discrimination against girls, with a 'care for girls' campaign in rural areas. Some commentators criticised the one-child policy on the grounds that it represented an infringement of a woman's control of her reproduction process 'since many women, whilst perhaps not wanting to have to go on until they have one or more sons, do wish to have at least two children' (Endicott, 1988: 179).

A further concern has been that the policy will completely transform the country's age structure, and in time will result in a declining workforce and a very aged population. The baby boom of the 1960s will eventually result in a large number of retired people in the 2030s. As Jowett comments:

> By then, over-65s could constitute more than 25 per cent of the population and thus, within a lifetime, the number of retired will have increased from one in twenty to one in four. Such a high level of old-age dependency is unprecedented even in today's developed countries where the over-65s generally constitute 10–15 per cent of a country's population.
> (Jowett, 1990: 121)

Concern about the implications of supporting a rapidly ageing population, where the 'over-60s' cohort is projected to increase from one-seventh to one quarter of the population by the early 2030s, led the Chinese government in 2014 to relax the one-child policy in certain provinces. Couples were allowed to have a second child if either parent was an 'only child', whilst in rural areas, couples could have a second child if their first child was a girl.

In spite of significantly reducing China's population growth rate, the one-child policy has received much criticism, not least because it represents a massive 'experiment' in social engineering.

Country	GNI per capita (US$)	Birth rate	Death rate	Infant mortality rate	Under-5 mortality rate	World rank	Life expectancy at birth
Bangladesh	1010	20	6	33	41	61	70
Brazil	11690	15	6	12	14	103	74
China	6560	12	7	11	13	108	75
India	1570	21	8	41	53	46	66
Jamaica	5220	15	6	14	17	88	73
Japan	46330	8	10	2	3	186	83
Mali	670	47	13	78	137	2	55
Sierra Leone	660	37	17	107	161	4	45
Sweden	61760	12	10	2	3	186	82
United Kingdom	41680	13	9	4	5	165	82
USA	53470	13	8	6	7	145	79
Zimbabwe	860	32	10	55	89	37	58

Source: World Bank (2012) World Development Indicators 2012. Washington: World Bank Publications.

Understanding population statistics

Changes in population growth rates over time are affected by a wide range of factors, but are essentially controlled by the changing relationship between birth rates and death rates. Table 5.2 presents population statistics for a sample of low-, middle- and high-income countries from across the world.

The crude birth rate is the most common index of the fertility of the population and is a ratio of the number of live births to the total population, usually expressed as so many per 1,000. Although the United Kingdom and the USA had birth rates of 13 in 2012, Mali and Sierra Leone in West Africa had rates of 47 and 37, respectively, indicating a decline from the figures of 51 and 49 for these African countries in 1970. The crude death rate is the number of deaths per 1,000 of the population. Considering the same four countries, the United Kingdom and the USA had death rates of 9 and 8 in 2012, whereas Mali and Sierra Leone recorded death rates of 13 and 17 in 2012 (World Bank, 2012b).

Two other important indicators of the quality of life and levels of development are infant mortality and life expectancy. The infant mortality rate measures the number of deaths of infants under one-year-old per 1,000 live births. This variable reflects general living conditions and also the health and nutritional status of pregnant and lactating mothers. Infant mortality rates in 2012 varied

from two in Sweden, four in the United Kingdom to 107 in Sierra Leone, one of the world's poorest countries. However, there is not always a direct relationship between wealth and infant and child mortality. For example, Vietnam, with a per capita GNI in 2012 of only US $4,892, had an infant mortality rate of 18, whereas Gabon in central Africa, with a per capita GNI over three times greater (US $16,977), had an infant mortality rate which was more than twice that of Vietnam (42) (UNDP, 2014).

Life expectancy at birth also reflects general living standards, nutrition and health care, and it reveals tremendous inequalities at the global scale. For example, as Table 5.2 shows, a child born in Japan in 2012 could expect to live for 83 years, but in Sierra Leone an average lifespan of only 45 years is all that a child could expect.

The demographic transition

The changing relationship over time between fertility and mortality rates is clearly demonstrated through the demographic transition model, which identifies four or five key stages that countries go through in their demographic history (Figure 5.2).

Stage 1 (high stationary or pre-transition phase) is characterised by high birth rates and high death rates, such that population growth is static or negligible. This situation applied to pre-eighteenth-century Europe and North America, but in many countries of the South this remained the position up to the Second World War.

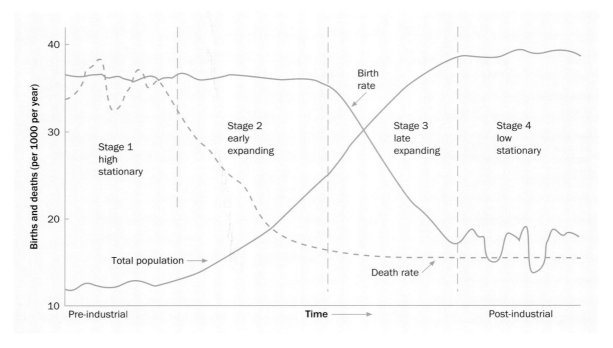

Figure 5.2 Demographic transition model
Source: adapted from Mayhew, S. (1997) *A Dictionary of Geography*. Oxford University Press. By permission of Oxford University Press, Inc.

In the next phase (Stage 2: early expanding or early transition) the death rate (mortality) begins to decline with better living standards, largely due to improvements in nutrition and public health. The incidence of famines and epidemics also falls. However, the birth rate (fertility) remains high, so population growth accelerates. In much of Africa, Asia and Latin America mortality did not begin to decline until the first half of the twentieth century. By the late 1960s the annual average death rate had dropped to 15 per 1,000, whereas the birth rate remained high at 40 per 1,000, resulting in an annual growth rate of 25 per 1,000 people or 2.5 per cent. In 1979 Kenya recorded an annual population growth rate of 4.1 per cent, one of the highest in the world. Some African countries today still have the highest birth rates in the world. Kenya's crude birth rate in 2012 was 36, whereas Uganda and Niger had even higher rates of 44 and 50, respectively (World Bank, 2012b). These growth rates are well above those observed in European populations when they were at the same stage in the transition.

Stage 3 (late expanding or mid-transition phase), occurs when improved technology in agriculture and

industry, together with better education systems and legislation controlling child employment, lead to a decline in the economic and social value of children. Furthermore, the breakdown of the extended family system places greater physical, emotional and financial costs on the parents. Couples start to use contraception to limit family size and the birth rate begins to fall. The death rate continues to decline and population growth at this point reaches its maximum. This stage occurred in countries of the North in the late nineteenth and early twentieth centuries. Elsewhere, in the last two decades there have been marked reductions in birth rates in East and Southeast Asia, due to a combination of family planning programmes and socio-economic development. Thailand had an annual population growth rate of 0.3 per cent for the period 2010-2014 and South Korea 0.4 per cent (World Bank, 2012b).

In Stage 4 (low stationary or late transition phase), the death rate reaches its lowest level and as fertility steadily declines, the rate of population growth begins to fall. Most countries of the South are currently in the mid- and late-transition stages. Some Caribbean countries, such as Cuba and Jamaica, have nearly completed the transition, and their respective population growth rates of 0.0 and 0.3 are lower than those of the UK (0.6) and USA (0.7) (World Bank, 2012b). Some writers, such as Bongaarts (1994), add a fifth stage to the model, known as the 'declining or post-transition phase'. This stage is characterised by a new equilibrium being achieved between births and deaths, such that population growth is close to zero; in some cases, there is even negative growth. Many European countries have now reached this stage. For example, average annual population growth rates for 2010–2014 are as low as −0.5 in Portugal, −0.2 in Spain and 0.5 per cent in Germany. Some of the most negative growth rates are found in the Russian Federation, −0.2 per cent for the same period, whereas in Hungary and Latvia the figures are −0.2 per cent and −1.0 per cent, respectively. The average figure for the 'more developed regions' over this period is 0.20 per cent (World Bank, 2012b).

Population policies

The reasons underlying the various changes reflected in the demographic transition are highly complex. It is unwise to blindly advocate the strict control of population growth in poor countries. As O'Connor argues in the case of the African continent:

> there is no evidence to suggest that rapid population growth is the main cause of poverty . . . which was just as widespread when the growth rate was much slower. In so far as the rapid growth results from high fertility it can be seen alternatively as a consequence of poverty.

(O'Connor, 1991: 54)

Population growth is undoubtedly a problem in some countries, but it is invariably a symptom of other problems such as poverty and lack of security. Having more children among poor families has traditionally been regarded as an insurance strategy to ensure household survival in places where infant and child mortality rates are high. Children frequently play a vital role in generating household income, as well as providing social security in the absence of any state provision, such as under structural adjustment programmes (see Chapter 3). The most successful initiatives to reduce family size start by tackling underlying causes and finding ways of ameliorating poverty and insecurity, and helping to improve the health of mothers and children. Experience has shown that, with such strategies, both fertility and mortality rates should begin to fall (Gould, 2009).

Some governments have, however, taken a strong interventionist line to control population growth. In some cases, these policies have been aimed at reducing population; whereas in others, pro-natalist policies have been adopted to increase population. The Nazi regime in Germany during the 1930s and early 1940s was strongly pro-natalist, generating much propaganda on the need to create a master Aryan race. A wide range of measures was introduced, such as generous family allowances and tax concessions for large families, taxes on unmarried adults and prosecution for induced abortions.

Romania under the Ceausescu regime also adopted a strong pro-natalist line, with abortion becoming illegal in 1966 and tight controls placed on the availability of contraceptives. In the following year, 1967, the crude birth rate almost doubled to 27 per 1,000, causing considerable pressures on education, employment and housing as the 1967–1970 bulge moved through the age groups.

Elsewhere in the world, Israel and Saudi Arabia have also encouraged population growth, primarily to strengthen their political power. Israel's average annual population growth rate in the period 1975–2004 was 2.3 per cent, whereas Saudi Arabia's rate was 4.1 per cent (UNDP, 2006), and reached as high as 5.2 per cent per annum during the period 1980–1990 (World Bank, 1996). The upsurge of Islamic fundamentalism has resulted in some states becoming pro-natalist. By introducing its New Population Policy in 1984, Malaysia reversed a longstanding policy of promoting family planning to encourage women to 'go for five', to catch up with more populous neighbouring states and to prevent ethnic Malays from being dominated by the Chinese population. In response to a shortage of labour, Singapore from 1987 adopted a more selective pro-natalist stance, encouraging educated and professional couples to 'have three, or more if you can afford it', rather than 'stop at two' (Drakakis-Smith et al., 1993). Singapore's average annual population growth rate was 2.2 per cent during the 1975–2004 period, and 1.6 per cent between 2010 and 2014 (World Bank 2012b).

However, with growing concern about the population–resource balance, anti-natalist policies are now rather more common than pro-natalist measures. India launched a family planning programme as early as 1951 (see Box 5.2), and during the 1960s many other countries followed in response to current development thinking and the production of the contraceptive pill and intrauterine devices. In 1965, US President Lyndon Johnson, addressing a United Nations audience argued, 'Let us act on the fact that less than five dollars invested in population control is worth a hundred dollars invested in economic growth' (Stycos, 1971: 115). The

United Nations began to provide advisory services to family planning programmes in 1965, and by 1976 some 63 countries in the South had initiated such programmes. The 1974 World Population Conference in Bucharest brought population issues and family planning initiatives under the political spotlight. At this meeting, countries of the North were strongly criticised by many from the South for placing too much emphasis on the population issue in development strategies, to the neglect of promoting social and economic progress.

BOX 5.2

Planning the growth of India's population

The population of India was estimated at 1,236 million in 2012, and is projected to increase at an average annual rate of 1.2 per cent to reach 1,400 million by 2026. The crude birth rate is projected to decline from 23.2 in 2005 to 16.0 by 2025 due to declining fertility. Problems associated with rapid population growth were recognised by the Indian government soon after independence in 1947, and since then there has been a succession of policies designed to control the burgeoning population. However, in 2012, India spent only 1.3 per cent of GDP on public health, compared with 7.8 per cent in the UK and 8.3 per cent in the USA.

India's Family Welfare Programme was introduced four years after Independence in 1951 and initially focused on improving the health of mothers and children. However, from the Third Five-year Plan period (1961–1966) there was a marked shift in emphasis from the welfare of women and children towards the objective of achieving population stabilisation. The 1977 Population Policy emphasised the need for an educational and motivational approach to strengthen the voluntary acceptance of family planning.

The International Conference on Population and Development in 1994 and the Beijing Women's Conference in 1995 had a significant effect on India's family planning policy, such that in 1997 the Community Needs Assessment Approach was introduced with decentralised participatory planning that was concerned primarily with addressing clients' needs. The Reproductive and Child Health Programme,

also launched in 1997, emphasised the principle of client satisfaction and the provision of high quality comprehensive and integrated health services. This Programme seeks to integrate services for the prevention and management of unwanted pregnancy, the promotion of safe motherhood and child survival, and the prevention and management of reproductive tract infections and sexually transmitted infections. Attention is directed particularly towards underserved and neglected population groups, including adolescents, and economically and socially disadvantaged groups, such as urban slum dwellers and tribal populations. For the first time in the history of the Family Welfare Programme attention is now focused firmly on gender concerns.

The National Population Policy (NPP), launched in February 2000, has supported the provision of client-based services, and provides a framework for achieving the objectives of population stabilisation and promoting reproductive health within the wider context of sustainable development. In the medium term, the NPP aimed to bring the total fertility rate down to replacement level by 2010, using strategies such as grassroots service delivery, empowering women, encouraging male involvement, meeting the need for family welfare services, addressing the needs of disadvantaged and underserved population groups and establishing public–private partnerships.

Various promotional measures have been introduced, not only for sterilisation, but linked to poverty, delaying marriage, antenatal and delivery care,

BOX 5.2 (continued)

birth registration, birth of a girl child and immunisation. More specifically, cash incentives are provided for women who have their first child after 19 years of age, and couples below the poverty line are rewarded if they postpone their marriage and have their first child after the mother reaches the age of 21. Rewards are also offered if parents adopt a terminal method after the birth of their second child. In some states stricter policies have been introduced, such as in Madhya Pradesh, where individuals who marry before the legal age are prevented from seeking jobs, gaining admission to educational institutions and applying for loans. Furthermore, couples with more than two children are prevented from contesting local elections. It remains to be seen whether such strategies will be effective in controlling population growth.

Indonesia, the world's fourth most populous nation, adopted family planning in 1970 as a key element in the drive for economic growth, and this policy was revitalised in 2012. Considerable success was achieved between 1970 and 1999, with the average number of children per woman falling from 5.6 to 2.5 (UNICEF, 2001). China's one-child policy (see Box 5.1) is probably one of the most well-known and most rigid anti-natalist policies, affecting one-fifth of the world's population and enforced through tight community control and a series of rewards and sanctions. As a result, the 1970 crude birth rate of 33 per 1,000 fell to 18 in 1979 and 12 in 2012 (World Bank, 2012b).

Other family planning schemes have commonly rewarded individuals with various tax concessions, with free or preferential medical treatment (South Korea), priority schooling (Singapore) or even a new sari (Bangladesh). It is in Asia that family planning programmes have been most widely implemented, whereas progress has been slower in Latin America, largely due to the proscription of 'artificial' methods of contraception by the Roman Catholic Church. Although evidence suggests that individual families frequently disregard the Church's views on birth control, government policy makers are likely to be more strongly influenced.

Another important factor affecting the size of families is the status of women in society. Although practice differs widely, Muslim societies are generally strongly patriarchal; men can have up to four wives and female education is often a low priority, since women are expected to stay in the home. The 1979 fundamentalist revolution in Iran swiftly overturned the Western-style policies introduced by the Shah, which had given a considerable degree of emancipation to women. Under the new regime a woman was required to gain her husband's consent to work, access to sterilisation and abortion was tightly controlled and the minimum age of marriage for women was reduced from 18 to 15 years. In the period from 1980 to 1990 Iran had an average annual population growth rate of 3.5 per cent (World Bank, 1996a).

Since such population policies led to shrinking family size in the world's most populous countries, one British newspaper in January 1998 claimed that the 'population bomb' had been defused (Figure 5.3), although many of the world's poorest nations, and particularly those in Africa, still continue to have rapidly growing populations. According to Figure 5.3, it is projected that in 2020 Africa's most populous country, Nigeria, will be one of the world's six largest countries (*The Independent*, 1998: 11).

Population structure

Key elements in the demographic transition process, together with the impact of disasters such as war, famine and disease epidemics are manifested in changes to the population structure. Typically, countries of the South with declining death rates, high birth rates and low life expectancy have youthful populations (Plate 5.3). Table 5.3 clearly shows how some of the poorer countries with high population growth rates have a large proportion of their populations under the age of 18. In Mali and Sierra Leone, respectively 50.7 per cent and 49.1 per cent of the populations are under 18, whereas in more developed countries these figures are much lower (Japan 15.9 per cent, Sweden 20.4 per cent). These statistics have implications for child welfare, especially educational provision.

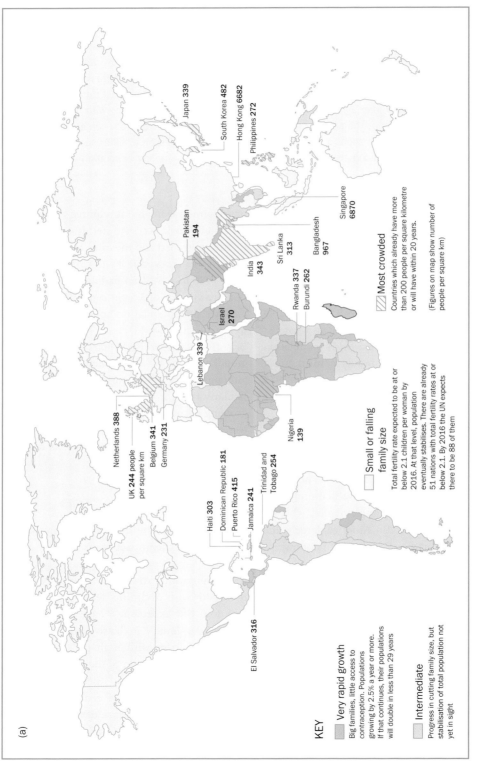

Figure 5.3 (a) Family sizes are shrinking rapidly, although human numbers are still soaring in many of the world's poorest nations. *The Independent*, 12 January 1998

Source: © reproduced by permission of *The Independent*

KEY

Very rapid growth
Big families, little access to contraception. Populations growing by 2.5% a year or more. If that continues, their populations will double in less than 29 years

Intermediate
Progress in cutting family size, but stabilisation of total population not yet in sight

Small or falling family size
Total fertility rate expected to be at or below 2.1 children per woman by 2016. At that level, population eventually stabilises. There are already 51 nations with total fertility rates at or below 2.1. By 2016 the UN expects there to be 88 of them

Most crowded
Countries which already have more than 200 people per square kilometre or will have within 20 years.

(Figures on map show number of people per square km)

El Salvador **316**

Haiti **303**
Dominican Republic **181**
Puerto Rico **415**
Jamaica **241**

Trinidad and Tobago **254**

UK **244** people per square km
Netherlands **388**
Belgium **341**
Germany **231**

Lebanon **339**
Israel **270**

Nigeria **139**

Rwanda **337**
Burundi **262**

Pakistan **194**

India **343**
Sri Lanka **313**
Bangladesh **967**

Japan **339**
South Korea **482**
Hong Kong **6682**
Philippines **272**

Singapore **6870**

(a)

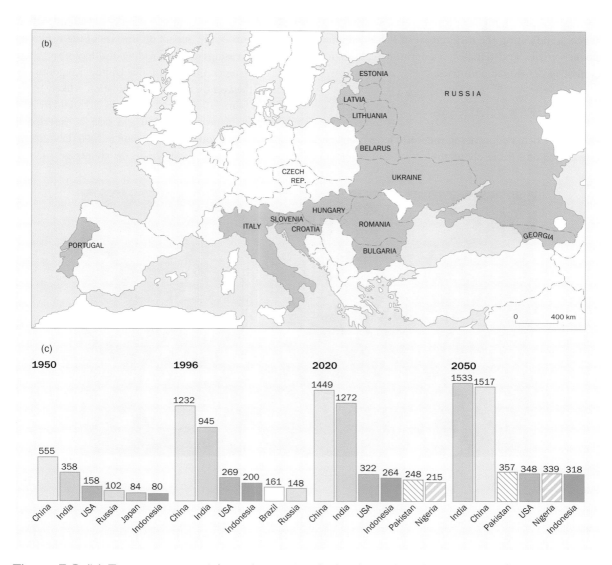

Figure 5.3 (b) European countries where population has already begun to fall
(c) The six biggest countries (in millions of people). The data are from the United Nations
Population division and the projections to 2050 are from the 'medium variant'
Source: adapted from *The Independent*, 1998

The structure of a nation's population is clearly revealed in an age–sex diagram, commonly known as a 'population pyramid'. The population pyramids for Ghana and the United Kingdom reveal quite different population structures (Figure 5.4a and b). In fact, only the diagram for Ghana actually resembles a pyramid, with a wide base indicating a youthful population and a steeply tapering top; there are fewer people in the older age groups due to an average life expectancy at birth of only 61 years. In sharp contrast, the diagram for the United Kingdom is hardly a pyramid, and is typical of a more stable population situation, with a smaller proportion of the population in the lower age groups and a greater proportion in the upper age groups, reflecting an average life expectancy that is 20 years greater than for Ghana. Interestingly, the UK figure also shows a higher proportion of women over 70 years, indicating the differential in life expectancy between males and females, a common feature in a number of developed countries.

Ageing populations

Many of the richer countries in the world have been concerned for some time about the social and economic implications of their steadily ageing populations, particularly in terms of the impact on the size of the workforce and the increasing cost of providing health care and social security to older groups. In the United Kingdom, for example, the average age of the population is likely to rise from 38.8 years in 2000 to 42.6 years in 2025, and by 2040 the number of people aged 80 and over is expected to double to 4.9 million from 2.4 million in 2000 (UN, 2013a). Some of the 'newly industrialising countries', such as

Plate 5.3 Children in The Gambia – a youthful population
(*photo*: Tony Binns)

Table 5.3 Proportion of the population under 18 years old in selected countries, 2009

Country	Total population (millions)	Population under 18 years (millions)	Proportion of total population under 18 years (%)
Bangladesh	162.0	61.1	37.7
Brazil	191.3	60.0	31.3
China	1331.2	335.9	25.2
India	1171.1	447.4	38.2
Jamaica	2.7	1.0	37.0
Japan	128.6	20.5	15.9
Mali	13.0	6.6	50.7
Sierra Leone	5.7	2.8	49.1
Sweden	9.3	1.9	20.4
United Kingdom	61.8	13.1	21.1
USA	307.7	77.3	25.1
Zimbabwe	12.5	6.0	48.0

Source: WHO, UNAIDS, & UNICEF (2012) *Global HIV/AIDS Response: Epidemic Update and Health Sector Progress towards Universal Access: Progress Report 2011*. Geneva.

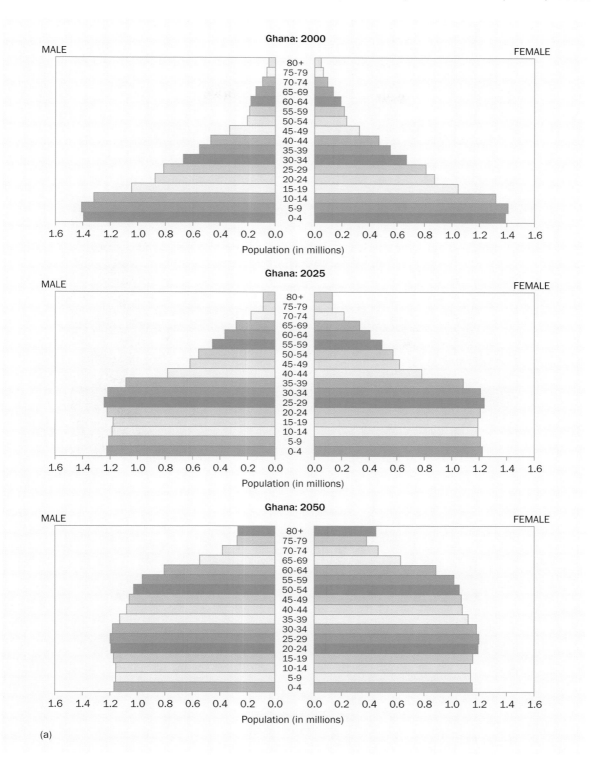

(a)

Figure 5.4 *(continued)*

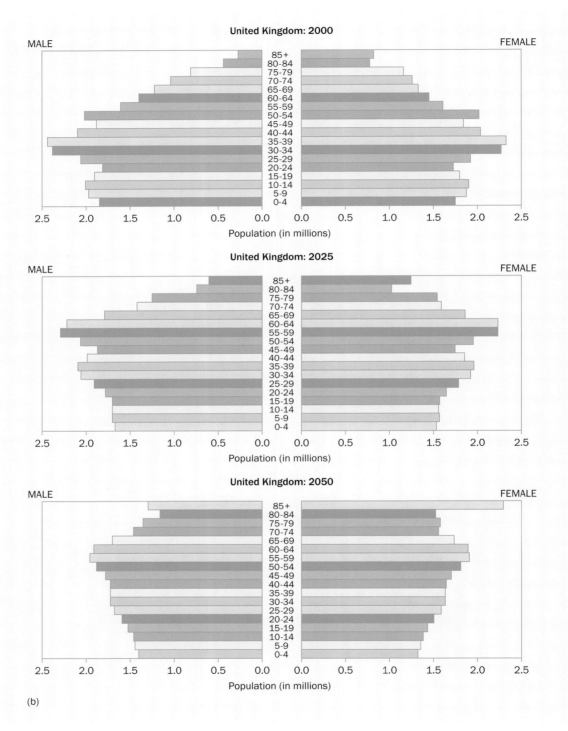

Figure 5.4 Population pyramids for: a) Ghana and b) the United Kingdom, 2000, 2025 and 2050

Source: adapted from http://populationpyramid.net/

Singapore and South Korea, are also experiencing a 'greying' of their populations, with an increasing proportion in the higher age groups. Globally, the number of people aged over 60 is the fastest growing section of the population, registering an increase of 63 per cent between 1960 and 1980, and with a predicted quadrupling of the size of this age group between 1955 and 2025 (UN, 2013a). Interestingly, between 1980 and 2000 the biggest increases in the elderly population occurred in Africa and Asia, despite their relative poverty and poorer health and welfare systems compared with many richer countries (Morrissey, 1999). The United Nations declared 1999 the International Year of Older Persons, advocating the fostering of a 'culture of ageing', that considers older persons as both beneficiaries and agents of development. While the ageing of populations in richer countries gives cause for concern, it is likely that many poorer countries, with multiple calls on limited funding, will experience even greater difficulty in meeting the needs of their elderly populations (Ageing and Development, 2002; Plate 5.4).

Critical reflection

Grey Power New Zealand

Grey Power is an effective lobby organisation in New Zealand which works to 'promote the welfare and well-being of all those citizens in the 50 plus age group'. The organisation's objectives and associated activities are indicative of the likely growing voice and influence of older people as national populations become older, particularly in the North.

Grey Power's aims and objectives

1 To advance, support and protect the welfare and well-being of older people.
2 To affirm and protect that statutory right of every New Zealand resident to a sufficient New Zealand Superannuation (retirement pension) entitlement.
3 To strive for a provision of a quality Health Care system to all New Zealand residents regardless of income and location.
4 To oppose all discriminatory and disadvantageous legislation affecting rights, security and dignity.
5 To be non-aligned with any political party, and to present a strong united lobby to all parliamentary and statutory bodies on matters affecting New Zealanders.
6 To promote and establish links with kindred organisations.
7 To promote recognition of the wide-ranging services provided by senior citizens of New Zealand.
8 To gain recognition as an appropriate voice for all older New Zealanders.

Source: http://www.greypower.co.nz/.
Accessed 13 February 2015.

Grey Power New Zealand has successfully raised the profile of issues and concerns affecting the country's older people and achieves a good amount of media attention. There are organisations such as Grey Power New Zealand in other developed countries which have been successful to a greater or lesser extent in giving older people a voice in shaping government policy and improving their quality of life.

What do you believe is the potential role for such organisations in poorer countries? From literature and internet searches, can you find any examples of such organisations in poorer countries?

Quality of life

Households

Sadly, the world is a very unequal place and not all people enjoy equal access to basic needs and a satisfactory quality of life. As we have already seen, variables such as life expectancy and infant mortality vary greatly from one country to another. We should be aware that national statistics produced by the World Bank, the United Nations Development Programme (UNDP) and other agencies also conceal marked

Plate 5.4 Supporting older people in Hong Kong
(*photo*: Elona Hoover, jesidewalks)

variations which exist within and between different regions in specific countries, within and between rural and urban areas and also between different communities and households. The household is still the key living unit in most countries of the Global South, which also usually controls production, consumption and decision making. Households have become an increasingly important focus of study in recent years, since it has been recognised that 'the very success of development policy is likely to be undermined by a failure to view the household and family in a holistic manner' (Haddad, 1992: 1). Households in the South are typically larger than those in the North, and rather than merely comprising parents and children, they may also include grandparents, unmarried aunts and uncles, as well as more distant relatives (see Chapters 9 and 10). The term 'extended family' is often used to describe such households. Urban-based households frequently retain strong links with their rural relatives, particularly those who live in the ancestral village, to which regular visits are common and where urban dwellers may have farmland.

Household development cycle

All households pass through a developmental cycle, during which their size and composition may change and the all-important ratio between workers and dependants changes over time. At certain stages in this developmental cycle, households may be under considerable pressure and this may directly impact on the quality of life, for example in terms of disposable income and nutritional intake. Households with a high proportion of very young or old members may encounter difficulties, since relatively few active workers in the household may have to support a large number of dependants.

Marked inequalities between households is also a characteristic of many countries of the Global South. More powerful households may be ethnically distinctive and better educated; they are key elements in the local, and possibly national, power structures, having good links with government officials, police, large landowners and traders; and they are frequently well endowed with assets and income. Poor households, however, are often less well educated, have poorer nutrition, are likely to be ignorant of the law and have few assets apart from their labour. Poor households are often vulnerable and susceptible to exploitation as they may become locked into cycles of debt, and they may depend upon the assistance of one or more richer patrons. The concept of social capital (as discussed in Chapter 3) is useful in recognising the levels of loyalty and response that a household can sometimes tap during vulnerable or hard times.

Household pressures, responsibilities and gender inequalities

Different pressures and responsibilities also exist within households. In some rural African societies, for example, husbands and wives may live in separate houses in a village compound, have very different household responsibilities and quite separate incomes. Age and gender differentiation in household labour inputs and expenditure patterns has long been appreciated, with women often displaying greater concern for others, particularly children (Barrett and Browne, 1995).

The gender of the household member who directly benefits from development policy interventions may be relevant to the intra-household distribution of wealth and resources, and there is a suggestion that 'enhancing and securing female earnings appears to make sound policy sense' (Kabeer, 1992: 51). In fact, women's ability to maximise both their own welfare and the welfare of their dependants may be severely constrained by power relations within the household.

There has been a strong call for 'mainstreaming' gender considerations in policy development and interventions. The signing of the Beijing Platform for Action in 1995 showed a commitment by many governments to achieving gender equality and the empowerment of women. The Council of Europe defines gender mainstreaming as 'the reorganization, improvement, development and evaluation of policy processes, so that a gender equality perspective is incorporated in all policies at all levels and at all stages, by the actors normally involved in policy-making' (Council of Europe, 1998: 15). However, the process of actually implementing gender mainstreaming is more complex, and evidence of this is rather patchy (see also Chapter 10). In Rwanda, Burundi and the Democratic Republic of Congo (DRC), where women constitute the majority of smallholder farmers, 'despite their importance in the agricultural economy of these countries, development projects focusing on their productive role in farming are yet to be integrated in national agricultural planning and policies' (Ochieng et al., 2014: 342).

The contributions of women to household income and welfare need to be much better understood. It is estimated that 70 per cent of the food of tropical Africa is produced by women, and yet far too frequently it is assumed that all farmers are men: 'Many of the most demanding farm jobs, such as hoeing, weeding and harvesting are done by women, in addition to taking care of young children, collecting firewood and water and processing and cooking food' (Binns, 1994a: 88; Plate 5.5; Figure 5.5).

An important report from the United Nations Food and Agriculture Organization (FAO) revealed a significant 'gender gap' in relation to agriculture – 'A large body of empirical evidence from many different countries shows that female farmers are just as efficient as their male counterparts, but they have less land and use fewer inputs, so they produce less' (FAO, 2011: 4). FAO contends that women have less access than men to key assets, inputs and services such as land, livestock, labour, education, extension and financial services and technology, and that 'if women had the same access to productive resources as men, they could increase yields on their farms by 20–30 percent' (FAO, 2011: 5). A study undertaken among smallholder farmers in Rwanda, Burundi and the Democratic Republic of Congo (DRC) found that, despite the importance of women farmers, their crop yields were often low and they had little control over crop management strategies. The study concluded that 'It is imperative to empower women with the monetary and technical support they need in order to enable them to play a larger role in crop management, and boost their agricultural productivity. Women must be provided with services that improve their control over land . . . and easier access to rural credit and extension services that are necessary for acquiring inputs for crop production' (Ochieng et al., 2014: 359).

Where modern contract farming exists it is generally the men who control the contracts, yet much of the farmwork is actually done by women. Research on contract sugar farming in South Africa indicated that on 70 per cent of the farms women were the main farmers (Porter and Phillips-Howard, 1997). In cases where women are in rural wage employment, it is often the case that women's work is seasonal, part-time and often poorly paid. Evidence from Bangladesh suggests that 80 per cent of women, but only 40 per cent of men, have low income jobs in the rural sector (FAO, 2011: 18).

A study focusing on the household and gender impacts of the introduction of Green Revolution technology in India suggested that the need for more cash to pay for costly inputs of high yielding crop varieties, tools and machinery has in many cases 'forced women to work as agricultural labourers, increased the need for unpaid female labour for farming tasks, thereby augmenting women's already high labour burden, and has displaced women's wage-earning opportunities through mechanization' (Satyavathi et al., 2010: 442). It is suggested that such impacts need to be considered early in the planning stage, with the development of 'a new agricultural research and extension agenda that integrates gender analysis into the technology generation and dissemination process. Gender equity should form an important variable in the holistic analysis of farming systems in future' (Satyavathi et al., 2010: 448).

Many development schemes have failed and tensions within households and communities generated through misunderstanding the different roles and responsibilities of women and men. Household analysis should take note of relationships between households (inter-household), as well as the composition of, and relationships within, individual households (intra-household). For example, in eastern Sierra Leone among the Mende, Leach (1991) found that in addition to working on the household farm, women and men undertake separately a range of productive activities. Whereas men gained independent incomes from selling bushmeat, palm wine tapping and undertaking day labour, many women made individual rice swamps, cassava and groundnut farms and vegetable gardens. Some women also traded commodities, such as salt and dried fish, from their homes or were active in local markets (Leach, 1991). In polygamous households, co-wives usually had separate individual enterprises and their consumption unit consisted of themselves and their own children.

Agricultural change has altered the division of labour between women and men, such that with the increasing production and sale of coffee and cocoa,

Plate 5.5 Women farmers harvesting rice in The Gambia
(*photo*: Tony Binns)

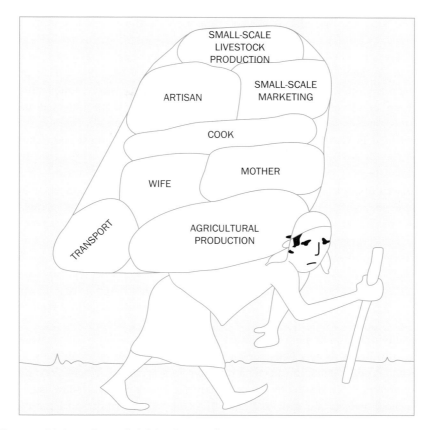

Figure 5.5 The multiple roles of Africa's rural women
Source: from www.coop.org/women/ica-ilo-manual/transparencies.htm. 2 May 2001.

'wives are expected to assist with harvesting and pro-cessing, receiving only a discretionary gift of cloth and the right to glean fallen produce in return' (Leach, 1991: 47). Women have also increased their work on the family rice farm, whereas work on tree crops was regarded as a woman's duty for her husband. These responsibilities could take significant time away from a woman's independent vegetable gardening or trading. However, Leach found that the life cycle of individuals and households was significant in that middle-aged men, who had built up resources through farming or trade, might relieve their wives' workloads by recruit-ing labour to help with the tree crop harvest or to plant rice, or might possibly help with clearing the swamp and the provision of trading capital. As Leach com-ments, 'Such wives tend to complain less of overburden, although they are just as concerned to maintain their own income streams' (Leach, 1991: 48).

In the south Indian state of Kerala, state government policies have significantly improved the position of women relative to other parts of India. It is common for women to inherit and own land, giving them financial independence and power of their own. Keralese women are regarded as an asset rather than a drain on a family's finances, such that instead of paying out an expensive dowry when daughters marry, parents in Kerala receive money from the bridegroom's family.

Although Kerala is one of India's poorer states, state government policies have led to a female life expec-tancy of over 75 years (compared with 68 years for India as a whole), infant mortality is only 14 per cent, and the female adult literacy rate of 87.7 per cent is the highest of any state in India. The average age of mar-riage for women in Kerala at 22 years is one of the highest in India and, together with the widespread use of contraceptives, this has led to an average household size of 4.3 compared with 4.8 for India as a whole (Global Eye, 2002).

The Sustainable Development Goals, launched by the United Nations in September 2015, and building on the Millennium Development Goals launched in 2000, place strong emphasis on the need for 'gender-sensitive' development strategies, whilst a specific focus is provided in Goal 5 'achieve gender equality and empower all women and girls' (UN, 2015b). The associated targets include the need to end all forms of discrimination against all women and girls, providing women with equal rights to economic resources, and recognising and valuing unpaid care and domestic work through the provision of appropriate public services, infrastructure and social protection policies (UN, 2015b).

Children

Just as gender inequalities need to be both recognised and addressed, there also needs to be a better understanding of the roles and needs of children and youth in households and communities. A frequently ignored aspect in many household budgets and survival strategies concerns the costs and benefits of having children, and especially the important work that they do (Box 5.3). As Ansell suggests, 'Child labour is often seen in the West as the unacceptable face of Third World poverty, yet in many societies it is considered entirely normal that children work' (Ansell, 2005: 158). In 1992, the International Labour Organization set up the International Programme on the Elimination of Child Labour (IPEC), whose aim is the progressive elimination of child labour and particularly the worst forms of this. Some progress has been made, with a decline of the number of children in child labour from 246 million in 2000 to 168 million in 2015. However, 85 million of these children are engaged in hazardous work (down from 171 million in 2000) (IPEC, 2015).

Pryer's study of some ultra-poor households in an urban slum in Khulna, Bangladesh, reveals how, faced with low, unreliable and seasonal incomes, households attempted to achieve a diverse employment profile with as many family members working as possible. The extreme poverty of the community is reflected by the fact that in 1984 no fewer than 67 per cent of children under five in the slum were second- or third-degree malnourished; that is, they were under 75 per cent of the expected weight for their age (Pryer, 1987: 133).

All seven severely undernourished households surveyed were deeply indebted, usually to landlords, employers, shops and neighbours. Since the only productive asset of these households is labour, all able-bodied adults and many of the children needed to do some form of paid work. Employment opportunities were invariably poorly paid in the informal sector, with men engaging in rickshaw pulling, petty trade, hawking and labouring on a daily basis. But during the monsoon months (June to September) less work was available. In two of the households women were major earners, typically engaged in domestic work or home-based piece-rate work, which involved long hours and was poorly paid both absolutely and in relation to male wages.

In the seven households, an average of 68 per cent of income was spent on food; the rest went towards fuel, rent and repayment of debt. Food intake was well below the recommended daily allowance.

One mother, whose husband died of tuberculosis, went out to work from 7 am to 4 pm and again from 6 pm to 11 pm every day, while her 10-year-old daughter assumed responsibility for childcare and domestic work. In another family, the wife, with a chronically sick husband who was unable to work, sold saris illegally on the black market, assisted by her 17-year-old niece, and her 12-year-old daughter was a servant in the main market. Given the family's circumstances, the wife was clearly the economic and social household head.

In both families, illness of the chief earners had led to sale of assets, indebtedness and deepening poverty, resulting in inadequate, unreliable and seasonal flows of food. One of the two women household heads was forced into heavy dependence on a patron who was her employer and landlord, while the other was engaged in illegal trading, both highly precarious strategies (Pryer, 1987). This study clearly illustrates both the different roles of members in attempting to ensure the household's survival, and the cycle of poverty and malnutrition from which it can be extremely difficult to escape.

BOX 5.3

Children: a neglected piece in the development jigsaw

Perceptions of children and childhood

Whereas children in developed countries can usually expect to be well fed, have good clean clothes, attend school until they are 16 or older, be well protected against ill-health and have a lifespan of well over 70 years, their counterparts in poor countries have few, if any, of these assurances. Furthermore, the welfare of children is a constant focus of attention in developed countries and a prime concern of many households, but children in countries of the South are themselves expected to help in maintaining the household in so many ways. Fetching water and firewood, scaring birds from the fields, processing food and selling items in the urban informal sector, are just some of the many tasks which children commonly perform. Yet, all too often, the vital contribution which children make to the welfare of households in poor countries receives remarkably little attention. As

Robson comments, 'By the age of 10–12 years, some children may contribute as much to household sustenance as adults' (Robson, 1996: 43).

Whereas in the last three decades there has been, quite appropriately, much debate and writing about the position and role of women, children still remain a somewhat neglected element in the development process. A report from Actionaid (1995) clearly shows that children and children's work have been neglected. Empirical research has also revealed the importance of this in different social and environmental contexts. The Actionaid report comments, 'The inclusion of children and their participation in the development process is as much their basic human right as is their right to health provision and protection from hazardous work and living conditions' (Actionaid, 1995: 5). With their numerous household responsibilities, so many children

Plate 5.6 Nursery school in Nepal
(*photo*: Lola Odessey Waters)

BOX 5.3 (continued)

in poor countries are denied the stereotypical 'childhood' which young people experience in rich countries.

However, there are complex moral discourses surrounding the nature of childhood and particularly the issue of child labour. Ansell concludes that, 'despite campaigns by NGOs and international organisations, it is increasingly recognised that depriving children of the opportunity to work can be damaging. There is a need to strengthen the bargaining power of those who sell their labour, either to ensure that they are better rewarded and work in better conditions, or that they are able to secure their livelihoods in alternative ways' (Ansell, 2005: 189).

Children in conflict situations

When children are caught up in conflict situations such as in Afghanistan and Sierra Leone, normal daily routines of school, work and play are completely transformed, and in some cases children (boys and girls) have been drawn into using weapons in combat scenarios. As Amnesty International reflects on the situation in Afghanistan, two decades of civil war from the 1980s meant that,

> Families have been torn apart in the fighting, many children have lost parents or siblings. Others have been forced to flee from their homes, either abroad or to other parts of Afghanistan. All have suffered from disrupted schooling and economic hardship. The physical, emotional and mental development of generations of Afghanistan's children has been severely affected by the ongoing fighting.
>
> (Amnesty International, 2002a: 1)

A study undertaken in Afghanistan by UNICEF in 1997 indicated that most of Kabul's children were suffering from serious traumatic stress, with 72 per cent of those children interviewed having experienced the death of a relative between 1992 and 1996. Virtually all the children had witnessed acts of violence, and two-thirds of them had seen dead bodies or body parts. As many as 90 per cent of the children feared they would actually die in the conflict (UNICEF, 1998).

Meanwhile, in Sierra Leone, an estimated 8,000 children under the age of 18 fought in the civil war (1991–2002). Many of these children were abducted from their homes and families and forced to fight. During the rebel invasion of the capital, Freetown, in January 1999, when some 2,000 civilians were killed, over 500 people had limbs severed and the raping of girls and women was widespread. It was estimated that some 10 per cent of the rebel combatants were children, who lived in constant fear of being beaten and killed, and their individual stories are often harrowing (Amnesty International, 2002b).

The UN Convention on the Rights of the Child (UNCRC), which provides the guiding principles for UNICEF, came into force in 1989 and has been ratified by 193 states. In February 2002, the Optional Protocol on the Involvement of Children in Armed Conflict was added to the Convention and has been ratified by 128 countries and signed by a further 28. The London-based NGO, 'War Child', established in 1993, is specifically concerned to raise the profile of children's issues in conflict situations (War Child, 2015).

The status and roles of children

Examining the status and role of children more broadly, research from a variety of different contexts has indicated that children need to be viewed as 'social actors', and the conventional model of childhood must be modified to support the notion of a 'plurality of pathways to maturity' (Save the Children Fund, 1995). In relation to this, gender is often important in determining children's roles and responsibilities. For example, a study in Jamalpur, a rural area in Bangladesh, revealed that boys are mainly involved in cultivating family plots of land and occasionally they go to neighbouring farms to work as wage labourers. They enjoyed their work and in earning cash from casual labour they felt that they were an asset to their families. Girls in the same area, however, were somewhat resentful that their work, which involved mainly household duties and looking after younger children, was invisible. The girls saw

BOX 5.3 (continued)

education as a way of earning greater respect from their families and communities. Both girls and boys agreed that they should work hard to help their parents and to contribute to family income and welfare (Actionaid, 1995: 49).

Children and education

For children in many poor countries, attending school is regarded as a privilege rather than a right. Commonly, far fewer girls than boys in the Global South go to school and this is reflected later in life in the form of a considerable differential in adult literacy rates between males and females age 15 and older. The West African state of Niger, with one of the poorest adult literacy records in the world, had an average male adult literacy rate in 2005–2013 of 23 per cent, while the rate for females was only 9 per cent (World Bank, 2015c).

Although levels of educational attainment are better in India, the gender differentiation is significant, with a female adult literacy rate of 65 per cent compared, with the figure for males of 82 per cent (World Bank, 2015c). This differential is also apparent in some richer countries where Islam is the dominant faith, and where girls are more likely to stay at home to assist their mothers with household chores rather than go to school. In Libya, whereas the male adult literacy rate is 96 per cent, the female rate is only 84 per cent. In Pakistan, the differential is greater, with a male adult literacy rate of 67 per cent, but only 42 per cent for women. In the mainly Muslim West African country of Chad, the

average female adult literacy rate in 2005–2013 was only 28 per cent compared with 47 per cent for adult males age 15 and older (World Bank, 2015c).

Whereas girls in poor countries may often attend the first few years of primary school, the proportion of girls in school classes frequently falls sharply among higher age groups (see Chapter 1). In Chad, for example, whilst the ratio of female to male primary school enrolment is 76 per cent, the ratio falls to 46 per cent for secondary school enrolment (World Bank, 2015c).

A study in the Kyuso area of Kitui district in eastern Kenya found that the major reason for school non-enrolment and drop-out was poverty and the high costs of school materials and uniforms. During drought conditions, parents frequently withdraw their children from school to assist with water collection and to look after younger children (Actionaid, 1994). In many countries, more and more children, particularly girls, are being withdrawn from school, as investment in their education is seen as being lost when they marry. Evidently, there is much concerning gender and the roles of children of different ages that needs to be much better understood.

Some progress has been made, notably through the International Year of the Child in 1979, the 1989 UN Convention on the Rights of the Child and the 1990 UNICEF-sponsored World Summit on Children. These were important landmarks in attempting to raise the profile of children in all communities, but in some countries there is still a very long way to go in improving the lives of children.

Culture, religion and development

The relationships between culture, religion and development are highly complex and have been explored in detail elsewhere (see, for example, Eade (ed), 2002). The term 'culture' is in itself highly contested, and there have been many attempts to define the concept. Two useful definitions are provided by Matsumoto (1996) and Spencer-Oatey (2008): '. . . the set of attitudes, values,

beliefs, and behaviours shared by a group of people, but different for each individual, communicated from one generation to the next' (Matsumoto, 1996: 16). Spencer-Oatey suggests that, 'Culture is a fuzzy set of basic assumptions and values, orientations to life, beliefs, policies, procedures and behavioural conventions that are shared by a group of people, and that influence (but do not determine) each member's behaviour and his/her interpretations of the 'meaning' of other people's behaviour' (Spencer-Oatey, 2008: 3).

In relation to development, culture has often been seen as inhibiting entrepreneurship and getting in the way of development interventions. Daskon and McGregor suggest that 'Development is accused of failing to confront the cultural-historical roots of development processes and for reducing other worlds to its own mirror image' (Daskon and McGregor, 2012: 550). As Eade comments, '*local* or *traditional* cultures are even now seen as a brake on development, while the international development agencies and their national counterparts regard themselves as culturally neutral – if not superior' (Eade, 2002: ix). Religion is often seen as an important element of culture by social scientists, but, as Tomalin suggests, religious leaders may object since 'this implies that it (religion) has been influenced and shaped by cultural processes, rather than being the timeless word of God, or reflecting the teachings of the original founder of the religious tradition' (Tomalin, 2013: 2).

In recent years there has been an increasing focus on the roles of culture and religion in development processes. Deneulin and Rakodi (2011) suggest that in light of the significance of religion in the lives of millions of people and the influence of religious organisations, 'religion needs to be "brought back in" to development research so that our understanding of challenging development issues can be improved' (Deneulin and Rakodi, 2011: 52). Following a detailed survey of the literature,

Khan and Bashar conclude that 'Most of the empirical studies point to a positive relationship between religion and economic growth and development' (Khan and Bashar, 2008: 7).

Daskon and Binns (2010) argue that much greater attention should be given to culture and religion when devising interventions aimed at promoting sustainable community development. They are particularly critical about the omission of 'cultural capital' from the Sustainable Livelihoods Framework (see Chapter 10). Daskon and Binns show how villages in the hinterland of the central Sri Lankan city of Kandy have longstanding cultural activities, such as metalworking, jewellery production, drum-making, dancing and music, which are all closely linked with the important Buddhist shrine of the Temple of the Tooth. When interviewed, community members stressed that 'traditional culture and livelihoods are inextricably linked, in that culture provides a common destiny based on collective customs, memories and values, and helps to mobilize and disseminate survival strategies among community members' (Daskon and Binns, 2010: 508).

Religion, culture and development can be seen coming together in Sri Lanka's Sarvodaya movement. Founded in 1958 by Dr A.T. Ariyaratne, the Sarvodaya movement is now Sri Lanka's largest non-governmental organisation. It is committed to community-based development, and strongly rooted in Buddhist and other

Table 5.4 Commitment to health: access, services and resources

Country	Public health expenditure (% of GDP)	Physicians (per 1,000 people)	Population with sustainable access to improved sanitation (%)		Population with sustainable access to an improved water source (%)
Year	2012	2011	1900	2012	2012
Bangladesh	1.2	0.4	20	57	85
Brazil	4.3	1.8	71	81	98
China	3	1.8	23	65	92
India	1.3	0.7	14	36	93
Jamaica	3.3	N/A	75	80	93
Japan	8.3	2.3	100	100	100
Mali	2.3	0.1	36	22	67
Sierra Leone	2.5	0.1	N/A	13	60
Sweden	7.9	3.9	100	100	100
United Kingdom	7.8	2.8	100	100	100
USA	8.3	2.5	100	100	99
Zimbabwe	N/A	0.1	50	40	80

Source: World Bank (2012) *World Development Indicators 2012*. Washington: World Bank Publications.

ancient Sri Lankan traditions, but is open to anyone whatever their religion, and encourages inter-religious cooperation. Sarvodaya has been involved in a number of development projects, such as helping survivors from the 2004 tsunami to re-locate and build new settlements away from the sea, including a 55-household eco-village designed by Australian permaculture experts (Westendorp (ed), 2010). Daskon and Binns quote the words of a villager from Henawela,

> Sarvodaya is closer to people's lives, because it is operated by Buddhist principles. We are Buddhist people, and we know the value of being kind and helpful for other people, without expecting anything in return. We all get together to discuss our problems and work together to get through all our difficulties. It teaches us the simple and peaceful way of getting away from our sorrows.
>
> (Daskon and Binns, 2012: 871)

Health and health care

The health status of a population, or elements of a population, can be crucial in the development process. It might be argued that a healthy population is more able to contribute to development efforts and will also be better placed to benefit from the fruits of these efforts. We have already seen that many countries of the South have high rates of child mortality and their life expectancy levels are well below those of richer, more developed countries.

Variables such as these are often a good reflection of the health status of a population and the quality of health care. In many poor countries of the South health facilities are inaccessible to a large proportion of the population, especially those living in remote rural areas. Where hospitals and clinics do exist, there are frequently shortages of trained health workers, drugs and basic equipment. With such shortages, it is often possible for disease to spread, as in the case of the Ebola outbreak in West Africa during 2014 and 2015. Ebola haemorrhagic fever, with a mortality rate of 50–90 per cent, was first recognised in the Democratic Republic of Congo in 1976 where it was named after a local river. The West African outbreak, principally affecting the three countries of Guinea, Sierra Leone and Liberia, has been the deadliest so far, with 25,000 reported cases and 10,000 deaths by March 2015 (UNDP, 2016).

Providing good health care for everyone is an expensive undertaking for the governments of poor countries. In many parts of the world, but notably tropical Africa, religious missions continue to play a crucial role in providing health care in certain areas, together with a variety of non-governmental organisations (NGOs). Many countries still cling to a top-down style of health care inherited from the colonial period, with a considerable proportion of health expenditure being allocated to a few key hospitals, particularly in the main towns and capital city, whereas the rural areas remain relatively neglected. Table 5.4 shows some key variables relating to the status of health care in selected countries.

The proportion of populations with adequate sanitation varies widely from 100 per cent in the richer countries to less than 30 per cent in parts of rural India. Of the 1 billion or so people in the world without a toilet, it is likely that some 600 million of these are in India. In 1999 only 44 per cent of Sierra Leone's population had access to essential drugs, while in India and Brazil the figures were even lower (India 35 per cent and Brazil 40 per cent). It should be remembered that these are countrywide figures and they therefore conceal considerable spatial and social inequalities in service provision. In terms of national expenditure on health, all the richer countries spend more than 5 per cent of their GDP on public health care, whereas in India it is only 4 per cent of GDP, 3.6 per cent in Bangladesh and 2.8 per cent in Chad (World Bank, 2015c).

In China under Mao Zedong various efforts to improve public health were introduced, particularly from 1968 onwards, when a central government document called the 'June 26th Directive on Public Health' demanded that the focus of medical and public health work should be transferred to the countryside. Mao suggested that although city hospitals should keep some doctors, a greater proportion should be sent to work in the villages (where 85 per cent of the population lived) to teach medical knowledge to the peasant youth (Endicott, 1988: 157).

Although these 'barefoot doctors', as they were popularly called, had a lot to learn, Mao believed they were better than 'fake doctors' and 'witch doctors'. Furthermore, he argued that villages could afford them, as medical funding was redistributed such that the bulk was directed to prevention and cure of the most common diseases. Village commune hospitals received much more finance, which could be used to purchase equipment such as X-ray machines, as well as to develop both Chinese and Western medicine. There was also a campaign to extend the recruitment of barefoot doctors, midwives and medical orderlies.

The effects of this campaign are partly reflected in statistics relating to the number of doctors for every 1,000 people (Table 5.4). In 2011, China had 1.8 doctors per 1,000 people, and in this regard China is well ahead of many other countries in the UNDP's 'high human development' group, which have significantly higher GDP per capita figures than China.

The impact of these policies in China was clearly seen in rural areas such as Shifang County in Sichuan Province:

> In three-month, sometimes six-month, courses, qualified doctors, sent down to the countryside by rotation during the Cultural Revolution, trained 658 barefoot doctors in basic first aid, Chinese medicine, acupuncture, the use of thermometers, the dispensing of vaccines by injection and drugs for influenza, stomach upsets and other common ailments. [As a result] the total number of medical personnel in the County rose from 592 in 1965 to 3420 a decade later . . . [The barefoot doctor initiative represented] . . . a good start on creating an accessible, experimental, non-elitist public health system biased in favour of prevention.
>
> (Endicott, 1988: 158)

A notable achievement in Shifang County's health programme was the virtual eradication of schistosomiasis (bilharzia), such that the number of people affected was reduced from 5,700 in 1959 to only four in 1982. By the end of the 1970s, 85 per cent of Chinese villages had a health station staffed by one or more barefoot doctors.

Health problems in the Global South are closely linked to poverty, notably inadequate or poor quality food and water and the lack of proper sanitation (see also Chapter 6). Children are particularly susceptible to diarrhea, and measles also claims many victims, whereas vitamin A deficiency may lead to blindness and infection, particularly after measles. Iron deficiency often leads to anaemia, causing weakness and particular risks for newborn children. Children are also very susceptible to a number of nutrition-related diseases such as pellagra, beriberi, rickets and kwashiorkor.

Diseases associated with water are a major problem in many countries of the South, and there is some evidence that the expansion of irrigated agriculture has encouraged their spread with large areas of slow-moving water in dams and reservoirs. Schistosomiasis is transmitted by snails in slow-moving water, whereas onchocerciasis (river blindness), which is endemic to large parts of tropical Africa, is also associated with water and is transmitted by the black fly.

Possibly the most serious threat to health in tropical regions is malaria, transmitted by mosquitoes which breed close to stagnant or slow-moving water. It is estimated that in tropical Africa alone as many as 200 million people are affected by malaria, which weakens victims and lowers their resistance to a wide range of other possible infections. Although draining swamps and spraying pools with insecticide might help, mosquitoes are becoming resistant to certain chemicals and anti-malarial drugs. Mosquitoes are also responsible for transmitting dengue fever and yellow fever.

Key idea

Malaria: the scourge of Africa

There were an estimated 627,000 global deaths from malaria in 2012, but 482,000 of these (77 per cent) were children under five in Africa (WHO, 2013). Malaria is the main cause of childhood mortality in sub-Saharan Africa – a child dies from malaria every 20 seconds in Africa. The economic and development costs of malaria are considerable, slowing economic growth by about 1.3 per cent annually and contributing to a decline in per capita GDP in many sub-Saharan African countries.

Malaria is a parasitic infection which is transmitted to humans through the bites of infected female

Key idea (continued)

Anopheles mosquitoes. The parasite spreads rapidly through the bloodstream to the liver and then settles in the red blood cells, where it multiplies and emerges in bursts of new organisms. The parasites can cause considerable damage to the kidney, liver and nervous system. Children and adults who have not recently been infected, and have therefore not developed natural immunity, can die in a short time from cerebral malaria, and others may later die from anaemia or liver and kidney failure. If left untreated, up to 20 per cent of infected persons will die.

A number of possible strategies exist for dealing with malaria:

➤ Controlling the breeding of mosquitoes by getting rid of stagnant water where they breed.

➤ Using chemical pesticides, but mosquitoes have in some cases developed a resistance to the pesticides.

➤ Limiting human exposure to mosquito bites, by using bed nets and window screens treated with insecticide. Bed nets treated with an insecticide (usually a pyrethroid) have proved to be effective.

➤ Using anti-malarial prophylactic drugs, particularly for travellers visiting infected areas for short periods of time. But mosquito resistance to the drugs is a common problem.

➤ Developing a vaccine to combat the disease. There is currently no commercially available malaria vaccine. Work on producing a vaccine has been going on for some time, but the complexity of the organism is making this difficult. A team of scientists is working on developing a vaccine through the European Malaria Vaccine Initiative (EMVI), which was started in 1998 with funding from the European Commission, Denmark, Ireland, The Netherlands, Norway and Sweden (http://www.emvi.org/). In 1999, another group, the PATH Malaria Vaccine Initiative (MVI) began work, funded by the Bill and Melissa Gates Foundation (http://www.malariavaccine.org/about-mvi.htm).

In the absence of complete protection against malaria, African communities have often developed their own strategies for dealing with the problem of malaria. For example, in the Tigray region of Ethiopia 'mother coordinators' have been trained to educate other mothers about the symptoms of fever and malaria. Mothers were provided with low-cost chloroquine and information on how to administer the drug. By educating mothers in this way under-five mortality has been reduced by 40 per cent, and the burden on hospitals in dealing with severe cases of malaria has been reduced (World Bank, 2004).

The health and nutritional status of households and household members may vary over time. For example, maternal health is an area of much concern and was the focus of the fifth Millennium Development Goal and the third Sustainable Development Goal. The 1994 International Conference on Population and Development (ICPD) held in Cairo transferred the focus on women's, and particularly maternal, health from a demographically driven approach to a human rights focus. It is estimated that between 250,000 and 343,000 women and 3 million babies die every year in pregnancy and childbirth, or soon afterwards (WHO, 2013). In 2009, globally, only an estimated 68 per cent of births were attended by skilled health personnel, but in poorer countries, most notably in sub-Saharan Africa, this figure is considerably lower (WHO, 2013). In Malaysia, where the government signed the Convention on the Elimination of all Forms of Discrimination Against Women in 1995, considerable success has been achieved in reducing the maternal mortality ratio, largely through home deliveries being conducted by trained community midwives, and by establishing a nationwide system to detect early complications in pregnancies and closely reviewing all maternal deaths (World Bank, 1999).

We have already seen how a particular stage in a household's life cycle may affect income and nutrition. This longer-term variation may be compounded by marked seasonal pressures in tropical countries, where the period of hardest work commonly coincides with the rainy season, which is also the time when the occurrence of many diseases, such as malaria, increases. Furthermore, in many communities, towards the end of the rainy season, but before the harvest, food stocks are often getting low and the quantity and quality of food intake declines. This time of year, sometimes called the 'hungry season', is associated with greater susceptibility to infection, though people still have to work hard in the fields. Certain elements of communities and households, such as pregnant and breast-feeding women and young children, may suffer disproportionately at such times.

HIV/AIDS

Since the early 1980s the HIV/AIDS pandemic has introduced a sinister new dimension to the world health scene, and it is unfortunately the poorer countries and people who have suffered disproportionately.

AIDS (acquired immune deficiency syndrome) is a disease in which the body's natural protection or immune system is damaged. Since the first AIDS case was reported in the USA in 1981, 'the world has been facing the deadliest epidemic in contemporary history' (UN, 2000: 76). The extensive spread of human immuno-deficiency virus (HIV), the aetiologic agent that causes AIDS, probably began as early as the 1960s, but spread rapidly during the mid to late 1970s and early 1980s. Two strains of HIV have been identified (HIV1 and HIV2), and infection occurs when blood from an infected person passes directly into another's bloodstream, and also through sexual intercourse. In almost all cases, those infected by HIV develop AIDS, which is inevitably fatal.

BOX 5.4

Entitlements, food security and nutrition

Much interest has been shown in recent years in the question of 'food security' – what it is, how it can be achieved, and the reasons why some individuals, communities and geographical areas are 'food secure', while others are not. This complex debate involves examining aspects of nutrition, vulnerability, coping strategies and what Amartya Sen has called 'entitlements'. There have been many attempts to define 'food security'. The World Bank (1986) suggested that it means, 'Access by all people at all times to enough food for an active, healthy life'. Kennes (1990), meanwhile, believes it is 'The absence of hunger and malnutrition'. Maxwell (1988: 10) provides a more detailed definition:

> A country and people are food secure when their food system operates efficiently in such a way as to remove the fear that there will not be enough to eat . . . In particular, food security will be achieved when the poor and vulnerable, particularly women and children and those living in marginal areas, have secure access to the food they want.

Whether or not individuals or communities are 'food secure' or 'food insecure' requires very careful investigation beyond the issue of merely quantifying food supply, and must take into account various 'entitlement'

relationships. Sen's important work on entitlements starts with the provocative statement, 'Starvation is the characteristic of some people not having enough food to eat. It is not the characteristic of there being not enough food to eat. While the latter can be a cause of the former, it is but one of many possible causes' (Sen, 1981: 1). The entitlement approach provides a useful framework for analysing the relationship between rights, interpersonal obligations and individual entitlement to things. An individual's 'entitlement set' is a way of characterising his or her overall command over things, taking note of all relevant rights and obligations.

Some of these entitlement relationships might include:

➤ 'trade-based entitlement', where an individual (or group) is entitled to own what they obtain by trading something that they own with a willing party;

➤ 'production-based entitlement', where an individual (or group) is entitled to own what they get from arranging production using their own resources, or resources hired from willing parties meeting the agreed conditions of trade;

➤ 'own-labour entitlement', where an individual (or group) is entitled to their own labour power, and thus to the trade-based and production-based entitlements related to that labour power;

BOX 5.4 (continued)

> 'inheritance and transfer entitlement', where an individual (or group) is entitled to own what is willingly given to them by another who legitimately owns it, possibly to take effect after the latter's death (if so specified by them) (Sen, 1981).

These relationships may exist and develop between individuals, or groups such as households. In relating this to food security, Blaikie suggests, 'there have been famines where the total food availability has not declined at all, but instead there has been a failure of effective demand (not need!) for food through the failure of their entitlements. People simply became too poor to afford food which is physically available' (Blaikie, 2002: 302).

The entitlement approach has helped in understanding the differential impacts of famines and how famines might occur at times when food is plentiful. It has also drawn attention to the functioning of markets and how certain catastrophic events (such as droughts or floods) do not necessarily lead to famine and food insecurity.

However, Devereux and Maxwell (2001) indicate some shortcomings of the entitlements approach, suggesting that in reality entitlements are often much less clear than the model suggests, and they may occur outside the legal framework suggested by Sen. The model has little to say, for example, about 'informal' or 'illegal' entitlements, which are often most important at times of food security crisis. Research has shown that food-insecure households are often remarkably resilient, adopting many ingenious coping strategies for securing nutrition, for example, borrowing food, gathering wild foods or disposing of assets such as livestock to purchase food. It is suggested that social capital, intra-household distribution and well-adapted social networks are also not sufficiently articulated in the entitlement approach, which gives prominence to formal exchange mechanisms.

Much recent work on food security has focused on individuals and households, examining the diversity of causes within different situations and the nature and effectiveness of the coping strategies adopted. In an attempt to reduce household vulnerability to nutritional insufficiency, food security planning has been moving away from a broad 'blue-print' approach towards developing flexible, locally based responses which build upon indigenous knowledge and skills (Maxwell, 1996).

BOX 5.5

Globesity

In some parts of the world, a new health problem is emerging – obesity. While this has long been a concern in the world's richer countries, recent evidence suggests that it is also becoming a major health issue in some poorer countries. Obesity is a disease with many causes that leads to an imbalance between energy intake and output, resulting in the accumulation of large amounts of body fat. It is most commonly measured as excessive weight for a given height, using the body mass index (BMI) – weight in kilograms (kg) over height squared (m^2). The World Health Organization (WHO) defines overweight as a BMI between 25.0 and 29.9 kg/m^2 and obesity as a BMI of 30.0 kg/m^2 or greater. The World Health Organization estimated that in 2014 approximately 1.9 billion adults worldwide were overweight, and at least 600 million adults, representing some 13 per cent of the world's population in 2014, were estimated to be obese, 11 per cent of men and 15 per cent of women (WHO, 2015).

Obesity is relatively rare in South Asia, and although generally rare in sub-Saharan Africa, it is becoming an increasing problem among urban and educated women. Some 44 per cent of black women

▶

BOX 5.5 (continued)

living in the Eastern and Western Cape provinces of South Africa were found to be clinically obese (Grummer-Strawn et al., 2000a). In Latin America, obesity was once restricted to those with high socio-economic status, but in Brazil and Mexico it is emerging as a feature in poor households. Childhood obesity is a problem because it generally leads to adult obesity (Grummer-Strawn et al., 2000b; Martorell, 2001). In 2013 there were globally an estimated 42 million overweight and obese children under the age of

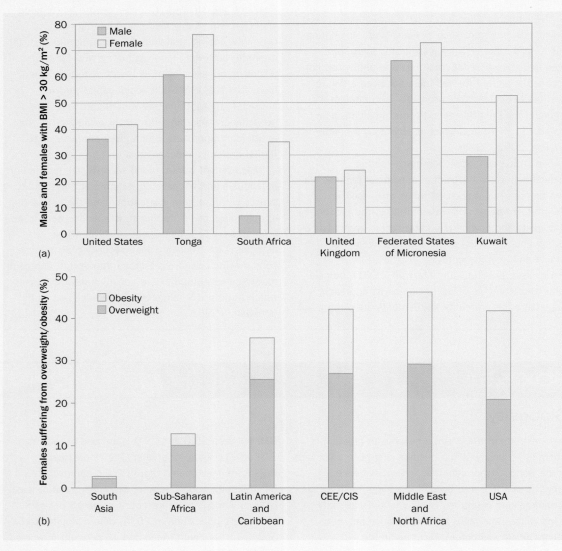

Figure 5.6 (a) Levels of obesity among men and women, according to selected countries
Source: from *The Independent* (2002)

(b) Overweight and obesity in women, according to world regions
Source: from Grummer-Strawn et al. (2000a) *European Journal of Clinical Nutrition*, 54(3), 250. Adapted by permission from Macmillan Publishers Ltd © 2000

BOX 5.5 (continued)

five (WHO, 2015). In China, the number of overweight people increased from less than 10 per cent to 15 per cent in three years. There is much concern in China that the one-child policy has led to overfeeding and obesity in children, particularly boys. Some of the Pacific islands have the greatest incidence of obesity, with an estimated 65 per cent of men and 77 per cent of women being obese in Samoa and Tonga.

Global rises in the numbers of overweight and obese people are due to a variety of factors, including a shift in diet towards a greater intake of foods which are high in fat and sugars, and a trend towards less physical activity due to the increasingly sedentary nature of lifestyles. Higher levels of obesity are leading to a greater incidence of diabetes, hypertension, stroke, cardiovascular disease and some cancers. Mortality rates from these diseases are

increasing in poorer countries, whereas they were once regarded as diseases of the richer countries. However, since the main focus continues to be on undernutrition in poor countries, the incidence of obesity and its link with chronic diseases has often received little attention. As early as 1992, the Singapore government, which had the necessary resources to deal with the problem, introduced a 'Trim and Fit Scheme', a ten-year programme involving teacher education, a reduction of sugar content in children's beverages and an increase in physical activity during the school day. More attention needs to be given to the problem of obesity with public health awareness campaigns, more recreational facilities in urban areas, nutrition labelling and agricultural research programmes that will lead to lower-fat meat and other products.

By December 2011, the Joint United Nations Programme on HIV/AIDS (UNAIDS) and the World Health Organization estimated that there were some 35 million adults and children living with HIV, some 67 per cent of whom are in sub-Saharan Africa (UNAIDS, 2012). As Table 5.5 shows, the bulk of those infected with HIV live in the poorer regions of the world (Africa; Central, South and Southeast Asia; Latin America; and Eastern Europe), with sub-Saharan Africa having by far the greatest infection rate (4.7 per cent). It is estimated that more than 7,500 Africans are newly infected each day (UNAIDS, 2012). Furthermore, with poor countries unable to afford expensive anti-retroviral drug treatments, deaths due to AIDS in sub-Saharan Africa during 2011 amounted to 1.2 million, or 75 per cent of the world total.

Table 5.5 also indicates that the main mode of transmission for adults varies in different parts of the world. In Western Europe and North America, for example, transmission is mainly through injecting drug use and sexual transmission among men who have sex with men. However, HIV in sub-Saharan Africa is mainly spread through heterosexual intercourse and perinatal transmission, which can occur *in utero*, during delivery or after birth through breast

milk. Table 5.6 shows the incidence of HIV/AIDS among adults aged between 15 and 49 in countries. Once again, the overwhelming dominance of sub-Saharan countries is apparent, with Zimbabwe showing a staggering, and very depressing, lead over other countries, some of which (for example, Mali and Sierra Leone), in relation to other development indicators, have both lower Human Development Indexes and levels of per capita GNP than Zimbabwe.

In June 2001, at a significant UN General Assembly Special Session on HIV/AIDS (UNAIDS, 2001) six main targets were agreed:

➤ To reduce HIV infection among 15–24-year-olds by 25 per cent in the most affected countries by 2005, and globally by 2010.

➤ To reduce by 2005 the proportion of infants infected with HIV by 20 per cent, and by 50 per cent by 2010.

➤ To develop national strategies for treatment, including the provision of affordable HIV-related drugs by 2003.

➤ To develop and implement by 2005 national strategies for supporting orphans and children infected and affected by HIV/AIDS.

➤ To formulate strategies by 2003 which will help reduce vulnerability to HIV infection, for example reducing poverty, sexual exploitation and by empowering women.

➤ To develop multi-sectoral strategies by 2003 which will help to reduce the impact of HIV/AIDS at the individual, family, community and national levels.

While these objectives were laudable, the chances of some or all of them actually being achieved seemed rather slim, particularly in the world's poorest countries. However, in February 2002 the World Bank approved an additional US $500 million for the second stage of its Multi-Country HIV/AIDS Programme for Africa (MAP), bringing the amount of its no-interest HIV/AIDS lending to Africa through this programme to US $1 billion in the 2001–2002 financial year (World Bank, 2002b). Steady progress has been made, and in 2013, funding for dealing with HIV/AIDS reached its highest level ever at $19.1 billion, with 47 per cent of spending directed to sub-Saharan Africa (Avert, 2015). Launched

in 2015, Goal 3 of the UN's Sustainable Development Goals aims to end the AIDS epidemic by 2030 (UN, 2015c). As UNAIDS 2016 Global Aids Update comments, 'The extraordinary accomplishments of the last 15 years have inspired global confidence that this target can be achieved' (UNAIDS, 2016: 1).

Sub-Saharan Africa faces the greatest problems since, on top of the general impoverishment and lack of any meaningful 'development' in many countries over the last two decades, HIV/AIDS adds further to the challenges which cash-starved African governments face today. In Botswana, Malawi, Zambia and Zimbabwe, AIDS is now considered to be the leading cause of death between the ages of 15 and 39. It was estimated in 1994 that in Nairobi (Kenya) and Abidjan (Côte d'Ivoire) the prevalence of HIV among prostitutes was well over 80 per cent (US Census Bureau, 1994). Although the problem is greatest in urban areas, it is not insignificant in rural areas. But given the fact that Africa is still mainly rural, in absolute numbers AIDS cases in rural areas predominate, though accurate data are difficult to obtain.

Table 5.5 Regional HIV/AIDS statistics and features, December 2012

Region	Epidemic started	Adults and children living with HIV	Adults and children newly infected with HIV	Adult (15–49) prevalence (%)	Adult and child deaths due to AIDS	Main mode(s) of transmission for adults living with HIV/AIDS
Sub-Saharan Africa	Late 1970s, early 1980s	25.0 million	1.6 million	4.7	1.2 million	Hetero
Middle East and North Africa	Late 1980s	260,000	32,000	0.1	17,000	Hetero, IDU
South and Southeast Asia	Late 1980s	3.9 million	270,000	0.3	220,000	Hetero, IDU
East Asia	Late 1980s	880,000	81,000	<0.1	41,000	N/A
Latin America	Late 1970s, early 1980s	1.5 million	86,000	0.4	52,000	N/A
Caribbean	Late 1970s, early 1980s	250,000	12,000	1.0	11,000	MSM, IDU, Hetero
Eastern Europe and Central Asia	Late 1990s	1.3 million	130,000	0.7	91,000	Hetero, MSM
Western and Central Europe	Late 1970s, early 1980s	860,000	29,000	0.2	7,600	IDU
North America	Late 1970s, early 1980s	1.3 million	48,000	0.5	20,000	MSM, IDU
Oceania	Late 1970s, early 1980s	51,000	2,100	0.2	1,200	MSM, IDU, Hetero
TOTAL		35.3 million	2.3 million	0.8	1.6 million	
Range		32.2–38.8million	1.9–2.7 million	0.7–0.9	1.4–1.9 million	

Source: WHO, UNAIDS, & UNICEF (2012), *Global HIV/AIDS Response: Epidemic Update and Health Sector Progress towards Universal Access: Progress Report 2011*. Geneva

Table 5.6 Incidence of HIV in selected countries and regions, 2010 and 2013

Country	Population ages 15–49 living with HIV (%)	
	2010	2013
Bangladesh	0.1	0.1
Brazil	N/A	0.6
China	N/A	N/A
India	0.3	0.3
Jamaica	1.9	1.8
Japan	<0.1	<0.1
Mali	1.0	0.9
Sierra Leone	1.6	1.6
Sweden	0.1	0.1
United Kingdom	0.3	0.3
USA	0.4	0.3
Zimbabwe	16.0	15.0

Source: UNAIDS (2013) *Report on the Global AIDS Epidemic 2013*. New York: Joint United Nations Programme on HIV/AIDS.

The HIV/AIDS epidemic has shifted south in Africa since the early 1980s, when the greatest incidence was in a band from West Africa across the continent to the Indian Ocean. But, while infection rates in West Africa stabilised at lower levels, by the late 1980s infection rates in southern African countries had increased, such that in 2002 they were the highest in the world (Daniel, 2000). According to the World Bank (2012b), no fewer than 21.9 per cent of adults in Botswana were infected with HIV in 2012, whilst Swaziland had a figure of 27.4 per cent, the highest level of infection in the world (Table 5.7). Although Botswana has a relatively small population of only 2 million, it was reckoned that between 1995 and 2015 there would be 385,000 additional deaths due to AIDS.

The significant effect of HIV/AIDS on life expectancy is also shown in Table 5.7 where, in the case of

Table 5.7 HIV/AIDS, prevalence and mortality in selected countries

Country	HIV prevalence (% ages 15–49) – 2012	HDI Rank 2012	Life expectancy at birth (with AIDS) – 2010	Years lost with AIDS – 2010	Deaths due to AIDS (thousands) – 2012
Swaziland	27.4	148	45.8	18.0	5500
Botswana	21.9	109	54.9	13.8	5000
Lesotho	22.9	162	45.3	17.4	15500
Zimbabwe	15.0	156	44.1	21.0	39500
Namibia	14.3	127	61.4	8.6	5000
South Africa	19.1	118	51.6	13.0	235100
Zambia	12.5	141	45.2	9.6	30300
Mozambique	10.8	178	47.8	7.9	76800
Malawi	10.3	174	52.9	11.4	45600
Central African Republic	3.8	185	46.9	4.6	11000
Gabon	3.9	112	60.3	4.7	2300
Cote d'Ivoire	2.7	171	57.2	5.2	31200
Uganda	7.4	164	52.4	6.2	63300
Tanzania	5.0	159	N/A	N/A	80000
Kenya	6.0	147	54.2	7.2	57500
Cameroon	4.3	152	51.0	4.6	34600
Congo	2.5	140	53.6	3.7	31700
Haiti	2.0	168	61.2	1.9	7500
Cambodia	0.7	136	60.9	1.1	2700
Ukraine	0.8	83	68.2	1.3	18100
India	0.3	135	63.5	0.5	135500
USA	0.3	5	79.2	0.4	17000
Brazil	0.6	79	72.3	0.6	N/A

Sources:

HIV prevalence: World Bank (2012)

HDI rank: World Bank (2012)

Life expectancy with AIDS: United Nations (2011)

Years lost to AIDS: United Nations (2011)

Deaths to AIDS: CIA World FactBook (2013)

World Bank (2012) *World Development Indicators 2012*. Washington: World Bank Publications.

United Nations, Department of Economic and Social Affairs, Population Division (2011) *World Mortality Report 2010*. New York: United Nations Publications.

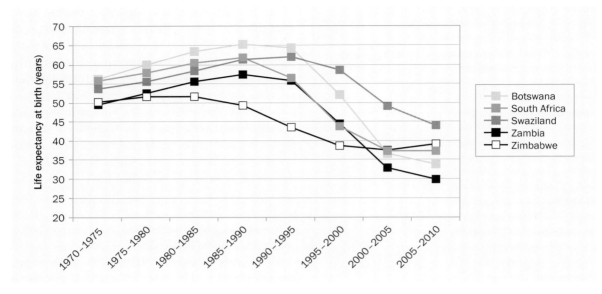

Figure 5.7 Impact of AIDS on life expectancy in five African countries, 1970–2010
Source: UNAIDS (2006) *Report on the Global AIDS Epidemic*

Zimbabwe, life expectancy with AIDS is only 44.1 years, representing 21 years lost to AIDS. In many African countries there was a steady increase in life expectancy before the 1980s, followed by a sharp decline due to the impact of HIV/AIDS (see Figure 5.7 above).

Uganda, one of the earliest countries affected by the epidemic, is unusual in having experienced an improvement in life expectancy since the mid-1990s, due to a decline in the overall prevalence of HIV/AIDS from 14 to 7.4 per cent between 1990 and 2012. This has resulted from a massive AIDS awareness programme, which was initiated in 1986, four years after AIDS was first recognised in the country. Political commitment has been at the highest level, from President Museveni downwards, such that every ministry has an AIDS Control Programme. The campaign has been remarkably open in attempting to demystify AIDS, involving religious and traditional leaders and being reinforced in schools, where young people were told of the merits of delaying sexual relations and engaging in safe sexual behaviour through the use of condoms. Although Uganda has achieved much success, the Ministry of Health estimated that in 2000 there were 1,438,000 people living with HIV/AIDS, and there were 838,000 deaths from AIDS, 83,000 of these being children (Evans, 2001). As Table 5.7 shows, by 2012 the prevalence

of HIV/AIDS among the 15 to 49-year-old age group had fallen to 7.4 per cent.

The HIV/AIDS epidemic is having a significant effect on population structure in some countries, as can be seen by comparing two countries with similar development indices, but where one country has a low HIV/AIDS infection rate, and the other has a high rate of infection. Morocco and Botswana are ranked 129 and 109, respectively, by UNDP in terms of the Human Development Index (UNDP, 2014). In economic terms, Botswana has a much higher per capita GDP of US$14,443 compared with Morocco's US$6878 (UNDP, 2014). However, in 2012, Botswana had an HIV/AIDS infection rate of 21.9 per cent among adults between the ages of 15 and 49, while the infection rate in Morocco was only 0.1 per cent (UNDP, 2014). Comparing population pyramids for the two countries, while there is a broad similarity in 2000, by 2025 population projections suggest that the Botswana pyramid has developed into what the US Census Bureau refers to as 'the population chimney' (US Census Bureau, 2002) (Figure 5.8).

Whereas the pyramid for Morocco has the 'normal' broad base, the Botswana pyramid has a much narrower base, since many sexually active HIV-infected young people die prematurely, while women may become infertile well before the end of their childbearing years, leading to fewer babies being born. Furthermore, as Barnett suggests, 'Up to a third of the infants born to HIV-positive women become infected themselves before or during birth, or through breast milk. Hence fewer babies survive to childhood and adolescence' (Barnett, 2002b: 393). The smaller number of females under 50 years old in the 2025 Botswana pyramid indicates the higher infection rate among young women than men.

Prothero (1996) has considered the possible effects of population migration on the transmission and diffusion of AIDS in West Africa, concluding that there is a need for more research on the complex interactions of socio-economic, cultural and biomedical mechanisms.

High rates of infection have been found among truck drivers, and the second stage of the World Bank's MAP programme, implemented from February 2002, targeted the Abidjan–Lagos transport corridor in West Africa which passes through Ivory Coast, Ghana, Togo, Benin and Nigeria (World Bank, 2002b). HIV/AIDS is also a significant problem among military personnel. UNAIDS reported that in peace time, infection rates of sexually transmitted diseases, including HIV, among armed forces are generally two to five times higher than in civilian populations, and in times of conflict, when mobility is greater and troops are often away from their families, the difference can be 50 times higher or more (UNAIDS, 1998).

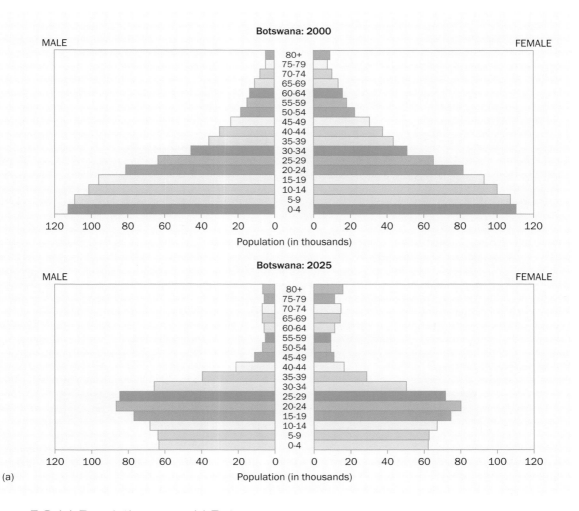

Figure 5.8 (a) Population pyramid Botswana
Source: From US Census Bureau (2002)

AIDS has now been added to the list of other child-killers in sub-Saharan Africa: diarrhea, malaria and measles. Browne and Barrett (1995) specifically examine the impact of the African AIDS epidemic on children and suggest that although more children still die from malaria, diarrhea and acute respiratory infections, the long-term effect on economic and human development at national, community and household levels gives much concern. HIV-infected children have a short life expectancy, with 80 per cent dying from AIDS-related causes by the age of five. In Zambia, the under-five mortality rate was 169 per 1,000 live births in 2000, due at least in part to AIDS-related causes.

However, in recent years, progress has been made in Zambia, with the under-five, mortality figure reducing to 87 per 1,000 live births in 2012 (World Bank, 2015c).

A further problem concerns the number of children orphaned as a result of AIDS, such that the rate of orphanhood has doubled in some countries. It was estimated in 1995 that in ten Central and East African countries there would be between five and six million orphans by 2000, representing about 11 per cent of the total 10–15-year-old child population (Browne and Barrett, 1995). A more recent estimate from UNAIDS suggests that in 2012 there were 15.5 million children in sub-Saharan Africa who had lost one or both of their parents (UNAIDS, 2012).

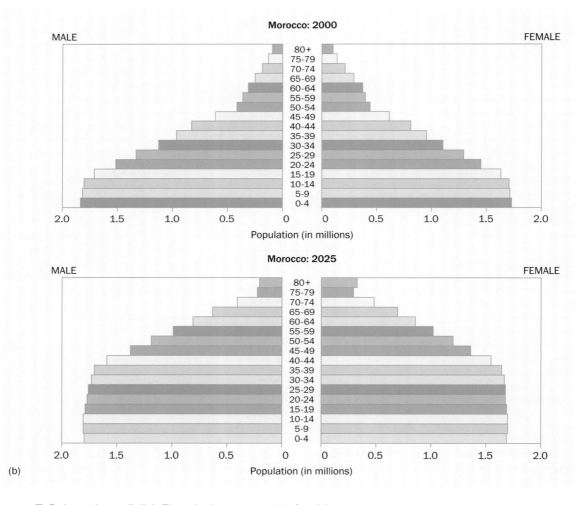

(b)

Figure 5.8 (continued) (b) Population pyramid for Morocco
Source: From US Census Bureau (2002)

AIDS could also have a wider impact on population growth rates, which are likely to fall, having a 'Malthusian effect' that could lead to an improvement in the ability of the world to sustain and feed itself. However, the spread of AIDS will increase the demand for curative health care, placing considerable pressure on poor African countries and perhaps meaning less health care for the rest of the population. For example, treating the estimated number of AIDS cases could represent 23 per cent of 1990 public health spending in Kenya and as much as 65 per cent in Rwanda. However, as Brown (1996a: 17) suggests, 'The most critical impact of AIDS is likely to be in the damage inflicted on the productive capacity of an economy and its potential to achieve food security through domestic production or economic access in world markets'. Increasing infection and mortality among the 20–40 age group has caused rising dependency ratios; some suggest an increase of between 18 and 29 per cent, leading to a significant reduction in the size of the economically active population (Gregson et al., 1994). What, sadly, does seem clear is that sub-Saharan Africa already has the dubious distinction of being the world's poorest region, and AIDS is likely to further exacerbate poverty as the poor lose access to what is often their only resource – their own labour.

BOX 5.6

HIV/AIDS in South Africa

South Africa has the dubious distinction of having the largest number of people infected with HIV/AIDS in a single country, with an estimated 6.1 million South Africans being HIV positive in 2012. The highest rate of infection is among female adults under 40 years of age, with women accounting for 80 per cent of those infected between 20 and 24 years old. In 2012, some 240,000 people in South Africa died of AIDS-related illnesses. Furthermore, life expectancy at the age of 20 with AIDS will be 13 years lower than without AIDS, while under-five mortality with AIDS is projected to be 98, whereas without AIDS it would be only 39 (UN, 2000). The high incidence of HIV/AIDS in South Africa is due to factors such as the long-established migrant labour system, which involves predominantly men leaving their families and moving to mines and cities for work where they often live in single-sex hostels. Other aspects of migration also play an important role in spreading infection. For example, KwaZulu-Natal province had South Africa's highest infection rate in 2008 at 15.8 per cent. One reason for this, it is suggested, is that Durban, its largest city, is situated on a major truck route from Malawi which has been called 'the highway of death', since 92 per cent of truck drivers visiting the city were infected with HIV (Webb, 1997).

The gravity of the situation in South Africa is reflected in a report published in May 2000, suggesting that:

➤ an estimated £720 million was spent on educating those of a productive age who died of AIDS in 1999–2000;

➤ by 2003, 12 per cent of highly skilled workers, 20 per cent of skilled workers and 27.2 per cent of low-skilled workers will be infected;

➤ medical aid claims are expected to rise rapidly and some schemes could face bankruptcy;

➤ it will cost the public health system £1690 a year to treat each AIDS patient (ING Barings, 2000).

Another report, published in 2000, considering the macro-economic impact of HIV/AIDS in South Africa, suggested that by 2008 the difference in real GDP growth rates between an 'AIDS scenario' and a 'no-AIDS scenario' could reach 2.6 per cent. However, due to a cumulative effect, it was estimated that real GDP by 2010 could be about 17 per cent below the level attained in the 'no-AIDS' scenario, as a larger proportion of the economically active workforce becomes infected (Arndt and Lewis, 2000).

In sharp contrast to Uganda, it has been suggested that, 'In the field of HIV/AIDS South Africa is a land of

▶

BOX 5.6 (continued)

missed opportunities and prevarication. One of the highest rates of HIV/AIDS infection in the world makes the tragic lack of political leadership so much worse' (Haffajee, 2001: 46). There has indeed been much controversy in South Africa over the AIDS issue. Former President, Thabo Mbeki, was strongly criticised for his stance, in which he was reluctant to accept the link between HIV and AIDS, and was less than enthusiastic about AIDS testing and the availability of anti-retroviral drugs. While the country's Anglican bishops agreed to be tested, Mbeki refused to have an AIDS test, saying it was 'irrelevant'. As the influential *Mail and Guardian* newspaper commented in May 2001,

> Rather than appearing as Solomonic wisdom, Mbeki's equivocation on HIV/AIDS, AIDS tests and antiretroviral drugs sounds like a dissident without the courage of his convictions . . . Government's schizoid attitude has already – and is now – taking a terrible toll, not only among the people smitten by HIV, but also among those in government trying to combat it . . . The underlying cause of AIDS is HIV. No one has provided a plausible opposing paradigm. Until Mbeki can either admit or rebut it, our advice to the president is to shut up.
>
> (*Mail and Guardian*, 2001a: 26)

A significant step forward was achieved in April 2001 after a protracted court case in which the Pharmaceutical Manufacturers' Association of South Africa (PMA) disputed the legality of the Medicines and Related Substances Control Amendment Act, which would allow the Minister of Health to take action to procure cheaper generic drugs for South Africa. Eventually, the PMA and 39 of its members dropped their court action, placing the ball firmly in the Government's court to implement major improvements in the health care system, especially for people with HIV/AIDS. As the *Mail and Guardian* commented, 'Now the world will see whether there is any truth in the pharmaceutical company arguments that high prices have simply been an excuse for lack of action by a government that in reality lacked the capacity or political will' (*Mail and Guardian*, 2001b: 2). In October 2001, Mbeki repeated in Parliament his view

that anti-retroviral drugs are toxic, asserting that they 'are becoming as dangerous to health as the thing they are supposed to treat' (*Financial Times*, 2001: iv).

The key question is how to deal with the AIDS crisis as swiftly, effectively and as economically as possible. Government policies have been generally successful in promoting awareness of the disease and most people know their 'ABC': Abstain, Be faithful, Condomise (Plate 5.7), but the chairman of the activist group Treatment Action Campaign (TAC), Zachie Achmat, commented, 'A model that pushes prevention without providing treatment is fundamentally flawed' (*Financial Times*, 2001: iv). The Government announced in November 2001 that it would increase spending on HIV/AIDS in the period up to 2004–2005 from £11 million in 2000 to £37 million. Yet, unlike neighbouring Botswana, South Africa had no plans to make anti-retroviral drugs available because of (according to government) the drugs' perceived toxicity, their excessive cost and the poor infrastructure to support their administration. Meanwhile, Nobel Peace Prize winner Desmond Tutu complained about the Government's 'dithering' and suggested that AIDS is 'the new enemy, the new apartheid' (*Financial Times*, 2001: iv). As we will see later, considerable progress has been made in South Africa since Desmond Tutu made his comments.

In light of earlier government indecision in South Africa, a number of NGOs became actively involved in campaigns to promote HIV/AIDS awareness. Soul Buddyz and Soul City media networks have been particularly effective in respectively targeting younger and older audiences. Another organisation, 'loveLife', supported by the former President's wife, Zanele Mbeki and other leading South Africans, and funded by such bodies as the US-based Henry J. Kaiser Family Foundation, sees itself as 'a new lifestyle brand for young South Africans promoting healthy living and positive sexuality', and has been active, through high-powered media publicity and outreach support programmes, in targeting the 15–20 age group (loveLife/Henry J. Kaiser Family Foundation, 2001). Another organisation, GIPA (Greater Involvement of People Living with AIDS), which started in 1997, has implemented the 'Workplace Model', which involves

BOX 5.6 (continued)

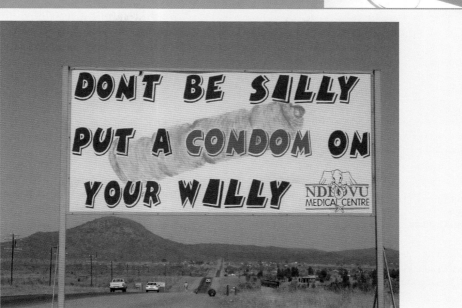

Plate 5.7 Roadside HIV/AIDS poster in South Africa
(*photo*: Bjorn Omar Evju)

placing articulate, open and often healthy HIV-positive people in workplaces to raise awareness and encourage debate (Haffajee, 2001).

The pressure group Treatment Action Campaign, founded in 1998, achieved a notable success in July 2002 when it won its court battle against the government to provide the anti-AIDS drug Nevirapine free of charge to all HIV-positive pregnant mothers in public hospitals. The Constitutional Court ruled the government's policy to be a violation of the constitution, a judgment that represents a landmark in the campaign for free antiretroviral drugs in South Africa. As a result

of pressure from the worldwide campaign for cheaper medicines in the Global South, pharmaceutical manufacturers have reduced significantly the price of many drugs, and it remains to be seen if and when the governments of other poor countries will be both willing and able to make anti-retroviral drugs freely available. Meanwhile, South Africa currently has the world's largest AIDS treatment programme, with some 2.4 million people receiving anti-retroviral therapy in 2014. Yet, in 2016 an estimated 2,700 South African men and women aged 15–24 become infected with HIV each week (BBC, 2016).

Education

If individuals and households are to fulfil their true potential, in addition to the provision of adequate nutrition and health care, it might be argued that an entitlement to education and freedom of expression should be key elements in the development process. Such an approach is embodied in Amartya Sen's 'development as freedom' perspective (Chapter 1). Like health care, education is an expensive item for poor countries and its quality and availability show considerable variations between and within countries, as does student attainment. Like health care, education systems are frequently a legacy of the colonial period, often totally inappropriate for the present-day needs of individuals, communities and nations. Indeed, there has been much debate on what is the most appropriate form and structure of educational provision in poorer countries. For example, what proportion of the budget should be allocated to the different sectors

Table 5.8 Primary school enrolment and literacy for selected countries, 2012

Country	Gross primary school enrolment ratio		Adult literacy rate	
	Male	Female	Male	Female
Bangladesh	111	118	62	55
Brazil	N/A	N/A	91	92
China	128	128	97	93
India	111	114	N/A	N/A
Jamaica	N/A	N/A	83	92
Japan	102	102	99	99
Mali	94	83	43	25
Sierra Leone	132	131	56	34
Sweden	102	101	99	99
United Kingdom	109	108	95	95
USA	99	97	94	94
Zimbabwe	N/A	N/A	88	80

Source: World Bank (2012) *World Development Indicators 2012*. Washington: World Bank Publications.

(primary, secondary and tertiary), and should more attention be given to non-formal education, such as farmer training and the acquisition of craft skills, rather than formal classroom tuition? Most commentators would probably agree, however, that providing everyone with basic primary education, especially literacy, should be the first priority of all countries. Table 5.8 shows how primary school enrolment and adult literacy rates in Mali, one of the world's poorest countries, are well below those of other countries. In many countries there is also a marked difference in the number of boys who attend school compared with the number of girls. Generally, fewer girls attend school, particularly in Muslim countries, and this is reflected in later years in male and female adult literacy rates (see Critical reflection box).

The 1990 World Conference on Education for All, held in Jomtien, Thailand, proclaimed the need for diverse, flexible approaches within a unified national system of education (UNICEF, 1997). The conference agreed a number of objectives for primary education:

➤ *Teach useful skills*. Courses should be relevant and linked to community life.

➤ *Be more flexible*. Use child-centred approaches; adjust school timetables to the daily routine and the seasonal farming calendar.

➤ *Get girls into school*. Be sensitive to social, economic and cultural barriers to ensure equal participation.

➤ *Raise the quality and status of teachers*. Improve pay and conditions and retrain those teachers with negative and stereotypical ideas.

➤ *Cut the family's school bill*. School fees and equipment charges deter participation; basic education that deters child labour must be free of such costs for poor families.

Global differences in enrolment ratios becomes greater at secondary and tertiary levels. As Gould (2009) has shown for secondary enrolment, Africa lags far behind other regions, whereas for South Asia the relatively higher proportion of the secondary age group enrolled in India is pulled down by much lower proportions in Bangladesh and Pakistan, both with populations of well over 100 million. Both Pakistan and Bangladesh are Muslim countries with low female participation in secondary education. At the tertiary level, although 40 per cent of the age group is enrolled in education in the high-income countries, an average figure of under 10 per cent is common in low- and middle-income countries, ranging from 5 per cent in sub-Saharan Africa to 11 per cent in Latin America and the Caribbean (Gould, 1993; UNESCO-UIS, 2006).

Some governments have introduced wide-ranging reforms to their education systems in an effort to make them more appropriate for national development needs. Whereas the small West African state of The Gambia in 1999 established its own university with Canadian and Cuban assistance, rather than sending students overseas for higher education, Africa's most populous state, Nigeria, has debated whether it should nationalise its extensive university system to reduce expenditure. Meanwhile, Ghana has also undertaken major educational reforms. In the 1950s the country probably had the highest proportion of its children in school in Africa, and this expanded further after independence. However, as the national economy deteriorated so did the schools and the quality of education, such that education spending fell from 6.5 per cent of GDP in 1976 to only 1 per cent in 1983. From 1985, under the Economic Recovery Programme of Jerry Rawlings' government, schools were encouraged to make a more positive contribution to economy and society. A single Ministry of Education and Culture was created along with decentralised planning in 110 districts. The school system was reduced from 17 to 12 years, the cost of boarding was passed on to pupils and student loans were introduced in the tertiary sector. The curriculum was restructured to emphasise practical and life skills rather than academic subjects. A strong emphasis was placed on expanding school enrolments, especially for girls (Binns, 1994a).

Investment in female education must receive top priority, not least because studies have revealed strong links between education and health, notably a strong correlation between high levels of infant and child mortality and low levels of maternal education, particularly basic literacy (see Critical reflection box).

Critical reflection

Educating girls

Sustainable Development Goals 4 and 5 are concerned with achieving universal primary education, promoting gender equality (especially in education) and empowering women. In many countries of the South far fewer girls attend school than boys, which is reflected in the difference between male and female adult literacy rates. Some North African, and predominantly Muslim countries, have among the highest disparities between male and female adult literacy rates. In Tunisia, a 'high human development' country, 88 per cent of males over the age of 15 are literate, but the proportion of females is only 72 per cent. In Niger, the country with the lowest Human Development Index in 2013, only 23 per cent of adult males could read and write, and just 9 per cent of females had these important skills (UNDP, 2014).

Numerous studies have clearly shown that educating girls has a significant impact on the health and welfare of households (Momsen, 2010). Educated girls generally marry later and are more likely to engage in economic activity outside the home. Furthermore, they tend to have fewer children and seek medical attention sooner for themselves and their children. They typically provide better care and nutrition for themselves and their children, which lead to a reduction in disease and lower child mortality. A reduction in child mortality over time leads to smaller families, increased use of contraceptives and smaller households. Childcare improves with smaller households and with lower fertility the school-age population gradually declines.

Examine some of the different strategies for improving the education of girls. What do you believe is the best way forward in the world's poorest countries?

Plate 5.8 Children using a computer in Tunisia
(*photo*: Jennifer Elliott)

Conflict, post-conflict, security and livelihoods

Periods of political instability and conflict can have a very significant and sometimes long-term effect on livelihoods (MacGinty and Williams, 2009). Normal routines of daily life can be severely disrupted, with household assets lost, food production and distribution interrupted, basic infrastructure damaged and deteriorating, whilst access to key services such as health and education can become difficult. Elsewhere in this book various issues relating to conflict and post-conflict scenarios are considered. The United Nations' peacekeeping role is examined in Chapter 7, whilst forced migration, as a common outcome of conflict situations, is considered in Chapter 8. Earlier in this chapter we examined the position of children in conflict situations.

In addition to the physical effects of conflict, it is important not to underestimate the psychological effects of conflict which can persist for many years after peace and stability have been restored. An NGO, 'Doctors without Borders' (Médécins Sans Frontières, MSF), conducted a psychosocial survey in Sierra Leone's capital, Freetown in May 1999 during the civil war, and discovered that,

> 99% of those surveyed suffered some degree of starvation, 90% witnessed people being wounded or killed, and at least 50% lost someone close to them. The intensity of the fighting is indicated by the numbers: 65% endured shelling, 62% the burning of their property, and 73% the destruction of their homes. Physical harm was also great: 7% had been amputated (typically a limb, hand, foot or ear), 16% had been tortured by a warring faction, 33% had been held hostage, and 39% had been maltreated in some way or another.
>
> (Doctors Without Borders (MSF), 1999)

The nature and level of violence can affect the re-building of livelihoods in the post-conflict period. During Sierra Leone's civil war (1991–2002), atrocities carried out by RUF (Revolutionary United Front) rebels included the brutal amputation of limbs of both adults and children, whilst in northern Sri Lanka some areas of farmland were planted with landmines which persisted

long after the end of the war in 2009. Reflecting on the experience of the Sri Lankan civil war, Korf (2004) comments that 'the psychological effects of such a situation of increased vulnerability are reported to be striking, and include lack of self-confidence, tendency to keep a low profile, frustration as a result of restricted life opportunities, fear and desperation' (Korf, 2004: 281).

In northern Uganda, the instability and conflict since the mid-1980s has led to loss of cattle, homes and assets, together with massive displacement of the local population. As Birner et al. (2011) comment, 'Some households were displaced due to fighting between the Ugandan People's Defense Forces and the rebel Lord's Resistance Army (LRA) and direct attack on civilians, but most became internally displaced persons (IDPs) as a result of the government's 2002 relocation order' (7). The movement of Acholi people to government camps in 2002 led to an increase in IDPs to 800,000 by the end of the year.

Mallett and Slater (2012) conclude that conflict can cause 'significant and long-lasting detrimental effects on human capital formation', and that 'certain segments of the population suffer worse and longer-lasting effects than others' (Mallett and Slater, 2012: 17). Vulnerable groups such as young girls, low income households, forced migrants and disadvantaged ethnic minority groups are particularly affected by conflict.

In a 2001 study of household livelihood strategies in four villages in the contested frontier area of northeastern Sri Lanka, a region occupied by the Liberation Tigers of Tamil Eelam (LTTE), migration, forming alliances, and receiving support from remittances and from extended family networks proved to be important factors in shaping household survival strategies (Korf, 2004). But poorer households with limited social networks had much less flexibility in terms of receiving support, and levels of success in coping with instability in the war zone varied considerably. In one Tamil village, Ithikulam, which was located between the rebel and army combat lines, households had to abandon traditional paddy cultivation and move to another area where they eventually developed a successful business in vegetable production, generating funds that were used to build houses. Meanwhile, in Vattam, a coastal fishing village where rebels often stole boats and the army controlled fishing locations, many households withdrew from fishing and became dependent on remittances from overseas relatives (Korf, 2004).

The post-conflict period is a crucial time for ensuring full disarmament, re-building livelihoods and getting over the trauma of conflict. The so-called DDR approach to peacebuilding is now widely accepted, which involves Disarmament, Demobilisation and Reintegration (Muggah, 2005). After the end of the civil war in Sierra Leone in 2002 the disarmament process was swift and effective, with some 72,490 combatants disarmed, and followed by time spent in demobilisation camps where they learned about civics and democracy. The process of re-incorporating ex-combatants into communities can be both delicate and complex. Re-settling former rebels into communities where they may have committed atrocities requires both empathy and understanding on the part of both the ex-combatants and community members. Since many of the rebels were disaffected and unemployed youths, it might be argued that the DDR process was trying to re-integrate people who had never been truly integrated in their communities.

In Sierra Leone, providing ex-combatants and other young people with gainful employment has been a key priority, which was reflected in the country's second Poverty Reduction Strategy Paper of 2009. Promoting vocational training and the generation of employment opportunities has been an important aspect of government and NGO policy, reflecting a genuine concern that large numbers of unemployed and disaffected youths could lead to further political instability. Although youth unemployment remains a serious problem, a study of vegetable and fruit growing in post-conflict Freetown, Sierra Leone's capital and largest city, revealed that large numbers of young people, many of them ex-combatants, are getting involved in such activities to supplement household food supply at a time of rising food prices, to generate income from market sales and to provide employment and empowerment (Maconachie et al., 2012).

Human rights

The Universal Declaration of Human Rights was a landmark agreement adopted by the United Nations General Assembly on 10 December 1948. After the trauma and atrocities committed during the Second World War, 50 representatives of member states agreed to the recommendations of a Drafting Committee chaired by diplomat, activist and former First Lady of the United States, Eleanor Roosevelt. The preamble to the Declaration states,

> Whereas the peoples of the United Nations have in the Charter reaffirmed their faith in fundamental human rights, in the dignity and worth of the human person and in the equal rights of men and women and have determined to promote social progress and better standards of life in larger freedom'.
> (UN, 1948: 1)

In the period following the Declaration, ideological differences between Western Liberal democracies and Socialist Eastern Bloc countries led to variations in interpretation and application of the 29 'articles', which include aspects such as the right to asylum, the right to freedom from torture, the right to free speech and the right to education (Elliott, 2014).

The Vienna Conference on Human Rights in 1993 also revealed significant differences in opinion on the nature of human rights and related policies. For example, some Asian countries questioned external criticism of their human rights records; in particular, they showed their resentment at having imposed on them a set of values based upon Western traditions (Drakakis-Smith, 1997). However, many would agree that an important issue affecting the quality of life is the ability of all people to voice their opinions freely and without fear of retribution. In some countries it is apparent that certain elements of the population, such as women, are denied complete freedom of speech because of religious and/or cultural attitudes. Across the world, there are many examples of repressive regimes, both military and civilian, which have clamped down with varying degrees of severity on any opposition.

China's continuing 'occupation' of Tibet is a source of much controversy. Although the extent and nature of Chinese influence and control over Tibet through history is disputed, in 1950 the People's Liberation Army clashed with Tibetan troops as the new Chinese government sought to integrate Tibet into the Chinese state. This policy was given a significant boost when, in 1954, China and India reached an agreement, whereby India recognised Tibet to be an integral part of China in return for China undertaking to respect religious and cultural traditions (Saich, 2011). However, in 1959 there was a rebellion in Tibet against Chinese control and the Tibetan Buddhist spiritual leader, the Dalai Lama, and many of his followers, fled to India, where they still remain. Meanwhile, China has steadily strengthened its control over Tibet, increasing the number of troops, introducing inappropriate policies and suppressing religious and cultural activity. China has even installed a young boy as its own 'puppet' spiritual leader in place of the Dalai Lama. In 1987, Beijing reasserted that 'Tibet is an inalienable part of Chinese territory' (*Beijing Review*, 19 October: 14).

In other countries, freedom of speech has been denied to specific racial groups, and nowhere was this more entrenched than under the apartheid regime in South Africa (Lester et al., 2000) (see Box 5.7).

BOX 5.7

Racial discrimination and separation in apartheid South Africa

In 1948, the same year as the Universal Declaration of Human Rights was signed, South Africa's National Party took power and formally introduced a policy of 'apartheid' or separateness. Apartheid was a policy based on fear, notably fear of the minority White population being dominated by the majority Black population. But the White regime was also well aware that economic survival was completely and unavoidably dependent on the plentiful supply of cheap non-White labour. The National Party government argued that different racial groups should be allowed to live and develop separately, each at its own pace and in accordance with its own cultural heritage, resources and abilities.

In reality, however, the regime was harsh and introduced a wide range of oppressive legislation to control the lives of non-White groups, which together comprised over 85 per cent of South Africa's population. The Group Areas Act of 1950 extended the principle of separate racial residential areas on a comprehensive and compulsory basis whilst, under the 1955 Natives (Urban Areas) Amendment Act, the rights of Blacks to live in a town were restricted to those who had either been born there or who had worked there for 15 years, or 10 years with a single employer. All other Blacks required a permit to stay for longer than three days.

Black political parties such as the African National Congress (ANC) were banned in 1960, police powers increased in 1962, Black newspapers suppressed in 1976 and censorship of political pamphlets introduced. A catalogue of legislation enforced what was known as 'petty apartheid', which took such forms as segregated transport, public toilets and even beaches. Meanwhile, the broader national development strategy known as 'grand apartheid' was manifested in the creation of homelands called 'Bantustans'. Through the 1959 Promotion of Bantu Self-Government Act, eight (later extended to 10) distinct 'Bantu homelands' were created, each with a degree of self-government and based largely on the historic homelands of different Black tribal groups. All Black South Africans were given the citizenship of a particular homeland in 1970, but then some subsequently lost their South African citizenship when four homelands were given 'independence': Transkei (1976), Bophuthatswana (1977), Venda (1979) and Ciskei (1981). Although these homelands had all the trappings of independent states, their independence was not recognised by any country other than South Africa (Lester et al., 2000).

Growing internal and international pressure, however, gradually forced the minority government to consider dismantling certain elements of apartheid,

BOX 5.7 (continued)

and this process was accelerated after F.W. de Klerk took power in 1989. In February 1990, an important and historic signal of intent was given to the world community when Nelson Mandela and several other ANC leaders were released from prison. The country's first democratic elections were held in April 1994, and the charismatic Mandela was proclaimed as first President of the 'new' South Africa. Mandela and the new ANC government then set to work on implementing a range of policies through its Reconstruction and Development Programme, designed to dismantle the structures of apartheid and address the practical problems facing one of the world's most 'unequal' nations (Binns and Robinson, 2002).

Conclusion

Returning to a point made at the beginning of this chapter, people are (or should be) central to the development process. Unfortunately, in recent years people have too often been a secondary consideration after the quest for wealth and profit. There is a need to reshape development strategies so that they place people at the heart of development. The Human Rights agenda and other brave calls to the world community have attempted to make this a reality, but sadly their impact has been small. For example, the Independent Commission on Population and Quality of Life (ICPQL, 1996) has argued that the world faces a linked crisis of environment, quality of life and population, and proposes a number of guiding principles in relation to population growth and improving the quality of life: equity, caring, sharing, sustainability and human security. The Commission takes issue with the prevailing concept of development, describing it as 'exclusively economic and obsessed with deregulation [it] . . . inevitably produces massive exclusion, inside every society, among nations, on all continents. This requires a shift in the way policies and measures are shaped and in how political decisions are made' (ICPQL, 1996: 4). The Commission argues that a number of issues must be tackled urgently, including

making life more liveable through improved individual and collective health and security; dealing with the scourges of poverty and exclusion; raising the levels of literacy, education and access to needed information; rationalising production and consumption in terms of what the planet's resources can continue to provide and bringing fairness and equity to all through better-balanced exploitation and use of these resources [such as keeping more profits from raw materials 'at home'; utilising them in a sustainable manner]; more effective policies of aid and assistance; and finding new funding mechanisms between North and South. And, last, but hardly least, caring for ourselves, our neighbours, and the environment by observing the rights pertaining to all of humankind.

(ICPQL, 1996: 286)

The Commission stresses the importance of not only environmental sustainability, but also social sustainability, and it emphasises the synergy between the two. Importantly, the Commission places much emphasis on improving the quality of life, which 'should become the chief focus of governments north and south'. It suggests:

We urgently need a new synthesis, a new balance between market, society and environment, between efficiency and equity, between wealth and welfare- a new balance between economic growth on the one hand, and social harmony and sustainability on the other.

(ICPQL, 1996: 16)

These are admirable sentiments, but given the lamentable record of national government and international community action following earlier well-intentioned initiatives, such as the Brandt Commission (1980) and the Brundtland Commission (1987), there is inevitably some scepticism about possible future progress. However, it remains to be seen how successful the people-centered Sustainable Development Goals will be in putting people first in future development initiatives (see Chapter 1).

Key points

➤ Improvement in the quality of life for all people should be at the core of development processes at all levels – internationally, regionally, nationally and locally.

➤ Relations between people and resources are often complex. Before development strategies are implemented it is important to understand these relationships in detail.

➤ Reliable data on population are essential for planning development interventions at all levels.

➤ Households are often the key unit of production, consumption and decision making. Household structure, dynamics and needs must be understood if appropriate development strategies are to be implemented.

➤ Achieving universal primary education for both girls and boys is one of the Sustainable Development Goals (SDG 4), and is a key priority for all countries.

➤ Access to good health care for everyone is an important goal, particularly in poor countries, and is reflected in several Sustainable Development Goals.

➤ Equality and empowerment for women and basic human rights for all are fundamental entitlements, but some countries still have a long way to go to achieve these objectives.

Further reading

Ansell, N. (2005) *Children, Youth and Development*. London: Routledge.
An excellent book, which examines the position and role of young people in different societies, with particular reference to the process of development in poor countries.

Binns, T. (ed) (1995) *People and Environment in Africa*. Chichester: John Wiley.
This collection of essays provides a number of very useful case studies of how people interact with and manage environment in Africa south of the Sahara.

Binns, T., Dixon, A. and Nel, E. (2012) *Africa: Diversity and Development*. London, Routledge.
This book covers many of the topics raised in this chapter in the context of Africa.

Boserup, E. (1993) The *Conditions of Agricultural Growth*. London: Earthscan.
A classic text, which is frequently cited and counters the Malthusian view concerning the relationship between population and resources.

Devereux, S. and Maxwell, S. (2001) *Food Security in Sub-Saharan Africa*. London: ITDG Publishing.
An important text which defines the concept of food security and examines aspects of food security with reference to case studies from Africa.

Gould, W.T.S. (1993) *People and Education in the Third World*. Harlow: Longman.

One of relatively few texts that focus on the importance of education as a key element in the process of development.

Gould, W.T.S. (2009) *Population and Development*. London: Routledge.
A useful overview of issues relating to demography, human resource development and population policies.

Momsen, J.H. (2010) *Gender and Development*. London: Routledge.
A frequently quoted book examining the significance of gender in the development process.

Websites

www.amnesty.org
Amnesty International.

www.earthsummit2002.org
Earth Summit 2002.

https://esa.un.org/unpd/wpp/publications/files/key_findings_wpp_2015.pdf
UNDESA (2015) *World Population Prospects: The 2015 Revision*, United Nations Population Division.

http://www.malariavaccine.org/about-mvi.htm
Malaria vaccine initiative.

http://www.unaids.org/sites/default/files/media_asset/global-AIDS-update-2016_en.pdf
UNAIDS (2016) *Global AIDS Update*. Geneva: UNAIDS.

http://hdr.undp.org/en/2015-report
UNDP (2015) *Human Development Report 2015*. New York: UNDP.

http://www.unicef.org/sowc2016/
UNICEF (2016) *State of the World's Children 2016*. New York: United Nations Children's Fund.

http://www.worldometers.info/world-population/
World Population Clock

http://www.warchild.org.uk/about
War Child

Discussion topics

➤ With reference to specific case studies, examine the relationships between people and resources. Evaluate the merits and problems of Malthus' and Boserup's perspectives.

➤ Select two countries, one with a pro-natalist population policy and another with an anti-natalist policy. Consider the reasons for the adoption of these policies and the likely effects on population growth and structure.

➤ Summarise the key features of the 'entitlement approach', and evaluate the advantages and problems of this approach in ensuring food security in specific countries or regions.

➤ Investigate the demographic, social and economic effects of high rates of HIV/AIDS infection in selected countries.

Chapter 6
Resources and the environment

This chapter investigates the relationship between development and the environmental resources of the globe. Since we live in a closed system in which matter and energy cannot be created or destroyed, there is no doubt that human societal development ultimately depends on the physical resource base. However, just as Part I has shown something of the diversity of opinion on normative questions of how wealth and well-being should be created and/or redistributed, this chapter reveals the substantial debate that persists as to the precise relationship between prospective development achievements and environmental resources. Questions of resource scarcity, of environmental degradation and global environmental change and the search for new patterns and processes of development that are more sustainable are major challenges currently in development studies and beyond.

This chapter:

➤ Identifies the core features and debates underpinning the notion of sustainable development;
➤ Details the key debates on the link between resources and development at the international scale;

➤ Investigates how new concepts of Planetary Boundaries and Ecosystem Services are shaping approaches to environmental management;
➤ Details recent patterns of resource use in key sectors of water, energy and raw materials to explore concepts of scarcity and equity in the challenges of more sustainable development;
➤ Examines the environmental impacts of development through core global issues such as deforestation, climate change and pollution;
➤ Illustrates the place-specific nature of the relationship between environment and development, but also how the challenges of sustainable development are shaped by processes operating at wider scales.

Introduction: the search for sustainable development

Debates concerning the relationship between human social development and the environmental resources of the globe are long standing. In 1945, for example, the geographer Huntington modelled resource inadequacies as the cause of underdevelopment in the tropical regions of the world (Huntington, 1945). In direct contrast, in 1968 Erhlich modelled development as having put 'mankind on the brink of extinction' (Ehrlich, 1968) through the ways in which it has led to environmental resource destruction. There is debate currently over the possibility of a new geological era being identified: the Anthropocene ('the human age'), such is the influence of human impacts in shaping nature (Monastersky, 2015).

Recent decades have been witness to a range of global environmental problems, many of which are worsening and inter-related and are closely linked to patterns of human development and human action (UNEP, 2012; MEA, 2005). As Barbier (2011) notes, economic development has delivered important benefits for human society, 'but the result has been profound alterations to the world's major ecosystems and the valuable benefits they provide' (234). The Millennium Ecosystem Assessment (MEA) (2005) reported that over 60% of the world's major ecosystem goods and services were degraded and/or being used unsustainably. It is also increasingly understood that environmental problems are inseparably linked to other social, economic and political challenges including poverty, inequality and political conflict as part of a single, complex 'social-ecological' system (ISSC/ UNESCO, 2013). However, the impacts of environmental change are in turn specific to the particular social, economic, political and cultural contexts in which people live.

The concept of 'sustainable development' has been central in fostering a more holistic and nuanced understanding of the complex linkages between environment and human development; how past patterns and processes of development cannot be sustained environmentally over time but also how degradation constrains opportunities now for people to live a life they have reason to value (see Elliott, 2013). The challenge for society is to 'secure a sustainable world through effective responses to today's interacting processes of environmental and social change' (ISSC/ UNESCO, 2013: 34).

This chapter investigates the global challenges of sustainable development in some detail. The first sections expand on the ways in which human society depends on the resources and ecosystems functions of the Earth and considers how natural resource 'limits' and 'planetary boundaries', for example, interact with concerns for social equity and justice in the future development of water, energy and mineral resources. The latter sections detail a number of key patterns of global environmental change that are substantially shaping the global challenge of sustainable development. Chapter 7 considers some of the responses to these challenges on behalf of institutions and actors in development. The outcomes in practice (the consequences of actions taken in response to these challenges) are the focus of Part III.

What is sustainable development?

It has been suggested that the concept of sustainable development can mean anything or everything you want (O'Riordan, 1995) such is the extent of writing, divergent interpretations and applications of the notion of sustainable development (and sustainability). The most often quoted definition of sustainable development dates back to the World Commission on Environment and Development of 1987: 'Development that meets the needs of the present without compromising the ability of future generations to meet their own needs' (WCED, 1987: 43). This apparently simple definition immediately raises questions including what constitutes 'needs', as quite evidently these will mean different things to different people, will change over time and people (can and do) define and meet their 'needs' in ways that exclude others. Further consideration is needed of what and how are the 'limits' to development set – by biophysical processes, human ingenuity and technological developments or by the underling values and social commitments of society? It also raises the question of what is it that one generation is passing to another and different disciplines engage in this debate with varied starting points. Ecologists, for example, may stress sustainability in terms of the future productivity of biomass; economists in terms of capital and natural environmental asset stocks; and sociologists in terms of cultural diversity and social justice (see Elliott, 2013).

The WCED definition raises very clearly the future aspect of sustainable development – the rights of future generations to meet their needs and aspirations – the principle of 'inter-generational equity'. The full report did much to illuminate also the '*intra*-generational equity' concerns underpinning the notion of sustainable development. This refers to the consideration of contemporary social equity across and between groups within the current generation and the rights of every person to a decent quality of life. Social and political scientists raise sustainable development as a moral concept where questions of intra-generational equity, justice and fairness are to the fore. 'Distributional equity', for example, considers how fairly the impacts of environmental change (including as a result of environmental management interventions) are distributed (see Walker, 2012). Table 6.1 points to a number of ethical concerns embraced in environmental change. Most recently, 'inter-species equity' has also been raised within sustainability debates, where the rights of nature and non-human species on an equal basis to human well-being are considered (Redclift, 2014).

In short, there are multiple entry points into, and varied interpretations of, the concept of sustainable development and many more (often deeply contested) ideas on how to put the concept into practice. As Redclift has suggested, the concept has a basic meaning that most people would not argue against; 'Like motherhood, and God, it is difficult not to approve of it' (1997: 438). Indeed, the attractiveness of the concept may lie in precisely the way in which it is used to support varied political and social agendas and practical initiatives. However, it is also a concept that is considered to have 'come of age' (Redclift, 2005), in that a number of shared concerns and principles can be identified 'out of the great diversity of theoretical formulations and applications' (Gibson, 2005: 39). These are identified in Table 6.2.

It is evident that the journey towards more sustainable patterns of development is a universal and globally linked challenge that requires ongoing critical consideration of the processes (means) of development and decision-making across inter-dependent spheres. There are no 'route-maps' (Adams, 2009) or blueprints for sustainable development – what it means will always be socially constructed, defined by

---

Table 6.1 The ethical challenges of global environmental change

Reasons for considering global environmental change as a matter of ethical responsibility include:

➤ The consequences of global environmental change are unevenly and unfairly distributed;
➤ The capacities to respond to the impacts of environmental change are unevenly distributed;
➤ Different groups in society vary in the extent to which they have contributed to environmental change and their reasons for doing so – this raises the issue of fulfilling basic needs as opposed to meeting luxury expectations;
➤ Greenhouse gas emissions will remain in the atmosphere for years to centuries and impact future generations – the issues of intergenerational justice are raised;
➤ Efforts to mitigate greenhouse gas emissions including technological interventions (such as geo-engineering and nuclear energy) and market mechanisms (such as payments for environmental services) involve unequal burden sharing within socieites.

Source: Compiled from ISSC/UNESCO (2013) World Social Science Report

---

Table 6.2 The shared principles of the concept of sustainability

The concept of sustainability is:

➤ A challenge to conventional thinking and practice
➤ About long term and short term well-being
➤ Comprehensive, covering all the core issues of decision making
➤ Recognition of the links and interdependencies, especially between humans and the biophysical foundations for life
➤ Embedded in a world of complexity and surprise, in which precautionary approaches are necessary
➤ Recognition of both inviolable limits and endless opportunities for creative innovation
➤ About an open-ended process, not a state
➤ About intertwined means and ends – culture and governance as well as ecology, society and economy
➤ Both universal and context dependent

Source: Gibson, 2005

societal choices regarding the kind of world we want to live in and to leave as a legacy for future generations. An international consensus on the desirability of (and need for) continued commitment and action on sustainable development was evident in the most recent United Nations Conference on Sustainable Development held in Rio De Janeiro in 2012. The Outcome Document was titled *The Future We Want* and was agreed by 188 participating nations. A common vision for the international community was set out, whereby;

> we recognise that poverty eradication, changing unsustainable and promoting sustainable patterns of consumption and production and protecting and managing the natural resource base of economic and social development are the overarching objectives of and essential requirements for sustainable development. We also reaffirm the need to achieve sustainable development by promoting sustained, inclusive and equitable economic growth, creating greater opportunities for all, reducing inequalities, raising basic standards of living, fostering equitable social development and inclusion, and promoting the integrated and sustainable management of natural resources and ecosystems that supports, inter alia, economic, social and human development while facilitating ecosystem conservation, regeneration, restoration and resilience, in the face of new and emerging challenges.
>
> (UN, 2012: 1).

The international community has recently committed to the Sustainable Development Goals (SDGs) as discussed in Chapter 1 as the 'Road to dignity by 2030: ending poverty, transforming all lives and protecting the planet' (UN General Assembly 2014). An integrated set of six essential elements frame and reinforce both the 'post-2015' sustainable agenda and the future delivery of the SDGs at a country level. These are Dignity: to end poverty and fight inequality; People: to ensure healthy lives, knowledge and the inclusion of women and children; Prosperity: to grow a strong, inclusive and transformative economy; Planet: to protect our ecosystems for all societies and our children; Justice:

to promote safe and peaceful societies and strong institutions and Partnership: to catalyse global solidarity for sustainable development (op. cit.).

Resources and development

All forms of productive activity make demands on the resource base, as raw materials and as energy sources in industrial and agricultural processes and in terms of the varied 'sink' functions that the environment provides in absorbing, dissipating and transporting the by-products of these activities. Resources are also consumed through human social activities associated with fulfilling the basic need for shelter, sustaining urban lifestyles and so on. Intrinsically, the environment supports life itself through the regulation of the Earth's temperature and atmosphere.

It is true that sections of the world's population now live in a 'post-industrial' society that has seen a decline in the traditional dependence on local or regional resources and environments (enabled by developments in transport and communications, in particular). However, the livelihoods of many more people around the globe remain very directly linked to immediate survival needs secured substantially through their local environmental resources (see Chapter 10). Furthermore, the apparent delinking or 'de-coupling' of development from the natural resource base in the more affluent nations has been referred to as a 'geographical illusion' (Emel et al., 2002: 338). The suggestion is that the increased spatial separation of production and consumption particularly through globalisation, whereby many peoples' lifestyles depend on long distance flows of resources, foodstuffs and material goods via such complex commodity chains, obscures the view of the political–economic, social and environmental patterns and processes through which production, exchange and consumption occur. Box 6.1 investigates the flows of carbon and water in the international trade of agricultural products. Making these processes more visible and exploring the benefits and costs of patterns of trade, for example, are central to the challenges of sustainable development and many initiatives towards changing consumption patterns at various scales. As Redclift (2014: 334) suggests, 'the processes through which we enlarge our choices, and reduce those of others, is largely invisible to people in their daily lives'.

BOX 6.1

Trade and embedded resources

Globalisation has been associated with rising volumes of international trade and closer integration of the world's regions (see Chapter 4). Production and consumption activities, particularly in the more industrialised/developed countries, increasingly depend on materials, energy, goods and services sourced from other world regions, the 'de-coupling' of production and consumption in post-industrial societies referred to above, with widespread and complex implications for sustainable development. The notions of 'embedded' materials, energy, carbon and water are now being used in attempts to analyse, and quantify, the full resource requirements associated with the production, transportation, consumption (and in some

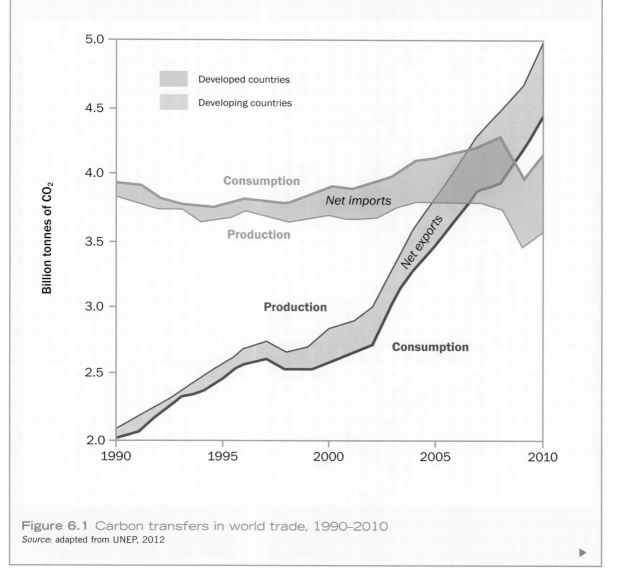

Figure 6.1 Carbon transfers in world trade, 1990–2010
Source: adapted from UNEP, 2012

▶

BOX 6.1 (continued)

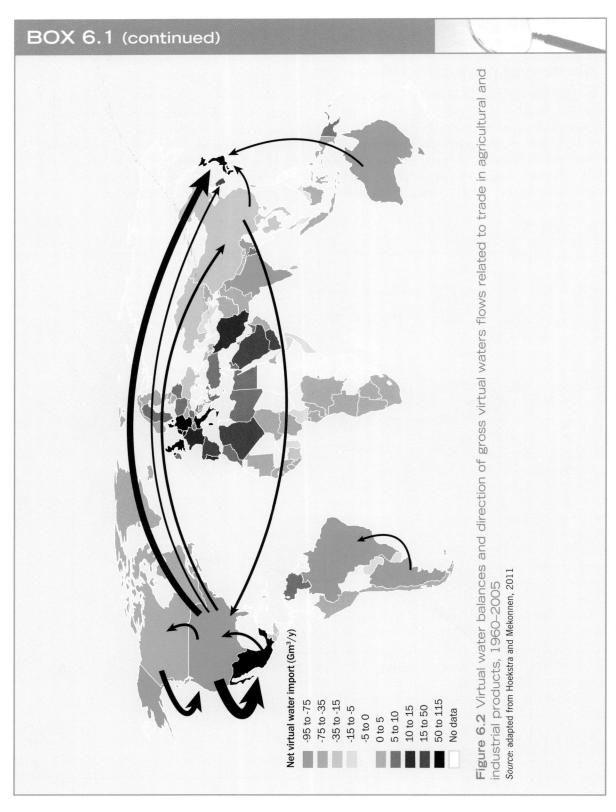

Figure 6.2 Virtual water balances and direction of gross virtual waters flows related to trade in agricultural and industrial products, 1960–2005

Source: adapted from Hoekstra and Mekonnen, 2011

Net virtual water import (Gm³/y)

-95 to -75
-75 to -35
-35 to -15
-15 to -5
-5 to 0
0 to 5
5 to 10
10 to 15
15 to 50
50 to 115
No data

BOX 6.1 (continued)

cases recycling) linked to the import and export of goods worldwide.

This kind of research is helping illuminate the geographic shifts in environmental burden (which locations carry the costs of resource degradation and pollution, for example) embraced in global trade. Figure 6.1 illustrates the 'transfer' of total carbon dioxide emissions between 'developed' and 'developing' countries as an outcome of trade balances. This is the difference between total goods and services imported and exported and the carbon embedded in the production, trading and consumption of those goods and services. Studies at the country level have shown that in Norway, for example, 61% of carbon dioxide embedded in household consumption impacted in foreign countries. In China between 2002 and 2007, between 8 and 12% of carbon dioxide emissions were attributable to exports to the United States (UNEP, 2012).

Analyses of embedded water, also referred to as 'virtual water', measure the volumes of water used, differentiating between 'green' rainwater; 'blue' surface and groundwater; and 'grey' water referring to

freshwater use, in the production of a good or service that are subsequently transferred elsewhere through international trade. Figure 6.2 displays the suggested 'global saving' of water associated with the import and export of agricultural products. It shows the largest savings (indicated by the size and strength of shading of the arrow) in water use through agricultural products consumed in the relatively water scarce countries of Mexico and Japan. These savings are made through the importation of agricultural products, mainly maize and soy bean.

This kind of research is proving useful in highlighting the global transfer of key environmental resources embedded in trade. It is the basis of measures of carbon and water 'foot printing' that, in turn, are being used in innovative schemes of consumer product labelling. Whilst not unproblematic, particularly in terms of providing the basis for policy development (see Wichelns, 2015), they are considered part of efforts to make 'more visible', including to consumers, the processes and patterns of environmental change that connect lifestyles across the globe.

Resource 'limits' in development?

The predominant view of resources is that they are given value by society in respect of the functions they can perform and according to the levels of development and aspirations of society. As Zimmerman (1951: 7) stated, 'Resources are not, they become'. However, there is also the view of environmental resources as stocks of substances or materials found in nature. The substantial debate concerning the adequacy of resources to support the demands of modern society flows from these conceptual differences (Mather and Chapman, 1995: 3):

If environmental resources are simply stocks of substances found in nature, then they are inevitably fixed and limited in quantity. Limits to resource use must inevitably exist. If, on the other hand, resources reflect human appraisal, then the conclusion is

quite different. In this case, their limits are not imposed by the non-human environment, but rather by human ingenuity in perceiving usefulness or value.

In Chapter 5, the doomsday predictions of Thomas Malthus were noted in which he considered that there were definite environmental limits (a fixed amount of land) to human development. Subsequently, influential publications such as *The Limits to Growth* (Meadows et al., 1972) promoted similar views of an ultimate limit on economic development presented by the availability of resources.

In contrast, authors such as Ester Boserup (1965) and Julian Simon (1981) were central in promoting the functional view of resources encapsulated in Zimmerman's definition, and in arguing against the inevitability of societal collapse. They point rather to the social, economic, institutional and technological factors that serve to extend the boundaries of development. In contrast to Malthus's emphasis on the physical limits of resources, these authors focused on the stimulus to, and opportunities for, innovations and developments in resource use which population growth brings. In particular, as resources become more physically scarce, market forces (signaled through price increases) would create the incentives to innovate, develop substitutes, and expand frontiers of production or to increase efficiency for example.

Human ingenuity is certainly displayed in the development of 'new forms of nature' – the new plants, animals and materials produced through the application of biotechnology. The potential of 'Genetically Modified Organisms' to deliver further increases in global food production (and some of the risks and costs involved) are discussed in Chapter 10. Human ingenuity is also illustrated in Case study 6.1 in terms of the characteristics of the irrigation technologies and agro-ecosystems which the Marakwet peoples in Kenya developed in order to sustain occupation and year-round agriculture within the arid Kerio Valley. It is an example of how the constraints of the physical environment are being overcome through technological innovation but also through new social institutions for management of the water and land resources.

Case study 6.1

Extending the ecological margins for development: indigenous irrigation in the Kerio Valley, Kenya

The system of stream diversion and canal networks along the east wall of the Rift Valley in Kenya, the 'Kerio cluster', has been referred to as the most complex and extensive indigenous water management system in Africa south of the Sahara (Adams and Anderson, 1988). Since the nineteenth century at least, the Marakwet peoples have applied considerable engineering skills to exploit the challenging ecologies of the Rift Valley, to enable permanent settlement and the cultivation of cereals and vegetables across the valley floor.

The Kerio Valley itself is an arid area lying around 1,000m above sea level, receiving less than 600mm annual rainfall and with scrub-like natural vegetation. However, less than 10 miles away, but separated by the precipitous Rift Valley escarpment, is the substantially different natural ecology of the Cherangani Plateau at 3,000m above sea level. This is a well-watered zone, receiving around 1,500mm of rainfall annually, supporting evergreen forests, and crossed by two major and several minor rivers and streams.

Over the years the Marakwet people have constructed dams, furrows, channels and terraces to divert and carry the water from the minor streams of the plateau to the fields of the valley floor. Earth and stone channels with simple brushwood and stone dams are used to modify the variable flow of the natural streams and to carry water to the majority of fields between the foot of the escarpment and the east bank of the Kerio River. Irrigation furrows are also used to irrigate kitchen gardens and fields among the villages of the hillsides (Adams and Anderson, 1988). Complex systems of water allocation for the maintenance of structures have developed within the Marakwet communities (Adams, 1996).

By the 1930s, the system of irrigation and livelihood was the focus of much commentary by outsiders, including colonial officials such as the district officer in the area at that time (Henning, 1941: 270):

> The plan of using streams at the top of the escarpment to water parched fields 3000 feet [1000m] below shows a practical imagination which has sometimes been supposed not to exist in the African.

Subsequently, there have been many different views concerning the environmental sustainability of the system and projects to modify and extend it. It is considered, however, that the current extent of cultivation and settlement along approximately 50 kilometres of the Rift Valley above the Kerio River is at least as extensive as it was in the early nineteenth century (Adams, 1996).

Concerns over physical resource scarcity at a global scale, and so called 'source-limits' for development, were prominent in the 1960s and 1970s with predictions of oil 'running out' and water shortages as a 'new oil crisis' (Biswas, 1993). Whilst these forecasts were not realised (in the timescales envisaged) current discussions over the notion and timing of 'peak oil' and 'peak minerals' discussed further below, point to the continued relevance of stocks of non-renewable resources in shaping future development. Box 6.2 expands on the different notions and key sources of

resource scarcity. In further sections, it becomes evident that questions of resource scarcity are shaped by many factors, not only of supply, but also of demand, the economics of the market and political decision making. Furthermore, what constitutes an environmental 'limit' on development is substantially set by the values and decisions of society; in defining 'acceptable' levels of resource degradation, for example, deciding which environmental resource functions are prioritised and which groups of people, where should bear the costs of degradation.

BOX 6.2

Different notions and sources of resource scarcity

The works of Malthus, Ehrlich and Meadows referred to above emphasised the limits to human development due to insufficient quantities of resources to meet demands. Their ideas were central in shaping the development of the concept of sustainable development (see Elliott, 2013) and continue to attract support and to be applied in contrasting socio-economic and historical contexts (see Chapter 5). The work of Malthus typifies the notion of 'physical resource scarcity', whereby resources and resource functions focus on those that are physically finite (non-renewable), and/or the rates of consumption of renewable resources are in excess of the rates of such renewal. In such circumstances, resources are predicted to become increasingly scarce and costly with conflicts over resources likely to increase.

It has been recognised for some time that 'threats to the sustainable use of resources comes as much from inequalities in peoples' access to resources and from the ways in which they use them as from the sheer numbers of people' (WCED, 1987: 95). Rather than absolute resource scarcity, it is evident that particular groups of people and locations have suffered, and continue to experience, resource constraints in development relative to others. The concept of resource scarcity also becomes much more complex when applied beyond the 'stock resources', such as non-renewable minerals and fossil fuels. Indeed, the physical existence itself of a resource does

not ensure its availability for development; access may be difficult or there may be a lack of sufficient capital or appropriate skills and technology to bring the location into production.

Furthermore, 'geopolitical' resource scarcity (Rees, 1990), may also be produced in circumstances where a resource is heavily localised and producing countries are able to restrict output and/or exports such as prompted by the OPEC countries in the early 1970s. A new kind of resource geopolitics is currently being seen in relation to land, with the large scale purchase, often referred to as 'land grabbing', of agricultural lands by overseas government and private interests (see section below).

Issues of human influence on resource 'scarcity' are also to the fore in models that conceive of resource scarcity in economic terms. Within such thinking, there is an optimism that before resources run out, 'economic scarcity' (as market forces lead to price increases) serve to incentivise human actions to promote resource efficiencies and substitution, through scientific and technological advances. Rees in 1990 forwarded a further category of resource scarcity, referring to scarce 'qualities' of resources, such as with respect to attractive landscapes, wildlife or clean air. Here quality may refer to aesthetics, in the case of valued landscapes, or physical characteristics such as the ability of the atmosphere to absorb pollutants. The recent development of the concept of ecosystem

▶

BOX 6.2 (continued)

services, as seen in the main text, has led to notion of 'ecological scarcity', referring to the loss of the benefits and services provided by ecosystems as they are exploited for human use and activity (Barbier, 2011).

Historically, market forces have not operated for these resource qualities, as they have with resources such as oil, to influence demand or to generate alternatives. However, this is changing as seen substantially through this chapter (see also Part III). There are now markets in carbon, created under the UN Kyoto Protocol, and payments to landowners to maintain certain kinds of uses and features, such as within the UN REDD+ scheme, for example.

It is suggested (see Dobbs et al., 2011), that the resource challenges in the next 20 years will be substantially different from any seen in the past, in five main ways:

➤ There will be up to 3 billion more middle class consumers in the global economy, particularly in China and India, with historically unprecedented

rises in wealth, demand for better nutrition and urban infrastructure developments.

➤ Demand is soaring, when finding new sources of supply and extracting them, are becoming increasingly challenging and expensive. A point has been reached where it is more difficult for supply to react quickly to meet rising demand.

➤ Resources are increasingly linked, shown by a closer correlation between resource prices currently than at any point in history. For example, the development of new energy resources often requires more intensive water use and additional resource inputs such as steel. Shortages and price changes in one resource can rapidly impact other resources.

➤ Environmental factors such as deforestation, excessive extraction of water and the risk multiplying effects of climate change are creating increasing constraints on the production of resources and on economic activity more broadly.

It has been questions of how development is currently impacting on a range of resource functions of the Earth related to environmental 'sink functions' that are to the fore in more recent discussion of resources and development. In these cases, the concern is less that resources will run out, and more in relation to the detrimental effects on human health and the operation of ecological systems, for example. This is most readily seen in relation to climate change, where past and current development processes have led to concentrations of greenhouse gases that exceed the natural capacity of the atmosphere to absorb these with impacts including unprecedented increases in average surface temperatures worldwide. Climate change presents complex global challenges for sustainable development that 'span science, economics and international relations' (UNDP, 2007:4), as considered further below (see also Chapter 7). Equity and justice concerns become key with the understanding that the emerging risks (and current impacts) 'fall disproportionately on countries that are already characterized by high levels of poverty and

vulnerability' (op. cit.: 25), and when considering responsibility for (and implications of) actions to respond to climate change. However, it is also substantially through climate change research that the complex interacting biophysical and social components comprising the Earth System are being understood. This includes exploring 'environmental limits' to the ability of the Earth System to absorb anthropogenic changes in terms of thresholds or 'tipping points', whereby abrupt and possibly irreversible changes to the life support functions of the planet could occur, rather than as the outcome of slower, more linear environmental changes.

Planetary Boundaries and a safe (and just) operating space for humanity

The concept of 'Planetary Boundaries' was first forward by Johan Rockström and colleagues at the Stockholm Resilience Centre in 2009. It was developed on the basis of understanding the interactions and non-linear dynamics of the complex components of the Earth System and mounting evidence that human actions have become the main driver of environmental change. In order to prevent human activities pushing the Earth System outside the Holocene state (the only era in the planet's history in which it is known that humanity can thrive) a set of key environmental processes that define a 'safe operating space for humanity with respect to the Earth System' (Rockström et al., 2009: 472) were identified. Central to the concept is that:

Although Earth's complex systems sometimes respond smoothly to changing pressures, it seems that this will prove to be the exception rather than the rule. Many subsystems of Earth react in a non-linear, often abrupt, way, and are particularly sensitive around threshold levels of certain key variables. If these thresholds are crossed, then important subsystems, such as a monsoon system, could shift into a new state, often with deleterious or potentially even disastrous consequences for humans.

(Rockström et al., 2009: 472).

On the basis of scientific understanding of these thresholds (and acknowledging uncertainties around critical levels and processes that may not exhibit threshold behavior), nine planetary boundaries were established at a 'safe distance' from the risks of abrupt, non-linear shifts occurring and in turn triggering 'unacceptable environmental change' (p. 472). As seen in Figure 6.3 (a), three of these interlinked Earth system processes are suggested to have already crossed their boundaries – climate change, rate of biodiversity loss and interference with the nitrogen cycle. Rockström et al. (2009) acknowledge that this is a 'first attempt' in representing the biophysical preconditions for human development and in 'tentatively quantifying' (p. 475) the safe limits outside which the Earth System cannot continue to function in a Holocene-like state. They also recognise that 'determining a safe distance involves normative judgements of how societies choose to deal with risk and uncertainty' (p. 473) and have adopted a 'precautionary approach' in selecting the lower end of the scientific uncertainty range.

The concept of Planetary Boundaries has also been developed by social scientists to recognise the social boundaries below which a range of resource deprivations also endanger human well-being. As Leach et al. (2013: 85) state:

Planetary boundaries propose the outer limits of pressure that humanity should place on critical Earth systems in order to protect human well-being. Yet at the same time, human well-being also depends upon each person having access to the resources needed to meet their human rights, such as food, water, health and energy. Just as there are planetary boundaries beyond which lies environmental degradation that is dangerous to humanity, so too there are social boundaries below which lie resource deprivations that endanger human well-being.

Figure 6.3 (b) integrates the nine Planetary Boundaries of Rockström et al. (2009) shown as an 'environmental ceiling' with eleven social boundaries identified as an inner 'social foundation' for humanity. The social boundaries are presented as illustrative, but are based on the priorities raised by governments at the UN Rio +20 conference in 2012. As such, all boundaries (environmental and social) draw on objective and subjective criteria and the process of setting them involves judgements about acceptable levels of risk and acceptable human outcomes and unacceptable human deprivations. The 'doughnut'-shaped space in the framework represents the 'safe and just' space within which 'all of humanity can thrive by pursuing a range of possible pathways that could deliver inclusive and sustainable development' (Leach et al., 2013: 85).

Ecosystem services and human well-being

Natural ecosystem processes support human lives (and economies) in a myriad of ways. The notion of ecosystem services centres on the benefits that ecological resources and ecosystem functions provide to human well-being. In 2001, the UN Secretary General launched a substantial investigation into the state of the world's ecosystems, the drivers of change and how these were linked to human well-being. The Millennium Ecosystem Assessment (MEA) reports were published in 2005, and combined existing research and information across a huge range of sources including from practitioners and local communities as well as scientific literature and for

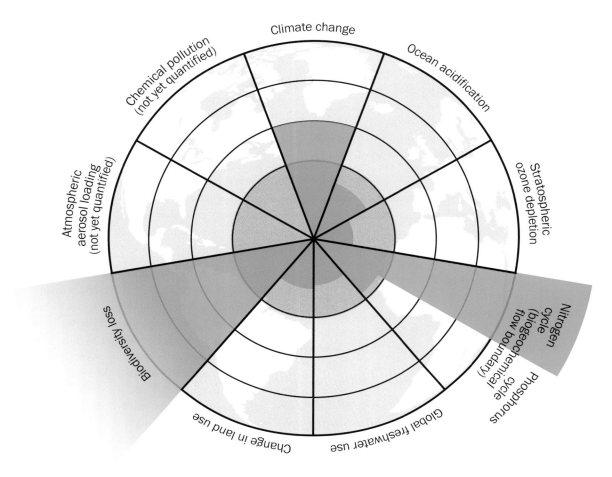

Figure 6.3a The nine Planetary Boundaries of the Earth
Source: adapted from Rockström et al., 2009.

all the major biomes of the world. The MEA has provided significant insight to the profound ways in which human actions have modified ecosystems worldwide, but also to the complex linkages between human well-being (and the multi-dimensional nature of poverty in particular) and 'natural' ecosystem processes. In turn, the findings have significant implications for the challenges of more sustainable development.

The research underpinning the MEA was guided by a Board that involved four working groups, five UN agencies, representatives from five international conventions, international scientific organisations, governments, private sector representatives, NGOs and indigenous groups. Over 2,000 reviewers were involved from 95 countries constituting a substantial undertaking. A people-centred view of ecology was taken, the aim being 'to assess the consequences of ecosystem change for human well-being and to establish the scientific basis for actions needed to enhance the conservation and sustainable use of ecosystems and their contribution to human well-being' (MEA, 2005: ii).

The 'ecosystem services' (in this case defined as the benefits which people obtain from ecosystems) were categorised in four ways, as seen in Figure 6.4. Ecosystems are seen to underpin human well-being through provisioning services such as in food production;

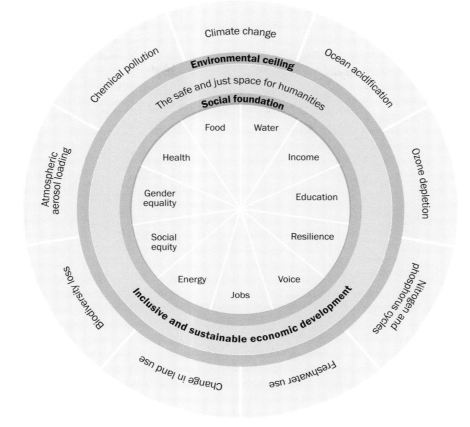

Figure 6.3b A safe and just space for humanity
Source: adapted from Raworth, 2012.

regulating services that maintain a benevolent environment and protect against environmental disturbances; cultural services reflected in religious or recreational values and practices, for example; and supporting services such as nutrient recycling that underpin the other services that ecosystems support. Figure 6.4 also shows that some aspects of ecosystem services can be influenced or 'mediated' by socio-economic factors to different degrees to shape human well-being. Obvious examples would be through engineering of flood defences and the quality of, and access to, health services. This confirms that the strength of the relationship between ecosystem services and human well-being will vary in different socio-economic and ecological contexts. The arrows portray the broad intensity of the linkages and potential for human intervention.

The MEA reported that approximately 60% of ecosystem services examined are being degraded and/or used unsustainably, including fresh water, fisheries, air and water purification and the regulation of regional and local climate, natural hazards and pests. Table 6.3 identifies those key ecosystems and services that have been enhanced or degraded over the last 50 years. Enhancement is defined as either increased production of, or change in, the ecosystem good or service that leads to greater benefits for people. Degradation is defined where use exceeds sustainable levels, or a reduction in the benefits obtained due to human-induced

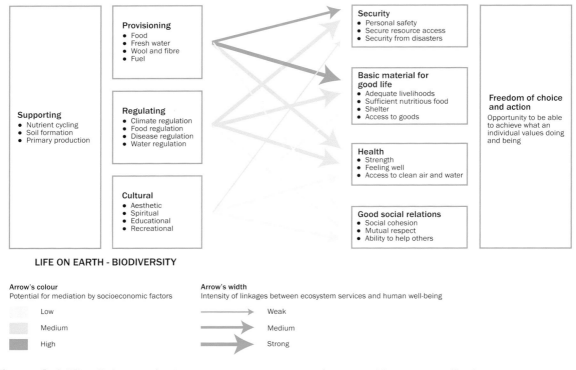

ECOSYSTEM SERVICES

CONSTITUENTS OF WELL-BEING

Supporting
- Nutrient cycling
- Soil formation
- Primary production

Provisioning
- Food
- Fresh water
- Wool and fibre
- Fuel

Regulating
- Climate regulation
- Food regulation
- Disease regulation
- Water regulation

Cultural
- Aesthetic
- Spiritual
- Educational
- Recreational

LIFE ON EARTH - BIODIVERSITY

Security
- Personal safety
- Secure resource access
- Security from disasters

Basic material for good life
- Adequate livelihoods
- Sufficient nutritious food
- Shelter
- Access to goods

Health
- Strength
- Feeling well
- Access to clean air and water

Good social relations
- Social cohesion
- Mutual respect
- Ability to help others

Freedom of choice and action
Opportunity to be able to achieve what an individual values doing and being

Arrow's colour
Potential for mediation by socioeconomic factors
- Low
- Medium
- High

Arrow's width
Intensity of linkages between ecosystem services and human well-being
- Weak
- Medium
- Strong

Figure 6.4 The linkages between ecosystem services and human wellbeing
Source: adapted from Millennium Ecosystem Assessment, 2005.

change or use exceeding its limits (MEA, 2005). Degradation and unsustainable changes have largely occurred as the result of growing and unprecedented demand for services such as food, fresh water, timber, fibre and fuel, confirming that the increase in provisioning services, particularly through the expansion of agriculture, has been met at the costs of other ecosystem services. Furthermore, these 'tradeoffs' were found to 'often shift the costs of degradation from one group of people to another or defer costs to future generations' (MEA, 2005:1) confirming the equity challenges of sustainable development.

The MEA also found evidence of potential 'tipping points' operating in the processes of ecosystem change. As identified above in relation to Earth Systems science more widely, the risks of nonlinear changes, including abrupt and potentially irreversible changes, are increasing through the changes being made in ecosystems, with profound implications for human well-being. Evidence reported in the MEA included

the creation of dead zones in coastal waters, shifts in regional climate and abrupt alterations in water quality. These processes are already causing significant harm to some people, particularly the poor, and will substantially diminish the longer term benefits that can be obtained from ecosystems.

Further confirmation of the distributive and equity challenges of sustainable development was the key finding that the persistent declines in the capacity of ecosystems to deliver services are being borne disproportionately by the poor in all regions and most overtly in sub-Saharan Africa. Ecosystem services are a dominant influence on the livelihoods of most poor people (MEA, 2005: 61), particularly through provisioning services that support food production, primary sources of energy and for protecting and providing water resources (see Chapter 10). As such, they are also highly vulnerable to ecosystem change through impacting on basic material needs, but also through impacts on other components of well-being. For example, freedom of

Table 6.3 The global status of key ecosystems services

Condition globally has been enhanced

➤ Crops
➤ Livestock
➤ Aquaculture
➤ Global climate regulation

Condition globally has been degraded

➤ Capture fisheries
➤ Wild foods
➤ Wood fuel
➤ Genetic resources
➤ Biochemicals, natural medicines and pharmaceuticals
➤ Fresh water
➤ Air quality regulation
➤ Regional and local climate regulation
➤ Erosion regulation
➤ Water purification and waste treatment
➤ Pest regulation
➤ Pollination
➤ Natural hazard regulation
➤ Spiritual and religious values
➤ Aesthetic values

Condition globally is mixed

➤ Timber
➤ Cotton, hemp, silk and other fibre crops
➤ Water regulation
➤ Disease regulation
➤ Recreation and ecotourism

Source: compiled from MEA, 2005.

choice and action (a core component of well-being seen in Figure 6.4) is compromised with environmental degradation, often for women and children who spend more time in the collection of water and fuelwood for basic household needs, thereby reducing time for education or employment. In addition, dependence on ecosystem services was found to increase with diminished well-being, creating further pressures on ecosystems and potential for degradation. The harmful effects of the degradation of ecosystem services were also found to be 'contributing to growing inequities and disparities across groups of people, and were at times, the principal factor causing poverty and social conflict' (MEA, 2005: 2).

In its recommendations for action, the MEA made substantial recourse to the role of economic and financial interventions to promote more sustainable use of ecosystems; 'because many ecosystem services are not traded in markets, markets fail to provide appropriate signals that might otherwise contribute to the efficient allocation and sustainable use of the services' (p. 21). The MEA urged the greater use of economic instruments and market-based approaches in the management of ecosystem services. This is consistent with what has been referred to as the market environmentalism/green capitalism approach to natural resource management that emerged through the 1990s and became mainstream in policy thinking and in much project planning in the space of a decade (Shaw, 2014). In part, this was due to the rising interest of economists in issues of environmental management, but was 'substantially a reflection of the mounting influence of neo-liberal thinking through this period, whereby the extension of market relationships into ever more arenas of society was considered the best way forward' (Elliott, 2013: 48). In short, there has been considerable expansion in efforts to put a monetary value on the range of goods and services provided by ecosystems, to create markets where they did not exist, most obviously in carbon, and in the development of market based mechanisms to deliver environmental improvement and conservation.

However, these market approaches are not uncontested in theory or practice. Many argue against the 'commodification of nature' that these approaches rest on, where whole ecosystems are broken down to the level of an ecosystem service; where natural resource 'services' are transformed into 'objects' as a means for trading as commodities; and how other ways of valuing nature or indeed the intrinsic value of nature, are pushed out in this thinking (see Shaw, 2014). The Key Idea of Payments for Environmental Services below presents some of the concerns regarding an internationally backed scheme which aims to reduce deforestation and degradation of forests towards enhancing their role in absorbing carbon (i.e. the global sink capacity for carbon). It rests substantially on putting an economic value on the role of forests in absorbing carbon and making payments to those land owners that manage those resources. However, there are concerns over environmental justice outcomes of this programme, and in particular, regarding the implications for the most marginalised and vulnerable members of society (see Chapter 10).

'Growing awareness of the impacts of development on natural ecosystems lends urgency to understand and value ecosystem services, as hard choices are faced between growing human populations and economies and shrinking reserves of natural assets and biodiversity' (Shaw, 2014: 360).

Key idea

Payments for Environmental Services

As understanding has risen of both the extent of ecosystem degradation worldwide and the range of valuable services that ecosystems provide, there has been a growing search for innovative solutions for conservation and more sustainable use of natural resources. Payments for Environmental Services (PES) are a tool that is increasingly used, in the Global South and more widely, to address a range of issues including biodiversity, carbon sequestration and watershed services. PES programmes are implemented at local, regional, national and international levels.

PES are based on the 'Beneficiary Pays Principle', which holds that those who use and benefit from environmental services, make payments to those who manage environmental resources, to restore or establish land uses with external benefits. They are a 'market-based mechanism' for natural resources management, in that they create markets for resource functions that may currently not be traded in formal markets, such as carbon sequestration. In putting a monetary value on those services and making payments to those who manage them, the thinking is that there is a financial incentive for local actors to provide and maintain those services that can then be integrated into their land management decisions.

One scheme that has had considerable attention is a global-scale PES programme known as REDD+. RED refers to Reduce Deforestation, the 'second D' to degradation and the '+' refers to the promotion of forest conservation and management. The programme is built on the recognition of the role of land use change and forestry status in the mitigation of climate change. It is a programme with widespread support from the UN and the World Bank, from many government and donors, from private sector interests (such as amongst the plantation, oil and gas

companies) and the Coalition of the Rainforest Nations. A range of pilot REDD+ initiatives are currently in operation, financed largely by bilateral aid, although international agreements on the full details of the programme are yet to be agreed.

The principal behind REDD+ acknowledges that there are powerful economic drivers of deforestation currently in the Global South, including for the conversion to agricultural use, oil palm expansion or industrial tree planting. The essential ideas behind REDD+ is that countries, companies, communities or individuals could be paid to manage forests and reduce deforestation through the transfer of finances from the beneficiaries of such action, i.e. the global community in this case who benefit in terms of the mitigation of climate change impacts. Beneficiaries would pay forest owners for the services that they are providing (maintaining global atmospheric systems) and compensate them for any additional costs and/or loss of income that taking such action to avoid deforestation involves.

Anticipated future funding for REDD+ could come through a direct carbon market, voluntary funds, international arrangements such as debt-for-nature swaps or the development of dedicated international finances such as the UN Green Climate Fund. However, the absence to date of agreement on a large scale funding mechanism, including in the context of wider problems of UN climate negotiations considered below, has slowed the full implementation of the scheme. Critics of REDD+ and payments for environmental services more widely, question the ethics of a market in carbon per se and also of payments being made to corporate interests who are able to continue to pollute or degrade elsewhere.

Water resources and development: scarcity for whom?

Water resources are central to human existence; they are the source of life itself and access to water is a basic human need and a fundamental human right. As identified in the MEA (2005), the 'services' provided to human well-being by freshwater and marine ecosystems are extensive and range from provisioning at the local and household level, water being a key input to the production activities that support livelihoods, through to regulating global climate and weather patterns. However, only approximately 3% of the world's water is freshwater and 2.5% of that is frozen, leaving 0.5% available for human use (UNESCO, 2015). In this way, freshwater resources are fundamentally limited and determined by the precipitation that falls. But mounting demand for, and competing uses of water across agricultural production, in industry and energy, transportation, for leisure and tourism and for domestic/municipal consumption, for example, are understood to have led to inequitable and unsustainable water demands in many countries (UNDP, 2007).

Past patterns and processes of human development have been closely linked to rising demand on water resources. Global water withdrawals accelerated throughout the twentieth century as seen in Figure 6.5 and at rates more than twice that of population growth (UNESCO, 2012). By 2050, global water demand is projected to increase by 55% (UNESCO, 2015), a rate that outstrips projected rates of population growth and will come principally through rising demands related to increased urbanisation and support to associated lifestyles in countries of the Global South. Yet 'business as usual' climate scenarios model a 40% global water deficit by 2030, and suggest that 1.8 billion people worldwide may live in water-scarce environments as regional and local precipitation patterns shift under climate change (UNDP, 2007).

It is this 'mismatch' between water demand and water supply that is the basis for long-standing sustainability concerns and fears of an impending water crisis.

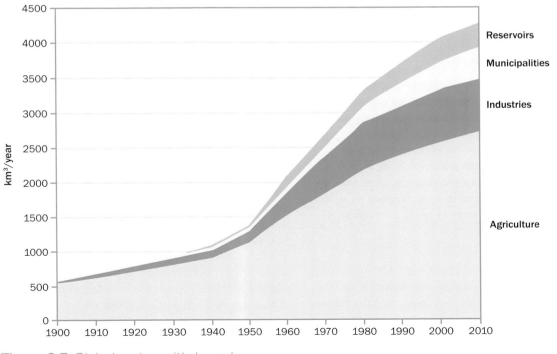

Figure 6.5 Global water withdrawals
Source: adapted from FAO Aquastats.

Fears that the increasing physical scarcity of water could lead to wars over water were prominent in the 1990s. Over 60% of the world's freshwater supply lies and 40% of global population live in 'transboundary' river and lake basins being shared by more than two countries (UNEP, 2012). The concern was that competition for scarce water could threaten already fragile ties between countries in key regions like the Middle East. Whilst outright 'water wars' have generally been avoided including through international treaties, many such agreements are regularly being tested (such as the Indus Water Treaty signed between Pakistan and India). Furthermore, 60 per cent of transboundary basins currently lack any form of cooperative framework to manage these resources (UNESCO, 2015), presenting substantial challenges of water governance as considered in Box 6.3. As competition over water rises with increased scarcity, there are also many examples of conflict at the local level where water needs are immediate (see Part III) and it is regularly people with the weakest rights such as small scale farmers and women who lose out (UNDP, 2007).

BOX 6.3

The challenge of transboundary water resources for international institutions in development

Although there is much progress to be made globally in the more efficient management of existing water sources to enhance supply, increasingly, and particularly in the Global South, the prospects of securing the water resources required to facilitate future development depend on the use of transboundary river and lake basins and aquifer systems (UNEP, 2012). The significance of the challenge was encapsulated by Biswas (1993: 167):

> Difficult though it is going to be to institute more rational and efficient management policies and practices for water sources that are contained wholly within the geographical boundaries of individual sovereign states for a variety of interrelated technical, economic, social, institutional and political reasons, the problem is likely to be intensified by several orders of magnitude when the management and development processes for water sources that are shared by two or more countries are considered.

Figure 6.6 highlights the predominance of transboundary river and lake systems within the Global South. Although the majority of international water bodies are shared by only two countries, there are nine river and lake basins which cut across more than six countries. Except for the Danube (12 countries) and the Rhine (eight countries), all of these systems – the Niger, Nile, Zaire, Zambezi, Amazon, Lake Chad and the Mekong – are in the Global South. The particular and challenging standing of Africa, as host to many of the largest river systems of the globe, is evident. There are 60 rivers and lakes extending into two or more countries on the continent, comprising 62% of the total land area (Wolf et al., 1999). Part of the explanation of the large number of international basins in Africa, is due to the characteristics of the political boundaries within the continent, which were 'drawn by the European powers with scant regard even for the physical geography of Africa, let alone the Africans' (Griffiths, 1993: 66).

International initiatives towards the improved management and governance of freshwater sources have proliferated in recent decades, with over 3,600 treaties relating to common rivers and water basins (UNEP, 2012). In many cases, however, these regulations have been disregarded or proven inadequate (Biswas, 1992). Many are in need of renegotiation (UNEP, 2012). In the Middle East, the Nile Water Agreements signed in 1959 between Sudan and Egypt is regularly ignored, with Egypt exceeding its quota for water extractions on an annual basis (Lee and Bulloch, 1990). Often it is conflict over quantities of flow and the creation of dams that are the basis for international cooperation and conflict (De Stefano et al., 2010). Syria and Iraq nearly went to war in 1975 after Syria and Turkey filled reservoirs behind two new dams, causing a sharp drop in the level of the

BOX 6.3 (continued)

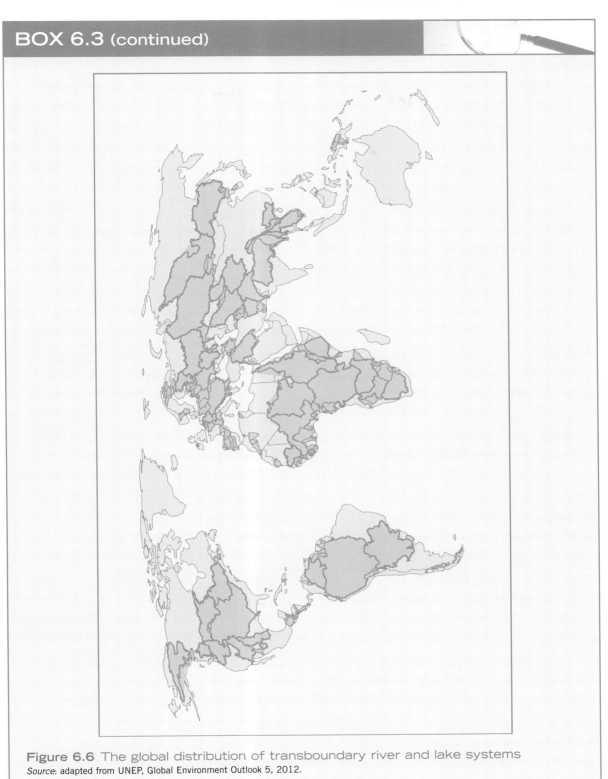

Figure 6.6 The global distribution of transboundary river and lake systems
Source: adapted from UNEP, Global Environment Outlook 5, 2012.

BOX 6.3 (continued)

Euphrates (Vesiland, 1993). Iraq depends on the Euphrates and the Tigris for its water, most of which originates in Turkey. The series of dams created by Turkey under its Greater Anatolia Project (GAP) has also led to diversions of water from the Euphrates and 'suddenly achieved what years of diplomacy had failed to do – the bringing together of Iraq and Syria' (Lee and Bulloch, 1990: 13).

The problems associated with individual transboundary water systems are very country-specific. They accommodate factors including fears over national sovereignty, political sensitivities, historical grievances and national self-interest. Political conflict continues to overshadow water relations between Israel and Palestine, for example, and compromise efforts to build functioning water sectors in these countries (Jägerskog, 2013). Water management issues were part of the Israeli-Jordanian peace agreement in 1994, through which cooperation on the transboundary management of the River Jordan has been relatively effective. However, it remains unclear concerning water allocation during (frequent) drought years (Jägerskog, 2013).

It is generally understood that that in large measure, cooperation outweighs conflict in international hydro-diplomacy (De Stefano et al., 2010). Most regularly, they exist side by side with continuous negotiations despite disagreements (Jägerskog, 2013). However, the majority of international river basins continue to lack any type of cooperative management framework (UNESCO, 2015). It is suggested that moves towards a single unified framework for the environmental governance of the world's transboundary water resources continue to evade the international community (Uitto, 2004), including for the politically sensitive nature of the issues.

Indeed, Biswas (2004: 81) suggests that 'water disappeared from the international political agenda in the 1980s and 1990s' and was 'confined to the wings' during the Earth Summit at Rio de Janeiro, as issues of climate change and biodiversity took centre stage. In 1997, the UN General Assembly adopted the convention on non-navigational uses of international watercourses after several decades of negotiations. It remains the only treaty governing shared freshwater resources that is of universal applicability. However, there are only 36 Parties to the convention to date.

Since 1996, 188 member organisations from 71 countries have been part of the International Network of Basin Organisations, whose objectives include: to develop permanent relations with the organisations interested in comprehensive river basin management and facilitating the exchange of experiences and expertise among network members; promoting the principles and means of sound water management in sustainable development cooperation programmes; promoting the exchange of information and training programmes for the different actors involved in water management. The network is open to public organisations managing large transboundary river basins and to bi- and multilateral development agencies. The network is membership based and is a non-profit organisation. It has 'special consultative status' with the United Nations Economic and Social Council (ECOSOC).

In 2000, the UN established the World Water Assessment Programme (WWAP) under UNESCO. Whilst not focused on the issues of transboundary water resource issues specifically, this is an initiative towards assisting national governments in the development and implementation of national water management programmes and capacity, to initiate a global monitoring system and to pool the perspectives of the various UN agencies involved. WWAP coordinates the influential triennial publication of the World Water Development Report, for example.

There is a further role for international institutions and bilateral organisations through the support and conditions on funding for capital-intensive water projects, with opportunities to promote the adoption of international treaties and the management of needs across the whole system. The Global Environment Facility (see Chapter 7) is considered to be a major facilitator of the implementation of international water agreements and of action plans around transboundary freshwater resources (Uitto, 2004).

Water scarcity and equity at the household level

There are currently 663 million people worldwide who do not have access to an improved drinking water source and a further 2.4 billion who lack access to improved sanitation (UNICEF/WHO, 2015). The global challenge of fulfilling the basic human right to safe water and ensuring greater equity in access to water as a foundation for human development was recognised in the targets on water and sanitation as part of the Millennium Development Goals. Whilst the target to halve the proportion of people without access to safe water provision was substantially met in 2015, there remain large inequities between rural and urban areas and by wealth, for example. The target on access to improved sanitation was not met as seen in Chapter 1 and remains a key challenge for more sustainable development. Figure 6.7 confirms the persistent challenges of meeting these basic human needs lies largely in two regions, sub-Saharan Africa and South Asia. Eight out of 10 people still without access to safe drinking water worldwide live in rural areas and almost 50% of the total rural population worldwide lack access to improved sanitation facilities (UNICEF/WHO, 2015).

Data regarding 'coverage' also does not capture the full inequities with continued disparities in quality and reliability of services or access by gender. For example, 'many people around the globe including women, children, the elderly, indigenous peoples and people with disabilities have lower levels of access to safe drinking water, hygiene or sanitation facilities than other groups' (UNESCO, 2015: 14). Such exclusion has long-term social and economic effects whereby these people are more likely to remain poor and lack opportunities for education, employment and social engagement (Plate 6.1).

The centrality of issues of access to safe water supply and sanitation in human health and development is confirmed in Table 6.4, which shows the global burden of major diseases attributable to water and sanitation and wider environmental factors. Such diseases are a function, not only of the presence of disease vectors (i.e. water quality), but also the quantity of water that a household can command (through public piped supply, purchase or collection), and the provisions for removal of water once used. Furthermore, water resource constraints operate in conjunction with other features of the urban environment – such as cramped housing conditions which make for the rapid transmission of disease and aggravate ill-health. The WHO estimates that one-tenth of the global disease burden could be prevented by improvements in water supply and sanitation (UNESCO, 2009). The benefits of improvements also go well

(a)

(b)

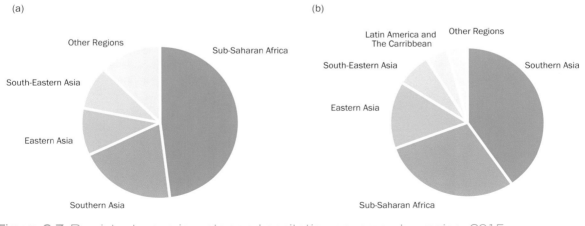

Figure 6.7 Persistent gaps in water and sanitation coverage by region, 2015
(a) Population without access to improved water
(b) Population without access to improved sanitation
Source: adapted from UNICEF/WHO, 2015.

Plate 6.1 Accessing water in the absence of piped supplies
(a) Kathmandu, Nepal (photo: Lola Odessey Waters)
(b) Shaanxi Province, China (photo: Elona Hoover, jesidewalks)
(c) Sirajgani District, Northern Bangladesh (photo: Phil Ashworth)

Table 6.4 Major diseases attributable to environmental factors

Disease	Annual global burden attributable to water, sanitation and hygiene		Percent of total burden attributable to environmental factors
	Deaths (thousands)	DALY * (thousands)	
Diarrhea	1,523	52,460	94
Malnutrition	863	35,579	50
Malaria	526	19,241	42
Lymphatic fiariasis	0	3,784	66
Intestinal nematodes	12	2,948	100
Trachoma	0	2,320	100
Schistosomiasis	15	1,698	100
Japanese encephalitis	13	671	95
Dengue	18	586	95

*Disability adjusted life year, a summary measure of population health. One DALY represents one lost year of healthy life.
Source: UNESCO World Water Development Report, 2009

beyond human health, in terms of the costs avoided for health care systems, the time saved in collection at the household level (giving more time for other economic and social roles), and enhanced dignity, privacy and safety at an individual level.

In 2006, the UN made the Global Water Crisis the focus for its annual Human Development Report. It was sub-titled 'Beyond Scarcity: power, poverty and the global water crisis', and was unequivocal in arguing that the 'the scarcity at the heart of the global water crisis is rooted in power, poverty and inequality, not in physical availability' (UNDP, 2006: 2). Too often, political processes and institutions in water management serve to disadvantage the poor and this is the underlying cause of the lack of access to water. There is a consensus, for example, that the privatisation of public services (under neo-liberalism) in many countries, and most notably in the water sector in countries of the Global South, has not led to any substantial improvements in access nor equity. Under neo-liberal thinking and within the aid conditionalities imposed by the International Financial Institutions, the expectation was that private sector companies, with commercial incentives, would be able to tap into large demand from unserved households who had the ability to pay as were currently buying expensive and unsafe water from informal vendors. In contrast, publicly provided services were deemed inefficient, were supported by overly large and often corrupt bureaucracies and lacked the resources to deliver to increasing demand. However, in practice,

much experience suggests that private contractors in fact 'picked off' the larger and wealthier cities in mainly middle income countries that had large proportions of middle and upper class residents and good existing infrastructures and political stability. The 'harder to reach' poorer countries, districts and customers were left substantially unserved (Budds and Loftus, 2014). Wide-scale social protest, particularly in cities of several Latin American countries, highlighting the basic human right to water has also led to the cancellation of contracts and moves towards alternatives to the neo-liberalisation of water governance (Harris and Roa-Garcia, 2013). The role of social movements in contesting the activities of the World Bank in wider development policy is considered further in Chapter 7.

Water scarcity and equity at the global level

Evidently there are deep inequalities in access to safe water at the household level and these deprivations in access have multiplier effects on human development. However, household requirements for water constitute a relatively small proportion of overall global water use as seen in Figure 6.5. At a global level, agriculture is the largest user of water (for irrigation, for livestock and for aquaculture) accounting for approximately 70 per cent of water withdrawals although there are significant variations across regions. Globally, five countries in Asia account for nearly half the world total groundwater use

(UNESCO, 2015). In 17 countries, the percentage of water withdrawals dedicated to agriculture are more than 90% and these are some of the poorest countries globally. Industry, including energy use, accounts globally for 20 per cent of total water withdrawals and municipal and domestic usage for 10 per cent as seen in Figure 6.5. Losses from large reservoirs in dry climates are also estimated to be close to 5 per cent of total water withdrawals and therefore represent a significant consumptive use of water worldwide.

Global averages evidently mask large discrepancies in water resources and withdrawals between and within countries, as well as temporal differences. In large countries such as China, water demands are concentrated in a few parts of the country, generally where demands for irrigated agriculture are higher and where industrial development are focused. Climate is also a factor in water use; water withdrawals are highest in arid and semi-arid areas, and are lowest in tropical countries reflecting the need for irrigation in agricultural production (UNESCO, 2009). However, this masks a range of factors, including economic, that influence the development of irrigation infrastructures. For the African continent as a whole, the current development of water resources is low in comparison to other regions, and only 5% of cultivated lands are under formal irrigation systems, with farmers remaining dependent on highly variable (and increasingly unpredictable) rain-fed systems of agriculture (see Chapter 10).

Water scarcity is already affecting all parts of the world as seen in Figure 6.8. Hydrologists typically assess water scarcity in terms of the ratio of water use/demand. This measures the amount drawn from the natural hydrological system in relation to the total amount of renewable water available. When annual water supplies drop below 1,700 cubic metres per person, an area is identified as under water *stress*; when it falls below 1,000 cubic metres per person, the population is considered to face water *scarcity*; and below 500 cubic metres, *absolute scarcity* (UNESCO, 2012: 124). However, it is acknowledged that large sectors of the global population currently face problems of accessing water, even in areas of low water stress. Hence, the UN defines water scarcity as 'the point at which the aggregate impact of all uses impinges on the supply or quality of water under prevailing institutional arrangements to the extent that the demand by all sectors, including the environment cannot

be satisfied fully' (op. cit.: 126). This definition thereby distinguishes between water 'stress' as a physical concept, and water 'scarcity' as a relative concept, that recognises that scarcity can occur at any level of supply or demand. Figure 6.8 uses the concept of 'economic scarcity' whereby access to water in regions such as central Africa, north eastern parts of South America and South-East Asia is not limited by resource availability. These regions have medium or low water stress, but 'human, institutional and financial constraints over the distribution of the resource to different user groups' (op. cit.: 126) underpins water access and in turn scarcity. On this basis, globally around 1.2 billion people live in areas of physical water scarcity and 500 million more are approaching this situation. A further 1.6 billion people face economic water shortage.

Evidently, water scarcity is both a natural and a human-made phenomenon. It is clear that the challenges of sustainable water development are strongly linked to agricultural futures and global food supply and the associated environmental changes which are discussed further below. They are also closely interdependent with issues of energy demand and climate change, with many of the impacts of climate change linked to water availability.

Energy resource developments: the search for efficiency and equity

Energy resources are fundamental to national economic development and a necessity for meeting basic human needs. Concerns over the future adequacy of energy supplies, the lack of access to improved household energy technologies, that undermine health and wider development opportunities, and the environmental damage occurring currently through the consumption of energy are all recognised global challenges for sustainable development.

World energy consumption in 2013 was over 13,500 Mtoe (Million Tons of Oil Equivalent) and is predicted to rise by a further one third over 2007 levels by 2030 (IEA, 2013). Much of the projected increase in demand will come from countries in the Global South and, on current trends, China and India will account for more than 40% of this global increase in energy use by 2030 (op. cit.). However, there are stark regional disparities in current consumption. 39% of total energy consumed in

Figure 6.8 Global physical and economic water scarcity

Source: UNESCO World Water Development Report 4 2012

Physical water scarcity

Approaching physical water scarcity

Economic water scarcity

Little or no water scarcity

Not estimated

2013 was in the OECD region and only 6% in Africa (OECD/IEA, 2015). The International Energy Agency estimates that the 20 million inhabitants of New York State use the same amount of electricity as 800 million people across sub-Saharan Africa. Furthermore, in many countries of the Global South as much as 90% of total energy supply comes from biomass sources such as fuelwood, charcoal and animal dung. 240 million people in India alone lack access to electricity (IEA, 2015). The implications for components of poverty and well-being are substantial, including through environmental degradation and the health impacts of indoor air pollution that are discussed in more detail below. The impacts of improved access to modern and reliable energy sources on small scale productivity (and educational achievement) are highlighted in Chapter 10.

Total energy consumption is influenced by many factors including climate, the size and population of a country and the structure of its economy. Past transformations of society from a predominantly agricultural and rural base to an urban and industrial base have been associated with a rise in total energy consumed, and an increased reliance on commercial fuels rather than traditional fuels such as wood, charcoal and other biomass sources. This pattern led to the classification of 'high- and low-energy societies' on the basis of the level and type of energy consumed (Mather and Chapman, 1995). However, more recent discussions have centred on the nature and challenges of the 'third energy transition' (Seitz, 2002) that the world now faces, the first being the transition from wood to coal, the second from coal to oil, as industry, governments and consumers now face the transition to a 'low carbon' global future. The transition to low carbon development is essential for mitigating the emissions that lead to climate change and for achieving development priorities such as poverty reduction, energy access and improved urban transportation (Tanner and Horn-Phathanothai, 2014). 80 per cent of total energy needs are supplied currently by fossil fuels such as oil, coal and gas (OECD/IEA, 2015), yet fossil fuel use is the principal source of the global increase in carbon emissions making this 'third' energy transition central to the challenges of climate change (see section below).

Fears concerning the finite nature of fossil sources of energy were paramount in the energy debates of the 1970s and 1980s, and indeed underpin many of the debates concerning the relationship between resources and development

and global future scenarios, as seen in the sections above. The concept of 'peak oil' is the theoretical point at which half or more of the world oil supplies are used up, and society moves into a new era when oil is more scarce, and new discoveries are more scattered and more costly to extract economically, environmentally and socially. Society is therefore challenged to end fossil fuel dependence (Prior et al., 2012). Geopolitical concerns are also central to the future security of energy supplies, given the turmoil in the Middle East and heightened international terrorism.

Raising the efficiency of energy use in production, and transportation and consumption, is central to the challenge of lower carbon development. 'Energy intensity' is an indicator of how much energy is required to yield set increases in GDP. Figure 6.9 displays the experience of a number of countries over time and through their energy transition associated with industrialisation. As seen in the case of the UK, the ratio of energy consumption to Gross Domestic Product rose and then fell associated with improvements in materials science and energy efficiency (Edge and Tovey, 1995). The maxima reached during these processes have also progressively declined, illustrated by the case of France peaking at lower energy intensity levels. In part, this has been due to the decoupling of energy growth from economic expansion. In Japan, for example, from the late 1970s, GDP rose much more quickly than energy use, and improvements in energy efficiency were important in explaining this pattern. However, it was also the era of rapid increases in oil prices, and there was a shift in the structure of the economy at this time, towards development based on less energy-intensive service industries and away from 'heavy' industry. The impact of this shift on global energy demands remained unchanged. As Edge and Tovey (1995: 325) point out

> The energy-intensive industries did not disappear; however, they went abroad, and to wherever the energy could be obtained cheaply. The energy is still 'used' by the Japanese economy, in the form of embodied energy imported as products.

The Key idea introduces the notion of global social metabolism as a way of understanding the international flows of energy and raw materials that characterise the global world economy and the way that China, for example, is following the pattern of many industrialised countries in substituting domestic energy and material extraction by imports from other world regions.

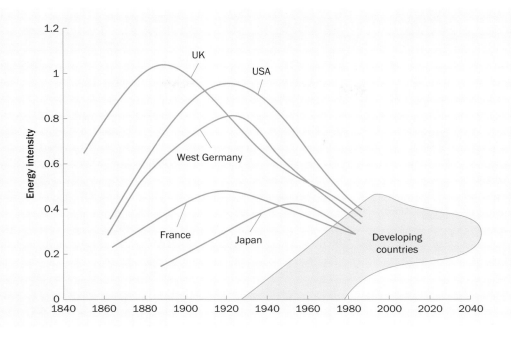

Figure 6.9 Energy intensity versus time
Source: adapted from Holdern and Pachauri, 1992.

Key idea

The global shift in social metabolism

The concept of social metabolism refers to the physical throughput of the economic system in terms of energy and materials as direct and indirect inputs and wastes. Muradian et al. (2012) suggest a new historical phase of modern capitalism in recent years, characterised by major changes in the size and geographic patterning of global social metabolism.

The 'biophysical size' of the world economy in terms of the flows of energy and materials associated with economic activities has grown. Core to this has been the very high rates of economic growth in the Asian region, and particularly in China. Whilst a global trend towards declining use of natural resources per unit of economic output had started to emerge at the global level, this trend has now been reversed. This is due to the rising material intensity of the Asian economies (domestic material consumption per unit of GDP) and much faster growth rates of per capita use of

natural resources in Asia than in other parts of the world. This is despite overall per capita consumption of resources remaining lower than most countries of the Global North.

China has moved very quickly to being the current resource consuming centre of the global economy. China is following many industrialised countries of the North in substituting domestic material extraction by imports from other world regions. In the space of two decades, China has become the largest importer of non-renewable resources worldwide (see Figure 6.10).

However, China's demand and search for natural resources has created both opportunities and threats, particularly for 'resource-rich' countries of the Global South. Higher prices for commodities have led to radical improvements in the terms of trade for many such countries in Latin America and Africa in the last decade, for example. The de-linking of commodity

▶

Key idea (continued)

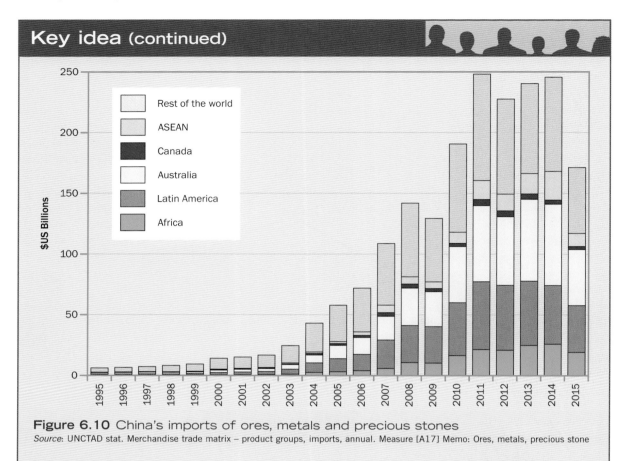

Figure 6.10 China's imports of ores, metals and precious stones
Source: UNCTAD stat. Merchandise trade matrix – product groups, imports, annual. Measure [A17] Memo: Ores, metals, precious stone

markets from the traditional economic cores, such as US, Europe and Japan that are now experiencing economic stagnation, has also enabled continued strong economic growth in many resource rich countries. However, many Chinese transnational companies (with substantial state investments and ownership) are involved widely in the extraction of natural resources in Africa and in wider large-scale land acquisitions. As discussed elsewhere in this chapter, these 'land grabs' are setting the conditions for new socio-environmental conflicts related to the distribution of economic and environmental costs and benefits of resource exploitation.

Figure 6.9 also models the trajectory of 'developing countries' in their transition towards declining energy intensity of production. There is optimism that countries of the Global South can achieve faster rates in improvement in energy efficiency than has been the case in the US and European countries. Global energy intensity has been declining over the past 30 years as seen in Figure 6.11, and China has shown the fastest decline in energy intensity of production of any country over that time (World Watch Institute, 2011). Whilst

China remains the biggest producer and importer of coal, with implications for carbon emissions as coal is a more carbon intensive energy source than electricity or gas, China has also invested heavily in recent years in renewable energy production, is moving away from heavy industry in its domestic production and has introduced energy efficiency standards across many sectors (IEA, 2015; Plates 6.2, 6.3). China is also introducing a carbon emissions scheme in 2017 that is anticipated to drive further energy efficiencies.

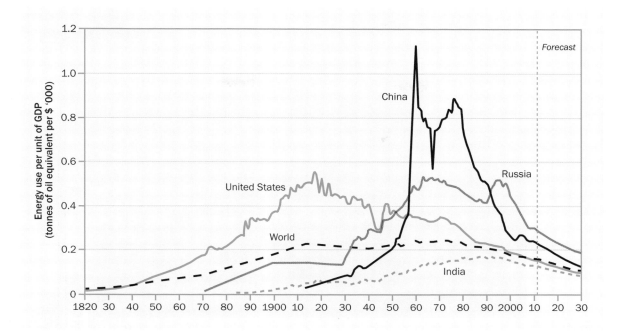

Figure 6.11 Change in energy intensity worldwide and selected countries
Source: adapted from http://www.economist.com/blogs/dailychart/2011/01/energy_use.
Accessed 18 April 2016.

Plate 6.2 Coal fired power station, China
(*photo*: Elona Hoover, jesidewalks)

Plate 6.3 Wind energy development, China
(*photo*: Elona Hoover, jesidewalks)

Energy policies are clearly important in shaping the link between energy intensity and development. The price of oil is also understood as a key determinant. This was seen in Figure 6.9 in understanding the structural shifts in Japan's economy in the late 1970s. It has also been demonstrated more recently, when the fastest declines in global energy intensity seen to date were in the years between 2004 and 2008, when oil prices were at unprecedented high levels (World Watch Institute, 2011). Global energy intensities then rose from 2008, reversing the 30-year trend of declining intensity, as oil prices fell and countries had to adjust to widespread economic recession, which they did through means including investments in energy intensive infrastructure projects.

Renewable sources of energy including hydroelectric, wind and solar, biofuels and nuclear power supplied approximately 17% of world energy supply in 2013 (OECD/IEA, 2015). The development of renewable sources of energy is an important part of the transition to lower carbon futures. Investments in renewable energy had been rising globally particularly through national commitments to climate change mitigation. However, renewable energy technologies are expensive to establish and often depend on government subsidies to develop

and implement. In late 2008, in the context of the global financial downturn, investments in clean energy fell and have fallen further with recent decreases in world oil prices and the rise of fracking technologies. Such volatility in economic conditions and political will underpins concerns as to whether the potential of renewables will be realised at a sufficient scale to address climate change.

Furthermore, the pressure on land for biofuel crops is understood as a key driving factor of the recent 'global land rush' (Scheidel and Sorman, 2012). The expansion of large-scale, cross-border land deals or transactions, typically by transnational corporations and on behalf of foreign governments, is understood to have complex drivers (see Chapter 10). These include the production of food for export to countries that are land and water short in the aftermath of food crisis of 2007–08. The impact of biofuel production on ecosystem functioning is considered further below. The wide reference to these transactions as global 'land grabbing', reflects the substantial conflicts that surround the unprecedented growth in demand for land in other countries (Zoomers, 2010), and confirms very starkly the global nature of the challenge of moving to energy efficient, lower carbon development.

Mineral resources: curse or cure for development?

Worldwide demand for raw materials has risen rapidly in recent decades, as seen in Figure 6.12. For any particular country, the presence of diverse mineral supplies can be a potential source of comparative advantage in economic development, as shown by the historical experience of Europe and North America.

Currently, mineral production is extremely important in the economies of many countries of the Global South as shown in Table 6.5. As well as contributing to the export earnings of a country, mineral development can assist in attracting foreign capital, in creating jobs and stimulating demand for local goods and services, in raising taxes, in prompting infrastructure developments and in providing options in industrial development (Plate 6.4). Yet evidence suggests that,

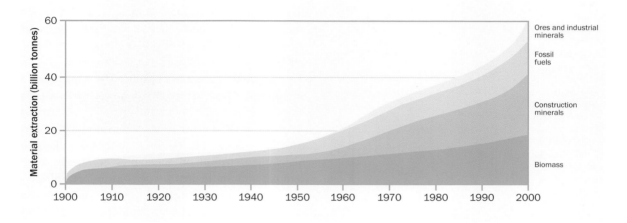

Figure 6.12 Global mineral extraction in the twentieth century
Source: adapted from UNEP, 2012.

Plate 6.4 Diamond mining, South Africa
(*photo*: Jennifer Elliott)

Table 6.5 The importance of mineral production in the economies of the Global South. Percentage of total merchandise exports via fuels, ores and metals for selected countries, 2014

Country	Percentage of merchandise exports via fuels, ores and metals
Algeria	96
Azerbaijan	93
Bolivia	80
Brazil	24
Chile	58
Colombia	39
Ecuador	71
Indonesia	39
Kazakhstan	87
Kuwait	94
Mexico	14
Nigeria	88
Papua New Guinea	56
Peru	60
Russian Federation	76
Saudi Arabia	88
Senegal	24
South Africa	37
Venezuela	98
Yemen	76

Source: compiled from World Bank (2015) World Development Indictors

since the 1960s, the 'mineral economies' of the Global South, defined as having over 40 per cent of their export earnings from the mineral sector, did not perform as well on conventional economic development indicators as was predicted, or in relation to the less well-endowed countries (Auty, 1993). Whilst the conventional view had been that favourable natural resource endowment could be particularly important in the early low-income stages of the development process, this has been increasingly challenged through the development of the idea of the 'resource curse' seen in the Key idea.

In 2004 Christian Aid undertook further comparative research of the economic, poverty and human development performance over four decades between six oil-producing nations (Angola, Iraq, Kazakstan, Nigeria, Sudan and Venezuela) and six non-oil-producers (Bangladesh, Bolivia, Cambodia, Ethiopia, Peru and Tanzania) that further confirmed the operation of a 'resource curse'. The oil economies were found to have achieved slower growth, an average of 1.7 per cent per annum, compared to an average annual growth of 4 per cent in non-producing countries. The military expenditures (and the size of armies maintained) within oil economies averaged 6.8 per cent per annum, against 2.9 per cent in non-oil economies, supporting suggestions that oil-producing countries are highly prone to conflict. Whilst the findings in relation to human development were less strong, both life expectancy at birth and literacy rates were found to have improved slightly more in non-oil economies than in oil economies. 'At the very least, they show that oil has done nothing to significantly improve the lives of ordinary people in oil-rich countries' (Christian Aid, 2004: 5).

Key idea

The 'resource curse thesis'

In 1993, Auty, in his book *Sustaining Development in Mineral Economies*, proposed the 'resource curse' to explain how and why high levels of resource endowment at a country level were not translating into higher levels of economic development and indeed, could explain the underperformance of such countries relative to those 'less well endowed'. The suggestion of a 'resource curse' was based on detailed research of the economic performance of countries from the 1960s through to the early 1980s, where exports of hard minerals such as copper, bauxite and tin accounted for more than 40 per cent of export earnings and at least 8 per cent of GDP. Whilst these countries sustained significantly higher levels of investment than the non-mineral economies, their GDP growth per capita was found to be lower and could not be explained by declining terms of trade for those products.

Key idea (continued)

The conclusion was that 'the cause of under-performance of the hard mineral economies lies not so much in a lack of investment resources, as in the inefficiency with which those investment resources were deployed' (Auty, 1993: 5). In particular, the roots of the underperformance were found to be in a number of characteristics of the mining sector and its production function. For example, mineral production is highly capital-intensive and is regularly controlled by a few multinational companies. In turn, there may be little impact on national employment and production is often heavily mechanised with expatriate labour being used to provide specialist skills. Mineral exploitation also shows marked enclave tendencies and may yield only modest local production linkages due to factors including the often remote location of mineral resources, the importation of specialist technologies and few local factories being established to supply imports or process ores prior to export.

The links between natural resource endowments and human development are undoubtedly complex. The geo-strategic significance of oil to capitalist development and US hegemony in particular, is a long-recognised part of the explanation for how high resource endowment can in fact undermine economic growth and be a source of conflict (see Peluso and Watts, 2001; Watts, 2004). Civil unrest and conflict in turn, may not be triggered by the presence of oil or minerals per se, but control over those resources may be key to financing and sustaining conflict and is very much part of current concerns for how favorable natural resource wealth can be host to conditions for terrorist activities. However, it is also understood that there are many more local struggles and conflicts currently occurring over natural resource extraction and use that have direct impacts on peace and stability within countries making environmental degradation central to the human security agenda (see Chapter 7).

The intensity of resource extraction within countries of the Global South rose rapidly from the 1990s under neo-liberalism, and the pressure for countries to seek private investment in the development of natural resources including oil and natural gas, mining and forestry, as well as biofuels as considered above. Many of the largest investments were in Latin America and in Peru, Chile and Argentina in particular (Bebbington et al., 2008). Accompanying this expansion in investment was 'an equally remarkable surge in social mobilization and conflict' (op. cit., p. 2889). In 2011, the Latin American Observatory of Mining Conflicts identified 155 ongoing mining conflicts affecting 205 local communities, for example, 26 of these were in Peru, 25 in Chile and 24 in Argentina (Muradian et al., 2012: 564).

Contestation by social groups over the current or future negative environmental and economic impacts of resource extraction have also risen through the recent era of high commodity prices and increased scarcity and competition for natural resources, substantially driven by demand in China and the Asian economies more widely as seen in Key idea above on the global shift in social metabolism. Furthermore, a distinctive feature of these types of conflicts have been that:

> they constitute a form of resistance, and use a language of contestation either with explicit reference to environmental claims, appealing to the dependency of local livelihoods on the threatened resources, or making use of religious/worldview concerns for defending natural ecosystems or the right to a clean environment.
>
> (Muradian, 2012: 564).

Whilst the way in which such social-environmental conflicts emerge and are organised are complex, research suggests that the rising global demand for energy and raw materials associated with economic activities are taking the 'commodity frontier' into new locations, and particularly areas of fragile ecosystems and dense human occupation. These issues are explored further in Chapter 10.

No simple resource – development–environment models

In summary, it is evident that resource constraints on development do exist; the persistence of poverty is testimony to the unresolved challenge of finding the means to overcome continued resource constraints in development at the local level. However, it is increasingly acknowledged that the persistence of these development challenges owes less to the geographical characteristics of the natural resource base than to issues of control, use and management of resources.

These factors also underpin much of the discussion of resource degradation in the following sections. Whilst the emphasis is on global patterns, the fundamental challenge for sustainable development in the future is in overcoming the resource constraints of the poorest groups in society, where options for development are most restricted. In Part III, it is seen that these groups often have a very close relationship with the physical resource base, live in some of the most impoverished environments of the world, and lack precisely the means required to prosper in those areas. The challenges for global environmental governance and the institutions and actors in development are the focus of Chapter 7.

Environmental impacts of development

Just as the characteristics of the resource base shape the challenges and opportunities for development, so development processes themselves impact on the environment and the varied functions it performs. Indeed, it has been understandings of the detrimental impacts of development, as well as resource scarcities, that have shaped environmentalism in the modern era. In the 1960s/1970s, environmentalists argued strongly that development was incompatible with conservation. Particularly in America, the undesirable side effects of industrial development, such as air and water pollution, were being experienced and an emerging environmental movement campaigning on these issues was fuelled by the generally anti-establishment middle class sentiments which prevailed at that time (see Elliott, 2013).

The notion of sustainable development considered at the outset of this chapter embraces the understanding that a lack of development can also be a prime factor in resource degradation. It has also exposed the complex and interdependent challenges of resource development and conservation, whilst at the same time delivering human well-being and opportunities for development equitably both now and in the future. However, better understanding of the increasingly global scale nature of environmental issues has also been fundamental to the search for more sustainable development. This includes the way that many environmental issues have a direct impact on globally functioning systems such as climate, and also the way that other environmental changes are experienced locally, but are increasingly reproduced at a worldwide scale, such as in the case of soil erosion. The next part of this chapter identifies briefly, the characteristics of past patterns and processes of development that underpin a number of key, and often inter-linked, global environmental issues.

Whilst it is easy to find patterns in the environment that suggest change for the worse over time, it is important to retain a consideration for how what is valued as a resource, and therefore what is considered degradation, are socially constructed. Previous sections have highlighted how the environment provides a number of interrelated resource functions for the development of society: as inputs into the economic system, as a sink for the waste products of economic production and in terms of 'services' such as the maintenance of the gaseous composition of the atmosphere, for example. These links between ecosystem functioning and services for human well-being were substantially illuminated through the Millennium Ecosystem Assessment. Subsequent sections confirmed that such functions are neither discrete nor time-bound. Resources may serve multiple ends, and the significance of particular functions may change with use, political interest or economic development. Critically, any discussion of environmental degradation needs to be not only in relation to particular resource functions at specific times and places, but also in relation to identified interest groups:

> To a hunter or herder, the replacement of forest by savanna with a greater capacity to carry ruminants would not be perceived as degradation. Nor would forest replacement by agricultural land be seen as degradation by a colonising farmer. Usually there

are a number of perceptions of physical changes of the biome on the part of actual or potential land-users. Usually too, there is conflict over the use of land.

(Blaikie and Brookfield, 1987: 4)

Deforestation

The removal of forests and woodlands through cutting or deliberate fire at rates in excess of natural regeneration processes is perhaps one of the most visible global patterns of resource degradation. Deforestation itself is not a new phenomenon. Much of Europe was largely cleared of forest in the Middle Ages, for example. However, it is the rates and extent of forest removal across the humid tropics in recent decades which have been unprecedented, and have been the focus of much global environmental concern. Annual rates of forest loss through the 1990s, were over 7 million hectares per year (FAO, 2001), and losses continue to be greatest in tropical countries as considered further below.

In part, the degree of scientific, popular and media interest in deforestation reflects the varied functions forest and woodland resources currently fulfil, and are expected to perform in the future. This includes for diverse interest groups and across all spatial scales. Indeed, forests and woodlands could be considered the archetypal multiple resource. They provide a range of raw materials, including fuel-wood, fruits and medicines and support employment. Forests also play a vital

role in the maintenance of global bio-diversity, and store carbon and modulate climate. Forests also perform a host of less obvious resource functions and services which are now acknowledged to be essential for societal well-being, including opportunities for recreational enjoyment (MEA, 2005; Pierce-Colfer et al., 2016).

Historically, forests have come under pressure from demands for shelter, agricultural land, meat production and fuel and timber extraction. Additional pressures in recent years have come through increased demands for agricultural expansion and biofuel production, and from rapid urbanisation and infrastructure development (UNEP, 2012). Furthermore, climate changes, such as rising annual mean surface temperatures and altered precipitation patterns, are leading to increased stress on forests globally.

Forests cover very nearly 4 billion hectares, approximately 31% of the global land area (FAO, 2015a). Fifty-two per cent of global forests are in tropical and sub-tropical countries. Between 1990 and 2015, total forest area declined by 3% and loss of forest area was largely in the tropics, as seen in Table 6.6. The biggest country losses by continent in the last five years have been in Brazil (South America), Indonesia (Asia) and Nigeria (Africa). However, the rates of forest loss in Brazil and Indonesia, for example, have declined to 2015 and are now around 44% slower than they were in 1990 (Keenan et al., 2015). Thirteen tropical countries including China, Chile and the Philippines, have moved from experiencing net forest loss to net forest gain, through

Table 6.6 Trends in forest area, 1990 to 2015, by sub-region

Sub-region	1990	2000	2005	2010	2015
Central America	26,995	23,448	22,193	21,010	20,250
Caribbean	5,017	5,913	6,341	6,745	7,195
East Asia	209,198	226,815	241,841	250,504	257,047
East-Southern Africa	319,785	300,273	291,712	282,519	274,886
Europe	994,271	1,002,302	1,004,147	1,013,572	1,015,482
North Africa	39,374	37,692	37,221	37,055	36,217
North America	720,487	719,197	719,419	722,523	723,207
Oceania	176,825	177,641	176,485	172,002	173,524
South America	930,814	890,817	868,611	852,133	842,011
South-Southeast Asia	319,615	298,645	296,600	295,958	292,804
West-Central Africa	346,581	332,407	325,746	318,708	313,000
West-Central Asia	39,309	40,452	42,427	42,944	43,511
Total	4,128,269	4,055,602	4,032,743	4,015,673	3,999,134

Source: Keenan et al., 2015, based on FAO Forest Resources Assessment, 2015.

expansion of planted forests. In China, over 32.5m hectares of planted forests have been created under the Natural Forest Protection and the Conversion of Cropland to Forest Programmes, substantially driven by concerns over soil erosion and flooding in the country (Payn et al., 2015).

The area of planted forests globally has expanded by 66% in the period 1990–2015, and accounts for approximately 7% of the total forest area worldwide (Keenan et al., 2015). Generally, planted forests have been for industrial purposes including timber, paper and rubber. However, they are also increasingly for the protection of ecosystems services, including carbon and water storage. The global area of forest under some form of protection in the name of environmental ends, including biodiversity, is increasing. This pattern is a further part of the debates concerning large scale land acquisitions in the Global South, or 'green grabbing', as it has been termed when the 'green credentials' are used to justify the appropriation of land and forests (Fairhead et al., 2012).

Understanding forest data and trends requires some caution. As Grainger (1993) suggested, all estimates of tropical deforestation rates are unsatisfactory in some sense, although some can be considered more unsatisfactory than others. The data in Table 6.6 is produced by the Food and Agriculture Organisation that is acknowledged to provide some of the most comprehensive information on global forest cover. However,

> estimates of forest area include natural forest and planted forest, and a reduction in net forest loss (which could result from a combination of loss of natural forest, and a gain in planted forest) is not the same as a reduction in deforestation.
>
> (Keenan et al., 2015: 19)

The Critical reflection below investigates these challenges of data in more detail. Making the uncertainties within, and differences between, data explicit in planning is essential. As Thompson and Warburton (1985) argued in relation to work in Nepal:

> If the most pessimistic estimates are correct, the Himalayas will become as bald as a coot overnight . . . if the most optimistic estimates are correct, they will shortly sink beneath the greatest accumulation of biomass the world has ever seen.
>
> (Thompson and Warburton, 1985: 116)

Critical reflection

Getting beneath the deforestation data

Since 1946, the Food and Agriculture Organization has been compiling data that is used by international agencies (including the UN Framework Convention on Climate Change and the UN Forum on Forests), governments, NGOs, the commercial sector, scientists and activists. Since 1990, it has undertaken a series of Global Forest Resources Assessments (FRAs) and is the basis of the time-series data in Table 6.6. But caution is required when considering this data. The FRAs depend on national forest inventories supplemented by satellite information and expert opinion. Yet in over half of the inventories used within the 2000 assessment, for example, the data used were over ten years old (Matthews, 2001) and of 137 countries included, only 22 had systems for continuous modelling and monitoring. Very often,

national data is sourced and reported over different time scales and in different ways, such that even national data sets are not completely comparable.

Importantly, the definition of 'forest land' used by the FAO has changed; in 1990 'forests' were defined as areas of more than 20 per cent canopy cover for higher income countries (defined on the basis of World Bank categories) and more than 10 per cent canopy within low income countries. In 2000 the definition was standardised as more than 10 per cent, but whilst this has given greater comparability, it has had the effect of 'revising upward' the extent of forest lands within higher income countries.

Interpreting trends over time in relation to forest status is also difficult. Changes in the extent of forests are often reported as aggregates of both natural and

Critical reflection (continued)

plantation forestry (as in the 2015 FRA), yet these are very different in terms of the biodiversity hosted, their productivity, management requirements and amenity value. Even where they are differentiated, it is now understood that there are very substantial problems in attempting to 'go back' to attest the extent of 'original' vegetation, including for the way in which such modelling depends on estimates of historical vegetation, population levels and activities, climate interrelationships and so on.

The work of James Fairhead and Melissa Leach is well known for their detailed research into environmental change, particularly in relation to forestry, within Guinea and the West African region more widely (see Fairhead and Leach, 1998). Drawing on data from oral histories, participant observation, archival sources and sequential aerial photography, they have revealed quite different understandings of forest change to that generated and sustained within official thinking, including within colonial policies and as portrayed within global assessments. They found in

Guinea, for example, that extensive 'forest islands' were created by human occupation and were being sustained by active agro-forestry management activities. This was in stark contrast to how such forest islands had been interpreted, as the last remnants of ancient forests, 'assumed' over long periods of time to be the natural vegetation of the region between the Equatorial belt to the south and the Sahara Desert to the north.

Their work has also promoted investigations into how and why certain narratives of environmental change, even when substantially erroneous, become so entrenched and continue to shape development interventions via the activities of government forestry departments and donor projects and programmes.

Critical reflection

Consider why we hear and see so much more in the academic literature and popular media about global patterns and processes of deforestation than local experiences of forestry and woodland change.

Complex drivers of deforestation

The driving factors behind deforestation are complex, yet often poorly understood (Carr et al., 2005; Grainger, 1993). In particular, there is a need to distinguish between the proximate and fundamental causes of deforestation. Population is regularly put forward as a proximate and underlying cause of deforestation, through a focus on particular groups such as shifting cultivators or on population growth per se. However, it needs to be understood how demographic drivers work, at various scales, in combination with political, economic and ecological processes to shape outcomes (Geist and Lambin, 2002). There is no single or ultimate cause of deforestation, rather a complex and dynamic mix of factors operating in any particular locality. Chapter 10 looks in more detail at the role of woodland resources in rural livelihoods and the complexity of forces in environmental transformations.

At a global level, conversion of lands for agriculture was a key factor in driving deforestation through the

1990s, accounting for approximately 70 per cent of world forest loss in this decade (FAO, 2001). This is predominantly under permanent rather than shifting agricultural systems although the patterns and scale of these differed regionally (UNEP, 2002). In South America, the conversion of land for agricultural use, and in particular for pasture production, was a key factor in the very rapid rates of deforestation experienced in the 1990s. At a country scale, large infrastructure developments, such as highways construction in the Rondonia region of Brazil, were also associated with forest clearance by impoverished farmers colonising the land alongside. However, whilst these farmers were certainly agents in enhanced deforestation rates, Colchester and Lohmann (1993: 15) point to the underlying failure of economic development planning as fundamental in the explanation of these patterns. They argue that agrarian reforms

have failed to achieve their targets, they have failed to alleviate rural poverty, they have failed to secure peasant tenure, they have failed to effect adequate redistribution of land, they have failed to stem the rising tide of landlessness and, above all, they have failed to respond to the needs and demands of the peasants themselves.

Latin America as a whole continues to suffer extensive deforestation and, whilst Brazil has been successful in decreasing the rates at which forest loss is occurring, as seen in Case study 6.2, forest conversion for pasture and cattle ranching continues to be a driver. Furthermore, soy production is now replacing pasture, and is understood as a further driving factor of deforestation in the region (UNEP, 2012). The principal use of soy is in cattle feed, and the key regions for its production in the tropics are in Latin America and the Caribbean. Globally, only 62% of crop production, on a mass basis, is currently allocated to food for human consumption, whereas 35% is for animal feed. If the area of land given over to pasture for stock rearing is added, then 75% of the world's agricultural land is devoted to raising animals in some way (Foley et al., 2011).

As we face the twin challenges of feeding a growing world while charting a more environmentally sustainable path, the amount of land (and other resources) devoted to animal-based agriculture merits critical evaluation.

(Foley et al., 2011: 338)

Case study 6.2

Controlling deforestation in the Amazon

The biggest forest losses in South America continue to be in Brazil. However, rates of deforestation have been reduced by 40% since 1990. In particular, the introduction of the Action Plan for Prevention and Control of Deforestation in the Amazon in 2004, has led to rapid reductions in the pace of deforestation. Policies associated with the Action Plan include:

➤ Creating new protected areas
➤ Establishing a monitoring programme
➤ Strengthening law enforcement which enables the apprehension and destruction of property
➤ Withholding public rural credit from producers who contravene environmental regulations

➤ Targets and obligations on municipalities to reduce deforestation rates and to register protected areas in a GIS database to make illegal deforestation apparent in a timely fashion

National associations in the oil and cereal industries in Brazil have also signed an agreement, substantially through pressure from Greenpeace campaigning, that they will not acquire soybeans from newly afforested areas.

Source: compiled from
UNEP (2012) Global
Environment Outlook, 5

Clearly, the drivers of deforestation are strongly linked to those of global food and feed production, and are increasingly shaped also by energy trends. Figure 6.13 shows the growth in area of land in the tropics given over to the cultivation of three key crops, including soy beans. The cultivation of sugar and oil palm production are substantially for use as biofuels. Biofuels as a renewable and lower-carbon source of energy than fossil fuels offer potential in addressing the challenges of future energy supplies and those of climate change, as seen above. However, as also seen, biofuels are a driving factor in the large-scale land acquisitions occurring in the Global South raising significant concerns including for social and environmental justice. The expansion of oil palm production for biofuels, and some food uses such as cooking oil and chocolate, is currently the most significant cause of deforestation in SE Asia (UNEP, 2012). Two-thirds of oil palm expansion in Indonesia has occurred through the direct conversion of rainforest. The clearance of forests

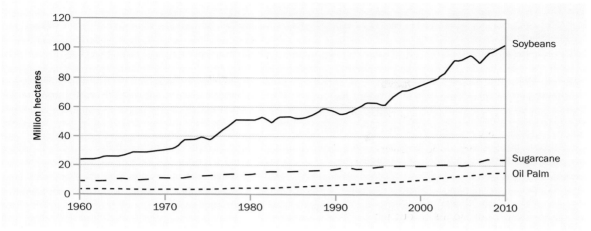

Figure 6.13 Areas under cultivation for selected crops in tropical countries, 1960–2010
Source: adapted from UNEP, 2012.

carries a carbon debt that will last for decades to centuries, and thereby undermines one of the main reasons for investing in biofuels. Whilst a moratorium on the clearance of primary forest for oil palm production was introduced by the President of Indonesia in 2011, this does not apply to existing contracts or to secondary forests (UNEP, 2012: 84).

The very direct impacts of deforestation, ranging from local livelihood options to global resource functions including climate change and biodiversity, are seen in subsequent sections and chapters. Less direct impacts have also been revealed recently in the increased vulnerability of coastal residents to cyclones and tsunamis in regions of mangrove destruction including in India, Burma, Madagascar and the Southern States of the USA (UNEP, 2012).

Soil erosion and desertification: local environmental issues experienced globally?

Soils are fundamental to life on Earth, but human pressures on soil resources are reaching critical limits (FAO/ITPS, 2015: 4). Soil-forming processes occur at slow rates (a few millimetres per century) and are controlled at the local scale by highly specific factors of geology, climate and topography. Soil degradation may occur naturally as a result of the action of wind and water over time, but accelerated rates of erosion occur through the interaction of human activities with such biotic agents. Land cover changes, such as the conversion of forest to cropland and pasture identified above, disturb soils and lead to the loss of soil nutrients (and declining fertility), to changes in soil properties (including structure and moisture retention) and to impacts on soil flora and fauna (soil biodiversity). A major consequence of deforestation is the loss of carbon from soils, a process regulated by microbial diversity, which has an important 'sink' function in terms of addressing climate change (FAO/ITPS, 2015).

Soil erosion has very direct impacts on agricultural productivity at all scales, where nutrient losses for example have to be replaced through artificial fertilisation, often at significant cost and assuming they are physically accessible. Soils also play a key role in global nitrogen and phosphorous cycles, and yet fertiliser use is a key factor in the disruption of those cycles, leading to a range of environmental and social concerns as considered in Box 6.4. Soil may also be 'quantitatively' degraded through its physical removal from one location to another, with significant costs in terms of sedimentation of water courses and siltation of reservoirs.

BOX 6.4

The disruption of global nitrogen (and phosphorous) cycles

Modern agriculture has had a major impact on global nitrogen and phosphorous cycles to an extent that an important Planetary Boundary (see discussion at outset of this chapter) has now been breached with globally significant environmental (and socio-economic) implications. Agricultural processes – largely the increased manufacture of fertilisers for food production and the growth of leguminous crops – converts approximately 120 million tonnes of nitrogen gas from the atmosphere every year into reactive forms (Rockström et al., 2009: 474).

However, 60% of nitrogen fixed by human activities is not being incorporated into food or products and is released back into the environment (UNEP, 2012). The increased release of reactive nitrogen and phosphorous underpins many significant environmental problems, including the pollution of ground and drinking water, hypoxia of water bodies and oceans, air pollution and climate change. Nitrogen deposition drives biodiversity loss through eutrophication, and nitrogen compounds are

precursors of atmospheric particulate matter that have impacts on human respiratory health. Nitrogen oxide is also one of the key non-carbon greenhouse gases and has a direct forcing effect (see the next section).

Soils play a key role as regulators of this leakage of nitrogen and phosphorous back into the hydrological and atmospheric systems. Soils are the largest pool of nitrogen and phosphorous within terrestrial ecosystems and nitrogen, for example, is cycled biologically through plant uptake, litter fall and is stored in organic form. Activities that disturb soil structure and organic matter therefore also affect nitrogen retention capacity.

Phosphorous is different in that it is a fossil mineral, but also has a key agricultural use in fertilisers. 20 million tonnes of phosphorous is mined every year, but approximately 9 million tonnes finds its way into oceans – a rate calculated to be eight times the natural background rate (Rockström et al., 2009: 474). Research suggests a link between past mass extinctions of marine life with the crossing of critical thresholds of phosphorous inflows to the oceans.

The quality of data on global soil and soil change is recognised to be poor and highly variable at a regional scale (FAO/ITPS, 2015). It has been suggested that estimates of land damaged or lost for agricultural use through soil degradation can range from 'moderate to apocalyptic' (World Bank, 1992: 55). There are substantial problems in translating global estimates of soil changes into accurate local erosion rates, as the processes are highly place-specific and dynamic over time. As Stocking (2000: 292) warned:

> Certainly, soil erosion and land degradation are serious in some places; equally, their degree and extent have been overstated, often for political ends. Rhetoric on soil erosion can be a useful device to displace people, point fingers of blame, promote the cause of environmental agencies and the professionals who work in them, and mobilise international aid.

However, what is known is that erosion rates on arable and intensively used pastoral lands are 100–1,000 times higher than natural background erosion rates and for soil formation; 'the large differences between erosion rates under conventional agriculture and soil formation rates implies that we are essentially mining the soil and that we should consider the resource as non-renewable' (FAO/ITPS, 2015: 103).

Soil erosion is one component of the wider processes of desertification. Desertification occurs wherever,

> land is periodically deprived of adequate moisture, where soils are infertile, or poor drainage leads to saline conditions, crusts or pans, if vegetation is present it will probably be easy to disturb and slow to re-establish. Because the end product often resembles desert the process has been termed desertification.
>
> (Barrow, 1995: 105)

However, desertification is not the actual expansion of deserts as can be commonly thought (see Table 6.7), nor is it an isolated process. There continues also to be substantial debate concerning the rate and extent of desertification (see Mortimore, 2016). Desertification is strongly linked to water availability and management and is a 'ubiquitous challenge in the dryland regions of the world' (UNESCO, 2012: 120). But the challenges of desertification and land degradation, and drought more widely, are increasingly occurring in all agro-ecological zones and are considered a global problem through their extent and impacts on environmental and social vulnerability. Research as part of the Global Land Degradation Information System (GLADIS) has reported that these interlinked challenges may affect 1.5 billion people globally, who currently depend on degrading areas for what are often basic livelihoods. Forty-two per cent of the world's poorest and most marginalised people live in these areas. An estimated 26% of these people live in India, 17% in China and 24% in sub-Saharan Africa (Nachtergaele et al., 2010).

Table 6.7 Key facts on desertification

➤ Desertification occurs through land degradation in arid, semi-arid and dry sub-humid areas resulting from various factors, including climatic variations and human activities.
➤ Desertification is not, as commonly thought, the actual expansion of existing deserts.
➤ Desertification affects nearly 1 billion people, or one-sixth of the world's population.
➤ Desertification is occurring in 70% of all drylands, or one-quarter of the total land area of the Earth.
➤ Desertification is responsible for the degradation of 73% of the world's rangeland.
➤ Desertification is especially severe in Africa, where two-thirds of the continent is desert or drylands, and where 73% of its agricultural drylands are already seriously or moderately degraded.
➤ Asia contains the largest amount of land affected by desertification of any continent – just under 1400 million hectares.
➤ Nearly two-thirds of Latin America's drylands are moderately to severely desertified.
➤ Desertification is estimated to cost the world more than US$40 billion a year in lost productivity.

Source: compiled from UNESCO (2012) World Water Development Report

Conserving soils

In large measure, the physical processes of soil erosion are well understood and 'the technology already exists to reduce erosion to acceptable levels under most circumstances' (FAO/ ITPS, 2015: 108). In 1985, Blaikie suggested that the most promising direction in terms of the explanation of continued soil degradation was that 'conservation is as much about social

Plate 6.5 Gully erosion, Zimbabwe
(*photo*: Jennifer Elliott)

processes as physical ones and the major constraints are not technical, but social' (Blaikie, 1985: 50).

This work did much to raise understanding of the individual land user (see Plate 6.5) and the wider political economic context in which resource management decisions have to be taken. For example, many colonial interventions in African agriculture were justified on the basis of the conservation of soil. Measures such as compulsory construction of contour banks and limitations on the number of stock owned, however, may have done more to protect settler interests in agriculture in southern Africa than they did to prevent soil erosion (Elliott, 1990). Many soil conservation programmes in countries of the Global South continue to be delivered through foreign aid institutions within which the implicit assumptions of this 'colonial model' may persist (Blaikie, 1985).

In 1977 the United Nations Environment Programme (UNEP) organised a World Conference on Desertification (UNCOD) in Nairobi, which was instrumental in forwarding desertification as a major contemporary environmental issue and in stimulating efforts to assess and address the problem of desertification (Plate 6.6). There are now 194 signatories to the 1995 UN Convention to Combat Desertification and an agreed assessment database on desertification. Images of advancing deserts have been refined, particularly as improved understanding

of dryland ecologies has forced a distinction between natural fluctuations and long-term degradation. It has also been recognised that many actions to combat desertification have been costly, focused on technical interventions, were largely initiated by the international aid community, and were rarely sustained beyond the initial donor input stage. Addressing the social dimensions of desertification, and assisting the most marginalised groups in drylands to cope with desertification, is now understood to be of paramount importance (UNEP, 2012; Mortimore, 1998; Toulmin, 2001). It has been acknowledged that progress in the implementation of the Convention to Combat Desertification has been mixed and a new ten-year plan to revitalise commitments was agreed in 2008 (UNEP, 2012).

In short, soil degradation and desertification are pervasive challenges with significance for global system functioning and for livelihoods worldwide. Complex and inter-related drivers, linked very strongly to agricultural practices and futures, ensure that measures to address soil degradation and desertification will need to be embedded in policies and programmes that support more sustainable agricultural systems (see Chapter 10). Furthermore, predicted climate warming scenarios discussed in the following section have major implications for soil and water resources, and in turn the functions and services that they support both now and in the future.

Plate 6.6 Dune planting to address desertification, Northern Nigeria
(*photo*: Jennifer Elliott)

Climate change

One of the most fundamental sink functions of the natural environment is in respect to the carbon cycle, within which oxygen is emitted through processes of photosynthesis and respiration as carbon is circulated between the atmosphere, oceans, soils and land vegetation. The amount of carbon dioxide in the atmosphere is a critical determinant of global surface temperature. The reradiation of solar radiation back into space (i.e. the amount of heat lost from the Earth's surface) is controlled by the insulating effect of 'greenhouse gases' in the atmosphere, in the presence of water vapour. These gases include carbon dioxide and also methane, nitrous oxide and a range of chlorofluorocarbons (CFCs). Carbon dioxide is identified as the principal greenhouse gas in that it provides the main warming or 'forcing effect' in the atmosphere (see Houghton, 2015; IPCC, 2015).

If there were no such insulation or 'greenhouse effect' from the atmosphere, then the average temperature of the Earth's surface would be at least 30°C cooler than at present (Kelly and Granich, 1995: 77). However, globally averaged surface and ocean temperatures have risen by 0.85°C since 1880, according to the Intergovernmental Panel on Climate Change (IPCC, 2015). The IPCC was established in 1998 by the World Meteorological Organization and the United Nations Environment Programme and is widely considered to be the most authoritative scientific body on climate change. Whilst natural ranging carbon dioxide concentrations 650,000 years ago (as established within ice cores) were between 180 and 300 ppm[3] (IPCC, 2007) atmospheric concentration of CO_2 exceeding 400 ppm have recently been recorded by the at the Mauna Loa Observatory in Hawaii (NOAA, 2016). The most recent report of the IPCC states that 'Warming of the climate system is *unequivocal,* and since the 1950s, many of the observed changes are unprecedented over decades to millennia' (2015: 2 *emphases added*).

Table 6.8 identifies a number of observed changes in the climate system as established by the IPCC. Whilst there is substantial debate regarding the direction of future climate change (Figure 6.14), including due to uncertainties in the science (discussed further below), climate change has been referred to as the 'mother of all development challenges' (Tanner and Horn-Phathanothai,

Figure 6.14 Debates continue over the direction of global climate change
Source: cartoon by David Hughes

2014). This includes for the way that it will impact on development outcomes, but also shape development choices in the future. In addition, 'some of the most important questions about how to respond to climate change . . . pertain to politics and ethics and are beyond science to answer' (op. cit.: 5). Climate change is certainly an archetypal 'global environmental issue' in that the causes and impacts extend across all boundaries. As Clayton (1995: 110) confirmed, 'a molecule of greenhouse gas emitted anywhere becomes everyone's business'.

Furthermore, climate change embraces difficult questions of inter-generational justice. As the IPCC (2015: 5) identifies, 'many aspects of climate change and associated impacts will continue for centuries, even if anthropogenic emissions of greenhouse gases are stopped'.

Causes and impacts

In 2007, the IPCC, drawing on 'new and more comprehensive data, more sophisticated analyses of data, improvements in understandings of processes and their simulation in models, and more extensive exploration of uncertainty ranges' (IPCC, 2007: 2), was able to assert 'very high confidence' that the globally averaged net effect of human activities has been one of warming. 'Discernible human influences' were also found to extend to other aspects of climate, including ocean warming, continental average temperatures, temperature extremes and wind patterns (IPCC, 2007: 8).

In 2015, the evidence for human influence on the climate system was considered to have grown (IPCC, 2015). Putting the scientific evidence into qualitative terms, the report states that 'it is extremely likely that more than half of the observed increase in global average surface temperature from 1951 to 2010 was caused by the anthropogenic increase in GHG concentrations and other anthropogenic forces together' (IPCC, 2015: 5).

Table 6.8 Observed changes in the climate system

Globally averaged land and ocean surface temperatures have warmed by 0.8°C since 1880

➤ The pH of ocean surface water has decreased by 0.1 corresponding to a 26% increase in acidity since the beginning of the industrial era
➤ The Greenland and Antarctic ice sheets have been losing mass; glaciers have shrunk worldwide and Northern Hemisphere spring snow cover continues to decrease in extent
➤ Global mean sea levels rose by 0.19 meters between 1901 and 2010 and the rate of sea level rise since the mid nineteenth century is larger than the mean rate during the previous 2 millennia

Source: IPCC, 2015

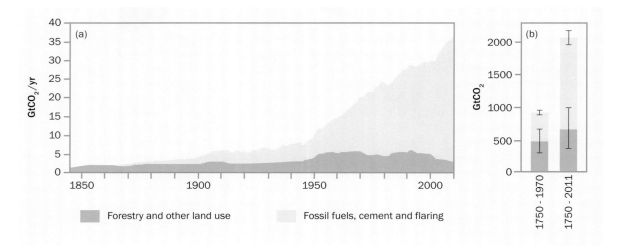

Figure 6.15 Global anthropogenic carbon dioxide emissions
(a) Annual carbon dioxide emissions
(b) Cumulative carbon dioxide emissions
Source: adapted from IPCC, 2015

Almost half of the anthropogenic CO_2 emissions between 1750 and 2011 have occurred in the last 40 years. Total anthropogenic CO_2 emission have continued to rise, with larger absolute increases in the last ten years, despite the growing number of climate change mitigation policies (IPCC, 2015: 5).

The major source of carbon dioxide production since the pre-industrial era has been the burning of fossil fuels. Development processes globally have required a progressive increase in per capita consumption of coal, oil and natural gas, as noted earlier in this chapter. Emissions from fossil fuel combustion and industrial processes contribute 78% of total emissions globally, as seen in Figure 6.15. There is greater uncertainty in the measurement of emissions from forestry, the burning of biomass, through crops and livestock and through degradation of soils. These were considered to account for approximately 10–15% of total emissions within the first IPCC report in 1990, but this share has been falling.

Table 6.9 identifies the projected impacts of climate change as put forward by the IPCC with 'high confidence' in relation to the underlying scientific evidence regarding the impacts on natural systems to date (summarised in Table 6.8). The IPCC is also involved in modelling different emissions scenarios into the future, known as Representative Concentration Pathways. These present varied pictures for the future according to different trajectories in what they consider the key drivers of anthropogenic emissions; population expansion, economic activity, lifestyles, energy use, land use patterns, technology and climate policy. One model includes a 'stringent mitigation scenario' that aims to keep likely global warming to below 2°C over pre-industrial levels. This is the level of warming that the IPCC identifies as the point at which the risk of large-scale human development setbacks and ecological catastrophe increase sharply. To reach it, global emissions need to be reduced by at least 80% over 1990 levels by 2050. 2°C is also the target used in the current international climate negotiations.

Clearly, the impacts of climate change in the future depend on 'the future state of the world' (Arnell et al., 2004: 3). Progress on international commitments to 'mitigate' climate change is evidently an important part of shaping this future (see Box 6.5). The impacts of climate change are also debated (and 'denied' in the case of some climate sceptics) due to the uncertainties of climate science. This refers not only to 'gaps in existing knowledge',

Table 6.9 The predicted impacts of global warming

Rising rates and magnitudes of warming and other changes in the climate system, accompanied by ocean acidification, increases the risk of severe, pervasive and in some cases irreversible detrimental impacts. Based on scientific understanding, there is 'high confidence' in a range of impacts, including:

➤ A large fraction of species face increased extinction risk
➤ Coastal systems and low lying areas are at risk from sea level rise, which will continue for centuries even if global mean temperature is stabilised
➤ Global marine species redistribution and marine biodiversity reduction will challenge the sustained provision of fisheries productivity and other ecosystem services
➤ There are large risks to food security globally
➤ Climate change will impact human health mainly by exacerbating health problems that already exist. Climate change is expected to lead to increases in ill-health especially in low income developing countries
➤ The combination of high temperatures and humidity in some areas for parts of the year is expected to compromise common activities including growing food and working outdoors
➤ In urban areas, climate change is projected to increase risks for people, assets, economies and ecosystems, including risks from heat stress, storms and extreme precipitation, inland and coastal flooding, landslides, air pollution, drought, water scarcity, sea level rise and storm surges
➤ Rural areas are expected to experience major impacts on water availability and supply, food security, infrastructure and agricultural incomes, including shifts in the production areas of food and non-food crops worldwide

Source: IPCC, 2015

but also to emerging understanding that elements of the climate system may have 'tipping' points, or thresholds, at which the system behaviour changes abruptly and irreversibly, rather than in a linear way. Deep ocean currents, for example, are driven by differences in the water's density, controlled by temperature and salinity. A non-linear response in the global ocean circulation could lead to the shutdown of the Gulf Stream, that is particularly vulnerable to changes in atmospheric temperatures and the hydrological cycle (Peake and Smith, 2009). Some of the complex ways in which the outcomes of climate change rest on the interdependencies of biophysical and human systems are confirmed in Figure 6.16.

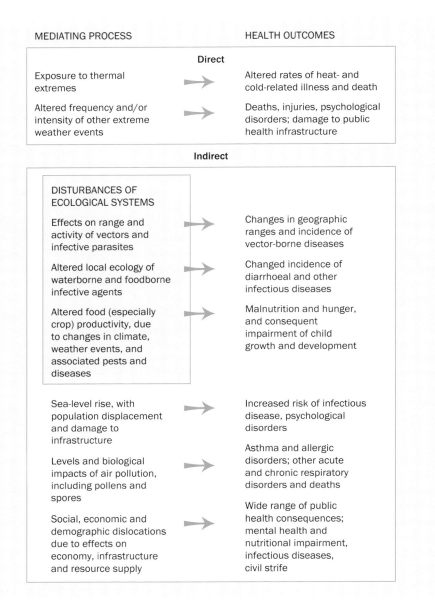

Figure 6.16 The direct and indirect health impacts of climate change
Source: World Resources Institute, 1998.

BOX 6.5

The development of an international framework on climate change: the UN Framework Convention on Climate Change

1992: The UN Framework Convention on Climate Change (UNFCCC) was adopted by 167 countries at the Earth Summit in Rio de Janeiro and came into force in 1994. It called on parties to voluntarily

BOX 6.5 (continued)

commit to the reduction of greenhouse gas emissions to their 1990 levels by 2000. Such mitigation was considered central to the stabilisation of emissions at a level which would prevent dangerous anthropogenic interference with the climate system. The UNFCCC is governed by the Conference of the Parties (COP) i.e. those countries that have signed the convention (currently 196). The UNFCCC provides the broad framework within which more legally binding protocols for action were to be developed through annual COP meetings.

1997: 113 signatories to the 'Climate Convention' agree to the Kyoto Protocol. This established the principal of legally binding targets for emissions reduction for 'Annex 1' countries, the OECD members plus countries of the former USSR and Eastern Europe. The Protocol moved to put into practice, the principle contained in the convention of 'common but differentiated' responsibilities for action on climate change, whereby developed countries should take the lead on the basis of their greater obligation and ability to do so. The Kyoto Protocol committed 'Non-Annex 1 Parties', the majority of the world's countries including the low income countries of the Global South but also including larger economies of China, India and Brazil, to monitor further and address their emissions towards climate change mitigation.

2001: The Marrakech meeting of the Conference of the Parties (COP7) formally recognises the challenges of adaptation to climate change and particularly for countries of the Global South. It calls for greater participation of these countries within future climate agreements and urges greater finances and technology transfers from richer nations to support their adaptation needs.

2005: The Kyoto Protocol becomes fully ratified and legally binding. Individual targets for 37 Annex 1 countries were negotiated, requiring an average 5.2% reduction of greenhouse gas emissions from 1990 levels to their average during 2008–12. The Protocol includes new mechanisms to enable

investments in actions to promote emissions reductions in countries of the Global South to 'count towards' Annex 1 country targets. By this time, however, the USA decided not to ratify the agreement. Australia also delayed ratification until 2011 and Canada withdrew its commitment in 2009 calling into question the legally binding nature of the Kyoto Protocol.

2009: The Conference of the Parties meet in Copenhagen (COP15) to confirm international agreement on actions to address climate change beyond 2012, when the first commitment period of the Kyoto Protocol will end. Negotiations were characterised by substantial divisions and acrimony and not solely between Annex 1 and Non-Annex 1 Parties as new alliances and different interests within and between these groupings emerged. There was also debate concerning the levels of action required, the science of the 2 degrees Celsius limit for the increase in global temperature, and how to account for efforts to reduce deforestation and degradation within targets (i.e. that support carbon sequestration). The meeting failed to reach international consensus on a binding agreement for emissions reductions beyond 2012. The 'Copenhagen Accord' was agreed by only 25 parties with the remaining countries noting the 'existence of the accord'. There was agreement on holding global temperature increases below 2 degrees Celsius, but no new emissions targets were set. A new form of agreement of 'pledge and review' was established, whereby parties in future would submit voluntary, 'nationally appropriate' targets for international review and monitoring. The Accord proposed US $30 billion to be made available in the short term to support adaptation activities in the Global South and established a High Level Panel to identify sources and mechanisms to deliver further finances in the longer term. This includes consideration of payments for the protection of forests.

2011: COP17 meets in Durban, South Africa. A new agreement – the 'Durban Platform' – is reached,

▶

BOX 6.5 (continued)

with the commitment that negotiations on the post-Kyoto future would be finalised by 2015 and put into practice by 2020. All countries were to be included in future agreements although with potentially different legal forms of agreement.

2015: COP21 meets in Paris, two weeks after terrorist attacks had killed 130 people in that city. Two key challenges for the international community were identified. Firstly, whether the voluntary pledges for emission reductions would be sufficient to prevent dangerous climate change in the future. A UN report had suggested that the aggregate effect of the 'Intended National Voluntary Commitments' submitted to date would not keep temperature increases below the critical 2 degrees limit. Secondly, in relation to equity and the continued debate concerning how the burden of cutting emission to 'safe' levels could and should be shared going forward. The Paris Agreement committed parties to the aim of keeping global temperature increases to below 2 degrees Celsius and pursue efforts to limit it to a 1.5 degree rise. All countries will submit new Nationally Determined Contributions by 2020 when the current

(Copenhagen) commitments end and again every five years with the expectation that each will be more ambitious in its emissions reductions than the previous. All will be part of a formal global stocktake to assess collective progress towards achieving the aim of the Agreement. Adaptation was recognised as a key component of the long term global response to climate change and an urgent need of developing country Parties. All countries are required to submit, and update periodically, a communication on adaptation priorities, needs, plans and action. The Copenhagen commitment on annual financing of US $100 billion by 2020 from developed countries to assist developing countries with their mitigation and adaptation efforts was extended to 2025, with a commitment to set a higher goal before 2025 and establish a clear process for reporting and accounting on these public financial contributions.

2016: The Paris Agreement on climate change enters into force in November.

Source: compiled from Sharma et al. (2016); Tanner and Horn-Phathanothai (2014); Elliott (2013).

In 2001, the IPCC identified that the impacts of climate change will not be manifested in the same way in all regions and that the countries of the Global South were more likely to suffer most from the negative impacts of climate change. This was due to their geographical location (in regions with high levels of existing climate variability, for example), and the economic importance of climate-sensitive sectors for national development and livelihoods. It was also acknowledged that they were more limited in terms of economic, institutional and human capacities to anticipate and respond to climate change. The IPCC confirmed that mitigation efforts will not stop climate change and urged greater international attention to the adaptation efforts. As such, this report was important in bringing the development agenda closer into the climate change arena. These key terms used by the IPCC are shown in Table 6.10.

Low-lying countries and small island states are particularly vulnerable to the impacts of climate change associated with sea-level rises (Plates 6.7 and 6.8). Whilst countries such as the Netherlands are vulnerable to coastal inundation, as a more wealthy nation they have already been able to undertake 'planned adaptations' including the construction of physical coastal defences against future storm surges (Barrow, 1995). Bangladesh is also a country dominated by low elevations above sea-level and substantially sited on the delta formed at the confluence of the Ganges, Brahmaputra and Meghna rivers. It is identified by the World Bank (2013a) as a 'potential impact hotspot', on the basis of the increased risks of coastal and river flooding and storm surges, and also of predicted higher extreme heats and more intense cyclone activity in the region. Unlike the Netherlands, Bangladesh has

Table 6.10 **Key terms in responding to climate change**

Mitigation: an anthropogenic intervention to reduce the sources or enhance the sinks of greenhouse gases

Adaptation: initiatives and measures to reduce the vulnerability of natural and human systems against actual or expected climate change effects. Various types are distinguished; anticipatory (pro-active), autonomous (spontaneous), reactive and planned, for example

Adaptive capacity: the whole of capabilities, resources and institutions of a country or region to implement effective adaptation measures

Resilience: the ability of a social or ecological system to absorb disturbances while retaining the same basic structure and ways of functioning, the capacity for self-organisation, and the capacity to adapt to stress and change

Vulnerability: the degree to which a system is susceptible to, and unable to cope with, adverse effects of climate change, including climate variability and extremes. Is a function of the character, magnitude and rate of climate change and variation to which a system is exposed, its sensitivity and its adaptive capacity

Source: compiled from IPCC, 2015.

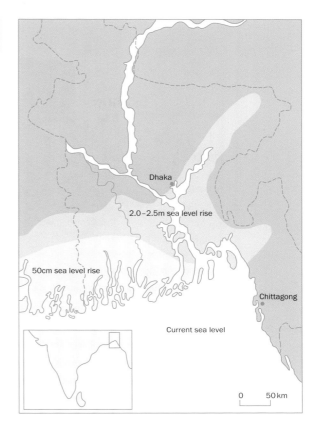

Figure 6.17 The inundation of Bangladesh under proposed sea level change
Source: adapted from Reading et al., 1995.

far fewer resources and capacities in terms of adaptation and responding to climate-related risks. The 'best-case' scenario for Bangladesh predicted by the IPCC, is for a 50-centimetre rise in sea level by the end of this century. A sea level rise of this magnitude would lead to substantial inundation, displacement of people and the loss of farmlands and infrastructures. Figure 6.17 illustrates the spatial extent of such impacts under even more serious scenarios. Moving to cities has already become a common coping strategy in the face of increased salinity of farmlands, flooding, river bank erosion and increased tidal-surge floods in Bangladesh (Black et al., 2011). In turn, the capacity of existing infrastructures in cities such as Dhaka, with a population of over 15 million, are becoming increasingly stretched. Recent research also suggests that people who are most exposed and vulnerable to the impacts of climate change are least capable of migrating and thereby suffer further injustice (Black et al., 2011).

Climate injustices and the challenge of adaptation

This pattern, whereby the current and predicted impacts of climate change fall disproportionately on countries that are already characterised by high levels of poverty and vulnerability (UNDP, 2007) raises substantial questions of 'climate justice'. As O'Riordan (2000: 171) summarised:

> The likely effects of human-generated climate change will be experienced almost in inverse proportion to innocence and blame. Those people and countries who contribute most to the emissions of radiative forcing gases are, for the most part, least likely to be most inconvenienced, impoverished or physically vulnerable to the consequences of their behaviour.

Plate 6.7 Mechanical approaches to flood protection, Bangladesh
(*photo*: Phil Ashworth)

Plate 6.8 Biological approaches to coastal protection: planting mangroves on Ambon Island, Indonesia
(*photo*: Alamy photos)

Figure 6.18 confirms that it is the richer nations that are responsible for the majority of historical carbon emissions. Historical emissions are important as climate change results from the cumulative build-up of greenhouse gases (GHGs) in the atmosphere over time, not emissions in any particular year. Climate justice principles suggest that the richer countries have an obligation to poorer nations on the basis of this 'ecological debt'. Concerns for climate justice also include the injustices of current approaches to addressing climate change, which are argued to have been dominated by mitigation strategies, focusing on future generations rather than justice concerns between groups within current generations, and focusing on 'false solutions' such as geo-engineering and carbon trading, that are asserted to maintain 'development as usual' and don't prevent further climate change or address poverty.

Concerns for climate justice are being taken up by many different 'grassroots' groups, and coalitions of organisations transnationally, that seek to understand climate change and the responses to it in terms of human rights and social justice (see Elliott, 2013). In short, these have demanded closer attention to questions of climate adaptation and the obligation of richer nations to do more in terms of transfer of finances to support climate resilient development in the countries of the Global South. Adaptation concerns the adjustments in natural or human systems in response to actual or expected climate change impacts, as identified in Table 6.10. It moves attention to the vulnerability of particular countries, communities or sectors to climate change impacts as the trigger for adaptation action. As such, there are close links between the concepts of adaptation and development, which both at their core, 'deal with social processes and issues of vulnerability, change and human agency' (Boyd, 2015: 343).

However, this also brings challenges in practice; 'not every adaptation intervention will necessarily reduce poverty' (Tanner and Horn-Phathanothai, 2014: 173), and processes of poverty reduction can increase vulnerability to climate change. There are problems also of establishing the 'additional impact' of climate change on development – in terms of its often uncertain future impacts – but also in relation to other sources of people's

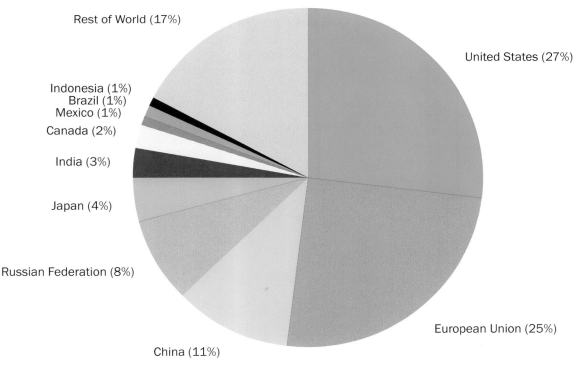

Figure 6.18 Cumulative CO$_2$ emissions, 1850–2011
Source: adapted from World Resources Institute, 2014.

vulnerabilities. As Tanner and Horn-Phathanothai (2014: 167) suggest, 'in reality, adaptation is usually a response to a wider set of changes that may include for example changes in prices, conflict, security or markets and globalisation'. As seen in Chapter 10, livelihoods are often built with a close understanding of, and in response to, a wide range of environmental and economic stresses and shocks. Furthermore, many people in the Global South have been adapting livelihood strategies and coping with uncertainties, including in weather patterns and extreme events such as drought and flooding, over centuries (Adger et al., 2003; Mortimore, 1989, 2016).

The concern is how climate change impacts may place increased pressure on coping strategies, which over time could erode capabilities into the future (UNDP, 2007). In recent years, the concept of resilience is being used to consider, not only people's abilities to 'bounce back' after a crisis, but also to adapt to reduce future vulnerability and risks. This concept draws together work on adaptation, disaster risk reduction, poverty reduction, food security and conflict, that are increasingly understood as overlapping issues with often common underlying drivers. 'Tackling "climate resilient development" is rapidly becoming a catch-all for tackling climate change impacts in a development

context' (Tanner and Horn-Phathanothai, 2014: 186) and is used, for example, by the latest IPCC (2015) report. Support to locally driven community-based adaptations 'operating on a learning-by-doing, bottom up, empowerment approach' (IPCC, 2014: 847) are considered particularly valuable in addressing the vulnerabilities of communities, by connecting climate change adaptation with non-climate needs. Table 6.11 identifies a range of community-based adaptions being undertaken in coastal regions. Further consideration of community-based approaches in rural development more widely are considered in Chapter 10.

The challenge of climate finance

Until the late 1990s, international policy responses to address climate change were largely focused on mitigation and the development of agreements on targets for countries to reduce future emissions (see Box 6.5 above). In 2004, when the Kyoto Protocol became legally binding on 'Annex 1' countries, a new principle was introduced that some emissions reduction required of these countries could be met by transferring to other countries, effectively introducing a market in carbon for the first time. Under the 'flexibility mechanisms'

Table 6.11 Community based adaptations in coastal and low lying regions

Impact	Type of Option	Measures
Increased salinity	New and diversified livelihoods	Saline tolerant crops
		Mangrove fruit production
		Rearing of crabs
	Structural	Raised foundations for houses
Flooding / Inundation	Socio-technical	Committees to discuss disaster preparedness
		Warning dissemination
	New and diversified livelihoods	Aquaculture
		Different vegetables
		Floating gardens
Cyclones/storm surges	Structural / hard	Retro-fitting houses
		Underground shelters
	Structural / soft	Fruit trees around homes
Sea level rise	Institutional	Education about insurance
Multi-coastal impacts	Institutional	Teacher training
		Coastal Zone Management
		Active female participation in institutions
	Structural / soft	Community led reforestation
	Institutional / socio-technical	Research centres / community monitoring

Source: adapted from IPCC, 2014.

identified in Table 6.12, 'permits to emit carbon', officially called 'certified emissions reductions', could be traded between countries and/or 'offset' through financing of projects in other countries.

The explicit aim stated in the Protocol, was that these mechanisms should assist Parties not included in Annex 1, to achieve sustainable development and to contribute to the overall global goal of lowering emissions. There was substantial faith in this development to deliver the transfer of technology and finances, from the North to the Global South, and to deliver global environmental benefits at least economic costs (see Stern, 2007). However, whilst some projects have led to significant emissions reductions, a key climate justice concern is that finances are not going to the poorest countries. 73% of CDM investments to 2009 were in China, for example, where costs of emissions abatement have been low (Boyd et al., 2009). In contrast, projects in countries within sub-Saharan Africa were less than 3% of all projects at this time. Projects have also been dominated by investments in gas captures at chemical and manufacturing plants, addressing emissions of NO_2 rather than CO_2 that has a greater forcing effect on climate. Further justice concerns include that corporate industry is able to be 'paid' for investing in pollution abatements that they should be investing in themselves, and that the CDM enables the pressure to be taken off the richer countries, through 'buying their way out', of more difficult domestic reductions in emissions. Furthermore, these mechanisms remain focused on mitigation interventions rather than delivering finances for adaptation. The Paris Agreement, reached at the recent meeting of the Conference of the Parties to the UNFCCC (see Box 6.5), suggests the continued support for voluntary cooperation between countries through such market-based approaches to achieve climate mitigation targets (Sharma et al., 2016).

In 2007, Parties to the Kyoto Protocol set up the Adaptation Fund (AF) to support adaptation activities that reduce adverse impacts of and risks posed to countries, communities and sectors by climate change. It was an innovative approach towards raising new, private, climate finances beyond the conventional sources of official development assistance or through the multilateral development institutions. Monies were raised through a 2% levy on CDM transactions (with some voluntary contributions from donors) and, as such,

Table 6.12 Flexibility mechanisms of the Kyoto protocol

1 Emissions trading: a developed country that has exceeded its Kyoto targets to reduce carbon dioxide emissions can sell its surplus reduction to another developed country that has failed to meet its target (Article 17).
2 Joint implementation: a developed country can fund a project in another developed country that will either reduce carbon dioxide emissions or enhance carbon sinks. The reduction of carbon dioxide in the atmosphere is allocated to the country financing the project (Article 6).
3 Clean development mechanism: a developed country can fund a project in a developing country that reduces emissions or enhances sinks. Such projects must produce reductions that are additional to any that would occur in the absence of certified project activity (Article 12).

Source: adapted from UN (1998) Kyoto Protocol to the UNFCCC.

rested substantially on the market for carbon to deliver funding for adaptation projects. The Adaptation Fund is governed by the UNFCCC secretariat, through which countries apply and schemes are administered. However, funds raised to date for the AF have been relatively limited, including due to the low price of carbon. Donors were also hesitant to support it initially due to some of its innovative features (Tanner and Horn-Phathanothai, 2014). Since 2010, UNFCCC efforts have centered on the development of the Green Climate Fund, with the intention that this fund should become the principal channel for multilateral funding in the future.

However, at the same time, there has been an expansion of climate change financing mechanisms such as the World Bank-led Climate Investment Funds that have attracted 'far greater financial contributions from donors than the UNFCCC funds' (Tanner and Horn-Phathanothai, 2014: 212). These funds provide loans and grants at concessional rates for investments that achieve development goals through supporting transition to lower carbon growth and a more climate resilient economy. These include in areas of clean technology, renewable energy and forestry. The aim is to integrate ('mainstream') climate change considerations across development cooperation activities – often referred to as 'climate-proofing' – rather than to focus support for adaptation through specific projects and programmes, as within the UNFCCC Adaptation Fund, for example. Support for these funds reflects the widespread understanding across development cooperation agencies that climate change impacts create risks for their investments and threaten the achievement of their development objectives. However, there remain concerns, particularly from countries within the Global South, about the continued dominance of existing ODA and international financial institutions in the governance and delivery of climate finances, given some of the previous conditions and relationships in past development cooperation (see Chapters 7 and 8). In the immediate term, large gaps continue in the funding available for adaptation responses in the Global South (IPCC, 2014).

Urban atmospheric pollution

Climate warming is a major atmospheric pollution problem which stems from the production of substances in quantities in excess of their absorption by natural processes, with implications for the functioning of the Earth as a whole. Additional atmospheric pollution problems, such as urban air pollution (Plate 6.9), may have quite local (largely industrial and transport related) sources and localised impacts, but are global environmental issues in the sense that all cities tend to experience similar problems.

Air pollution is now considered as one of the world's worst environmental health risks (UNEP, 2014). The World Health Organization has long-established, and continuously monitored and developed, guidelines on air quality. These seek to set internationally recognised threshold levels of air pollution above which deleterious effects, established through health science research, on human health could be expected. Yet, more than half of the global population monitored across 1,600 cities in 91 countries, is exposed to levels of air pollution over 2.5 times higher than the guidelines (WHO, 2014a). These statistics combine different types and sources of 'particulate matter' of less than 10 microns within the atmosphere. Particulate air pollution is a complex mixture of small and larger particles of varying origin and chemical composition, including smoke and dust, but also soot from vehicle exhausts (often coated with chemical contaminants or metals). Data is only available for those cities that collect and report on air quality. As such, it is likely to underestimate the situation globally, and furthermore, the situation in some cities and for some pollutants may be more hazardous in terms of human health. In Kathmandu, Nepal, for example, exposure to PM_{10} was over 500 micrograms per cubic meter (UNEP, 2014), whereas WHO guidelines on safe levels are 20 micrograms per cubic meter.

Plate 6.9 Smog enveloping Mexico City
(*photo*: Mark Edwards, Still Pictures)

In most cities worldwide, air pollution is getting worse overall. Areas of the City of London exceeded WHO guidelines for average nitrogen dioxide levels just a few days into 2016. It is evident that contemporary patterns and processes of development are compromising future development prospects very directly through air pollution, but particularly in countries of the Global South. Ambient (outdoor) air pollution was the cause of 3.7 million premature deaths globally in 2012 (WHO, 2014a). This includes through its contribution to stroke and heart disease, chronic pulmonary diseases, lung cancer and acute lower respiratory diseases. Eighty-eight per cent of these deaths are in low and middle income countries and a large proportion live in SE Asia and the West Pacific region (op. cit.). The implications for health services in particular cities are substantial. Research within Jakarta, Indonesia, indicates that 1,400 deaths, 49,000 Emergency Room visits and 600,000 asthma attacks could be avoided every year if particulate levels were brought down to WHO standards (World Resources Institute, 1998).

Furthermore, indoor air pollution was the cause of 4.3 million premature deaths worldwide in 2012 and these deaths were almost exclusively in countries of the Global South (WHO, 2014b). In SE Asia alone, there were 1.7 million premature deaths linked directly to indoor air pollution. The principal cause of these deaths was the burning of coal and biomass sources for cooking and associated heating and lighting. Gender roles within the household, whereby women take key responsibility in domestic cooking and spend most time indoors including in caring and self-employment, means that women and children suffer more from the health impacts of air pollution. An estimated 60% of premature deaths from indoor air pollution in 2008 were women and 44% were children (UNDP/WHO, 2009). This suggests that solid fuel use within the home is the second biggest environmental contributor, behind unsafe water and sanitation, to ill health worldwide.

Sulphur dioxide is probably the best-known urban pollutant, with most industrial cities having been subject to sulphurous smogs at some point (Elsom, 1996). The primary sources of sulphur dioxide production are the smelting of metallic ores, fossil fuel use in power production and heating, and in transport. The key health effects are through its contribution to particulate matter and include the impairment of respiratory function, including the aggravation and/or causation of bronchitis, asthma and emphysema, and the subsequent strain on the heart, leading to premature death. Sulphur dioxide also has an impact on terrestrial and freshwater system quality and functioning through acidification and on cultural heritage, for example, through the corrosion of building materials (UNEP, 2012).

Global emissions of sulphur dioxide were dominated by the US and Europe until 2000, but have subsequently been overtaken by East Asian emissions. 'Ceilings' on emissions through national legislation and regional directives, such as the EU National Emission Ceiling, have led to reductions in sulphur emissions. The actions to address energy efficiency in countries including China (discussed above) are also supporting the slower growth in emissions. However, critical loads of sulphur dioxide are still exceeded in many freshwater ecosystems including across Europe and North America (UNEP, 2012). Figure 6.19 confirms the continued challenge of air pollution within cities of the Global South.

The increase in private vehicles, the poor state of public transport and inefficiencies in energy use, are all key contributors to these challenges of air pollution (WHO, 2014a). As seen above and in Chapter 8, there is a strong link between economic growth and increased movement of goods and services through international trade, and long distance shipping is relatively unregulated in terms of air pollution (Viana et al., 2014). 15% of global nitrogen dioxide and up to 8% of Sulphur dioxide emissions are attributable to ocean going ships. 70% of sulphur dioxide emissions occur within 400 km of land, making this form of transport a significant contributor to air quality and degradation in coastal areas and busy ports in particular.

Ozone is a further aspect of urban air pollution that constitutes significant risks to human health and development opportunity, particularly in countries of the Global South. 'Tropospheric ozone' in the lower atmosphere is a factor in climate warming. Ozone is not emitted directly, but is formed when nitrogen oxides from fuel combustion react with other 'volatile organic compounds' (VOLs) in the atmosphere. 'Surface ozone' refers to concentrations at ground level and is a major component of photochemical smogs in urban areas. As a powerful oxidant, ozone reacts with most biological tissues and, as such, has widespread health implications. The impact of surface ozone on human health is

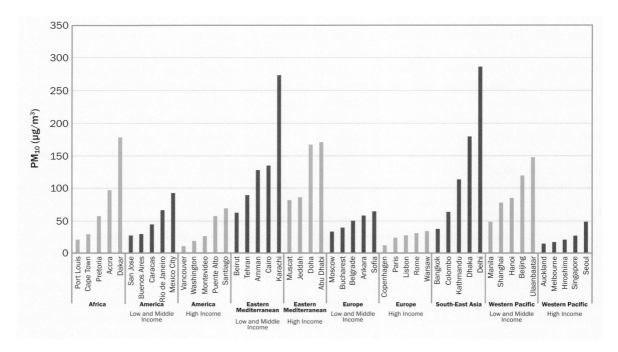

Figure 6.19 PM₁₀ levels for selected cities by region, 2008–12
Source: adapted from WHO, 2014c.

considered second only to particulate matter (UNEP, 2012: 48). Surface ozone concentrations also have a major impact on vegetation and are a major cause of diminishing crop yields and forest productivity.

Biodiversity loss

Biodiversity is essentially the variety of life on earth and has evolved over the planet's approximate 5 billion year history (UNEP, 2012). Species extinction is a natural process that would occur without human action. For example, five major extinction events have been identified through fossil records and linked to natural upheavals and planetary change (UNEP, 2012). However, the rate of biodiversity loss and species extinction has increased rapidly through the last century to an extent that the current biological diversity loss can be considered the sixth global extinction (op. cit.: 196). The Millennium Ecosystem Assessment (2005) reported that human actions over the last few hundred years have increased species extinction rates by as much as 1,000 times the background rates that were typical over Earth's history. Future extinction rates are predicted to be ten

times higher than current and with an increasing risk of abrupt (non-linear) changes. Climate change is expected to become more important as a driver of biodiversity loss though this century, with up to 30% of all mammal, bird and amphibian species under threat (Rockström et al., 2009: 474). It is also recognised that in the longer term, these extinction rates may well alter 'not only biological diversity but the evolutionary processes by which diversity is generated' (UNEP, 2012: 196).

However, there are problems of data regarding biodiversity and predictions of future species loss and their impacts. For example, only a small proportion of the Earth's species have been identified to date; species concepts have also been developed with respect to studies of invertebrates and insects that may not be relevant when considering micro-organisms such as fungi; and there is substantial debate even concerning what constitutes a 'species' (Dolman, 2000). Biodiversity can also be considered in terms of ecosystems, species and genetic material (Mather and Chapman, 1995). The Convention on Biological Diversity agreed at the UN 'Earth Summit' in 1992 now has 193 signatories (see Chapter 7 for a full discussion of the UN in Sustainable

Development). The Convention defines Biological Diversity as the 'variability among living organisms from all sources including, inter alia, terrestrial, marine and other aquatic ecosystems and the ecological complexes of which they are part; this includes diversity within species, between species and of ecosystems'. The significance of species variability to biological diversity is elaborated in Table 6.13.

The Millennium Ecosystem Assessment did much to introduce the idea of 'ecosystem services', the multitude of benefits that ecosystems provide for humanity, into widespread use and have been embraced within biodiversity policies at all scales. However, whilst it is recognised that a rich mix of species underpins the functioning of ecosystems, and the subsequent 'services' that they provide to human well-being, there is much that is not known regarding how biodiversity is linked to ecosystem services (Science for Environment Policy, 2015). There is a concern that the 'anthropo-centric' (i.e. human focused) emphasis of the concept of ecosystem services may not guarantee the protection of biodiversity (op. cit.). It is also acknowledged that further research is needed to understand 'how much and what kinds of biodiversity can be lost before (ecosystem) resilience is eroded' (Rockström et al., 2009: 474).

The MEA also confirmed (and as seen in Figure 6.4) that biodiversity can be valued for many different reasons, and the impacts of biodiversity loss have to be considered at multiple scales and for particular groups of people. Impacts are currently seen very directly at the local level, where consumptive or productive uses are compromised by loss of food or fish stocks. Wild-harvested food and medicine also form very important parts of food security, health and cultural identify for many people in the Global South. But biodiversity loss is also now recognised to have pervasive impacts at a global level, including through how ecosystem services such as in climate regulation and nutrient cycling interact with other Planetary Boundaries (Rockström et al., 2009). For example, loss of biodiversity can increase the vulnerability of terrestrial and aquatic ecosystems to changes in climate. However, the loss of biodiversity to date is one of the planetary boundaries that are considered to have already been transgressed through human activity (see Figure 6.3a). Whilst there are considered problems of establishing a boundary on biodiversity, 'we can say with some confidence that Earth cannot sustain the current rate of loss without significant erosion of ecosystem resilience' (Rockström et al., 2009: 474).

Biodiversity is deteriorating at the level of populations, species and ecosystems (UNEP, 2012). Populations of vertebrate species have declined on average by 30% since 1970. The proportion of species under threat of extinction, as monitored by the IUCN Red List, has also risen in recent decades and is particularly rapid amongst coral species. At a habitat/ecosystem level, approximately 13 million hectares of forest are being lost annually and over 20% of mangroves and 38% of coral reefs have been destroyed since 1980 (UNEP, 2012).

Table 6.13 The significance of species variability

Species variability is key to biodiversity in a number of senses:

➤ The variability between species including the relative abundance between species
➤ Variability within species, i.e. aspects of genetic diversity for example
➤ Diversity of functional traits, i.e. the properties of species that define their ecological role and in turn their impact on ecosystem functioning and services
➤ The variability of ecosystems themselves at a landscape level, i.e. variation across and within major vegetation types for example

Source: compiled from Science for Environment Policy, 2015.

Sources of biodiversity loss

The key pressures on biodiversity come through habitat loss and degradation. As such, the expansion and intensification of global agriculture is the principal underlying driver. The key patterns of forest conversion for agriculture were considered in the section above, with major implications for habitat loss and fragmentation. This includes that tropical forests are particularly species diverse in that they occupy less than seven per cent of the Earth's surface, but account for between 50 and 90 per cent of all known plant and animal species (Mather and Chapman, 1995: 122). The impacts of agriculture on biodiversity also include the manipulation of the gene pool of species (and the introduction of new species into land and freshwater environments), the increased use of pesticides and the over exploitation of animal species such as through hunting. Genetic diversity has declined at a global level and particularly amongst cultivated species (MEA, 2005). So-called 'genetic erosion' has occurred as modern agriculture has become based on the manipulation of a very small number of plant varieties for intensive production. Genetic erosion is also associated with the increased vulnerability of crops to predation by bacteria or aphids which, 'unlike their genetically uniform prey, are constantly evolving' (Murray, 1995: 22). Fears for the further loss of plant genetic diversity are also a principal concern of opponents to the adoption of genetically modified crops (see Chapter 10).

Wetland habitats worldwide are also increasingly under threat from agricultural intensification and through urban developments. Wetlands include areas of marsh, fen, peatlands, swamp forests, estuaries and coastal zones. They provide many resource functions, including direct use value in terms of supporting agriculture, fishing, tourism and transport. Wetlands also have indirect hydrological uses, including groundwater recharge and discharge, sediment trapping and flood protection (Hughes, 1992). Their biodiversity function is in the diverse habitats supported for aquatic species, waterfowl and other wildlife (Plate 6.10). In mangrove swamps alone, it is estimated that there are 60 species of

trees and shrubs and over 2,000 species of fish, invertebrates and epiphytic plants that depend for their survival on those wetland environments (Maltby, 1986). However, over half of the world's mangrove forests may already have been destroyed (MEA, 2005) and coastal wetlands continue to decline by more than 100,000 hectares a year (UNEP, 2012). Whilst the rate of loss of mangroves globally has slowed a little, more than half of the global totals of mangrove systems are in the Asia and Pacific regions where mangrove losses have been accelerating in recent years (UNEP, 2012).

The regulation of water and drainage for agricultural purposes has widespread implications for wetland habitats and species variability. Dams, irrigation schemes and aquaculture all have major implications for key ecological components and hydrological processes within rivers, lakes, floodplains and wetlands fed by ground water. Most overtly, dams influence the amount of water discharging into the oceans and alter the water flow throughout the river basin. Dams also block the flow of sediments and nutrients for plants and fish and can disrupt migratory and breeding patterns. In altering the flow, the habitats provided by particular rapids or floodplains may be removed with the disappearance of whole ecosystems. Habitat is also removed very directly where water flows submerge areas of land.

Whilst there are long-established concerns regarding the negative environmental and social costs of dam

Plate 6.10 Biodiversity in New South Wales, Australia
(*photo*: Chris Joyce)

construction and water regulation more widely, construction has expanded rapidly in the last decade, particularly in countries of the Global South, and demand for reservoirs of all sizes is expected to rise, including with rising water scarcity under climate change and the search for lower carbon energy futures. 589 large dams were built in Asia in just two years to 2001 (UNESCO, 2009). 243 dams are currently in planning stages for the Amazon basin with huge implications for the rivers and forests (Webster, 2016). Further planned dam construction on the lower Mekong River in Laos is raising serious concerns about the possible impact on local people who depend on the river's rich natural biodiversity and fish as a source of subsistence and income generation (Pillay, 2013).

Riparian and coastal zones have long been favoured areas for human population and settlement, particularly in arid zones. Although low-elevation coastal zones account for just two per cent of the world's total land area, they host approximately 13 per cent of the world's urban population and many of the world's largest cities (UN-Habitat, 2016). One of the most powerful contemporary forces of wetland degradation globally is the encroachment of urban, industrial and infrastructural developments. The impacts of such development on biodiversity may be very direct, such as in the case of eastern Kolkata, where 4,000 hectares of inland lagoons have been filled to provide homes for middle class families, but also include less direct impacts via altering water flows, enhancing siltation and aggravating pollution (World Resources Institute, 1996). However, distinct agricultural systems have also evolved to exploit the productive habitats of wetlands such as in aquaculture, recessional cultivation and wet rice cropping. Further consideration of how agricultural systems have modified riparian ecologies, and hydrologies, and the impacts on environmental and social change are considered in Chapter 10.

Conclusion: towards sustainable resource management

This chapter has confirmed that development patterns and processes are intrinsically related to natural resources, ecological systems and their functioning. It is this interrelationship of environment and development that is central to the notion of sustainable development. Development challenges are environmental challenges and one end will not be achieved without the other. However, there are deep challenges in ensuring equitable outcomes across current and future generations. The chapter has also shown that the nature of the challenge is highly specific both in time and space. For example, it was seen that how resources are valued changes as development occurs. The significance and implications of resource constraints, scarcity and degradation were also seen to be highly conjunctural at the local level.

There has been unprecedented growth in recent years in the demand for natural resources including land, energy and minerals, with major changes in the geographical patterning of flows of these materials, including with the growth of emerging economies particularly in Asia. Production and consumption in any place increasingly depend on materials, energy and goods sourced from other world regions. This creates opportunities for 'resource-rich' countries in the Global South in addressing economic development priorities, but carry significant threats in terms of new socio-environmental conflicts that impact particularly on poorer groups.

New research, including within climate science, confirms the very complex ways in which biophysical and human system functioning and health are inter-connected, as well as the profound changes that are already being observed. Finding cost-effective, resource-efficient, lower-carbon and more equitable trajectories to meet development aspirations into the future are seen to challenge international institutions, national governments, business and civil society sectors. In short, this chapter has illustrated areas of research and understanding that have been important in overcoming ideas of any simple, deterministic link between resources and development and has alluded to some of the ways in which new processes and patterns of development need to be found. Part III of the text provides insight into how these challenges are being variously taken up, shaped and resisted by the activities of different organisations involved in influencing development policy and action within particular places and spaces.

Key points

➤ Past patterns of human development have been closely linked to the exploitation of environmental resources. New understandings of the impacts of such patterns suggest that 'planetary boundaries' may have been crossed and even a new geological era of the 'Anthropocene' can be identified.

➤ The notion of sustainable development centres on the interdependence of environment and development into the future and highlights why past patterns and processes of 'development' cannot be sustained in environmental, economic and social terms.

➤ Ecosystem resources and functions are essential to human well-being through a range of 'services' that they provide, but the majority are being degraded and/or used unsustainably.

➤ Whilst human society as a whole has not experienced the absolute resource scarcities that have been predicted, there are many dimensions of resource scarcity that are experienced currently which shape closely the opportunities for many people, particularly in the Global South.

➤ In recent years there have been major changes in the size and geographical patterning of flows of energy, materials and inputs into the economic system, including through the rise of emerging economies such as China and India.

➤ Questions of the future availability and management of water and commercial energy sources are global resource considerations that present complex challenges particularly of social and distributional equity.

➤ There are a number of global environmental changes, such as climate warming and the decline of biodiversity, that are widely understood to be underpinned by human actions that challenge current systems of global governance.

➤ The persistence of poverty and rising inequality are major constraints on the prospects for sustainable development in the future.

Further reading

Adams, W.M. (2009) *Green Development: Environment and Sustainability in the Third World*, 3rd edn. London: Routledge.
Presents a thorough analysis of the evolution of environmental thinking of both mainstream ideas of sustainable development and their opponents, and how development in practice has been influenced by such 'Greening'.

Elliott, J.A. (2013) *An Introduction to Sustainable Development*, 4th edn. London: Routledge.
An accessible introduction to the challenges and opportunities of sustainable development, with particular reference to the Global South.

Houghton, J. (2015) *Global Warming: The Complete Briefing*, 5th edn Cambridge: Cambridge University Press.
An accessible text on the latest science of climate change, as well as the physical and human impacts.

Middleton, N. (2013) *Global Casino: An Introduction to Environmental Issues,* 5th edn. London: Routledge.
An accessible introduction to a range of core global environmental issues.

Millennium Ecosystem Assessment (MEA) (2005) *Ecosystems and Human Well-Being: Synthesis.* Washington: Island Press.
The summary document that confirms the linkages between ecosystem services and the multi-dimensional

aspects of human well-being and how these are changing with degradation and unsustainable use.

Tanner, T. and Horn-Phathanothai, L. (2014) *Climate Change and Development*, London: Routledge.
Clear exposition of the linked challenges of and responses to under-development and climate change.

United Nations Environment Programme (2012) *Global Environment Outlook 5: Environment for the Future We Want.* UNEP.
An authoritative look at the current state of the global environment.

Websites

www.ipcc.ch
Site of the Intergovernmental Panel on Climate Change. Hosts a wealth of technical, scientific and socio-economic information regarding understanding and responding to climate change including the latest 2015 reports.

www.maweb.org
Site of the Millennium Ecosystem Assessment project that reports on five years of work by over 1,000 scientists to report on conditions and trends of global ecosystems and consequences for human well-being. Five synthesis reports on biodiversity, wetlands and water, desertification, health, business and industry can be accessed in full.

www.iied.org

Site for the International Institute for Environment and Development, which is an independent non-profit organisation promoting sustainable patterns of development. Gateway to substantial research and policy studies in areas of climate change, forestry, agriculture, biodiversity and mining.

https://sustainabledevelopment.un.org/

The central platform for the United Nations work on the post-2015 development agenda and the development of the new Sustainable Development Goals.

Discussion topics

➤ This chapter has focused on global patterns of the complex interrelationships between resources, the environment and development. Compile a list of evidence that you can find locally, regionally and nationally for this relationship.

➤ What is more damaging to the environment, poverty or affluence?

➤ Research in more depth the problems of data accuracy in relation to deforestation, biodiversity or soil erosion.

➤ Investigate the notion of 'common but differentiated responsibilities' within the ongoing development of the international agreements on climate change. What do you think should be the responsibilities of poorer countries of the Global South in future mitigation actions?

➤ Do you think that targets on greenhouse gas emissions should be legally binding?

➤ Investigate in more depth current energy policies in India and China – what factors do you think are key to the prospects for lower carbon development in these countries?

Chapter 7
Institutions of development

Decision-making in development is undertaken by various individuals, agents, bodies and organisations. Historically, this role most frequently fell to governments in defining and implementing policy and planning at a national level. However, the role of the state has altered substantially over time including through processes of economic globalisation. This chapter introduces a range of institutions within the arenas of state, market and civil society that now characterise the institutional landscape of development. It focuses on how the activities of these institutions are changing, particularly in relation to global challenges of economic regeneration and sustainable development, and how they are increasingly working together in new partnerships to promote development. The outcomes of these activities are the focus for Part III.

This chapter:

➤ Identifies a range of key institutions and organisations involved in development planning and practice;
➤ Describes the responsibilities and operations of the core institutions of global governance including the United Nations, the World Bank and the World Trade Organization;

➤ Critically considers the 'fitness for purpose' of these global institutions, particularly from the perspective of the Global South;
➤ Explores the rise of non-state actors in development and, in particular, civil society and the private sector;
➤ Investigates the ways in which multilateral institutions, the state, business and civil society increasingly 'work together' in new alliances and networks for development;
➤ Considers the impacts of economic crises and the search for sustainable development, as drivers of change for these institutions and alliances in development.

Introduction: the changing institutional landscape of development

Whilst 'doing development' was for a long time the preserve of governments, the capacity of governments to shape the trajectories of human and resource development within the boundaries of the state has changed substantially and particularly across the decades spanning the millennium. As considered in Part I, significant forces of change through the 1990s included those associated with increasing globalisation, the end of the Cold War, and the mounting influence of the international financial institutions (IFIs), such as the World Bank and the International Monetary Fund in driving new strategies for development. As discussed in Chapter 1, economic liberalisation came to dominate the theory and practice of development from the late 1980s, but was increasingly challenged into the new millennium, including by broad-based social reaction, both within the Global South and North, the 'anti-globalisation' movement discussed in Chapter 4. As Craig and Porter (2006: 4) suggested, 'development's lead institutions had to be recast as more "inclusive", more responsive and "participatory", and thereby, somehow more legitimate'. Indeed, civil society came to have a much more prominent role in international policy debates and global problem-solving than had previously been seen (Edwards, 2001a), including for its role in holding states more accountable to their citizens and for their potential to deliver better outcomes for the poor.

Furthermore, what are now considered to be over-simplistic dualistic discussions of 'state' or 'market' were also replaced by those concerning strengthening state capacities and building institutions for markets (World Bank, 2002a) as the critique of market-led strategies for development mounted. Neo-liberal ideology has again been called into question since 2008 and the onset of Global Financial Crisis (GFC). This 'nightmare on Wall Street' (Silvey, 2010: 829) has reinvigorated discussions of the role of the state in leading development in recent years.

The institutional landscape of development continues to be characterised by these three pillars of state, market and civil society, and 'conceptualisations of what constitutes and best promotes "development" have evolved and continue to evolve alongside changing perceptions of the relative roles of these three pillars' (Banks and Hulme, 2014: 182). However, there are now many new actors and alliances within these three pillars. For example, alongside the more 'traditional' actors in development, of governments, of international organisations like the World Bank, and Non-Governmental Organisations, newer actors now include private foundations, such as the Bill and Melinda Gates Foundation, consumers and even celebrities (see Richey and Ponte, 2014). There has also been substantial growth in the number and impacts of Southern, Gulf and Central/Eastern European countries, both as donors and sources of private finance (see Mawdsley et al., 2014, and Chapter 8). The recent global economic crisis has confirmed the intensification of economic interdependence of countries worldwide and the significance of new global powers, including China and India, in driving global agendas. Furthermore, understanding of the global nature of environmental challenges, particularly of climate change, has also required extensive changes to the international institutional framework to better address the needs and participation of countries of the Global South.

The institutional landscape of development is also characterised by new alliances or ways that institutions are working together in development. For example, NGOs are now working with governments, as well as with the World Bank, the United Nations and even with private corporations, such that they may be 'simultaneously viewed as market based actors and central components of civil society' (Desai and Potter, 2014: 536). Businesses are engaging in new roles, with an interest in countries of the Global South and not solely as sites of investment, production or trade. For example, businesses (not unproblematically) now link consumers within the Global North to international development causes through initiatives like Fairtrade, discussed further in Chapter 8. The Critical reflection considers a more recent initiative, ProductRed, that links consumers with iconic brands including Apple, Gap and Starbucks, to 'help' those suffering AIDS, TB and Malaria, particularly in Africa. A proportion of the profits made through such shopping is then disbursed through an innovative international public-private financing mechanism that is supported by the World Health Organisation and the G8 countries. It is suggested to have launched a new frontier for development aid, in which private financing is becoming more important, and confirms a new role of business as a social actor in development, beyond the 'traditional' role, in which business was 'active but not responsible for development outcomes' (Richey and Ponte, 2014: 7).

Critical reflection

ProductRed

ProductRed was the idea of the Irish rock-star Bono, and was launched by him, at the 2006 meeting of the World Economic Forum, that comprises many of the world's top business leaders and global politicians. ProductRed is a brand created to link consumers with red-branded products developed by major international companies, including American Express, Apple, Microsoft, Gap, Armani, Starbucks and Hallmark. These companies commit to a multi-year partnership with ProductRed and pay a license fee to be involved. A percentage of the profits from the sales of their red-branded profits are then transferred to the Global Fund. The Global Fund is an international mechanism for raising and channelling public and private finances to address the global health challenges of HIV/AIDS, TB and malaria.

The Global Fund was set up in 2002, substantially through the work of the UN Secretary General, calls from the World Health Organization to scale up finances to achieve global health targets, and through the commitments of the G8 countries to raise levels of official development assistance, particularly to African countries. It is the second largest pool of donor funds globally, after the UN, and draws approximately 5% of its funds through private sources, including the Bill and Melinda Gates Foundation. To date, ProductRed has raised over US $350 million for the Global Fund. The Global Fund is not an implementer of projects, but disburses finances to Principal Recipients, that can be government ministries, community based organisations or private sector organisations, for example, identified through Country Coordinating Mechanisms and Local Fund Agents.

ProductRed has been termed 'Brand Aid' (Richey and Ponte, 2008, 2014) and is considered a distinct form of wider 'cause-related marketing', for the way in which it targets specific development causes and involves celebrities in its launch, mediation and management. Celebrities, for example, are central to creating and guaranteeing or validating, the 'caring/cool' brands, in shaping the representations of distant 'Africans' in need of help, and in selling the products to consumers 'as the means to achieving development for recipients and good feelings for consumers simultaneously' (Richey and Ponte, 2014: 10). This contrasts with wider cause-related marketing, such as Fair Trade products, where consumers are provided with more transparent information about the processes of production, the conditions of exchange and the 'certification' of the products. With Brand Aid, consumers are linked, not with the workers or producers of the red-branded products, but with the (passive) recipients of help.

Critical reflection

Have you bought a red-branded product? What were your motivations/thoughts? On what information did you base your decision? Is ProductRed a helpful initiative for engaging more people with aid and development issues? Could it provide a model for further ways to raise money to assist development in the Global South? To what extent can it be considered a genuine alternative? Does it help address the underlying factors of poverty or challenge how we frame and represent the challenges of development? The chapters in the Special Issue of the journal Third World Quarterly (2014, Vol. 35, No.1) dedicated to *New Actors and Alliances in Development* will help you consider these questions further.

Discussions of institutions in development also include less 'tangible' institutions that may lack a specific organisational form, but are understood as often critical in mediating the processes through which people construct their livelihoods. These institutions include the regularised patterns of behaviour between individuals and groups, which are structured by 'unwritten codes' and norms that have widespread use in society. These informal institutions may have as much influence over human action, decision-making and what happens in terms of development as formal institutions governing markets or the activities of the state, for example. Many insights into the operation and impacts of these kinds of institutions have come through work concerning natural resource management (see Chapter 10). It is also through this kind of thinking that the importance of gender relations as institutions structuring the lifestyles and livelihoods of individuals has been illuminated (see Chapter 5).

The concept of 'governance' is often used to recognise the range of institutions, participants and rules that operate currently in complex networks and across scales to 'steer, control or manage sectors or facets of society in certain directions' (Evans, 2012: 4). The concept is used widely and particularly by social scientists. It helps understand the range of institutions and relationships, beyond government and state activities, for example, that are involved in the processes of governing. It also highlights the complex and contested processes through which actors at different scales develop and implement action and how these evolve and change.

Evidently, institutions in and of development are dynamic and the alliances and relationships between them are complex. This chapter identifies (inevitably rather briefly) the principal characteristics of a number of key institutions in the development landscape. It highlights in particular, how their roles and activities are changing, including as new alliances are formed in response to the global economic crisis, the challenges of sustainable development and towards recognising the role of countries and peoples of the Global South in current systems of governance. The contested nature of the outcomes on the ground of these activities is considered more fully in Part III.

In any discussion of the role of institutions in development it is important to consider that institutions across all scales are not neutral factors in the development process; 'they represent values, which in turn represent the interests of some political or social group' (Sharp, 1992: 55). As such, there is a need for ongoing critical analysis of institutions, not just for the ways in which they 'do development', but also for the way in which they may present barriers for particular groups and social actors and because of the 'power' they exert over the development process.

The rise of global governance

International institutions are created by states, usually as a 'means of achieving collective objectives that could not

be accomplished by acting individually' (Werksman, 1996: xii). At the end of the Second World War, the challenges of ensuring peace, of the resurrection of the global economy, avoiding a return to the national protectionism which created the Great Depression of the 1930s and of reconstruction in Europe in particular, prompted the creation of new forums, such as the United Nations and the International Bank for Reconstruction and Development (IBRD or, as commonly termed, the 'World Bank'). The intention was the development and coordination of international efforts towards achieving the collective goals of preserving peace, resolving conflicts and promoting social and economic development.

Since the end of the Second World War, a system of global governance has continued to evolve, whereby actors at the international and national level seek to 'cooperate to achieve commonly accepted goals and to address global challenges' (Massa and Brambila-Macias, 2014: 555). Whilst the economic reconstruction of Europe and peace in that region has been substantially secured, poverty and armed conflict persist particularly across countries in the Global South. There are also new global challenges to address, including the need to resolve development aspirations across the globe within the limits of natural resources and the environment (see also Chapter 6).

The concept of 'global governance' refers to the institutions and organisations, the relationships between them, that are often based on partnerships rather than hierarchy, and the rules of international conduct put in place (Williams et al., 2014). There is substantial debate currently concerning the 'fitness for purpose' of a number of international institutions within the global governance system (see Massa and Brambila-Macias, 2014). Concerns include whether these institutions are able to change quickly enough to cope with the pace and nature of new global challenges, such as climate change or international migration and terrorism. In the following sections, the slowness of decision making and policy setting in both the United Nations and in the World Trade Organisation, where decisions depend on consensus are identified. There are also debates around the effectiveness and legitimacy of some international institutions in meeting the development needs of the Global South, and in recognising the role for, and participation of those countries, particularly in the context of recent shifts in global economic power.

In short, institutions of global governance are highly varied in terms of their shape and function, the rules and practices concerning their activities, and their power to influence the behaviour of other organisations. Fundamentally, the pursuit of collective goods demands some devolution of sovereign power, but the capacity of international institutions to take on characteristics and powers distinct from the states which created them, depends on the willingness of those states to make such investments (Werksman, 1996). This provides the context for any critical analysis of the operation and development outcomes of these institutions.

The United Nations system

To be sure, the UN has made many changes over the years, but rarely have these been enough to solve the institutional weaknesses. The UN is still hamstrung by pre-Cold war structures, redundant agencies, inadequate personnel policies, a lack of accountability, and inadequate resources.

(Mingst and Karns, 2012: 50)

The Charter of the United Nations (UN) was signed in San Francisco in June 1945, by 51 countries as the successor organisation to the League of Nations created in the inter-war years. The UN was a more complex and ambitious undertaking than the League of Nations, intended to go beyond merely ensuring stability in international relations, and to 'systematise the promotion of change' (Righter, 1995: 25; Plate 7.1). The UN today is a complex web of institutions, many with overlapping responsibilities, but retains the original broad purposes, including a commitment to equal rights for people of all nations, to free succeeding generations from the scourge of war and to promote social and economic progress. Over the course of its history, and as it has evolved, the UN has been the focus of substantial debate and uncertainty regarding its role, operations and future, as highlighted by the statements in Table 7.1 and discussed more fully in the following sections.

Since 2000, the Millennium Development Goals have substantially directed the development activities of the UN, as well as bilateral donors, states, private investment and NGOs. They have been referred to as

Table 7.1 Debating the future of the United Nations

➤ Disillusion with the UN has become one of the clichés of our time. The reality is much more complex (Ignatieff, 1995)

➤ The UN's governance problem is that it relies to an excessive degree on time-honored but cumbersome processes of intergovernmental consultation in the quest for solutions (Browne, 2014: 1853)

➤ The world wants more of the UN and the organization is only able to deliver less (former deputy Secretary-General cited in Browne, 2011: 116)

➤ Our resources are simply not commensurate with our global tasks (Kofi Annan, 2000)

➤ The UN was set up to recognise the supremacy of the nation state; it now needs to factor in the impact of globalisation on the system (Dodds, 2002: 293)

➤ As the gap between rich and poor continues to widen and as a spiral of poverty, environmental degradation and violent conflict become all but a way of life in some regions, the difference between what the UN enshrines and what it is able to accomplish threatens its legitimacy (Whitman, 2002: 467)

➤ In Iraq a tipping point has been reached. After going to war in 1991 and overseeing the massacre of untold thousands of Iraqis, the UN became complicit in the slow death of thousands (Ransom, 2005: 11)

the UN's greatest achievement in galvanising actions towards a more poverty-focused approach to human development and in terms of the outcomes seen on the ground. These successes include the number of people lifted out of poverty and removed from living in slum conditions (as seen in Chapter 1). However, the MDGs have been criticised for their relative silence on issues including inequities in the rules of global trade and international finance that have been longstanding agendas for countries of the Global South. As Fukuda-Parr (2012: iii) suggested, the MDGs promote a discourse of development 'that has no room for understanding poverty as related to underlying power relations within and between countries and asymmetries in the global economy'. Despite the inter-related nature of the goals, it has also been suggested that the MDGs took the focus off the more holistic and complex sustainable development agenda (Dodds et al., 2012). In 2016, the UN adopted a new set of Sustainable Development Goals, to build on and supersede the MDGs. The failure of the MDGs to capture the integrated nature of sustainable development was acknowledged by the UN itself:

to fulfil our vision of promoting sustainable development, we must go beyond the MDGs. They did not focus enough on reaching the very poorest and most excluded people. They were silent on the devastating effects of conflict and violence on development. The importance to development of good governance and institutions that guarantee the rule of law, free speech and open and accountable government was not included, nor the need for inclusive growth to provide jobs. *Most seriously, the MDGs fell short by not integrating the economic, social and environmental aspects of sustainable development as envisaged in the Millennium Declaration.*

(UN, 2013b: 7 *emphasis added*)

This section identifies the key characteristics of the United Nations as it operates currently in relation to a number of its core commitments and particularly in relation to sustainable human development. Inevitably, the discussion is brief and is only a partial insight to the complexities of the UN system as a whole. The emphasis here is on those parts that are most centrally involved in the governance of sustainable development, on the most recent reform processes within the institution, and on the way that the UN works with other actors in development.

Core characteristics and functions

The UN system illustrated in Figure 7.1, includes the United Nations organisation itself, comprising six main organs as shown, various programmes and funds, such as the United Nations Environment Programme, a range of functional commissions, five regional commissions, numerous standing and ad hoc committees, plus a number of specialised agencies including the International Labour Organization and the World Bank Group. It also includes varied associated, but autonomous bodies and institutions, such as the World Trade Organization, which liaises closely with the UN. Evidently, the UN system constitutes a 'formidable array' (Williams et al., 2014: 89)

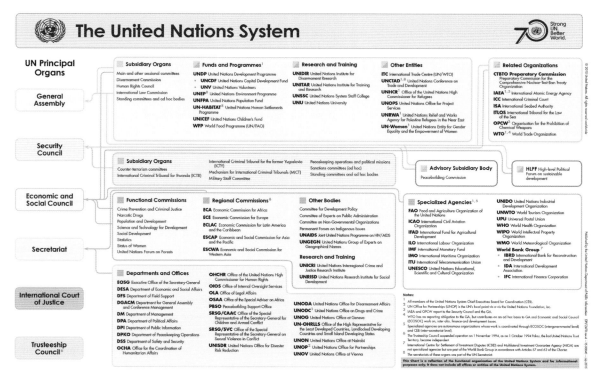

Figure 7.1 The UN System

Source: http://www.un.org/en/aboutun/structure/pdfs/UN_System_Chart_30June2015.pdf. Accessed 18 April 2016.

of institutions. This presents challenges for coordination of its activities, for streamlining its operations and for strengthening its partnership working, that are all part of ongoing processes of institutional reform at the UN and are considered through the sections below.

Almost every country in the world, a total of 193, is now a member of the UN. Its headquarters are in New York and it is funded through a mixture of member state assessments and voluntary contributions. This lack of an independent source of money has contributed to longstanding financial problems as considered in the Critical reflection. In the current context of global economic crisis and declining commitments to official development assistance (ODA), the UN recognises that many traditional sources of multi-lateral funding are under pressure and there is a need to diversify its funding base. In 2010, for example, 17% of contributions to the United Nations came from NGOs, from public-private partnerships and other multinational organisations (OECD, 2015a).

Critical reflection

Financial problems at the United Nations

The United Nations depends largely on its member states for finance through assessed and voluntary contributions. Assessed contributions are used to fund the core UN agencies and functions, including the General Assembly and peacekeeping activities. Voluntary contributions are, by definition, at the discretion of each member state and are used to finance many of the UN development agencies, including UNDP, UNICEF and the World Food Program.

The assessed contribution made by each nation is on the basis of ability to pay, reflecting a country's Gross National Income, but also their debt commitments and adjustments are also made for very low per capita incomes. A maximum ceiling on contributions is set at 22% of the total UN budget, aimed at ensuring that the UN is not unduly dependent on any one member state. A 'floor-rate' minimum contribution is also set at 0.001%. However, funding of the UN is dominated by a limited number of rich countries; 57% of total resources in 2008 came from countries within the OECD (Browne, 2011). Figure 7.2 confirms that the USA remains the largest contributor to the UN, although smaller countries tend to contribute more per citizen.

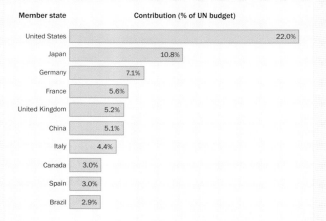

Figure 7.2 The top ten contributors to the UN budget

Source: adapted from 'Assessment of Member States' contributions to the United Nations regular budget for 2015'. UN Secretariat. Accessed 24 July 2015.

Critical reflection (continued)

Whilst country commitments to the multi-lateral institutions remain high in the current context of falling levels of Official Development Assistance (OECD, 2015a), the concern is that the share going to UN core activities is declining. This is important as the UN has the power to control the disbursement of its core funding as it sees fit in relation to its Charter, whereas donors retain a degree of control of those finances that flow to non-core activities. In consequence, Browne (2011: 119) suggests that the activities of the UN are likely to reflect the donor's agenda;

> Within every UN organization and agency, secretariats instinctively 'follow the money'. Wherever it has become clear that donors are willing to fund a particular initiative or program, a suitable proposal is sure to follow.

There are also long-standing concerns for the limited size of the UN budget overall. The total UN budget for 2014–15 was US $5.492 billion (UN, 2014a). In comparison, Kofi Annan (the Secretary General to 2006), noted that the budget for the UN core activities is about 4% of the annual budget of New York City and almost a billion US dollars less than that of the Tokyo Fire Department (cited in Mingst and Karns, 2012: 57/58). Many International NGOs such as Oxfam, CARE, Médécins Sans Frontières and Save the Children currently have annual budgets over US $500 million (Desai and Kharas, 2009: 1112).

Furthermore, there are issues of arrears and non-payment, particularly with poorer nations often not being able to afford their full assessment to the UN. In other cases, there have been problems of delaying or withholding payments. Questions of the scale and timing of finances, all influence the ability of the UN to carry out its activities. During the 1980s, the US began withholding parts of its dues to the UN, in relation to concerns over particular UN policies and the politicisation of many agencies (Mingst and Karns, 2012). In the 1990s, the UN faced its most serious financial crisis, with 85 members failing to pay their legal obligations and the US owing over two-thirds of its due assessment (Mingst and Karns, 2012). In the case of the arrears of the US, the media mogul, Ted Turner, stepped in to address some of his country's shortfall. More recently, further voluntary contributions to the UN have come from other major philanthropists, including from the Bill and Melinda Gates Foundation.

Critical reflection

International Non-Governmental Organisations now together distribute more development aid than the entire UN system (Mingst and Karns, 2012). Consider the challenges and opportunities that this presents. Is the UN target that richer countries should allocate 0.7% of their annual Gross National Income to official development assistance still relevant and/or appropriate, given the rise of private finance in development and 'austerity pressures' within the more developed economies domestically?

Each member state of the UN is represented on the General Assembly (GA), with equal voting power irrespective of the size, population or economic power of that country. The GA is the main representative and policy-making body of the UN and was designed as the central hub of the organisation. It has responsibility for coordinating and supervising the extensive bodies and it also controls the budget and staffing levels across the UN system. The GA serves largely as a 'forum for forging consensus and influencing state behaviour' (Werksman, 1995: 11), since decisions taken by the GA, unlike those of the councils, have no legally binding force for governments. Such decisions do, however,

'carry the weight of world opinion' (Buckley, 1995: 4), with many resolutions being subsequently incorporated into international treaties such as the UN Framework Convention on Climate Change Convention (UNFCCC) discussed in Chapter 6. The GA also shares with the Economic and Social Council (ECOSOC) responsibility for authorising major meetings, summits and conferences. These are an integral part of global governance and for mobilising attention and action on cross-cutting development issues, not just within the UN and member states, but amongst transnational networks of NGOs, scientific and other expert groups, as well as private corporations (Mingst and Karns, 2012).

The GA also elects the nonpermanent members of the Security Council. The Security Council is the body that deals with security issues and can request UN members to undertake military action, for example. Since its formation in the 1940s, it has had the same five permanent members (China, the USA, Russia, the UK and France), reflecting 'the world of 1945, not the world of the twenty-first century' (Mingst and Karns, 2012: 50). Whilst additional members can be voted onto the Security Council for short periods, it is only the permanent members that have the power to veto, and there are longstanding concerns regarding its legitimacy, given the absence of representation from Latin America or Africa. It is suggested that 'no UN reform issue is as controversial as the question of changing the Security Council's membership and voting rules' (Mingst and Karns, 2012: 51).

Peace and security

At the time of the formation of the General Assembly and the Security Council, the key threats to international peace were considered to be external acts of aggression coming from outside particular countries. The UN had no remit under its Charter to intervene within domestic jurisdictions. However, UN peacekeeping activities have evolved to more regularly involve conflicts *within* states, as well as activities in peace-building, enforcement and conflict prevention (Plate 7.1).

During the Cold War era, the power of veto served to limit substantially the UN's peacekeeping role, as the USA or the former Soviet Union would vote against any substantive proposal. By the mid-1980s, the number of peacekeeping operations rose significantly as the UN committed to stabilising security situations and implementing new peace agreements. There were only 13 UN peacekeeping operations in the first 50 years of the organisation, whereas 20 new operations were sanctioned between 1989 and 1994. The number of peacekeepers involved rose from 11,000 in 1989 to 75,000 in 1994 (un.org/en/peacekeeping/operations). This expansion of operations and the rising costs of UN peace and security, substantially underpinned international concerns for the future financing of the UN as seen in the Critical reflection box above.

Questions over the ability, power and willingness of the UN to force changes within national states, have been the focus for substantial academic and popular debate, as well as discussions within the organisation itself. The UN has been criticised for failing to act in

Plate 7.1 Repatriation of Cambodians from refugee camps in Thailand under UN protection
(*photo*: Teit Hornbak, Still Pictures)

relation to the genocide in Rwanda in 1994 and being too quick to intervene in Libya in 2011, for example (Schaaf, 2013). The relevance of a multi-lateral system for ensuring global peace and security has also come under scrutiny, including as countries (along with certain allies) have undertaken military action without UN support, such as in the case of the USA and the UK invasion of Iraq in 2003.

The international terrorist attacks on New York City in November, 2001, as well as more recently in London and Paris and widely in the Global South including in Tunisia, India, Kenya and Pakistan, have brought a renewed focus on the threats of organised violence from outside to physical state security. However, the concept of 'human security' is now increasingly used within the UN to embrace the variety of interrelated threats to individuals, vulnerable groups and states that go beyond physical violence. Such threats include poverty, infectious diseases and environmental degradation, as well as genocide, nuclear weapons, terrorism and transnational organised crime. The challenges of poverty, health and environmental degradation are longstanding, rather than new, concerns for the UN, as discussed further below. However, as Mingst and Karns (2012: 248) summarise:

> What has changed is recognition that failure to address either environmental degradation or major threats to health has a fundamental impact on human security. They can also have a direct impact on peace and stability within and between states. In short, issues once perceived as 'merely environmental' or 'merely social' have far-reaching security implications when people rather than states become the primary concern.

Tackling poverty

The central UN forum for addressing economic and social development is the Economic and Social Council (ECOSOC), effected through the nine functional commissions and five regional commissions shown in Figure 7.1. From the outset, it was envisaged that ECOSOC would also take the key role in coordination of the operational activities of the specialised agencies including the World Bank, the World Health Organisation (WHO), the Food and Agriculture Organisation (FAO),

the International Labour Organisation (ILO) and the UN Educational, Scientific and Cultural Organisation (UNESCO). These specialised agencies are organisations established by separate international agreements, with their own charters, memberships and budgets. All have global responsibilities and undertake activities related to economic and social advancement. They are formally affiliated to the UN through agreements with ECOSOC and the GA. The activities overseen by ECOSOC encompass the majority of the human and financial resources of the UN system, accommodating as much as 75% of the UN efforts through the 1980s and 1990s (Buckley, 1995). The challenge of coordination of those activities is evident in Figure 7.1, in terms of the number of commissions and specialised agencies involved and the range of economic and social activities encompassed. A key way in which ECOSOC seeks to enhance coordination and to stimulate cooperation amongst countries has been through the five regional commissions. ECOSOC also has a key role in undertaking research and convening conferences. It is the UN body with which many NGOs have consultative status. Further complexity to its role is added as new entities are created under the GA that also report through ECOSOC. Most recently, the High Level Political Forum on Sustainable Development was formed in 2015 and its role is considered further below.

The UN Development Programme (UNDP) remains the largest subject area for ECOSOC and is central to UN development activities. It was established in 1965 to mobilise technical assistance and facilitate development solutions. UNDP remains the UN's central funding agency for technical assistance activities and is the principal in-country representative of the UN. However, the UNDP in particular has suffered from the wider financial problems of the UN, as well as the test of tackling the cross-cutting nature of social and economic development challenges on the ground. UNDP is a programme of the UN, rather than a principal body or organ. It therefore depends largely on voluntary funding from member states. It came under considerable financial pressure through the 1990s, as Official Development Assistance became diverted to areas of humanitarian relief rather than longer term development assistance (Thomas and Allen, 2000). This was also the era when the international financial institutions became more involved in areas of economic development within countries of the Global South. By the mid-1990s, the World Bank had become a larger funder of technical assistance to developing countries than the UNDP (Gwin, 1995). For many observers, the UN organisations in this period were being 'outperformed' by the international financial institutions.

As seen in the Critical reflection above, the UN as a whole and bodies such as UNDP are increasingly taking a multifaceted strategy in their activities, collaborating as much with private enterprise as with governments, other international and bilateral donor agencies and in supporting measures to promote capacity building within the business sector. The Critical reflection box below, in the section on the World Bank, highlights the role of UNDP in implementing the Global Environment Facility. This is an initiative in conjunction with the World Bank and private finance, to support low-income countries to tackle issues of global environmental significance. Like other UN organisations, UNDP has moved in recent years to being more of an implementing agency for other aid sources in order to maintain its activities (Browne, 2014). The two largest sources of current funding for UNDP are the EU and the Global Fund. The Global Fund, as seen in the Critical reflection box on ProductRed above, is an international financing organisation set up in 2002 to raise and disburse funds to fight HIV/AIDS, Tuberculosis and malaria. It has a range of public (bi-lateral donors) and private sources of funding, including the Bill and Melinda Gates Foundation. The Global Fund identifies UNDP as its key recipient for work in 40 countries (Browne, 2014).

Despite problems of funding, UNDP is understood to have a significant role in challenging dominant paradigms in, and yardsticks of, development (Browne, 2011) particularly through its annual Human Development Reports. The first report in 1990 introduced the concept of 'human development' as a process of enlarging people's choices (see Chapter 1). The concept and report was conceived by two distinguished economists from the Global South, Mahbub Ul Haq and Amartya Sen. It was developed in response to the adverse impacts of macro-economic adjustment in many countries at that time and has had huge influence subsequently; 'By putting "people at the centre of development", the concept provided "an integrated intellectual framework for catalyzing a new system-wide approach to economic and social development"' (Mingst and

Karns, 2012: 182). Successive Human Development Reports are also considered to have been central to the modernisation of UNDP and its transformation into a more comprehensive and 'fully fledged' development agency (Browne, 2011: 63). UNDP now has a reputation for high quality research and support for global knowledge networks, including on human rights policy and on gender, as well as on the MDGs.

However, the development impacts of UN activities, both within and beyond UNDP, are considered to have been limited by the number of agencies competing for the same monies and what has been termed the UN's 'butterfly' approach: 'thousands of mini projects working on mini objectives' (Righter, 1995: 59). Problems of duplication and a lack of coherence in UN programmes, and often supported by excessive bureaucracies, have been the target for critics and the focus for institutional reform. The UN response in times of humanitarian crises is often highlighted, whereby different UN agencies have historically taken distinct functional responsibilities; 'the UNHCR manages refugee camps, UNICEF handles water and sanitation, the WFP is responsible for food supplies and logistics, and WHO handles the health sector' (Mingst and Karns, 2012: 59). The UN Joint Programme on HIV/AIDS (UNAIDS) is an example of an explicit attempt to foster stronger partnerships working across UN agencies, as well as with other agencies. It was created in 1996 by UNICEF, UNDP, UNESCO, WHO and the UN Fund for Population Activities (and was to be led by the World Bank). However, UN agencies and programmes continue to perform poorly in relation to other multi-national sources within assessments of aid effectiveness, with persistent concerns over fragmentation and limited overall resources (OECD, 2012; DFID 2013).

One response from within the UN towards strengthening the synergies and efficiencies across the UN organisations and increasing the impact of programmes was the formation of the UN Development Group in 1997. This united 32 UN funds, programmes, agencies, departments and offices. UNDP continues to have responsibility for coordination of these activities through its role as Chair. Further integration of UNDP activities within the UN system as a whole was fostered by the common agenda around poverty and the adoption of the Millennium Development Goals in 2000.

The turn of the millennium was a key point for reinvigorating commitments to the UN system in general and for actioning a more integrated poverty-focused approach to development. The 'Millennium Summit' was a special gathering of member countries convened by the Secretary General Kofi Annan and attended by 189 world leaders. The Declaration that emerged was designed to reaffirm faith in the organisation and its Charter and identified a number of key objectives for the UN community, including reform of the Security Council and the strengthening of ECOSOC. The meeting also committed members to work towards development and poverty eradication, peace and security, environmental conservation, democracy and human rights. A concrete action plan was set, with measurable goals and a clear deadline, the basis of the Millennium Development Goals agreed in the following year (see Chapter 1). In 2001, Kofi Annan was awarded the Nobel Peace Prize, shared with the UN itself, in recognition of his 'pre-eminent role' in bringing new life to the UN (Usbourne, 2001).

In 2005, a High Level Panel on UN System-wide Coherence was formed to explore how the UN system could work more coherently and effectively in the areas of development, humanitarian assistance and the environment. One of the key suggestions was that the UN should consider 'delivering as one' at a country level, i.e. a strategy based on having a single lead, programme, budget and office (where appropriate) in each country. Table 7.2 identifies the considered value of this approach. An independent evaluation of the pilot of eight countries confirmed positive outcomes, particularly on cross-cutting issues such as gender equality and HIV/AIDS. A further 28 countries have since adopted the approach. However, the evaluation suggests that:

> bolder measures may be required to put the UN on a more comprehensive track of reform, including rationalisation of the number of UN entities; reform of mandates, governance structures and funding modalities; and a new definition of the range of development expertise expected from the UN system.
> (UN General Assembly, 2012: 32)

'Delivering as One' continues to be central to the UN's post-2015 agenda, within which further integration of the UN and its activities is recognised as essential to address the multi-dimensional and inter-linked challenges of

Table 7.2 The value of 'Delivering as One'

➤ Improving the UN system's focus on working together towards achieving national development results
➤ Aligning UN activities with national priorities and avoiding duplication
➤ Making best use of the mandates and expertise of the entire UN system to deliver results
➤ Creating integrated policy solutions and responses needed to address multi-dimensional challenges
➤ Promoting the values, norms and standards of the UN in a coherent and consistent manner
➤ Increasing the transparency, predictability and accountability of the UN system
➤ Using the convening role of the UN to facilitate the inclusion of all relevant stakeholders, including global and regional practitioners and non-state actors
➤ Reducing transaction costs for governments, development partners and, based on new Standard Operating Procedures, also for UN country teams
➤ Establishing a clear division of labour based on comparative advantages and capacities of each UN agency
➤ Achieving efficiency gains and cost savings through harmonised business practices and integrated operational support services

Source: compiled from UN (2014b) Delivering as One on the MDGs and the Post-2015 Agenda

sustainable development. The following section identifies a number of recent reforms that have addressed the challenges of sustainability governance explicitly.

The UN and the governance of sustainable development

The United Nations has played a very significant role in the development of structures and processes of global sustainability governance. Whilst environmental issues did not feature at the time of the origins of the institution, certainly from the early 1970s the UN has had a major role in the development of the international environmental policy framework and in developing new standards in development amongst governments, business and public sector organisations. It has also been in the area of sustainability governance that some of the most significant changes have been seen in terms of addressing the needs and raising participation of countries of the Global South (Williams et al., 2014; Dodds et al., 2012).

In 1972, the UN sponsored its first major conference on the Human Environment (UNCE) held in Stockholm, Sweden. It was in response to growing political, scientific and public concerns, largely in the US and Europe, over the environmental impacts of development processes. Whilst countries of the Global South were cautious about participating, their concerns at the time being '"too little industry" rather than too much' (Elliott, 2013: 43), 113 countries attended, including Brazil, India and the Republic of China (attending its first major conference since entering the UN). Whilst the conference was 'only partly, and belatedly' (Adams, 2009: 59) concerned with the environmental and development concerns of the 'developing' countries at that time, the conference is acknowledged to have been a key event in evolving the concept of sustainable development and in understanding the integration of human development and environmental concerns as a global challenge. It established environmental issues firmly on the UN agenda (see also Chapter 6).

The UN has sponsored a plethora of conferences and summits since Stockholm, addressing specific issues such as population (1974, 1984), and women (1975, 1980, 1985, 1995). There have also been a number of summits focusing explicitly on sustainable development. These were the UN Conference on Environment and Development in 1992 – the 'Earth Summit' – held in Rio de Janeiro; the World Summit on Sustainable Development of 2002 in Johannesburg and Rio+20 in 2012. Whilst the role of 'mega-summitry' is a regular source of debate, including for their cost and often rather anodyne outcome documents, there is a consensus that they have a key role in initiating processes of institutional development, within and beyond the UN.

For example, multilateral environmental agreements that are often agreed at these conferences, are the key way in which countries commit to achieving global environmental goals. The Convention on Biodiversity and the UN Framework Convention on Climate Change were agreed at the 1992 UNCED meeting, for example. Agenda 21 – a forty chapter 'action plan' for the global community towards the implementation of sustainable development in practice, was also adopted.

Furthermore, UN conferences provide opportunities for the involvement and networking of NGOs, scientific and technical experts, as well as private business. This constitutes an important space for strengthening the capacity of individual organisations within those networks, for generating new understandings of the demands of global sustainable development, and for developing new ways of working in practice. Over 8,000 representatives of NGOs and other organisations were involved in the formal meetings at WSSD in 2002. A decade earlier at the Earth Summit, only 200 such organisations had participated and this was confined to parallel forums rather than within the main body of the conference (Mingst and Karns, 2012). Box 7.1 identifies how the UN is working collaboratively with civil society organisations and businesses to develop globally accepted standards for reporting on economic, social and environmental performance. The Global Compact is explicitly based around developing and sharing good practice across different kinds of organisations with the aim of aligning the activities of non-state actors in development (principally large corporations) more closely with the principles and values enshrined in UN-inspired agreements, such as the Universal Declaration on Human Rights and Agenda 21.

BOX 7.1

The Global Compact

The Global Compact was initiated by the Secretary General of the United Nations, Kofi Annan, and launched by him in 2000. The aim was to promote more responsible business and investments, in the context of rapid globalisation, widening imbalances between rich and poor, and increasing concern regarding the values on which global markets were operating. It was also a chance for the UN to assert a more proactive role in the field of economic globalisation, after some years of marginality relative to the World Bank and the World Trade Organisation, for example (see sections below).

▶

BOX 7.1 (continued)

The Global Compact invites private sector companies, particularly multinational corporations, to commit voluntarily to the integration of a set of ten principles, covering human rights, labour, environment and anti-corruption, into their business strategies and operations. It also involves them in a collaborative network, including with UN organisations but also with NGOs, trade unions and academic institutions, to develop shared understandings and practice in corporate responsibility, to progress partnership projects and to take further action towards advancing the wider social goals of the UN including the Sustainable Development Goals.

All the ten principles are those that already exist within UN-inspired, international agreements, including the Universal Declaration on Human Rights and Agenda 21. As such, the Global Compact is an innovative approach by the UN to engage social actors beyond governments, in the promotion and implementation of those international principles. It is an example of a cross-sectoral, multi-level global governance network.

Currently, there are over 8,000 private companies involved in the Global Compact. Many are large corporations, but it also includes small and medium sized enterprises and from across the world. More than 4,000 other stakeholders are also involved in the networks.

In sum, the Global Compact is based on principles that were universally endorsed by governments, expressing aspirational goals of the entire international community. It enlists the corporate sector and civil society to help bridge the gap between aspiration and reality – to become agents for the promotion of community norms. And it is entirely network based. Thus apart from constituting an innovative UN 'program' to change corporate behaviour, the Global Compact is also an experiment in devising fundamentally new forms of global governance.

(Ruggie, 2003: 312/3)

In 2012, questions regarding the institutional framework for sustainable development and whether the current system of international conventions, agencies and programmes were 'fit for the future', was one of the two overarching themes for the Rio+20 conference. The second theme was the challenges of moving to a Green Economy. Of particular concern were two UN organisations, the UN Environment Programme dating back to 1972 and the Commission on Sustainable Development formed in 1992. Both organisations have been central to the integration of environmental work within and across UN activities and have achieved important successes. However, as Dodds et al. (2012: 15) identify, 'the world has changed drastically over the last 40 years, and both organisations – for different reasons – seem no longer capable of delivering what they had been expected to or what is now needed'. Because of the significance of these two organisations within the overall international institutional framework for sustainable development, the following sections look at their activities in operation in more detail.

UNEP was formed in 1992 to promote international coordination on environmental activities, and to provide an 'environmental watchdog' and 'early warning' function through the monitoring and reporting of global environmental change. Its headquarters are in Nairobi, Kenya, and it was the first UN agency to be based in the Global South. As established above, UNEP has a key role in sustainable development governance globally as the UN organisation that oversees the negotiation and management of multilateral environmental agreements (MEAs). MEAs are the international agreements and treaties that set the principles and rules for how individual states should act in relation to cross-boundary environmental problems. Table 7.3 identifies just a small number of these MEAs. UNEP has also become an influential and authoritative source for environmental information and on environmental law (Mingst and Karns, 2012), through its monitoring and evaluation roles and its publications such as the annual State of the Environment Reports.

UNEP has, however, had problems of coordination with other UN agencies and in integrating environment with economic and social development, thereby compromising its role in sustainable development in practice.

Table 7.3 Selected multi-lateral environmental agreements (MEAs)

MEA	Purpose	Entry into force
CITES – Convention on International Trade in Endangered Species of Wild Fauna and Flora	To ensure that international trade in wild plants and animal species does not threaten their survival in the wild, and specifically to protect endangered species from over-exploitation	1975
UNCLOS – United Nations Convention on the Law of the Seas	To establish comprehensive legal orders to promote peaceful use of the oceans and seas, equitable and efficient utilisation of their resources, and conservation of their living resources	1994
Basel Convention – Convention on the Control of Transboundary Movements of Hazardous Wastes and their Disposal	To ensure environmentally-sound management of hazardous wastes by minimising their generation, reducing their transboundary movement, and disposing of these wastes as close as possible to their source of generation	1992
UNFCCC – UN Framework Convention on Climate Change	To stabilise greenhouse gas concentrations in the atmosphere at a level preventing dangerous human-induced interference with the climate system	1994
CBD – Convention on Biological Diversity	To conserve biological diversity and promote its sustainable use, and to encourage the equitable sharing of the benefits arising out of the utilisation of genetic resources	1993
Aarhus Convention – Convention on Access to Information, Public participation in Decision-Making, and Access to Justice in Environmental Matters	To guarantee the rights of access to information, public participation in decision-making, and legal redress in environmental matters	2001

UNEP is not an implementing agency and has a relatively small professional staff and budget. These have been stretched, for example, as the number of MEAs proliferated from the 1980s. As French (2002: 177) observed, 'each environmental treaty creates its own mini-institutional machinery' with their own offices and secretariats, located in various capitals around the world, and treaty members to convene regularly and oversee implementation. Furthermore, the relationship between these mini-institutions and UNEP often remained unclear (Sandbrook, 1999). The effectiveness of UNEP has also been called into question by its inability to resolve the contradictions and overlap amongst different MEAs (see Biermann, 2013).

There have been repeated calls within policy and academic debates for the replacement of UNEP by a fully-fledged, 'world environment organization' with specialised agency status within the UN, towards strengthening global environmental governance and increasing the coherence of UN activities across all three pillars of sustainable development. This was supported by the EU and the African Union and a number of countries of the Global South at the Rio+20 conference

in 2012. However, there have been longstanding concerns (amongst some countries of the Global North), that UNEP is too heavily influenced by the interests of the Global South (Mingst and Karns, 2012). At Rio+20, plans for strengthening UNEP were resisted heavily by the US, Japan and even Brazil. However, one reform that was agreed was regarding the representation of countries of the Global South in the governing Council of UNEP. Formerly, 58 governments based on regional representation were members of the Council, but this was extended to all countries being represented making UNEP more similar to other agencies with 'specialised status' at the UN.

The Commission on Sustainable Development (CSD) is a further UN organisation that has been an important part of global sustainability governance. It was formed in 1992 to ensure effective follow-up to the UNCED conference, to review progress on the implementation of Agenda 21 and to integrate environment and development activities across the UN system. The recommendation at the time, was for a body at the 'very apex of the UN' (Jordan and Brown, 1997: 274), chaired by the Secretary General, with the capacity to assess, advise, assist and report on progress of sustainable development and with supreme powers to create inter-agency commitment to, and coordination for, sustainable development. However, 'in the event, the Rio conference fudged this issue' (Jordan and Brown, 1997: 274), creating a lower ranking body placed under the ECOSOC. As such, it had no legal authority to compel states to act, nor power to require actions on behalf of other UN agencies (Dodds et al., 2012). The CSD also struggled to mobilise the cooperation of governments and other intergovernmental bodies and to integrate environment into development activities. For example, government representatives on the CSD tended to be environment ministers, 'with little influence over their more powerful colleagues in trade and industry departments' (Jordan and Brown, 1997: 275).

However, the CSD is acknowledged to have been important in providing a forum for review, exchanging information, building political consensus and for forging partnerships. Every two years, it has met to discuss particular themes and cross-sectoral issues (covering the major elements of Agenda 21). It has had a mandate to foster the participation of NGOs, industry, scientific and business communities and has been important in increasing the access of these non-state actors into the UN system (Mingst and Karns, 2012). Whilst these are notable successes of the CSD (Dodds et al., 2012), there have been repeated calls for the strengthening of its standing within the overall UN system, and in turn, higher level commitments from member governments to the institution in future. A stronger standing within the UN was achieved in 2015, when the CSD was replaced by the High Level Political Forum on Sustainable Development (HLPFSD). Under this new body, all UN members will be included and multilateral financial and trade institutions, such as the World Bank and the World Trade Organisation, are also invited to participate. Table 7.4 identifies the aims and role of the new forum.

It is evident throughout the sections above that the constituent institutions of the UN system are currently undergoing substantial change as a result of, and to respond to, a world context its founders never envisaged (Ignatieff, 1995). A key challenge remains that the logic of the UN is built on the idea of members that are nation

Table 7.4 The aims of the High Level Political Forum on Sustainable Development

➤ Provide political leadership and recommendations for sustainable development
➤ Follow-up and review progress in implementing sustainable development commitments
➤ Enhance the integration of economic, social and environmental dimensions of sustainable development
➤ Have a focused, dynamic and action-oriented agenda
➤ Consider new and emerging sustainable development challenges
➤ From 2016 take on the functions of the ECOSOC Annual Ministerial reviews on the post-MDG/Post-2015 Sustainable Development Goals

states. However, it is clear that many other actors now influence the agenda and activities of the UN and indeed, the role of the state in shaping development within their own territories is under considerable change, including through the activities of the international financial institutions.

The World Bank Group and the International Monetary Fund

The World Bank and the International Monetary Fund are multilateral development banks (MDBs) through which countries come together to provide financing and professional advice for the purposes of development. Other 'Regional' MDBs include the African Development Bank, the Asian Development Bank and the Inter-American Development Bank Group. All have broad memberships of both borrowing and donor countries and in the case of the Regional Development Banks, are not confined to countries within that region. All are complex organisations and perform a wide variety of tasks according to different ideologies, mandates and structures. However, the World Bank and the IMF are among the world's most powerful international institutions and have been key 'institutional anchors' for the post-Second World War order (Boas, 2014). As such,

Plate 7.2 World Bank headquarters in Washington
(*photo*: Getty Images/News)

they are given substantial emphasis through the following sections of this chapter.

The World Bank Group consists of five closely associated institutions, as identified in the Key idea box. It was formed at the Bretton Woods Conference in 1944, convened to establish a new framework for world economic stability after the economic crisis of the 1930s and the Second World War. The World Bank is owned by its member countries that are represented by a Board of Governors and a Washington-based Board of Directors (Plate 7.2). There are currently 188 member countries of the World Bank, each with a representative on the Board of Governors. A smaller group, the Board of Executive Directors, is responsible for general operations and policy making within the group, the Chairman being the World Bank President who by tradition, is a national of the largest share-holder, that being the US.

Key idea

The World Bank Group

Figure 7.3 identifies the five institutions that comprise the World Bank Group. The first institution to be established was the International Bank for Reconstruction and Development in 1945. It was founded on the principle that many countries in Europe after the Second World War would be short of foreign exchange for reconstruction and development activities, but would be insufficiently creditworthy to borrow all the necessary funds commercially. In contrast to individual countries, IBRD as a multilateral institution, with share capital owned by its member countries, could borrow on world markets and lend more cheaply than commercial banks. The IBRD raises monies through selling bonds and other securities to individuals, other banks, corporations and pension funds around

▶

Key idea (continued)

The World Bank Group

The World Bank

IBRD	IDA	IFC	MIGA	ICSID
International Bank for Reconstruction and Development	**International Development Association**	**International Finance Corporation**	**Multilateral Investment Guarantee Agency**	**International Centre for Settlement of Investment Disputes**
Established 1945 189 countries own/ subscribe to its capital	Established 1960 173 members	Established 1956 184 members	Established 1988 181 members	Established 1966 151 members
Lends to governments of middle income and creditworthy low-income countries based on high real rates of economic return	Lends at a favourable rate to poorer and economically at risk countries	Assists economic development by promoting growth in the private sector	Assists economic development through promoting foreign direct investment	Provides facilities for the concilliation and arbitration of disputes between member countries and investors who qualify as nationals of other member countries

Figure 7.3 The World Bank Group
Source: compiled from World Bank, 2015. www.worldbank.org/en/about

the world. It lends money over 15- to 20-year periods, and loans are subject to interest.

The International Development Association (IDA) is the Bank's concessional lending window, providing no-interest loans to the poorest countries. It is one of the world's largest sources of aid and is of particular importance to the world's poorest countries. IDA finances averaged over US $18 billion in each of the three years to 2014 with over 50% going to countries within Africa (www.worldbank.org). The IDA cannot raise funds on capital markets as the IBRD does, so it depends entirely on wealthier nations for finance (supplemented by a portion of general World Bank profits). IDA loans are repaid within 25–38 years often with a 5–10-year grace period. Figure 7.4 illustrates where IBRD/IDA finances went geographically and by theme in 2015. IDA finances have been an important source for investments in basic health, primary education and environmental improvements including water and sanitation and rural electrification, for example, that are key elements in terms of prospects for meeting the MDGs.

The International Finance Corporation of the World Bank Group lends directly and exclusively to the private sector. Its role is to mobilise capital and expertise to support private sector development and help overcome constraints of finances, technical and skills capacity for example. The Multilateral Investment Guarantee Agency also promotes private investment in developing countries through providing political risk insurance guarantees to overseas private sector investors and lenders and thereby attracting them to what can be considered 'difficult operating environments' (www.miga.org/who-we-are). Such guarantees could be against non-commercial risks such as war or nationalisation. Both IFC and MIGA are legally and financially independent and have different owners, clients, mandates and operational procedures from the IBRD and IDA. Hence, it is the IBRD and IDA combined that are commonly referred to as the 'World Bank' and is the convention used in this chapter.

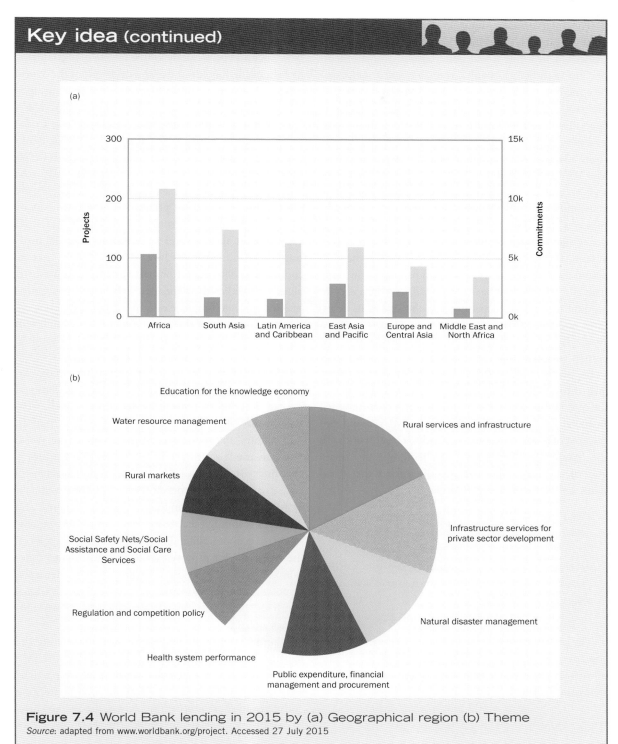

Figure 7.4 World Bank lending in 2015 by (a) Geographical region (b) Theme
Source: adapted from www.worldbank.org/project. Accessed 27 July 2015

The International Monetary Fund (IMF) was also created at the Bretton Woods conference and is closely associated with the World Bank Group. To gain membership to the World Bank Group, a country must first be a member of the IMF. The World Bank and the IMF are part of the UN system, as seen in Figure 7.1, being specialised agencies reporting to ECOSOC. In practice, however, they function as institutions very separate from and with little accountability to the UN system. The World Bank and the IMF work closely together, as well as with an expanding range of other actors and stakeholders. Traditionally, the primary distinction between these two institutions was that the IMF was concerned with the health of the international monetary system, and may lend (from subscriptions) to member countries briefly to overcome short-term financial instability. Each member of the IMF pays in a certain amount to the fund depending on the size of its economy, and can borrow from the fund on a short-term basis. Historically, the World Bank had been more concerned with the financing of longer term development in the poorer countries of the world. However, particularly through the 1980s, concerns that the insolvency of the middle-income debtors threatened the international financial system as a whole, led to the IMF moving into the area of lending to members and to closer work with the World Bank regarding rescheduling. In consequence, the distinctions between the roles of the World Bank and the IMF became less clear:

> The Fund had begun to worry about longer-term development, and the Bank was taking a new interest in short-term macro-economic policy . . . in one developing country after another, the two institutions devised overlapping programmes of economic reform and backed them with cash.
>
> (Crook, 1991: 4)

These international financial institutions have considerable influence over the development agenda, as well as the global economy, as seen through the following sections.

The World Bank as a development actor

Although only 'peripherally conceived as a development agency' (Righter, 1995: 187), since its inception, the World Bank has increasingly lent monies to governments of the South. It has been a very important source of finance and particularly for the low income countries, as seen in the Key idea box. The decisions of the World Bank are also a central influence on the lending decisions of other public and private institutions. Many lenders and investors link their own spending to the presence in those recipient countries of World Bank/IMF programmes of economic reform. Standards developed by the World Bank for environmental and social risk management, known as the Equator Principles, are used as prerequisites for private sector investments by 71 banks and financial institutions worldwide, 32 OECD export credit agencies and 15 European financial institutions (World Bank, 2012a: 25). Access by low income countries to debt relief from the Paris Club of industrialised nations has also depended on having a programme of economic and financial reform with the IMF. As such, the World Bank and the IMF remain hugely important in shaping the ability of countries of the Global South to attract international capital.

The World Bank is also an important actor in development due to the way that it influences national development policy, in terms of directing research, technology transfer and other forms of institutional support. The country and sector reports drawn up by the World Bank, are used by commercial lenders and aid agencies to plan their own activities. The annual *World Development Reports* are also an important source of information and opinion for academics and practitioners. Certainly, and particularly through successive prescriptions and requirements for economic liberalisation and governance reform, the World Bank has moved far beyond its original function as a credit institution to become quite fundamental in policy determination and planning within the Global South and is a major player in shaping development outcomes globally.

There has been substantial debate concerning the legitimacy, and role, of the World Bank and the IMF in the context of the global economic crisis, particularly regarding the under-representation of emerging countries in these institutions, given the recent shifts in economic power. In 2008, the IMF Board of Governors made the decision to increase the voting share for emerging economies. As a result, China is now the third largest member country in the IMF and India and Russia are in the top ten (Massa and

Brambila-Macias, 2014). At the World Bank, decision making has been very largely by member countries according to the financial contribution of that nation to the Bank (known as the system of 'one dollar one vote'). These 'quota votes' have recently been reformed towards enhancing the voice and power of 'developing' countries, as categorised by the Bank using economic indicators, in the World Bank's governing body. This is discussed further in the Critical reflection. Since its inception, there has also been a system for allocating 'Basic votes' to all members, in the same amount, as a means to ensure voting power for the smaller and poorer members of the World Bank. However, the share of these basic votes in terms of overall decision making is less than 3% (Vestergaard and Wade, 2013) and typically, most of the poorer countries have had less than 0.1 per cent of quota votes.

Critical reflection

The Voice Reform process and outcomes at the World Bank

In 2010, the outcomes of the process of 'voice reform' at the World Bank were announced. Commentators, particularly from within the World Bank, suggested a major shift in favour of developing countries, embracing a modernised World Bank Group and reflecting the economic realities of the early twenty-first century. The headlines were that the voting share of developing and transition countries was to increase from 42.6% to 47.19% and that of developed countries to decrease from 57.4% to 52.81% through the reforms, suggesting a move towards 50% voting parity between the categories.

However, critics point to the categories used to classify countries and their voting share; the World Bank reported, for the first time, a new grouping of 'developing and transition' countries, rather than its normal classification of high, middle and low income. In practice, this categorisation thereby included several high income countries and which do not in fact borrow from the World Bank (Vestergaard and Wade, 2015). If the conventional country categorisation was used, the voting share of 'developing country' members would have increased from 34.67% to only 38.8%, and the high income countries would retain more than 60% of votes. It is also suggested that the changes made to specific country voting power to reflect their current economic weight were generally very minor and also varied between countries, with the suggestion that a very conservative indicator for economic weight was chosen.

> The scale of the reform for individual countries was such that only 22 of the 187 member countries were subject to a change of voting power of more than 0.1 percentage points, only eight countries to a change of more than 0.5 percentage points, and only two countries (China and Japan) to a change of more than one percentage point.
>
> (Vestergaard and Wade, 2015: 156).

The assertion is that whilst the reforms have been much trumpeted by the World Bank and made

Table 7.5 Changes in voting power within the World Bank (shareholding in percentage)

	Before voice reform	After voice reform	Total percentage change
Low income countries	3.45	3.84	0.39
Middle income countries	31.22	34.54	3.32
High income countries	65.33	61.62	-3.71

Source: compiled from Vestergaard and Wade, 2015.

▶

to appear substantial, in fact change has been minor, as seen in Table 7.5. 'Developing' countries 'remain severely under-represented relative to their weight in the world economy, both collectively and many individually' (Vestergaard and Wade, 2015: 153).

Critical reflection
Has the World Bank gone far enough, do you think, in its reform processes given the current distribution of economic weight in the world economy today and in the light of the recent global economic crisis?

The World Bank and sustainable development

In 2012, the World Bank published a new environment strategy entitled '*Towards a Green, Clean and Resilient World for All*' (World Bank, 2012a). It was the outcome of a consultation process that had included over 2,300 World Bank Group (WBG) stakeholders and an independent review of progress since its first environment strategy of 2001. The call for a more sustainable economic development path, and for new partnerships to deliver on the challenges of poverty, environmental degradation and equity, are evident in Table 7.6.

Table 7.6 New challenges and partnerships for sustainable development

'In consultations for this strategy, all WBG stakeholders said clearly that the world needs to rethink the current growth model and move towards greener development pathways' (World Bank, 2012a:7).

'More than ever before, all development partners – public, private, and civil society – need to come together to achieve sustainable growth. Addressing the challenges for a green, clean and resilient world requires leveraging the comparative advantage of all development partners' (World Bank, 2012a: 13).

'The current economic model, driven by unsustainable patterns of growth and consumption, is clearly putting too much pressure on an already stretched environment. Current unsustainable and inefficient growth patterns highlight the need for inclusive green growth' (World Bank, 2012a: 2)

Source: compiled from World Bank (2012) *Toward a Green, Clean, and Resilient World for All: A World Bank Environment Strategy 2012–22*, Washington: World Bank Group

Table 7.7 details the notions of 'Green, Clean and Resilient' development in more detail.

Whilst for some commentators the World Bank is currently positioning itself as a key source of expertise on sustainable development (see Bugalski and Pred, 2013), the World Bank more regularly, has been a key target of environmental critics. Through the late 1970s and 1980s, the role of its lending in causing environmental destruction was taken up by environmentalists, particularly in the USA. Large infrastructure projects in mining, transportation and energy were a particular focus of concern. The World Bank has also been a long-standing 'lightning rod for criticisms of the international economic system' (Nelson, 2006: 706). Media exposure and public pressure, including from NGOs, have been important drivers of change at the World Bank, its work with an expanding range of actors, and efforts to increase transparency and accountability. As Nelson (2006) identified,

NGOs have pressed the World Bank to become more generous, egalitarian, and responsive to gender and minority concerns; more transparent and open to effective civil society participation; and more sensitive to natural resource use and human rights standards.

(Nelson, 2006: 706).

By the turn of the millennium, it can be considered that the World Bank was substantially embracing the notion of sustainable development. For example, the annual *World Development Report* had focused on poverty in 1990 and on the environment in 1992. However, the persistence of poverty and the emerging understanding of the multidimensional nature of the challenges, led to poverty being the focus again in 2000/01 (World Bank, 2001a). This report is considered to have been

Table 7.7 The Green, Clean and Resilient vision of the World Bank Environment strategy

'GREEN' refers to a world in which natural resources, including oceans, land and forests are sustainably managed and conserved to improve livelihoods and ensure food security. It's a world in which healthy ecosystems increase the economic returns from the activities they support. Growth strategies are focused on overall wealth rather than gross domestic product (GDP) as it is currently measured. Governments pursue regulations that encourage innovation, efficiency, sustainable budgeting, and green growth. Biodiversity is protected as an economically critical resource. In this world, good policies enable the private sector to use natural resources sustainability as part of good business, creating jobs and contributing to long-term growth.

'CLEAN' refers to a low-emission world in which cleaner air, water, and oceans enable people to lead healthy, productive lives. It is a world where development strategies put a premium on access alongside options for low-emission, climate-smart agriculture, transport, energy, and urban development. Rural women no longer spend their days hauling wood because they have access to cleaner fuels. Cleaner production standards spur innovation, and industry is encouraged to innovate for new, clean technologies that provide jobs and support export-led, sustainable growth. Companies and governments are held to account on their low-emission, low-pollution commitments, and innovative financing helps spur change.

'RESILIENT' means being prepared for shocks and adapting effectively to climate change. In a resilient world, countries are better prepared for more-frequent natural disasters, more-volatile weather patterns, and the long-term consequences of climate change. Healthy and well-managed ecosystems are more resilient and so play a key role in reducing vulnerability to climate change impacts. Climate resilience is integrated into urban planning and infrastructure development. Through effective social inclusion policies, countries and communities are better prepared to protect vulnerable groups and fully involve women in decision making.

Source: compiled from World Bank (2012) *Toward a Green, Clean and Resilient World for All: A World Bank Group Environment Strategy 2012–2022*, p. 1.

instrumental in defining the international consensus on poverty reduction into the twenty-first century (Maxwell, 2004). The 2000/01 report was informed by participatory poverty assessments that were carried out with various groups of people in 60 countries, the 'voices of the poor' project (Narayan et al., 2000). The report emphasised the multidimensional nature of poverty and it was suggested that poverty was the principal global challenge for sustainable development.

The World Bank also produced its first Environment Strategy in 2001, *Making Sustainable Commitments* (World Bank, 2001c). A report by the independent Operations Evaluation Department, had concluded that despite significant progress within the World Bank's environmental work, there was a need to instill the environment as integral, rather than as an 'add on' to, the concerns for sustainable development and poverty reduction. Mainstreaming the environment through the work of the Bank was at the center of the new strategy, based on 'an understanding that sustainable development, built on a balance of economic growth, social cohesion, and environmental protection, is fundamental to the Bank's core objective of lasting poverty alleviation' (2001c: 6).

The World Bank has had an Environment Office since 1973. However, it had a minimal staff and it was not until 1993, that a strategic environmental agenda for the Bank was identified. The key components of the 'four-fold environmental agenda' are shown in Table 7.8. Supporting member countries to build and strengthen their institutional and policy frameworks for environmental management and to address the inter-related economic, social and environmental concerns at a country level remain central to the current World Bank strategy. For example, in the early years of the Rio process, the World Bank supported countries in the development of National Environmental Action Plans that aimed to integrate environmental considerations into a nation's overall economic and social development strategy over the longer term. More recently, the World Bank has developed the use of Country Environmental Analysis (CEAs) as a tool to engage country borrowers in discussions aimed at improved understanding of linkages between poverty and the environment, and how productivity and livelihoods for particular groups of people can be undermined by degradation. These CEAs have become an important means for the World Bank to improve its own environmental analytical work and ultimately for strengthening the integration of environmental concerns into lending decisions.

Table 7.8 The four-fold environmental agenda of the World Bank, 1994

1 Assisting member countries in setting priorities, building institutions and implementing programmes for sound environmental stewardship
2 Ensuring that potential adverse environmental impacts from bank-financed projects are addressed
3 Assisting member countries in building on the synergies among poverty reduction, economic efficiency and environmental protection
4 Addressing global environmental challenges through participation in the Global Environment Facility

Source: World Bank (1994) © International Bank for Reconstruction and Development/The World Bank

Through the generation of information on the state of the environment, on poverty linkages within the country, and on aspects of the specific institutional and policy context, CEAs can be seen as part of the World Bank's commitment towards more country-driven and evidence-based approach to their work more broadly in recent years. They form an important stage in the processes of developing Country Assistance Strategies and Poverty Reduction Strategy Papers (PRSPs), for example (see Chapter 1). PRSPs are the key WB mechanism for operationalising poverty reduction (and achievement of the MDGs/SDGs) at the country level and are considered further below.

Targeted finance for environment and natural resource management

Assisting member countries to establish and build programmes for the environment through financial resources for targeted, primarily environmental, projects, such as in pollution control, biodiversity and water management, has been a long-established part of the World Bank environmental agenda, as seen in Table 7.8. Raising new monies to address global challenges, including climate change, remains an important strategic concern for the World Bank. Figure 7.5(a) shows how World Bank commitments to address these environmental themes have grown to US $6.3

billion in 2011 (equivalent to 14.3% of lending). Figure 7.5(b) shows that about half of that spending has been in areas of climate change and pollution management. However, some caution is required in that these figures include both targeted environmental projects and those that have environmental objectives within them. Furthermore, an increased proportion of lending to environment and natural resource management is now being managed in non-environment sectors such as in energy, mining and water (Figure 7.5(c)). In these cases, finance may be for the creation of protected areas, or environmental offset programmes, that are not uncontested in terms of potential environmental and social benefits, and costs, as illustrated in chapter 10.

Some caution is also required in considering the World Bank's involvement with the Global Environment Facility, the fourth element of the agenda identified in Table 7.8. GEF is a programme that was developed in 1991, initially in conjunction with UNEP and UNDP, aimed at creating new finances to support the 'additional costs' for the least developed countries to tackle environmental problems and explicitly in areas of the global commons. There are six focal areas: biological diversity, climate change mitigation and adaptation, international waters, land degradation (primarily desertification and deforestation), ozone depletion and persistent organic pollutants. GEF currently involves the World Bank in partnership with ten UN agencies, several other multilateral development banks, numerous NGOs and the private sector (Plate 7.3). The role of the World Bank in GEF remains as a trustee of the funds, an implementing agency for GEF financed projects and hosting the GEF Secretariat. GEF has allocated more than $13 billion in grants and concessional loans, embracing over 700 projects across 120 countries (Independent Evaluation Group, 2013). Over two-thirds of this finance has been to climate change and biodiversity-focused activities. However, there are continued concerns over the financing of GEF and the role of the World Bank within its operation as identified in the Critical reflection. The 'international competition' over the control of climate finance was considered further in Chapter 6.

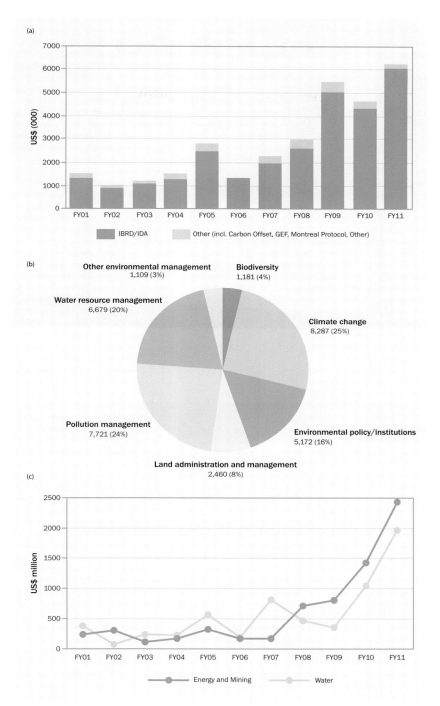

Figure 7.5 Targeted finances for the environment and natural resource management 2001–2011
(a) Lending commitments
(b) Lending by theme
(c) Commitments in non-environment sectors
Source: adapted from World Bank, 2012 *Toward a Green, Clean and Resilient World for All*

Plate 7.3 Institutional partnerships for conservation
(*photo*: Jennifer Elliott)

Critical reflection

Questioning the World Bank-GEF partnership

There has been concern since the outset of GEF as to the influence of the World Bank in its activities; membership of GEF is dominated by those Northern countries wealthy enough to contribute the minimum US $4 million required; the chair of GEF is appointed and employed by the World Bank and during the pilot phase to 1994, 80 per cent of projects were linked in some way to larger World Bank projects. Although this proportion has fallen through successive phases to 23% in the GEF-5 term (2010–2014), this constitutes approximately $150 million of GEF commitments being implemented by the World Bank (IEG, 2013).

Jordan and Brown (1997: 278) referred to GEF having adopted many of the failings of its 'administrative parent' and to 'profound discrepancies' between the ways in which North and South perceive the need, role and scope of additional financial transfers to GEF. Many consider that the monies within GEF are fundamentally too small to have a significant

impact on global environmental concerns and there remains a lack of consensus regarding how NGOs can and should participate in GEF projects.

These problems are not unrecognised within GEF or within the World Bank. In 2012, an independent review of the World Bank Group's partnership with GEF, confirmed the ongoing 'mutual relevance and compatibility' of the mandates and strategies of the World Bank Group and the GEF (IEG, 2013). The World Bank considers the GEF as a key contributor to innovative and risk sharing approaches to tackling global environmental issues. The World Bank is considered by GEF as having the experience and leverage in financing and implementing larger scale environmental projects. However, the review also acknowledges that a number of developments have 'diminished significantly' that partnership (IEG, 2013: xviii). This includes that the number of agencies, internationally and nationally, now able to access GEF and related funds, has risen tremendously. This has led to competition amongst implementing agencies and problems of coherence and coordination. Controversies have also arisen in managing the dual project cycles involved in World Bank-GEF projects. There was evidence of reduced trust amongst GEF staff of the World Bank's ability to generate good projects and amongst World Bank staff, regarding the attractiveness of GEF projects. World Bank implemented GEF projects were found to progress more slowly through the cycle than other World Bank environment projects, and their average performance had declined over time and in relation to other similar projects. A further recent development has been the

expansion of funding alternatives to the GEF that have emerged for the World Bank, particularly in relation to climate change and the new Climate Investment Funds (see Chapter 6).

Critical reflection

Using the materials of Chapter 6 on Resources, and the environment consider whether the GEF may be fundamentally limited in the way that it fosters a 'Northern' rather than a 'Southern' environmental agenda. Sources such as Adams (2009) and Elliott (2013) will also be useful in considering this debate concerning the core environment and development concerns of the Global South.

Reducing environmental and social impact

A further key area of activity and strategic priority for the World Bank in relation to sustainable development has been the development and strengthening of its own 'safeguard policies'. These are the mandatory policies that have to be followed by World Bank operations on the ground, towards ensuring protection of the environment and some of the world's most vulnerable peoples. Since 1989, the World Bank has had mandatory procedures for assessing and mitigating the potential adverse environmental impacts of its project lending. In short, 'Operational Directive 4' required that, prior to the approval stage of a proposed investment, it was the responsibility of the country borrower to ensure that projects were 'screened' for prospective environmental impacts. Proposed projects were then assigned to one of four categories, on the basis of the nature, magnitude and sensitivity of environmental issues, which then required varying levels of subsequent environmental analysis before approval. Further Operational Directives were developed subsequently, including on involuntary resettlement and indigenous peoples. It is often failings in these policies that have been the focus for critics and protest. In 1992, for example, the USA threatened to withdraw its contribution to the Bank in response to adverse environmental and social impacts of the Bank-sponsored Narmada River dam project in India.

Fierce and prolonged protest from environmental groups within the USA, international NGOs and from the Narmada Peoples Movement within India, led to the World Bank withdrawing from the project.

The need for continuous review of safeguard policies as the nature of the Bank's activities and the context in which it works change has been recognised in successive environment strategies. In the late 1990s, the World Bank started to convert Operational Directives (ODs), that combined elements of policy, procedure and guidance, into separate statements of mandatory policy, mandatory instructions for carrying out the policy and advice on good practice. In relation to environmental assessment, Operational Policy 4.01 replaced OD 4.01, and a new category was added to include the screening of projects that involved Bank funds going through a financial intermediary or 'sub-borrower'. Environmental assessment procedures for structural adjustment loans, those for policy reforms rather than projects, were also introduced as these came to form an increasing part of World Bank activities.

Since 2012, the World Bank has been in the process of undertaking a review and update of its safeguard policies. It is considered the most extensive consultation that the World Bank has ever had, and is in response to the significantly changed environmental and economic context for borrowing countries and for the Bank in recent years. In the second phase of drafting, it involved 65 countries, eight dedicated Indigenous Peoples consultations, five expert consultations (on biodiversity, labor, non-discrimination, LGBT/SOGIE and cultural heritage) and consultations with development partners, including other multilateral development banks, the International Labour Office and the World Health Organisation.

Table 7.9 shows the proposed Environmental and Social Framework, in its 3rd draft at the time of writing. A key change is the move from ODs to a set of 'standards'. The former OD on Environmental Assessment, for example, now becomes the Environmental and Social Standard ('ESS1') that also becomes the overarching standard for the framework as a whole. As such, it provides a strengthened emphasis on the *integrated* nature and assessment of environmental and social risks and outcomes over previous directives. ESS1 also requires both the borrower and the World Bank to agree on an Environmental and Social Commitment Plan once the environmental and social assessment has been carried out. Responsibility is on the borrower to monitor and report on that plan and a further key change is that these are extended to the *entire* project lifecycle, with the aim to ensure better risk management as the project progresses and to respond to unforeseen circumstances. This reflects the commitment in the 2012 Environment Strategy to active risk avoidance and management towards more sustainable (and resilient) development outcomes.

A further key improvement of the Framework over previous safeguard policies, is the provision for Free, Prior and Informed Consent within the Indigenous Peoples standard. If such consent cannot be shown, then a project does not proceed. Former operational directives had only required 'informed consultation'. The standard on Involuntary Resettlement also now includes much more detail on planning for resettlement and support to restore and improve livelihoods where resettlement cannot be avoided. Furthermore, compensation must always be paid *before* displacement. All the provisions within the new framework are mandatory for borrowers and Bank staff and for all investment projects. It is suggested that these changes will align World Bank procedures more closely with those of other development actors, including bilateral donors and private credit agencies,

Table 7.9 The World Bank proposed Environmental and Social Framework: the constituent standards

ESS1 Assessment and Management of Environmental and Social Risks and Impacts

ESS2 Labor and Working Conditions

ESS3 Resource Efficiency and Pollution Prevention

ESS4 Community Health and Safety

ESS5 Land Acquisition, Restrictions on Land Use and Involuntary Resettlement

ESS6 Biodiversity Conservation and Sustainable Management of Living Natural Resources

ESS7 Indigenous Peoples

ESS8 Cultural Heritage

ESS9 Financial Intermediaries

ESS10 Information Disclosure and Stakeholder Engagement

Source: World Bank draft standards, http://consultations.worldbank.org. Accessed 06 August 2015.

enabling more effective joint financing and stronger partnership working in the future; 'increasingly partnerships have become essential in a fiscally constrained world faced with major environmental challenges' (World Bank, 2012a: 2).

International financial institutions (IFIs), debt and economic development

It is probably in relation to debt and economic crisis that the most significant changes within the activities and roles of the World Bank and the IMF can be identified. In particular, the debt crisis of the early 1980s was seen to require comprehensive solutions and close cooperation between the two institutions. Through the subsequent decades, strategies and programmes that these institutions have financed towards addressing those challenges, came to profoundly influence the development agenda for countries of the Global South (see Chapter 3). Most recently, the IMF in particular, has come under close critical attention in relation to the reforms required, typically termed 'austerity packages', in order to access further lending in countries including Greece, Portugal and Ireland. As Susan George, a well-respected and oft-cited writer on debt and its impacts, states, 'now it's Europe's turn' (2013: 20).

The term structural adjustment programmes (SAPs) is used generically to describe the activities of the World Bank and the IMF in the design and support of packages of broad-based policy reform that became the central mechanism to address the economic crisis developing through the 1980s in many countries of the Global South. At a time of world recession and declining terms of trade, particularly for non-oil commodities, the World Bank noted that any developmental progress from its traditional portfolio of project-based lending was 'being swamped by macroeconomic imbalances in most of its client countries' (Reed, 1996: 9). At the same time, the IMF was looking beyond 'crisis management' in the monetary and financial sectors of countries of the Global South, towards assisting countries in building up productive capacity.

The first SAP was initiated in Turkey in 1980 and by the end of the decade, 187 SAPs had been negotiated for 64 developing countries (Dickenson et al., 1996: 265). By 1994, 30 per cent of World Bank lending was not to projects, but to programmes of broad-based policy reforms, rising to over 50 per cent by the end of the decade (Brown and Fox, 2001). The specific instruments of structural reform were varied, but typically included those listed in Table 7.10. All confirm a close association with the principles of neo-liberal development thinking discussed in Chapter 3. In short, redefining the role of the state in

development and enabling a greater role for the market as an actor in development, are key to neo-liberal ideas and to the requirements of SAPs.

The impacts of structural adjustment

Evaluating the outcomes of macro-economic adjustment is difficult, not least due to the far-reaching implications of the different elements of the 'package' shown in Table 7.10. Many countries were also subject to complex and phased programmes of reform over time. Debating the outcomes of neo-liberal approaches to economic development has also resurfaced in the context of the recent global economic crisis. It has been suggested that neither the World Bank, nor the IMF themselves, were able to demonstrate a 'convincing connection in either direction' between SAPs and economic growth (Killick, 1995, cited in Mohan et al., 2000: 58). Interest in monitoring the economic outcomes of SAPs was also not a priority in the early years. Mohan et al. (2000: xiv) point to how the first 15 years of structural adjustment was:

> relatively insidious, taking place in distant and impoverished places that were always in trouble and usually too complicated to comprehend. Once these distant places began to melt down (Russia, Indonesia, Brazil) in the mid 1990s and threaten 'our' development we began to take note.

Latin America and sub-Saharan Africa were the two regions where SAPs were implemented most stringently and yet the total amount of debt as a proportion of GDP rose markedly through the 1980s and 1990s. Indeed, it remained very high in the case of sub-Saharan Africa until the mid-2000s. As Schaaf (2013: 100) suggests, this raises 'clear questions concerning the effectiveness and relevance of the macroeconomic strategy advocated by the IFIs and adopted by developing countries'. Box 7.2 considers some of the social and environmental impacts of structural adjustment programmes. Further illustration of the outcomes of adjustment and the impact, for example, of the privatisation of environmental resources on which some of the poorest groups in society depend, is discussed in Chapter 10.

Table 7.10 The principal instruments of structural adjustment programmes

- Currency devaluation
- Monetary discipline
- Reduction of public spending
- Price reforms
- Trade liberalisation
- Reduction and/or removal of subsidies
- Privatisation of public enterprises
- Wage restraints
- Institutional reforms

BOX 7.2

The social and environmental impacts of structural adjustment programmes

It is widely considered that Structural Adjustment Programmes had specific and 'probably negative' impacts on women, 'given the complexity of gender relations, the invisibility of women's work both in the rural and urban sectors, and the multiple and complex roles women actually perform' (Pearson, 1992: 309). In short, there is substantial research that confirms how SAPs were in fact gender 'blind', rather than 'neutral', as assumed by the international financial institutions. There was no consideration of the gender division of labour, or gendered power relations within the household and how these would shape the socio-economic outcomes of adjustment for different genders and groups of people (see Elson, 1995; Schaaf, 2013). Some of the negative impacts of SAPs on women can be understood in terms of accepted gender roles, whereby women generally assume greater responsibility for household reproductive tasks. Women as a result, are intensive users of health services, as are children, and as government spending in health declined under adjustment, women tended to suffer more. Not only had the services on which women relied, such as clinics and maternity care, been reduced (necessitating greater travel and more expense for women), but women themselves had to supplement those public services through their own labour (Pearson, 1992).

Similarly, gender role analysis has exposed how women's unpaid work often increased under adjustment, whilst SAPs assumed implicitly that women's time was infinitely elastic (Sparr, 1994). The greater unemployment, decreased purchasing power and cutbacks in social services resulted in women adopting strategies to make funds go further. This included increase in time spent in shopping for cheaper alternatives, purchase of foods that have had less processing (leading to increased food preparation time) and supplementing income through the growing of vegetables for household and/or sale. Similarly, the

shift to export crops encouraged by SAPs often did not benefit women, the explanation for which requires an analysis of gender relations whereby women may produce and trade more in local and potentially non-monetary markets, for example. The 'gender-neutral' stance of SAPs was encapsulated by the way in which they did not require any significant reform in terms of enhancing women's access to land, credit or other inputs, yet these are fundamental gender inequalities that impede economic efficiency, for instance.

Evidence that economic adjustment may be at the cost of environmental sustainability also mounted through the 1990s. Ghana was widely heralded by the World Bank as one of its success stories in terms of progress with economic adjustment, with average annual growth in GDP of 3.8 per cent throughout the 1980s (Rich, 1994). However, timber exports increased from US $16 million in 1983, to US $99 million in 1988 under the trade liberalisation required by structural adjustment. As a result, the forest area within Ghana was reduced to 25 per cent of its original size by the late 1980s (Rich, 1994). In Cameroon,

Table 7.11 Explaining environmentally blind SAPs

➤ The World Bank and other lenders did not consider the environment to be a priority at the time
➤ Those borrowing from the major lenders were also more concerned with pressing fiscal issues and did not specifically request funding for environmental protection
➤ Sustainable development in its broadest sense was not high in the public consciousness so that environmental protection was not an obvious policy element
➤ Environmental protection would incur further state expenditure which was the antithesis of adjustment programmes

Source: Mohan et al, 2000

BOX 7.2 (continued)

the IMF recommended export tax cuts accompanied by devaluation of the currency under structural adjustment in 1995. This led to a substantial economic incentive to export timber resources from that country; the number of logging enterprises increased dramatically and lumber exports grew by almost 50 per cent in the two years after the export cuts were implemented (IMF, 1998).

Mohan et al. (2000) assert that SAPs were substantially 'environmentally blind' for the first decade of their design and implementation. Table 7.11 identifies a number of features of the wider context of the period that help explain this pattern. Fundamentally, further state expenditure, such as on environmental protection, was contrary to the core of neo-liberal thinking encapsulated in SAPs and it took ten years before proponents and architects of SAPs 'gradually realised' their environmental impacts.

Addressing the limitations of structural adjustment

In 1999, Poverty Reduction Strategy Papers (PRSPs) replaced structural adjustment programmes as the strategic documents around which the World Bank, IMF and other donors coordinate their assistance to low-income countries. The core principles of the PRSP approach are identified in Table 7.12. The PRSP approach was introduced by the World Bank and IMF in recognition of the limitations of SAPs, and in particular the need for greater country ownership and an enhanced poverty focus. PRSPs were seen as the key tool for operationalising the World Bank's approach to poverty and for implementing the MDGs at a country level. They remain the prerequisite for low income countries to access World Bank/IMF concessional lending and for debt relief under the Heavily Indebted Poor Countries Initiative (see Chapter 8).

PRSPs are written by national governments and should be formulated through broad participatory processes as seen in Table 7.12. Participation should involve civil society and domestic stakeholders, including from the private sector, as well external donors and the World Bank and IMF. PRSPs are required to set out coherent macro-economic, structural and social sector reform programmes, focused on country circumstances and priorities for poverty reduction and to identify the financing needs and sources. They should have clear links with other national action plans and

Table 7.12 Core principles of the PRSP approach

Country driven and owned: PRSPs should involve broad-based participation by civil society and the private sector at all stages, including formulation, implementation and outcome-based monitoring

Results-oriented: PRSPs should focus on outcomes that will benefit the poor

Comprehensive: PRSPs should recognise the multidimensional nature of poverty and the scope of actions needed to effectively reduce poverty

Partnership-oriented: PRSPs should involve the coordinated participation of development partners, including bilateral and multilateral agencies and non-governmental organisations

Based on medium- and long-term perspectives: PRSPs should recognise that sustained poverty reduction will require action over the medium and long term as well as in the short run

make explicit reference to MDG outcomes. As the key mechanism through which the MDGs were to be implemented at a country level, PRSPs were a significant development for the World Bank in terms of linking their activities and staff to other bilateral and multilateral donors and UN agencies.

One advantage of PRSPs is considered to be the way in which they open capacity for civil society actors to be involved in the development and implementation of programmes of policy reform that had not been present within the SAP process. However, there remain questions over the level of participation, and by whom, in practice. Research suggests that participation is often limited to consultation stages and it tends to be the more educated and wealthier member of civil society who have access to the process. This is considered further in the next section.

Enhancing 'country ownership' and garnering broad-based public support for PRSPs, is also considered central for more relevant and successful outcomes of policy lending and for overcoming the much criticised 'one size fits all' approach of SAPs. However, the highly prescribed framework within which PRSPs are developed, and the ultimate control that the World Bank and IMF have in terms of approving or rejecting the plans, continues to be a concern. Hulme (2010: 23) suggests that the process is so tightly overseen by the World Bank/IMF, that the very notion of country ownership is a 'joke in developing countries'. His concern extends to the potential for global goal-setting in future, such as within the Sustainable Development Goals considered in Chapter 1, unless genuine country authority and responsibility in linking national policies, plans, budgeting and accountability can be ensured. Hulme suggests that a cultural shift will be needed at the World Bank and IMF; 'they will need to adopt "arrogance reduction strategies" and learn not to believe that they know precisely what are the best policies for each specific country' (p. 23).

As seen, PRSPs were also to be the key mechanism through which the MDGs would be implemented at a country level and a key means for better alignment and effectiveness of donor support. A review of 40 countries with PRSPs to 2005 concluded that the PRSP approach had been important in putting poverty as a stronger focus within government and for enhancing coordination of donors (Driscoll and Evans, 2005). Fukuda-Parr (2010) reviewed 22 PRSPs and found a high degree of commitment to the MDGs as a principle, but also that PRSPS were selective in incorporating particular goals and targets, 'consistently emphasizing income poverty and social investments for education, health and water but not other targets concerned with empowerment and inclusion of the most vulnerable such as gender violence of women's political representation' (p. 26).

There is also evidence that the PRSP process continues to be compromised in terms of key social and environmental outcomes. Schaaf (2013: 105) suggests that the PRSP experience confirms that 'the World Bank and IMF continue to struggle to fully recognize how gender relations and inequalities interact with poverty'. A review by the World Resources Institute (2005) urged an 'environmental overhaul' of PRSPs, if the central role of ecosystems in the lives of the poor and their potential to reduce rural poverty is to be secured. Similarly, Bojo et al. (2004) have looked at how poverty–environment linkages were mainstreamed or not into PRSPs, and the extent to which consultation and participation had allowed environmental concerns to be heard with the process. In their review of 53 PRSPS, only 14 had any explicit target aligned to the MDG7 on environmental sustainability. The fragmented nature of that particular MDG, in failing to provide a comprehensive picture of the complex connections between poverty and environment or across the interlinked social, economic and environmental dimensions of sustainable development has been noted, including by the UN, as discussed above (UNDG, 2010).

Most fundamentally, critics of the PRSP process have questioned whether these programmes actually represent any real shift beyond neo-liberalism of the previous decade (see Chapters 1 and 3). Fukuda-Parr (2010), on the basis of a review of 22 PRSPs and 21 bilateral aid policy statements, concludes that PRSPs reflect a continuation of the neo-liberal agenda of the 1980s/90s and the programmes of funding they access, 'follow the same macroeconomic policy prescriptions of the Washington Consensus as did the Structural Adjustment Programmes' (p. 34). In the continued emphasis given to engaging with the globalised economy and rolling back the state, it is external factors such as international finance and trade that are seen as fundamental to overcoming poverty, rather than part of the dynamic of poverty creation. In turn, this continues to place responsibility on government and society of countries of the Global South for both the causes and outcomes of poverty (Fairhead, 2004).

Working with non-governmental organisations

In continuity with the UN, the World Bank has a long-stated commitment to work with civil society, including as a means of fostering local empowerment and the accountability of official institutions:

The aims should be to empower ordinary people to take charge of their lives, to make communities more responsible for their development, and to make governments listen to their people. Fostering a more pluralistic institutional structure – including non-governmental organisations – is a means to these ends.

(World Bank, 1989: 54–5)

The final section of this chapter includes a more detailed discussion of civil society organisations as institutions in the current development landscape. NGOs, as a subset of civil society, are diverse and multi-dimensional organisations. For example, they vary in terms of financial and technical capacity and in values and political ideas (see Nelson, 2006). This affects how they engage with all other actors and institutions in development. This section focuses on the changing ways in which NGOs engage with the World Bank and in particular, how they have prompted change in the activities of the World Bank.

Nelson (2006) identifies three principal forms of NGO-World Bank engagement as cooperation within projects, critical advocacy and consultations on policy issues. Project collaboration between NGOs and the World Bank grew rapidly in the 1980s and 1990s, principally as many governments' service delivery capacity decreased under structural adjustment programmes, and as NGOs were attracted by the funds available from the Bank. Through that period, most World Bank projects with activities at the community level had some form of collaboration with NGOs (Nelson, 2002). By 1993, 30 per cent of all projects were reported to involve collaboration, rising to 82 per cent in 2010–12 (World Bank, 2013b). Whilst the Bank systematically encourages such operational collaboration, the role of NGOs may be quite minor – limited to 'implementing projects designed and negotiated by government and World Bank officials' (Nelson, 2006: 706). Malena (2000: 22) has queried the nature and impact of such involvement, which:

could indicate anything from the genuine and sustained participation of a large number of NGOs through all stages of the project cycle, to the contracting of an NGO for purposes of service delivery, to an informal lunch meeting with the local Oxfam representative.

However, it is more generally accepted that the activities of NGOs have established significant concessions through their 'confrontational' involvement with the World Bank, particularly in the fields of environmental and social policy. Although the 'least frequent' form of NGO–World Bank engagement (Malena, 2000), the most visible roles are where NGOs intervene in opposition to World Bank/government activities, to block or modify a planned project (typically infrastructure projects). Such activities often involve coalitions of affected groups and national or international NGOs who share their concerns. A variety of political strategies may be used, including direct action at project sites, media campaigns and communication with Bank staff. The successful role of international NGOs in getting the World Bank to withdraw its funding of the Narmada dam projects, on the basis of environmental impacts and processes of involuntary resettlement was seen above. Other examples include confrontations over debt relief (see Chapter 1). It is these kinds of activities that many advocacy-based International NGOs are keen on, in that they combine policy dialogue with the World Bank, with collaborative or confrontational actions at the field level through community based organisations. As Nelson (2006) identifies, it is the World Bank's political influence that often attracts NGOs seeking to influence the Bank itself and/or the actions of borrowing governments.

Extended criticism of the World Bank by NGOs has also been important in promoting change within the institution, towards becoming more transparent, participatory and accountable (Tussie and Tuozzo, 2001; Woods, 2000). Both World Bank and independent reviewers have found evidence of changes in World Bank practice as a result of the 'high-volume encounters' between NGOs and the World Bank, for example in the area of involuntary resettlement (Woods, 2000). It was proposals from environmental NGOs on the basis of the Narmada case that led directly to the development of the World Bank's information disclosure policies and the formation of the independent inspection panel in 1993. This has now made most project-related documents available to the public and has given citizens of the Global South the forum to make grievances against the World Bank independently of their governments. The Inspection Panel now represents a formal and fully institutionalised mechanism for contacts between the WB and civil society.

Such critical advocacy by NGOs has also helped cement what has been referred to as a 'culture of consultation with NGOs' that now exists within the World Bank (Nelson, 2006). Significantly, there is now greater consultation and involvement of NGOs in policy discussions, such as in the preparation of PRSPs and the Country Assistance Strategies that guide lending. The World Bank Civil Society Forum also provides a standing consultative mechanism for NGOs, and there is support to bring officers of these organisations to annual meetings of the Bank to engage in policy development. Invited consultations on controversial issues and specific themes, such as water privatisation, dam construction and forestry, have also 'become the norm' (Nelson, 2006).

There remain concerns as to which NGOs are invited to consult and work with the World Bank, which governments it supports, the nature of the consultation processes and the outcomes of those (see Malena, 2000). The World Bank recognises the complex nature of civil society and the relationships between civil society and government in some countries of the Global South that has led to uneven levels of their engagement (World Bank, 2013). Annual reporting of engagement now includes considerations of the institutional mechanisms in place to ensure that collaboration is sustained. The need to extend engagement with specific constituencies such as indigenous people is also acknowledged (World Bank, 2013b).

The World Trade Organization

International trade is the most important aspect of the global economy and a determining factor in the social and economic development of nations. International trade has grown faster than world economic output in every decade since 1950, and flows of foreign direct investment (FDI) have grown faster than international trade since the mid-1980s (Neumayer, 2001; see also Chapter 4). Global trade grew on average by 7% annually in the years preceding the 2008 financial crisis, when it slowed to 4% in 2013–14 (World Bank, 2015e). Global investments also fell during the crisis, but have been growing again since 2012. FDI grew by 9% in 2013 and 54% of the total flows were to 'developing countries' (UNCTAD, 2014). The geography of global trade is discussed further in Chapter 8 (see also Dicken, 2015).

The majority of world trade takes place according to a set of rules administered by the World Trade Organization (WTO). The WTO was formed in 1995, although its origins go back to the General Agreement on Tariffs and Trade (GATT) of 1948. In the immediate post-Second World War context, the 50 founding members of the United Nations had envisaged the creation of an institution, the International Trade Organization that would regulate world trade and international investment towards economic recovery and international stability. It would also serve to limit the restrictive and protectionist business practices that had brought about the Great Depression of the 1930s. However, the charter drawn up proved unacceptable to many countries, particularly the USA, and led to 23 of the richest and most powerful countries withdrawing and forming the GATT.

Membership of the World Trade Organisation is now almost universal, with 161 member countries. Its remit now extends beyond cross-border 'physical' trade issues (relating to manufactured goods) into areas related to trade, such as services (including telecommunications and banking) and intellectual property rights and patents. The increased membership, scope and depth of affairs now involved, ensures that the WTO agenda has substantial political and social significance (Reiterer, 2009). Its decisions impact significantly on domestic policy and economies, throughout environment, agriculture and health, for example. For some commentators, such as the networks of civil society organisations within the anti-globalisation movement, the WTO is the 'ultimate villain' in global governance. Chapter 8 discusses in some detail how trade rulings can work against the needs of marginalised groups across societies. For others, the WTO, through providing a platform for negotiations, agreements and dispute settlement, is 'the instrument to harness globalization for building global governance' (Reiterer, 2009: 360). This section identifies the structure and key activities of the WTO. It highlights questions of the current legitimacy and power of the WTO to address the needs of countries of the Global South, and its capacity to deliver more sustainable patterns of economic development in particular.

Key structures and activities

The structure of the WTO is shown in Figure 7.6. The Ministerial Council is open to all members and can take decisions on any matter of the trade agreements. Its Secretariat is based in Geneva. The ongoing work of the WTO is undertaken by representatives of all member countries through the General Council that meets, under different terms of reference, as the Dispute Settling Body and the Trade Policy Review Body. Three further councils identified in Figure 7.6 handle the different broad areas of trade and report to the General Council. In turn, their work is carried out by a set of smaller committees.

The WTO is a much stronger institution than GATT and it has a legal status similar to the UN. All member countries commit to two key principles that date back to GATT and are designed explicitly to encourage free trade, undistorted competition and prevent the protectionism that had plagued the international economy in that post-war era. The first principle refers to 'national treatment', under which all countries must treat participants in their economies the same as domestic firms, and the second to the 'most favoured nation', which aims to ensure that any concession granted to one trading partner is extended to all. These rules are binding on members and the Dispute Settlement Body shown in Figure 7.6 monitors and enforce the principles and agreed rulings. The system does support tariffs and other forms of protection in limited circumstances, such as to protect consumers or prevent the spread of disease (WTO, 2011). Trade sanctions and compensation can be made as penalties if member countries do not follow decisions under the dispute settling mechanism.

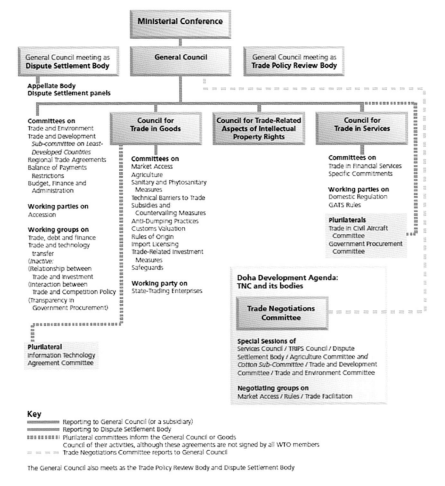

Figure 7.6 The structure of the World Trade Organization
Source: adapted from World Trade Organization, 2011.

The WTO hosts a series of multilateral trade negotiations, known as 'rounds', within which arrangements are negotiated and disputes resolved. Voting within the WTO is unweighted, in that each member receives one vote. Whilst decision making is generally based on consensus, and there are provisions for majority voting in certain instances, 'it is often "states" market share (that) is the primary source of influence' (Mingst and Karns, 2012: 173).

The length of each round gives insight into the challenges of achieving international consensus on trade matters. For example, the Uruguay round took eight years to complete (1986–1994) and it then took a further seven years to agree to the *shape* for the subsequent current round of deliberations (that being finally agreed in Doha, Qatar, in November 2001). The Doha round was to be a 'Development Agenda' (DDA). There was optimism at the time of its launch, that WTO agreements 'could and should be made better to accommodate the development dimensions of trade and give a stronger role for developing country members in negotiations' (Elliott, 2013: 156). Whilst there were some early successes, such as around intellectual property rights that have lowered the costs of patented medicines used in the treatment of HIV/AIDS, the Doha round has been substantially stalled since 2008 (see also the Key idea in the next chapter on the collapse of the Doha Agenda).

Enhancing the participation of countries of the Global South

The politics and economics of trade negotiations are complex, as are the negotiating mechanisms (Reiterer, 2009). The external environment in which negotiations have to occur has also changed markedly with the recent economic crisis that has emphasised the economic inter-dependence of countries globally. However, it is suggested that the WTO has been more responsive to recent shifts in the balance of economic power globally than the World Bank or IMF has been, and that the deadlock of the Doha round 'should not be mistaken for stasis in the WTO' (Narlikar, 2011: 717).

As seen above, the WTO is a member driven institution and all councils and committees are open to all members. However, increasingly, countries group together to form alliances and coalitions outside these formal meetings to seek consensus and confirm common negotiating positions. Over 20 such coalitions have submitted proposals in the agricultural negotiations, for example (WTO, 2011) and the number of coalitions now including countries of the Global South has grown significantly in recent years. Since 2005, Brazil and India have been identified as 'major members' of the WTO and part of the 'G-6' that includes Australia, the EU, Japan and the US, in working to break the deadlock of the Doha negotiations, particularly in agriculture. In 2008, the G-6 was extended to 7, with the inclusion of China. This has been an important step in enhancing the legitimacy of the WTO, whereby its decisions potentially reflect better the current balance of global economic power. In addition, India has a long history of activism in GATT and the WTO (Narliker, 2011) and as such brings experience and capacity, in terms of skills, information-sharing and research, for example, that can support greater engagement of other countries of the Global South and more widely within the WTO.

However, reaching agreement across these alliances can still be difficult. Some argue that it is now differences across countries of the Global South, in terms of their levels of economic development and interests/needs, that has caused the deadlock on the DDA and has compromised further the credibility of the WTO. As Schaaf (2013: 184) notes,

> so while the BICs *(Brazil, India and China)* have become more involved and less satisfied, the EU and USA have engaged less with the process and the rest of the developing world has become less content, resulting in overall disillusionment and deadlock.

There remain serious questions regarding the relevance and effectiveness of the WTO, particularly as it seems unable to control the persistent use of large scale subsidies in agriculture by the EU and US. As Narliker (2011: 724) summarises: 'unsurprisingly, when faced with interminably long rounds and no political support for them at home, politicians are turning to the more populist, cheaper and quicker alternatives of bilateralism, regionalism and protectionism'.

World trade and the environment

> Environmental collapse and deepening inequity are a visible, tangible, audible calamity everywhere on Earth. The liberalisation of world trade is the most active agent in this calamity.
>
> (Ransom, 2001: 28)

The WTO is an established focus for environmentalists who fear that progress towards sustainable development is being compromised through the liberalisation of trade generally and in particular, through WTO rulings. There is no explicit attention within the WTO mandate to the relationship between trade policy and other major policy areas, such as the environment. However, there are articles in the agreement granting exceptions to the general free-trade requirements, where the protection of human, animal or plant life or health, or the conservation of exhaustible natural resources are concerned.

Any such measure must be non-discriminatory (applied to domestic as well as foreign firms) and it needs to be established that the purpose is for conservation or health ends and not as a protectionist device. Furthermore, WTO rulings refer to the product being traded and not the processes of production. 'Thus, tuna fish caught with nets which also take dolphin have to be treated in the same way as those caught with dolphin-friendly methods' (Buckley, 1994: 6).

In 1995, the WTO established a Committee on Trade and the Environment (CTE). There had been a 'Group on Environmental Measures and International Trade' under GATT since 1971, although the group was supposed to convene upon request and there was no such request until 1991 (Neumayer, 2001). The terms of reference of the CTE are: to identify the relationship between trade measures and sustainable development; to make appropriate recommendations on whether the multilateral trading systems should be modified; and to assess the need for rules to enhance the interaction between trade and the environment, including avoidance of protectionist measures and surveillance of trade measures for environmental purposes (Williams and Ford, 1999). However, the impact of the CTE and the outcomes of their meetings are considered disappointing (Williams

and Ford, 1999; Neumayer, 2001). As Ransom (2001) noted, the WTO, as a 'key player in the neo-liberal project', is fundamentally concerned with environmental measures as distortions to free trade and the possibility of countries using such interventions to protect domestic firms. As the WTO itself identifies:

> The WTO is only competent to deal with trade. In other words, in environmental issues its only task is to study questions that arise when environmental policies have a significant impact on trade. The WTO is not an environmental agency. Its members do not want it to intervene in national or international environmental policies or to set environmental standards. Other agencies that specialize in environmental issues are better qualified to undertake those tasks.
>
> (2011: 65)

Table 7.13 highlights some of the key areas in which free trade and environmentalist views are divergent concerning the relationship between market economics and environmental protection. A key ongoing concern remains the power of TNCs within global trade. Whilst TNCs are not members of the WTO, they make very large contributions to the economic prosperity of particular, largely Northern, countries, such that their concerns are 'practically guaranteed' to be listened to at a national

Table 7.13 Competing ideologies on trade and the environment

Environmentalists	Free trade policy analysts
➤ Trade liberalisation creates unchecked growth and pollution	➤ Protectionism is inefficient and leads to even more wasteful use of resources
➤ Environmental costs must be internalised into all WTO activities and decisions	➤ Trade distortions and protectionist intentions of environmental measures
➤ Consideration of production processes must be part of WTO decisions	➤ Trade can create finances for design and enforcement of environmental measures
➤ Environmental solutions need to reduce consumption	➤ Well-targeted environmental policy can control environmental impacts of free trade

level and taken forward within the WTO (Taylor, 2003). TNCs, by definition, are 'non-place-based actors' and therefore it could be suggested they have no loyalty or accountability to any community, government or place.

There are also longstanding concerns from within the Global South and amongst INGOs, regarding the substantially unregulated nature of TNC activity and the lack of an internationally binding agreement on corporate responsibility. Whilst many TNCs now have well-developed corporate strategies on the environment (Plate 7.4) and new initiatives such as the Global Compact, seen above, seek to align business practices more closely to internationally agreed values and principles including on the environment and human rights, there continue to be questions regarding the effectiveness of such voluntary measures. This has been the focus of an ongoing campaign by Friends of the Earth International, for example. In reference to the failure of the WTO to raise the issue of TNCs in international trade at all at its ministerial meeting in Doha in 2001, a representative of Christian Aid suggested that 'it is like a conference on malaria that does not discuss the mosquito' (cited in Madeley, 2001: 27).

There is also a concern that existing multilateral environmental agreements (MEAs) may become subordinate to WTO rulings in future (Biermann, 2013; Bigg, 2004). Whilst the Doha mandate includes a commitment to launch negotiations on the relationship between WTO rulings and specific trade obligations set out in MEAs, as well as a proposal for closer working between the Trade and Environment Committee with MEA Secretariats, those negotiations remain stalled as identified above. Some MEAs, such as the Convention on the Control of Transboundary Movements of Hazardous Wastes and their Disposal and the Convention on International Trade in Endangered Species of Wild Flora and Fauna, evidently place restrictions of some kind on trade and could be seen as strictly violating WTO principles. In 2013, the US brought a complaint against India to the WTO in relation to its solar energy policy. This was in relation to a 'domestic content' requirement that violated the 'national treatment' principles of the WTO and discriminated unfairly against imported solar cells. To incentivise the expansion of solar production, the Indian government has an agreement to assure producers of a certain price for energy,

Plate 7.4 Corporations committing to environmental responsibility
(*photo*: Jennifer Elliott)

Figure 7.7 The WTO rules against India
(*Cartoon*: Courtenay Lewis)

but is conditional on the producer using domestically sourced inputs such as solar cells and modules. The Indian government argued that the development of its solar industry was key to meeting its climate commitments under UNFCCC and to addressing the global challenge of lower-carbon development. In 2016, the WTO ruled against India, rejecting that domestic policy in violation of WTO rules could be justified on the basis that they fulfil international climate commitments such as UNFCCC (Figure 7.7).

The chapters in Part III illustrate further a number of concerns regarding the impacts of trade liberalisation in delivering more sustainable development and addressing the needs of the poorest. For many countries of the Global South, engaging in world trade and increasing their foreign exchange earnings means expanding the export of primary products and raw materials. Some of the negative impacts of such resource dependence for development prospects were considered in Chapter 6 in terms of the 'resource curse'. 'Commodity dependency' is also discussed in Chapter 8, yet commodities remain outside current WTO rulings. The volatility of both fuel and non-fuel commodity prices seen in the last decade

has emphasised the difficulty for many countries, particularly in the Global South. Unstable prices for commodities is widely considered to be among the most powerful influences that prevent trade from working for the poor (see Box 8.5).

Fundamentally, markets are diverse and complex institutions which rarely operate to provide equal benefits to all participants. As seen, WTO rulings do not distinguish between corporations, companies, individual producers, petty traders or consumers, nor do they recognise their differential power in accessing markets, which themselves are not uniform even within a region. It is on this basis that INGOs and wider social movements continue to seek change within the WTO.

The role of the state

The state is a network of government, quasi-government and non-government institutions that coordinate, regulate and monitor economic and social activities in society (UNDP, 1997). As such, it is a wider category than government, including the civil service, the police and the military and the legal system, for example.

Box 7.3 details further the concepts of state and government. The state takes many different forms worldwide. As Johnston (1996: 146–7) identifies, 'individual states have developed through conflict and accommodation, as various interest groups have contested for power within society'. States also do not operate in any particular or predetermined way including as the 'ensemble of political institutions' comprising the state, 'may not always act as one or in concert' (Thomas and Allen, 2000: 191).

BOX 7.3

Concepts of state and government

State, in its wider sense, refers to a set of institutions that possess the means of legitimate coercion, exercised over a defined territory and its population, referred to as society. The state monopolises rule making within its territory through the medium of an organised government

    Government has different meanings in different contexts:

➤ the process of governing, the exercise of power
➤ the existence of that process, a condition of ordered rule
➤ the people who fill the positions of authority within a state
➤ the manner, method or system of governing in a society, i.e. the structure and arrangement of offices and how they relate to the governed

Source: World Bank (1997)

The role taken by the state in any arena of activity is influenced by a host of forces including inter- and intra-state conflicts and the decisions of international finance institutions as considered above. Further factors include pressure from civil society organisations as seen recently and very overtly in many North African countries with the political changes that accompanied the 'Arab Spring'. The final section of this chapter considers the role of civil society organisations as 'democratizers of development' in more detail. However, mobilising the financial resources necessary to achieve its public functions, including environmental stewardship and addressing the needs of poorest groups, remains a key role for the state. The following sections look briefly at the changing ways in which the role of the state has been considered in development (see Chapter 3 for more detail), and in particular the pressures for reform that have been associated with accessing finances for development. How these reforms have shaped the ability of the state to deliver on key aspects of its environmental stewardship and development roles are identified. Further illustration of the environmental and social outcomes of these activities is detailed in Part III.

Debating the role of the state

The role of the state as an actor in the development landscape is longstanding as Mackintosh (1992: 61) suggested:

> The very subject of 'development' was built on the idea of the state as the main lever for changing the economy and society. The ideology of 'developmentalism' and the concept of the interventionist state were inseparable in the optimistic post-war beginnings of development theory.

Throughout the 1960s, many, often newly independent, nations built up large state enterprises including in public utilities, and nationalised mining and agricultural enterprises to lead industrial development and drive economic growth. It was a stage of 'great optimism' (Mackintosh, 1992: 68) concerning both the benevolence and the competence of the state to work in the 'public interest' that only became seriously challenged in the early 1980s (Thomas and Allen, 2000). In short, government expenditures within the developing world through the 1970s grew faster than GDP. Further state investment was therefore only enabled by borrowing from commercial and multilateral sources that were easily available at that time. However, the economic performance of many countries remained poor at the end of that decade and the state was beginning to be seen as part of the problem rather than the solution.

By the 1980s, the capacity of national governments in the Global South to continue to make investments in development were severely limited by rising oil prices, mounting debt burdens and recession within the global economy. Through the 1990s, substantial reforms of the state were held as being central to global economic recovery and as conditions for the receipt of further development assistance from multilateral and bilateral sources (the era of structural adjustment programmes discussed above). As Banks and Hulme (2014: 183) summarise: 'neoliberal growth models categorized the state as part of the problem of under-development, arguing for a reduction in its size, influence and 'interference' as a precondition for growth take-off and acceleration'.

Whilst the poverty-focused development agenda of the new millennium reasserted an important role for the state in targeting poverty, and in raising the accountability and responsiveness of state institutions to the needs of the poorest, questions regarding reform of the state persisted. As Naim identified in 2000,

> Early in the 1990s, the fashionable code words commonly used by politicians, experts and journalists commenting on economic reforms were 'macroeconomic stabilisation' and 'structural reforms'. *'Governance', 'transparency' and 'institutions' have now replaced these terms* . . . The obsession with crushing inflation, common in the late 1980s and early 1990s, has been substituted by the obsession with the need to curb corruption.
>
> (p. 521, *emphasis added*)

Since 2008 and the onset of the global economic crisis, which many commentators suggest has undermined the credibility of the neo-liberal approach irreversibly, there has been substantial reconsideration of the role of state and the market (and the relationship between them) in development (see Chapter 3). As Silvey (2010: 829) comments, many states worldwide have 'scrambled to rescue

national economies', including through public support to the private banking sector. The dramatic economic growth in China in recent years, built on strong government control in directing development, has also reinvigorated discussions of the relative role of the state and policy approaches that 'deviate' from 'Washington Consensus' norms (Hochstetler and Montero, 2013). Elements of the 'developmental state' are now reappearing in countries including Brazil, Vietnam, Korea, India, Venezuela, Mozambique, Malawi and Uganda (see Williams et al., 2014). In Brazil, Hochstetler and Montero (2013) suggest 'renewed developmentalism', in that considerable continuities with earlier state-led development approaches, such as import-substitution industrialisation, can be identified. For example, from 1985, the first democratically elected Governments embarked on some privatisation of state firms and trade liberalisation, but retained a strong industrial policy combined with efforts to support innovation and global competitiveness amongst domestic firms. Through the presidency of Lula Da Silva (2003–10) in particular, there has been a strong role for the state-controlled banks in partnerships with firms and private companies, whereby public funding has prioritised the development and application of new technologies and subsidies, taxation and credit are used to direct private investments. Furthermore, growing numbers of Latin American and Asian states are now actively not borrowing from the IMF and the World Bank and thereby avoiding 'buying into' a liberal view of the state embraced in the conditions of borrowing from those institutions (Schaaf, 2013).

Reforms of the state: the conditions for accessing development finance

It was in response to the economic crises of the 1980s that potentially the most far-reaching changes in the activities and operations of state institutions were promoted. A new economic orthodoxy, termed 'market triumphalism' by Peet and Watts (1996), was gaining the sympathy of leaders in the industrialised nations and was rapidly transferred to the countries of the Global South, particularly through the lending conditions of the international financial institutions. Within this thinking, it was the market rather than the state that is seen as the prime instrument of economic development. The state was conceived as a block to development, rather than a protector of the public interest or a force for development. This agenda also included rediscovering civil society; 'the expressed aim of the neo-liberal project is to free the entrepreneurial potential of civil society from the omnipotent and omnipresent hostile state' (Zack-Williams, 2001: 218).

The implementation of Structural Adjustment Programmes became the conditions for borrowing countries to access further finances from the IFIs, as well as from other donors and private investors. Table 7.10 above identified the principal instruments of SAPS. The conditions for internal reforms of the state included deregulation, such as giving up public

monopolies in education, and cost recovery including the use of fees for services such as health, aimed at cutting demand and promoting efficiency. A further means of saving on tax revenues, and thereby assisting with balance of payment difficulties, was to devolve the activities of the state and its decision making to other institutions such as in the private or voluntary sectors. External policy reforms, including currency devaluation and the removal of tariffs and quotas, were designed to encourage foreign investment and expand exports. In short, the state function in development under adjustment was reduced to one of co-ordination, 'or more vaguely, an "enabling role"' (Mackintosh, 1992: 83). Mohan et al. (2000: xiv) refer to the irony of a theory that 'posits the "freedom" of the markets and

Plate 7.5 Promoting good governance in Botswana
(*photo*: Jennifer Elliott)

the limited use of state power' that in fact 'required massive amounts of political interference to do so'.

It has been suggested that the issues that dominated in the 1980s, concerning states that were too strong, were replaced by concerns that states may be too weak by the millennium (see Naim, 2000). For example, the World Bank, since 1997, has monitored and reported on 'good governance' worldwide, on the basis of six dimensions shown in Table 7.14. The suggestion is that they had 'universal development relevance for all cultures and societies in the modern world' (Leftwich, 1993: 605). For the World Bank, their interest in promoting good governance was influenced, in part, by the experience of structural adjustment, where progress was seen to depend, not only on macro-economic stability and good policies, but also the quality of the structures through which policies are developed and implemented. The notion of good governance has many implications for the institutions and activities of the state (Plate 7.5). There are concerns that the World Bank's principles reflect the values of western democratic models, in the definition of government effectiveness, for example, and remain rooted in neo-liberal assumptions such as that the state's role is to promote private sector development.

There are also concerns that governments of the Global South may have become more accountable to donors than to their own citizens in the strategies and process of poverty reduction, given the continued dependence on official development assistance (ODA) and finances through institutions like the World Bank, and when 'the aid which they receive is tied to certain conditionalities that seek to address externally identified governance problems' (Banks and Hulme, 2014: 183). ODA remains a key source of finance, particularly for the poorer countries, despite the generally rising role of overseas private investments for some countries of the Global South. Furthermore, 'private capital flows are not necessarily invested in countries most in need and in sectors necessary for sustainable development' (UN, 2015b: 66).

Chapter 8 looks in more detail at the changing landscape of aid and official development assistance (ODA). There is also much contemporary discussion around the role of philanthropic sources of finance to address shortfalls in future government spending in development, including in the context of economic crisis and declining public commitment internationally

Table 7.14 The World Bank dimensions of 'good governance'

1. **Voice and Accountability (VA)** – capturing perceptions of the extent to which a country's citizens are able to participate in selecting their government, as well as freedom of expression, freedom of association, and a free media.
2. **Political Stability and Absence of Violence/Terrorism (PV)** – capturing perceptions of the likelihood of political instability and/or politically-motivated violence, including terrorism.
3. **Government Effectiveness (GE)** – capturing perceptions of the quality of public services, the quality of the civil service and the degree of its independence from political pressures, the quality of policy formulation and implementation, and the credibility of the government's commitment to such policies.
4. **Regulatory Quality (RQ)** – capturing perceptions of the ability of the government to formulate and implement sound policies and regulations that permit and promote private sector development.
5. **Rule of Law (RL)** – capturing perceptions of the extent to which agents have confidence in and abide by the rules of society, and in particular the quality of contract enforcement, property rights, the police, and the courts, as well as the likelihood of crime and violence.
6. **Control of Corruption (CC)** – capturing perceptions of the extent to which public power is exercised for private gain, including both petty and grand forms of corruption, as well as 'capture' of the state by elites and private interests.

Source: World Bank, 2015b

for ODA. There is a long history of private philanthropy, or charitable giving in the public interest, but typically, this was given in the past within national borders. Currently, it is working internationally and increasingly according to business principles, so called 'philanthrocapitalism' (McGoey, 2014; Edwards, 2011). The Bill and Melinda Gates Foundation is one of the most prominent foundations currently (see Key idea below). However, there are concerns regarding the role of the state in these relationships;

We must try to understand the repercussions of a situation in which charitable foundations have a greater sway in health policy than health ministries in some developing countries, setting agendas by their global priorities and values rather than in-country needs, and thereby displacing the roles of state and civil society in designing, implementing and contesting policies and programmes. With global foundations lacking accountability and responsiveness to stakeholders in recipient countries, this also leaves no role for civil society to hold them to account for their developmental policies and outcomes.

(Banks and Hulme, 2014: 187)

Key idea

Private foundations in international development

There are estimated to be over 176,000 foundations in the US and Europe alone. Their numbers continue to grow, including within middle-income countries such as Brazil, India, China and South Africa. They are also increasingly working outside national borders. In 2009, foundations worldwide provided nearly US $10 billion to international development activities, two-thirds of which came from the USA.

The largest contributor is the Bill and Melinda Gates Foundation (BMGF), which spent US $2.5 billion in 2009 on global health and development. It spends more on global health annually than the World Health Organisation. It is run by a board that includes three family members and Warren Buffet, who has pledged to give away 99 per cent of his immense fortune on his death and largely to the BMGF.

However, at a global level, foundations provide approximately 29 per cent of total grants given by voluntary agencies (that also include NGOs, charities and faith based organisations). In total, this forms less than 7 per cent of all development assistance, such that in these terms so called 'Big' philanthropy could be considered quite small.

Foundations are diverse in terms of philosophy and activities. They are considered to offer the potential for addressing the longer-term and deeper dimensions of human wellbeing/social change, in that they are not under pressure to continually find new funds (financed as they are, through the interest on the substantial endowments). They are also free from political pressures to follow particular priorities.

However, concerns include that they are often championed by entrepreneurs who have made their fortunes in the worlds of finance and technologies and are bringing the values and tools of the business world into philanthropy. The suggestion is that they are turning it into a lucrative industry in itself, one of 'philanthrocapitalism'. Fears include the tendency to take a 'Grand Challenge' approach to development, centred on technical solutions, innovative financing models, performance metrics and issues that are amenable to rapid 'scaling up'. The concern is that there is insufficient consideration of local contexts and alternative trajectories within development.

Source: compiled from Edwards, 2011; McGoey, L., 2014

The state in sustainable development

The Brundtland Report identified a key role for the state in fostering more sustainable patterns and processes of development worldwide (WCED, 1987). Governments, as seen in sections above, are key actors in the continued development of multilateral environmental agreements and international trade rulings, that substantially shape the global prospects for more sustainable development outcomes. Table 7.15 identifies a range of ways in which governments specifically can influence environmental outcomes within national territories that encompass key environmental stewardship and resource development roles. In short, governments through these roles in establishing the policy, regulatory and institutional frameworks within a country, have substantial impacts on the prospects for sustainable development within their own boundaries (Elliott, 2013).

However, it has been asserted that 'rather than being an actor with possible solutions to environmental problems, the state has typically contributed to exacerbating

Table 7.15 Government's role in environmental outcomes

➤ Establishing and enforcing laws that determine who has the right to use the environment and the duty to protect it
➤ Managing natural resources including state-owned and collective environmental goods
➤ Determining which environmental uses are to be taxed or subsidised
➤ Restricting environmental threats posed by individual or corporate behaviour
➤ Defining and enforcing the rules of formal markets
➤ Allocating funds for conservation and development
➤ Redistributing resources between groups in society

Source: compiled from World Resources Institute (2003)

those problems' (Bryant and Bailey, 1997: 55). This includes through bureaucratic resistance and corruption that have limited its stewardship role. It may be, for example, that the most powerful groups have accessed that strength through their control over environmentally damaging activities, such as in mining and energy generation, which they are reluctant to give up. The stewardship role of governments in the Global South has also been compromised by often close associations between political leaders and business interests. Aspects of these 'failings' of the state and government in respect to sustainable development were considered in more detail in Chapter 6. More positively, the chapter also illustrated how several countries from within the Global South are now leading on national commitments to greener energy development.

International institutions are influencing national policy development in sectors that are key to achieving more sustainable social and environmental outcomes. The capacity of the state to respond to environmental problems was regularly undermined through the processes of structural adjustment, for example, via the pressure to cut the budgets and staffing of environment departments. Many governments of the Global South continue to lack the fundamental finances to provide the kinds of investments, services and environmental controls to ensure healthy environments and particularly for the poorest groups in society (see Elliott, 2013). In the urban sector (as illustrated further in Chapter 9), it has been increasingly private, and often overseas, companies and corporations that now shape access and

opportunity in key resource sectors such as water supply and sanitation. There is ongoing concern that privatised service provision is neither equitable nor environmentally sustainable (Budds and McGranahan, 2003), and remains a key driver in civic unrest and focus for public action (Larner and Laurie, 2010).

The state has historically been a key driver of conservation, particularly through its role in the establishment and running of protected areas and the formulation of natural resources policy more widely. However, a 'neo-liberalisation' of conservation can also be identified over recent decades, in which the role of the state as an actor in conservation has been 'rolled back', as in economic arenas, with a greater role for NGOs and other private sector interests in running protected areas, for example. It is also confirmed by the increased use of 'market mechanisms' to find ways for preserving natural resources and ecosystem functions (Holmes, 2012; Elliott, 2013). Ecotourism (discussed in Chapter 8) is an example of raising private finance through tourist receipts to cover the additional costs of preserving valued flora and fauna and can be initiated by private interests at various scales. The role of community-based natural resource management initiatives is discussed in Chapter 10. In Chapter 6, pilot initiatives such as the UN supported REDD+ programme was seen to be based on 'payments for environmental services' that rest on market mechanisms to transfer finances to those who manage forest resources, from those that use and benefit from the environmental services associated with standing forests (biodiversity, water regulation and carbon sequestration, for example). Leading conservation NGOs are now taking over roles in environmental stewardship that were formerly held by the state (Holmes, 2012), and many of these NGOs in turn, are increasingly working with large business interests, and taking on a culture of business, as discussed in the final section of this chapter.

Civil society, NGOs and development

It has been suggested that the last decade of the twentieth century witnessed the 'rise and rise of civil society' (Edwards, 2001b: 2). Certainly through the

1990s, there was a rapid growth in the volume and depth of writing on civil society, from which were to come 'agents of change to cure a range of social and economic ills left by failures in government or the marketplace' (Van Rooy, 2002: 489). To this was subsequently added a political development role for civil society actors as part of the good governance agenda. This 'rise to prominence', whereby NGOs now work in association with a host of different actors in development, 'has itself been based on a set of general arguments about their strengths and distinctive competences as providers of "development alternatives" that offer more people-centered and grassroots-driven approaches to development' (Banks et al., 2015: 708). However, there are also concerns that some of those distinctive strengths may now be being undermined.

It has already been seen that the role of NGOs in the direct provision of key services within countries of the Global South expanded rapidly through periods of macro-economic adjustment as the capacity of many governments in this arena declined. Numerous autonomous associations in civil society have also been identified as a characteristic of, and a route to, more democratic societies. Whilst not unproblematic, the positive role of NGOs in these processes of political change is widely taken as 'axiomatic' (Mercer, 2002: 6). The role of international advocacy groups was also seen above to vital in prompting institutional change within the international financial institutions.

These brief examples hint at the diversity of actors encompassed within this arena of 'civil society' and the varied ways in which they work with other actors in development. This is part of the explanation for the proliferation of writings on civil society. The examples also point to how the 'interest' in, or of, civil society to promote development changes can be contrasting and as Edwards (2001b: 1) cautioned; 'Civil society is an arena, not a thing; although it is often seen as the key to future progressive politics, this arena contains difficult and conflicting interests and agendas'.

This section looks at the key characteristics of civil society and NGOs, in particular. It identifies their 'traditional strengths' especially in relation to sustainable development and in promoting democracy, but also how their roles are changing through new alliances with other actors more recently. Further illustrations of the outcomes of these activities in practice are in Part III.

What is civil society?

The concept of civil society is not easily defined, as discussed in Chapter 3. Most commonly, it is identified as an arena for association and action that is distinct and independent from both the state and the market: a voluntary, self-regulating, 'third' sector in which citizens come together to advance their common interests (excluding business). It includes both formal organisations, such as religious bodies, cultural societies, professional associations, trade unions and NGOs, as well as more informal types of association, including a host of informal networks and mutual support groups. For Banks and Hulme (2014: 189) 'it is not the participating civil society organisations themselves, but the space in which they are formed and participation in dialogue and negotiations to advance their interests, that constitutes "civil society"'.

However, while some interpretations stress the 'form' of a certain part of society, other definitions stress the 'norms', or particular characteristics of a society deemed 'civil'. Such interpretations focus on the social values and attributes, including trust, tolerance and cooperation, that characterise 'civil' ways of being and living in the world that are 'different from the rationality of either state or market' (Edwards, 2001b: 5). It is in this sense that discussions of civil society are closely aligned to debates concerning social capital, referring to the networks and norms of behaviour that link people to each other and within communities.

The terms 'civil society' and 'non-governmental organisation' are often used interchangeably. However, NGOs are only part of civil society and, as already seen, 'any particular selection of non-governmental organisations may very unequally represent a society' (Woods, 2000: 835). Box 7.4 looks at the diverse characteristics of NGOs in more detail. Social movements are also part of civil society, but are not equivalent to NGOs. The term tends to be used to refer to coalitions and networks that are less institutionalised than NGOs, although NGOs may provide an organisational focus for these movements. Social movements, such as environmentalism and feminism, are often referred to as 'new', in that they have mobilised people around issues of natural resources and gender relations that are distinct from the 'old struggles' concerning class and labour (Routledge, 2002). A common feature of new social movements is that they seek to challenge existing systems and structures and tend to operate outside the organised political sphere (see Chapter 1 and Plate 7.6). For Ford (1999: 73), the central distinction between new social movements and NGOs is that the former tend to reject engagement with mainstream institutions to advocate a deeper, more radical challenge; 'it is not just about influencing the agenda but fundamentally altering the system and building a new agenda that puts people and the planet first'.

Plate 7.6 Contesting airport expansion, UK
(*photo*: Julie Doyle)

BOX 7.4

NGOs introduced

Conventionally, the principal defining feature of NGOs has been that they are 'not government', but private organisations operating on a 'not-for-profit' basis. Further primary distinctions are often made between NGOs according to the scale of their operation, or between those that exist for members' or mutual benefits as distinct from those that exist for public benefit.

▶

BOX 7.4 (continued)

Some of the most 'well-known' NGOs, such as Greenpeace or Oxfam, are examples of NGOs that operate for public benefit at the international scale, that are based in the North, but have branches in the Southern countries in which they work. Such International Non-Governmental Organisations (or 'INGOs' as they are often referred to as seen in Table 7.16) are relatively permanent and institutionalised and are staffed by paid professionals. Many have very large budgets. It is suggested that Oxfam, CARE, Médécins Sans Frontières and Save the Children all have budgets over US $500 million and together distribute more development aid than the entire UN system (Desai and Kharas, 2009: 1112)

Typically, public benefit NGOs work in two main areas: in campaigning and policy advocacy work, or in service delivery (Greenpeace and Oxfam are illustrative of these kinds of work, respectively). At times, NGOs that were originally set up for advocacy work may move into service provision where this complements their promotional or lobbying work.

In recent years, there has been an expansion of NGOs at a national level within the Global South, working in both campaigning and service delivery for public benefit. Typically, they centre on particular issues, such as human rights or conservation, or assisting particular groups, such as landless labourers or women. Many international NGOs increasingly work in partnerships with such national and provincial, particularly service providing, organisations.

A further category of NGOs is those that form around, and exist for, members' interests. These are typically local and issue-based, reflecting the goals and immediate concerns of members. For these reasons, they are often termed 'grassroots' or 'community-based' organisations. Examples would include work teams, burial societies, village cereal banks and squatter associations. They may have varied degrees of formality, their formation may or may not have been stimulated from within or outside those communities, and they may be quite short-lived and 'may dissipate once their immediate concerns have been addressed' (Desai, 2014: 568).

It is important to note that many of the 'conventional distinctions' between NGOs, such as according to size or whether they are recipients or donors of aid, have been blurred in recent years by the substantially different ways of working and new alliances with other actors.

Table 7.16 NGOs come in all stripes

INGO – International NGO

BINGO – Big international NGO

TANGO – Technical assistance NGO

CONGO – Corporate-organised NGO

DONGO – Donor organised NGO

GONGO – Government-organised NGO (not really an NGO)

PANGO – Party NGO (set up by a political party, not really an NGO)

Briefcase NGO – NGO set up only to draw donor funds

CBO – Community-based organisation

Source: compiled from Godrej, 2014.

There has been an expansion in recent years (see Chapter 4) of social movements developing quite rapidly and operating transnationally, enabled by social media and ICT, as people across global regions are acting increasingly, not on behalf of others as in the past, but in solidarity with each other as their common interests are recognised.

The role of NGOs in sustainable development

The search for sustainable processes and patterns of development has been a primary force in the mounting attention given to NGOs at a variety of scales (see Elliott, 2013; Edwards and Gaventa, 2001). At a local scale, promoting the empowerment of communities, whether through new or existing local institutions, is key to more sustainable development, given that resource use decisions are ultimately made at the household level (in the context of wider environmental, political-economic and social forces). As Pye-Smith and Feyerarbend (1995: 304) noted, 'an essential element of sound resource management is a local body that discusses, organises, plans, takes action and responds at a human scale'. It is also widely understood that poverty, as a symptom of the disempowerment of local people, is a major constraint on sustainable development in the future (WCED, 1987; Elliott, 2013). It has become evident that much presumed 'lack of care' regarding the environment at the local level arises because 'people do not feel in charge of or, indeed, do not have the power to act' (Pye-Smith and Feyerarbend, 1995: 303).

It is widely acknowledged that NGOs and community benefit organisations have a number of characteristics that potentially make them particularly suited to effecting more sustainable development outcomes. These include their 'grassroots orientation' (Banks et al., 2015), their ability to innovate and adapt to local context, their 'relative smallness' and the recognition of local needs, values, knowledges and realities (Chambers, 1993). In addition, their social proximity (Malena, 2000), the tradition of working with the poorest groups, with women as well as men, and from the grassroots (Craig and Mayo, 1995), and the calibre, commitment and continuity of staff (Conroy and Litvinoff, 1988) have proven to be essential characteristics in developing the relationships with local peoples and shaping the prospects for more sustainable patterns and processes of development.

Further discussion of the importance of the local context in sustainable development is provided in Part III. However, the conditions for sustainability extend beyond this level. For example, the power of particular groups at a local level is shaped also by broader social and political structures, including patriarchy at all scales. Global scale processes also underpin substantially the privatisation of environmental resources that is occurring widely at a local scale (see Chapter 10). There are many examples of projects which aim to foster com-

munity participation but have served to aggravate inequalities (see Guijt and Shah, 1998, *The Myth of the Community*). Although community empowerment necessarily involves the challenging of social structures, it cannot be assumed that all interests are served equitably through 'community development efforts'. The challenge of changing wider structures for more sustainable outcomes is also confirmed by the growing range of southern based social movements that have developed in recent years in response to widespread social and environmental conflict due to the loss of local control over environments, natural resources and indigenous land rights (see Martinez-Alier, 2002).

At an international scale, it was seen that large 'INGOs' have historically been important through their advocacy roles in challenging multilateral organisations, including the World Bank and the WTO, and corporate interests over their environmental and social impacts/performance. Indeed, Godrej (2014) notes that some of the most activist INGOs have been in the environmental arena. However, large charitable organisations are now working in very different ways, including as competition for financial support has increased in the context of global economic crisis. An increasing proportion of their funding, for example, now comes from governmental and inter-governmental aid agencies and from corporate donors (Godrej, 2014). Business thinking and a wider corporate culture now characterises many of these larger NGOs, and many are headed by people from the business world. Concern is that the 'not-for-profit' characteristic of NGOs becomes compromised, as they 'have to survive as bureaucracies, something which requires considerably more finance than that which is spent on their supposed beneficiaries' (Thomas and Allen, 2000: 210). The links between NGOs and corporations can be longstanding. CARE in the US, for example, has collaborated with Coca-Cola for over 30 years (Brown, 2014). However, there are mounting concerns that such relationships are compromising the historic ability of INGOs to hold big business to account, as considered in the Critical reflection. Furthermore, it is in the environmental arena that 'some of the most corporate friendly and compromised INGOs are found' (Godrej, 2014: 15).

Critical reflection

NGO-corporate linkages

Since 2001, Save the Children has been in partnership with the pharmaceuticals giant GlaxoSmithKline (GSK). GSK has a commitment to reinvest 20 per cent of its profits into projects strengthening health care infrastructure, and research into child-friendly medicines within the Global South (Brown, 2014). Save the Children has a programme with GSK that seeks to improve the lives of a million children in Africa. However, GSK was fined 3 billion dollars by the US government in 2012, for activities including bribing of doctors, and encouraging the prescription of Paxil (an antidepressant) to children even though the drug had not been approved for this use and was unsuitable. Save the Children have been quoted as being 'aware of the reports on the historic issues relating to Paxil . . . but our belief is that the risks are outweighed by the benefits of the partnership' (cited in Brown, 2014: 16).

Oxfam has a 'Behind the Brands' campaign that aims to provide people with the information needed to hold some of the largest global food and beverage companies to account. However, they are also in a partnership with one of these companies, Unilever, through its 'Corporate engagement' programme. The suggestion is such programmes, in fact, seek to incorporate thousands of smallholder farmers into Unilever's global supply chain (Brown, 2014). The Head of Oxfam's private sector team has identified Unilever as a 'vocal advocate for tackling climate change and new business models that benefit poor farmers' and confirms that Oxfam 'will continue to engage with Unilever and other companies because reducing global poverty and inequality is good for business and us all' (cited in Brown, 2014: 17).

Critical reflection

Consider the opportunities and problems associated with the close association of companies and charities. Have the charity and corporate worlds become too close?

Furthering democracy through civil society organisations

There is also an increasing interest in NGOs in terms of their roles in promoting more democratic processes of development (see Desai, 2014: Mercer, 2002). This centres on their existence as autonomous, self-regulating actors, and their potential political role in development. Banks et al. (2015) suggest that the perceived advantages of NGOs as grassroots 'democratizers of development' is so widespread that it could be considered their 'defining' characteristic. In short, NGOs are considered to provide opportunities for association and collective action, and to provide channels for representation and political participation (Banks et al., 2015). NGOs are also considered to have a comparative advantage over other institutions for promoting democratic processes through their defining principles and structures. As Edwards and Hulme (1992: 14) pointed out, membership of NGOs is more often based on a commitment to a normative purpose than to a narrow self-interest. Their organisational frameworks also tend to be more democratic than hierarchical; 'simple, human concern for other people as individuals and in very practical ways is one of the hallmarks of NGO work'. Table 7.17 expands on the range of considered roles for NGOs in promoting more democratic development.

However, Mercer (2002: 6) cautions the uncritical consideration of the positive role of NGOs for democratic development as a serious issue, 'not least because of the key role NGOs now play in donor-, government- and even World Bank-funded development projects and programmes'. As seen above, NGO activity expanded rapidly though the 1980s, in the context of economic and political liberalisation, and the increased funding available for NGOs working in services and social welfare provision, for example. NGOs were set up, and/or changed their key activities, according to this availability of funds and donor priorities. As service providers,

Table 7.17 The role of NGOs in promoting democratic development

➤ Expand and strengthen the institutional arena by bringing more democratic actors into the political sphere
➤ Increased opportunities for a wider range of interest groups to have a voice
➤ More autonomous organisations that can act in a watch-dog role over state activities
➤ More opportunities for networking and fostering alliances that can channel public opinion, put pressure on the state and bring about reform
➤ Can strengthen the state through participation in measures to improve the efficiency of government services, to fill gaps in service provision and to help government foster links with grassroots groups, for example
➤ Can have a key role during and after democratic transitions

Source: compiled from Desai, 2014.

NGOs were increasingly required to operate in more market-driven ways and to be commercially competitive. Many smaller and more community-based organisations were driven out of that market (Malena, 2000). In this context, it is recognised that NGOs face significant constraints and contradictions in their ability to strengthen civil society, to maintain a political agenda, to represent the interests of their beneficiaries or to tackle longer term structural issues that underpin poverty (see Banks et al., 2015; Mercer, 2002).

Whilst national and local political environments are diverse across the Global South, the relationship between NGOs and the state is understood as being important in shaping the extent to which NGOs can act politically and/or engage in processes of institutional change. States can work to substantially compromise and restrict the space for NGOs to organise, network and campaign, for example. A recent example has been the Indian Government blocking access of Greenpeace India to foreign funding on the basis that Greenpeace campaigns, on Genetically Modified Organisms and extractive industries, are a threat to India's national development (Bunsha, 2014). Another case is the accusations of corruption and forced resignation of Mohammed Yunus from the Grameen Bank (seen in Chapter 10), that is widely understood to be linked to

his attempts, subsequent to him being awarded the Nobel prize, to create a new political party and foster political change within Bangladesh (Banks et al., 2015). Perspectives on the political role of NGOs have also changed substantially since 9/11, and amidst concerns that varied civil society organisations could be being used as a front for terrorism both nationally and internationally (Shaw, 2014).

It is evident through this section, that there are many varied expectations in development being placed on NGOs and CBOs, and these are likely to continue into the future. NGOs have grown in size, number and capacity, and their impacts and ways of working have expanded to include engagement in global policy processes. Concerns regarding the accountability of NGOs to local beneficiaries and their effectiveness in terms of ability to impact at a significant scale, are quite longstanding. It is some of the newer alliances being made, particularly with private sector interests, that are now leading concerns for the capacity of NGOs to deliver 'real alternatives' in development practices (Banks et al., 2015).

Conclusion

This chapter has identified the nature and activities of a range of institutions that variously set and shape development policies, deliver investments and widely influence the directions and outcomes of development policies, programmes and projects. Assessing the role of these institutions has been set in the context of continued debate concerning the relative role of the three pillars of state, market and civil society to best promote development. It is very evident that multiple institutions, mechanisms and relationships at various scales are involved in the processes of steering societal concerns. It is also clear that there are many new actors in the development landscape currently and significant change in the way that different actors are now working in new alliances to address the challenges of governance globally. Many of these relationships involve the flow of people, finances and natural resources and this is the focus of the next chapter. In Part III, the outcomes of the activities of these institutions in development are considered in more detail.

Key points

> The institutional landscape of development is characterised by a range of organisations, bodies, agencies and individuals. All these institutions are dynamic and under continued change, as is the relationship between them.

> Institutions are not neutral factors in development processes, rather they are engaged in inherently political activities, creating both opportunities and barriers for particular groups and individuals in development.

> Recent decades have seen an increasing role for international financial institutions, transnational business and civil society in shaping development outcomes, but also new alliances between them.

> Significant changes in the distribution of economic power globally in the last decade have led to the questioning of the legitimacy and effectiveness of key institutions of global governance, including the UN and the World Bank, and have challenged them to recognise the role and participation of countries of the Global South.

> Finding responses to global challenges of sustainable development and economic crises has required significant changes in the roles of, and the relationship between, the spheres of the state, the market and civil society.

> Ongoing critical analysis of institutions and the relationships between them is needed, not just for the ways in which they 'do development', but also for the way in which they may constrain development opportunities and present barriers for particular groups and social actors.

Further reading

Desai, V. and Potter, R.B. (2014) (eds.) *The Companion to Development Studies*, 3rd edn. London: Routledge.
11 succinct chapters in this volume are given to the consideration of Governance and Development making an excellent starting point for the debates raised in this chapter

Edwards, M. and Gaventa, J. (eds) (2001) *Global Citizen Action*. London: Earthscan.
Provides a very good overview of the processes underpinning the rise of civil society in shaping development practice

Mohan, G., Brown, E., Milward, B. and Zack-Williams, A.B. (2000) *Structural Adjustment: Theory, Practice and Impacts*. London: Routledge.
A readable text that draws together the economic, social, political and environmental impacts of the adjustment experience and raises a number of alternatives to structural adjustment.

Mingst, K.A. and Karns, M.P. (2012) *The United Nations in the 21st Century*, 4th edn. Boulder: Westview Press.
A readable overview of the range of institutions and activities comprising the UN system and the pressures for change.

Schaaf, R. (2013) *Development Organisations*. London: Routledge.
A useful introduction to the range of institutions, organisations and actors in development.

Third World Quarterly (2014) Volume 35, number 1.
Special Issue: New Actors and Alliances in Development.

A full journal issue dedicated to considering how development is currently shaped by a wide and more complex range of actors and relationships including business and consumers; NGOs and celebrities; philanthropic organisations and the state; and new donors and governments of the Global South.

World Bank (2001) *World Development Report*, 2000–2001. Oxford: Oxford University Press.
The publication considered to be a landmark in the development of an international consensus concerning the new poverty agenda in international development.

Websites

http://web.worldbank.org/WBSITE/EXTERNAL/TOPICS/ CSO/
Link to information on the ways that the World Bank engages with civil society and materials for CSOs.

https://sustainabledevelopment.un.org/
The central platform for the United Nations work on the post-2015 development agenda and the development of the new Sustainable Development Goals.

www.gatesfoundation.org
Website for the Bill and Melinda Gates Foundation that is one of the key philanthropic organisations now working in international development, particularly in health.

www.oxfam.org
Website of long-established international nongovernmental organisation (INGO). Hosts

substantial materials relating to issues of international trade and debt alleviation, for example, from a more broadly Southern perspective.

https://red.org/

Website for ProductRed – an initiative that seeks to deliver an AIDS-free generation through linking consumers with red-branded products and the Global Fund to Fight AIDS, Tuberculosis and Malaria.

www.unrisd.org

Website of the autonomous United Nations agency, the UN Research Institute for Social Development. Hosts research, information and publications relating to social and equity dimensions of contemporary development concerns, including around corporate responsibility, economic transition, gender, human rights and sustainable development.

Discussion topics

➤ How important do you consider the 'mega-summitry' hosted by the United Nations, such as the Earth Summit in 1992 and the Rio+20 conference in 2012, has been in changing patterns of development worldwide?

➤ How successful do you think the Millennium Development Goals have been?

➤ In what ways could good governance be a means or an end in development?

➤ Has the Global Financial Crisis since 2008 undermined the international financial institutions irrevocably?

➤ Can further trade liberalisation deliver environmental conservation?

➤ Review the arguments that NGOs may be best placed to promote more sustainable development processes. Consider the major contemporary challenges for these institutions to deliver in this way.

PART III

Spaces of development: places and development

Chapter 8
Movements and flows

This chapter examines the movements and flows of people, commodities and finance across the world and particularly in relation to countries of the South. These movements and flows are numerous and often complex, but the chapter attempts to unravel some of the complexities and draws upon case study material to illustrate particular concepts and situations.

The main topics covered in this chapter are:

➤ Population movements – different types of population movements are discussed, including the relationships between rural and urban areas and the impact of migrants' remittances on their home communities;

➤ Tourism and development – tourism is a form of voluntary migration which has accelerated rapidly in recent years and contributes significant amounts of revenue to some countries of the South. The future role and nature of tourism are considered, including possibilities for pro-poor tourism and ecotourism;

➤ Forced migration – sadly the world has no shortage of forced migrants and refugees often living in desperate conditions. Some resettlement programmes are examined, and the effects of civil unrest on communities and livelihoods are considered;

➤ Transport – the world is shrinking as communications improve, yet for many people in the South the basic necessities of life are still not available;

➤ World trade – the concept of an 'interdependent world' is examined, yet poorer countries have relatively little influence on world trade. The World Trade Organization is critically examined, and issues surrounding fair and ethical trade;

➤ Transnational corporations – the large companies operating in the world trading system have considerable power. Other players are strengthening their positions, notably from the BRICS countries (Brazil, Russia, India, China and South Africa). Meanwhile, many transnational companies are giving greater attention to corporate social responsibility in response to consumer criticism of their operations;

➤ The debt crisis – many countries in the South are faced with crippling levels of debt. The nature of this debt and how it might be reduced are examined, including the Heavily Indebted Poor Countries (HIPC) Debt Relief Initiative;

➤ Aid to poor countries – the quantity and quality of overseas development assistance (aid) given by the rich countries to the poor countries is examined.

Introduction: unravelling complexities

In addition to examining the nature of specific development variables in particular locations, geographies of development need also to consider relationships between people, environment and places in different locations and at a variety of different scales, ranging from the micro-level, such as the individual or the household, through the local community level to the regional, national, international and, ultimately, the global level. These relationships are often complex and highly dynamic. The nature and relative significance of these relationships are changing constantly, both through time and space, and are themselves determined to a large extent by complex movements and flows of people, commodities, finance, ideas and information.

This chapter aims to demystify and explain some of these complex and interrelated movements and flows. Starting with a real-world example, in order to illustrate some of the inter-linkages and flows which take place over time and space, we will then consider movements of people, before examining flows of commodities and finance through trade, aid and debt.

Movements and flows in the 'real world': growing coffee for export

Reference to a real world example should help to demonstrate some of the many possible interconnections between people, commodities and finance across the world. Let us consider the case of a resource-poor farming household in Ivory Coast (Côte d'Ivoire), West Africa, whose main income comes from growing coffee for export. Although Ivory Coast is Africa's third largest producer of coffee, and in 2014 was the world's twelfth largest producer (1.5 per cent), world coffee production in 2014 continued to be dominated by Latin American countries such as Brazil and Colombia, which produced, respectively, 32 and 8.8 per cent of the world crop, and also by Vietnam, which produced 19.4 per cent (ICO, 2015). The expansion of coffee cultivation in Ivory Coast dates from the French colonial period when, both after 1930 and again in the 1950s, France assured a guaranteed market at very high prices for large quantities of coffee.

The producer household in Ivory Coast is heavily dependent on receiving a good return from cash crop sales in order to buy food and clothes, pay school and medical bills and hopefully, over time, steadily improve its standard of living. But there is a wide range of factors which can affect household income in any given year. Some of these factors are environmental, but others are social, political and economic.

Inadequate rainfall, declining soil fertility and pest attacks are common, and usually unpredictable, environmental factors. Small farmers would generally receive little, if any, advice and practical help from agricultural extension officers, and they often lack the necessary finance to buy pesticides and fertilisers to raise productivity.

The availability of labour is another key element, perhaps the most important factor in poor households with low levels of technology. Such farmers can rarely afford to hire wage labourers and are often totally dependent on family labour. Family members between the ages of 15 and 40 years are likely to be the fittest and therefore particularly valuable for working on the farm. But if at crucial times in the cropping cycle just one key member becomes unwell, or perhaps decides to leave the village to seek work in the city, then this withdrawal of labour can have a major impact on the productivity and therefore the general well-being of the entire household.

Rural producers are also affected by a range of economic and political decisions that are well beyond their control. For example, many farmers and others have been affected to a greater or lesser extent since the mid-1980s by structural adjustment programmes (SAPs) imposed by major international donors such as the World Bank and the International Monetary Fund (IMF) (see also Chapters 3 and 7). In fact, it might be suggested that 'not since the days of colonialism have external forces been so powerfully focused in shaping Africa's economic structure and the nature of its participation in the world system' (Binns, 1994a: 163). Currency devaluation, raising interest rates and the removal of subsidies and price controls are just a few of the measures that were commonly introduced by SAPs (Mohan, 1996: 364).

In the case of Ivory Coast, with primary products representing over 75 per cent of exports, the country had a total external debt of US $8.96 billion in 2013, and government debt to GDP ratio of 54.1 per cent

(World Bank, 2015c). As far as the coffee farmer is concerned, currency devaluation can also have a significant effect on returns from coffee sales. In fact, shorter or longer term fluctuations in the prices which producers receive for commodities such as coffee can have a major impact on household economy and well-being.

With the dominance of Brazil and Colombia in world coffee production, one or more of a variety of factors affecting production in these two countries could have a significant effect on the world coffee price. In simple terms, overproduction could lead to lower world prices, whereas a fall in production, perhaps due to changes in the Brazilian climate, might result in higher world coffee prices. This happened in early 1997, when prices reached a 20-year high due to extremely cold weather in Brazil, forcing producers to relocate entire coffee plantations to warmer areas. More recently, in 2009, the daily weighted average price of Brazil Arabica coffee was 116.55 cents per pound, but by 2011 the average price had risen to 248 cents per pound. But in reality the factors affecting world prices are complex. Among farmers in the South, the decision to invest in the production of 'cash crops' such as coffee is usually taken when prices are high. It may involve a major reorientation of household activities and a significant switch of labour inputs from food to cash crop production. There is evidence to show that in some cash crop producing areas family nutrition has actually suffered due to a relative neglect of food production (Kennedy and Bouis, 1993). Furthermore, by the time the first cash crops are harvested, which may be up to 10 years after planting, prices may well have fallen below the levels which existed at the time of planting.

The situation is further compounded by the fact that producers in the South generally only receive a small fraction of the final selling price of commodities such as coffee. Within producing countries there are usually networks of buyers, agents and sub-agents, each taking their share of the price, to say nothing of the substantial element taken by large transnational companies who process the final product in Europe or North America. An Oxfam study in 1993 revealed that in Uganda, where coffee accounted for 90 per cent of all exports, coffee growers received the equivalent of £0.08 (just 5 per cent) of the final value of a jar of coffee which was sold in UK supermarkets for £1.60. In sharp contrast, the shippers and roasters, who are generally part of one transnational corporation, received 65 per cent of the final selling price (Oxfam, 1994).

To reduce the impact of fluctuating world coffee prices on small producers, Oxfam's Bridge programme provided a market for producers from the South, paying Fairtrade prices and purchasing through organisations which ensure that the bulk of the price actually reaches the producers. Bridge is involved with three other trade organisations in marketing 'Cafedirect', where the coffee is purchased directly from small farmers, who receive a price linked to the minimum floor price set by the International Coffee Organisation. As Oxfam points out:

> When Cafedirect was launched (1989) during the trough in world coffee prices, producers were paid $1.20 per lb. Had they been selling in the international market, they would have been paid around 65 cents per lb.
>
> (Watkins, 1995: 148)

Cafedirect is now the UK's largest Fairtrade hot drinks company, and has links with 40 producer organisations in 14 countries, 'ensuring that over a quarter of a million growers receive a decent income from trade' (http://www.cafedirect.co.uk/smallstory/our-history/, 2015).

The purpose of presenting this case study, which is typical of so many situations, is to demonstrate that the smallholder coffee producer in Ivory Coast is just one element in a complex system of relationships involving local, national and international movements and flows of people, commodities, finance, ideas and information (see Critical reflection). Too often in the past, researchers have considered just one element in the system without appreciating the interconnectedness at different scales. As we have seen in earlier chapters (especially Chapter 4), globalisation is one of the most significant features of the late twentieth and early twenty-first centuries. With the increasing speed and frequency of international air travel since the 1960s, and most especially with the 'great leap forward' during the 1980s and 1990s in the transmission of information through satellite communication and the internet, the world is indeed becoming a 'global village' in one sense. Unhappily, however, as in so many communities (and particularly those in poor countries), there is a wide and ever growing disparity between the wealth and living standards of the 'haves' and the 'have-nots' (Chapter 4).

Although it would be impossible to identify, let alone discuss, the many movements and flows across the globe, this chapter aims to shed light upon some of those which involve people, commodities and finance. We will first examine movements of people, and then consider trade, aid and debt, emphasising wherever possible the changing nature of these movements and flows over time and space.

Critical reflection

Rooibos tea production in Wupperthal, South Africa

Rooibos (red bush), a form of herbal tea that is indigenous to the Cape Floral Region in South Africa's Western Cape Province, is believed to possess health-giving properties; notably it is caffeine free, has a low tannin content and contains compounds which act as antioxidants. As a result, *rooibos* enjoys a rapidly growing international market. *Rooibos* production only occurs in a mountainous region some 200–300 km north of Cape Town, where micro-climates and soil conditions are particularly favourable. A community of 400 families that has benefited from *rooibos* tea is Wupperthal, located in a remote area among the high valleys of the Cedarberg mountains. During the 1990s, the community was struggling economically, and an unemployment rate of 80 per cent caused a steady stream of young people to head for Cape Town, since the only local work available was in vegetable farming, local shoe and glove factories and seasonal farm labouring.

In the 1990s, an NGO called A-SNAPP (Agribusiness in Sustainable Natural African Plant Products), visited the area to conduct a 'needs assessment', and began to develop a highly successful relationship with the community. A-SNAPP operates in nine African countries and helps community-based agribusinesses to compete in international markets. Grants worth £50,000 were accessed from various South African government departments and agencies. The funds were used to resuscitate the old 'tea court' in Wupperthal, buy a tractor, lay a new sheet of concrete in the tea-drying area, enlarge the drying floor to 1,000m², extend the storage shed and build a new store. These developments enabled the community to process their tea locally, rather than having to transport the raw material 70km to Clanwilliam, the nearest town.

The community's customers have included European and North American Fair Trade distributors, such as TopQualiTea and Equal Exchange. Prices are favourable, since the high altitude of Wupperthal ensures good quality tea, which is also produced organically. The community gained accreditation from the Fairtrade Labelling Organisation (FLO) in 2005, which set minimum standards for economic dividends and opened up more market opportunities.

Who benefits?

The Wupperthal initiative has achieved a significant level of success, such that since 1998 the number of farmers has increased from 25 to 170, while annual *rooibos* production has risen from 16 tonnes to over 100 tonnes in good years. Incomes for farmers have risen noticeably. Cooperative members are now able to add value to the product that they grow by utilising their own tea court for processing. The establishment in March 2006 of the Fair Packers packaging venture in Cape Town further strengthened the community's control over downstream elements of the value chain.

This expansion of the *rooibos* enterprise has already generated employment for Wupperthal migrants, as well as providing producers with an increased share of the value of their product. Most farmers now employ up to four labourers, and an additional 14 people work at the tea court. Furthermore, labourers are now able to gain employment locally without having to circulate around other farming regions in search of seasonal work. In this way, Wupperthal-sourced *rooibos* operates through an increasingly separate supply network to that of the vast majority of Cedarberg *rooibos*, which is produced on plantation style farms owned by white farmers, where opportunities for black people rarely extend beyond low-paid farm labour.

Funding from *rooibos* sales, which is boosted by guaranteed Fairtrade prices and the Fairtrade premium, has also been invested in farming equipment and the local school. Furthermore, the community's sense of self-determination has increased substantially and reflects the widespread benefits that have been derived from tapping into a niche consumer market for a product that is healthy, environmentally friendly and ethically produced.

What are the likely advantages and disadvantages of communities such as Wupperthal linking with global trading organisations?

Source: see Bek et al. (2006) for further reading.

People on the move

Population movements, or migrations, have been taking place in various shapes and forms for centuries, and there are many detailed studies and publications on this topic. As was recognised in Chapter 5, the movement of people within and between countries has played an important role in determining population growth rates and in affecting other factors such as ethnic composition and the spread of disease, including HIV/AIDS. In Chapter 10, the significance of migration (and the remittances 'back home' by family members) in shaping contemporary rural livelihoods is discussed.

In broad terms, population movements may be divided into 'forced' and 'voluntary', but then more detailed classifications commonly focus on such aspects as the distance covered and the frequency and time span over which the migration occurs. Some writers differentiate between 'migration' and 'circulation' (Drakakis-Smith, 1992; Gilbert and Gugler, 1982; Gould, 2009). Migrations are usually more permanent or irregular and can involve a lengthy change of residence, whereas circulations are generally shorter, sometimes daily, periodic or seasonal. Much interest has also been shown in the decision making which is involved in the migration process, and in the consequences of migration for the well-being of the migrant and the migrant's family, as well as the problems and benefits which migration causes in both the source and reception areas.

Seasonal migration and circulation

Although some population movements have a long history, there seems little doubt that colonial policies played a key role in accelerating the process. In Africa, the introduction by the colonial powers of taxation in the form of cash payments, together with the creation of many new towns, mines and cash-cropping areas, led to large-scale migration of wage labourers. In West Africa, for example, the movement of Mossi men from Burkina Faso to help with the cocoa harvest in Ghana and Ivory Coast has been going on for many years and the money they earn provides a vital addition to their poor villages in Burkina.

In northern Nigeria, with a long dry season when little can be cultivated on non-irrigated farms, there is a tradition of seasonal migration which is known by local Hausa people as *cin rani*. Since the great majority of migrants in this strongly Muslim region are men, they are more correctly known as *masu cin rani*, 'men who while away the dry season' (Prothero, 1959). Commonly, men leave their homes in the dry season to visit relatives and/or to engage in craft industries, trade or irrigated farming.

Before the 1930s, Prothero reports that there was little reference to seasonal migration in the Sokoto region of north-western Nigeria, but a traffic census in 1928 recorded 3,500 migrants per month passing southwards through Yelwa on the River Niger and heading mainly for the large towns of Yorubaland in south-western Nigeria. Dry season migration seems to have accelerated during the 1930s, such that the *Annual Report for Sokoto Province* in 1936 noted that 'there has been a large seasonal migration to the Gold Coast [Ghana] and elsewhere by men in search of money to pay their tax and support their families' (Prothero, 1959: 22).

A later survey, undertaken in Sokoto Province in the dry season of 1952–53, enumerated some 259,000 predominantly male migrants, with south-western Nigeria and Gold Coast (Ghana) as their main destinations. Some 92 per cent of migrants were seeking to supplement their income in various ways, through such occupations as labouring, petty trading, fishing and craft work. It seems likely that, on their return home, migrants probably brought more money into Sokoto Province than they could have created without migrating (Prothero, 1959). But much time is spent in travelling, and Prothero argued that the Province would gain a great deal if this labour could be diverted to local productive work, for example in the expansion of cotton and groundnut production for export. A particularly significant point, which has relevance for other poor migrant source areas, is that 'the total number of migrants away from the Province for several months of the year must go a considerable way towards conserving [food] supplies in the home areas' (Prothero, 1959: 34).

Seasonal migration is well established in other parts of the South. For example, much of the labour force for cutting sugar cane in north-west Argentina comes from neighbouring areas of Bolivia, where unemployment and poor wages provide an incentive to migrate. Whereas this generally involves migration on a seasonal basis, migrants have sometimes settled in Argentina, moving to cities such as Buenos Aires, where there are better employment opportunities (D. Preston, 1987).

Rural–urban migration

One particularly significant form of migration in many countries of the South is from rural areas to towns and cities, for reasons such as advancing education or to obtain specialist health care (see Chapters 5 and 9). Young people are frequently attracted to towns by the 'bright lights' syndrome – the idea that the towns have modern facilities compared with what are often perceived as being backward and traditional rural areas. In many parts of the South, economic reasons play the most important role in drawing people to the cities. For many, and particularly for young males, a spell in the big city is seen as an opportunity to earn a good income and is also regarded as an initiation into adulthood and Western culture.

In Central America, Mexico City's population grew from 14 million in the 1980s to a massive 20 million by 2015. Now the largest city in North America, much of this growth was due to migration. Meanwhile, on Mexico's once predominantly rural Yucatan Peninsula there has been rapid development of tourism since the 1970s, which led to the city of Merida tripling its population in 25 years, to reach 650,000 in 1992, representing almost half of the state's total population. Ninety per cent of migrants to the city have been drawn from Yucatan's rural areas, whereas villages surrounding Merida have become dormitories for commuters working in the city (MoBbrucker, 1997).

A fascinating Indian study of some 50 years of migration from the rural village of Sugao, in Maharashtra State, to the city of Bombay, over 150 miles away, revealed some interesting features about both the migrants and the process of migration (Dandekar, 1997). Significantly, over a long period of contact between village and city, a valuable city-based network of village relatives and friends was established, and this played a key role in locating jobs and providing shelter for newcomers. Most urban employment continued to be in the textile industry, though its relative importance has declined in recent years. Few rural families remained untouched by the migration process, which has been overwhelmingly male-dominated. Remittances from city workers have had a major impact in improving conditions back in the village, such that almost half the households have piped water and more than two-thirds have electricity. However, very few men actually left Sugao permanently, and generally returned home when their productive working life was over and it became too expensive to remain in Bombay (Dandekar, 1997).

International migration and remittances

In the last four decades, international migration has increased significantly from about 76 million in 1960 to an estimated 232 million migrants in 2013. The rise in international migration is a key characteristic of the increasingly interconnected world and migration for economic reasons are often significant in overall flows (see Willis, 2014). The number of skilled migrants from the Global South has also increased dramatically in recent decades, providing many positive benefits at the family level. In 2004, some 55 per cent of migrant Nigerian workers in OECD countries were regarded as highly skilled, whilst the corresponding figure for South Africans was 48 per cent. The main destinations for skilled migrants from the Global South are the USA, European Union, Canada, Australia, some Middle East countries, India and some other Asian countries (Page and Plaza, 2006).

The significance of remittances sent by migrants to their families back home should not be underestimated. Remittances may take the form of various goods and commodities, as well as money, and they can have a significant impact on household livelihoods in the South. Flows of remittances have become significantly easier in recent years with developments in international money transfer services, ICT generally and transport improvements. In 2010, an estimated US $325 billion was sent in remittances to countries of the Global South, representing a significant increase on the two previous years which were affected by the Global Financial Crisis (World Bank, 2010a). Such events as the Global Financial Crisis (GFC, 2008–2012) and the earlier Asian financial crisis in 1997 undoubtedly had a significant impact on the value of remittances reaching the South. In 2010 India (US $55 billion) and China (US $51 billion) were the two largest recipients of migrant remittances. In terms of the value of remittances as a share of a country's GDP, the figure for Tajikistan (35 per cent) was the highest, followed by the Pacific island state of Tonga (28 per cent) and the small southern African country of Lesotho (25 per cent) (World Bank, 2010a).

Many small Pacific island countries depend heavily on imported goods and finance, which is all too evident on flights from Auckland to Apia, the capital of Samoa, with travellers carrying large quantities of electrical goods, clothes, food and other items. Whilst the population of Samoa in 2013 was 190,000, there were a further 144,000 Samoans living in New Zealand. In fact, it is often claimed that Auckland is the largest Samoan city! New Zealand Samoans have a material standard of living which is twice as high as Samoans living in Samoa. In 2010 an estimated US $143 million was sent in personal remittances from overseas Samoans to their families, churches and schools in Samoa. This figure represented 21.7 per cent of GDP and about three times what the country received in foreign aid. The biggest sources of remittances were the USA (39 per cent) and New Zealand (31 per cent). The flows of income to Samoa and other Pacific islands are in fact substantially higher than most official records suggest, since visiting relatives frequently carry large quantities of cash, especially during the Christmas period.

In West Africa, a survey was undertaken in 1996 in eight villages close to Kayes in the Senegal River valley of Mali, a region which supplies large numbers of migrants to France. The Soninke migrants from Mali and neighbouring Mauritania and Senegal have been settling in France since the 1920s. Among the 305 households surveyed, there was an average of 2.6 migrants from each household, remitting about US $1,500 in 1996 to their households in Africa. As Azam and Gubert comment,

> The amounts at stake are considerable: using the World Bank's poverty line of $US1 a day, remittances received per household represent on average no less than the annual consumption expenditures required for keeping three individuals just above the poverty line . . . It is far from certain that these 2.6 migrants on average would have been able to produce an output worth that amount, had they stayed with their family. It is almost certain that they would not have been able to produce such a surplus over and above their own consumption.
>
> (Azam and Gubert, 2006: 446)

Azam and Gubert conclude that remittances play a crucial role in the economies of the households which they studied, and in those households where there was at least one member living overseas, remittances represented a very significant 50.8 per cent of total gross household income (Azam and Gubert, 2006).

Attempts have been made to examine the impact of international migration and remittances on poverty. Adams and Page, after studying data from 71 countries in the Global South, conclude that, 'on average, a 10 percent increase in the share of international migrants in a country's population will lead to a 2.1 percent decline in the share of people living on less than US$1 per person per day' (Adams and Page, 2005: 1660). Evidence also suggests that in those households receiving remittances from migrant family members children generally receive more schooling and households experience better health care (Page and Plaza, 2006: 286).

On the other side of the migration equation, whilst benefits can fall at the family level, there are concerns for the loss of resources at a country scale, often referred to as a 'brain drain', where those who have been trained in their home countries take their labour and skills overseas in search of better incomes and working conditions. As Willis (2014: 213) notes, 'more educated, skilled and dynamic individuals are over-represented within economic migrant flows'. The departure of health professionals from poor countries has been a particular concern. As Page and Plaza observe in the case of Zimbabwe, 'three-quarters of all doctors emigrate within a few years of completing medical school' (Page and Plaza, 2006: 294). Such losses have to be weighed up carefully against income from remittances, return migration and the creation of trade and business networks. The latter are important and often undervalued, and it has been suggested that 'recent attention has shifted from analyzing the impact of skilled migration on sending country labour markets, to a broader agenda that also considers the possible channels by which migrants promote trade, investment and technological acquisition' (Page and Plaza, 2006: 295).

Growing urban populations

Many towns and cities in the Global South are growing rapidly, in many cases more rapidly than overall national population growth rates (see Chapter 9). Although Africa is still overwhelmingly a rural continent, with some 70 per cent of the population in sub-Saharan Africa living and working in rural areas, the average annual urban growth rate of 4.3 per cent between 1990 and 2005 was more rapid than for any other part of the world, and much of this growth was due to rural–urban migration (UNICEF, 2006). In 2013, six out of the ten countries with the highest annual rates of urbanisation were in sub-Saharan Africa, with several exceeding 5 per cent – Niger, 5.1 per cent; South Sudan, 5.2 per cent; Tanzania, 5.4 per cent; Uganda, 5.4 per cent; and Rwanda, 6.4 per cent (World Bank, 2015c). In the immediate post-independence period, rapid rural-urban migration was fuelled by significant increases in urban formal sector wages. It is estimated that real average urban wages increased by 40 per cent in Zambia between 1964 and 1968, compared with only a 3 per cent increase in farmers' incomes. In Tanzania, the real urban minimum wage increased nearly fourfold between 1957 and 1972 (Jamal and Weeks, 1994).

Concern has been expressed about feeding these growing urban populations and the availability of employment, and terms like *over-urbanisation* have been used (Gilbert and Gugler, 1982: 163; Gugler, 1997: 114–23). For example, in Ghana during the first decade after independence (1957–1967), the urban population grew by 6.6

per cent, but employment in the modern sector increased by only 3.3 per cent, whereas registered unemployment rose by as much as 9.3 per cent each year (Knight, 1972). Another early study by Gutkind in Lagos estimated that in 1967 approximately 21 per cent of all males over 14 were actively seeking work (Gutkind, 1969). While searching for work, many migrants relied on the support system provided by friends and relatives, who could assure a level of survival not radically different from that experienced in the rural village. Work is often gained through such ethnic and kinship links and the higher wages earned by a few manage to 'trickle down' to support those marginally employed and even unemployed. Others will in time find employment in the highly diverse 'informal sector', which might involve working in a family tailoring or carpentry workshop, or perhaps more likely begging or hawking on street corners, or even illegal activities such as prostitution and theft.

Governments and academics have given much thought to strategies for controlling rural–urban migration, notably the reduction of urban–rural differentials through the improvement of living standards in the rural areas and the redistribution and generation of more urban employment opportunities (Becker and Morrison, 1997). However, Riddell concluded in the late 1970s that

> there is no easy remedy for spatial differentials: urban incomes cannot be lowered because of the severe economic and political implications; jobs in the modern sector cannot be created in sufficient numbers because of the limitations upon the national economy; and rural agriculture cannot be transformed because of the scale of the problem and the very limited results likely to accrue.
>
> (Riddell, 1978: 260)

In South Africa, under the oppressive apartheid regime, rural–urban migration was tightly controlled, Black migrants were forced to carry identification passes and their movements were closely regulated by police and security forces. However, during the 1980s and 1990s, rural–urban migration in South Africa accelerated considerably with the progressive relaxation of apartheid controls.

In the 1980s and 1990s the situation changed dramatically in many countries, with structural adjustment programmes, falling urban incomes, deteriorating urban services and public sector retrenchments leading to a massive decline in urban living standards, which has resulted in urban growth rates and migration processes adjusting to urban economic conditions, in some cases leading to people actually moving back to rural areas (Chapter 9). The rural–urban income gap collapsed in the 1970s and 1980s, and by the 1980s it seems that a 'new urban poor' had developed in many African cities (Jamal and Weeks, 1994). In Ghana, indexes of real minimum wages showed a rise from 100 in 1970 to a peak of 149 in 1974, then a massive decline to 18 in 1984. In Tanzania, there was a rise from 100 in 1957 to 206 in 1972, then a fall to 37 by 1989.

The gap between rural and urban incomes in many countries either vanished or actually shifted in favour of the rural sector. In Sierra Leone before the 1990s civil war the average non-agricultural wage in 1985–1986 was estimated to have been 72 per cent less than average rural household incomes (Jamal and Weeks, 1994). Riley suggests that by 1986 the urban poor in Sierra Leone were 'a deprived group with fewer income or equivalent earning opportunities than the rural poor', which had adverse effects on levels of infant mortality and malnutrition (Riley, 1988: 7). Households have often responded by engaging more in informal sector activity, with wage earners taking on additional cash-earning activities, and by growing food on any available pieces of land (see Case study 9.3).

Jamal and Weeks (1994) suggest that in Uganda another coping strategy is for urban residents, particularly from non-local ethnic groups, to migrate to rural areas. The 1980 Zambian census revealed a slowing down of urban growth rates and indicated a significant increase of urban–rural migration. Surveying the evidence, Potts suggests that a form of counter-urbanisation has been taking place in a number of African countries, 'where the number of urban residents opting to leave the city and move to rural areas has exceeded the number of rural–urban migrants' (Potts, 1995: 259). These 'return' migrants are often the poor and unemployed who are moving back to their rural homes, and this movement seems to be over and above the patterns of circulation between rural and urban areas which are such a long-established feature in many African countries.

International tourism and the Global South

Another type of population movement is represented by the phenomenal growth in international tourism since the Second World War, from only 25 million tourist arrivals in 1950 to 800 million in 2005 and 1,087 million in 2013 (WTO, 2014). Although Europe remains the dominant source and destination of international tourists, the expansion of air travel and the quest for adventure and exotic places has led to a massive increase in long-haul travel, particularly to the Caribbean and Central America, to Asian countries such as China, Hong Kong, Malaysia, Thailand and to African countries such as Morocco, The Gambia, Tunisia, Kenya and South Africa (see Chapters 4 and 6).

Tourism makes a valuable contribution to the economies of some countries in the South (Table 8.1). For example, tourist arrivals in Thailand have grown over 5 per cent per annum since 2000, with 26.5 million arrivals in 2014 generating receipts of over US $46 billion. In 1988, tourism actually earned more for Kenya than either of the two traditional exports of coffee and tea, and the 676,900 tourists who arrived in the country contributed no less than US $404.7 million to the economy. By 1995, despite exchange rate fluctuations, tourism accounted for 16 per cent of GDP and brought gross receipts of US $486 million, compared with US $350 million from tea. Almost half of the international visitors to Kenya in 1995 came from Germany and the United Kingdom (Binns, 1994a: 146). The systemic effects of the 11 September 2001 terrorist attacks in New York led to international tourist arrivals in 2001 being 4 million down (−0.6 per cent) on the 2000 figure. The most affected regions were South Asia (−6.3 per cent), the Americas (−5.9 per cent) and the Middle East (−3.1 per cent). Europe registered a decrease of −0.6 per cent, while Africa and the Eastern Pacific region experienced an increase in tourists of 3.8 per cent and 5.5 per cent, respectively (WTO, 2002).

Tourism also provides a considerable amount of employment, both directly within hotels and also indirectly through taxis and transport, craft industries, restaurants and entertainment. The spectacular tourism development on Mexico's Yucatan Peninsula since the 1970s has transformed a once sparsely

Table 8.1 International tourism receipts and tourist arrivals in selected countries (with large or fast-growing tourist industries)

Country	International tourism receipts (US $million) – 2012	International tourist arrivals (1000s) – 2012	Average annual growth in tourist arrivals (%) – 2008–2012
Angola	711	528	79.5
Armenia	487	843	51.0
Australia	34130	6146	10.0
Cambodia	2000	3584	68.6
China	54937	57725	8.8
Costa Rica	2544	2343	12.1
Egypt	10823	11196	–8.9
France	63530	83013	4.7
Kenya	2004	N/A	N/A
Mexico	13320	23403	2.1
Mongolia	480	476	6.7
Morocco	8491	9375	18.9
New Zealand	5467	2473	4.3
South Africa	11201	9188	–4.2
Thailand	37740	22354	53.3
Uganda	1105	1197	41.8
Ukraine	5988	23013	–9.8
United Kingdom	45966	29282	–2.9
USA	200092	66969	15.5
Yemen	1057	1174	14.7

Source: UNWTO (2012) *UNWTO Tourism Highlights 2012 Edition* [online], [cit. 2012-07-04], http://mkt.unwto.org/en/publication/unwto-tourism-highlights-2012-edition. Accessed 15 Jan 2015.

settled agricultural region around Cancun and has resulted in considerable in-migration, which is linked to work opportunities both in the construction industry and servicing the growing tourist population (MoBbrucker, 1997).

In many countries of the South there is considerable potential for strengthening the linkages between the tourist sector and local food and drink production and supply systems, thus reducing the need for expensive imports. However, in Fiji, the linkages have been limited due to high imports of goods, hotel furnishings and services, and the repatriation of substantial profits by airline companies and foreign-owned hotels, which account for almost 60 per cent of bed capacity (Lockhart, 1993; see also Scheyvens, 2011). In some countries there is an increasing trend towards providing all-inclusive tourist packages, whereby visitors receive all their meals and refreshments in hotels, and they therefore have little need to use local bars and restaurants (see Critical reflection box).

Critical reflection

Are all-inclusive tourist packages a good idea?

An all-inclusive package is when tour operators provide all food and beverages inside the hotel, in addition to providing transport and accommodation. The price paid by tourists is usually significantly lower than if they have to purchase their own meals and beverages at restaurants and bars outside the hotel. With the convenience and affordability of such all-inclusive holidays, there has been a marked growth in demand for this type of package over the past two decades. However, in many countries of the Global South there has been considerable debate about the merits and problems of all-inclusive packages.

Hoteliers and tour operators point to a range of benefits, such as:

Critical reflection (continued)

➤ Increased hotel earnings which lead to an increase in government revenues

➤ More employment opportunities and greater job stability in hotels

➤ If tourists spend most of their time within the grounds of the hotel, there is less risk of them facing crime and harassment

However, a number of disadvantages of such packages are also apparent:

➤ Tourists with all-inclusive packages are likely to arrive with less spending money when their meals and beverages are included in the overall package price

➤ They are less likely to venture outside the hotel to spend their money in local bars and restaurants and in purchasing locally made crafts and souvenirs

➤ This can have a negative impact on local business revenue and employment

➤ It might also be suggested that tourists on all-inclusive packages have much less direct contact with local people, so there is less chance of breaking down stereotypical views of the country and its people

With reference to particular case studies, do you consider that all-inclusive packages are a good way forward in promoting tourism in the Global South?

There are several concerns relating to the growth of tourism in poor countries. Hotel owners are often expatriates and a large proportion of tourism-related jobs are low paid; the wages of Kenyan hotel staff are lower than in many other sectors of the economy, except possibly agriculture and domestic service. Tourism may also be a strongly seasonal activity, such that during slack seasons staff may be laid off without wages. The impact of tourism on environment and society is a further controversial issue. The loss of valuable farm and grazing land and the 'dilution' of local cultures, with the transference of Western values and patterns of behaviour, are among the major concerns (see also Chapter 4). In small countries such as those of the Caribbean and the islands of the Pacific and Indian Oceans, along with states such as The Gambia in West Africa, there is a danger of large numbers of tourists overwhelming the country and its people (Plate 8.1). The small Caribbean island of St Lucia has a population of only 186,730, yet in 2015 it attracted 1,073,017 visitors, of whom 344,908 were stay-over tourists, while the majority of the rest (677,394) were cruise ship passengers (St Lucia Tourist Board, 2015).

In Africa, The Gambia is the smallest mainland country and one of the poorest, with an average life expectancy in 2013 among its 1.8 million people of only 59 years. South of the capital, Banjul, the 30-kilometre Atlantic coastal strip is being steadily taken over for hotel building, to cater for the growing number of tourists wanting to escape the European winter. In 2013, some 157,000 tourists visited the country and numbers are growing, particularly with stability restored after the July 1994 coup. However, following the coup, 1995 proved to be a low point for the Gambian tourist industry, which in the late 1990s contributed 12 per cent of GDP and provided direct and indirect employment to about 10,000 Gambians.

The great majority of The Gambia's tourist infrastructure is still confined to the coast, with most tourists seeking a beach holiday with the occasional day excursion. There are a few 'up-country' camps catering for more adventurous travellers, but so far they have had a limited impact on the rural hinterland. Indeed, there is some concern within the country about the possible negative effects of encouraging the penetration of larger numbers of tourists into the poor, remoter rural areas. Theft, begging and prostitution are already commonplace in the coastal area, as relatively wealthy visitors, invariably with little local knowledge, are seen as easy prey to those who are desperate to make a living. Similar problems are evident on the Kenyan coast.

In Kenya, farmers and pastoralists have had their traditional lands incorporated into national parks, where wild animals have caused damage to crops and livestock. The traditional pastoral economy of the Masai has been severely constrained, whereas some critics have questioned the profitability of allocating large areas of Kenya for wildlife-based tourism. Like other countries

Plate 8.1 Globalisation and international tourism: a tourist hotel in The Gambia
(*photo*: Tony Binns)

which are experiencing increasing pressures from tourism development, Kenya is keen to promote ecotourism which, in theory at least, is designed to have a more sensitive and sustainable approach to people and the environment. It remains to be seen whether this happens (Box 8.1).

BOX 8.1

Pro-poor tourism and ecotourism

The literature on the developmental impacts of tourism, mainly in the South, but to a certain degree also in the Global North, has in recent years sought to identify whether tourism can actually be regarded as, and encouraged to become, a 'pro-poor' development strategy (Binns and Nel, 2002; Scheyvens, 2011). Poverty alleviation/elimination is the core focus of 'pro-poor tourism' (PPT). But there is often some confusion as to how PPT relates to other tourism concepts such as 'ecotourism', 'sustainable tourism' and 'community-based tourism'. In an attempt to clarify the situation, the Pro-Poor Tourism Project explains:

> PPT also overlaps with both ecotourism and community-based tourism, but it is not synonymous with either. Ecotourism initiatives may provide benefits to people, but they are mainly concerned with the environment. Community-based tourism initiatives aim to increase local people's involvement in tourism. This is a useful component of PPT. But PPT involves more than a community focus – it requires mechanisms to unlock opportunities for the poor at all levels and scales of operation.
>
> (Pro-Poor Tourism, 2002: 1)

As Ashley and Roe (2002: 61) argue, 'despite commercial constraints, much can be done to enhance the contribution of tourism to poverty reduction, and a pro-poor tourism perspective assists in this endeavour'. In support of this approach, Sharpley (2002: 112) argues that, 'tourism has long been considered an effective catalyst of rural socio-economic development and regeneration'.

Sharpley does, however, question whether tourism can in fact be regarded as a developmental panacea.

BOX 8.1 (continued)

Even though positive evidence of the impact of tourism-based development on communities can be found in localities such as Taquile island in the Peruvian section of Lake Titicaca (Mitchell and Reid, 2001), the reality is that in many countries control often remains vested in the hands of outsiders, such that local communities are often only incorporated at a subservient level. This can easily lead to negative effects, such as resource depletion and the loss, or commodification, of culture. As Tourism Concern Director, Patricia Barnett comments on Belize,

It now has a highly competitive tourism industry, more interested in marketing a product than ensuring that it is environmentally sound, or that the people are benefiting from it. Local people are marginalized as outsiders buy up the land. Locals are angry that they can no longer access their own forests, which have been their natural home for generations and their islands are sold out to American ecotourism developers.

(Tourism Concern, 2002: 2)

As Weaver (1998: 91) has shown, also in Belize, although ecotourism has spawned development initiatives in local communities, 'the overall number of local residents affected is probably quite low, due to the limited number of parks that accept significant visitor numbers and the tendency of groups to visit on a day-only basis'.

The Gambia in West Africa is attempting to restructure its tourist industry so that both poor people and the environment achieve greater benefits. For example, the government is opposed to 'all-inclusive' deals in hotels, since they limit many opportunities for local service providers to earn a living from tourism (see Critical reflection box above on all-inclusive

tourist packages). The country's rich cultural heritage and its wildlife, particularly birds, are an important feature of the tourism development programme, and in 1998 an Ecotourism Task Force was established. An ecotourism map of the country has been produced and various sites have been identified as having good potential.

In 2000 one of the first ventures, the Tumani Tenda Ecotourism Camp, received an award from the German Institute for Tourism and Development as being a good model of community-based ecotourism. The camp, accommodating some 40 visitors in huts built from local materials, is located about 500 metres from a small village alongside a tributary of the River Gambia and adjacent to Kachokorr Community Forest, protected by, and for, the community since the mid-1980s. Meals are produced entirely from local ingredients, while water is provided by a solar-powered pump. Target groups are ornithologists and study groups who can take guided forest walks, canoe trips on the River Gambia to accompany fishermen or help women with oyster collection, and there are a variety of workshops such as batik production, traditional healing practices, and the production of vegetables and medicinal plants. The project has enhanced environmental awareness, as well as alleviating poverty among the local community. In the two years following its establishment in 1999 the project raised over £14,500 for the community, which was used to finance the village kindergarten and school. The entire village has been involved in the project, from designing and building the camp to arranging tourist programmes, while useful links have also been developed with Tourism Concern Gambia and the UK organisation Voluntary Service Overseas.

Perhaps Kenya and other countries could learn from the experience of the Central American state of Costa Rica, where ecotourism has been successfully developed. The Monteverde Cloud Forest Reserve (MCFR) in western Costa Rica was designated in the early 1970s and is an area of great biological diversity. Visitor numbers increased rapidly from only 471 in 1974 to 49,552 in 1992. With annual visitor numbers (2000–2014) of around 70,000, the MCFR is now one of the main ecotourism destinations in Costa Rica, and the tourism industry has led to the creation of over 80 different businesses, of which a large percentage are locally owned, including hotels, restaurants, craft shops and bookstores. Additionally, tourism has led to the improvement of local education and the conservation of natural resources, and successful community participation has resulted in Monteverde becoming one of the most prosperous and successful communities in Costa Rica.

Forced migration

In the case of forced migration, the decision to relocate is made by people other than the migrants themselves. The Atlantic slave trade was one of the largest forced migrations in history when, from the late sixteenth to the early nineteenth centuries, over 10 million Africans were transported to work on plantations in North and South America and the Caribbean (see Chapter 2).

In the 1980s, in West Africa, Nigeria shocked its neighbours by expelling 2 million foreign workers in 1983, and a further 700,000 in 1985. The purpose of the expulsion was supposedly to reduce unemployment among its own people during the slump following the 1970s oil boom, but other members of the Economic Community of West African States (ECOWAS), notably Ghana, whose nationals constituted the majority of those expelled, were appalled at Nigeria's action and argued that it contravened the 'spirit' of earlier ECOWAS agreements.

A further example of migration, where there is some controversy about the level of force involved, concerns the movement of over 6 million Indonesians from densely settled Java, where 57 per cent of the national population lives on 7 per cent of the land area, to some of the other 13,000 less populated islands and national territories. Population resettlement began in 1905 under Dutch colonial rule, but accelerated after Indonesia gained independence in 1945, and became even more intensive in 1969 under the government's aggressive 'transmigration programme'. Hancock (1997: 234) has described this migration as 'the world's largest ever exercise in human resettlement'. Furthermore, it has been supported by funding from a number of national and international development agencies. Between 1976 and 1986, the World Bank committed US$600 million to the programme, and further assistance has been given by the governments of the Netherlands, France and Germany, as well as USAID, UNDP, EEC, FAO, the World Food Programme and Catholic Relief Services.

The programme has been highly controversial in many ways, including migration to Irian Jaya (West Papua), the name given by the Indonesian authorities to the western half of the island of New Guinea, which they formally incorporated in 1969 with the approval of the UN. Land was taken by force for settlers from Java, which has fuelled a growing conflict between Indonesian armed forces and nationalist Irianese (Papuans). Reports suggested that villages have been bombed, people tortured and shot dead, with over 20,000 Irianese fleeing their homes and seeking refuge in neighbouring Papua New Guinea. Additionally, the Indonesian government wants to settle and 'assimilate' all Indonesia's tribal peoples, including moving (with force if necessary) Irian Jaya's entire indigenous population of 800,000 tribal people into resettlement sites on the island (Hancock, 1997: 235; UNPO, 2014).

Transmigration has also happened elsewhere in Indonesia, with East Timor being seized by the Indonesian army in 1975, to provide for further resettlement from Java. An estimated 150,000 indigenous inhabitants of East Timor were either killed in fighting or died of hunger. In October 1999, the United Nations Transitional Administration in East Timor (UNTAET) was established, leading to East Timor eventually gaining its independence on 20 May 2002 under the democratically elected government of President Xanana Gusmã o.

Other examples of forced migration in Southeast Asia (Plate 8.2) are the massive outflow of Khmer and Lao fleeing genocide and invasions in the late 1970s and early 1980s, and the many refugees escaping from Vietnam during the 1980s, in some cases as 'boat people' journeying to places such as Hong Kong in search of asylum. Meanwhile, in 1990s Africa streams of refugees fled into neighbouring countries to escape civil wars and state collapse in Liberia, Sierra Leone, Rwanda, Burundi and Mozambique (Allen, 1999) (see Box 8.2).

After the Soviet invasion in 1979, Afghanistan lost millions of its people, fleeing mainly to neighbouring countries such as Iran and Pakistan. By 1990 there were an estimated 6.3 million Afghans in exile, over 3 million in each of Pakistan and Iran and some further afield. Following the overthrow of the Taliban regime in November 2001, the Afghan Transitional Authority and the United Nations High Commission for Refugees

(UNHCR) successfully repatriated more than 1.3 million refugees in the five-month period from March to August 2002 (UNHCR, 2002).

Migration overseas is often preceded by internal displacement within the home country, and some countries have large numbers of internally displaced people (IDPs) who have fled from their homes to seek greater security (see Box 8.2). In 2011 there were an estimated 26.4 million IDPs around the world, of whom 15.5 million were under the care of UNHCR in 26 countries (UNHCR, 2015). In Syria and Libya in 2014, as a result of ongoing instability and associated violence, there were respectively 6.5 million and 140,000 IDPs. By early 2015, an estimated 50,000 Syrians had sought asylum in some 90 countries, mainly in Europe (UNHCR, 2015). Ongoing instability in places such as Libya, Eritrea and Somalia has led to a steady stream of migrants and asylum seekers crossing the Mediterranean from North Africa and landing in southern Europe. In 2012, a total of 15,000 migrants landed in Italy and Malta, some 13,200 of these arriving in Italy. Crossing the Mediterranean, often in small and overcrowded boats, has led to many tragedies, and in 2012 some 500 migrants were reported dead or missing at sea (UNHCR, 2015).

In recent years, the issue of 'environmental migration' has received increasing attention, particularly, though not exclusively, in relation to the impact of climate change on small and low lying island states, which are seen as being vulnerable to sea level rise and an increasing frequency of extreme climatic events such as storm surges and flooding (Chapter 6). One of the earliest references to 'environmental refugees' was by El-Hinnawi, in a 1985 paper from the United Nations Environment Program (El-Hinnawi, 1985). The Intergovernmental Panel on Climate Change (IPCC) has advocated further research on the issue of environmental migration, suggesting that, 'some adaptation measures appear to be advocated, particularly for small islands' (IPCC, 2007: 711–2).

The South Pacific state of Tuvalu is an example of a country where climate change could have a serious impact on livelihoods. The country comprises five low lying atolls and four coral islands, with no place higher than 4.5 metres above sea level. Whilst the country's territory covers an area of 750,000 sq km, the land area is only 24.4 sq km, inhabited by a population of about

11,000. Tuvalu is becoming increasingly vulnerable to storm surges and a gradual rise in sea level (Shen and Binns, 2012). The country has longstanding and harmonious relationships with New Zealand and receives significant amounts of international aid from New Zealand. Over 2,000 Tuvaluans live in New Zealand, 81 per cent of them in the largest city, Auckland.

The issue of whether Tuvaluans can migrate to New Zealand should conditions on the islands become intolerable due to the effects of climate change, has been raised on many occasions, but the New Zealand Ministry of Foreign Affairs and Trade has taken a firm stance on this matter, stating that,

New Zealand does not have an explicit policy to accept people from Pacific island countries due to climate change. Stories circulated in the media stating that New Zealand has an agreement with Tuvalu to accept people displaced by rising sea levels due to climate change are incorrect. The Government of Tuvalu has acknowledged that there is no such agreement with New Zealand. New Zealand has no such arrangement with any other Pacific Island country.

(NZ MFAT, 2015)

Those Tuvaluans who have managed to migrate and settle in New Zealand have generally been more educated, better skilled and more wealthy than those who remain in the islands, raising concern about the steady 'brain drain' from such a poor country with limited resources (Shen and Binns, 2012). The New Zealand government is aware that a number of other Pacific island countries like Tuvalu are also vulnerable to the effects of climate change, for example Kiribati and Tokelau, though the latter is a territory of New Zealand. In response to this the New Zealand Ministry of Foreign Affairs and Trade has issued a statement recognising,

that climate change poses a significant threat for our neighbours in the Pacific, including the many small island developing states that are most vulnerable to its impact. The New Zealand Government's efforts are focused on providing a range of assistance to support Pacific-identified priorities in addressing climate change. New Zealand has made a voluntary commitment of NZ$5 million per year

Plate 8.2 Refugee camp for Rohingya Muslim refugees from Burma in southeast Bangladesh
(*photo*: Howard J. Davies, Panos Pictures)

to assist with climate change projects in developing countries, and much of this is directed to the Pacific, including through NZAID's Pacific Regional Environmental Programme.

(NZMFAT, 2015)

Vulnerability to climate change has also been uppermost in government policies in the Maldives, an Indian Ocean state comprising 26 atolls, where 80 per cent of the land inhabited by some 400,000 people is less than one metre above sea level. Since 2004 the country has

been developing a National Adaptation Programme of Action to address the most vulnerable elements of the country's population and environment (Maldives Government, 2009).

There is a need for more detailed understanding of the relationships between environmental degradation and forced migrations, and the United Nations and other organisations should be ready to provide humanitarian aid, particularly when entire communities are displaced (Renaud et al., 2007).

BOX 8.2

Civil war and forced migration in Sierra Leone

Over the last three decades, the small West African state of Sierra Leone has become synonymous with political instability, economic devastation and a brutal civil war that lasted most of the 1990s. The protracted conflict ravaged much of the country, and brought immense suffering to its people, with an estimated 50,000 deaths and the displacement of over half of Sierra Leone's 5 million population. Many towns and villages were completely

evacuated, particularly in the diamond mining areas of the country's Eastern Province, where fighting between RUF (Revolutionary United Front) rebels and government troops was most intense. The population of Freetown, the capital city, mushroomed during the conflict as refugees sought a safe haven and support from aid agencies.

As massive dislocation occurred, economic activities were severely disrupted, much of the country's

BOX 8.2 (continued)

infrastructure was destroyed or badly damaged, and poverty became widespread and deeply entrenched. Consequently, Sierra Leone, over 10 years after the civil war ended in 2002, had the dubious distinction in 2014 of being ranked 183 out of 187 countries according to the UN's Human Development Index (UNDP, 2014).

Since the completion of the disarmament process in January 2002, significant progress has been made towards peace and recovery in Sierra Leone, including the extension of civil authority throughout the country, peaceful parliamentary and presidential elections, and the return home of thousands of internally displaced persons (IDPs). Although these are encouraging signs, much remains to be done to improve livelihoods and to set the country on a path towards sustainable development. The government has joined with national and international partners to make a concerted push towards reconstruction and development, and a National Recovery Strategy launched in 2003, based on needs assessments conducted in all districts, aimed to provide a framework for these recovery efforts.

The causes of the debilitating conflict were complex, but it is commonly agreed that the origins of instability extend back well beyond the last 25 years, and embody a mixture of factors including bad governance, the denial of fundamental rights, economic mismanagement and social exclusion. The Eastern Province towns of Kayima and Panguma are typical of many settlements that felt the brunt of the war and its associated atrocities. A post-conflict survey in 2004 found that the proportion of demolished buildings was 34 per cent in Kayima and 32 per cent in Panguma, but vandalism was widespread and indiscriminate during the RUF incursions, such that very few buildings were left totally unscathed. The RUF also destroyed bridges, schools, hospitals, markets, community halls, water pipes, and in the case of Panguma, the electricity supply and sawmills. Several times during the conflict both communities had to be completely evacuated.

Although residents have been steadily returning since 2002, housing shortages are still a major problem. In addition to the widespread physical destruction of infrastructure during the civil war, the impact on the social fabric of rural society was equally damaging. Considerable efforts are now urgently needed to rebuild community cohesion and institutions, and to rehabilitate rural livelihoods in remote rural areas.

Source: see Binns and Maconachie, 2006.

The impact of migration on environment and health

The Indonesian resettlement programme has destroyed vast areas of rainforest in one of the most biologically diverse areas of the world. Sumatra alone has lost 2.3 million hectares of rainforest and the cleared land has rapidly become severely degraded. More than 30 per cent of Sulawesi has been reduced to a similar state. Hancock (1997: 237) suggested that by 1996 some 300,000 people were estimated to be living in 'economically marginal and deteriorating transmigration settlements', and were recognised by the Indonesian government itself as 'a potential source of serious political and social unrest in the future'. Infrastructure in the shape of clinics, schools and roads was often inadequate and the settlers suffered from malaria and other diseases.

The land became so impoverished that many people moved back to the towns and cities. In recent years, although transmigration has been reduced from its aim of settling 20 million people, the scheme still continues, with private companies running enterprises such as the Barito Pacific plywood factory on Mangole Island, and the creation of new settlements to supply cheap labour for agribusiness, the timber industry and mining.

The potential environmental impact of the large-scale displacement of populations can be considerable, as was the case during the Ethiopian crisis in the 1980s (Box 8.3). However, two studies undertaken in the mid-1990s among Mauritanian refugees in the Sahel region of the middle Senegal River valley in Senegal (Black, 1997), and in areas of settlement by Liberian refugees in the remote forest zone of eastern Guinea (Black, 1996), revealed some decrease in woodland areas, but remarkably little other negative impact on the environment. In the Senegal study, Black questions whether changes in the fragile environment can indeed be attributed entirely to the influx of 50,000 refugees, and concludes that because the refugee population became dispersed over a large area and good relations were maintained with local communities, there was little conflict over natural resources between the two populations. In Guinea, a similar number of refugees were also spread over a wide area and, as in Senegal, they were largely of the same ethnic groups as the local populations. Black (1996: 37) could find 'little or no evidence that refugees are using natural resources in a more "wasteful" manner than local people'. In both studies it seems that the degree of dispersal of refugees, the generally good relations between refugee and host populations and the existence of strong local institutions seem to have been key factors in minimising environmental impact.

BOX 8.3

The 1980s refugee crisis in Ethiopia

Some of Africa's poorest people are the millions who have been forced to flee from war, terrorism, persecution or natural disasters such as drought. It was estimated that in 1991 there were about 4 million refugees in tropical Africa (O'Connor, 1991), and in the same year Oxfam warned:

> In Africa as many as 27 million people now face starvation as a result of drought and war . . . The famine threatening millions of Africans is on a greater scale than the famine of 1984/85.
>
> (Oxfam, 1993: 20)

Famine and refugees in 1991 were associated with Liberia, Angola, Mozambique, Ethiopia and Sudan, but since then people have been forced to leave their homes in Somalia, Sierra Leone and in the Great Lakes region of central Africa, most notably the small and densely settled states of Rwanda and Burundi.

Mohamed Amin's film and Michael Buerk's commentary from Korem, Ethiopia, in October 1984 produced what was probably one of the most powerful pieces of television documentary ever; to millions of comfortable homes around the world it brought images of starving refugees. Here is part of the commentary:

> Dawn, and as the sun breaks through the piercing chill of night on the plain outside Korem, it lights up a biblical famine, now, in the 20th century. This place, say workers here, is the closest thing to hell on earth. Thousands of wasted people are coming here for help. Many find only death. They flood in every day from villages hundreds of miles away, felled by hunger, driven beyond the point of desperation. Death is all around. A

> child or an adult dies every 20 minutes. Korem, an insignificant town, has become a place of grief.
>
> (Harrison and Palmer, 1986: 122)

This report had a significant global impact and was instrumental in generating such popular fundraising efforts as Band Aid and later Live Aid, which took place simultaneously in London and Philadelphia in July 1985 and broke new ground in worldwide satellite communications, raising over US $100 million by mid-1986.

The causes and effects of Africa's continuing refugee problem are highly complex and each case has its unique features. Nowhere is this more evident than in the case of Ethiopia in the early 1980s, where drought, rural impoverishment and armed conflict all played a role in generating a serious refugee problem (see Figure 8.1). Ethiopia has a long history of famines. The great majority of rural Ethiopians in the 1960s were living in conditions which were similar to those of European peasants in the Middle Ages. Feudal landlords exacted heavy taxation and other obligations from their subjects; quite apart from the sheer volume of produce leaving the peasants' hands, the amount of time spent working for the landlord cost dearly in lost production.

It was the repercussions from droughts in Wollo during 1965–1966 and 1972 that eventually brought to an end the 44-year rule of Emperor Haile Selassie in September 1974, with the takeover of the Provisional Military Government of Socialist Ethiopia, known as the Derg. A land reform programme was quickly introduced, but in the years immediately following the revolution, food and cash crop production

BOX 8.3 (continued)

was disrupted by the many uncertainties caused by the radical transformation in land tenure arrangements. A poor distribution of surplus grain supplies, combined with an inadequate transport infrastructure, severely hampered redistribution to food deficit areas.

But the origins of the refugee problem which developed in the 1980s must also be examined in the context of the Derg's heavy military expenditure and its involvement in a series of costly and protracted conflicts. The civil war in Eritrea was ongoing, having begun in 1962 when Haile Selassie dissolved the

Figure 8.1 Map of Ethiopia in the 1980s
Source: adapted from Oxfam, 1984.

▶

BOX 8.3 (continued)

federation between the two countries and annexed Eritrea to Ethiopia. The war in Tigray started in 1975, and was concentrated in the densely settled central highlands and the important agricultural region in the west of the province. To compound the situation further, the Derg's forces were engaged in a war with Somalia in 1977–1978 over the disputed Ogaden region. American military aid was withdrawn and Ethiopia requested Russian and Cuban aid, which had the effect of alienating many Western governments. In addition, the Derg massively increased its defence spending to US $378 million in 1981, representing a higher per capita military expenditure than any other country in sub-Saharan Africa, and giving Ethiopia the second best equipped army on the continent, after South Africa (Harrison and Palmer, 1986: 94).

Against this background of conflict, poor rains in the early 1980s resulted in hardly any harvest in the northern regions of Wollo, Eastern Gondar and parts of Tigray in 1982 (see Figure 8.1). Refugees abandoned their homes and flooded across the Sudan border to await relief supplies. The main rains in July 1983 also failed, and it was estimated that more than 2 million people in Tigray and Eritrea were seriously affected by the drought and needed emergency assistance. The relief supply situation in both regions was further complicated by the lack of security, due to the separate armed conflicts with the government of Addis Ababa. The liberation fronts accused the government of withholding relief supplies and aid donors were also criticised for channelling all their relief through the government, when many of the people at risk were actually in areas not under government control.

The Relief and Rehabilitation Commission (RRC) of the Ethiopian government reported in May 1984 that the official population of 7,800 in the Wollo town of Korem had been swelled by some 35,000 displaced people gathering at the feeding centre there, with a further 110,000 people registered to receive emergency food supplies from the RRC store in Korem.

The RRC argued that it was too stretched to distribute seeds to ensure people could plant a crop during the July rains, and other seed distribution schemes were ineffective due to the security situation.

One long-term solution to the droughts in northern Ethiopia tried by the government was to move people out of the highlands to new RRC settlements in the south. However, this policy proved unpopular since highland farmers were reluctant to leave their lands and, when they did move away, they would require food and other subsidies for some years before they could regain self-sufficiency. The situation in Ethiopia deteriorated during 1984 as the central highlands and areas near the Kenyan border in the south were also affected by drought. In the eastern province of Harerge, close to the Somali border, the RRC estimated that some 350,000 people, mostly pastoralists, were at risk.

The Ethiopian refugee crisis, which reached its peak in 1984, was caused by an inability to break the constant cycle of drought–famine–emergency feeding, largely due to the continuing conflicts in the northern provinces and the Derg's heavy military expenditure. Both relief aid and long-term development projects were severely hampered by the conflict situation, but there was also a need for the improvement of basic infrastructure, particularly roads, health services and water supplies, and for the introduction of better agricultural techniques and conservation measures such as terracing and reafforestation to reduce people's vulnerability during future droughts.

In April 2000 Ethiopia was once again in a crisis situation, with 8 million people facing food shortages and over half the country's population living on less than US $1 a day. In May 1998 the governments of Ethiopia and Eritrea declared war over a border dispute. As a result, over £600,000 a day was spent by Ethiopia on funding the conflict, having serious effects on the country's economic and social progress and undermining the food security situation (Department for International Development, 2000c).

Migrants and disease

Population movements can have a significant impact on disease transmission and health. Prothero (1994) has demonstrated the significance of interactions between a variety of diseases and population mobility in tropical Africa, just as the spread of *falciparum* malaria, which is resistant to chloroquine, has been facilitated by movements of people, particularly of refugees, in South and Southeast Asia (Prothero, 1994). In African refugee camps, disease and high death rates have been associated with overcrowding, poor accommodation, inadequate water supply, sanitation and waste disposal, as well as the amount and quality of food available. More than half the deaths in the 'emergency phase' are due to measles, diarrheal diseases and acute respiratory infections.

Malaria is a major hazard when refugees from areas of low endemicity are forced to move into areas of high endemicity. Health problems were caused by forced resettlement in Ethiopia and Somalia, where people were moved from the relatively malaria-free Ethiopian plateau above 2,000 metres to lower areas in the west and south-west where malaria was endemic. Irrigation projects at altitudes below 2,000 metres also extended areas of endemic schistosomiasis (bilharzia). In addition, more contact between Ethiopian pastoralists and agricultural settlers increased pastoralists' risk of infection with schistosomiasis. Migrants also experienced nutritional problems, since the traditional cereal crops of the Ethiopian plateau could not be grown at lower altitudes (Prothero, 1994).

The spread of AIDS and sexually transmitted diseases can also be linked to population mobility (Chapter 5). In Burkina Faso, from where there is much migration to Ivory Coast, AIDS is known as *la maladie (ou la diarrhée) de la Côte d'Ivoire*. In Abidjan, Ivory Coast's largest city, some 25,000 deaths occurred from AIDS-related illnesses between 1986 and 1992. The incidence of AIDS along important national and international routes in Ivory Coast, Mali and The Gambia has been reported as being generally much higher than elsewhere in these countries, and lorry drivers, itinerant traders and prostitutes have higher than average levels of infection (Prothero, 1996). In Uganda, Cliff and Smallman-Raynor (1992) examined a number of possible factors underlying the spread of AIDS, including proximity to major roads and migrant labour. They found that the recruitment and movement of Ugandan soldiers in the 1970s and 1980s, and their contact with prostitutes, were key influences in the diffusion of AIDS.

The spread of the highly infectious Ebola virus in the West African countries of Liberia, Sierra Leone and Guinea in 2014 and 2015 was exacerbated by population mobility and direct contact with infected persons. The earliest Ebola cases in Sierra Leone were along the main east–west road from the Liberian border, thorough the city of Kenema and further west to the capital city, Freetown. In an effort to control the spread of the disease, the Sierra Leonean government closed schools and introduced curfew periods when people had to stay in their homes (MSF, 2015).

Communications and transport

In the early twenty-first century we find ourselves in a world where people living and working in rich Northern countries can increasingly perform their business and everyday activities without even leaving their homes, through an ever changing array of technology, including telephone, fax, electronic mail (e-mail) and the World Wide Web (WWW). Virtually instant contact by e-mail is now possible across most of Europe and North America, and the WWW serves the needs of millions by providing vast quantities of information for business, education and entertainment. So-called 'telecommuting', where people work mainly from home, is being actively encouraged by governments and employers in crowded European countries in an attempt to reduce the number of car journeys and the associated pollution.

For many in the privileged North the world is shrinking day by day as innovations come on stream. As we have seen in Chapter 4, the 'globalisation' of a wide range of processes and transactions was a key feature of the last decades of the twentieth century, which is continuing and indeed accelerating in the new millennium. Meanwhile, in West Africa, one of the world's poorest regions, but only six hours' flying time from Europe, millions of people are still without electricity and fresh water supplies; their health and education services are inadequate; and they must work long hours in the fields using low-level technology to produce enough food to satisfy family needs. For many poor people in rural areas of the Global South, their main means of communication, in the absence of television and newspapers, is still word of mouth; such is the 'digital divide' explored in Chapter 4. However, in most countries it is fair to say that the transistor radio has had a considerable impact in the transmission of knowledge and information.

One important development that has massively transformed communication across the Global South is the increasing use of the mobile phone. With poorly maintained and even non-existent land-line telephone systems in many areas, there has been a phenomenal growth in the use of mobile phones in the first decade of the twenty-first century. In Africa alone, the growth in mobile phone use has been staggering, from an estimated 10 per cent using mobile phones in 1999, to 60 per cent in 2008 and well over 80 per cent in 2015. Between 2000 and 2010 Kenya's largest mobile phone company, Safaricom, saw a 500-fold increase in its subscriber base. A study undertaken in 2008 found that South Africa and Botswana had the largest number of subscribers as a proportion of the total population, whilst levels of subscription were lowest in Burundi, Ethiopia and Eritrea (Aker and Mbiti, 2010). Even the poorest households, for whom the cost of buying and using a mobile phone will likely represent a large proportion of their disposable income, frequently rely heavily on phone-based communication.

Mobile phones can play a key role in accessing markets, examining price variability and managing supply chains, which can be important both for farmers selling produce and for market traders securing supplies of agricultural and other commodities. With access to the internet, mobile phones are also used for banking, and the MPESA system launched by Safaricom in Kenya in 2007 for money transfer and micro-financing has proved particularly popular, with 17 million accounts registered, representing more than a third of the total population. Other common uses of mobile phones are for entertainment, education and for social networking. In the so-called 'Arab Spring' pro-democracy uprisings across North Africa in 2011, mobile phones played a key role in promoting activism and opposition to unpopular regimes such as in Egypt, Libya and Tunisia (Aker and Mbiti, 2010).

Despite these significant technological advances, with the high cost and lack of motorised transport, many poor people are still forced to cover thousands of miles each year on foot, often carrying heavy loads. A 1980s study in Ghana estimated that rural households typically spent some 4,830 hours per year in transport activities, particularly collecting water and fuelwood, with most of this work being done by women (Porter, 1996). In such communities there has generally been little tangible improvement in living standards, and certainly no evidence of a shrinking world (Plate 8.3). It is astoundingly difficult at times to appreciate that people with such contrasting lifestyles actually inhabit the same planet!

It was during the colonial era that the first railways and surfaced roads were constructed in many countries of the Global South (see Chapter 2). In Africa and elsewhere, railways were built to ensure strategic and military control, but more especially to extract raw materials, whether cash crops or mineral resources, and typically linked major source areas with coastal ports. English, French and Portuguese colonial powers, far from collaborating in the development of transport infrastructures to 'open up' Africa, were actively competing with each other, such that rail links between neighbouring anglophone and francophone countries never materialised. Despite ambitious plans, single unconnected lines were common within countries, and only states such as Morocco, Nigeria and South Africa can be said to have anything resembling a rail 'network'.

Today, in many African countries, rail transport suffers from a lack of investment and maintenance, and in relative terms is much less important than in the colonial period. For example, the 1,146-kilometre line which links Abidjan in Ivory Coast with Ouagadougou in Burkina Faso carried 3 million passengers in 1988, but only 760,000 in 1993, due largely to the poor condition of the rolling stock. Freight tonnage also fell from 800,000 tons in 1980 to 260,000 tons in 1993 (Economist Intelligence Unit, 1996a).

In Africa's most populous country, Nigeria, the rail system was effectively closed down in 1995, awaiting rehabilitation by a team of Chinese rail engineers.

However, since 2010 there has been some significant progress. In 2012 the Nigerian government signed a US $1.49 billion contract with the state-owned China Civil Engineering Construction Corporation to build a railway between the economic capital, Lagos, and the city of Ibadan. A year later, in February 2013, the 1,100 kilometre line linking Lagos, and the north's largest city, Kano, was eventually re-opened at a cost to the Nigeria Railway Corporation of US $153 million. In Latin America, by 1940 the railway systems of Argentina, Brazil and Mexico accounted for 75 per cent of the region's network, and in these three countries there was significantly more interlinkage of lines than in African countries. The railway system in São Paulo, Brazil, was a key element in the state's industrialisation, facilitating the advance of the coffee frontier, increasing exports and the development of engineering enterprises linked to the railways.

Since the Second World War, road transport has increased in importance, and with growing populations and less traffic carried by rail, roads now have to shoulder a much greater burden (Plate 8.4). In many countries of the Global South the road networks are similar to those constructed during the colonial period, although new capital cities such as Abuja (Nigeria), Brasilia (Brazil) and Islamabad (Pakistan) have necessitated further highway construction. In Nigeria, funds generated by the oil boom in the 1970s had a significant effect on the upgrading of the country's road network; but in the 1990s, like other African countries, and despite an injection of monies from the Petroleum Trust Fund for the rehabilitation of some major trunk roads, general road quality steadily deteriorated. The stringencies imposed by SAPs in countries such as Ghana and Nigeria have had a major impact on road transport, with less road maintenance, fewer vehicles and a severe shortage of spare parts (Porter, 1996).

In tropical regions, road surfaces quickly become pot-holed in the rainy season, and unpaved roads can become completely impassable. Many governments in the South face the difficult dilemma of whether to invest limited funds in building a few all-weather highways to connect the main towns or, alternatively, constructing and upgrading many more kilometres of unpaved rural

Plate 8.3 Cyclists in Kunming, southern China
(*photo*: Tony Binns)

Plate 8.4 Crowded street in Freetown, Sierra Leone
(*photo*: Tony Binns)

feeder roads, which could actually improve the lives of a greater proportion of the population in connecting them with clinics, schools and markets. In reality, it is probably most effective to try to achieve a balance between the two strategies.

For many rural producers, their main concern is how to transport their often perishable produce to markets as easily and quickly as possible. Women vegetable farmers in The Gambia, while praising the assistance from the NGO Action Aid in sinking wells and supplying tools and seeds, were concerned about the lack of reliable and refrigerated transport to carry

their produce to large urban markets (Binns, personal interview, 1997).

North and South: an interdependent world

We live in an interdependent world where links and relationships have developed over time and space and where flows of commodities and finance reinforce these links. But it is also an unequal world, and many would argue that issues such as trade, aid and debt are crucial in perpetuating inequalities both between and within countries.

Plate 8.5 Mobile phone hub in Botswana
(*photo*: Jennifer Elliott)

An important landmark in considering the ramifications of an 'interdependent' world was the Brandt Commission, established in 1978 under the chairmanship of Willy Brandt, former Chancellor of West Germany, and its influential report, entitled *North–South: A Programme for Survival* (Brandt, 1980). Possibly the most memorable thing about this report was the world map on its cover, across which a black line divided the rich North from the poor South (Chapter 1). One of the main themes running throughout the report is the mutual interest of rich and poor countries in a better regulated world economy.

The Brandt Commission covered many issues, but its most important conclusions concerned the international monetary system, the transfer of resources from North to South, better trading opportunities for countries of the South and the nature of aid. A well-argued critique of the International Monetary Fund was presented, with the Commission proposing a system that would place less severe restrictions on borrowing countries and also establish greater stability in exchange rates. Brandt argued for a massive increase in resource transfers between rich and poor countries, with the aim of Northern governments first reaching, and then

substantially surpassing, the target of allocating 0.7 per cent of their GNP to aid. A special initiative was proposed to cope with the world's 30 poorest countries, with a programme of long-term and flexible financial and technical assistance. Within poor countries, Brandt recognised the need for social and economic reforms to reduce inequality.

Reviewing the question of food aid, Brandt suggested that the best long-term solution to food shortages is for food production in poor countries to be increased to meet most of their own needs. Meanwhile, external aid should be devoted mainly to improving the capacity for local food production, rather than shipping in food supplies which, whether free or subsidised, compete with local production and may actually discourage it by depressing prices. The report concluded that the governments of poor countries must devote a large part of their development effort to increasing agricultural production.

Brandt was also concerned that rich countries, while reducing trading restrictions among each other, should consider dismantling trade barriers affecting the import of goods from poorer countries. A new set of trade rules and the negotiation of new commodity agreements were advocated, and both rich and poor countries were urged to liberalise their trading policies.

Brandt recognised the powerful position of transnational corporations (TNCs) within the world economy, which in 1980 controlled somewhere between one-quarter and one-third of world production, with just a few corporations controlling production, marketing and processing of important food and mineral commodities (Brandt, 1980). Brandt advocated the establishment of a new mutually agreed 'investment regime' to ensure that host countries, as well as TNCs, benefited adequately from investment, through contractually agreed arrangements covering such aspects as foreign investment, transfer of technology and the repatriation of profits, royalties and dividends. In addition, the Commission favoured the introduction of legislation in each country to regulate the activities of TNCs in matters such as ethical behaviour, disclosure of information, restrictive practices and labour standards.

The Brandt Report received much attention at the time of its publication, and was regarded as visionary, though somewhat unrealistically idealistic, in the light of the strength and entrenched position of TNCs and other key actors on the world stage. In fact, its recommendations fell victim not only to apathy and intransigence, but also to international recession in the early 1980s. Just three years later, a sequel to the report commented:

> Three years have passed since the publication of the Brandt Commission's Report: *North–South: A Programme for Survival* – years which have brought increasing economic hardship to the industrial countries, and little short of disaster to much of the developing world . . . The Commission offered hope. It expressed the belief that national problems could be solved, but only with a degree of collaboration and wider vision which is still lacking in international affairs . . . The Cancun Summit [October 1981], which brought world leaders together to consider North–South issues, was the first of its kind and was a direct result of the Report. The leaders present felt that their exchanges had been valuable, but while the Summit helped to keep alive the process of global negotiations within the United Nations, it did not make any immediate contribution to resolving the problems of developing countries; nor did it set up any continuing procedure to accelerate negotiations. Now, more than a year later, there is still little sign of action. The North–South dialogue remains much where it was when the Commission reported . . . Meanwhile the world economy continues its dangerous downward slide, and the desperate situation of many developing countries finds no new hope of relief.
>
> (Brandt, 1983: 11–12)

Crisis and commodity dependency

Despite the good intentions of the Brandt Report, it certainly seems that little progress has been made in the world's poorest continent, Africa. An Oxfam report in 1993 presented an extremely depressing view, commenting:

> Sub-Saharan Africa is on a knife edge. For more than a decade the region has been locked in a downward spiral of economic and social decline. That decline, unlike the tragedies of famine and drought, which dominate news coverage of the region, has been largely invisible to the outside world. Yet it has spread human suffering and misery on an unprecedented scale. Hard-won gains in health and education have been reversed; living standards, already among the lowest in the world, have fallen; hunger is on the increase. And the tragedy is set to deepen. On current trends, the ranks of the 218 million Africans already living in poverty will increase to 300 million – equal to half the region's population – by the end of the decade (2000).
>
> (Oxfam, 1993: v)

So what has gone wrong? Earlier in this chapter the case of the Ivory Coast coffee producer was examined and the widespread implications of changing coffee prices for both national economies and poor rural households considered. In fact, it is the long depression in world commodity markets that has had such a profound impact on African economies, and therefore on the quality of life of Africa's people. The situation has been particularly serious where countries are heavily dependent for the generation of foreign exchange on a limited range of primary agricultural and mineral commodities such as coffee, cocoa, cotton and copper. Between 1992 and 1997

Uganda gained over 85 per cent of its export earnings from primary commodities, with coffee being the largest contributor at over 50 per cent. In certain countries a single product dominates export earnings; tobacco provided 59.7 per cent of Malawi's total export earnings, whereas cotton generated 47.7 per cent of Mali's earnings.

The prices of such primary commodities fell dramatically during the 1980s, but import costs continued to rise, leading to a fall of about 50 per cent in the purchasing power of sub-Saharan Africa's exports in the decade from the early 1980s. The situation in some countries was much worse than the average picture:

> In 1986, coffee provided Uganda with US$365 million in foreign exchange earnings and financed about 70 per cent of its imports. By 1991 it yielded only US$115 million, and financed less than a quarter of imports . . . Overall, the slump in commodity prices cost Africa US$50 billion in lost earnings between 1986 and 1990 – more than twice the amount the region receives in aid.
>
> (Oxfam, 1993: 7)

The collapse in commodity prices and the deteriorating terms of trade, together with rising debt-service payments and a reduction in foreign investment, have made it even more difficult for many countries in the South to purchase imports. Furthermore, these trends have seriously undermined structural adjustment programmes sponsored by the World Bank and the International Monetary Fund, which were so dependent on increasing exports. SAPs have probably exacerbated the situation by encouraging countries with a narrow range of exports to increase their production, depending on markets which are already saturated and have fixed levels of demand. This can be seen in the case of increased cocoa exports from Africa, the world's major producing region, which led to the collapse in world prices (Oxfam, 1993). Oxfam suggests that Africa's trading prospects can only be improved by establishing an African Diversification Fund to promote the increased processing of raw commodities in African countries, plus reducing protectionist barriers against Africa's exports as well as ending the subsidised disposal of agricultural surpluses on world and regional markets (Oxfam, 1993).

BOX 8.4

A stronger voice for Africa

Africa, the poorest, and arguably the world's most marginalised, continent, desperately needs a stronger voice which is listened to more seriously by the world community. In an attempt to achieve this, in July 2002, African leaders met in Durban, South Africa, for the Inaugural Summit of the African Union (AU), which replaced the frequently ineffective Organisation of African Unity (OAU). The OAU was formed in 1963 'essentially as a vehicle for pan-African unity and the coordination of the struggle against colonialism' (*Sunday Times,* 2002: 17).
It has been suggested that, 'A major weakness . . . [of the OAU] is that member states have not found it easy to delegate their individual or collective powers to the OAU and the organization's role in the international system has therefore been limited' (Binns, 1994a: 165).

All countries on the continent are members of the new AU, with the exception of Morocco, which withdrew from the OAU in 1982 over the OAU's recognition of the Saharawi Arab Democratic Republic, following Morocco's invasion of Western Sahara in 1976. The aims and objectives of the African Union go well beyond those of the OAU and include:

> acceleration of the political and socioeconomic integration of the continent; promoting democratic principles and institutions, popular participation and good governance; and, establishing the necessary conditions which enable the continent to play its rightful role in the global economy and in international negotiations.
>
> (African Union, 2002: 3)

The AU aims to move away from the overly state-centric character of the OAU and the lack of civil

▶

BOX 8.4 (continued)

participation, and is loosely based on the model offered by the European Union.

Much of the drive behind the establishment of the African Union and the New Partnership for Africa's Development (NEPAD) since 1999 came from Thabo Mbeki, former President of South Africa, supported by Nigeria's Olusegun Obasanjo, Senegal's Abdoulaye Wade and Algeria's Abdelaziz Bouteflika. Mbeki raised the issue of the motivation for an 'African Renaissance' when he was Vice-President in May 1996. A year later, in a landmark speech delivered to the US Corporate Council on Africa, Mbeki argued that an African Renaissance was a real possibility in which the current period of crisis might be seen as a time of opportunity, 'which the New Africa must seize for its own advantage' (Akosah-Sarpong, 1998, quoted in Lester et al., 2000: 281). Mbeki envisaged the African Renaissance leading eventually to the emancipation of women and the mobilisation of youth, and he expressed 'hope for [achieving] sustainable development, together with the broadening, deepening and sustenance of democracy, with decision-making "trickling down" to the level of the actual people affected' (Lester et al., 2000: 281).

The NEPAD initiative developed from Mbeki's call for an African Renaissance, and is envisaged as a long-term vision of an African-owned and African-led development programme. NEPAD is, basically, an appeal to the West's conscience for help, although the initial presentation of NEPAD to the G8 Summit in June 2002 received a somewhat lukewarm response.

However, former British Prime Minister Tony Blair publicly spoke about the need to move Africa higher up the world political and economic agenda. At the Labour Party Conference in September 2001, Blair said,

The state of Africa is a scar on the conscience of the world. But if the world as a community focused on it, we could heal it. And if we don't, it will become deeper and angrier.

(*The Independent*, 2002: 10)

The proposal from Africa's leaders asserts that NEPAD,

is a pledge by African leaders, based on a common vision and a firm and shared conviction, that they have a pressing duty to eradicate poverty and to place their countries, both individually and collectively, on a path of sustainable growth and development and, at the same time, to participate actively in the world economy and body politic.

(NEPAD, 2001: 1)

The proposal suggests that the continued marginalisation of Africa, 'from the globalisation process and the social exclusion of the vast majority of its peoples constitute a serious threat to global stability' (NEPAD, 2001: 1).

There is much in the 70-page NEPAD document about Africa's historical legacies and the poor living standards of many Africans today. It is suggested that Africa's impoverishment is due to, 'the legacy of colonialism, the Cold War, the workings of the international economic system and the inadequacies of, and shortcomings in, the policies pursued by many countries in the post-independence era' (NEPAD, 2001: 1).

NEPAD argues that there is now greater democracy in Africa, and takes support from the UN Millennium Declaration of September 2000, which confirmed the global community's readiness to support Africa's efforts to address the continent's underdevelopment and marginalisation, and its commitment to enhancing resource flows to Africa by improving aid, trade, debt and private capital relationships between Africa and the rest of the world.

In essence, NEPAD calls for a 'new global partnership' and the importance of Africa negotiating a new relationship with its development partners. Such a relationship, it is argued, should lead to conflict prevention, debt reduction, increased development assistance to meet the 0.7 per cent of GDP target, progress in education and health with better access to inexpensive drugs, technical support and private sector investment. This is an ambitious agenda and the Heads of State present at the launch of the African Union in Durban reinforced a shared commitment to NEPAD, saying

BOX 8.4 (continued)

We do not underestimate the challenges involved in achieving NEPAD's objectives, but we share a common resolution to work together even more closely in order to end poverty on the continent and to restore Africa to a place of dignity in the family of nations.

(NEPAD, 2002: 10)

Cynically speaking, both NEPAD and the African Union might be accused of generating yet more political rhetoric about a continent which is a lost cause. However, being more optimistic, there is also a real sense that a group of African leaders is genuinely committed to achieving a fresh start for Africa and, rather than merely talking among themselves, they have engaged at the highest level with the leaders of the world's most powerful countries in a carefully planned dialogue.

One outcome of this dialogue was the launch in early 2004 by UK Prime Minister Tony Blair of the 'Commission for Africa', which brought together a task force of 17 people, including politicians, business people and pop star Bob Geldof, to define the challenges facing Africa, and to provide clear recommendations on how to support the changes needed to reduce poverty. The Commission first reported in March 2005 and its key recommendations were:

➤ Building capacity in Africa, with better education systems and vocational training;

➤ Improving accountability in government and management, with greater transparency and less corruption;

➤ Building capacity to prevent and manage conflict;

➤ Investing in people, reducing poverty and rebuilding health and education systems;

➤ Encouraging entrepreneurship and investment in infrastructure, agriculture, small enterprises, women and young people;

➤ Improving Africa's capacity to trade by reducing tariffs and other non-tariff barriers to African products;

➤ Supporting an additional US $25 billion per year in aid to Africa, to be implemented by 2010.

(Commission for Africa, 2005)

Following the Commission's report, Africa was put at the top of the agenda at the G8 Summit in July 2005 held in Gleneagles, Scotland. The Summit agreed to increase aid to the South by $50 billion and to write off the debts of Africa's 18 poorest countries, although African nations had called for all African debts to be cancelled.

Since the Commission for Africa and the Gleneagles Summit, Africa has been changing rapidly, with economic growth fuelled by massive investment from China and India. However, in many African countries, economic growth is not yet translating into significant reductions in poverty. Aid needs to be delivered in such a way that it does not undermine African institutions. Perhaps most important is that Africa needs to be treated as an integral part of the global community. With increasing global investment in the continent, it should be recognised that if things go wrong in Africa there could be repercussions throughout the world.

World trade: the changing scene

There were major changes during the twentieth century in the geography of international trade. At the beginning of the century, Europe and the USA dominated the world scene. The European powers relied on their colonies in the developing world, but also places such as Australia, Canada and New Zealand, to produce raw materials to supply growing industries at home, industries that produced manufactured goods which could then be traded for more raw materials. Strong trading links still remain between many former colonies and their former European masters. For example, Jamaica still exports most of its bananas to the United Kingdom; and in Africa there is still much trade between francophone countries and France and between the former British colonies and the United Kingdom. The association between colonialism and export economies was emphasised by the concentration of the large-scale export trade in the hands of a few large, mostly European firms and by transnational corporations (see also Chapter 2).

Although there have been colonial links between Western Europe and Pacific-Asia – the British colony of Hong Kong was only returned to China in 1997 – international trade in the Pacific region is dominated by Japan, China and the USA. It has been suggested that 'the West Europeans withdrew from Pacific-Asia in the post-war decades not just politically and militarily, but also economically' (Shibusawa et al., 1992: 30).

GATT and the WTO

Two of the key organisations governing the movement of commodities between countries, namely the General Agreement on Tariffs and Trade (GATT) and the World Trade Organization (WTO), were introduced in Chapter 7 as global 'institutions' that form an important part of the contemporary development landscape and have widespread implications for development processes and outcomes. Here we will focus on some of the concerns about the WTO and how it operates.

The General Agreement on Tariffs and Trade (GATT), was signed in Geneva by 23 nations on 30 October 1947, and came into effect on 1 January 1948 at a time of world reconstruction after the Second World War. GATT was designed to bring some order to world trade and prevent the instability of the inter-war years, at the same time advocating the pursuit of free-trade policies (see Chapter 7). The reduction of tariffs, prohibition of quantitative restrictions and other non-tariff barriers to trade, together with the elimination of trade discrimination, were the main objectives of GATT. The Uruguay round of GATT negotiations began in September 1986 and only concluded in April 1994, after which GATT was replaced by the World Trade Organization (WTO). The talks focused more on debates between Europe and the USA on agricultural subsidies, whereas issues of greater relevance to poor countries, such as gaining better access to developed world markets, were sadly rather neglected.

The expansion of commerce through the deregulation of markets is the main aim of the WTO, and trade liberalisation, in the shape of measures such as removing tariff barriers, quotas, price supports and subsidies, is also increasingly central to economic policy in many countries of the Global South (see Chapter 1 and 7). The WTO has come under much attack in its relatively short history. As Watkins observes, 'issues of sustainable resource management, the regulation of commodity markets, and poverty reduction strategies, are conspicuous by their absence from the international trade agenda' (Watkins, 1995: 32). Others are critical of how during WTO's ministerial meetings rich countries tend to lobby hard to shape the rules in their favour and, because poorer countries are less able to field delegates from powerful large companies, they suffer as a result. Christian Aid is critical of the WTO agreement on investment where;

> developing countries are often prevented from favouring domestic investors over foreign ones, [and] . . . developing countries are also unable to provide short-term subsidies to help their agriculture and industry become competitive, again because of WTO rules that forbid favourable treatment to domestic over foreign firms.
>
> (Curtis, 2001a: 12)

WTO rules have also changed the way that large multinational companies are able to tap into markets in poor countries, for example in agricultural trade and in services, and through foreign investment and securing patent rights to natural resources (Box 8.5). Curtis argues that new trade rules should be formulated which target the eradication of poverty and cover the activities of powerful multinational companies, as well as of governments. These rules, he suggests, should be decided democratically and carefully monitored (Curtis, 2001b).

In a 2002 report, Oxfam, a tireless campaigner for fair trade, stated that

> World trade has the potential to act as a powerful motor for the reduction of poverty, as well as for economic growth, but that potential is being lost. The problem is not that international trade is inherently opposed to the needs and interests of the poor, but that the rules that govern it are rigged in favour of the rich.
>
> (Oxfam, 2002: 3)

Like Christian Aid, Oxfam is keen for poor countries to have a stronger voice in the WTO and is particularly critical of such issues as the agreement on Trade-Related Aspects of Intellectual-Property Rights (TRIPs) (see Chapters 4 and 7). It is suggested that

> More stringent protection for patents will increase the costs of technology transfer. Developing countries will lose approximately US$40 billion a year in the form of increased licence payments to Northern-based TNCs, with the USA capturing around one-half of the total. Behind the complex arguments about intellectual-property rights, the TRIPs agreement is an act of institutionalized fraud, sanctioned by WTO rules.
>
> (Oxfam, 2002: 14)

BOX 8.5

Christian Aid's 'Seven deadly WTO rules'

Christian Aid has argued that seven specific trade rules have a significant impact on poor countries:

1. *Rule one:*   WTO limits protection against cheap food imports
   Developing countries are restricted from intervening in order to raise adequate barriers against cheap food imports, while export subsidies by rich countries are allowed to persist.

   The outcome: *a flood of food imports into developing countries which undermines or threatens to undermine the livelihood of many poor people.*

2. *Rule two:*   WTO limits government regulation of services
   Countries which agree to sign up must open up their services sectors to foreign suppliers by abolishing restrictions on access to those markets.

   The outcome: *the renegotiation of the WTO's services agreement may result in health, education and water services being run and controlled by profit-driven foreign corporations.*

3. *Rule three:*   WTO limits regulation of foreign investment
   The WTO's investment agreement bans policies and regulations favouring the use of domestic over foreign products.

   The outcome: *poor countries are denied some important ways of supporting the development of viable local industries over foreign producers. A new investment agreement would further strengthen this rule.*

4. *Rule four:*   WTO limits use of agricultural subsidies
   Developing countries are limited in their freedom to increase subsidies to agriculture. Some (the non-least developed countries) are required to reduce them. Particular types of subsidy are banned altogether. Meanwhile the EU and US are still permitted to spend huge sums on agricultural subsidies themselves.

   The outcome: *poor people's food security is being undermined by restrictions on subsidies which deny poor countries an important tool in development.*

5. *Rule five:*   WTO puts limits on industrial subsidies
   Governments are prevented from using industrial subsidies to promote the manufacture of domestic products over imported alternatives. Some subsidies of special use to rich countries are permitted.

   The outcome: *poor countries' industrial development is being hampered by taking away a critical policy tool to help develop their own industrial sector.*

6. *Rule six:*   WTO blocks exports from developing countries
   Rich countries can retain high import barriers or other restrictions against key exports from developing countries.

   The outcome: *poor countries lose much needed export revenues and the economic growth rates of affected poor economies will suffer potential losses.*

7. *Rule seven:*   WTO gives business rights over knowledge and natural resources
   This WTO rule requires countries to introduce effective patenting laws, including plant varieties and seeds, which can give TNCs rights over those products for 20 years. This in effect legalises biopiracy of natural resources and knowledge.

   The outcome: *poor people's food and health security can be threatened if TNCs are successful in securing monopoly control over knowledge and natural resources.*

Source: Curtis, 2001b

Oxfam is particularly concerned about the effects of reinforced patent protection on the costs of medicines in poor countries. The WTO, Oxfam argues, 'is old before its time, [and] . . . behind the façade of a "membership-driven" organisation is a governance system based on a dictatorship of wealth' (Oxfam, 2002: 15). More specifically, Oxfam advocates a number of reforms to the WTO, notably: an end to the universally applied intellectual-property blueprint, so that poor countries can maintain shorter and more flexible systems of intellectual-property protection; a commitment to put public health priorities before the claims of patent holders; a prohibition on patent protection for genetic resources for food and agriculture and the ability of poor countries to develop more appropriate forms of plant-variety protection and protect farmers' rights to save, sell and exchange seeds; to prioritise development objectives and strengthen national sovereignty; to strengthen WTO provisions for the 'special and different treatment' of poor countries; and to remove restrictions on governments to regulate foreign investment and protect their infant industries (Oxfam, 2002: 14–15). Ransom suggests that, 'the WTO must shrink, divest itself of "trade related" issues like services, patents and investment, open itself up to democratic control and close itself off from corporate manipulation' (Ransom, 2001: 28).

The WTO refutes the suggestion that it is undemocratic, saying that decisions are usually made by consensus with every country having a voice, and that WTO trade rules were in any case ratified in members' parliaments. Furthermore, it asserts that freer trade creates more jobs than are lost and that, 'while about 1.5 billion people are still in poverty, trade liberalization since World War II has contributed to lifting an estimated 3 billion people out of poverty' (World Trade Organization, 2000: 239). Adding to the debate, Clare Short, then UK Secretary of State for International Development, in a speech to the WTO meeting in Seattle in November 1999 commented:

> those who make blanket criticisms of the WTO are working against, not for, the interests of the poor and the powerless. International trade can be unfair and exploitative. The strong can deceive and defraud the weak. That is precisely why we need an institution like the WTO which is membership-based and rules-based – to prevent fraud, monopoly, predatory pricing and other abuses. Just as we need rules on these issues at the national level, so we need them at the international level.
>
> (Short, 2000: 11)

However, the influence of countries such as the USA, the European Union and Japan within the WTO, continues to be debated and particularly in relation to the collapse of the WTO Doha Development Trade Round in July 2006 (Key idea box). Measures to enhance the participation of countries of the Global South within the WTO structures and processes are considered further in Chapter 7.

Key idea

The collapse of the 'Doha Round' trade talks

The so-called 'Doha Round' of WTO trade talks was launched in Doha in the Middle Eastern state of Qatar in November 2001 and was due to be concluded by December 2006. The talks aimed to prioritise the development of poor countries and were therefore referred to as the 'development' round. Subsequent meetings were held in Cancun, Mexico in 2003, Geneva (2004), Paris (2005), Hong Kong (2005) and Geneva (2006). It was in Geneva in July 2006 that the talks failed to reach an agreement about reducing farm subsidies and lowering import taxes. A successful outcome of the Doha Round seemed unlikely as the broad trade authority granted under the US Trade Act of 2002 to President George Bush expired in June 2007. A further meeting held in Potsdam in June 2007 failed to break through the impasse between the US, the EU, India and Brazil in relation to opening up agricultural and industrial markets and how to reduce rich nation farm subsidies.

As India's commerce minister, Kamil Nath, commented following the Geneva conference in 2006,

Key idea (continued)

This is a Development Round, completing it is extremely important, but equally important is the content of the Round. The content has to demonstrate new opportunities for developing countries, primarily market access of developing countries into markets of developed countries. This Round is not for perpetuating the flaws in global trade especially in agriculture, it is not to open markets in developing countries in order for developed countries to have access for their subsidized products to developing countries. We say the Round should correct the structural flaws and distortions in the system, and there should be fair trade, not only free trade. The USA say 'we want market access and only if we get it the way we want it can we correct the structural flaws.' There is no equity in that argument.

(Kamal Nath, quoted at http://www.globalissues.org/TradeRelated/FreeTrade/dohacollapse.asp, 28 July 2006)

The so-called 'Doha Development Agenda' (DDA) was re-visited at a finance ministers meeting in Bali in December 2013, but Oxfam's Senior Policy Advisor, Romain Benicchio, was rather sceptical about the meeting's achievements;

The Bali package is hardly going to make a difference for poor countries, but at least it keeps the negotiations on food security alive. However, a peace clause can't be the end of the story and negotiators now have to find a long term solution to change the rigged rules that stand in the way of developing countries food security policies.

(Oxfam, 2013)

Fair and ethical trade

The issues of fair and ethical trade have received much attention in recent years and there have been serious attempts, particularly by charities and pressure groups, to influence the working conditions and remuneration of workers in poor countries (Hughes, 2001; Fairtrade International, 2014).

For example, in September 1999 *The Independent*, a UK-based newspaper, launched its 'Global Sweatshop' campaign to increase awareness about the sale of 'sweatshop' goods in British high-street stores. The newspaper revealed that 13,000 workers in 32 garment factories on the US-administered Northern Mariana Islands in the western Pacific were producing 'designer' shirts and other garments for well-known retailers in the USA under appalling working conditions, long hours of work and poor wages (*The Independent*, 1999). Another report by the charity Christian Aid revealed that plantation workers growing bananas in Costa Rica commonly received only 5.5 per cent of the average price of a banana, while on tea plantations workers' wages accounted for just 7 per cent of the final price (Christian Aid, 1996).

There has been a strong call for retailers to report annually on their codes of conduct, to make compulsory the country-of-origin labelling on all imported clothes,

and to introduce an 'ethical trade kitemark' funded by retailers but independently monitored, indicating acceptable standards of workers' pay and working conditions (*The Independent*, 1999).

Such fair trade 'kitemarking' is more advanced in relation to food crops, where a distinctive label is used to denote commodities which have been produced by workers receiving a fair wage and working under acceptable conditions. As the Fairtrade Foundation comments:

Fairtrade is about better prices, decent working conditions and fair terms of trade for farmers and workers. It's about supporting the development of thriving farming and worker communities that have more control over their futures and protecting the environment in which they live and work.

(Fairtrade Foundation, 2016: 1)

The first Fairtrade Label was created in the Netherlands in 1988, and by 2002 there were 17 Fairtrade Labelling Organizations, including related initiatives in the UK, USA, Japan, Netherlands, Germany and Switzerland. The UK Fairtrade Foundation was established in 1992, with support from development agencies such as Christian Aid, CAFOD, New Consumer, Oxfam,

Traidcraft Exchange and the World Development Movement. In 1997 Fairtrade Labelling Organizations (FLO) International was established, which is an association of 20 national labelling initiatives that promote and market the Fairtrade label in their countries. FLO is the worldwide standard setting and certification body for labelled Fairtrade (see www.fairtrade.net).

In 2001 alone there was a 21 per cent increase in UK sales of Fairtrade marked commodities, such as coffee, tea, chocolate, honey, sugar, orange juice, bananas and mangoes. In 2005 the entire range of UK high street retailer Marks & Spencer's coffee and tea, totalling 38 lines, switched to Fairtrade in a move which was estimated to increase the value of all Fairtrade instant and ground coffee sold in UK supermarkets by 18 per cent and that of Fairtrade tea by approximately 30 per cent. Over 1.5 million farmers and workers are currently participating in Fairtrade certified producer organisations, over 50 per cent of farmers being located in low-income countries in Africa and the Middle East (Fairtrade Foundation, 2016).

Recent trends in world trade

Two important trends in world trade developed during the 1980s and 1990s. First, with the end of the Cold War, the collapse of Soviet communism in 1991, and the expansion of the European Union, trade between Eastern Europe and the Western capitalist countries accelerated with western investment playing an important role in the restructuring of the former Communist bloc countries. In the early 1990s, over 400 agreements were signed between Western businesses and bodies in the newly democratised Czechoslovakia, Poland and Hungary, much of this investment going to the major cities and heavily industrialised regions.

A second and very significant development in world trade was the increasing power and participation of the export-oriented 'newly industrialising countries' (NICs), such as Hong Kong, Malaysia, South Korea, Singapore and Taiwan, in addition to the already powerful Japan (see also Chapter 4). Industrial employment in South Korea increased by 77 per cent between 1974 and 1983, and by 75 per cent in Malaysia during the same period.

Trade, trade and more trade was what propelled the so-called Pacific Rim states out of agrarian destitution or post-World War II destruction and decline into world economic prominence.

(Aikman, 1986: 10)

The growth of international trade in the countries of the western Pacific Rim in the 1980s and 1990s was remarkable (Figure 8.2). From 1982 to 1988 the growth in export volume from East Asia (even excluding Japan) was over 12 per cent per annum, a rate almost double that of South Asia, three times that of the Middle East, North Africa and Latin America, and about six times higher than in sub-Saharan Africa (Hodder, 1992: 67). The western Pacific Rim's share of world trade increased from 14.3 per cent in 1971 to 22.8 per cent in 1984. This reflected the success of export-led growth strategies and the readiness of the peoples of these countries to undertake programmes of rapid structural adjustment, the development of new products and the exploitation of new markets (Dicken, 1993).

However, in 1997 and 1998 many of the Asian NICs suffered a serious economic downturn which had widespread implications both domestically and internationally. In South Korea, for example, the crisis was precipitated by a growing concern in 1997 about heavily indebted and overextended companies with weak profitability that were borrowing heavily to finance long-term investment. Banks were also borrowing heavily, such that in November 1997 the USA made it difficult for three large South Korean banks to continue borrowing from abroad to lend at home. Despite the South Korean government trying to restore foreign and domestic confidence in the country, the problems continued and the stock market fell sharply, while external liabilities were estimated to be as high as US $200 billion. Negotiations took place with the IMF and a rescue package of US $20 billion was announced, with a further US $40 billion coming from the World Bank, the Asian Development Bank, Japan, the USA and other lenders. World reaction to this was mixed. The South Korean currency was allowed to float freely from mid December 1997 and some confidence was only restored when the IMF brought forward part of its assistance package. However, South Korea's economy bounced back in 1999–2000, such that GDP grew by 10.9 per cent in 1999 and 8.6 per cent in 2000, representing the fastest growth rates since 1987. In the following year, despite recession in South Korea's important export markets of USA and

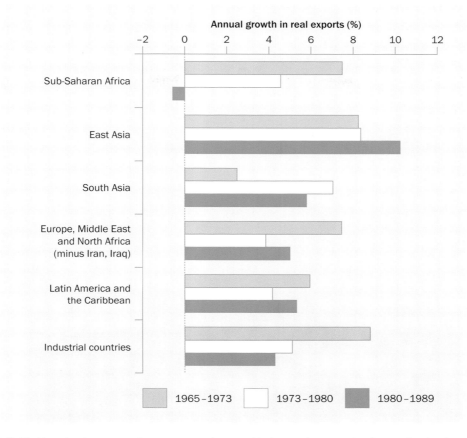

Annual growth in real exports (%)

Figure 8.2 Estimated percentage annual growth in real exports for selected regions, 1965–1989
Source: adapted from Hodder, 1992.

Japan, economic performance at home was strong. GDP in 2001 grew by 3.3 per cent, while Taiwan and Singapore experienced sharp falls in output (Economist Intelligence Unit, 2002b).

International trade as a whole was dominated in 2013 by four countries – China, USA, Germany and Japan (see Table 8.2). China's share in world exports has increased massively from just 1.9 per cent in 1990 to 11.7 per cent in 2013, whereas Japan's share has more than halved in the same period, from 11.5 per cent in 1990 to 3.8 per cent in 2013. In terms of imports of manufactured goods in 2013, 32.6 per cent of the world's imports of manufactured goods was accounted for by the European Union, followed by USA (12.3 per cent), China (10.3 per cent) and Japan (4.4 per cent) (World Trade Organization, 2014).

The western Pacific Rim countries conduct most trade with the USA and Canada. In most of Southeast Asia, except Singapore, there is still evidence of the colonial pattern of trade, in which countries export raw materials and primary products and import most of their manufactured goods. In the case of Hong Kong and South Korea, a clear majority of both imports and exports are manufactured goods (Hodder, 1992; Plate 8.6).

As the Chinese population gets more wealthy, there is considerable potential for tapping further into the vast Chinese market, and Southeast Asia's 'overseas Chinese' have established a close network of business links with the Chinese in Taiwan, Singapore and Hong Kong, and they are well placed to take full advantage of potential business opportunities. Hong Kong has provided about 80 per cent of investment in southern China's Guangdong

Table 8.2 Leading world exporters and importers, 2013

	Exporters		Importers	
	Value US $billion	Share %	Value US $billion	Share %
China	2209	11.7	1950	10.3
USA	1580	8.4	2329	12.3
Germany	1453	7.7	1189	6.3
Japan	715	3.8	833	4.4

Source: adapted from World Trade Organization (2014) *International Trade Statistics, 2014*. WTO.

Plate 8.6 Container port, Kowloon, Hong Kong
(*photo*: Tony Binns)

Province, which has experienced massive industrial development (Box 8.6), while Taiwan has invested heavily in Fujian Province, opposite Taiwan on China's eastern coast.

Whereas in the 1960s and 1970s the USA was the dominant world trading power, in the 1990s a 'multipolar' system developed, with power concentrated in three blocs: North America, Europe and, increasingly, the Pacific Rim. Trade relations are being transformed by such features as increased flows of foreign investment, the globalisation of production under the auspices of transnational corporations and trade liberalisation in the Global South. Institutional structures have also changed, such as the customs union between Brazil, Argentina and Uruguay created in 1995, and the

Asia-Pacific Economic Cooperation (APEC), established in 1993, leading to links between the Pacific Rim states (Japan, China, South Korea, Malaysia, Philippines and Thailand) and the North American Free Trade Agreement (NAFTA), comprising the USA, Mexico and Canada (Watkins, 1995: 113).

Transnational corporations

It is often assumed that trade is an activity which is conducted between countries, each of which controls its own economic destiny. However, as noted in Chapter 4, world trade flows are in reality dominated by incredibly powerful transnational corporations. Dicken has examined the nature of TNCs and concludes that because these big companies are often based in a single country, though they operate in at least two countries, including the firm's home country, they are now usually termed 'transnational' rather than 'multinational'. All multinational corporations are transnational corporations, but not all transnational corporations are multinational corporations.

(Dicken, 1992: 47)

The role of transnational corporations in world trade should not be underestimated – indeed they are vital actors in the global economic and trading system. However, the impacts of trade liberalisation in general and the particular role of large business corporations in social and environmental outcomes are highly contested as considered further in Chapter 7 (see also Critical reflection below).

BOX 8.6

Migration and economic development in China

The reforms introduced since 1979 under Deng Xiaoping's rule have had a major impact on population movements within China. Although migration did occur before 1979, it was generally involuntary and much more centrally controlled than in recent years. Resettlement programmes took place, most notably from the densely populated provinces of the east to the sparsely populated western regions. In the case of Xinjiang Province in the far northwest of China, there was a deliberate government policy to change its ethnic balance. Xinjiang has many minority groups, but in-migration of Han Chinese from the east increased the proportion of Han within the population from under 10 per cent in 1949 to 40 per cent in 1982. This process has continued and many Han have been appointed to important administrative and political posts in Xinjiang, so Beijing is able to maintain strong central control over the region.

Another wave of migrations occurred during the period of the first five-year plan (1953–1957), when millions of peasants moved into towns looking for jobs during a phase of intensive reconstruction and industrialisation after the Second World War and the subsequent civil war. As a result, between 1949 and 1957 China's urban population increased by 60 per cent, whereas the rural population grew by only 13 per cent (Jowett, 1990).

During the Great Leap Forward (1958–1960), despite a strong emphasis on rural industrialisation, this initiative was thwarted by widespread famine in 1959–1961, leading to 'surplus' population being moved back into the countryside. Later, during the

Cultural Revolution of the 1960s and 1970s, the Chinese government imposed strict controls on rural–urban migration, and urban youths were sent to work in the countryside in the so-called 'rustication' programme. During this period the country's largest cities scarcely grew through migration; for example, there was a relatively small net gain of 350,000 migrants in Tianjin during the 30 years between 1950 and 1980, and China's largest city, Shanghai, actually experienced a net loss of 1 million people through out-migration during the same period.

The reforms of 1979, however, had a major effect on population movements within China. Probably the most important reform was the replacement of people's communes with individual farming units under the 'household responsibility system'. This new approach to agricultural production led to the collapse of collective farming and gave rise to abundant rural surplus labour, due to a substantial increase in the efficiency and productivity of the agricultural sector. Controls on internal migration were relaxed, such that surplus rural labour could move freely without the need for permanent registration. The late 1970s and early 1980s were characterised by increasing migration, and it was estimated that in Shanghai alone there was a net in-migration in 1979 of 264,800 (Jowett, 1990).

A second significant element in the reforms of 1979 was the establishment of the first four special economic zones (SEZs). Located on China's southeastern coast, close to Hong Kong and Taiwan, and with a series of tax inducements, these areas were

▶

BOX 8.6 (continued)

designed to attract foreign investment and 'joint ventures' between Chinese and overseas companies, to manufacture export goods which would generate foreign exchange. The SEZs were also seen as 'social and economic laboratories, in which foreign technological and managerial skills might be observed and adopted' (Phillips and Yeh, 1990: 236).

Two of the first SEZs, Zhuhai and Shenzhen, are located in the Pearl River Delta zone of Guangdong Province. Shenzhen, the largest SEZ (327.5 square kilometres) is situated adjacent to the Hong Kong border less than an hour's travel from the 'throbbing heart of capitalism' in Kowloon and Hong Kong Island. It has grown spectacularly since the 1980s, from being just a small rural town to an ultramodern city with a population approaching 15 million in 2015. China's southern coast has become an innovative capitalist periphery for the new international division of labour

and capital flowing into the region from all over the world (see Figures 8.3 and 8.4).

Female migration to southern China

These two factors – the changes in the rural production system and the creation of the SEZs – have provided an important stimulus for the massive increase in migration which China has experienced in recent years. The 1990 population census revealed there were 525 million population movements during 1982–1985, 740 million during 1985–1987 and 660 million during 1987–1990. Whereas in many countries of the South, migration is usually dominated by males, China's 1990 census indicated that 56 per cent of migrants were male and 44 per cent female. However, if intra-provincial migration alone is considered, females were in the majority at 66 per cent, due

Figure 8.3 Province-level administrative divisions of China (Xinjiang, Tibet and Inner Mongolia are autonomous regions)
Source: adapted from So, 1997

BOX 8.6 (continued)

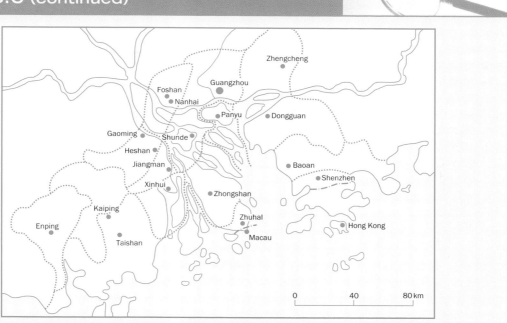

Figure 8.4 The major cities in Guangdong Province
Source: adapted from So, 1997

largely to migration for marriage, since brides commonly move to their husband's home. Yet aggregate data mask striking differences at the local level and, in fact, females dominate migration from some counties of the vast, and predominantly rural, Sichuan Province (China's most populous province), to the growing industries of Guangdong Province, particularly in the Pearl River Delta region (Davin, 1996). Regulations relating to labour migration were further relaxed from 1984, and from July 1985 peasants were allowed to be temporary residents in urban areas, applying for six-monthly permits through their work units. As a result, in Guangdong Province the 'temporary resident' population rose from 280,000 in 1982 to 3.3 million in 1990, representing nearly a 12-fold increase (So, 1997).

A study undertaken in the mid-1990s of female migrants from the rural areas of Sichuan to the industries of Guangdong found that only 12 per cent of household heads were strongly against the migration of their female members (So, 1997). The decision for a household member to migrate was taken by the entire family, but migration was seen as important in generating cash income to pay for such items as education, marriage, consumer goods, farming inputs, house building and maintenance. Migration was also seen as a 'risk aversion' strategy to diversify sources of income (So, 1997: 161).

The considerable attraction of migration is summed up in a popular Chinese phrase, *dongnanxibeizhong, facaidao Guangdong* – 'east, south, west, north or central; to get rich, go to Guangdong Province'. However, rural households were concerned about the social problems of cities, such as prostitution, robbery and rape, and the potential vulnerability of their women in a strange environment. In relation to the income of rural households, the economic cost of migration can be considerable, with very long journeys by bus and train. A typical journey from Sichuan to Guangdong in the mid-1990s would take up to three days and cost more than 100 yuan, a considerable financial outlay for poor rural households; 1 yuan = US $0.12 (12 cents) in 1996.

Food and accommodation in Guangdong were provided by the factory, although the employer might charge for certain services. It appears that female

▶

BOX 8.6 (continued)

migration had little effect on the rural household's productivity. On the contrary, the income from migrants' remittances far outweighed the impact of the loss of labour. Furthermore, the status of migrant women improved after they engaged in wage labour, and young migrants felt they had 'grown up' by learning new skills, experiencing a different environment and earning their own wage before getting married. The great majority of female migrants (79 per cent) were between the ages of 16 and 24, and a similar proportion were unmarried (So, 1997: 174, 189).

In the late 1990s the Chinese government started to regulate the flow of labour migration by coordinating efforts between the migrant-sending and migrant-receiving provinces, in order to relieve pressure on the transport system and reduce social problems. Coordinating offices were established from 1991 to regulate the flow of labour from Sichuan and other provinces to Guangdong, and factories recruited migrant workers through local labour bureaux. Potential migrants found out about job prospects through labour offices or industrial enterprises, which could even contact their villages. Well over half (57.8 per cent) of female migrants interviewed in 1994 found out about job opportunities through families and friends, and many already had contacts in Guangdong, who played a key role in helping migrants adjust to the new ways of living and working (So, 1997: 180).

Employment was mainly in producing electrical goods, toys, clothing and shoes, many of the products being destined for the export market. Working conditions were difficult and the work was manual and highly repetitive, with many industrial accidents. Women migrants typically worked for 70 hours or more in a seven-day week and additional overtime at a rate of 1 or 2 yuan per hour was common. Wages averaged 10–15 yuan per day, with a typical monthly income of between 250 and 450 yuan, including bonuses. Factories then often deducted as much as 100 yuan for provision of meals and accommodation (usually in dormitories),

leaving a monthly net income of 150–350 yuan. The migrants were seen by the indigenous population as poor peasant workers and in a much inferior position compared with local residents, who invariably earned higher wages and held more responsible positions in the factories. Upward mobility for migrants was therefore very difficult, and workers coped with the poor conditions through a mutual support network known as the *tongxiang* system (people from the same village or county).

Migrants retained strong links with their villages by exchanging letters. However, the Chinese New Year (Spring) holiday provided a valuable opportunity for migrants to return to their villages, taking money, consumer goods and much information about life and work in Guangdong. Between 70 and 90 per cent of Sichuan migrants returned home at least once a year, usually for the Spring holiday, which lasts about 60 days around the New Year period (Davin, 1996). However, transport costs increase at this time and there is much competition for places.

Typical remittances from migrants varied between 100 and 200 yuan per month (1,200–2,400 yuan per year), which is quite considerable in relation to the average annual net income in 1993 of only 698 yuan for a Sichuan peasant. An estimated 5 billion yuan was remitted each year to Sichuan province from migrant workers, a substantial proportion of whom were working in southern coastal cities, predominantly in Guangdong (So, 1997: 237).

The advantages and problems of migration on such a massive scale within China are highly complex, and the extent to which these factors are reflected in the fortunes of individuals and their rural households needs further careful investigation. However, one is inclined to agree with Davin's conclusion that

migration in the form it takes at present in China has the potential to return human and financial resources to the villages, and thus helps prevent the gap [between the poor countryside and the prosperous urban areas] becoming even wider.

(Davin, 1996: 665)

Many TNCs have their origins in the colonial period (Chapter 2). Walter Rodney (1972: 182) traced the development of the large TNC, Unilever, as what he calls 'a major beneficiary of African exploitation'. Originally founded in 1885 by William H. Lever, the firm of Lever made soap from palm oil imported from West Africa. Large concessions were also obtained in the Belgian Congo and, through a series of mergers, the company (renamed Lever Brothers) gained a foothold in every colony in West Africa. Lever bought the Niger Company in 1920, and then in 1929 further company takeovers led to the establishment of the new United Africa Company (UAC).

Yet more mergers took place with Dutch soap and margarine companies, and in 1930 Unilever Ltd (registered in Britain) and Unilever NV (registered in Holland) were formed, with the UAC subsidiary supplying the oils and fats. With further takeovers the organisation grew from strength to strength. As Unilever's information division commented, 'Unilever's centre of gravity lies in Europe, but far and away its largest member (the UAC) is almost wholly dependent for its livelihood . . . on the well-being of West Africa' (quoted in Rodney, 1972: 182).

In the second decade of the twenty-first century, Unilever is still a major operator on the world commercial stage, with a total turnover in 2014 of €48,517 million and an operating profit of €6,903 million. Unilever's stated mission is 'to add vitality to life – we meet everyday needs for nutrition, hygiene and personal care with brands that help people feel good, look good and get more out of life' (Unilever, 2006a; see Chapter 4).

Until the 1960s most TNCs were of either US or UK origin, but in recent years Japanese, German and other companies have become important on the global scene. In the future, it is likely that companies based in the BRICS countries will become increasingly significant (see Key idea box on BRICS). Although TNCs are by no means homogeneous, they typically have their headquarters or strategic base in one country, but with a variety of production sites and subsidiary operations in other countries (Plate 8.7). TNCs also generally have a good amount of geographical flexibility, enabling them to shift resources and operations from one global location to another as production factors change, in order to seek new competitive advantages.

Key idea

BRICS and the global economy

Jim O'Neill, an economist at Goldman Sachs, a global investment banking and management firm, was probably the first to use the term 'BRICs' in 2001, to refer to Brazil, Russia, India and China – a group of rapidly developing economies which were becoming progressively more important in international investment trends (Wilson and Purushothaman, 2003). O'Neill suggested that in less than 40 years the BRICs economies could become larger than those of the world's six most developed countries, possibly leading to a significant shift in the global balance of power. It is predicted that by 2050, of the current six largest economies, only the USA and Japan will remain in the top six. Just as Germany and Japan experienced massive economic growth after 1945, so it is argued

that the BRICs countries are capable of achieving similar success.

India has the potential to show the fastest growth over the next 30 and 50 years, with an estimated average annual growth rate of about 5 per cent. China's annual economic growth rate averaged 7.7 per cent between 2005 and 2013, but it is expected that this rate may slow down to an average of 3.5 per cent, whilst Brazil's growth rate slowed to 2.5 per cent in 2013 from a rate of 7.5 per cent in 2010 (World Bank, 2015c). In fact, in August 2015 it was declared that Brazil had entered recession following a 1.9 per cent contraction of the economy between April and June 2015, largely due to falling global commodity prices. Meanwhile, Russia's growth projections are hampered by its shrinking population and fluctuations

▶

Key idea (continued)

in oil revenue, but by 2050 it will probably have the highest per capita GDP in the BRICs group, and comparable to other countries in the G6. Russia's economy is expected to overtake Italy in 2018 and the UK in 2027.

As the number of people in the BRICs countries with an annual income over a threshold of US $3,000 increases, this is likely to lead to a massive increase in the size of the middle class in these nations and a corresponding increase in demand for higher priced consumer goods. However, by 2050 individuals in the BRICs countries are still likely to be on average poorer than in the G6 economies, though Russia should catch up with the G6 during this period. In China, however, per capita income in 2050 is likely to be approximately where the developed economies are now (Wilson and Purushothaman, 2003).

The Goldman Sachs thesis has generated much debate, for example in possibly underestimating the level of economic growth in China and India. Meanwhile, Brazil's economic potential has long been recognised, but so far it has failed to achieve investor expectations. Other factors such as human rights issues, civil unrest, poor governance, disease and terrorism could have an effect on the economic progress of one or more of the BRICs countries during the period up to 2050.

The four BRICs countries admitted a new member, South Africa, to the group in December 2010, and the group formally became known as BRICS. In March 2013, South African President, Jacob Zuma, hosted the annual BRICS Summit in Durban, when it was agreed to establish a BRICS development bank, located in Shanghai, as an alternative to the World Bank. Jim O'Neill was apparently somewhat sceptical about the addition of South Africa to the group, suggesting that a number of other high growth countries, notably South Korea, might be more appropriate members. In January 2014, the former Goldman Sachs economist suggested that the next economic giants after BRICS could be the MINT group, comprising Mexico, Indonesia, Nigeria and Turkey, all with strong economic growth and large and youthful populations (*Thomson Reuters*, 2014).

However, the earlier upbeat reports about the rapidly growing BRICs economies have been tempered in 2015 and 2016, as these countries have experienced significant changes in their fortunes. As Foroohar comments;

The BRICS – those once hot emerging markets including Brazil, Russia, India and China- have been beleaguered for some time. Brazil and Russia are in full-blown recessions, China is trying to stave off a big slow down, and India, while still of interest to global investors, is struggling to put through the economic reforms that would help it reach its full potential.

(Foroohar, 2015: 1)

In November 2015, Goldman Sachs, whose Jim O'Neill originated the BRICs idea in 2001, actually closed its BRIC Investment Fund, which had declined in asset value by 88 per cent since 2010. As Foroohar suggests, 'The BRICs, it seems, are finally broken' (Foroohar, 2015: 1). With political scandal facing the presidents of both Brazil and South Africa in 2016, and state-condoned corruption in Russia, Simon Tisdall argues that, 'A common factor for all BRICs countries as they struggle economically is institutional weakness, in particular a lack (or in some cases, a total absence) of democratic accountability, transparency in public life, and independent media scrutiny of official behaviour' (Tisdall, 2016: 2).

China and Africa

China's strengthening relations with Africa illustrate the global activity of just one of the BRICS countries. In October 2000, the Forum on China-Africa Cooperation (FOCAC) was established in Beijing at the first Ministerial Conference involving the Chinese Ministry of Foreign Affairs and the African diplomatic community based in Beijing. One element of the lengthy Beijing Declaration announcing FOCAC stated:

We decide to vigorously promote further China-Africa cooperation in the economic, trade, financial, agricultural, medical care and public health, scientific and technological, cultural, educational, human resources development, transportation, environmental, tourism and other areas on the basis of the principles enshrined in this declaration and the Program for China-Africa Cooperation in economic and social

Key idea (continued)

development adopted at the Forum so as to promote the common development of China and Africa.
(Forum on China-African Cooperation, 2000: 5).

There seem to be two contrasting, but somewhat simplistic, viewpoints relating to China's increasing interest and involvement in Africa. One view is rather critical, suggesting that China is pursuing a neo-colonial approach, with its objectives primarily concerned with the exploitation and extraction of natural resources and the growth of markets for Chinese manufacturing goods. Another viewpoint is more positive, suggesting that China's involvement in African countries is generally beneficial, in some cases superseding longstanding links with Western countries and potentially playing a vital role in the future development of the world's poorest continent. In reality, both viewpoints are probably relevant, but it is important to avoid making sweeping conclusions since Chinese involvement in Africa is both dynamic and highly complex and the local context of each case needs to be examined carefully.

Since the inauguration of FOCAC in 2000, the Chinese government and Chinese companies have become much more active in Africa. There are currently over a million Chinese living in the continent, many involved in small and medium sized businesses in the retail sector. There has been some criticism, both of China's diplomatic support and military sales to regimes such as Sudan, and also health and safety issues concerning working conditions in Chinese owned businesses in countries such as Zambia (*Diplomatic Courier*, 2013).

As Alden explains, 'Essentially China-Africa economic relations are managed bilaterally, led by the Ministry of Commerce and the policy banks (primarily China Export-Import Bank and China Development Bank), while diplomatic conduct is handled by the Ministry of Foreign Affairs' (Alden, 2012: 704). In 2000, two-way trade between Africa and China amounted to just over US $1 billion, but by 2013 trade between China and African nations had reached US $200 billion and included a 44 per cent increase in Chinese direct investment in African countries, with the largest amounts going to Ghana (US $11.4bn), Nigeria (US $8.4bn), Sudan (including South Sudan) (US $5.4bn), and Ethiopia (US $5.4bn) (Rotberg, 2014). In 2012 some 29 per cent of China's exports to Africa were machinery and electrical goods (*The Economist*, 2013). China is investing heavily in African infrastructure and construction projects, and particularly in oil exploration in countries like Angola, Equatorial Guinea and Sudan, in order to meet its rapidly growing petroleum needs. At the G20 Summit in France in November 2011, Chinese President Hu Jintao announced that China would give tariff exemption on 97 per cent of exports to China coming from the less developed countries which have diplomatic ties with China (Forum on China-Africa Cooperation, 2011). Also in late 2011 China gave a US $500 million loan to the East African community for the development of trade and infrastructure. As Alden comments, 'With infrastructure projects being accepted as a key part of the regional development corridors, China's recognized ability to build roads, railroads and port facilities in a short span of time may prove to be the catalyst required to realize the requisite economies of scale needed for accelerated development in binding the economies of a region more closely together' (Alden, 2012: 703).

China's involvement in African development initiatives is likely to further accelerate in the foreseeable future, and it will be important to understand both changing government to government relationships, as well as the experience of specific development initiatives at the local level.

The relocation of operations to countries in the South may often be because labour costs are cheaper, there is generally less militancy among labour unions and fewer health and safety restrictions in the workplace. Abundant, low-cost and largely illiterate workforces, with little industrial tradition, are very attractive. Nike, for example, is a large, disaggregated TNC which subcontracts out production of its footwear and apparel to 700 factories around the world (Chapter 4). The company originally produced goods in the USA, but when production costs there rose, it subcontracted production to Taiwan and South Korea and then to other countries of the Global South. In 2014 Nike's global net income was US $2.69 billion, higher than the GNP of many sub-Saharan African countries (Nike, 2015).

Foreign direct investment (FDI) is when one firm invests in another firm and/or country (for example, in an overseas subsidiary) with the intention of gaining some control in that firm's operations (Dicken, 2015). In order to attract TNC investment, governments frequently offer tax breaks, lax regulations, low minimum

Plate 8.7 TNC regional headquarters: Lonrho building, Nairobi, Kenya
(*photo*: Tony Binns)

wages, cheap rent and, if necessary, military assistance to crush any labour unrest. Governments establish export-processing zones (EPZs) with the intention of attracting foreign investors, who then stay and hopefully make the development permanent (Gwynne, 2002). The level of FDI in 2007, before the Global Financial Crisis, was nine times that of international development aid and about 100 TNCs accounted for all FDI in the Global South (Madeley, 1999; World Bank 2007). By the end of the 1990s, 38 per cent of global FDI went to countries of the Global South, but one-third of this went to China alone, making that country the single largest host of inward investment, with at least 18 million people employed in 124 EPZs (Hoogvelt, 2001; see also Chapter 4).

Schneider and Frey (1985) and Clayton and Potter (1996) found that other factors, such as the size of the home market, price and exchange rate stability, and political and institutional stability, were also important considerations in TNC overseas investment decisions. The power and influence of TNCs continue to grow, facilitated both by governments withdrawing controls on foreign investment, and thus encouraging the greater mobility of capital, and also through government support of WTO trade rules, which limit the rights of governments to control TNC activities.

TNCs have been hailed by some as the new development agents, as they can provide assistance to countries of the South in the shape of economic, technical and managerial resources. Furthermore, the World Bank believes that 'private sector investment is the most important source of growth in developing economies' (World Bank, in Madeley, 1999: 24). In contrast, dependency theorists argue that TNCs represent 'core' countries exploiting 'peripheral' countries, and that TNC investment leads to the international division of labour, foreign indebtedness, capital monopolisation and economic impoverishment (Bury, 2001). Curtis is particularly critical of TNCs and the effects of their operations, suggesting that

> Under TNC-led globalisation, the evolution of the world economy continues to be driven by expanding inequalities in wealth both between and within most countries. Income differentials are generally widening, skewing wealth distribution towards the middle classes and the rich. The result is that markets, products and services are increasingly focused on supplying the needs of these powerful and dominant consumers.
>
> (Curtis, 2001b: 115)

In reality, the impact of a TNC on a specific country will partly depend on the nature of the employment generated. The low-skill production work that Nike provides has particular negative implications for development. Employment will not necessarily be beneficial for workers in terms of pay, working conditions or skills enhancement; the low-tech nature of the work does not hold much scope for useful technology transfer; nor will it bring many local linkages, since few local suppliers are used; trade advantages will be moderate, as the country is mainly being used as an export platform and the government may provide tax incentives; positive impacts may be unsustainable, since investment is often insecure and short-term, and there is frequently a lack of provision for social services, such as education and healthcare. Much of the literature has evaluated the impact of TNCs internationally and at the level of the state, but there is also an urgent need to focus on individual households as a key unit of analysis (Bury, 2001).

Critical reflection

TNCs and corporate social responsibility

As a result of adverse media attention about the activities of certain TNCs in countries of the South, most major firms have been through a process of re-conceptualising their relationship with broader society. Many firms now employ 'corporate social responsibility' (CSR) managers, whose tasks include promoting their firm's role as corporate citizens, and assisting in the publication of annual reports detailing

▶

Critical reflection (continued)

the firm's contributions to the societies within which they operate (Jones et al., 2007; Seyfang, 2002).

According to the European Commission, 'Corporate Social Responsibility (CSR) refers to companies taking responsibility for their impact on society. As evidence suggests, CSR is increasingly important to the competitiveness of enterprises. It can bring benefits in terms of risk management, cost savings, access to capital, customer relationships, human resource management, and innovation capacity' (European Commission, 2015). In July 2013, the EC inaugurated the European CSR Award Scheme by making awards to 63 small, medium and large companies which have initiated partnership projects demonstrating CSR principles in 30 European countries.

In the case of UK retail firms (such as Tesco, Sainsbury's and Marks & Spencer), there has been more careful attention in recent years given to ensuring that working conditions at the site of production meet acceptable standards, for example that farms in the South do not use child labour, that their pay levels are in line with national legislation and that proper health and safety equipment is provided. International codes of practice are used to confirm that appropriate standards are being met.

For some companies these approaches represent a defensive role, as they attempt to protect themselves from external criticism which could be potentially damaging to their business operations. Other companies are more proactive and seek to promote responsible practice as a central component of their corporate brand image, as illustrated by this statement by Marks & Spencer's Chief Executive in the firm's 2006 CSR Report:

We believe that being a responsible business is the right thing to do, but we also believe that it makes good business sense. Put simply, it helps us to attract shoppers to our stores, recruit and retain the best people, form better partnerships with our suppliers and create greater value for our shareholders.

(http://www2.marksandspencer.com/the company/invest relations/downloads/2006/ complete_csr_report.pdf, 27 February 2007)

There have been a number of cases which have tested the CSR credentials of large transnational companies with production activities in the South. For example, the sudden collapse of the eight-storey Rana Plaza building in Bangladesh in April 2013, which led to over 1,000 deaths and many injuries, received worldwide publicity, not least because a number of overseas companies were using the building for garment production. The UK-based company Primark was one such company which, following media pressure, agreed almost a year after the disaster to provide compensation amounting to US $12 million to families who lost relatives in the disaster (*The Guardian*, 2014). Campaigners were hoping that other companies using the building would follow Primark's actions in giving compensation.

However, other cases of claims for compensation from transnational companies have not been so quickly addressed. For example, the gas leak from the Union Carbide pesticide plant in Bhopal, India, over 30 years ago in December 1984, left thousands of poor local residents dead or severely incapacitated, but some 93% of the victims have still received no compensation from the US-based company (see Chapter 9).

Many tourism-based businesses are now giving more attention to CSR issues. As Kalisch comments, tour operators now have a 'role and responsibility for creating the conditions for positive dynamics in the locations where they operate' (Kalisch, 2002: 19). A study of tourism businesses in Livingstone, Zambia, discovered that CSR initiatives are occurring on a variety of scales. One backpacker lodge was supporting a local orphanage through donating clothes and organising football matches and a Christmas party. At the other end of the business spectrum, the large South African-based Sun International corporation with two hotels in Livingstone in 2011 had a CSR budget of US $250,000, and had established a number of community projects for vulnerable groups – 'Successful projects include a vegetable-farming scheme that has been set up with blind members of the local community, a worm-farming scheme that is run with vulnerable women suffering from HIV/AIDS, a

Critical reflection (continued)

large-scale fish farming scheme that involves both local schools and community members, and a community-based bee-keeping scheme which produces honey' (McLachlan and Binns, 2014: 106).

Why do you think large companies are showing an interest in corporate social responsibility (CSR)? Examine some company policy statements to see what reasons are motivating companies on CSR.

TNCs and the globalisation of fresh food

During the 1990s, with trade liberalisation and the associated change in the global regulatory network, improvements in transportation technology and changing consumer demand resulted in an increasingly integrated global food production system dominated by TNCs. Overproduction of staple crops in the European Union under Fordist production systems and favourable government subsidies through the Common Agricultural Policy (CAP) meant that, during the 1980s, trade declined in cereals and sugar, as well as tropical beverages from the Global South (Dixon, 1990).

One element of the global food trade that has shown a spectacular increase in the last three decades is the export of high-value crops, such as fresh fruit, vegetables and cut flowers. Between 1989 and 1997,

the value of exports of fresh vegetables from sub-Saharan Africa to the EU increased by 150 per cent (Dolan and Humphrey, 2000). In 1989 the trade in these items comprised 5 per cent of global commodity trade and was equivalent in volume to trade in crude petroleum (Jaffee, 1994; Watts, 1996). Countries of the Global South contributed one-third by value to this lucrative trade, twice the value of their traditional agricultural exports of cocoa, coffee, cotton, sugar, tea and tobacco.

In 1990, 24 low- and middle-income countries, mainly in Asia and Latin America, exported annually in excess of US $500 million worth of high-value, fresh horticultural products. The main producers were Chile, Argentina, Brazil and Uruguay in South America, and Malaysia and Thailand in Asia. Elsewhere, in order to maintain their foreign exchange earnings, as well as to diversify their economies, some African countries have

Plate 8.8 Rose-growing for export, south of Nairobi, Kenya
(*photo*: Tony Binns)

been giving more attention to the production and export of high-value horticultural produce, most notably in Egypt, Kenya, post-apartheid South Africa, Zambia and Zimbabwe. Africa has been part of the global food market for centuries, with efficient and well-integrated marketing chains developing from the late nineteenth century to move cash crops such as tropical beverages, sugar, cotton and tobacco from African producers to consumers in Europe. However, these traditional marketing chains are not suitable for the export of highly perishable items such as fruit, vegetables and cut flowers (Plate 8.8). New chains have therefore evolved which, perhaps more than anything, reflect the considerable power of the large European retailers in responding to changing consumer demands (Box 8.7).

Until the beginning of the twentieth century, urban populations in Europe and the temperate regions of North America could only eat fresh produce seasonally and had to rely on canned and, later, frozen foods. The major change came with bananas, a tropical fruit that could withstand a long transportation link between producer and consumer, provided the temperature could be controlled. Early experiments in the banana trade began in the 1870s, when nationally based British, French and US specialist firms produced bananas in their tropical colonies, or 'semi-colonies' in the case of the USA, for consumption in Europe and the USA. As the banana industry grew, the US firms became extensively involved in the internal politics of states such as Cuba and the Central American 'banana republics' (Friedland, 1994).

Three firms involved in the early production and trade of bananas are Dole, Chiquita and Del Monte Tropical Products. All three firms also have major stakes in food labelling and transportation, with refrigerated cargo ships. Dole is a US-based transnational, known until 1991 as Castle & Cooke. It originally began as a merchant firm in the Hawaiian Islands and then became involved in food processing, real estate and fresh fruit and vegetable activities. Chiquita is also originally US-based and was formerly known as United Brands, and before that as the United Fruit Company. The Del Monte Fresh Produce Company, originally a US-based company, was known as Del Monte Tropical Products until late 1992.

Although bananas were important in the early history of these companies, they have, like other TNCs, diversified considerably since the Second World War. Chiquita bought seven lettuce-producing firms in California in 1969 and integrated them into a single subsidiary, Interharvest, which dominated US lettuce production and distribution. The Dole Food Company emerged in its modern form in 1961, when Castle & Cooke acquired the Dole Company, a pineapple producer. It expanded into bananas from 1964, as it bought an increasing share of the Standard Fruit Company, a banana producer for the North American market. In 1967, when Dole owned 87 per cent of Standard, Standard supplied 31 per cent of North American banana requirements. Ten years later, in 1977, Dole followed Chiquita into lettuce production by purchasing Bud Antle, the second largest lettuce producer in the USA. Subsequently, it was from the Bud Antle base that Dole expanded into a wide variety of other commodities.

BOX 8.7

The globalisation of food: horticultural exports from Kenya

Trade in fresh fruit, vegetables and flowers from sub-Saharan Africa to the EU increased dramatically during the 1980s and 1990s (Barrett et al., 1999; Bek, Binns and Nel, 2013; Dolan and Humphrey, 2000; Hughes, 2001). The European consumer now demands high-quality fresh commodities throughout the year. With a flight time of about nine hours from Europe to Kenya, major supermarket chains have established links and organised production to ensure these items can be on their shelves in less than 24 hours after harvest.

Exports of fresh horticultural produce from Kenya have grown steadily since independence, such that in 2000 they accounted for 16 per cent of total export earnings and were the second most important export after tea (Economist Intelligence Unit, 2001). The value of Kenyan horticultural exports rose more than

BOX 8.7 (continued)

five-fold from Ksh 3,780 million (about US $66 million) in 1991 to Ksh 21,216 million (about US $360 million) in 2000, and more recently has increased to Ksh 28,200 million (about US $480 million) in 2004, and reached Ksh 105 billion (about US $1.1 billion) in 2013.

Over the last two decades the horticultural industry has undergone dramatic change, coinciding with economic liberalisation. Huge private investments have been made, particularly by the country's ten largest producers in the cut flower and pre-packaged vegetable sectors. This has been in response to increased demand from Europe, and especially to attract and keep lucrative supply arrangements with large UK supermarkets. Kenya is a major supplier of green beans, mange-touts, avocados, mangos and cut flowers, as well as a significant range of Asian vegetables. Green beans are the most important vegetable crop exported, although quantities declined in 1995–1996. However, this decline was compensated by adding value to green bean exports through sorting and packaging in Kenya. The country faces increasingly stiff competition from other producers, such as Egypt, for green beans, South Africa for avocados, cut flowers and mangos and Israel for avocados and cut flowers.

The ongoing troubles in Zimbabwe, leading to serious disruption of that country's horticultural exports, have provided a gap in the market which Kenya, Zambia and other African countries have been filling. The growth of the Kenyan cut flower sector has been spectacular, and in 1996 Kenya overtook Israel to become the leading supplier of cut flowers to the Dutch auctions. In 1995, the tonnage of cut flower exports exceeded that of vegetables for the first time (Barrett et al., 1997, 1999; Hughes, 2001). In 2014, an estimated 125,000 tonnes of flowers were exported, earning some US $531 million. Kenya exports most of its fruit and vegetables to the United Kingdom and France, whereas cut flowers are destined for the Netherlands and Germany, as well as the United Kingdom.

The growth of the Kenyan horticulture industry has been due in no small measure to government support

since the late 1960s. The Horticultural Crops Development Authority (HCDA) was formed in 1967, through which state policy and support for the sector have been channelled. The government has generally restricted itself to the role of facilitator and has not interfered with market mechanisms or pricing policy, a role which has been endorsed by a series of structural adjustment programmes since 1979. *Sessional Paper 1, 1986* specifically emphasised that agricultural growth was to be achieved by higher productivity, the expansion of high-value crops (such as fruit and vegetables) and improved export competitiveness.

The promotion of the horticultural industry is seen as a partnership between government departments, quasi-parastatal organisations, such as the Export Promotion Council, and the main growers, such as Sulmac – Brooke Bond's flower-growing subsidiary and the country's largest producer of cut flowers – and Homegrown, the largest producer of vegetables. Meanwhile, under structural adjustment, the influence of agricultural marketing boards has been greatly reduced. Duty exemptions have been particularly helpful, for example from 1991 the exemption of imported packaging materials used in the industry, and from 1994 the exemption of fertilisers, tools and greenhouse sheeting.

Two distinct marketing chains can be identified in the Kenyan export horticulture industry. One chain, which has developed since the 1960s, involves mainly small and medium-sized growers, and in the mid-1990s accounted for 31 per cent of Kenya's horticultural exports. Small farmers may either supply medium growers, who then sell on to exporters or, alternatively, sell to intermediaries and agents who then sell to exporters. There is some criticism at various points in this chain about the quality and reliability of produce supply. This chain supplies large quantities of vegetables for the Asian market and strong links have developed between Asian exporters in Kenya and Asian importers and retailers in the United Kingdom. Importers of Asian vegetables are keen to have a wide variety of produce, but in smaller quantities than the supermarkets. Consumers are

▶

BOX 8.7 (continued)

concerned with flavour and value for money rather than presentation or packaging. Produce for this market is generally imported and sold loose, not in pre-packs, and it does not have to meet strict supermarket specifications (Barrett et al., 1997, 1999).

In sharp contrast, a fully integrated chain, which has developed since 1990, links Kenya's largest producers to major companies in the EU. Virtually all their vegetable produce is sold under contract to supermarket chains, mostly in pre-packs, which are processed in packing stations where standards exceed EU requirements. The packs use approved materials, and are bar-coded and priced in Kenya as directed by the supermarkets, which supply the pricing and other stickers. Many flowers are also sold to supermarket chains, and bouquets are made up in pack-houses on the farm. The rest of the flowers are sent in bulk to Dutch flower auctions, where they constitute over 25 per cent of all flowers sold. The major producers have all invested heavily in EU-standard pack-stations, refrigerated trucks and cold stores.

The large UK supermarket chains are at the top of the power hierarchy in this business, but shoulder few of the risks until produce actually reaches their shelves. Supermarkets depend on UK importers, through their associated exporting companies in Kenya, for getting produce out of Kenya and into the United Kingdom. The requirements of the UK Food Safety Act (1990) have had a major effect on production and marketing, since the Act calls for 'due diligence', requiring importers to know exactly where and how the crops were produced (including fertilisers and pesticides used), and there must be documentation to prove it. Traceability is now as crucial in the horticultural trade as quality, reliability and price, and logistically this favours dealing with a few large commercial farmers who can maintain strict standards and detailed records, rather than with many smallholder producers among whom there could be much variability. UK consumers are highly sensitive to issues concerning toxic chemicals, or the perceived exploitation of local labour.

Two factors are absolutely crucial in exporting horticultural produce: the freight space and the cold chain. The larger exporters have more control than smaller exporters over freight space, because they can negotiate guaranteed space on aircraft and either fill it with their own produce or sell it on. Kenya's largest horticultural exporter has a pre-booked arrangement for cargo space on British Airways' nightly airfreight service to London. Maintenance of the cold chain is also vital in dealing with such highly perishable goods in a tropical climate. Exporters with their own dedicated cold storage facilities, at Jomo Kenyatta International Airport in Nairobi, run much less risk of breaking the cold chain than if they have to rely on using the general cold-store facilities.

If Kenya's export-oriented horticulture industry is to expand further these constraints need to be addressed, particularly in relation to the possible incorporation of more small-scale producers into the trade. In addition, the improvement of road infrastructure and the expansion of airport facilities are necessary. In the late 1990s a new international airport at Eldoret was completed, which could both reduce the pressures on Nairobi airport and also create potential for exporting more produce from the country's northwestern region. Other possible measures might include the establishment of an agency to monitor controls and standards for all export crops, including banning sales of chemicals not permitted under EU regulations. Codes of conduct between growers, exporters and freight agents might also be enforced by trade associations, which also work to promote the industry.

But in the context of a poor country, such as Kenya, surely a key question is the extent to which poverty can be reduced among small producers engaged in export-oriented production. If horticultural production is to have a meaningful impact on poverty alleviation in Kenya, then more attention needs to be given to small-scale producers – perhaps coordinated within producer groups that help them gain access to export markets – as well as controlling quality, post-harvest handling and marketing techniques.

During the 1980s Chiquita, Del Monte and Dole all expanded substantially into global sourcing and distribution based on their banana operations. The recipe for success of these TNCs has involved: (1) attracting capital from investors to make the initial purchases; (2) continuously generating new capital and demonstrating good profit levels; and (3) making good acquisitions, which have to fit into an overall strategy. Acquisitions should ideally be clustered geographically rather than be spread all over the world, and should be fully consolidated before venturing into new areas (Friedland, 1994).

Critical reflection

Should we be reducing 'food miles'?

There have been massive changes in the production and supply of food in the post-war period and particularly in the last 30 years. With globalisation of the food industry and the setting up of supermarket regional distribution centres, food is travelling greater distances by air, road and rail to reach the consumer – a trend which has led to some concern about 'food miles'. Steadily increasing food miles from the farm to the consumer have led to increased carbon dioxide emissions, air pollution, congestion, accidents and noise. Air transport increased by 140 per cent between 1992 and 2002. Although air travel in 2002 only represented 0.1 per cent of total vehicle distance travelled, it contributed 11 per cent to greenhouse gas emissions. It is estimated that CO_2 equivalent emissions from all food transport increased by 12 per cent between 1992 and 2002.

In reflecting on the issue of food miles, we might ask ourselves: are organic bananas really worth the cost of the jet fuel that carried them from the West Indies? Does an apple grown a few hundred miles away taste better than one grown 3,000 miles away? Is it better to support the local green bean producer than farmers in Kenya? What would happen to the economies of the world's poorest countries if food exports to richer countries were cut back? And how would richer, but distant, countries such as New Zealand manage such changes given the key importance of exported meat, fruit and milk products to the national economy?

The food miles issue is not straightforward, as an article in The Economist suggests:

> Obviously it makes sense to choose a product that has been grown locally over an identical product shipped in from afar. But such direct comparisons are rare. And it turns out that the apparently straightforward approach of minimising the 'food miles' associated with your weekly groceries does not, in fact, always result in the smallest possible environmental impact. The term 'food mile' is itself misleading. A mile travelled by a large truck full of groceries is not the same as a mile travelled by a sport-utility vehicle carrying a bag of salad. It is more helpful to think about food-vehicle miles (i.e. the number of miles travelled by vehicles carrying food) and food-tonne miles (which take the tonnage being carried into account).

> (© The Economist Newspaper Limited, London, 7 December 2006)
> (see also DEFRA, 2005).

What are your views about the 'food miles' issue? Choose one supermarket item that you eat regularly and that has been transported over a long distance. Examine the feasibility and implications of sourcing a similar product more locally.

The Global South and the debt crisis

The total external debt stocks of countries in the South more than doubled from US $2,352,002 million in 2005 to US $5,032,074 million in 2012. According to World Bank statistics, the four countries with the largest total external debt stocks in 2013 were China (US $874,463,286,000), Brazil (US $482,469,814,000), Mexico (US $443,012,459,000) and India (US $427,561,868,000) (World Bank, 2015c).

The origins of the debt crisis are complex, but undoubtedly major factors were the long-term effects of rising oil prices in the 1970s, compounded by countries in the North adopting monetarist policies in the late 1970s following the 'second oil shock' of 1979, which forced up interest rates on debt repayments (Corbridge, 2002b). Added to this was the collapse of commodity prices in the early 1980s, such that in 1993 prices were 32 per cent lower than in 1980; and in relation to the price of manufactured goods they were 55 per cent lower than in 1960. As a result, there was a sharp deterioration in the terms of trade affecting countries of the Global South (ICPQL, 1996). Facing massive debt repayments, the IMF and World Bank, which were created in part to transfer the savings of surplus countries to deficit countries, then imposed structural adjustment programmes on these countries, which required deep cuts in public spending, often with little concern for local circumstances and human welfare (see Chapters 1, 3 and 7). As Watkins observes,

> In Latin America, the epicentre of the debt crisis, average incomes fell by 10 per cent in the 1980s and investment declined from 23 per cent to 16 per cent of national income, causing widespread unemployment and poverty.
>
> (Watkins, 1995: 174)

The debt crisis occurred suddenly in the early 1980s, with the financial collapse of Mexico in August 1982, and affected other middle-income countries which were heavily dependent on commercial lending, particularly Brazil and Argentina. The poorest countries were also badly hit, but since commercial banks had been reluctant to lend to them, most of their borrowing has been through public sector aid programmes. During the 1980s, the question of rescheduling the massive debts of certain countries became a major issue, since some were unable to repay the interest on the sums borrowed, let alone reduce the basic sum.

As we saw earlier, the newly industrialising countries of East and Southeast Asia did not experience such problems due to the relative buoyancy of their economies, although in 1997 and 1998 many Asian NICs registered a serious downturn in their economies. Countries such as South Korea, while borrowing heavily, have been able to service their debt due to a high level of exports. During the 1990s private and often highly speculative capital flows, mainly in the form of direct foreign investment, benefited China and middle-income countries such as Argentina, Malaysia, Mexico and Thailand. Furthermore, in 1989 the Brady Plan assisted middle-income countries by recognising that commercial debt could be reduced with IMF and World Bank support and by extending repayment periods.

However, the world's poorest countries, particularly those in sub-Saharan Africa, continue to suffer from a huge debt crisis, and are heavily dependent on official aid flows for their financial survival. As the flow of aid declines in real terms, trade and debt reform assume a greater importance. Between 1980 and 1999 sub-Saharan Africa's debt more than tripled to around US $216 billion and, although considerably less than that of Latin America (US $813 billion), the region's debt increased from the equivalent of 28 per cent of its GNP to 72 per cent, compared with 40 per cent for Latin America. Between 1985 and 1992, Africa disbursed US $81.6 billion in debt payments, diverting government funds from vital expenditure on education, health and other urgent priorities (Oxfam, 1993: 13). A number of countries have had to reschedule their debts, which has contributed to the steady buildup of arrears. Between 1989 and 1991 the official creditors cancelled some US $10 billion worth of debt to sub-Saharan countries, but the debt problem remains severe.

So what can and should be done about Africa's plight? As Oxfam observed,

> It is difficult to avoid being struck by the contrast between the urgency with which Western governments have responded to the financial problems of Eastern Europe and Russia, and their neglect, for more than a decade, of Africa's far deeper problems.
>
> (Oxfam, 1993: 17)

Oxfam advocates a fresh approach on the part of Northern governments, arguing that Africa's problem is not temporary, but rather a serious matter of bankruptcy which must be recognised 'in placing debtors' *ability to pay* above the claims of creditors'. Furthermore, Oxfam called on the industrialised countries to 'agree to the cancellation of between 90 and 100 per cent of *all* non-concessional debt' (Oxfam, 1993: 17).

Oxfam is also highly critical of the IMF, stating that it is not an instrument for providing long-term concessional development finance; and it is governed by apparently immutable orthodoxies entirely inappropriate to African conditions. The time has come therefore either fundamentally to reform the IMF, or to extricate it from Africa. In either case, measures to write off obligations due to it from low-income African countries are long overdue.

(Oxfam, 1993: 17)

It seems that the recovery of Africa will depend on substantial investment of foreign capital, since in 2005 sub-Saharan African countries together only received about 1.7 per cent of worldwide foreign direct investment, compared with the 8 per cent received by China alone. In 2015, Foreign Direct Investment (FDI) inflows to Africa fell by 2015, with most of the decline in the Sub-Saharan region. Nigeria experienced a decline in FDI of 27 per cent with the drop in oil revenues, whilst in South Africa FDI in 2015 fell significantly by 74 per cent (UNCTAD, 2016: 5). With the lack of private investment, Africa is particularly dependent on government and multilateral agency development assistance There is no doubt that some real progress was made in the late 1990s and early twenty-first century in alleviating the debt crisis in Africa and elsewhere among the world's poorest countries. The call from Oxfam and other influential charities and NGOs for urgent attention to be given to the debt problem was taken forward by targeted anti-debt pressure groups, most notably 'Jubilee 2000', and with pressure also from the world's most powerful leaders, the World Bank and the International Monetary Fund launched the significant HIPC initiative in 1996 (Box 8.8).

Jubilee 2000 proved to be particularly successful, and originated when a number of major development-focused charities decided in 1996 to petition political leaders of the rich countries to 'cancel the unpayable debts of the poorest countries by the year 2000 under a fair and transparent process' (Jubilee 2000, 2002: 2). The petition grew to become a major international campaign, such that by the end of the campaign some 24 million signatures had been collected for the Jubilee 2000 petition, the first ever global petition. The campaign brought the issue of debt in the South to ordinary people across the world, through similar campaigns in 60 countries. The decision to introduce the Enhanced

Initiative for HIPC countries in 1999 was undoubtedly a sign of the power and influence of Jubilee 2000 (Roodman, 2001). Worldwide concern about the debt crisis in poor countries by no means ended in 2000. From early 2001 Jubilee split into a number of campaigning organisations across the world, such as Jubilee Research, Jubilee Debt Campaign and Jubilee Scotland based in UK and the Jubilee USA network based in Washington.

Aid to the Global South

In 1970, through Resolution 2626 in the International Development Strategy for the Second United Nations Development Decade, the UN General Assembly set out for the first time agreed targets for finance resource transfers and flows of overseas development assistance – aid. The UN urged developed countries to achieve an allocation level of 0.70 per cent of their gross national product in overseas aid by 1975. As we have already seen, this figure was subsequently emphasised in the Brandt Report in 1980, and has been reaffirmed at numerous world gatherings such as the Earth Summit in Rio de Janeiro in 1992, the Conference on Population and Development in Cairo in 1994 and the World Summit on Social Development in Copenhagen in 1995.

However, there has unfortunately been little progress on this, and in some cases governments in the North, which are members of the Development Assistance Committee (DAC) of the Organisation for Economic Co-operation and Development (OECD), have actually reduced their aid budgets substantially. For example, the United Kingdom's allocation of overseas development assistance reached an all-time high in 1979 at 0.51 per cent of Gross National Income (GNI), but then declined steadily to an all-time low of 0.27 per cent in 1990. There was a slight increase to 0.32 per cent in 1991, but at the time of the Labour Party's general election victory in May 1997 the UK aid budget had fallen again to 0.26 per cent. Since the incoming Labour government pledged not to raise key taxes for two years, there seemed little prospect of an increase in the UK aid budget before the year 1999. However, in 2000 there was a significant increase in UK Official Development Assistance (ODA) to 0.32 per cent of GNI and an even greater increase to 0.48 in 2005. In 2013, for the first time, the UK's ODA reached, and indeed exceeded, the

0.7 per cent target with a figure of 0.72 per cent of GNI (Figure 8.5a and b). More recently, in March 2015, the UK parliament took a very significant step in passing a bill which enshrined in law a commitment to spend 0.7 per cent of GNI every year on overseas aid. In making this important decision, the UK became the first of the powerful G7 nations to meet the UN's aid target (*The Guardian*, 2015b).

BOX 8.8

The Heavily Indebted Poor Countries (HIPC) Debt Relief Initiative

The Heavily Indebted Poor Countries (HIPC) Debt Relief Initiative was launched by the World Bank and the IMF in 1996 and represented a recognition of the significant effort needed to bring about a once and for all reduction in the debts of some of the world's poorest countries. According to the World Bank,

> It was the first comprehensive approach to reduce the external debt of the world's poorest, most heavily indebted countries, and represented an important step forward in placing debt relief within an overall framework of poverty reduction.
>
> (World Bank, 2001b: 1)

The experience of some of the first countries to qualify for HIPC debt relief led the UK government to push for a thorough review of the initiative, which started in January 1999.

> The [UK] Government believed it would have to be redesigned to ensure that it provided poor countries with a permanent solution to their debt problems and freed up resources to tackle poverty.
>
> (Department for International Development, 2000b: 2)

This was supported by the leaders of the Group of Seven (G7) at their summit in Cologne, Germany, in July 1999, and in September 1999 the World Bank and IMF approved an 'enhanced initiative' as an integral part of the new poverty reduction strategy. This strategy was designed to link external support to domestically formulated, results-based poverty strategies and also to improve relations between the World Bank, IMF and recipient countries.

In 2005, in order to help speed up progress towards achieving the Millennium Development Goal, for countries completing the HIPC initiative process, the Multilateral Debt Relief Initiative (MDRI) was added to the HIPC initiative, which allowed for 100 per cent of relief on debts from three specific multilateral institutions – the International Monetary Fund, the World Bank and the African Development Fund. At the end of 2013, the value of the new HIPC framework, in providing assistance to the 39 countries which were eligible, was about US $75 billion, compared with US $12.5 billion under the original HIPC Initiative. To be eligible for HIPC Initiative assistance, a country must meet four criteria:

➤ Be very poor (as defined by the World Bank and IMF), and therefore eligible to borrow from the World Bank's International Development Agency which gives interest-free loans and grants, and from the IMFs Poverty Reduction and Growth Trust, which provides loans to low-income countries at subsidized rates;

➤ Face an unsustainable debt burden that cannot be addressed through traditional debt relief mechanisms;

➤ Have established a track record of reform and sound policies through IMF and World Bank-supported programmes;

➤ Have developed a Poverty Reduction Strategy Paper (PRSP) through a broad-based participatory process in the country policies – macro-economic, structural and social policies consistent with poverty reduction and sustained growth.

(International Monetary Fund, 2015)

In response to problems with the original initiative, the enhanced HIPC Initiative aims to provide:

BOX 8.8 (continued)

➤ Faster debt relief, beginning immediately or soon after the 'decision point';

➤ Stronger links between debt relief and poverty reduction strategies, formulated with civil society participation;

➤ Deeper and broader debt relief, with a reduction of US $50 billion in external debt servicing.

By February 2006, some 33 countries had reached their 'decision point' under the enhanced HIPC Initiative, and six countries had reached the 'completion point' under the original HIPC Initiative. At that time, the 33 countries were receiving debt relief amounting to some US $38.2 billion (WB-IEG, 2006).

By March 2015, (as Table 8.3 shows) 35 countries were at a 'post-completion-point' stage and were receiving full debt relief, one country (Chad) was between decision and completion point and had received some interim debt relief, whilst three countries (Eritrea, Somalia and Sudan) were at the 'pre-decision-point' stage and had been

identified as potentially eligible for HIPC Initiative assistance. It should be noted that a large proportion of the countries listed are in sub-Saharan Africa.

In June 2001 Bolivia became the second HIPC country to reach completion point after Uganda, the latter being the first country to receive approval in May 2000. The conditions which Bolivia had to meet in order to receive assistance were: first, continued implementation of strong macro-economic and structural policies; second, the establishment of a fully defined Poverty Reduction Strategy Paper (PRSP); and, third, confirmation of participation in the enhanced HIPC framework from Bolivia's other creditors.

Bolivia met virtually all of the financial requirements in its programme with the IMF and, in addition, reformed its customs and internal revenue agencies; introduced a new tax procedure code to strengthen tax administration; and launched a new financial management information system to increase

Table 8.3 Countries that have qualified for, or are eligible, or potentially eligible, and may wish to receive HIPC Initiative assistance (March 2015)

Post-completion-point countries (35)

Afghanistan	Ghana	Mozambique
Benin	Guinea	Nicaragua
Bolivia	Guinea-Bissau	Niger
Burkina Faso	Guyana	Rwanda
Burundi	Haiti	São Tomé & Príncipe
Cameroon	Honduras	Senegal
Central African Republic	Liberia	Sierra Leone
Comoros	Madagascar	Tanzania
Republic of Congo	Malawi	Togo
Democratic Republic of Congo	Mali	Uganda
Côte d'Ivoire	Mauritania	Zambia
Ethiopia		
The Gambia		

Interim countries (between decision and completion point) (1)

Chad

Pre-decision-point countries (3)

Eritrea	Somalia	Sudan

Source: International Monetary Fund (IMF) (2015) *Debt relief under the Heavily Indebted Poor Countries (HIPC) Initiative*. Factsheet, 15 Apr 2015. http://www.imf.org/external/np/exr/facts/hipc.htm, Accessed 7 May 2015.

▶

transparency and accountability in the administration of public expenditure. Including assistance provided under the original 1996 Initiative, Bolivia received debt service relief of over US $2 billion. As a result of HIPC assistance, Bolivia's total external debt has been reduced by 50 per cent, and annual debt service payments in the ten years from 2001 were reduced by some US $120 million per year.

Sierra Leone, which in 2002 emerged from over a decade of civil war and internal turmoil, was admitted to the Enhanced HIPC Debt Relief Initiative in March 2002. The country's government formulated a detailed plan for the transparent and accountable use of funds received, with emphasis placed on education, health and rural development.

HIPC has been effective in channelling additional resources to qualifying countries, and transfers to HIPC countries increased from US $8.8 billion in 1999 to US $17.5 billion in 2004, while transfers to other low-income countries grew by only a third. The requirement for countries to implement a poverty reduction strategy at the same time as receiving debt relief has been an important and beneficial outcome of the programme.

The aid giving record of the USA, the world's largest economy, has been rather disappointing. Despite giving the largest total amount of overseas aid in absolute terms in 2013 (US $31.55 billion), the proportion of GNI given as aid was only 0.19. Although this represents an increase on the 0.13 per cent figure for 2002, this is one of the lowest figures among OECD countries. In 2013, only five countries – Denmark, Luxembourg, Norway, Sweden and the United Kingdom – had reached, and indeed exceeded the 0.70 target. Norway, with 1.07 per cent of GNI, was followed closely by Sweden (1.02) and Luxembourg (1.00). The increase was particularly significant in the UK, which reached 0.72 per cent in 2013, but which in 2004 only gave 0.36 per cent of GNI as aid. In 2013, the UK gave US $17.88 billion in aid, second only to the USA in absolute terms.

In the case of some European countries there is evidence of cut-backs in overseas aid from 2008, possibly due to the Global Financial Crisis. For example, the Netherlands, Austria, Ireland, Italy, Spain and Greece all gave lower proportions of Gross National Income as aid in 2013 compared with 2008.

The politics of overseas aid

In addition to examining the quantity of overseas aid, it is important to consider the nature and direction of the aid and the reasons for giving it. Whether overseas development assistance takes the form of short-term disaster relief, longer term development aid, food aid or military aid, each has many complex ramifications and implications, both in relation to the successful alleviation of poverty in the Global South and also in relation to the priorities, and frequently ulterior motives, of donor countries.

There are many interesting examples where international or local political perspectives have affected donor-recipient relationships. For example, a study by Dreher et al. (2009) found that World Bank projects have often been 'funneled to politically important developing countries, such as those serving a term on the UN Security Council' (Dreher et al., 2009: 14). For example, in 1970 Argentina had no new World Bank projects, but in 1971 when Argentina joined the UN Security Council (UNSC), two new projects were started. When Argentina was again elected to the Security Council in 1986, the number of new World Bank projects doubled in that year. A similar pattern occurred in Ghana, which was elected to the UNSC in 1986, and in the following year eight World Bank projects were approved (Dreher et al., 2009). The USA, France, Germany, Japan and the UK can exert considerable pressure on funding decisions made by the World Bank, for example, in 1991 when the US 'supported a World Bank loan for China in exchange for China's support of the Security Council resolution to deploy armed forces in Iraq' (Dreher et al., 2009: 4).

The overseas aid policies of particular donor countries frequently reflect prevailing political perspectives and objectives. For example, during the 1980s and early 1990s, Britain tied a higher proportion of its aid than most donors, and 74 per cent of bilateral aid in 1991 was

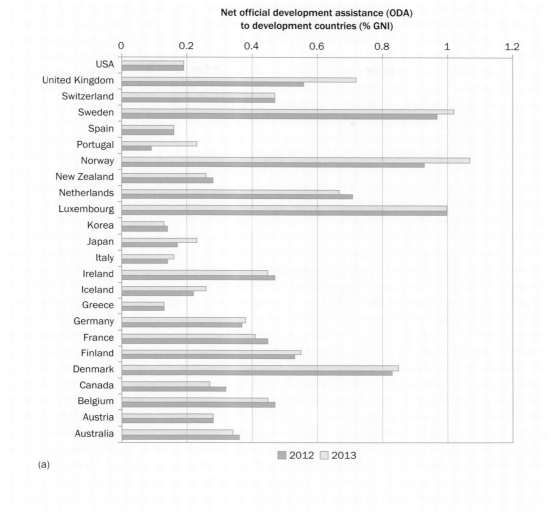

Net official development assistance (ODA) to development countries (% GNI)

Figure 8.5a Net official development assistance (ODA) 2012–2013: by donor country (% GNI)
Source: World Bank, 2012b

tied to the purchase of British goods and services (German and Randel, 1993). The construction of the controversial Pergau Dam in Malaysia in the early 1990s, costing US $350 million, was the largest single project ever financed under the UK aid programme. However, critics argued that it was an expensive and inefficient source of power and a waste of money for both Malaysian consumers and British taxpayers. Nevertheless, the project went ahead, because it was linked to selling large quantities of British exports to Malaysia, including over US $1 billion of arms exports.

From 1 April 2001 all UK development assistance became fully untied with the Department for International Development, commenting that;

Tying aid protects donor exporters from international competition for contracts. This leads to higher costs and lower quality, and consequently reduces the impact on poverty. The World Bank estimates that tying aid reduces its effective value by as much as 25 per cent.

(Department for International Development, 2001b: 1)

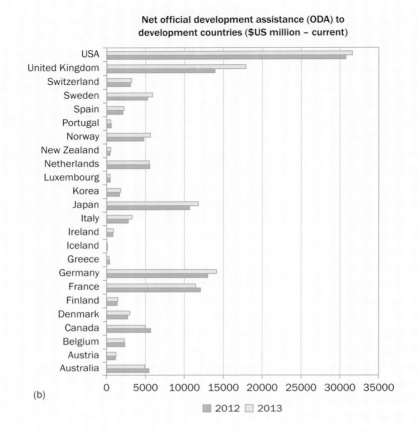

Net official development assistance (ODA) to development countries ($US million – current)

(b)

■ 2012 □ 2013

Figure 8.5 (continued) (b) ODA by donor country ($US million)
Source: OECD (2006)

The UK government has encouraged other governments to untie their aid, and on 1 January 2002 the OECD's *'Recommendation on Untying Official Development Assistance to Least Developed Countries'* came into effect, representing an important step forward.

A report written in 1993 by German and Randel, and reflecting on the policies of the Reagan and Bush administrations in the USA, noted that US aid was generally directed to two broad categories of countries: countries of strategic importance, and poor, but 'politically correct', countries. Egypt and Israel, both of strategic importance, respectively received 32.1 and 8.3 per cent of US aid in 1990–91. During the civil war in El Salvador, Central American countries received about US $1 billion of bilateral aid from the USA each year. One-third of US bilateral aid in 1991 was spent on food aid. Interestingly, the primary stated purpose of US aid is to 'advance US interests by helping co-operating countries to expand their economies and the opportunities they offer their people' (German and Randel, 1993: 59). In the 1980s poverty alleviation was not a specifically stated goal of US aid, though it was an element of certain programmes.

Since the 1990 *World Bank Report on Poverty*, some governments have made a stronger commitment to poverty alleviation, and the DAC is keen to monitor donor performance in this area. NGOs are concerned that too much aid is used to promote exports and subsidise domestic industry rather than to benefit the poorest people of the Global South. Even Norway, with a significant proportion of Gross National Income allocated to aid, and with a strong poverty alleviation focus, was keen in the early 1990s to expand Norwegian commercial interests. With the then Prime Minister Gro Harlem Brundtland's high-profile involvement on the world development stage, environmental issues became a particularly important element in Norwegian development aid.

In its White Paper on International Development, published in December 2000, the UK government stated its aim to focus development assistance on 'systematic poverty reduction':

> In 1999/2000 we spent 74 per cent of the UK's development assistance in low income countries, up from 68 per cent in 1996/97. We will further increase the focus on low income countries over the next three years . . . [and increase] our capacity to provide more resources to countries that implement pro-poor policies by establishing policy and performance funds for Africa, Asia and for the multilateral development institutions.
>
> (Department for International Development, 2000a: 87)

More recently there has been an increasing focus on governance, as reflected in the UK government's 2006 White Paper titled *Governance, Development and Democratic Politics* in which there was a strong focus on making politics work for the poor. The UK White Paper strongly endorses the 'Paris Declaration on Aid Effectiveness' which was signed in 2005 by over 100 donor and recipient country governments, donor agencies and development banks.

Aid effectiveness

The Paris High Level Forum on Aid Effectiveness, organised in February 2005 by the OECD and hosted by the French government, was an important landmark in discussions about aid policies, and particularly aspects of aid management, application and governance. The Paris Declaration contained 56 partnership commitments designed to improve the effectiveness of aid and listed 12 indicators to track progress. Further High Level Forums on Aid Effectiveness were subsequently held in Accra, Ghana (September 2008) and in Busan, South Korea (November 2011).

The 'Paris Declaration on Aid Effectiveness' outlined five key principles for making aid more effective:

1 **Ownership**: That countries in the South should lead their own development policies and manage the implementation of these on the ground, with support from donors in building local capacity.

2 **Alignment**: That donors should line up their aid strategies behind the priorities outlined in the national development strategies of countries in the South.

3 **Harmonisation**: That donors should give more consideration to better coordinating development work among themselves to avoid unnecessary duplication and to ease the pressure on governments in the South in having to deal with numerous field missions.

4 **Results**: That all organisations should give greater attention to achieving tangible results from aid which make a difference to the lives of poor people.

5 **Mutual accountability**: That donors and countries in the South should be open and transparent in accounting to each other for the use of aid funds, and should explain to citizens and parliaments about the impact of the aid which has been received.

(OECD, 2008)

In examining the significance of governance issues in the Paris Declaration and the future agenda set at the Paris meeting, Armon poses the question, 'So does the governance resurgence, built on the Paris agenda, herald a sea-change in the way aid agencies go about their work?' (Armon, 2007: 656). Whilst Armon is cautiously optimistic about the increasing focus on political governance in the giving, receiving and application of aid, he is concerned that policies should have tangible development impacts. He argues that 'If the politics of development begin to obscure the morality of development, we will lose much of our focus and vigour' (Armon, 2007: 656). Hyden examines the implications of the Paris Declaration in terms of governance issues and changing power relationships between aid donors and governments in the South. He suggests that 'by giving these governments more say over how donor funds are spent, the straitjacket that foreign aid has often been for recipients is removed. They are now expected to be able to make long-term policy commitments and thus become more effective in pursuing development goals. This growing control over foreign aid resources by partner governments has implications for power relations within the state as well as between state and civil society' (Hyden, 2008: 268).

Types of aid

Food aid continues to be significant in commodity flows between countries and, although most food aid is provided bilaterally on a government-to-government basis, the creation of the World Food Programme (WFP) in 1961 added a significant multilateral dimension, such that it is now the main provider of international food aid for development and disaster relief. Food aid is a controversial form of development assistance, since political and economic motives may be significant in sustaining flows and determining their direction (Shaw and Clay, 1993). Food aid may be divided into three types:

➤ *Programme food aid* is usually given as a grant or a soft loan on a government-to-government basis to fill the gap between the demand and supply of food from domestic production and any commercial imports. Such aid may reduce the amount of foreign exchange a country needs to spend on buying imports, and if the food is sold it provides additional local currency for the government.

➤ *Project food aid* is primarily aimed at satisfying the nutritional needs of the poor, mainly in rural areas, and is given as a grant, with the food aid closely targeted. Although the WFP is the main provider, other government and NGO bodies may also be involved. WFP is also involved in a variety of rural projects concerned with health centres for mother-and-child care, primary education and training, and food-for-work programmes.

➤ *Emergency food aid* is a response to sudden disasters such as drought, floods and pest attack, as well as civil war. Emergency food aid is provided both bilaterally and multilaterally, mainly by the WFP. The 1980s crisis in Ethiopia, the severe floods in Bangladesh and the refugee crisis in Africa's Great Lakes region in the 1990s, and the Nepal earthquake in 2015, all triggered large quantities of emergency food aid. In the period 1987–1991 Bangladesh dominated the recipient countries, followed by Pakistan, India and Tunisia.

(Shaw and Clay, 1993)

The world food aid system is highly complex and diverse, with the USA being the largest single provider; some of the other countries involved are Canada, Australia, Japan, Norway and Sweden. The European Union operates a union-wide programme, in addition to separate national programmes.

Much has been written about the merits and problems of food aid. Although most commentators would agree with the importance of food aid as part of a disaster-relief package, there is more concern about longer term food aid, which might affect local production and disrupt food-marketing systems. It is suggested that food aid can lower local food prices, encourage governments to neglect the drive to food self-sufficiency, create a dependency mentality and change eating habits. However, although potential problems in moving to food self-sufficiency are recognised, 'the widespread professional view of practitioners and economists [is] that disincentive effects are avoidable' (Shaw and Clay, 1993: 15).

Military assistance

With the end of the Cold War, it had been suggested that some of the so-called peace dividend might be allocated to overseas development assistance aimed at poverty alleviation, rather than on military expenditure. It is both ironical and deeply disturbing, however, that although military expenditure within countries in the North has fallen, the sale of arms and military hardware to the poorer countries of the world is still big business. In 1987 the USA gave US $5.4 billion in worldwide military assistance, and the former Soviet Union gave US $13.5 billion. These figures declined to US $3.4 billion (USA) and zero (former Soviet Union) by 1993, but there was still a total military assistance of US $4.6 billion, some 74 per cent of this coming from the USA. In 2013, US foreign military assistance amounted to US $5.6 billion, with the largest recipients being Israel and Egypt, followed by Jordan and Pakistan.

The United Nations Development Programme (UNDP) has argued that

military assistance to the Third World formed one cornerstone of the Cold War . . . and also had commercial motives, helping sustain the output of the arms industry by subsidizing exports and unloading outdated weaponry.

(UNDP, 1994: 53)

Military assistance has many damaging effects for poor countries. Even after conflicts are resolved, large quantities of weaponry within countries pose a continuing threat to internal stability, and considerably strengthen the army and its ability to seize power.

UNDP advocates the phasing out of military assistance and tighter controls imposed on the arms trade. In 1994, 86 per cent of conventional weapons exported to countries in the South came from (in descending order): the former Soviet Union, the USA, France, China and the United Kingdom, all permanent members of the UN Security Council. Two-thirds of these arms were sold to ten countries in the South, including Afghanistan, India and Pakistan.

A comprehensive policy for arms production and sales is urgently needed, with special emphasis placed on cutbacks in the production of chemical weapons and landmines (UNDP, 1994). In Angola and Cambodia it is estimated that millions of landmines have been planted, causing continual suffering among local populations. The landmine issue came to the fore in 1997, and many governments, including the UK government, have now agreed to ban their sale overseas.

Aid: quantity and quality

There needs to be a significant improvement in the quality as well as the quantity of overseas development assistance if poverty alleviation, and ultimately poverty eradication, is to be achieved throughout the world. There have been proposals to make development assistance obligatory, perhaps by introducing a form of international tax on the rich countries (Watkins, 1995). Another proposal is a tax on international currency transactions, which would deter vast flows of speculative capital, estimated at US $1 trillion per day, which are destabilising economies in both the global North and South. The so-called 'Tobin Tax' is considered in some detail in Chapter 4. National and international action would be needed to bring financial markets under more effective control. Some reform of the IMF is also necessary to help poor countries with serious foreign exchange shortages to increase their reserves without resorting to deflationary measures or constraining growth by cutting essential imports (Watkins, 1995).

Aid should target the poorest people in the poorest countries, and the nature of future development assistance must place greater emphasis on key aspects such as health and education, rather than emphasising the potential for exports from donor countries. There is a need to discuss aid and development priorities with local communities, and also to reduce the costs of delivering aid through an army of relatively well-paid expatriate consultants and developers (Oxfam, 1993). Perhaps most important of all, development assistance should concentrate more on achieving a sustainable improvement in the quality of life.

There are so many questions relating to aid, and much detailed evidence is available to support the many different perspectives in the ongoing debate. It is impossible to cover all aspects here. But, we might ask, does aid actually work? Why, for example, are so many sub-Saharan African countries worse off now than they were at independence in the 1960s, despite having vast amounts of development assistance pumped into them? It is a sobering thought that the number of Africans living below the poverty line actually increased from an estimated 217 million in 1987 to 291 million in 1998, and primary school enrolment fell by 1 per cent (Reality of Aid, 2002). A survey undertaken in Zambia in 2012 found that, in a country which is rich in natural resources, over 60 per cent of the population was living on less than US $1 a day (DFID, 2015). These trends have occurred at the same time as countries in the North have experienced an information technology revolution and steadily improving standards of living.

The issue of conditionality is of great significance. As we have seen in the case of the HIPC Initiative, the World Bank and IMF expect recipient countries to fulfil a number of conditions before they will be assisted in relieving their debt burden. UNICEF reports on another case where, in 1998,

the IMF, the World Bank and other international agencies loaned Indonesia more than US$50 billion. But with the loans came stringent restrictions . . . [such that] the IMF-imposed austerity measures exacerbated the mushrooming social crisis . . . Between 1997 and 1998, according to the World Bank, the number of Indonesians living in poverty doubled.

(UNICEF, 2000: 36)

In many cases the consultants who undertake the research which might subsequently lead to the formulation of aid packages are expatriates, who during their commonly all-too-brief field visits fail to understand local situations and are conditioned by donor country approaches and priorities. As the Reality of Aid report comments, with reference to the experience of NGOs in Uganda, 'even when countries have developed their own national strategies for addressing poverty, donors insist on additional processes which undermine the very ownership and accountability that donors are claiming to promote' (Reality of Aid, 2002: 9).

Perhaps understandably, evidence of good governance has become a prerequisite for the receipt of much overseas development assistance. As the UK Government's White Paper comments,

> Effective governments are needed to build the legal, institutional and regulatory framework without which market reforms can go badly wrong, at great cost – particularly to the poor . . . Effective governments are also needed to put in place good social policies . . . [to] ensure the provision of key public services.
>
> (Department for International
> Development, 2000a: 24–5)

But does good governance as a prerequisite for the receipt of aid necessarily lead to development and poverty alleviation? The UK White Paper also speaks of

> Making political institutions work for poor people [which] means helping to strengthen the voices of

the poor and helping them to realise their human rights. It means empowering them to take their own decisions, rather than being the passive objects of choices made on their behalf.

> (Department for International
> Development, 2000a: 27)

Further discussion of the how the notions of good governance, empowerment and effectiveness are being taken up by key institutions in development (including private organisations) can be found in Chapter 7.

Conclusion

As we have seen, there is a complex network of movements and flows between the Global North and South and also within and between particular countries. It is quite impossible to catalogue all such movements and flows, simply because of their diversity and complexity. It is hoped that, through the use of real examples, this chapter has clarified some of the key concepts and important issues which need to be monitored in the future. Furthermore, it is impossible to fully appreciate the character and underlying causes of different geographies of development without an understanding of the ways in which people and places are connected through movements of people themselves, as well as flows of commodities, finance and knowledge.

Key points

➤ Producers in poor countries have very little control over the prices they receive for their commodities and world price fluctuations can have significant effects on their livelihoods.

➤ Migrants' remittances can have a valuable impact on the quality of life in their home communities and countries.

➤ Tourism makes valuable contributions to the economies of some countries in the South, but the possible negative effects of having large numbers of international visitors need to be fully appreciated in planning for the expansion of tourism.

➤ We live in an interdependent, but unequal world. Many poor countries are heavily dependent on producing just a single commodity for world markets and are therefore vulnerable to changes in the terms of trade.

➤ World trade policy and institutions are dominated by the world's richest countries. Countries in the South should be given a larger role in decision making, and fair trading policies should be strengthened.

➤ Transnational corporations play an important role in world trade. Criticisms of some poor working practices have encouraged TNCs to show a greater interest in corporate social responsibility.

Key points (continued)

➤ The so-called BRICS countries (Brazil, Russia, India, China and South Africa) are playing a significantly greater role in world trade and investment, but their governments and economies have encountered some problems in recent years.

➤ Although some progress is being made in reducing the crippling debt burden in the world's poorest countries, there is still much to be achieved.

➤ It is not just the amount of overseas development assistance (aid) that richer countries give to poorer countries that is important, but also the nature and conditions associated with that assistance.

Further reading

Curtis, M. (2001) Trade for Life: Making Trade Work for Poor People. London: Christian Aid.
A thought-provoking study of world trade and its role in poverty alleviation.

Department for International Development (2000) Eliminating World Poverty: Making Globalisation Work for the Poor, White Paper on International Development. London: DfID.
The UK government's official statement on the importance of eliminating poverty within the broader context of globalisation.

Dicken, P. (2015) Global Shift: Mapping the Changing Contours of the World Economy, 7th edn. London: Sage.
A key text which examines how economic globalisation arises from the dynamic interplay between transnational corporations as prime actors and nation states as regulators, facilitated by processes of technological change.

Hoogvelt, A. (2001) Globalization and the Postcolonial World: The New Political Economy of Development, 2nd edn. Basingstoke: Palgrave.
An important and thought-provoking text on the ramifications of globalisation.

Jenkins, R., Pearson, R. and Seyfang, G. (eds) (2002) Corporate Responsibility and Labour Rights: Codes of Conduct in the Global Economy. London: Earthscan.
A collection of papers examining issues relating to the operating activities of companies in light of corporate social responsibility.

Madeley, J. (2008) Big Business, Poor Peoples: The Impact of Transnational Corporations on the World's Poor, 2nd ed. London: Zed Press.
A fascinating study of how poor people are affected by the operations of transnational companies.

Roberts, J.T. and Hite, A.B. (eds) (2007) The Globalization and Development Reader. Oxford: Blackwell.
An excellent collection of papers, which were originally published elsewhere, but have now been assembled in this collection. Includes classic works of Marx, Engels, Weber and Rostow, as well as many more recent contributions on the theme of globalisation.

Websites

http://www.cafedirect.co.uk/
This Cafedirect website provides a useful insight into the operations of a successful Fairtrade organisation involved in the purchase and marketing of tea and coffee from some 37 producer organisations in the Global South.

http://www.ico.org/history.asp
The International Coffee Organization site includes useful details and statistics on world coffee production and trade.

http://www.CarnegieEndowment.org
The Carnegie Endowment for International Peace website contains some helpful papers on world trade.

http://www.commissionforafrica.org/
This website has details on the establishment of Tony Blair's Commission for Africa in 2004 and includes a copy of the Commission's Report published in March 2005.

http://www.fairtrade.net/
The Fairtrade International site is wide-ranging website on the Fairtrade movement, with statistics and case studies relating to Fairtrade.

http://www.worldbank.org/en/topic/debt/brief/hipc
The official website of Heavily Indebted Poor Countries (HIPC), concerned with building the capacity of HIPC governments to conduct debt strategy analysis and negotiate debt relief and new financing.

https://www.oxfam.org/en/research
Contains detailed statements on Oxfam policies and reports on particular countries and projects where Oxfam is involved.

www.propoortourism.org.uk

Pro-poor Tourism Partnership website includes a range of research reports and studies that focus on how tourism can contribute more to poverty reduction.

http://www.unhcr.org/cgi-bin/texis/vtx/home

The UNHCR (United Nations High Commission for Refugees) is the key international organisation concerned with the condition and relief of refugees.

http://www.worldbank.org/

World Bank website, with information on economic policy and debt issues.

Discussion topics

➤ Select a single commodity which is produced in a poor country and is traded internationally. Examine the significance of the commodity in the producing country's economy, and suggest how improved terms of trade might lead to a fairer return for both the producing country and those engaged in production.

➤ How might governments in countries in the South ensure that local people gain greater benefit from the development of international tourism?

➤ What do you feel are the implications of the greater involvement of the BRICS countries in world trade and investment?

➤ Investigate the significance of debt with reference to selected countries in the South. Suggest some possible strategies for overcoming the debt burden.

➤ Examine the levels of aid given by different countries and the progress in achieving the 0.70 per cent target of Gross National Income for aid to poor countries. What types of aid do you feel should receive priority in the future?

Chapter 9
Urban spaces

Since 2007, over half the world's population has been urbanised. This reality, together with the most rapid rate of urban growth in human history which is now occurring in many parts of the South, is placing enormous challenges on urban planners and governments in the South. While many countries in the North are experiencing low or even static urban growth rates, and many parts of Europe and North America are witnessing the phenomenon of 'shrinking cities', this is not the reality for most of the South. In contrast, the challenges of burgeoning slums and the inability of cities to provide adequate shelter, employment and services has probably become the world's biggest development challenge.

The chapter starts with the global setting in stressing the apparent relationship which exists between rapid urbanisation and poor nations. This is manifest in the location of the largest and fastest growing cities to be found in the world today. Moving down a scale, the regional role of cites is then considered, in respect of the generic approaches that can be used in efforts to change urban circumstances by urban and regional planners and policy makers. It is noteworthy that whilst, in many cases, urbanisation in the North was generally associated with industrial development, the same has seldom been the case in the South,

with many large cities growing because of their administrative and service role, not because of rapid economic expansion. In the North, this growth provided the employment opportunities and economic capacity to absorb the urbanising populations. The suggestion that the urban and the rural are closely interlinked and that new forms of urban–rural relations are characterising cities in the Global South in the twenty-first century is then explored. Attention is then directed at individual urban areas, in respect of their structure, and the important role which the informal sector plays in providing both jobs and homes. To conclude, the pressing nature of environment–urbanisation issues is discussed, with a strong accent on the need to promote more sustainable forms of urbanisation. Specifically, the chapter:

➤ Shows how in the twenty-first century rapid urbanisation is characteristic of many Southern countries. Indeed, it has been occurring at rates that exceed those that were experienced in Northern countries when they experienced rapid urban growth in the nineteenth and twentieth centuries;

(continued)

(continued)

➤ Discusses how rapid growth has caused severe development challenges related to the growth of slums and burgeoning urban poverty;

➤ Explores the occurrence of urban primacy and unequal development, and emphasises how these often have to be examined and understood at the regional rather than the national scales;

➤ Reviews the generic strategies that can be employed by states as part of urban and regional planning, these approaches being referred to as 'national urban development strategies';

➤ Considers the relations between urban–rural areas and looks at the argument that new forms of urban–rural relations and zones can be recognised in the South;

➤ Stresses the ways in which the informal and self-help sectors have provided both homes and jobs for the majority poor in cities in the South;

➤ Reviews the links between urbanisation and environment in respect of the Brown Agenda.

Urbanisation and development: an overview

Over recent history it has generally been assumed that urbanisation – defined as an increase in the proportion of a given population that is to be found living in urban spaces – goes hand in hand with the process of 'development'.

Over time, and since the emergence of the first cities some 6,000–9,000 years ago (Pacione, 2009; Potter and Lloyd-Evans, 1998), it has generally been assumed that urbanisation, industrialisation and development occur together as joint processes. For this reason, it can be argued that urbanisation is one of the most significant processes affecting societies through the late twentieth and early twenty-first centuries (Devas and Rakodi, 1993; Drakakis-Smith, 2000; Gilbert and Gugler, 1992; Lloyd-Evans and Potter, 2008; Potter 1992a, 2000; Potter and Lloyd-Evans, 1998; Satterthwaite, 2008).

As stressed in Chapter 3, dualistic conceptualisations regarded the development process as endeavouring to change what are regarded as traditional, rural, agrarian-based societies into so-called modern, urban–industrial ones, based on the model provided by European nations. Hence, urbanisation and industrialisation were conflated as being essentially synonymous processes. This was the case in Europe and North America, and to a lesser degree in South America, parts of SE Asia and the Caribbean, but is not the case in the rest of the South (UNDESA, 2014). Watson (in Woodrow Wilson International Centre, 2007) argues that in the case of Africa, economic

development has been delinked from the rapid urbanisation which is taking place. It is, however, apparent that by comparison, certain upper middle income countries, such as China, Mexico and Brazil have urbanised and developed economically at rates faster than the rest of the South, and are currently 63% urbanised as a group (UNDESA, 2014). It is anticipated that the upper middle income urbanisation rates will accelerate faster than other regions for the next two to three decades. By contrast, the lower middle income and low income countries lag in terms of this score, and in 2014 these countries had average urbanisation levels of 39% and 30% respectively, figures which are expected to rise to 57% and 48% in 2050, with little current prospect of commensurate economic growth taking place (UNDESA, 2014).

Dwyer (1975: 13) observed that 'in all probability we have reached the end of an era of association of urbanisation with Western style industrialisation and socio-economic characteristics' (Plate 9.1). This is best illustrated by the disparity which characterises the relationship between levels of urbanisation and industrialisation in the Global South. In 1970, the non-communist, less-developed countries, taken as a whole, showed a level of urbanisation of 21 per cent, whereas only 10 per cent of the economically active population was employed in manufacturing, yielding an excess of urbanisation over industrialisation of 110 per cent (Bairoch, 1975; see Critical reflection on urban definitions). Europe in the 1930s showed a 32 per cent level of urbanisation, but at this point some 22 per cent of the active population were engaged in manufacturing.

Thus, the excess of urbanisation over industrialisation was appreciably lower, at around 45 per cent.

Moving from industrial employment to broader economic activities it is apparent that the mismatch also exists at a broader level. Figure 9.1 indicates the association between per capita GDP and the percent of national populations living in urban areas. The figure clearly shows that for some countries there is an association between GDP levels and urbanisation levels, such as in Luxembourg, the USA, Qatar and Singapore. There are, however, clearly many countries which have low GDP levels yet growing levels of urbanisation, such as China and Sierra Leone, which do not conform to the expected correlation and, potentially face challenges in terms of sustainably managing urban growth.

As we know from the consideration of global shifts provided in Chapter 4, the industrial expansion that has occurred in developing countries is being concentrated in just a few nations, mainly in Asia, with there being particularly rapid recent growth in China and India. In contrast, the majority of poorer developing nations in the South now account for a reduced proportion of total world manufacturing output. Thus, for many poor nations, urbanisation currently has little to do with industrialisation, but rather is linked with the creation of jobs in the service sector. This trend will be fully considered later in this chapter. The difference between urban growth and economic growth has led to the use of the terms 'hyperurbanisation' or 'overurbanisation', in which cities are perceived to be growing at faster rates than economic and social facilities can accommodate them. While these arguments have been disputed, the challenges posed by rapid growth remain critical issues of global concern (Chant and McIlwaine, 2009; Knox and McCarthy, 2012).

Given that such a significant proportion of the global urban growth is now focused in cities in the South, how they manage that growth will prove to be critical to the future wellbeing of humanity, as the United Nations

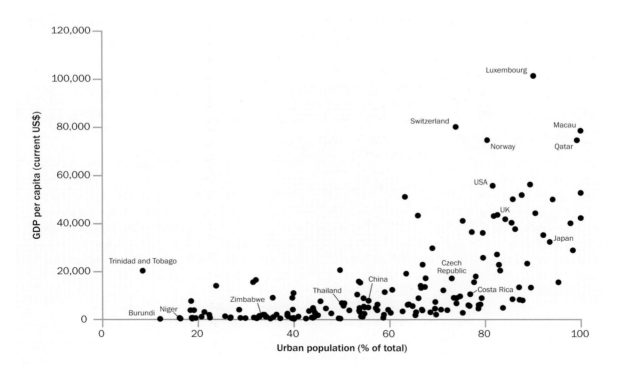

Figure 9.1 Urbanisation and economic development, 2015

Source: The World Bank. Urban population: http://data.worldbank.org/indicator/SP.URB.TOTL.IN.ZS; GDP per capita (current US$): http://data.worldbank.org/indicator/NY.GDP.PCAP.CD

Plate 9.1 Ulan Bator, Mongolia
(*photo*: Elona Hoover, jesidewalks)

Population Fund (in Knox and McCarthy, 2012: 137) argue: 'What happens in cities of the less developed world in coming years will shape prospects for global economic growth, poverty alleviation, population stabilization, environmental sustainability and, ultimately the exercise of human rights'.

Critical reflection

Urban definitions and characteristics

Urbanisation may be defined as the proportion of the population of a nation or region that is to be found living in towns and cities, and is generally represented as a percentage. But, of course, the measure depends on a prior categorisation of what exactly constitutes an urban settlement. In fact, each and every nation exercises its own judgement in determining urban status. Indeed, different criteria and thresholds are used, involving variations on total population size, density of population, predominant economic activity and even legal definition. Bearing this in mind, what do you normally expect of a town or a city? Do you think in terms of a given threshold size of population, or are there key facilities that you expect to be present and which therefore define urbanity in your eyes? Are you aware of the definitions of urbanity that are used by countries around the globe?

Urbanisation and regional differences: the urbanising South

In 1950 an estimated 30% of the world's population was urbanised; by 2014 this figure had risen to 54% and is expected to reach 66% in 2050, with the most rapid growth occurring in Asia and Africa. Figure 9.2 shows just how striking the transition to an urban world has been and the degree to which, over the next few decades, urban populations are expected to increase significantly

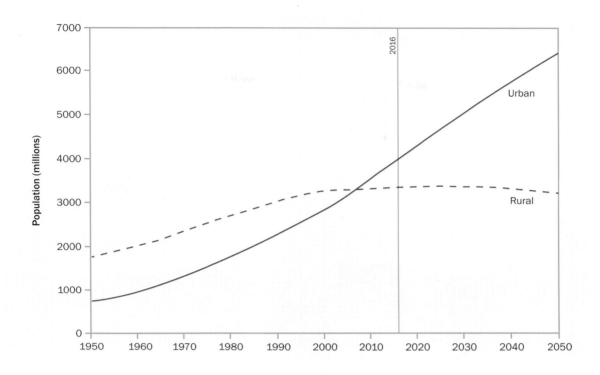

Figure 9.2 The world's urban and rural populations, 1950–2050
Source: adapted from UNDESA, 2014: 7.

while that of rural areas plateau and may even decline. It is expected that the world rural population will probably peak at 3.4 billion after 2025 and could decline to 3.2 billion in 2050. By contrast, the world urban population rose from 700 million in 1950 to 3.9 billion in 2014 and is expected to reach 6.3 billion in 2050 (UNDESA, 2014).

Historically, the countries of the North experienced the most rapid rates of growth, but today it is the countries of the South that are experiencing the fastest rates of urbanisation and, as this chapter will demonstrate, their urban populations are increasing much more rapidly than those of European countries at their fastest growth phase.

Such rapid growth is shown in the series of world maps reproduced in Figure 9.3. As these maps show, in 1950 the North was already highly urbanised, and up to 2014 significant urbanisation had taken place in Latin America and East Asia. Over the next few decades, up to 2050 these regions will strengthen their urbanisation levels, while Africa and the rest of Asia will grow significantly. As can be predicted, growth will continue at a

significant and perhaps an accelerating rate in some parts of these latter regions after 2050.

During the 1980s, through to the end of the 1990s, the Global South was characterised by annual growth rates of urban population well in excess of 2 per cent per annum. Indeed, considerable tracts of both Africa and Asia were, for the last two decades of the twentieth century, characterised by urban growth rates higher than 4 per cent. It is, however, noteworthy that even though all regions are experiencing and, will continue to experience, urbanisation, that the rate of increase is slowing down (see Figure 9.4), albeit that the fastest growth rates will be in Asia and Africa. This slowing is perhaps to be expected when over the half the population is urbanised and the rural population is static or declining. The rate of urbanisation is naturally not the same as the rate of urban growth, as a result of which cities will grow at a faster rate as a result of natural increase, particularly in countries with young populations.

As a result of natural increase and urbanisation the world will become significantly more urbanised in the

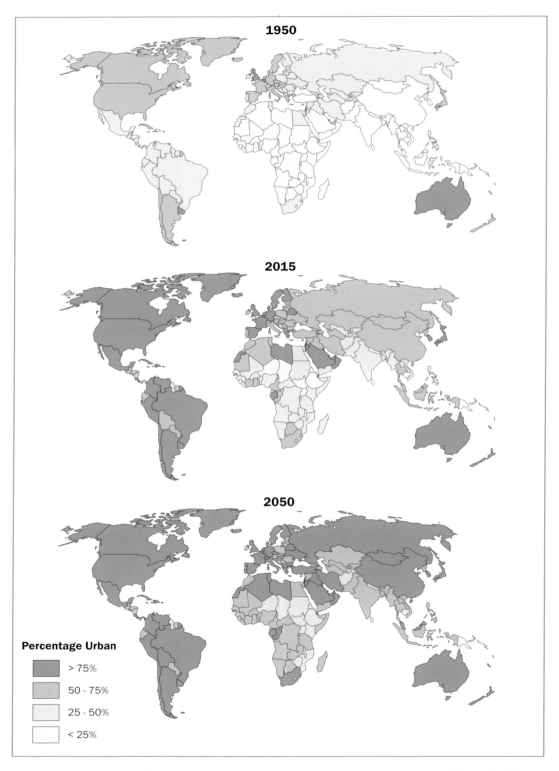

Figure 9.3 Percentage of the world's population living in urban areas, 1950–2050

Source: adapted from https://esa.un.org/unpd/wup/CD-ROM/WUP2014_XLS_CD_FILES/WUP2014-F02-Proportion_Urban.xls.

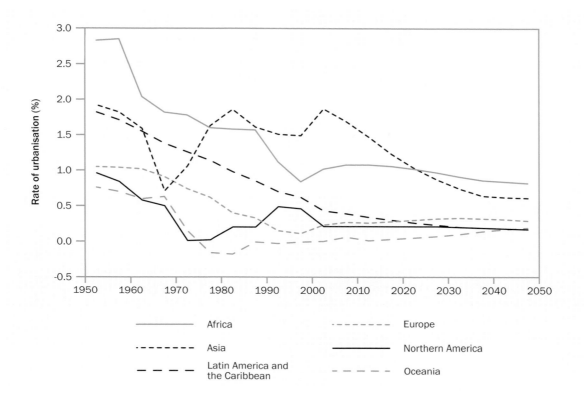

Figure 9.4 The rate of urbanisation by major world region, 1950–2050
Source: adapted from UNDESA, 2014: 11.

next three or so decades. As the statistics in Table 9.1 show, significant growth will occur in Asia and Africa, with much lower growth levels anticipated in other regions. The Table makes for interesting reading with regards to both differential urban growth patterns around the world and the degree to which the South will increasingly dominate the world urban profile, a factor which will feature below in the overview of where the world's biggest cities are. Important patterns which can be discerned from Table 9.1 include:

➤ The total world urban population will nearly double between 1990 and 2050.
➤ In what is indicated as the more developed countries (i.e. the North), the urban population will probably only increase by 133 million between 2014 and 2050.
➤ In the same time period in the less developed countries (the bulk of the South), there will probably be 1.7bn more urban residents, with an additional 0.6bn

in the least developed countries, giving a total of 2.3bn extra residents in the South.

➤ Urban growth rates (2010–15) in the least and the less developed countries are nearly four to five times higher than those in the developed countries.
➤ In Asia and Africa the percentage of the national population living in urban areas will double or near double between 1990 and 2050, while in other parts of the world the percentage will increase between 10–20% and Oceania will remain static.
➤ In terms of absolute numbers, the urban population of Asia is expected to triple between 1990 and 2050, while that of Africa may increase seven-fold.

A striking feature of rapid urbanisation in the South is the degree to which the relative balance between the percentage of the world's total urban population in various regions of the world is altering and will alter still further in the future. Even though all regions are experiencing

Table 9.1 Urban population as a percentage of regional populations, 2014–50

	Total urban numbers (bn)			% Urban			Annual rate of change
Region	1990	2014	2050	1990	2014	2050	2010–15
World	2.285	3.880	6.338	43	54	66	0.9
More developed	0.830	0.980	1.113	72	78	85	0.3
Less developed	1.346	2.615	4.329	37	52	67	1.3
Least developed	0.107	0.283	0.895	21	31	49	1.7
N America	0,212	0.291	0.390	75	81	82	0.2
Europe	0.505	0.545	0.581	70	73	82	0.3
Latin America	0.313	0.495	0.673	71	80	86	0.3
Asia	1.036	2.064	3.313	32	48	64	1,5
Africa	0.196	0.455	1.338	31	40	56	1.1
Oceania	0.019	0.027	0.041	71	71	84	0.0

Source: UNDESA, 2014

growing urban population (allowing for the reality that is some countries, mainly in the North, there is also the reality of 'shrinking cities'), the relative percentage of the global urban population in the North is falling rapidly, while that in the South is increasing (see Table 9.2). Figure 9.5 shows the share of the world population according to regions in 2010. The dominant position of Asia, and the relatively small contribution made by the North, is evident in this Figure. Significantly, by 2050, it is anticipated that 52% of the world's urban population will be in Asia and 21% in Africa.

Urbanisation in China is generally regarded as one of the most dramatic movements of human population in history. Figure 9.6 vividly illustrates the dramatic transition from a rural to an urban society which China has undergone. In 1970, less than 100 million people in China were urbanised. By 1990, this had tripled to 300 million, and by 2010 had more than doubled again to reach nearly 700 million, while the rural population has declined in absolute terms since the 1990s. This rapid growth is associated with China's defined pursuit of state capitalism and the attraction of foreign investment to existing or newly created cities,

Table 9.2 Relative shifts in the percentage of the global urban population, 1950–2050

Region	1950	1990	2014	2050
North	59.5	36.6	25.3	17.6
South	40.5	63.6	74.7	82.4

Source: UNDESA, 2014

primarily on the eastern seaboard as part of the country's 'open-door' policy which has profoundly impacted on the locus of global economic activity and the associated growth of what are now some of the largest urban centres in the world.

The development challenges of the cities of the South

In 1920, UN data indicate that less than 10 per cent of Africans and Asians and only 22 per cent of Latin Americans were urban dwellers (UNCHS, 1996). By 2000 there were two city dwellers in the South for every one in the North, and by 2050 the ratio will increase to nearly five to one. This fact stresses once more the degree to which, in numerical terms at a global level, urban living in the modern era has come to be associated with the poorer countries of the globe.

By 2025 it is believed that just under 60 per cent of all Africans will be living in urban settlements, as will just over half of all those living in Asia. In the same year, nearly 85 per cent of all Latin Americans will be living in towns and cities.

Politicians, planners and development experts from all over the world must grapple with these facts during the coming decades of the current millennium. As illustrated above, this very rapid rise in urban living is occurring in the regions of the world where socio-economic conditions are generally at their poorest and where industrial production is relatively low.

In these areas, resources are often very limited, so enormous pressure is being exerted on existing

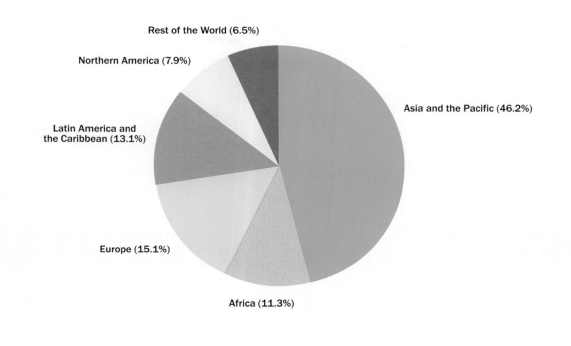

Figure 9.5 Regional shares of the world urban population, 2010
Source: adapted from http://www.forbes.com/sites/davidferris/2012/08/31/the-stark-environmental-challenge-of-asias-megacities/. Accessed 18 April 2016.

socioeconomic systems, and especially on the children, women and men who live in such poor areas and regions. Indeed, dealing with the challenges that are presented by these fundamental changes represents one of the major tasks faced by planners and politicians in the twenty-first century. Despite the urgent nature of the development challenges which cities in the South face, it is a worrying reality that, according to the Cities Alliance (2006, 5), 'few local and national governments have done anything to prepare for urban population growth and, on the contrary, most governments have been in denial about urban growth, resulting in a refusal to plan or prepare for orderly expansion'.

As a direct result of the preceding, and the rapid urban growth of the cities in most of Asia and Africa in particularly one of the major development challenges of the twenty-first century will clearly be the pursuit of

development interventions which can help to ensure sustainable urban development.

Weaker local economies, and the often poor levels of housing, health, education, services and infrastructure pose the reality that a globally unprecedented level of support will be required to assist urban areas in the South to cope with the significant development challenges which they face.

In 2012, UN Secretary General Ban ki Moon commented that 'Our struggle for global sustainability will be won or lost in cities' (Moon, 2012). Whether the world's nations and population have the capacity and willingness to provide for current and future sustainable urbanisation is a critical question which will impact on human well-being, concerns of equity and global well-being. Should the needs of the burgeoning urban population of the South not be met, sadly, the development gap between the North and the South, alluded to

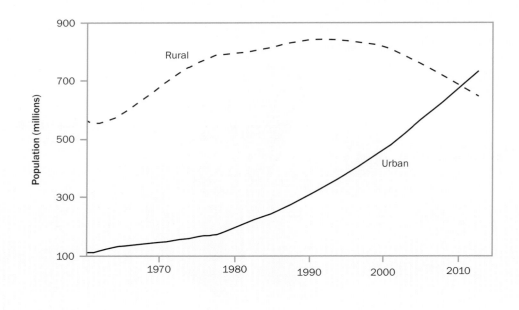

Figure 9.6 China's urban and rural populations
Source: adapted from http://www.citymetric.com/politics/china-strictly-controls-urbanisation-and-limits-migrant-workers-rights-all-could-be. Accessed 18 April 2016.

in Chapter 1, will grow, as will the gap between the haves and the have-nots in most countries in the world.

Rapid growth, planning failures to date and looming future challenges, require concerted community, state and international interventions to respond to a series of core challenges to which attention now turns, including the challenges posed by the rapid development of cities, slums within them, burgeoning urban poverty and inadequate housing supply and employment provision.

A focus on cities

The rapid growth of major cities in the South

The urbanisation processes discussed in the previous section have led to the rapid growth of urban centres in all size classes across the urban hierarchy. It is, however, important to note that not only have the absolute number of cities increased dramatically since the 1950s, but also that the most dramatic growth has been in the South – both in terms of the absolute number of cities, but also in terms of the sheer number of urban residents.

The very rapid growth of towns and cities that has been occurring in the South over the last 70 years can be illustrated in a number of different ways. One way is the increase that has occurred in cities that have a population of a million or more persons. Statistics show that in the 1920s, 24 of the world's cities had more than 1 million inhabitants, by the 1940s this had risen to 41, by 1960s there were 113 and, by the early 1980s, the number of such cities had increased to 198 (Potter, 1992a). By 2014 there were 488 cities with more than a million residents (UNDESA, 2014).

If one examines statistics, it is noticeable that the fastest growing cities are all located to the south of the line that divides the rich 'North' from the poor 'South'. Thus, large cities such as Mexico City, São Paulo, Lagos, Cairo, Delhi, Bangkok, Manila and Jakarta grew rapidly after 1970, as did numerous smaller agglomerations such as Zibo, Surabaya, Pune, Bangalore, Casablanca, Caracas and Porto Alegre. The salient point is that these cities will continue to grow rapidly into the future. In fact, cities are growing so fast in many parts of the South that in certain areas they are merging together to form large linked or 'compound' urban regions, a point which is elaborated later in this chapter (Potter and Lloyd-Evans, 1998). These large urban systems, such as Mexico City, São Paulo, Lagos and Cairo are variously termed *mega-city*, *super-city*, *giant city* and *conurbation* to indicate these large, sprawling and complex urban regions.

Since the early 1990s the expression 'extended metropolitan region (EMR)' has increasingly been used to describe new urban forms, especially in the Asian context. The nature of these large urbanised tracts of land is examined later in the chapter when the focus is placed on the changing form of urban and rural linkages in developing countries.

The distribution of major cities in the world with more than 300 000 people is shown in Figure 9.7. The map shows the major cities in the world in five distinct cohorts, and for 1990, 2014 and the anticipated situation in 2030. Outside of Western Europe and northeastern America, the largest concentration of million cities occurs in Asia, and particularly in China and India, and there are also concentrations in South and Central America with increasing concentrations in Africa. The substantial number of million plus cities south of the North–South global divide is plain to see from the Figure. The rapid growth of all cities, but particularly in Asia and Africa, echoes the discussion in the previous sections. Figure 9.8 indicates the differential growth rates of cities of different class sizes from around the world. The relatively modest growth rates in all classes of cities in many parts of the North is immediately apparent from the Figure. Higher rates of growth are evident in Asia and Latin America, with the highest growth rates being noted in Africa and parts of Asia. Some African cities, such as Abuja in Nigeria, have growth rates exceeding 5% p.a.

One of the most notable features of rapid recent urban growth has been the emergence of a set of key 'mega-cities', i.e. places with populations of more than 10 million people. In 1950 there were two such cities, both in the North – Tokyo and New York. By 1990, there were 10 such centres (four cities were in the North), and this had risen to 28 in 2014 (with six in the North), hosting 7% then 12% of the total world urban population respectively in 1990 and 2014. By 2030 it is estimated that there will be 41 mega-cities and of these only four will be in the North – Tokyo, Osaka, New York and Los Angeles.

Table 9.3 details the number of cities according to size classes in 1990, 2014 and 2030. Between 1990 and 2030 it is estimated that the number of cities in the world with more than 500,000 people will more than double from 564 to 1393. In most cases these will not be new cities, except in the case of numerous examples in China, but rather the growth of pre-existing cities to above the 500,000 threshold. The near tripling of the number of cities with less than 1 million residents indicates that growth is spread across the urban hierarchy and we are not seeing a sole focus on the largest classes of settlements. The latter consideration is an important factor which Satterthwaite (2008) has commented on in his overview of global urbanisation. While the growth is not solely focused on the largest centres, the fact that secondary cities are often growing even faster poses particular challenges, as these places are not national capitals and, given the weak resources and finances of many such cities in the South, they are generally less able than the capital cities to cope with the challenges posed by rapid urbanisation.

Table 9.4 shows the 15 largest cities in the world in 2014, their anticipated growth rates and size to 2030, and their relative rank in terms of city size. Whilst

Table 9.3 Number of major cities by size classes: 1990, 2014 and 2030

Class	1990	2014	2030
Megacities of +10mn	10	28	41
Large Cities 5–10mn	21	43	63
Medium Sized Cities 1–5mn	239	417	558
Cities 0.5–1mn	294	525	731
Total	564	1013	1393

Source: UNDESA, 2014

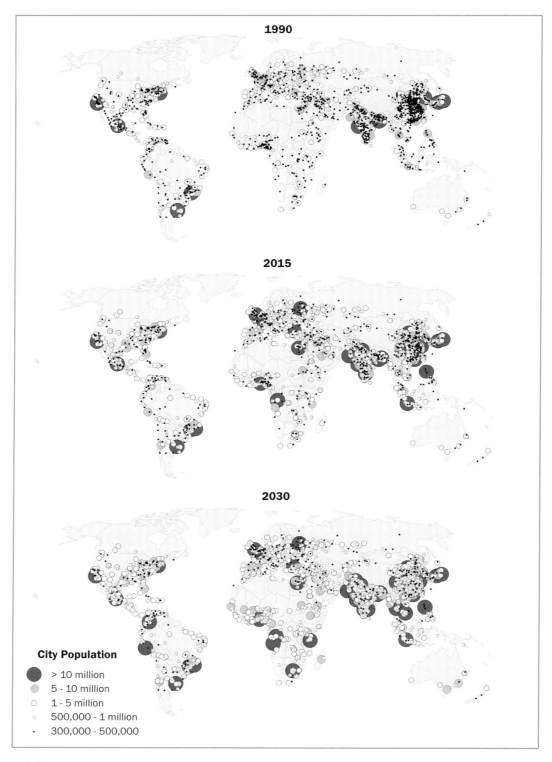

Figure 9.7 The world's cities by size classes: 1990, 2014 and 2030
Source: adapted from https://esa.un.org/unpd/wup/CD-ROM/WUP2014_XLS_CD_FILES/WUP2014-F12-Cities_Over_300K.xls.

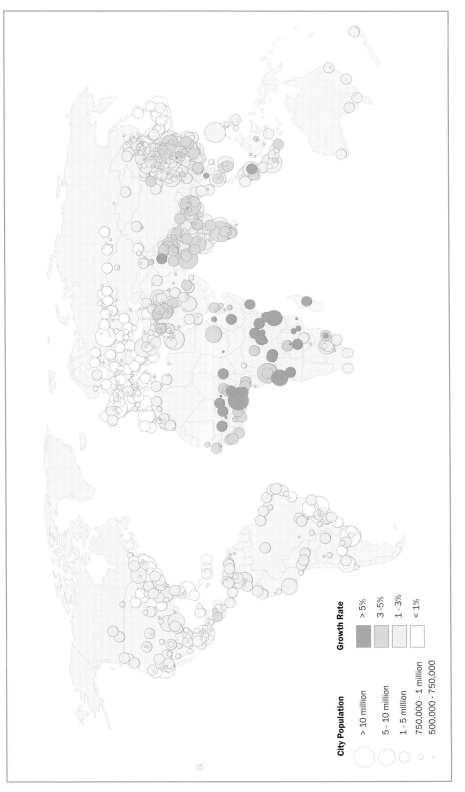

Figure 9.8 Urban growth rates according to city classes, 2014

Source: adapted from https://esa.un.org/unpd/wup/CD-ROM/WUP2014_XLS_CD_FILES/WUP2014-F14-Growth_Rate_Cities.xls.

City Population

> 10 million

5 - 10 million

1 - 5 million

750,000 - 1 million

500,000 - 750,000

Growth Rate

> 5%

3 - 5%

1 - 3%

< 1%

Tokyo will remain the world's largest city, it will probably lose people, whilst Delhi will rapidly catch up to it in size with a growth rate of 3.2% p.a. Significant readjustments in the membership of the largest 15 cities will take place, with Buenos Aires and Istanbul losing their places in this league and, significantly, being replaced by two African cities, Lagos and Kinshasa, both of which are expected to experience rapid and sustained growth over time, reflecting the delayed but significant urbanisation rates in that continent compared with other parts of the world. Once major cities in terms of size, Moscow, London and Paris are no longer in the league of the major 15 cities in terms of size, but this in no way diminishes their economic and social significance as key world cities, since sheer size is not necessarily a surrogate for economic size or global influence.

The growth of slums

A stark reality of the inability of cities in the South to absorb and adequately house and cater for the economic and social needs of rapidly urbanising populations leads to the challenge posed by burgeoning urban slums. It is estimated that some one billion people currently live in slums – variously referred to as *favelas*, *bustees*, informal settlements, shacks and slums in different parts of the world. The unifying theme in this terminology is the sub-standard nature of the available shelter, which often is owner-built out of scrap material, and with generally minimal service provision and compromised living standards. While the enormity of the urban crisis regarding slums has long been appreciated, the publication of the UN-Habitat report entitled 'The Challenge of Slums' in 2003, helped focus attention on the enormity of the challenge, its causes and how little had been achieved to improve conditions through interventions over the preceding 30 years. The reality in many countries is that slum growth has outpaced urbanisation, with between 80%–90% of new migrants to cities such as Delhi and Nairobi settling in slums. In many cities, but particularly those in Africa, such as Luanda, Addis Abba and Mogadishu it is estimated that up to 80%, or more, of the urban population are living in accommodation of this type. According to UN-Habitat (2015), in 2010 32.7% of urban residents in the South lived in slum conditions (827.7 million), with average incidence rates varying from 13.3% in North Africa to 61.7% in sub-Saharan Africa. Latin America's average is 23.5%, while Asia varies from 28 to 35%. According to Davies (2006)

Table 9.4 The fifteen biggest cities in the world, 2014–2030

City	Population (thousands) 2014	Population (thousands) 2030	Rank 2014	Rank 2030	% growth p.a.
Tokyo	37833	37190	1	1	0.6
Delhi	24953	36060	2	2	3.2
Shanghai	22991	30751	3	3	3.4
Mexico City	20843	23865	4	10	0.8
São Paulo	20831	23444	5	11	1.4
Mumbai	20741	27797	6	4	1.6
Osaka	20123	19976	7	13	0.8
Beijing	19520	27706	8	5	4.6
New York	18591	19885	9	14	0.2
Cairo	18419	24502	10	8	2.1
Dhaka	16892	27374	11	6	3.6
Karachi	16126	24838	12	7	3.3
Buenos Aires	15024	16956	13	18	1.3
Kolkata	14776	19092	14	15	0.8
Istanbul	13954	16694	15	20	2.1

Two newcomers to the ranks of the fifteen biggest cities in 2030:

Lagos	12619	24239	19	9	3.9
Kinshasa	11146	19996	22	12	4.2

Source: UNDESA, 2014

there are more than 200,000 slums on earth, with the large South Asian cities such as Karachi, Mumbai, Delihi, Kolkata and Dhaka alone containing more than 15,000 slums. In many cities 'mega-slums' are discernible, such as Dharavi in Mumbai, made famous in the film *Slumdog Millionaire*, where up to a million people are estimated to be living in an area of just one square mile. In cities such as Rio de Janeiro and Nairobi the reality of slum conditions is equally significant (Plate 9.2).

According to the Cities Alliance (1999: 1):

Hundreds of millions of urban poor in the developing and transitional world have few options but to live in squalid, unsafe environments where they face multiple threats to their health and security. Slums and squatter settlements lack the most basic infrastructure and services. Their populations are marginalised and largely disenfranchised. They are exposed to disease, crime and vulnerable to natural disasters. Slum and squatter settlements are growing at alarming rates, projected to double in 25 years.

Slums are the products of failed policies, bad governance, corruption, inappropriate regulation, dysfunctional land markets, unresponsive financial systems and a fundamental lack of political will. Each of these failures adds to the toll on people already deeply burdened by poverty.

Trying to address the challenges of slums was incorporated into the MDGs and the goal of striving to achieve 'Cities without Slums' has been set by the Cities Alliance (1999) which has devoted considerable effort to seeking ways to alleviate the realities and challenges of informal housing. Despite this, it is estimated the number of slum dwellers will rise commensurate with the rapid urbanisation patterns detailed above, such that by 2025 there could be 500 million slum dwellers in Africa, 200 million in Latin America, 900 million in Asia and 90 million in the Middle East, totalling nearly 1.7 billion (see Figure 9.9). This clearly is a daunting challenge, particularly since that figure will equate to over 30% of the anticipated global urban population.

The growth of slums is the result of a coalescence of a range of negative variables, including the rapid growth of cities, the absence of adequate economic and social infrastructure to absorb that growth, poor national economic performance, coupled with low earnings and savings rates, and the absence of national policies designed to provide mass housing. In parallel, rural challenges, including limited opportunities and the perceived benefits of urban life, have encouraged urban movement, often to slum areas. The harsh effects of structural adjustment in the 1980s, which incapacitated many countries and their ability to more effectively manage urban growth, and the frequent pursuit of policies which are not conducive to the effective and humanitarian absorption of new urban residents have aggravated the situation. Figure 9.10 summarises the causes of rapid slum development.

Policies of removal which have been commonplace in many countries, but in particular in Brazil (more recently in Rio de Janiero in association with the Olympic Games redevelopment), India, Zimbabwe, Nigeria and Indonesia. These action are ostensibly in pursuit of 'redevelopment' which normally benefits the middle class, despite claims to the contrary have frequently aggravated conditions, destabilised communities and family life and led to the establishment of new slum settlements elsewhere.

Attempting to respond to the challenges posed by slums features prominently in policy and academic discourse. From 2000–2015 MDG (Goal 7, Target 11) strove to reduce the number of slum dwellers globally by 100 million. While more than this number were rehoused, these gains were outweighed by the movement of many more millions to new urban slums in the corresponding period. Academic debates regarding the nature and fate of slums have variously articulated arguments, ranging from the perspective that slums can be places for self-improvement, to the contradictory argument that these places are locked in a hopeless and desperate struggle of human survival. The arguments of 'slums of hope' and 'slums of despair' no doubt both share elements of the truth based on the complex diversity of urban life and settlements around the world. Earlier arguments from Lloyd (1979) and de Soto (in Satterthwaite and Mitlin, 2014) about the positive aspects and potential for self-improvement and nascent capitalism in such areas, are contested by the stark realism argued by Davies (2006) in his key study 'Planet of Slums', which argues that despite interventions, the benefits are selective and the challenges cities face continue to grow.

From a policy perspective, as noted above, the objective of 'Cities without Slums' is a key strategic focus for

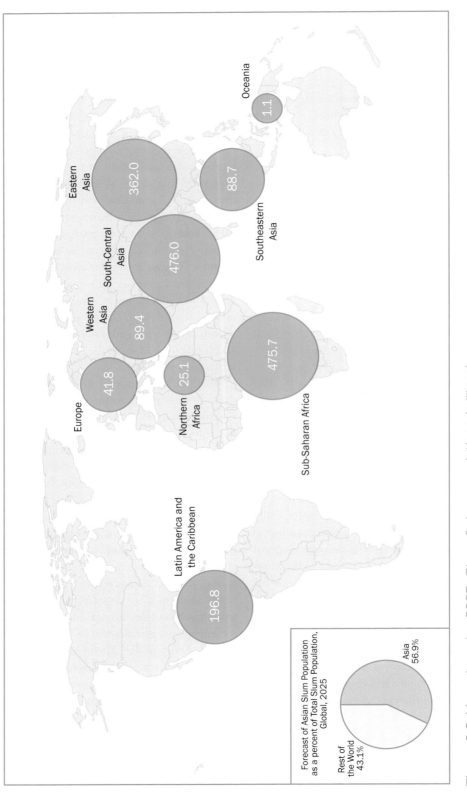

Figure 9.9 Megaslums by 2025. Size of slum populations (millions)

Source: adapted from http://www.slideshare.net/FrostandSullivan/frost-sullivan-mega-trendsurbanisation-city-as-a-customermanijames. Accessed 18 August 2016.

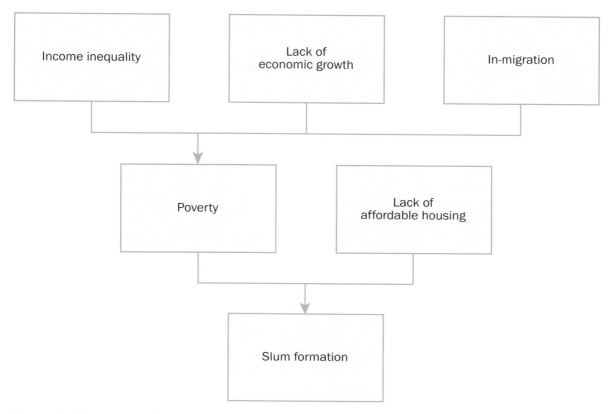

Figure 9.10 Causes of slum formation
Source: adapted from UN-Habitat, 2003.

Plate 9.2 Mathare Valley Slum, Nairobi, Kenya
(*photo*: Tony Binns)

the Cities Alliance (1999), which has encouraged projects including urban farming, transport improvements and water and sanitation support in slum areas. This builds on interventions from the 1970s when, with World Bank support and encouragement, many cities around the world actively started engaging in policies of slum upgrading – improving facilities and services in slum area – and site and service schemes, where serviced sites are provided to new residents who build their homes which are normally still shacks, but they at least have access to basic services and often legal title. These programmes have been pursued, with varying degrees of success in cities around the world often through the actions of NGOs. While there is evidence of improved urban services and water supply in countries such as Venezuela through direct involvement of citizen groups, in other countries limited resources have meant that schemes fail to achieve all that they set out to do and only partially address the scale of urban need. Limited investments made often translate into poor implementation on the ground and an inability to fully address the scale of the needs which exist (UN-Habitat, 2003). Arguments by de Soto that property titling will encourage proto-capitalism in such areas (in Satterthwaite and Mitlin, 2014), are countered by mounting evidence of landlordism and over-crowding, with density rates of over 13 people per room being noted in some Indian slums (Davies, 2006).

Given the continued and rapid growth of cities and slums in particular, and the failure of national and international organisations to effectively address the scale of the challenge which exists, Davies (2006: 19) had these sobering words to say about urban life in the future:

Thus, the cities of the future, rather than being made out of glass and steel as envisioned by earlier generations of urbanists, are instead largely constructed out of crude bricks, straw, recycled plastic, cement blocks, and scrap wood. Instead of cities of light soaring towards heaven, much of the twenty-first-century urban world squats in squalor, surrounded by pollution, excrement, and decay.

This stark reality should not be seen as a criticism on the positive success which some cities have achieved in dealing with the challenge of slums, rather it should be seen as a challenge to the world to deal more effectively, and on a much larger scale, with the huge and growing backlog which exists. UN-Habitat (2003) argues that, as a way forward, development priorities must be reconsidered and the quest for 'inclusive cities' must be actively pursued. In order to achieve this objective, UN-Habitat argues the need for:

1) A move from slum upgrading to cities without slums, which draws on participatory processes to encourage employment, effective governance, supports social capital, provides safety nets, draws in finance and uses pro-poor mechanisms and policy to bring about effective change.

2) The provision of tenure security.

3) Improving transport and accessibility.

4) Encouraging empowerment and employment.

5) Mobilising finance.

6) Improving urban policy to ensure inclusive development.

Urban poverty

As noted in Chapter 1, poverty and its persistence, particularly in the poorest countries, remains one of the key barriers to human development. Inevitably, with more than half of the world's population now living in cities, the issue of urban poverty has become more distinctive and often desperate. In 2003, the UN-Habitat, in their report on 'The Challenge of Slums', warned of the worldwide catastrophe of urban poverty. As with the challenges posed by slums, urban poverty is one of the most pressing urban development challenges. While there is some evidence that averaged national poverty levels are reducing, this does not in any way mitigate the reality that hundreds of millions of urban dwellers are eking out a living well below national income averages and below poverty lines, however calculated.

The nature, incidence, scale and responses to urban poverty have become a major focus of attention for policy makers and academics, and key recent work in this area includes the writings of the Cities Alliance (2006), the Woodrow Wilson International Centre (2007), the World Bank (2009b) and writings by Stevens et al. (2006), Mitlin et al. (2013) and Satterthwaite et al. (2014). The focus of the MDGs on poverty reduction has been a key catalyst in attracting attention to this issue.

It is estimated that nearly one billion people now live in poverty in cities of the South, often living in slums without access to key resources such as education and formal shelter to try and improve their condition (Mitlin et al., 2013). This is a significant increase from the 746 million in 2002 who lived under the questionable measure of $2/day in cities (Woodrow Wilson International Centre, 2007). Understanding the true nature and extent of poverty is complicated by the questionable value of using a poverty line of $1/day or higher as a gauge of urban survival in widely differing contexts and conditions around the world. World Bank estimates of poverty can be extended by the use of surrogate measures of poverty such as access to shelter and water which, in their absence, skew up poverty scores from an estimated 495 million by the World Bank in 2000 to nearly a billion in that year. Based on localised costs of food supply, Mitlin et al. (2013) estimate that urban poverty in much of eastern Africa ranges between 40–56% of the urban population, while in DR Congo it is 61.5%. In Haiti, the poorest country in the western hemisphere, the estimate is 76%, while in Latin America it ranges from 33–53% varying according to country

and often city. A more nuanced understanding of urban poverty also requires consideration of key issues such access to transport, education, shelter and water, while inequality within cities both raises questions over averaged statistics and reflects the persistence of social and structural barriers to change. Figure 9.11 shows gini-coefficient scores for a range of cities in the South. A gini-score measures the scale of inequality, usually in terms of the distribution of wealth in a society on a scale from 0 to 1, or from zero to extreme inequality. The existence of significant social and economic inequality within cities indicates the stark reality of poverty.

The multiple and intersecting causes of urban poverty are reflected in Figure 9.12, which shows the degree to which a multitude of economic, service, infrastructure and social deprivations intersect to reinforce urban poverty and the powerlessness of hundreds of millions of urban residents.

The persistence of urban poverty is increasingly being recognised as an issue of long-term concern. While it is generally regarded that urban poverty levels are not as bad as those in rural areas, evidence from India indicates that the gap between urban and rural poverty is narrowing as

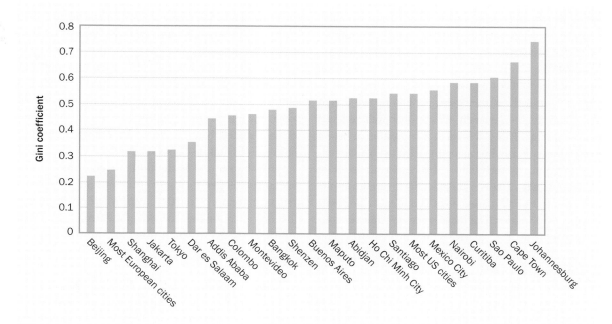

Figure 9.11 Gini-coefficient for selected cities in the South
Source: adapted from Mitlin et al., 2013.

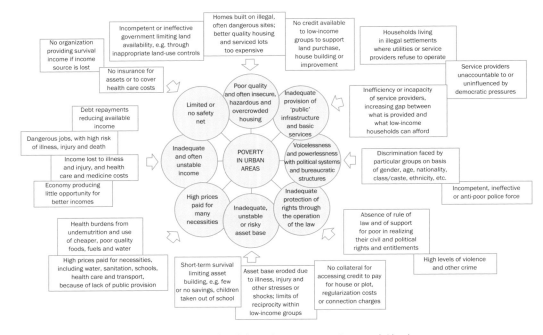

Figure 9.12 Deprivations associated with urban poverty and their causes
Source: adapted from Mitlin et al., 2013.

the situation in urban areas worsens. It is also important to note that in smaller urban centres, i.e. those with less than 50,000 people in India, poverty levels are generally far higher than in larger centres where more concerted interventions have been undertaken and economic opportunities are general better (Government of India, 2009).

Despite the very real challenges which cities face, as the Cities Alliance (2006) argues, cities can be regarded as 'engines of growth', as they generate 80% of world economic activity and generally have higher welfare levels than rural areas. This places them in a position to have a potentially significant impact on the selection of interventions to reduce poverty and enhance overall levels of economic activity. The World Bank (2009b) argues for the need to improve city management and to make pro-poor policies city priorities. The Bank argues for interventions which improve the macro-economic environment, enhance slum upgrading endeavours, prioritise poverty alleviation and put safety nets in place for the poorest of the poor. Encouraging the economic development of cities and investment within them, and facilitating market access to land and finance, are seen as critical to addressing poverty and laying a basis for sustainable development.

However, as Stevens et al. (2006) argue, interventions need to go further than the issues raised above, and

actively focus on supporting sustainable livelihoods through interventions which recognise and do not marginalise the role and place of existing local organisations and social networks. While advocating the pursuit of the sustainable livelihoods approach (see Chapter 1) Stevens et al. (2006) argue the need to ensure that issues of governance, access to space and infrastructure, support for community organisations and recognition of the diverse nature and sources of urban incomes must be embedded in any intervention. Within this context, the pursuit of Integrated Urban Development linking the various interventions and strategies is advocated.

Satterthwaite and Mitlin (2014) argue that accountable and effective local government and governance structure are a critical first step in addressing urban poverty. Responses to poverty from the state and other sources, which these authors identify and critique can include:

1) Welfare transfers, such as the *Bolsa Familia* scheme in Brazil and the social welfare transfers in South Africa, which both transfer state funds to vulnerable social groups, appear to have gone some way to providing a basic urban safety net and which are being extended to other parts of Latin America.

2) A second approach is that of urban management and state led development. While this may extend infrastructure and services, it often unwittingly marginalises the poor in terms of the restricted access to services which the inevitable requirement for the payment of user charges for services leads to.

3) Participatory governance and budgeting, as demonstrated successfully in Brazil, and in Porto Alegre in particular, can provide for empowerment and the better targeting of state support. While this can increase accountability and improve decision-making, it can also marginalise the least vocal constituencies.

4) Rights-based approaches which uphold the position of residents and producers can protect the interests of the poor from being marginalised, but they do not necessarily improve conditions.

5) Improving market access is a long-argued for intervention from a neo-liberal perspective. Access to micro-credit and finance and housing improvements are seen as a way to break the cycle of poverty. Evidence suggests that while this can lead to positive outcomes, higher income groups tend to derive the greatest benefit, whilst lower income groups lack the capacity to fully benefit from what is available.

6) Social movement and advocacy can help articulate local needs and demands and give the marginalised a voice. This, however, does not guarantee a way out of poverty.

7) Aided self-help has a long history in terms of the work of the World Bank and advocates of support for the informal sector. While having some benefits, limited state support and difficulties which the poor experience in accessing the services and support to help them 'better themselves' have restricted the outcomes of this approach.

8) Clientelism, or the use of patron-client networks by the poor to improve their situation. This is particularly important in areas lacking in services and housing where the poor depend on relationships with the more powerful to improve their situation. Gains however tend to be limited, they encourage dependence and seldom benefit the poorest.

Satterthwaite and Mitlin (2014) go on to argue that if urban poverty is to be effectively addressed, then new ways of thinking about providing finance and access to services are critical which do not disempower the poor. Equally important is the need for the poor to actively engage in the process of change and to give greater voice to local institutions. At a broader level, global economic inequalities, which tend to reinforce dominance-dependence relationships between the North and the South, tend to maintain and reinforce lower levels of income in the South, and these must be addressed if realistic progress is to be made.

Migration and the cause of rapid urbanisation

As already noted, urbanisation can be defined as the process which leads a higher proportion of the total population of an area to live in towns and cities (Potter and Lloyd-Evans, 1998). Urbanisation is thus a relative measure, recording the percentage of the total population of a nation or a region that is to be found in towns and cities. This should not be confused with the absolute growth of urban areas and urban populations. These are best described by the term *urban growth*.

Throughout the South, people are migrating from the rural areas to towns and cities. It is suggested that often about half the growth of cities reflects rural-to-urban migration. For example, during the 1960s, the World Bank estimated that migrant related increase, as a percentage of total population increase, amounted to 50 per cent in Caracas, 52 per cent in Bombay, 54 per cent in Djakarta, 50 per cent in Nairobi and 68 per cent in São Paulo.

In the Philippines in the 1970s the in-migration rate to cities was 1.9 per cent per year, out of an annual urban population growth rate of 3.9 per cent, with the balance being accounted for by natural increase within cities. For Brazil, during the same decade, in-migration accounted for 2.2 per cent per annum out of a total growth rate of 4.4 per cent per annum (Devas and Rakodi, 1993; UN, 1989). High rates of natural increase tend to be accounted for by the generally youthful nature of populations in the South and of the cities in particular, given that it is often the young, who are in the reproductive cohort, who leave rural areas and move to cities where they raise their families. Since 2007, the number of people living in urban areas has exceeded the population of rural areas, which will, gradually, lead to a slowing down of urbanisation at a global level. While this is happening in Latin America, in much of Africa and Asia the rural population still exceeds the urban, and high rates of urbanisation will continue in these areas for several decades.

But why have migrants been moving to cities in the South in such large numbers? This mainly stems from the widespread existence of poverty, unemployment and deprivation in the rural areas of many countries in the South, coupled with the perceived benefits which cities have to offer, such as potential or perceived access to jobs, education and health care. While these benefits may not be realised by all urban migrants, relative to living in rural areas the potential access to services is generally better. Additional factors include pressure on rural dwellers to earn money to pay taxes, support families and to be able to buy commercially produced goods. In certain countries, employment opportunities, or at least the perceptions that there are opportunities in industrial estates, serves as an additional catalyst. What emerges has been termed the 'push-pull' relationship, which describes a situation in which poor opportunities in the rural areas, 'the push', match the attraction of urban areas 'the pull' encouraging migrants to make the transition to the cities (Pacione, 2009).

Data show that where jobs do exist then rates of pay are higher in urban areas, and also that average incomes increase with city size in a progressive manner. In addition, social and health facilities are better in the principal towns and cities, although access to them is a major problem for the poor in society. Urban migration takes many forms – it can be temporary, permanent or circulatory, i.e. related to seasonal opportunities. Increasingly, migration is taking on an international dimension, e.g. workers from South India moving to cities in the Middle East in search of employment opportunities (Potter and Lloyd-Evans, 1998; Pacione, 2009).

History, culture and even the nature of communication and transport systems, all have a role to play in the decision to migrate. Certainly, the last of these factors has induced considerable change in the nature of both internal and international migration. With regard to internal migration, in most countries it is almost as cheap and easy to access the major cities as it is to move to smaller local centres; consequently, the smaller local centres are often bypassed in the rural–urban migration process.

This has drawn attention to the role that small and intermediate towns can and should play in the development process (Aeroe, 1992; Baker and Pedersen, 1992). Despite the validity of this focus, the attention of most governments and development agencies has been diverted away from small towns per se, and towards the immediate challenges posed by the phenomenon of mega-urbanisation.

In the previous section, the emergence of extended metropolitan regions was considered, whereby vast compound urban–rural zones are the outcome. Some writers refer to mega-urbanisation as the process which leads to rapid urban expansion along major lines of communication, enveloping villages and villagers *in situ*, and creating multi-nodal settlements, where rural and urban become blurred and indistinguishable, obfuscating the precise nature of movements between the two (McGee, 1989; McGee and Robinson, 1995; Potter and Unwin, 1995).

One of the reasons why mega-urbanisation is occurring in countries with rapid economic growth is the expansion of international urban migration. In Pacific-Asia, the waves of economic growth which have rippled from Japan through the four tigers to the industrialising ASEAN (Association of South East Asian Nations) states and the Middle East, have been followed by streams of job-seekers moving in search of work in manufacturing and tertiary activities.

However, there is more to the demographic aspects of sustainable urbanisation than the nature and management of migration, not the least of which is the two-way relationship between urbanisation and fertility. For example, living in the city not only raises the cost of rearing children, but also increases access to family planning programmes, and yet cities in the Global South have overwhelmingly young populations, with cities as geographically different as Bogotá, Delhi and Jakarta all having half their populations aged 15 years or less.

On the other hand, in some of the cities of Pacific-Asia, ageing populations, and their impact on the labour force and social welfare, provide different, but equally pressing issues.

Other demographically linked issues related to sustainable urbanisation can involve considerations of household composition and the roles of women in generating income and meeting basic needs, or of ethnicity and the ways in which migration has created more complex situations in the competition for limited urban resources (see Box 9.1).

BOX 9.1

Urban migration and ethnicity

The fact that migration to cities is being drawn from increasingly extensive geographical areas has often resulted in a broader diversification of ethnic groups. In most countries this ethnic complexity is spontaneous, as people from economically, geographically and ethnically marginal regions are drawn to capital cities. Almost two-thirds of the migrants to Bangkok, for example, are from the Lao-dominated northeast of Thailand. But in Malaysia, increased urban ethnic diversity has been the consequence of deliberate government policies designed to increase Malay participation in urban economic activities (Eyre and Dwyer, 1996).

Although some might argue this process has occurred in Malaysia without increasing ethnic tension, it was in fact prompted by ethnic tensions in the first place. In other cities where ethnic mixing has accompanied migratory growth, tensions have increased markedly, for example in many African cities where national politics reflect tribal antagonisms.

This growing urban ethnic diversification and its consequences have been exacerbated by the increased internationalisation of labour movements. In Southeast Asia, this has produced a particularly complex pattern of movements. Singapore was the initial magnet for migrants from Malaysia, Indonesia and the Philippines, for factory work and domestic work. More recently, construction labour has come from Thailand and India. And as it has developed its own economy Malaysia has recruited both legal and illegal workers from Thailand and, more particularly, Indonesia. There are now an estimated 1 million Indonesians working in Malaysia, most of whom are illegal, and local resentment at narrowing access to jobs has increased substantially. Meanwhile, illegal workers from the transitional socialist economies of Southeast Asia are also beginning to flow across weakly policed borders into the regional capitals of Thailand, which have lost migrants to Bangkok.

This increasingly complex pattern of ethnodevelopment is threatening urban sustainability in a variety of ways. Although it may provide a larger labour pool for economic growth, it is also leading to growing ethnic and class antagonism and exploitation.

The implications of growth: emerging city systems and urban models

In order to understand patterns and processes of urban change various models have been put forward which focus on the size disparities of cities and their differing rates of growth, relative to changes in the demographic situation in the host countries.

Urban primacy and city size distribution

Later in this chapter, socio-economic conditions within cities in the South are examined in detail. Before that we will focus attention on some of the most important discussions about the sets of towns and cities which make up the so-called 'urban system' of nations and regions. Indeed, the idea of an urban system can just as easily be applied at the continental and global scales. An urban system can be defined as a set of interrelated towns and cities which together comprise the urban settlement fabric of an area.

It has frequently been argued that urban primacy – the eminence of one or more cities – is characteristic of urban systems in the countries of South. Multiple examples of countries exist in which a single city, usually the capital, is often home to a significant proportion of the national urban population and usually has an above average concentration of national wealth, services and industries.

In the mid-1990s, 15 per cent of the global urban population was to be found living in capital cities globally; this fraction is considerably higher for several of the world's countries in the South. The proportion of the total urban population living in the capital was as high as 33 per cent for sub-Saharan Africa, and approximately 25 per cent for Latin America, the Middle East and North Africa. Extreme cases of primacy are city states such as Singapore, the Hong Kong autonomous area and Macau, where nearly 100% of the urban population live in the single city. These are naturally unique cases given the small size of the city states and their unique political contexts. Other cases do, however, emphasise the point. Guatemala City is 125 times the size of the country's second city, while Manila hosts 60% of the Philippines manufactures (Chant and McIlwaine, 2009). In 2014, 42 urban agglomerations contained more than 40% of the urban population of their respective countries, with some of the most significant primate cities being Brazzaville, Djibouti, Conakry. Kuwait City, Panama City and Ulaanbaatar (UNDESA, 2014).

But despite this broad association, when we turn to the level of urban primacy recorded in individual countries, the issue becomes more complex. In a pioneering paper, Berry (1961) showed that, at the level of nation states, there is no clear statistical relationship between a nation's city size distribution and, either its level of urbanisation or economic development, as measured by GNP per capita. In the face of these negative findings, Berry speculated that a whole complex of forces serve to influence relative city size distributions. In particular, it was posited that if a few strong forces operate, a primate distribution will be the outcome (Figure 9.13a). The figure shows the context of a small country with a single dominant centre and a limited number of significantly smaller secondary centres.

It was argued that fewer forces are likely to influence the urban situation in the case of a smaller country, which has a shorter history of urbanisation, a simpler economic and political life, and a poorer overall degree of socio-economic development.

The opposites of these cases suggest that in a larger country it is likely a range of specialised cities performing a variety of functions will develop. The smooth distribution of cities that results can be called a rank–size distribution (as opposed to overwhelming dominance of the 'primate' city) (Figure 9.13b), or a log-normal city size distribution, which looks nor at actual population number but the city rank in a hierarchy (Figure 9.13c). These situations arise in countries where there might be a single major city, but there are several cities only slightly smaller and often an increasing number of cases, e.g. in the USA, New York is the dominant core, then smaller but more numerous at the secondary level are cities such as Chicago and Los Angeles, then at the tertiary level there are centres such as San Francisco, Atlanta, Miami, etc., i.e. the rank–size distribution of settlements.

Berry's line of argument was followed up in several research papers, notably those by Mehta (1964) and Linsky (1965), both of whom took essentially the same approach, correlating a number of variables against the degree of urban primacy for a sample of nations. Linsky pre-specified the predicted relationships between urban primacy and six variables. He suggested that primacy was positively associated with the degree of export-orientation of the nation, the proportion of the workforce employed in agriculture and the overall rate of population growth. The areal extent of areas of dense population was envisaged as being negatively correlated with primacy. Finally, somewhat curiously perhaps, an open verdict was initially pronounced on the association between primacy and former colonial status.

The empirical analysis showed that all the hypothesised associations between the variables and urban primacy were as expected. In addition, former colonial status was positively related to levels of urban primacy. This might be expected, for colonial status generally involved a strong coastal–mercantile orientation in the siting of cities, and the attendant urban polarisation that goes with this, as mapped into the mercantile and plantopolis models of settlement evolution in developing countries (Chapter 3).

Thus, Linsky's work was significant in confirming that, although urban primacy is characteristic of small nations which have low per capita incomes, a high dependence on exports, a former colonial status, an agricultural economy and a fast rate of population growth, it is certainly not precluded elsewhere. For example, contemporary Thailand exhibits few of these features, yet it presents extreme urban primacy.

A few years later, Vapnarsky (1969) in an historical–empirical study of Argentina argued that the primate and rank–size distribution patterns are not to be seen as the extremes of a continuum, that is, separate and mutually exclusive.

Rather, he argued that the two distributional types are produced by different sets of circumstances. On the evidence offered by Argentina, Vapnarsky (1969) regarded urban primacy as being positively associated with the degree of closure of the economy i.e. the

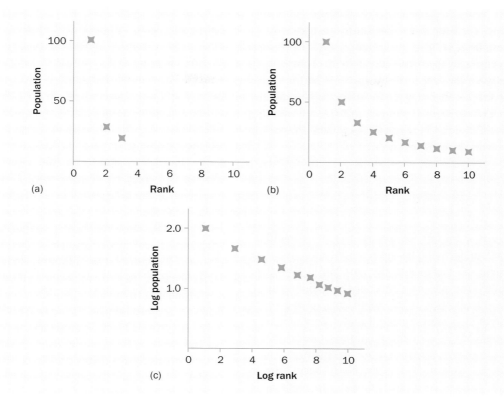

Figure 9.13 Urban settlement distributions: (a) primate (b) rank–size (c) log-normal

degree of dependence on overseas trade – which generally favours the growth of a single major trading city, usually a port city.

With increasing closure, urban primacy was believed to reduce, other things being equal. In contrast, Vapnarsky saw the urban distribution pattern as being affected by the level of interdependence existing in a country – i.e. the extent to which its various regions are interlinked by virtue of flows of people, goods, capital, etc.

It was believed that as internal interdependence increases, the smooth or log-normal pattern will progressively be approached. The classic primate distribution is seen as the outcome of low closure together with low interdependence; this may prevail for longer in small countries than elsewhere.

Undoubtedly the most important point, is that primacy really does occur and should therefore be examined at the regional scale. Large developing countries such as India, China and Brazil display low levels of primacy at the national scale, precisely because they are comprised of several primate regional urban areas, such as Kolkata, Mumbai, Delhi and Chennai, in the case of India. Thus, primacy should be seen as one expression of the wider existence of regional inequalities and spatial polarisation in development.

As reviewed in detail in Chapter 3, the mercantile model shows how global trade and capitalism since the 1400s have led to development being articulated through coastal gateway cities. Such places are the concentration points of social surplus product.

Despite the clear evidence of how significant urban primacy was for many countries in the South in the twentieth century, there is evidence that the rate of growth of the largest cities is now lower than that of secondary cities (Cohen, 2004), and is likely that the majority of new urban migrants will move to smaller cities (Knox and McCarthy, 2012). According to Chant and McIlwaine (2009) this reflects a range of key issues, including the negative effects of congestion, protracted travel times and the fact that the largest cities have been hard hit in terms of economic crises and neo-liberal restructuring. The net result is that future urban growth, in most countries, is likely to be more evenly spread across all centres in the urban hierarchy than was the case previously. The UN (UNDESA, 2014) has established that the number of primate cities has declined from 50 in 1970 to 47 in 1990 to 42 in 2014, reflecting greater diversification in the urban system and the significant growth of secondary cities.

Modelling change: demographics of birth and death rates and the cycle of urbanisation

Another very important factor in explaining rapid urban growth in the South has been the enhanced medical provision and facilities in the post-World War II period, while birth rates have remained at traditionally high levels. Thus, cities in the South are growing by what are often high rates of natural increase, as well as by migration, although the relative proportions of the significance of each varies from region to region.

This was not true of cities in the North during the Industrial Revolution. Such areas though experiencing high rates of urbanisation, often as a direct result of industrial development and the attraction of employment, tended to be far less healthy than the surrounding countryside, and were often regarded as deathtraps due to insanitary conditions, poor health care and dangerous working conditions in the mines and factories. Overall rates of natural increase fell when incomes improved, and living conditions improved from the late nineteenth century with the introduction of sanitation and pollution controls, leading to an identified correlation between increasing wealth and lower rates of natural increase resulting in reduced family size in the North. This theme was elaborated in Chapter 5. Populations in the South are now growing at an average of 2 per cent per annum.

These sorts of demographic features of contemporary urbanisation are shown if the demographic transition model and what is referred to as 'the cycle of urbanisation', are juxtaposed (Figure 9.14).

The countries of the North experienced a gradual process of demographic change, as a result of urbanisation and industrial development in the nineteenth and early twentieth centuries as mentioned above.

Figure 9.14a and c show just how gradual this has been. Birth and death rates both fell relatively gradually from 1800 onwards as medical changes slowly made a difference and living standards gradually rose. In the South, the birth rate has, until recently, generally continued at traditional levels of 40–45 per 1,000 of the population. But, since around 1950, crude death rates have often fallen very dramatically, as a result of medical advances leading to very rapid rates of total population increase – shown by the growing gap between the two lines on Figure 9.14c. This is frequently known as the 'telescoping of the demographic transition' in the South.

Figure 9.14 also shows that, in a similar fashion, urbanisation is occurring at a much accelerated rate in the South. The gradual increase in urbanisation, which occurred in the North, is described as the 'cycle of urbanisation' mentioned above. This takes the form of an attenuated or squashed S-shape curve (Figure 9.14c). The downward trend in recent years in the North reflects counter-urbanisation, or movement to rural areas from the cities. However, urbanisation is occurring much more rapidly in the South. The very rapid rise in the urban proportion occurs at the same time as the massive spurt in population growth.

Real growth statistics for several nations are graphed in Figure 9.15. The urban proportion for England and Wales increased gradually from around 25 per cent in 1800 to approximately 80 per cent in 1975. The swiftest rise came in the period 1811–1851, and the rate of increase dropped somewhat after that.

In comparison, countries such as Brazil, Egypt, South Korea and India have shown very rapid rates of urbanisation in the relatively short period since 1945.

Rural–urban interrelations in the South

Just as Chapter 3 has shown that in the past too much of a distinction has been drawn between the categories 'developed' and 'developing', along with 'core' and 'periphery', the same can be said about the terms 'urban' and 'rural'.

Although definitional exercises involve the recognition of a gradual transition between rural and urban settlements (that relates to the existence of a rural–urban

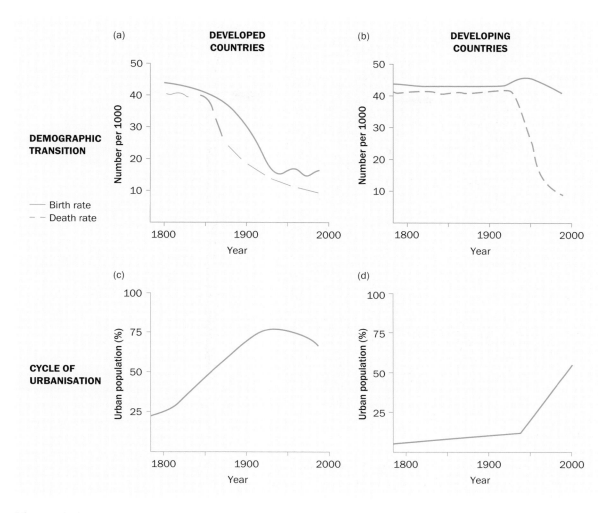

Figure 9.14 The cycle of urbanisation and the demographic transition for the North (developed) and the South (developing countries)
Source: adapted from Potter (1985, 1992a).

continuum); the politico-administrative need to define hamlets, villages, towns and cities has involved the imposition of clear thresholds and boundaries, which do not always mesh with the realities of people life, lifestyle, employment and movement, and which differ, often significantly, between countries.

It seems that the same sort of categorical thinking has come to affect the identification of rural and urban zones in many respects. In other words, all too frequently, writers have implied that the urban and the rural are essentially discrete and separate entities, in both physical and functional terms. The aim of the present section is to show that in respect of urban policy and

urban management, this is a very simplistic and essentially unhelpful view.

Work over the last two decades or so has stressed how closely interrelated urban and rural areas are. This theme is fleshed out below under three headings: (i) rural–urban interaction in the South, (ii) the nature of peri-urban zones and (iii) extended metropolitan regions. Several of the themes raised here are picked up and further developed in Chapter 10, which considers predominantly rural landscapes and development.

In short, there are multitudes of interactions which occur between urban and rural areas, relating to the movement of goods, services and people, and the

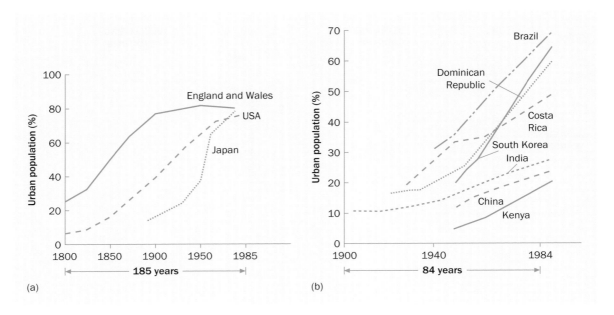

Figure 9.15 Examples of urbanisation curves for the North and South
Source: adapted from Potter (1992a).

degree to which urban areas are also conduits for links and trading relationships between rural areas and the wider regions.

Rural–urban interaction in the South

While there is a natural tendency to regard and treat rural and urban areas as separate, unrelated entities, the reality is that there are high degrees of interaction and engagement between the two. The division between the two is often blurred by improved transportation systems, ICT and communication, migrancy and commuting, dependence of rural areas on urban services, and the blurring of the physical boundaries between the two, as a result of the growth of 'peri-urban' areas. Peri-urban areas can be considered a zone of transition often characterised by a blend of semi-rural lifestyles and farming with high levels of dependence on urban services and employment and increasing residential occupation by people from the city. Furthermore as considered in Chapter 10, many people currently engage in both rural and urban lives, building 'multi-local livelihoods' (Zoomers, 2014) based around the opportunities of rapid urbanisation and the enhanced mobility afforded by communication and technology.

An additional overlay complicating the simplistic dichotomies is the degree to which both areas are influenced by identical processes, as suggested in Figure 9.16. These processes include the impact of globalisation, structural adjustment and economic change, and are complicated by issues such as urban primacy and the mediating role which cities play in such relationships.

Some of the first efforts to contest dichotomous thinking about the urban and the rural occurred in the 1980s. Several works have focused attention on the fact that strong and complex interactions occur between rural and urban areas, and that these underpin many aspects of the development equation (see Dixon, 1987; Potter and Unwin, 1987).

Just like the argument about development and underdevelopment being opposite faces of the same coin, so it can be stressed that the differences between urban and rural at their extremes are maintained by the strong functional interlinkages which exist between them on a day-to-day basis. For example, much of the cheap food produce sold on urban stalls and in urban markets is picked and transported by rural dwellers who then transport such goods to town. Some of these will be

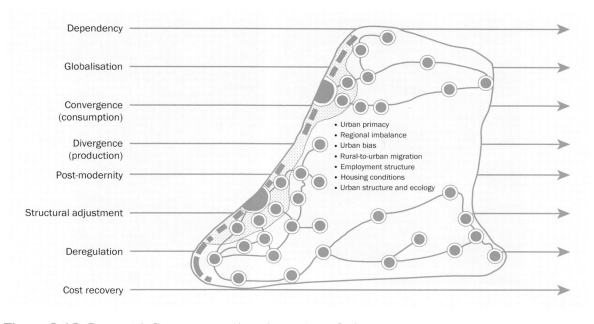

Figure 9.16 Current influences on the character of city systems
Source: adapted from Potter (1995a).

part-time rural agriculturists. Via processes of unequal exchange and urban bias, the relative low prices of agricultural products (compared with imported produce) serve to reduce the costs of city life. Urban bias is examined further in Chapter 10. Other urban–rural flows involve trips to shop, to visit offices and to health and education facilities. All of these movements serve to etch out what are major differences between rural and urban zones. Rural–urban interactions are also considered further in Chapter 10 and many of these factors are important to consider in relation to resource degradation and sustainable livelihood opportunities as examined in Chapters 6.

The nature of peri-urban zones

Another rural–urban topic which has commanded a mounting volume of attention among geographers and others interested in development studies have been debates on the zone where the urban and the rural meet. This has principally involved recognising the social, economic and environmental salience of the areas that exist at the very edges of cities in the Global South. These tracts of land are frequently referred to as 'peri-urban' zones or interfaces, and include areas of active assimilation of agricultural lands into the urban network (see Allen, 2003, for example). As such, these zones show a mixture of land uses. For example, the recent growth of urban population is reflected in the existence of large peripheral squatter settlements and shanty towns, often on land held by traditional tenure systems such as communal tenure, which impacts on the capacity of local authorities to either intervene or service such land, as has happened in many parts of Africa. At the same time, these very areas are often the locales for intensive agricultural production in order to supply the food needs of the rapidly burgeoning urban populations (Lynch, 2005). Such urban-based agriculture is common in many cities of the Global South. Case study 9.1 looks at the peri-urban zones of Kano, Nigeria (see also Plate 9.3, showing the Kano close-settled zone, Nigeria).

The research that is being done on such urban agriculture is examining the advantages and limitations of such production. The 'cons' are perhaps far less obvious than the 'pros'. They include the potentially worrying possibility of the use of polluted groundwater for intensive agricultural production.

Plate 9.3 Traditional Hausa village in the Kano close-settled zone, northern Nigeria
(*photo*: Tony Binns)

Case study 9.1

Urban and peri-urban agriculture in Kano, Nigeria

Nigeria, with a total population exceeding 173 million, is Africa's most populous country. The country has an average annual population growth rate of 2.9 per cent and the annual growth rate of the urban population was approaching 5 per cent, leading to 47 per cent of the total population being urban-based by 2014 (UNDESA, 2014). As in many countries in the South, there is an increasing demand for fresh foodstuffs in Nigeria's cities, and large quantities of food are now being produced within the urban and periurban areas.

The city of Kano, with an estimated population of more than 3 million, dominates northern Nigeria. Located in the semi-arid savanna belt, with an annual average rainfall of under 700mm, and a long dry season from late September to May, the region experiences considerable variation in both the amount and frequency of rainfall from one year to the next. Dry season cultivation is dependent upon irrigation, and low-lying areas in river valleys and

depressions, where the water table is close to the surface (known locally as *fadamas*), are valuable locations for such cultivation. The construction in the last 30 years of a number of dams and associated irrigation schemes in Kano State, together with the sinking of wells and boreholes, has resulted generally in more water being available for dry season cultivation. However, where facilities such as abattoirs and tanneries discharge their effluent into rivers and drains, pollution of water sources can be a serious problem, particularly during the dry season when rainfall that might dilute and flush out toxic elements is absent (Lewcock, 1995).

A survey undertaken in 1996 discovered considerable amounts of fruit and vegetables being produced in and around Kano, within 10km of the walls of the old city (Figure 9.17), and mainly located near major routes. Fruit and vegetables were also piled high along the roadside, waiting for collection and passing trade. The production, transporting and marketing of

Case study 9.1 (continued)

such fresh produce is a significant income-generating business, as well as satisfying the basic needs of the urban population. While wealthy households and businessmen see fruit trees as a form of investment, 'resource-poor' cultivators grow mainly vegetables, with some fruit, for home consumption and sale. As the Figure shows, many plots are actually located in built-up areas, with limited amounts of cultivation even within the walls of urban family compounds, in some cases undertaken by women who, under Islamic tradition, are in seclusion. Plots in the built-up area are typically small, ranging from 0.01 to 0.40 hectares, while in the peri-urban area they are generally larger, between 0.1 and 2 hectares. Most growers outside compounds are men between the ages of 30 and 70,

with little, if any, formal education. Traditional tools such as hoes and cutlasses predominate, though some farmers use water pumps and apply chemical fertilisers and pesticides, when available, as well as manure and compost. The most common vegetable crops grown are spinach, maize, okra, lettuce, onion, tomato, carrot, sorrel, pepper and sugar cane, while the main fruits are mango, guava, cashew, orange and pomegranate.

A particularly important area of vegetable production in Kano lies underneath the transmission masts of the Federal Aviation Authority (FAA), on the southern side of the old city and just across the main road from the city walls (RTA on Figure 9.17). The site covers an area roughly 1 by 0.5 km, and draws its main water supply from a drain leading from the old city (Binns and Fereday, 1996). This area was opened up to cultivation in the early 1980s, when the civilian government under President Shagari gave permission under its 'Green Revolution' initiative that all vacant public lands within urban areas could be used for cultivation without charge. However, this permission has never been formalised, so tenure of such land is by no means secure. The Federal Aviation Authority is generally satisfied that farming activities have improved the condition of the site and there seems to have been little negative impact on the environment. The area is divided into two sections; the first, located alongside and as far as 200 metres to the west of the main drain, uses irrigation for the year-round cultivation of vegetables and grains, such as lettuce, spinach, okra, maize and rice, while the other section of the site grows rainfed staple crops, such as sorghum and millet during the wet season.

Prospective cultivators must first seek permission from the Aviation Authority's officers and land is allocated on a 'first-come, first-served' basis. There is stiff competition for plots, and those acquired more recently are generally smaller than those occupied earlier. Plot size in the irrigated area is between 0.01 and 0.4 hectares, while plots located in the rainfed cultivation section are generally two to four times larger. During the dry season there is considerable competition for water, such that farmers may even

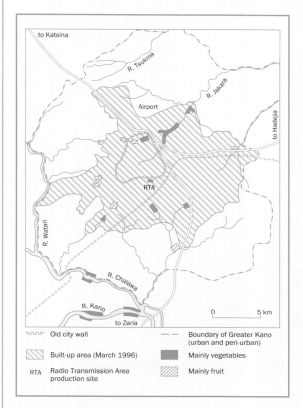

Figure 9.17 Main horticultural production sites, Kano

Source: adapted from Bayero University Kano Survey map.

▶

Case study 9.1 (continued)

irrigate at night. Buckets are mainly used to raise water and those farmers with plots situated away from the drain have in some cases sunk shallow wells to tap rather less polluted groundwater, though FAA officials were concerned about possible damage to underground transmission cables.

Most farmers use a combination of family and hired labour. There are three cropping seasons for vegetables: the dry season with full irrigation lasts from November to March; a transition season starts in April, and continues into the rainfed cropping season in June; wet season cropping usually begins in early June and continues until late September. Some chemical fertiliser is used, but farmers experienced difficulty in acquiring it, many using ash, household refuse and animal manure instead to maintain soil fertility, although there is also often some difficulty in acquiring these items, as shown in Plate 9.4 (Lewcock, 1995). Farmers generally received little, if any, advice from extension workers, and a 'self-help' credit association collapsed because of the lack of transparency in the way its leaders managed the funds. Over 75 per cent of those interviewed on the FAA site said that they relied on horticultural production to supplement earnings from their main occupation and that horticultural production was more lucrative than growing rainfed staples.

Vegetables and fruit were generally head-loaded or transported by bicycle to a local market on the southern edge of the production site. However, in some cases crops were sold directly to local consumers or to market traders and middlemen. Sometimes, an entire plot of maize or carrots, for example, will be sold to a trader who first visits the farm to negotiate a price, and then arranges for the harvest and transport of the produce to the larger city markets. The largest quantities of vegetable crops are sold in the dry season, when growing conditions for crops such as tomato and pepper are more favourable.

The most common marketing chain goes from the producer to the major wholesaler, to the lesser wholesaler, the retailer and, finally, to the consumer. However, some farmers sell produce such as leafy vegetables directly to local consumers or street traders.

Plate 9.4 Boy with donkey conveying urban waste to peri-urban fields around Kano, northern Nigeria
(*photo*: Tony Binns)

Case study 9.1 (continued)

Given the perishability of fruit and vegetables, ease of movement between production sites and the main fruit and vegetable markets is important. Transportation seems to be the responsibility of whoever owns the crop at the time of transport. Large (about nine tonne) trucks, minibuses, taxis, motorcycles, bicycles and sometimes donkeys are the main forms of transport.

Some markets sell a wide range of fresh products and manufactured goods, while others are more specialised, such as Yan Kaba market which sells vegetables, Yan Lemo fruit and Bachirawa market onions. Market traders identified the lack of cold storage facilities, the high cost of transport and communication difficulties between producers and buying agents as the main problems in dealing with fruit and vegetables.

Urban agriculture in Kano is a significant form of land use, employment and food supply. In terms of the future sustainability of urban and peri-urban agriculture, Kano respondents identified two important concerns; first, the heavily polluted nature of much of the water used for irrigation and, second, the uncertainties surrounding security of tenure in many crop production locations (Lynch et al., 2001). These and other issues need careful consideration, but there is divided opinion among urban authorities on the merits of encouraging the further development of urban and peri-urban agriculture. Urban planners are concerned about such issues as land-use conflicts and possible disease transmission when irrigated areas are closely juxtaposed to dwellings.

Extended metropolitan regions (EMRs) / City regions

Recently, some analysts have suggested that what amount to new rural–urban complexes are developing, and that the nature of the urbanisation process and urban structures are thereby changing fundamentally. This idea has been presented by Terry McGee (1991, 1995) (see Key thinker box) among others, in the context of Asian cities.

Key thinker

Plate 9.5 Terry McGee

Terry McGee's contribution to development studies has been summarised by Lea (2006). Terry McGee (Plate 9.5) was born in Cambridge in North island of New Zealand in the heart of the Waikato agricultural area. After a teaching diploma, he took a degree specialising in geography at the Victoria University of Wellington, New Zealand.

His first academic appointment was to a lectureship in Geography at the University of Malaya in Kuala Lumpur in 1959 and he remained in this position for six years, during which time he undertook a PhD on Malay migration to Kuala Lumpur City and travelled extensively through Southeast Asia. This led directly to the publication of his book *The Southeast Asian City: A Social Geography of the Primate Cities of Southeast Asia* in 1967. In this book, McGee saw urbanisation in the region as being characterised by conspicuous consumption and the extraction of surplus from the countryside (see Chapter 3). He employed the term 'pseudo-urbanisation' to imply that urbanisation was acting as a brake on effective and progressive development. In the 1970s, McGee's research

▶

Key thinker (continued)

focused strongly on the contribution made by the informal sector in cities of the Global South.

Urban–rural differences became a topic of particular concern to Terry McGee during the 1980s, and this gave rise to the identification of what have come to be known as Extended Metropolitan Regions (EMRs) – areas within which new urban–rural forms are to be found mixed together. In the mid-1980s, with Warwick Armstrong, McGee published *Theatres of Accumulation*, which proved to be influential, not least in stressing the relevance of the concepts of convergence and divergence in relation to patterns and processes of urbanisation in developing nations.

Stated simply, the approach stresses the fusion of urban and rural, as cities extend along corridors of transport and communications. McGee (1995) referred to regions of extended urban activity surrounding the core cities of many Asian countries as evidence of this process. McGee originally called these 'kotadesasi', and later 'desakota' (Indonesian for city-village). Such forms are now referred to in more generic terms as 'extended metropolitan regions' (EMRs).

The early diagram used by McGee to explain the nature of such EMRs is reproduced here as Figure 9.18. Five principal zones were identified as making up a hypothetical Asian country. These consisted of:

(i) first, the major cities, which generally amount to one or two large urban places in the Asian context;

(ii) these are surrounded by peri-urban zones, which are defined as those within daily commuting reach of the city;

(iii) the *desakota* areas are identified beyond the peri-urban zones, and witness the intense mixing of agricultural and non-agricultural activities, along major national corridors. Many are associated with intensive wet rice cultivation;

(iv) on their periphery are the densely inhabited rural areas;

(v) and these in turn are surrounded by the less populated frontier agricultural regions.

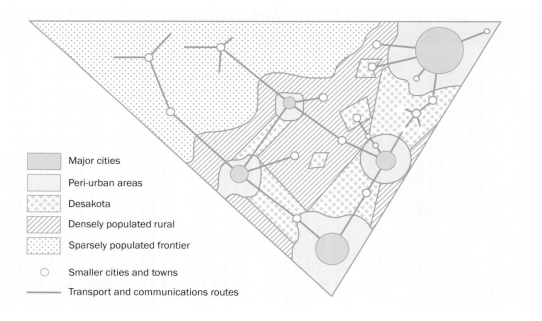

Major cities

Peri-urban areas

Desakota

Densely populated rural

Sparsely populated frontier

○   Smaller cities and towns

——   Transport and communications routes

Figure 9.18 A simplified depiction of desakota regions within a national space-economy
Source: adapted from McGee, 1991.

Thus, urban and rural type settlements become juxtaposed and enmeshed within one variegated area, and localities with high agricultural employment counts exist within what ostensibly appears to be a major urban zone. Throughout these areas, the overall population density is high.

McGee identified a range of desakota zones in Asia, and these are shown in Figure 9.19. In so doing, three different types of desakota region were recognised, according to their processes of formation and development over time.

The first were those associated with rapid rural–urban shifts, but where agriculture has remained important, such as in Japan and South Korea.

The second type were identified as being based on rapid changes in economic activity, involving the transition to secondary economic activities. The Taipei–Kaohsiung corridor in Taiwan was given as an example, where the proportion of the workforce engaged in agriculture declined from 56 to 20 per cent between 1956 and 1980. The Bangkok–Central Plains region of Thailand, and the main coastal cities of China were given as further instances of this type of development. Examples of different regions in Asia are indicated on Figure 9.19.

Third, urban zones characterised by high population growth, but slower rates of economic change, were identified, resulting in underemployment and self-employment

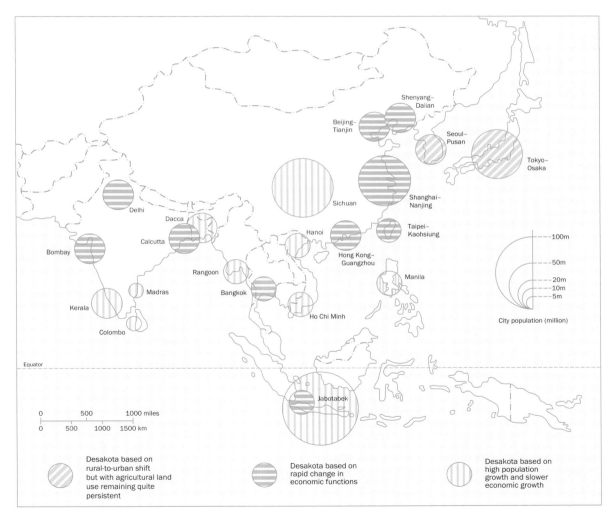

Figure 9.19 The distribution of different types of desakota regions in Asia
Source: adapted from McGee, 1991.

in unpaid family work and enterprises. Such trends were identified in respect of Kerala and Tamil Nadu in India.

Another major feature of the EMR is the formation of multiple nuclei, as major functions decentralise into special zones for business, recreation, finance, production, entertainment and tourism. As a prime example of this, Drakakis-Smith (2000) used the case of Hanoi, Vietnam. With growth, the wider city of Hanoi is showing marked signs of regionalisation. Notably, several of these developments reflect the input of international finance. These include the development of the Noi Bai export processing zone (EPZ), and the Noi Bai golf course and entertainment resort, both joint ventures between Malaysia and Hanoi. A range of developments are giving rise to a multiple-centred urban zone.

City regions and world cities

To a considerable extent, the emergence of EMRs can be recognised as the southern equivalent of what the geographer Jean Gottmann (1961) had much earlier referred to as 'megalopolis' in the context of the North. Urban sprawl, suburbanisation and improved transport have led to the coalescence of urban areas in numerous parts of the world into vast metropolitan areas.

The term 'megalopolis' was first applied to the continuously urbanised northeast seaboard of the USA, stretching from Boston in the north to Washington in the south (the so-called 'Boshwash' megalopolis), and later to other major linked metropolitan regions. These included those in Brazil based on Rio de Janeiro and São Paulo, and China based on Shanghai (Gottmann, 1957).

In more recent work, Rimmer (1991) and Evers and de Vries (2013) have considered EMRs and city regions surrounding the Pacific Ocean and in Europe, and including major American urban systems such as the Pacific Northwest corridor (Vancouver to Seattle), plus the Californian corridor (based on San Francisco, Los Angeles and San Diego), as well as the East Asian, Southeast Asian and European corridors. In most respects these can be seen as evolving megalopolitan forms in the way Gottmann originally envisaged. According to Aguilar et al. (2003) a key feature of city region development is the emergence of poly-centric systems and the associated growth of 'edge-cities'.

Also in the 1960s, the Greek scholar Doxiadis (1967) suggested that such urban complexes would coalesce into chain-like forms. It was ventured that these urban lineaments would eventually connect all of the urban cores in South America, Africa and Asia. Doxiadis (1967) referred to this as the 'inevitable city of the future', and the development of extended metropolitan regions in the North and South can be seen as the major ingredient, and one which will witness the progressive functional integration and physical inter-digitation of the urban and the rural through the twenty-first century.

World cities and the South

Since Friedmann's (1986) identification of the importance of a set of key 'world' or 'global cities' which dominate the world economically and political, there has been significant attention devoted to the identification and analysis of these cities and the key factors which determine their global significance (Sassen, 2002, 2011). Criteria such as international connectivity, the presence of stock exchanges and the headquarters of transnational corporations are generally employed as yardsticks to gauge global city rankings. Inevitably, this privileges cities in the North for entirely logical economic reasons. In so doing, however, it is apparent that being a mega-city, in size terms, does not necessarily equate to having a significant impact on the world economy. Figure 9.20 shows the key cities, based on connectivity measures, and by implications access to and control of world wealth and production. It is immediately apparent that, with the exception of New York and Tokyo, none of the other 15 mega-cities shown in Table 9.4 are in the league of being 'global command centres' in the economic sense. As the map shows, the cluster of 'control' is primarily in Europe and secondarily in North America and SE Asia/China.

A significant critique of what has been termed the 'world city hypothesis' has been undertaken by authors such as Robinson (2006). She argues that we need to recognise the status of 'ordinary cities', and she reminds us of the fact that all cities are integrated into the world economy in different ways, and having fewer corporate offices or airline connections in no way diminishes a city's global and national roles.

A significant challenge to the traditional role of the 'leading' cities in the North, comes from the growing global significance of key cities in the South such as Shanghai, Beijing, Dubai, Singapore and São Paulo.

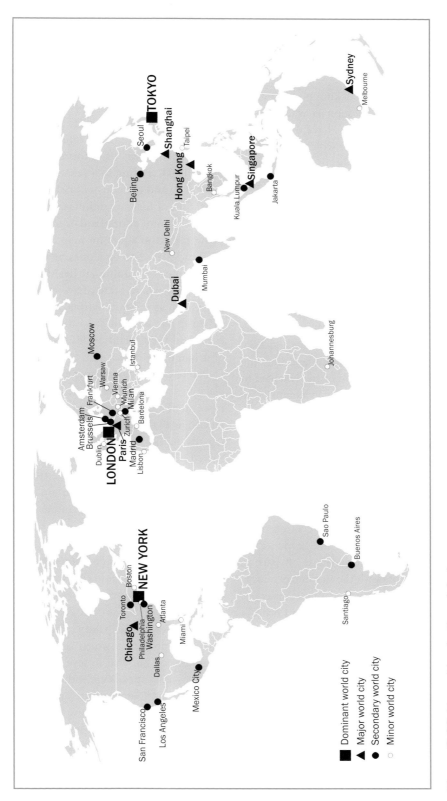

Figure 9.20 Key cities in the global economy

Source: adapted from Knox, Agnew, and McCarthy, 2014.

Urban and regional planning in countries in the South

Urban planning

Given the rapid growth which is taking place in cities around the world, a crucial question is whether city administrators and planning systems have the capacity to manage such growth in a manner which is both sustainable in terms of a range of social and economic scores, but also equitable in its outcomes.

Key issues in this regard relate to questions of: how is urban growth understood and managed at a national level? And, secondly, within local areas, what are the allocation processes and mechanisms in place to help ensure that land, services and housing are provided at a level which both meets demand and does not compromise health and safety considerations?

In terms of the second issue, an unquestionable challenge, over and above the enormous challenge posed by rapid growth, is the degree to which in Africa and Asia, in particular, inherited colonial planning and building standards norms and strategies have often remained in place for decades after independence in countries as diverse as Kenya and India. Failure to formally permit the use of traditional building materials for homes, despite the often prohibitive cost of building according to 'European norms' for the average urban resident in many cities in the South, is one of the challenges of unquestioningly adopting alien norms and standards. An equally significant challenge is that many colonial cities in the early and mid-twentieth century were planned based on what was known as 'Garden City' planning, geared towards the extensive use of space in dispersed urban settlements with the significant allocation of space to private gardens and public reserves. Though cities such as New Delhi, Lusaka and Nairobi developed as well planned and attractive settlements, the fact that they are transport dependent cities has imposed significant and long-term cost burdens on working classes in terms of personal transport expenses, and on urban authorities in terms of the need to maintain and service spatially extensive cities, creating long-term planning challenges. As late as the 1980s, new town planning schemes for Lusaka were still employing the same colonial principles, despite the apparent need in many such centres to incorporate processes such as

densification, improving accessibility and connectivity and adapting building standards.

Equally problematic in many parts of the South, and in Latin America in particular, have been the persistence of restrictive policies related to land access and ownership which do not allow for the accommodation of the large numbers of urban residents who cannot afford land purchases and whose urban occupation of informal shacks becomes *de facto* illegal, leading to a sense of impermanence and insecurity and the constant risk of displacement. The operation of formal land markets often leads to people who cannot afford land or formal accommodation being forced to squat on marginal land, for example on flood plains, steep slopes or near rubbish dumps, which imposes additional health and security risks. That said, where states have provided land to the poor, such as in South Africa, the land is often on the urban fringe at significant distances from the urban cores and their facilities, leading to yet another layer of urban marginalisation.

Practices of urban regeneration, which are commonplace in the North, are limited in scope to a few core cities in the South, such as Cape Town and Rio de Janeiro, with the 2016 Olympics being a key driver with regards to the latter. Housing interventions (as discussed below), in the form of site and service schemes and the upgrading of informal settlements, are some of the few interventions which certain cities pursue.

A slow and gradual shift in urban planning procedures has seen the move into more inclusive and participatory planning approaches, often with a focus on how to improve conditions in low-income cities. Based on the principles of civic engagement and empowerment local governments, particularly in Latin American cities such as Porto Alegre and Belo Horizonte, have embraced participatory planning and participatory budgeting processes, which seek to both engage with communities, but also to give them a say in planning decisions and expenditure within the constraints of limited resources (Satterthwaite and Mitlin, 2014). These processes will hopefully allow for bottom-up responses and sensitivities to local needs. However, the risk is that there may be 'elite capture', a focus on the interest of the most influential and articulate, and an inability to meet the expectations of all citizens.

Urban bias in development

The perceived advantages of living in large urban places are of great importance to most of the residents of the South. This is because in the past, where they did exist, factories, roads, infrastructure and other facilities focused on the major urban areas. Similarly, efforts to plan the urban system in many nations have likewise stressed the key role played by urban areas.

Sometimes this so-called 'urban bias' in development has been attributed to the outcome of rational–Western forms of development planning, as discussed in Chapter 3 (Jones and Corbridge, 2008; Lipton, 1977). This key concept is elaborated in the Key idea box below.

Key idea

Urban bias in development

A strong argument is mounted by some commentators that development, due to its western origins and orientation, has in the past always favoured the urban over the rural. It is argued that this has been the result of explicit development politics that have emphasised urban industrialisation, and is thereby also reflected in the operation of day-to-day processes in society.

Michael Lipton has been a leading figure in this arena and, since the 1970s, has championed the role of small-scale agriculture in development (Harriss, 2006). In a book published in 1977 under the title *Why Poor People Stay Poor: A Study of Urban Bias in World Development*, Lipton stressed what he referred to as 'urban bias' in development (see also Jones and Corbridge, 2008)

Over time, as noted in Chapter 3, the presumption has been that developing nations should follow a path to industrialisation starting with import-substituting industrialisation. Thus, Lipton argued that agriculture tends to be neglected in the allocation of public investment, whereas the aim of policy should be to reduce the riskiness of agriculture (see Harriss, 2006). It is argued that urban bias in the past has acted against what would be more efficient and equitable ways of using public resources in the agriculture sector, rather than in the urban-industrial sector.

Lipton argued that the urban classes, both rich and poor, have a vested interest in forming a powerful political alliance to ensure the maintenance of urban bias. They have an interest in keeping the prices of agricultural goods cheap, and in the transfer of productive resources out of agriculture and into urban-based activities. In this way, urban bias is maintained.

Urban bias arguments, while having merit, have been critiqued for focusing on countries in their phases of rapid urbanisation, and not giving recognition to the unequal power relations and dependency in the world between the North and the South, which ultimately impacts on policy choice (Knox and McCarthy, 2012).

Critical reflection

Bearing in mind the diverse range of theories and strategies of development reviewed in Chapter 3, how do you respond to the thesis of urban bias? Which approaches to development theory and practice reviewed in Chapter 3 seem to support the thesis of urban bias, and which appear to run counter to it? Is it right to argue that states get the urban–rural space-economies that they sign up for in the first place? Can you bring the experience of particular nations with which you may be familiar to bear on the issue of urban bias in development?

Regional planning

Equally important to consider is the issue of regional planning, which tends to fall under the ambit of national policy planners in most countries. The relative balance between urban and rural development, similar to direct urban planning, often still retains residues of colonial thinking in some countries which was grounded on efforts to promote rural development as a counterweight to urban development. In some parts of the world, such as Southern Africa, colonial policy had often sought to restrict urbanisation through legal processes and quotas and return 'illegal' migrants to rural areas.

Chant and McIlwaine (2009) quote the example of India which in 2005 introduced the National Rural Employment Scheme in an endeavour to reduce urban growth. Though costly, some countries have also tried to divert growth from the largest cities through the pursuit of policies of decentralisation and the establishment of new towns. The former was actively pursued in Peru and Mexico from the 1970s, with the effect of distributing urbanisation in Mexico. In most cases, however, the cost of supporting development in multiple centres is simply too expensive to implement. Countries such as Malaysia and South Korea have also actively pursued new town development policies, while in Brazil, Nigeria, Tanzania and Malawi, efforts to dilute urban primacy have focused on the development of new capital cities. In most cases, new developments have proven to be extremely costly, often creating 'white elephants' which have administrative purposes, but few economic reasons for their existence and they seldom alter the urbanisation streams to the largest centres.

The role of the state in urban development

The degree to which the state should become involved in regulating urban growth, and redirecting it at the regional and national scales, is a crucial development planning issue for debate (Potter and Lloyd-Evans, 1998). Many social commentators have inferred, or stated overtly, that only socialist states have seriously endeavoured to reduce urban and rural imbalances in national development. For example, avowedly anti-urban policies were implemented in South Vietnam between 1975 and 1980, and policies of zero urban growth were followed in China periodically from the late 1950s. But it is Cuba, since the socialist revolution in 1959, that is frequently cited as the best example of redressing the urban–rural imbalance (Case study 9.2).

It is vital to recognise that urban and regional planning policies must be based on economic, political, and even moral and ethical considerations, not just on economic foundations. Indeed, although Richardson argued from a strongly pro-large-city standpoint, in reviewing national urban development strategies in the early 1980s, he noted for the first time that the key goals were the same as societal goals in general, and that such strategies need to be highly country-specific (Richardson, 1981). In other words, there is no panacea or general solution to urban and regional problems.

Case study 9.2

Cuba: urban and regional planning in a revolutionary state

Cuba, the largest of the Caribbean islands, was discovered by Columbus in 1492 at the dawn of the mercantile period. With the exception of a brief spell of British rule in 1762, Spain retained its colonial power over Cuba until defeated in the Spanish-American War of 1898. This represented the start of a period during which the island was dominated by the United States of America, first militarily and then economically, after independence in 1902.

During the first half of the twentieth century the country was governed by a series of dictators, the last one being Fulgencio Batista, whose corrupt regime ruled the country from 1933. After a two-year guerrilla campaign, law student Fidel Castro and his followers ousted Batista from power in 1959. It is generally accepted that the leaders of the revolution were not initially communists, but fervent nationalists who were opposed to the corruption and inequalities that had existed before. But the antagonistic stance taken by the United States after the revolution resulted in the Cubans increasingly turning to the Soviet Union. Before the revolution, Havana, the capital, was a classic primate city. Most of the wealth and activities of the country were concentrated there. However, it was also characterised by shanty towns, poverty, gambling and vice. By 1953 the Greater Havana area had grown to 1.2 million people, containing 21 per cent of the country's total population. At this time 75 per cent of all industry was found in Havana, and 80 per cent of the nation's exports passed through the port, serving to stress the

Case study 9.2 (continued)

dependent relation of the country to the United States. Most of the country's health care facilities, schools, colleges and cultural organisations were also situated in and around Havana.

Castro and his followers regarded the city as representing capitalist (American) interests and over-privilege. From around 1963, Havana was increasingly discriminated against. Its physical fabric was left to decay, so as to make it less attractive to potential rural migrants. Two key policies were adopted: the decentralisation of people and activities from Havana, and the reduction of the striking differences which had come to exist between the urban and rural areas of the nation.

Thus, since 1959, promoting a more even geographical pattern of development has been the express aim of the state. The growth of provincial towns having populations between 20,000 and 200,000 has been encouraged. At the next level down, the regrouping of villages into rural new towns (*comunidades*) has occurred. Each rural new town has been developed with its own food and clothing stores, nurseries, primary schools, small clinic, social centre, bookshop and cafes. By 1982, some 360 *comunidades* had been created. Control has also been exercised over migration,

with ministerial permission being required in order to move to a job in Havana.

Most importantly, massive efforts have been made to develop primary, secondary and tertiary health care facilities throughout the country. Treatment at the centres is free. Primary health care is available throughout Cuba, whereas secondary and tertiary facilities are located in towns and cities. There have also been great improvements in education. In 1971 only seven out of 478 secondary schools were to be found in rural areas; by 1979 this had changed to 633 rural schools out of a total of 1,318. All students are expected to work in agriculture at some stage, in an effort to reduce elitist attitudes and values.

Today, some 77 per cent of the total population of Cuba is to be found living in urban settlements (UNDESA, 2014). Cuba has done much to reduce the differences between town and country, although critics of the Marxist approach which has been followed suggest that the same could have been achieved without the state apparatus that controls all sectors of the economy. Critics also argue that much unemployment is disguised, that rural–urban differences still exist and that elite privileges have re-emerged.

Source: Potter (1992a)

Richardson (1981) documented the wide range of policies which can be employed by governments in the South, prior to the 1980s, which sought to decentralise people, jobs and social infrastructure away from primate cities and congested core regions.

The variety of policy reactions is shown in Table 9.5. These range from three policies of continued concentrated urbanisation, to seven representing genuine interregional deconcentration and decentralisation.

The first policy of concentrated urbanisation is the *laissez-faire* (or free market) policy of letting the market take its course. If, however, problems of congestion and imbalance are recognised in the primate city, efforts may be made to decentralise, though merely within the core region. Thus, a polycentric pattern of growth on the edge of the primate city emerges, or a form of leap-frog decentralisation to the edge of the existing core, may be envisaged (Table 9.5).

Table 9.5 Richardson's categorisation of national urban development strategies

Concentrated urbanisation
1. Free market or do nothing
2. Polycentric development of the primate city
3. 'Leap-frog' decentralisation within the primate city

Deconcentration and decentralisation
4. Development corridors and axes
5. Growth poles and growth centres
6. 'Countermagnets'
7. Secondary cities
8. Provincial capitals
9. Regional centres and hierarchy
10. Small service centres and rural development

Source: Richardson, H.W. (1981) National urban development strategies in developing countries. *Urban Studies*, 18, 267–83; permission from Taylor & Francis, www.tandf.co.uk/journals

Strategies of genuine deconcentration can be categorised into seven generic types, as shown in the Table. Development corridors or axes can be designated, leading from the core region, and growth can be focused upon them. Alternatively, growth may be channelled into what are regarded as dynamic growth poles or growth centres. A variation on essentially the same theme sees the strengthening of a few distant major nodes as countermagnets. Other forms of decentralisation can be created by the promotion of a limited number of secondary or intermediate cities, or the establishment of provincial state and departmental capitals.

Yet another variant involves the promotion of regional metropolises and an associated hierarchy of urban places. At the far end of the spectrum, a dispersed policy of small service centres and associated rural development throughout the periphery may be pursued.

Of course, these strategies are not mutually exclusive and several of them are very similar. Various elements of these strategies can be combined into any number of hybrid forms. Examples of the ways in which Cuba and Nigeria have applied national urban development strategies like these are provided in Case studies 9.2 and 9.3.

In conclusion, it is re-emphasised that arguments about urban and regional systems planning cannot sensibly be based on economic reasoning alone. As demonstrated by Case studies 9.2 and 9.3, strategic social, political and ideological issues are just as important in the equation. The choices are socio-political and

moral, so once again we encounter a classic position where it must be accepted that there are many urban and regional geographies of the future which may be promoted by the state or other responsible agencies. In addition, much of the literature over the past 10–15 years has stressed the importance of bottom-up and grassroots approaches to national planning. Despite this logic, the World Bank, the United Nations Development Programme and the Cities Alliance have been returning to the argument that urban growth and large cities are the keys to development and change, and that development should increasingly be left to market forces (UNDP, 1991; World Bank, 1991; Cities Alliance, 2006).

This argument is strongly based on the success of the Asian newly industrialising countries (NICs), and on what is regarded as the overall failure of rural-based development programmes. Neo-liberal policies involving deregulation, privatisation, the rolling back of the state, export-based programmes of industrialisation, structural adjustment programmes (SAPs) and poverty reduction strategies (PRSs) are all signifiers of what some have called the urban management programme of the World Bank or the 'Washington consensus' (Drakakis-Smith, 2000; Potter, 2000), which most countries in the South have generally been obliged to follow. Given the compromised state of the finances of most countries in the South, and the large development backlogs, it is debatable whether a free market approach will realistically address the challenges which exist, particularly for the poorest of the poor.

Case study 9.3

Nigeria: urban and regional planning in a top-down context

Nigeria is the largest nation in Africa and currently has a population of 173 million. In 1471 the Portuguese were the first Europeans to visit what is today the Nigerian coast, and they were followed by visitors from other European countries. British colonial rule dated from 1900. From the colonial era to the present, policies have tended to be top–down or from above, and development has been concentrated into a limited number of areas. Planning strategies, since their introduction in 1946, have been essentially

market-oriented, concentrating on the production of agricultural crops for export and import substitution industrialisation. Investment and industrial plants have focused on the cities.

Today the 12 major cities of Nigeria account for nearly 77 per cent of all industrial establishments in the country and 87 per cent of the total industrial employment. However, in 1985 only 23 per cent of the population lived in towns and cities, rising to 46% in 2013. Of the total employment in manufacturing,

Case study 9.3 (continued)

76 per cent is to be found along the coastal belt (see Figure 9.21). The largest city, Lagos, accounts for well over 50 per cent of the nation's industrial wages, nearly 60 per cent of its gross output, 49 per cent of all industrial employment and 38 per cent of total industrial plants. Within each of the states making up the country, services and jobs are also strongly concentrated in the state capital. For example, in the north of the country, in Kano State, the Kano metropolitan area contains the majority of the state's industries and banks.

In such circumstances it is perhaps not surprising that rural-to-urban migration has been very strong and the main cities have grown extremely quickly. For example, during the period 1952–1963, Port Harcourt grew at the exceptional rate of 10.5 per cent per annum, whereas Lagos and Kano increased their populations at 8.6 and 7.6 per cent per annum respectively. A long search for oil proved to be successful in the mid-1950s, and by 1963 oil accounted for 3 per cent of government revenues. In 1982 oil represented 90 per cent of the value of the country's exports. However, many people maintain that the oil monies have been used inefficiently, leading to massive imports of expensive foreign goods.

Although many agree that the Nigerian economy, now the largest in Africa, has grown, others maintain that it has not developed. They suggest that the majority of the population are not better off and that deep regional inequalities still characterise the country. These critics claim there have been relatively few 'trickle-down' effects of growth from the urban areas to the rural areas. Too much emphasis has been placed on sectoral growth – the promotion of different areas of the economy, such as industry – but little regard has been paid to the geographical consequences. Agriculture has been neglected, the drift from the land to the cities has not been reduced, and the country remains strongly dependent on the nations of the West.

Source: Potter (1992a)

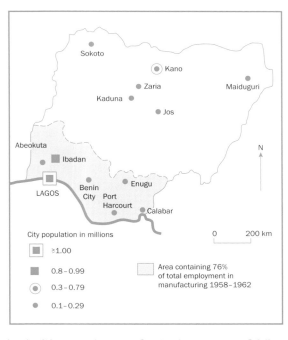

Figure 9.21 The principal cities and manufacturing zone of Nigeria
Source: adapted from Potter, 1995.

Planning and global institutions

Concerns over the need to sustainably manage urbanisation processes and improve urban living conditions have become key foci of international attention. Key international agencies engaged with efforts to try and find solutions to urbanisation challenges include: UN-Habitat (the United Nations Commission for Human Settlements) and the Cities Alliance, which has links with the World Bank and UN-Habitat.

UN-Habitat has been active in a strategic and advocacy role seeking appropriate responses to key urban development challenges. Key publications include in 2003 *The Challenge of Slums* report (UN-Habitat, 2003) and the semi-regular *State of the World's Cities* Report (UN-Habitat, 2012), which documents current trends and best practices and makes numerous recommendations on interventions, such as improving inclusivity, addressing tenure challenges and improving economic well-being.

The Cities Alliance, which enjoys support from a range of international organisations and national and local governments, has identified two core foci for its activities, namely the pursuit of: 'City Development Strategies' and 'Cities without Slums'. Over the last 15 years the Cities Alliance has actively supported cities around the world to draft strategy responses to better cope with the twin challenges of ensuring that cities are able to develop and prosper, but also that they are able to address the significant challenges which slum development presents. Key City Development Strategy foci include:

➤ Developing long-term visions
➤ Incorporating the contributions of the poor
➤ Supporting local business growth
➤ Networking with other cities and knowledge sharing
➤ Promoting local economic development
➤ Supporting local leadership
➤ Focusing on implementation (Cities Alliance, 2006).

To address slum challenges, the Cities Alliance/World Bank Action Plan (2013), identifies the key role which must be played by good governance, ensuring tenure security, accessing finance and enabling community participation. Significant emphasis is placed on slum upgrading interventions, shared learning and support for in-country capacity development. Whether these interventions have the capacity and necessary levels of support to deal with the magnitude of the slum development challenges, as discussed in the section on slums, is a key global development challenge.

In 2015 the Cities Alliance and UN-Habitat co-produced a key document entitled *The Evolution of National Urban Policies: A Global Overview* (Cities Alliance, 2015). The objective of this overview was to encourage joint learning between countries, and to foster national level support and responses to the key urban challenges which countries face. Key issues which emerge from this document are:

➤ The need for coordinated approaches within countries to the challenges of planning and managing cities;
➤ The development of legal and financial instruments to design and build more resilient and livable cities;
➤ The pursuit of compact and inclusive urban growth;
➤ The need to increase land provision in urban core areas and along transport corridors;
➤ To promote land and infrastructure development in advance of settlements; and
➤ Adopting a broader planning perspective which considers the city and its hinterland in planning decisions.

While recommendations like these have the potential to make a difference, they do require significant national-level commitments, international support and local capacity on the ground to implement and afford the interventions required. There is the constant risk that the speed of urbanisation, particularly in Africa and Asia, is exceeding the capacity of national and local urban systems to respond to the development needs which exist, particularly given the limited number of qualified planners in many parts of the South.

Sustainable urban development

In order to understand fully the range of problems faced by urban managers and the processes which give rise to such issues, we need a more comprehensive and flexible conceptual approach. Such a perspective started to emerge in the 1990s and is concerned with 'sustainable urbanisation' (Satterthwaite, 1999, 2008; Elliott, 2013; Mitlin and Satterthwaite, 2013).

This must not be confused with sustained growth, in which the city is seen to have a pivotal role in initiating and maintaining national economic growth. Economic growth is a vital component of sustainable urbanisation, but it is only one in the array of interlinked processes which make up the contemporary city.

Sustainable urbanisation can and should constitute an important goal for any urban management team, irrespective of the level and nature of economic development. Figure 9.22 indicates some of the major components of sustainable urban development. Drakakis-Smith (2000) has given these issues fuller consideration – and, more importantly, the ways in which they interlink, illustrating the complexity of many urban problems faced in towns and cities.

Thus, the economic dimension of urban development is not just related to the role of the city in the national economy, but also to the repercussions of the economy on the residents of the city in terms of employment, incomes and poverty at the household level, as well as its impact on the urban environment and social issues, such as workers' rights.

The main components which need to be considered comprise demographic factors, economic factors, social, political and environmental factors. The management of urban development in order to achieve sustainable, rather than just sustained, growth is clearly a complex task. Many of the issues raised by such an approach have been carefully researched over the past two decades, though often separately rather than in an interlinked manner.

Moreover, urban management for sustainable urban development requires a new set of attitudes towards the objectives of intervention. So, in addition to seeking to create and sustain economic growth, there must be other, equally important priorities. These might be enumerated as including:

➤ The pursuit of equity and social justice
➤ The satisfaction of basic needs
➤ The recognition of social and ethnic self-determination and human rights
➤ Environmental awareness and integrity
➤ Appreciation of the inter-linkages across space and time

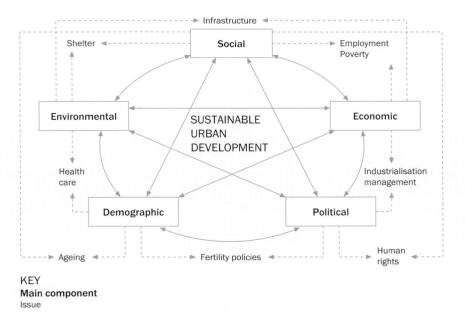

KEY
Main component
Issue

Figure 9.22 The main components of sustainable urbanisation

Inside the cities of the South

Understanding the processes and the patterns

Although many towns and cities in the South exhibit the signs of urban growth discussed earlier in this chapter, their individual characteristics vary enormously according to a wide range of factors, not least their ability to provide adequate shelter, employment and services. Within this context, cities range from the sophisticated SE Asian cities of Singapore and Seoul which have experienced remarkable growth, full integration into the world economy and the provision of high quality housing and employment opportunities for many of their residents. This is in contrast to other cities such as Luanda (Angola) and Addis Ababa (Ethiopia), where the majority of urban residents reside in informal housing, or Mogadishu (Somalia) which has experienced the effective collapse of urban service provision. As a result, generalisations about what is happening in the cities of the South have to be made with caution. These considerations are impacted by the legacy of colonialism, and the role which cities and nations play in the broader regional and global economies, as shown in Chapters 2 and 4.

The economy and employment

Since colonial times, there has been a small, but significant, employment base in administration, manufacturing, services and trade in cities in the South. In the colonial period many imperial administrations imposed controls on urbanisation, confining the majority of populations to rural areas, and ensuring that cities remained relatively small and had high degrees of employment. With independence, controls were lifted and rapid urban growth ensued as we have seen above, however, rapid urban population growth has seldom been associated with economic growth in most of the South, as discussed earlier in this chapter. This mismatch has generally been translated into the informal provision of housing and employment. Structural adjustment, and the barriers which many countries face economically in trying to integrate from a position of comparative weaknesses and limited economic capacity, have often seen job loss and retrenchment in the areas of administration

and manufacturing, particularly when countries face the challenge of cheap overseas imports.

Countries which have experienced significant urban and economic expansion since World War II include China, most of SE Asia and leading Latin American countries such as Mexico and Brazil. These countries collectively known as the Newly Industrializing Countries (NICs) have received significant levels of foreign investment. High skills, low labour wage levels, state support and incentives and access to global transportation networks, have enabled this group of countries to achieve higher levels of employment, integration into global production chains and economic growth than the rest of the South. Countries such as South Korea, China and Brazil have become leading industrial countries as a direct result, and are part of the limited group of countries in the South which are fully integrated in what is known as 'global production networks', linking manufactures and consumers in the North with selected countries in the South (Coe and Yeung, 2015; Chapter 4). The remarkable growth of cities such as Shanghai and Guangzhou in China, which have become key centres of global manufacturing and, more recently, service provision, is emblematic of highly successful but selective urban and economic growth in the South. On the downside many of these countries in the South have experienced significant economic growth, but suffer from low wages (particularly in South Asia), low levels of worker protection and civil rights (in East and SE Asia), and ultimately many are incorporated into the global system in an inferior position as suppliers of produce for the North.

For most countries in the South, however, there is only limited scope for employment in what is known as the formal sector, i.e. employment in western-style firms, administration, industries, banks, shops, etc. Africa, for example, is home to some 12% of the world's population, but only produces 1% of global manufacturing. Where manufacturing does exist in cities outside of the NICs, it often has a focus on producing goods for domestic consumption, e.g. food, textiles and metal products, since local industries generally cannot compete in costs terms with the NICs in the global market place (Stock, 2013). In capital cities such as Dodoma, Abuja, and Lilongwe, state employment is often the largest form of regular, paid employment, which as a sector that is dependent on taxing other sectors is reliant on the general health of the economy, and which by implication will be constrained in the world's weaker economies. Outside of capital cities, state employment levels fall dramatically with employment in manufacturing often also falling in parallel way from the larger centres.

The informal sector

For the majority of urban residents, the key employment options generally lie in the area of self-employment and micro-businesses, or what is known as the 'shadow economy' or informal sector. The term 'informal sector' became widely used in the development lexicon from the 1970s, following the key work undertaken by Hart and the International Labour Organization, which sought to understand how residents of the cities of the South were earning a living, despite the apparent limited capacity of local manufacturing, administrative and service positions. In the colonial period it was argued that people in cities not employed in western style employment, belonged to the traditional market economy, i.e. the production and sale of craft goods and food

in traditional market places. As cities grew in the post-independence period, the inadequacy of such a dualistic understanding was recognised, as was the reality that a whole parallel economy existed alongside the 'western' styled 'formal' one. The result was the recognition that the 'informal' sector was a key source of livelihood and employment in cities in the South (Pacione, 2009; Stock, 2013; Desai and Potter, 2014).

While both the term and the role which the informal sector plays have been disputed, it nonetheless has been used as a key lens to understand the employment and livelihoods of what is often the majority of urban residents in cities in the South. While getting accurate statistics on the scale of the informal sector is difficult to secure, particularly in cases where employment is in an illegal or black-market activity, according to Knox and McCarthy (2012) the number of jobs which the informal sector provides varies from approximately one-third of all jobs (in the case of Jakarta) to over two-thirds (in the case of cities such as Surabaya and Conakry). Figure 9.23 indicates the significant role which the informal sector plays as a source of employment provision in a range of cities.

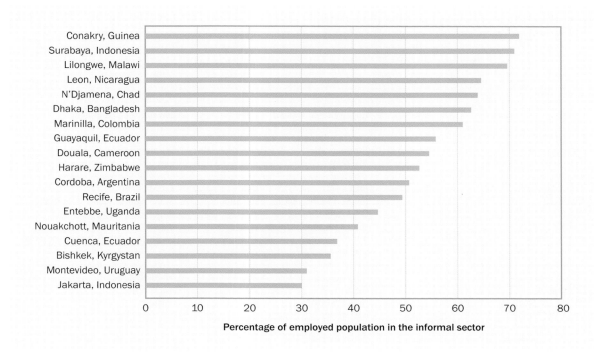

Figure 9.23 The scale of informal sector employment in selected cities in the South
Source: adapted from Knox and McCarthy, 2012.

What is the informal sector?

The informal sector, sometimes called the 'shadow economy' is also called the 'tertiary refuge sector', and is made up of jobs such as street hawking, shoe shining, car washing, taxi driving and many others (see Plates 9.7–9.12) (Lloyd-Evans and Potter, 2008; McGee, 1979; Portes et al., 1991; Desai and Potter, 2014). While the sector may suffer from being 'unregulated' and operating informally, its benefits include ease of entry, low skills and finance barriers to start operation and an ability to quickly adapt to new opportunities.

Initially, the informal sector was understood as being part of a dual economy, i.e. an economic structure in which some jobs, in the western-style sector, were regarded as the 'formal sector' – i.e. they are provided by employers which are legally registered, have formal labour contracts, pay regular wages and operate from formal business premises. Examples of the latter include employment in government, banks, main-street shops and services, and manufacturing firms. By contrast, the informal sector lacks legal recognition and formal employment contracts; employment is generally through self-employment or informal contracts; the premises occupied are often unlicensed; and the products and services supplied generally lack official recognition. In addition, the use of traditional technology and their family owned and focused nature have been traditional hallmarks of the sector.

The informal sector encompasses a wide range of activities from retail (i.e. selling western or traditional goods, often from the pavement or informal shelters), to providing services (such as hair-dressing, and fixing cars and electronic goods), to the small-scale manufacturing of goods for community use (such as clothes and furniture), as well as illegal activity such as fraud, theft and prostitution. This dualistic perspective was modified over time to recognise what were termed the 'upper and lower circuits' of the urban economy (i.e. the formal and informal) (Santos, 1979). This conceptualisation is shown in Table 9.6, which indicates just how different the two sectors are in terms of their economic operations and legal status.

Over time it has been recognised that that a dualistic division was not realistic. This is because there is a cross-over of activity between the formal and the informal sectors, i.e. both can sell each other's products, and the informal can maintain products of the formal, e.g. cars. For example, many trishaw owners

Table 9.6 Characteristics of the two circuits of the urban economy

	Upper circuit (formal)	Lower circuit (informal)
Technology	Capital-intensive	Labour-intensive
Organisation	Bureaucratic	Primitive
Capital	Abundant	Limited
Labour	Limited	Abundant
Regular wages	Prevalent	Exceptional
Inventories	Large quantity and/or high quality	Small quantity and poor quality
Prices	Generally fixed	Negotiable (haggling)
Credit	Banks and institutions	Personal and non-institutional
Profit margin	Small per unit, but large turnover and considerable in aggregate	Large per unit, but small turnover
Relations with customers	Impersonal and/or on paper	Direct, personalised
Fixed costs	Substantial	Negligible
Advertising	Necessary	None
Re-use of goods	None (waste)	Frequent
Overhead capital	Essential	Not essential
Government aid	Extensive	None or almost none
Direct dependence on foreign countries	Considerable	Small or none

Source: Santos, 1979

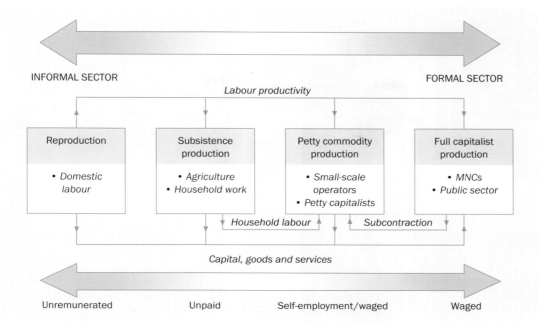

Figure 9.24 The informal–formal sector continuum
Source: adapted from Potter and Lloyd-Evans, 1998.

Plate 9.6 Tricycle taxi, Sri Lanka
(*photo*: Tony Binns)

Plate 9.7 Informal sector furniture production, Castries, St Lucia
(*photo*: Rob Potter)

Plate 9.8 Female hawkers in Georgetown, Guyana
(*photo*: Rob Potter)

work in the formal sector and rent their machines out to the riders, whereas domestic outworkers are often essential to small businesses in helping them absorb fluctuations in demand.

Instead, it is more realistic to consider a continuum from the formal to the informal (see Figure 9.24). This Figure recognises that there is a continuum from unpaid work (e.g. child-minding and working for the family) through to waged employment. It also recognises different production elements in the employment economy and the links between them, such as through subcontracting (e.g. a registered builder sub-contracting work to unregistered bricklayers). At its extreme, the informal sector is associated with reproduction and domestic labour, and is unremunerated or unpaid. It then links to subsistence production (for example, in agriculture and household work) and, in turn, to petty commodity production by small-scale operators. Finally, one moves to waged employment in the formal sector. Examples of informal sector activity can be seen

on Plates 9.9–9.14 and are considered in the Critical reflection below.

Approaches to the informal sector

For many years the activities of the informal sector, although clearly useful, have been anathema to urban planners and management, as they are seen by some as 'marring' the modernising image which the city is trying to create in order to attract investment. In both the pre- and post-industrial periods municipal regulations have sought to keep the informal sector in check, despite the 'unconventional wisdom' of the 1970s, which saw support for the informal sector as a way of improving basic needs provision (Richards and Thomson, 1984). The International Labour Organization, amongst other organisations, has tried to support the informal sector, arguing that it is a sector, which if properly supported, can help emerging entrepreneurs graduate into more regular and formal employment and lay a basis for capitalists expansion. The South African government is a

Critical reflection

The informal sector

As already noted, Plates 9.6–9.10 show various activities in the informal sector of several cities. Specifically, these show a taxi driver, furniture maker and street-side retailers. In what ways do these activities appear to be essentially similar to those you might encounter in your home locality, or in towns and cities that are well known to you? And in what principal ways do they appear to differ from similar types of activities in other places that are well known to you? What advantages do informal

sector activities have over more formal ones? And what challenges might informal sector activities pose for local policy makers and environmentalists? As we shall see later in this chapter, houses are also frequently built within the informal sector. Are you aware of the construction of what may be regarded as informal sector homes in your locality – both in the past, as well as currently? Or, alternatively, are you aware of informal sector homes constructed in other localities that are well-known to you?

case in point, where support is provided to hawkers to set up formal stalls, and advisory and financial assistance is provided to small and emerging businesses.

From a neo-liberal perspective, the informal sector is seen as a trajectory which can assist emerging entrepreneurs to join the formal business sector. Neo-Marxists, by contrast, argue that few people ever 'break-out' of the informal sector, and that the limited scale of support it receives actually perpetuates the sector and does not

address structural inequalities and unequal social and economic relations within societies (Potter and Lloyd-Evans, 1998).

In practice, few urban governments have been as enthusiastic as the experts, and relatively little has been achieved through support for the informal sector, particularly in the field of improved employment opportunities. However, the first decades of the 2000s are witnessing a revival of interest in the informal sector,

Plate 9.9 Street barber in Kashgar, Kashi, western China
(*photo*: Tony Binns)

Plate 9.10 Street traders in central Johannesburg, South Africa
(*photo*: Tony Binns)

particularly in the wake of the reduced employment opportunities and reduced incomes which have followed structural adjustment programmes, particularly in Africa.

The pursuit of poverty reduction strategies in many countries has also prompted a growing interest in the sector. As poverty is often shaped by limited job access and as the informal sector seems capable of creating employment, it is reasoned that removing some of the constraints on the informal sector (through deregulation) would help to expand work opportunities and reduce poverty. However, this approach has not yet been the success it was hoped, and there is a limit to the capacity of the informal sector to create employment and income.

On the negative side, very few small informal firms have the capacity to upgrade and 'formalise' on their own without assistance from the state. In short, as Parnwell and Turner (1998) note, the urban informal sector does not equate with the flexible specialisation that has emerged in the West, despite structural similarities; it is much more a survival mechanism than an engine of growth. The main consequence of these urban labour market problems has been increasing poverty.

Whilst arguments advocating support for the informal sector are appealing, the reality is, that in the absence of effective and comprehensive support, successful transition has been limited and many micro-entrepreneurs, because of factors ranging from competition, to lack of skills, lack of support, and under-capitalisation, remain at the fringes of urban employment. Evidence from many countries suggests that, rather than being a conduit to formal employment, the informal sector has often been a downward path of access for the unemployed and the retrenched from the formal sector, leading to scenarios of disguised employment and underemployment.

The result, according to Davies (2006) are the 'myths of informality'. In his critique, he argues that the sector's supporters are semi-utopian, arguing that support for the informal sector is compromised by a series of interlocking challenges, which include:

1) The sub-subsistence nature of many informal sector enterprises, which has grown commensurate with the decline of formal sector opportunities.

2) The unregulated nature of the informal sector often locks participants into economic contracts which verge on exploitation, while the employees of informal sector employers seldom rise above subsistence. This applies particularly in the case of women and children.

3) High interest rates demanded from micro-credit lending agencies restrict the growth prospects of informal sector enterprises.

4) Increased competition in the sector depletes social capital and weakens self-help networks.

5) At a broader level, the persistence of the informal sector maintains a significant number of people in low-waged conditions which depresses wage demands in the formal sector.

Whatever the debates over the effectiveness of support for the informal sector, the reality is that this sector is a key source of employment and livelihood support in the cities of the South, and one which will continue to play a key role in the foreseeable future for urban employment and survival.

Gender, child labour and urban survival

Women have been incorporated into the urban labour market in many different ways, depending on local economic and social conditions. However, as McIlwaine (1997) has noted, access to work has not always reduced gender inequalities in society in general or within the household. It is often the case that women occupy the most vulnerable positions in the employment structure – even in the informal sector, such as hawking goods from pavement shelters (Desai and Potter, 2014).

The changing links between gender and urban economic growth need therefore to be followed through to other dimensions of urban sustainability, such as those related to basic needs provision and human rights.

Children also form an identifiable group whose specific needs must be taken into account in any review of sustainable urban development. The value of child labour is well recognised and is often exploited by employers. Unfortunately, informal production systems in South Asia often rely on child labour in the marginal textile and light manufacturing sectors. Low levels of policing and inadequate social service provision exacerbate the practice. For example, it has been estimated that in Thailand the child labour force is approximately the same size as the female labour force. One-third of these 1.5 million working children are employed in urban factories where they receive about half the adult minimum wage. Although it is true that in many developing countries children are often important income earners in the family (Clifford, 1994; Gilbert, 1994), there are ways in which their conditions of work and their life as a whole can be improved without threatening household survival strategies (Lefevre, 1995; Desai and Potter, 2014).

It must not be thought, however, that those who find themselves disadvantaged in the labour market are passive acceptors of their fate. Low-income households practice a wide range of coping mechanisms, in addition to participating in the informal sector (Rakodi, 1995), some of which are indicated in Table 9.7 and growing their food in the urban area (see Plate 9.11). These strategies variously draw on household capacities and economic opportunities to ensure survival within the urban context

Not all strategies are available to all households, depending on individual and local circumstances, but the ways in which poor families sustain themselves in the city ought to be the basis on which policy responses are formulated and developed.

Table 9.7 Urban household strategies for coping with worsening poverty

Changing household composition

➤ Migration
➤ Increasing household size in order to maximise earning opportunities
➤ Not increasing household size through fertility controls

Consumption controls

➤ Reducing consumption
➤ Buying cheaper items
➤ Withdrawing children from school
➤ Delaying medical treatment
➤ Postponing maintenance or repairs to property or equipment
➤ Limiting social contacts, including visits to rural areas

Increasing assets

➤ More household members into workforce
➤ Starting enterprises where possible
➤ Increased subsistence activity such as growing food or gathering fuel
➤ Increased scavenging
➤ Increased sub-letting of rooms and/or shacks

Source: Rakodi (1995)

Plate 9.11 Urban farming in Zambia
(*photo*: Tony Binns)

Providing shelter

Housing in the South

The inability of most cities in the South to offer their residents safe, permanent dwellings is a reflection of the relative poverty of the state, limited formal employment opportunities and structural inequalities (Desai and Potter, 2014). Broadly speaking, housing exists in three relatively distinct categories:

1) The State – i.e. public housing. While most countries attempted to build such housing in the post-independence period, limited funds and rising demands often put paid to such schemes. Some of the most well-known public housing schemes in the South have been in the wealthier NICs, e.g. Singapore and Kuala Lumpur (see Plate 9.12), Hong Kong, China and Venezuela. Often however, well intentioned low-income schemes become housing for the middle class, as costs rise and user charges are required to be paid (Chant and McIlwaine, 2009).

2) Private Sector – i.e. generally middle and upper income housing, which tends to be relatively limited in scale in most cities, relative to the size of the population. There has occasionally been evidence of the supply of housing by private companies, e.g. by mining houses on the Zambian Copperbelt, although much of that stock has now been privatised. Rental housing forms a small component of this dimension of the housing market, particularly for people with a regular income, who are unable to afford their own private dwellings (Chant and McIlwaine, 2009).

3) Popular Housing – this refers to the self-provisioning of housing, generally by the poor, and normally without legal sanction in terms of both building standards and land access/tenure. Commonly referred to as 'slums', the term encompasses both makeshift dwellings constructed out of wood, plastic and scrap metal, and once formal dwellings which have become sub-standard and generally overcrowded over time (see Plate 9.13). In order to secure land access, what is known as 'land invasion' is a common and often

orchestrated process of land take-over to ensure relatively large scale occupancy of private or public land, to diminish the chances of eviction and forced relocation (Pacione, 2009). At the lower end of the socio-economic spectrum are those who sleep on the streets, or who rent tenements and slums (Drakakis-Smith, 2000).

As noted above, more than one billion people now live in slums, and the informal nature of their housing and their marginal access to water and other services constitutes a key urban development and humanitarian challenge.

Responses to housing challenges

Housing poverty (Pugh, 1996) has been well researched since the 1960s, when John Turner (1967, 1982) and William Mangin (1967) first drew attention to the positive qualities of squatter settlements (illegal settlements) and shanty towns (poorly built settlements). Associated with the discussion on slums above, essentially these writers argued that such housing should be seen as a solution to the housing shortage, rather than as a problem. Turner

(1967) in particular argued that if security of tenure was provided, and if real incomes are rising, then self-help houses will improve year by year and little by little. Both Mangin and Turner showed how squatter settlements often house residents who have a job, and who are trying to make their own way in the urban economy and that they are not necessarily an 'undesirable' element in the city as they were often portrayed in the local and international media.

Thus, self-help housing was not seen as leading to slums, but rather to sites of incremental improvement over time. Work in Mexico and Brazil and other parts of the world indicated that in places where there are both reasonably steady levels of employment and community organisation, self-improvement and the gradual formalisation of housing can occur and services can be slowly provided – either by the local state, or community organisations, or through joint action. This is shown as 'consolidation' on Figure 9.25, and in Plate 9.14, which in turn can be encouraged by external support, shown in the Figure as 'Aided Self-Help'. It was argued that the role of the state in this context is to help the poor to help themselves, by promoting aided self-help schemes, for

Plate 9.12 Public housing in Kuala Lumpur
(*photo*: Etienne Nel)

Plate 9.13 Low-income settlements in Cape Town, South Africa
(*photo*: Rob Potter)

example through providing tenure security, subsidised material and building advice. A variant is to be found in South Africa where there has been the mass roll-out of basic state housing (see Plate 9.15) but this is done in such a way to allow residents to later extend or upgrade the unit.

While consolidation did occur in the investigated cases of Brazil and Mexico, it has been argued that it

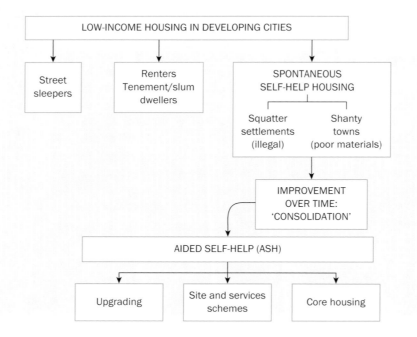

Figure 9.25 Different types of low-income housing in cities of the Global South
Source: Adapted from Potter, 1992a.

Plate 9.14 Self-help housing in Caracas, Venezuela, undergoing consolidation
(*photos*: Rob Potter)

took place in a time of relative prosperity which has not been repeated, and that community buy-in at the time was crucial to ensure success. Neo-Marxists argue that era of relative prosperity has passed, and that low levels of support, and the limited capacity of the poor to significantly improve their condition, serves to maintain inequality within society (Drakakis-Smith, 2000).

Aided self-help consists of upgrading, that is improving existing slum areas, and developing site and service schemes, where new lands are opened up, often with World Bank and national government support. Upgrading for slums or favelas in Brazil though often controversial, is a well-documented example of significant efforts to improve physical infrastructure and service access in low income areas (Pacione, 2009). Site and service normally involves the provision of serviced plots of land, normally with tenure, water, sewerage and road access, which low income settlers can occupy and build their shelter on. The ideal is that over time they will 'consolidate', and residents will build a more formal structure given their secure tenure and better access to services. Sometimes the core of a new house is also provided on the site which residents may later extend.

The choices which low income residents make about where they want to live may lead to several movements as residents seek to improve their situation and as their economic and family status alter. Research about this reality shows that rural migrants often initially locate in rental housing in the city when they first arrive in the city and are finding their feet, and only move out to squatter settlements once they have a solid foothold in the urban economy which, over time, can 'consolidate' into more formal dwellings. Many new urban residents first settle in the inner-city, often with relatives, while they adapt to their new environments. When some income is earned and family needs alter, this often leads to movement to 'independent' self-constructed dwellings on the periphery. Finally, a few who experience real income growth, might move to more formal housing areas, either in the inner-city or on the urban periphery (Drakakis-Smith, 2000).

Current housing approaches and debates

In spite of almost four decades of many varied responses to shelter needs, the problems seem to be as widespread as ever. It is generally believed that at least 20 per cent, and perhaps even as high as 50 per cent, of the world's population lack decent housing. Although much of the statistical information on housing poverty is unreliable and incompatible, what information is available serves a

Plate 9.15 Low-cost housing at Cradock, Eastern Cape Province, South Africa
(*photo*: Tony Binns)

useful role in illustrating trends over time and between regions.

In some cities, renting is far more usual and acceptable than ownership, yet the policy responses over much of the last 30 years have been based on the assumption that tenure security through ownership is the fundamental desire of most low-income populations.

Certainly, the discussions about shelter itself have evolved into a type of dualism. On the one hand are the debates about the role of shelter provision in the development process as a whole, a debate which in recent years has increasingly been conducted at the global rather than the national level, with the main international development agencies dominating the discussion, the funding and hence the policy.

Increasingly distinct from these processes are the national and urban debates about devising appropriate programmes and projects for the real world. In recent years, this has tended to focus upon the practical ways that the various stakeholders involved can help improve access by the poor to better housing. As noted above, for many years the debate on practical responses to housing poverty has revolved around aided self-help programmes, in which the energies and ambitions of the poor themselves are combined with providing tenure,

building material and land inputs by the state to produce developments which are largely self-built, but which have the support and approval of the state (Chant and McIlwaine, 2009).

Although many low-income households have benefited substantially from such schemes, the schemes were nevertheless subject to considerable criticisms. Pinches (1994: 118), in particular, claimed that aided self-help schemes 'served the narrow economic interest of states, elites and international agencies', by offering cheap solutions to demands for housing, containing restive populations and formalising part of the informal sector. The failure to provide or to access adequate shelter or land often results in densification of the urban area, with squatter shacks in-filling spaces in the more formal housing areas in an effort to accommodate growing numbers of residents. This takes place with or without the consent of property owners and is known as 'shack farming'. A further negative factor is that low income housing interventions, often end up being middle class housing, due to the imposition of user charges, such as rents, which the poor often cannot afford (Chant and McIlwaine, 2009; Pacione, 2009).

Since the 1990s enthusiasm for these housing interventions has diminished substantially, partly because there was an enforced retreat of the state from welfare programmes under structural adjustment, partly because the scale of the housing problem was not reducing substantially, and partly because funds from the international agencies dried up.

As urban populations have continued to grow, so housing poverty has remained an important issue related to sustainable urbanisation. In some cities, particularly in Africa, this has meant a resurgence of squatter settlements; in others, market forces have produced a rapid expansion of renting and sharing. The growing research interest in these phenomena has revealed the existence of a wide range of circumstances which have emerged in response to housing challenges.

In Latin America, for example, Gilbert (1992) argued that most landlords operate on a small scale and are not exploitative; but in many African cities there is widespread exploitation of shack tenants in gardens or yards attached to formal housing, conditions are cramped and there are grossly inadequate washing and toilet facilities (Auret, 1995; Grant, 1995). Essentially, this witnesses the privatisation of housing, the benefits of which usually filter upwards through a hierarchy of landlords and owners.

It is increasingly recognised that two key elements are critical to ensuring the stability of low income housing residents and giving them an assisted stake in the urban environment, namely the need to ensure access to secure tenure and finance. Tenure insecurity means that slum dwellers are unlikely to improve their dwellings because of the risk of eviction, and they generally lack the collateral which secure tenure provides when seeking housing finance. Provision of micro-finance through community banking and state sources has been an important element in housing support in parts of Latin America and Asia (Pacione, 2009).

State responses to the continued housing crisis have been strongly influenced by the neo-liberal trends in international development, and have shifted away from the more direct subsidies of aided self-help to the formulation of partnerships between the national and local governments, together with a variety of local agencies, such as non-governmental and community-based organisations (NGOs and CBOs). The focus for these partnerships is on facilitating the access of households to land or credit through the removal of existing constraints – i.e. helping the poor to help themselves. The 'Cities with Slums' agenda of the Cities Alliance and

UN-Habitat's 'Slum Upgrading Facility' seek to mobolise local resources public, private and community to develop sustainable financing mechanisms, reduce poverty and improve access to tenure, employment and services (Chant and McIlwaine, 2009).

However, the poorest and most needy households are often not capable of the organised and sustained collective action required to improve their housing, health care or education. Enablement programmes are often used by the authorities as an excuse to abandon many of their social responsibilities, privatising them to the NGOs and CBOs. Since the 1990s, therefore, the pursuit of adequate shelter as a human right has proceeded in theory, rather than in practice.

Reliance on market forces has widely resulted in a mounting, but often hidden, problem that is liable to create social and political tensions for many years to come (see also Potter, 1994; Potter and Conway, 1997).

Urban services: health, water and waste

It is estimated that some 600 million urban residents live in conditions that continually threaten their health. For most families, simply trying to feed themselves takes up most of their income, so there is little money for shelter or health care. Many are forced to live in squatter settlements or tenements that exhibit a range of environmental problems. The second United Nations Centre for Human Settlements (Habitat) Report (UNCHS, 1996) highlighted four particular problems: water, sewerage, overcrowding and air pollution.

Of all basic needs, access to clean water is probably the most important, and yet some 660 million people continue to lack access to safe and reliable potable (drinkable) water near their homes (UNICEF, 2015). For example, in Indonesia, only one-third of the urban population has access to safe drinking water. Moreover, those with such access are usually the better off. The poor, who can least afford it, are forced to buy their water from vendors at much higher prices, which often constitutes a significant percentage of their limited household income. Water and sanitation considerations are examined further in Chapter 6, particularly in relation to their associated pollution and health related outcomes (see also Desai and Potter, 2014).

Little wonder that the poor are often forced to resort to contaminated water with disastrous consequences for their health. With rising populations some cities have been forced to overexploit their aquifer resources, so cities such as Bangkok and Mexico City have experienced widespread land subsidence as aquifers are depleted.

Even where, as in Amman, the capital of Jordan, water supply connections exist to virtually every dwelling, water is often rationed and issues of social inequity mean that the poor have to spend more time and proportionately more of their income to get adequate water, especially in the summer months (see Case study 9.4).

Case study 9.4

Urban water supply issues – the example of Amman, Jordan

Amman, the capital city of Jordan, is in one of the ten most water scarce nations in the world (see Potter, Barham and Darmame, 2007; Potter, Darmame and Nortcliff, 2007; Potter *et al.*, 2007). In 2004, the total water consumption for the city area was 105 million cubic metres and local resources were insufficient to meet this. In its *National Water Master Plan* 2004, the Jordanian government stressed that the first priority is to meet the basic needs of the people. Indeed, as the population of the city has grown, various strategies have been implemented, most notably the transfer of waters from the Jordan Valley, from distant reservoirs and aquifers and the recycling of wastewater.

Today, Amman receives around 50 per cent of its water from the Jordan Valley. Water is pumped from −225 metres altitude from the Jordan Valley to a modern treatment plant at Zai, which is located to the northwest of the city at an altitude of 1035m. The remaining water demands of the city are met from the Al-Mafraq well, the Azraq aquifer (some 70km east of Amman), and from Qatrana, Swaqa and Wala to the south of the city. Looking to the future, providing the city with adequate water is a priority for the government. One of the major projects to achieve this is the Disi Project. This involves the proposed construction of a 325km pipeline from the Disi aquifer that lies on Jordan's border with Saudi Arabia. This will provide the city with around 100 million cubic metres per year for the next 100 years at an estimated base capital cost of US $600 million.

Unlike many cities in the Global South, 98 per cent of households in Amman are connected to the water supply network. However, since 1987 the supply of water to households has been rationed. For most parts of the city, water is supplied on just one or two days of the week, and the problem for households is one of storage. Wealthy families have been able to invest in large underground storage tanks or cisterns, whilst less wealthy families have been dependent on the ubiquitous 2 cubic metre rooftop storage tank. For such consumers, purchasing a second tank is likely to be very costly, amounting to around 90 Jordanian Dinar (approximately US $130).

The rationing of the urban water supply system in Amman reflected not just the relative scarcity of water, but also the generally dilapidated physical state of the network. Until 1999, 54 per cent of the water entering the city's distribution system was classified as 'unaccounted for', with half of this being lost through leakage. This situation reflected the fact that over time, extensions to the network have not generally been planned and have consisted of small diameter pipes. Over the years, operators have generally responded to problems of water pressure by increasing pump size rather than by reinforcing the network, thereby increasing overall pressures within the system. The remaining 'unaccounted for water' has been due to inadequate billing, lax payment collection and the illegal use of water, which in 2004 amounted to over 30,000 instances. The Water Authority of Jordan calculates that on average an illegal user of water consumes two to three times more water than a legal subscriber.

In order to meet the demand, especially in the dry summer months, various sub-markets for urban water have developed, such as private water tankers, water bottled from private wells and distilled mineral water derived from small reverse osmosis machines. In this context, household income and family size are

Case study 9.4 (continued)

vitally important variables. The cost of purchased water, storage tanks, pipework and filters are prohibitive for poor households in the eastern and southern areas of Amman. This is one of the reasons for the low average domestic water consumption of 94 litres per head per day in the city. Not surprisingly, the social polarity that characterises Amman is also reflected in patterns of water consumption within the city (Potter, Barham and Darmame, 2007).

In respect of management, Amman's water supply system was placed in the hands of the private sector in February 1999. At this time, a four-year contract was granted to ONDEO, the commercial arm of Suez Environmental, of which Lyonnaise des Eaux, France is a leading subsidiary. A local company known as LEMA was created, owned 75 per cent by Suez Environmental and 25 per cent by Arabtech Jardaneh (Jordan) and Montgomery Watson (UK). LEMA operated with an operational investment fund of US $25 million for urgent maintenance and repairs. The contract was extended twice and continued through to December 2006.

LEMA operated over an area of 3,000sq km, supplying 2 million people and managing 350,000 accounts. It is generally acknowledged that LEMA's major contribution has been in improved billing and debt collection, customer service in general, and in the regulation of rationing. For instance, in winter 2006 continuous supply was introduced to 15.8 per cent of LEMA's customers, and it is clear that some technical sources feel that the entire system should move toward continuous supply both for technical and supply reasons. However, it seems equally clear that at the present time government does not feel this is a step in the right direction – or at least, one they wish to follow (see Potter, Darmame and Barham, 2007).

After much debate during the period 2005–2006, the era of privatisation came to an end in January 2007, and the management of Amman's water was placed in the hands of a 'public company' named *Meyahona* ('Our Water'). This is owned by the Water Authority of Jordan (WAJ), but was to be run on the lines of a private company. This is exactly the model that has been in operation in the second city, Aqaba, since 2004 and is being presented by the Ministry of Water and Irrigation as a crucial alternative to private sector involvement in the water sector in Jordan. In this sense, sources in the Ministry stress that while the water system of Amman may no longer be privatised, it will remain commercialised.

Closely linked to water provision is the problem of solid waste removal and liquid waste through sewerage systems (Pernia, 1992). Again, in many countries of the Global South because of increasing populations this situation is worsening. During the 1980s alone the number of urban residents without access to adequate sanitation increased by 25 per cent (World Bank, 1992). Current estimates are that one in three people globally do not have access to adequate sanitation facilities (UNICEF, 2015).

Human waste, therefore, often lies untreated around the household, increasing health risks, and is eventually washed into waterways, lakes or seas, polluting aquifers and poisoning aquatic resources (Stren et al., 1992; UNEP, 2012). The health problems created by poor water and sanitary conditions are often exacerbated by poor diets and by overcrowding and poor ventilation, which intensifies the risk of respiratory infections, especially where biomass fuels are used. Those who are more involved in domestic activities (women and children) are therefore more prone to tuberculosis or bronchitis, which are still major killers in the cities of the South (Satterthwaite, 1997).

The city environment

The problems experienced in and around the household can be compounded by city-wide issues that often reflect the particular setting of the settlement. For example, many cities are located in hazard-vulnerable zones, and it is usually the poor who are forced to live in the most marginal areas, such as on steep slopes or flood-prone lowlands (Drakakis-Smith, 2000).

All too often the impact of natural disasters is intensified by poor urban management in allowing such areas to be settled without providing adequate safeguards. In Rio de Janeiro in 1988 the floods and landslides which followed torrential rain were partially caused by neglected, blocked or inadequate drainage systems in the *favelas* (World Bank, 1993).

In the same way, Case study 9.5 demonstrates how the increased incidence of landslides and mudslides in Caracas, Venezuela, has been attributed to the growth of informal rancho areas (Jimenez-Diaz, 1994; Potter, 1996).

Governments contribute to these environmental problems as a result of the inadequate supervision of economic growth, and their reluctance to enforce what few regulatory controls they have for fear of discouraging foreign investment in industrial activity.

As a result, industrial air and water pollution from uncontrolled discharges increasingly contaminate cities in the South as discussed further in Chapter 6. The air pollution challenges and high incidence of lung cancer experienced in China's industrial and mining cities and in Beijing have unfortunately become legendary, with interventions such as efforts to restrict the numbers of vehicles on the roads not fundamentally altering the root causes of problems caused by unrestricted and poorly managed economic and urban growth.

The most infamous example of such pollution remains the Union Carbide plant in Bhopal, India, where in 1984, poisonous gases killed some 3,300 people and seriously injured another 150,000. Most were from poor households living adjacent to the plant

(Gupta, 1988). The disastrous explosion occurred in a storage tank containing methyl isocyanate gas at the plant. The Bhopal plant was an unprofitable operation, which Shrivastava (1992: 3) suggests was for the most part 'ignored by the top Union Carbide officials'.

This, combined with the unregulated development of two large slum areas across from the plant, these housing several thousand residents, gave rise to the preconditions for a major disaster. Over 30 years later, many are still suffering from serious health problems stemming from the incident. More recent preventable urban disasters include clothing factory fires in Lahore and Karachi in Pakistan in 2012, and the 2010 chemical factory explosion in Nanjing in China and in 2015 in Dongying in China. These disasters killed hundreds of people and reflect on poor management and safety standards which have been compromised in the quest to raise profits, with little cognition shown of the environmental implications of these practices.

Increasing vehicle ownership and extensive use of fossil fuels are also contributing to air pollution widely in cities of the Global South. In Bangkok, 26 million workdays are lost annually through respiratory problems. Figures suggest that the incidence of lung cancer in Chinese cities is up to seven times greater than in the country as a whole. However, we must put this into global perspective, including that the three leading global producers of carbon emissions per capita are the USA, Canada and Australia as considered in Chapter 6.

Case study 9.5

Urbanisation and environment: the case of Caracas, Venezuela

Caracas is the primate capital city of Venezuela, and as such exhibits many of the features discussed earlier in this chapter. It may be recalled that in developing his ideas about core–periphery relations in transitional societies, John Friedmann (1966) specifically used Caracas and the rest of Venezuela as his case study (Chapter 3). The city grew very rapidly indeed following the development of the oil industry in the early part of the twentieth century. In 1950 it housed a population of just over 500,000; but by 2013

over 3 million people were living in the metropolitan district.

One of the most conspicuous features of Caracas is its location in a very narrow east-to-west valley (see Plate 9.14). With rapid urban growth, the sites for new development have become increasingly scarce. Like many cities in the Global South, since the 1950s a very high proportion of the growth of the city has been accounted for by self-help low-income settlements. These are referred to locally as *barrios*. Within

Case study 9.5 (continued)

these areas, many individual houses may start as relatively poor dwellings, but the majority undergo reasonably rapid improvement, upgrading and consolidation.

By the mid-1980s, over 61 per cent of all homes in Caracas were self-built informal sector dwellings.

Given the geography of the city, it was inevitable that many of these new informal dwellings were to be found located on steep slopes. It is estimated that some 67 per cent of the total area occupied by *barrios* were on land which was unstable enough to justify the legal eviction of the residents.

Records for Caracas suggest that before 1950 landslides were comparatively rare events. Although it is always possible that some were not recorded, only 12 were documented between 1800 and 1949. But the records then show that by the 1950s and 1960s landslides were occurring at the rate of one a year. Thereafter, research shows that failures increased

dramatically, from an average of 25 per year in the 1970s, to 35 per year during the first half of the 1980s (Jimenez-Diaz, 1994).

However, the most important fact is that up to the 1960s the majority of slope failures recorded in Caracas were associated with the occurrence of earthquakes as the initiating mechanism. However, from 1970 onwards, slope failures and mass movements became associated with heavy rainfall events rather than seismic activity. Spatially, it is noticeable that slope failures have tended to occur in the *barrio* areas. The areas with significant landslide events between 1974 and 1979 correspond almost exactly with the main barrio areas of the city. As an example of the outcome, when Tropical Storm Bret hit Caracas in August 1993, over 150 are believed to have been killed and thousands more lost their homes as a result of the major mudslides which occurred in the hilly low-income settlements.

Solid waste disposal compounds these problems for most cities. City-wide collection services are a rarity, and where they exist they are often confined to the wealthier districts. For example, in Lusaka in Zambia only about 10% of solid wastes are collected by the municipality from areas where residents can afford to pay for services. The majority of solid waste is simply dumped adjacent to living areas and burnt, causing related health and pollution challenges.

Sometimes private garbage removal services do exist, not necessarily provided by companies but by groups of people traditionally associated with such activities. Again, however, the fees necessary for such services often restrict them to those households that can afford them.

Ironically, it is the poor themselves who often recycle solid waste, saving and selling bottles, cans or paper. Sometimes families even live on the city garbage dumps, as in the famous Smokey Mountain site in Manila, where some 20,000 scavengers live and work.

Regional environmental impacts of cities

The regional environmental impacts of cities have now spread far beyond their immediate hinterland. Food,

fuel and material goods are drawn into cities from all over the nation and the world, affecting the lives of many.

The area that the city affects by its waste output has also grown – its so-called footprint (see Elliott, 2013). Indeed, the wealthier the individual or the city, the more distance they can afford to put between themselves and their waste. This is most clearly illustrated by the export of toxic and noxious wastes from the North to the more poverty-stricken parts of the South.

It is useful to divide the regional impact of cities in the South into two zones: (1) the immediate peri-urban area around the city where the urban footprint looms large and heavy; and (2) the broader region beyond this.

Peri-urban zones exhibit two broad areas of concern (Satterthwaite, 1997):

➤ *Unplanned and uncontrolled urban sprawl.* Often in the form of squatter settlements and illegal small-scale industries beyond the city boundaries, these areas can also contain large-scale municipal uses such as power stations.

➤ *Liquid waste disposal.* Untreated sewage and industrial effluent enters rivers, lakes or aquifers, making peri-urban areas concentrations of intense contamination.

Large Latin American cities such as Lima and Mexico are notorious for their inability to process the amount of liquid wastes which these cities generate, leading to significant water pollution risks, the contamination of rivers and the seas, loss of aquatic life and very real risks of water-borne diseases.

The impact of these processes is worsened by the fact that the peri-urban area is often a zone of major importance for recent migrants, offering land for shelter and agriculture and perhaps for wood fuel. The destruction and pollution of the peri-urban area is thus viewed rather differently by urban and peri-urban residents.

Further afield, in terms of regional impact, the urban footprint is becoming more marked every year, altering the traditional links between the city and its hinterland. Meeting the energy needs of the city has often created environmental problems, such as denudation of biomass, or expansion of coal mining and associated waste tipping. There are many other examples of regional urban footprints; the growing demand for cement and bricks have led, respectively, to quarrying and pollution, or to loss of valuable soil resources (see also Chapter 6).

Water demands too can affect regions way beyond the city, particularly for cities in semi-arid areas. Bulawayo in Zimbabwe is seeking funds to draw on the waters of the Zambesi. If this succeeds, what will be the impact on the fragile ecosystems of this part of southern Africa? The Three Gorges Dam on the Yangtse is also partly designed to provide energy for urban industry but will have enormous environmental effects on the 600 km of the new lake between Chongqing and Ichang. As noted previously, Amman, Jordan is bringing water some 325 km from the Disi aquifer in southern Jordan (Potter, Darmame and Nortcliff, 2007).

Understanding and responding to environmental issues: the brown and green agendas and climate change

For many people, urban sustainability in developing countries equates only to environmental issues. Moreover, this environmental agenda tends to prioritise those issues which are of greatest concern to the North, such as climate change and the rapid use of finite resources. For many governments and cities, managing these issues have become a major area of concern. Green agenda issues relate to ecosystem health, soil, water and air quality, while brown agenda items relate to the impacts of industrial and other urban activities on human well-being and health. The impacts of the green and brown agenda issues as summarised in Table 9.8 exercise a decisive influence over the quality of life within settlements, and seeking ways to mitigate negative effects, though a high priority, are generally compromised by low available budgets and the challenges which many cities in the South face simply in terms of coping with the rate of growth (Elliott, 2013). These issues are further discussed in Chapter 6.

The environmental problems facing such cities vary enormously according to the local combination of contributing factors. In broad terms, these encompass the following:

➤ The nature of the urbanisation process itself – the rate, scale and degree of concentration of growth;
➤ The ecosystem within which the settlement is located;
➤ The level and nature of the development process, which affects the ability of the family and the state to respond to problems;
➤ The development priorities of the state.

Table 9.8 The brown and green agenda for urban environmental improvement

Problem/Issue	Brown Agenda Focus	Green Agenda Focus
Key impact	Human health	Ecosystem health
Timing	Immediate	Delayed
Scale	Local	Regional / Global
Worst affected	Lower income groups	Future generations
People	Work with	Educate
Environmental services	Provide more	Use less
Water/land	Inadequate access	Overuse / loss

Source: adapted from Government of India, 2009; and McGranahan and Satterthwaite, 2000.

Within the development process, urban environmental problems usually emanate from two principal sources. The first is environmentally irresponsible or poorly managed economic development. Despite the arguments of development economists, the market has responded poorly to environmental problems created by the philosophy of 'grow now and clear up later', unless coerced by the enforcement of regulatory legislation. In general, such controls have been weak, often because urban managers themselves are frequent beneficiaries of uncontrolled development. Net results include severe environmental pollution, contamination of soils and water (above and below ground), the generation of toxic wastes and, as a result, compromised human health (Pacione, 2009).

The second major contributor is poverty and vulnerability, which forces low-income households to survive as best they can, leaving the environment to look after itself, creating a range of critical outcomes which impact on human well-being and environmental sustainability. Overcrowding, compromised water quality and risks of disease have extremely negative human impacts. Equally important is the inability to adequately process waste products and sewerage which poses risks of a variety of water-borne and other diseases (Pacione, 2009). This does not mean that the poor are unaware of the environmental consequences of their actions, rather that they have other more immediate survival orientated priorities. The implication is that improvements to the urban environment must be strongly linked to poverty alleviation, as well as the regulation of industry. This is another area where poverty reduction/amelioration have become of great salience.

This combination of contributory factors to the brown agenda also varies spatially and in terms of scale – from the household scale to the regional and global scales. In general, the concerns of the household, workplace or community are more immediate and relate primarily to health and to equality of access to basic services (Table 9.9). At the regional and global levels, the problems are more long term in nature and are linked to the impact of resource use on future generations – the major concerns of the North. Between these sets of concerns lies the city itself, combining all these issues in a complex situation that requires careful management to ensure sustainable urbanisation. These issues will impact to an ever increasing degree on cities and their residents as time progresses.

Table 9.9 Spatial dimensions of the brown agenda

Principal service infrastructure	Problem issues
Household/workplace	
Shelter	Substandard housing
Water provision	Lack of water, expensive
Toilets	No sanitation
Solid waste	No storage
Ventilation	Air pollution
Community	
Piped water	Inadequate reticulation
Sewerage system	Human waste pollution
Drainage	Flooding
Waste collection	Dumping
Streets (safety)	Congestion, noise
City	
Industry	Accidents, hazards, air pollution
Transport	Congestion, noise, air pollution
Waste treatment	Inadequate, seepage
Landfill	Unmonitored, toxic, seepage
Energy	Unequal access
Geomorphology	Natural hazards
Region	
Ecology	Pollution, deforestation, degradation
Water sources	Pollution, overuse
Energy sources	Overextended, pollution

Source: Bartone et al., 1994. © International Bank for Reconstruction and Development/The World Bank

Clear future environmentally-related challenges also exist, particularly in the face of climate change. Particularly vulnerable areas include the towns and cities of small islands states in the Pacific and Indian Ocean areas, and low-lying river delta areas such as in Bangladesh. Floods, El Nino events, extreme weather and earthquakes and tsunamis have unfortunately become commonplace events in countries such as Ecuador, Chile, India, Bangladesh, Mozambique, Fiji and Vanuatu, all of which have suffered from natural disasters in 2014–2016 impacting on human survival, destroying physical assets and negatively impacting on livelihoods.

Preparing for disasters through developing the capacity to respond to them when they occur, and ensuing people avoid living in low-lying areas is a key urban priority (Bicknell et al., 2009). Equally important are measures to reduce pollution risks, and to improve urban drainage and sanitation. Citizen engagement and involvement in these processes is critical, as evidence from cities such as Durban (South Africa) has shown in helping communities better manage their resources and enhance their disaster preparedness (Bicknell et al., 2009). Equally important, as the Government of India (2009) has identified, is the need to promote sustainable practices through low technology interventions focusing on energy saving technologies, recycling and waste reduction initiatives.

Final comments: urban management for sustainable urbanisation

The above discussion of the brown agenda reveals some of the main challenges of urban management for sustainable urbanisation, including false priorities, lack of adequate legislation, self-interest, poor knowledge and training and a susceptibility to external influences, both benign and malign. Furthermore, a lack of public awareness of appropriate policy responses, coupled with the fact that protests have often been fragmented (and easy for authorities to contain) has meant that most pressure for change in urban management towards greater responsiveness to problems of sustainability in cities of the Global South have come from external sources.

Institutional responses to these challenges have mirrored the emergence of neo-liberal development strategies in general (see Chapters 1 and 3), with an emphasis on market-led solutions and limited interference by the state, with many urban management policies being substantially shaped by national governments in conjunction with their external advisers.

Municipal governments thus have to work within limits set by agencies beyond their control, although even within the city there are often more specific management problems too. Many would claim that overall the shift to the market economy has simply resulted in the transfer of responsibilities from the state to the poor, largely by removing the constraints on letting them help themselves.

Certainly, the poor have taken advantage of such moves in the development of their coping mechanisms, but these are essentially small in scale and focused on the household. Collective and larger scale responses are difficult without proper knowledge,

training and funding. Recycling waste is possible for the poor, constructing a sewerage system is not.

Increasingly, intermediaries have become involved in order to 'improve local capacity'. However, of the private sector, the embodiment of the market, has been slow to respond to the needs of sustainability. Although there are some examples of the private sector meeting some basic needs in large Latin American and Pacific-Asian cities, they are far from universally replicable and, unsurprisingly, tend not to affect those in greatest need of assistance. Indeed, the role of the private sector in water vending has increased the exploitation of the poor (Choguill, 1994).

Despite early pessimism, community participation and cooperation have emerged on a substantial scale, perhaps due to growing competition for resources by increasingly diverse ethnic and social groups. In this context, the role of NGOs and CBOs as facilitators of urban community development have also been apparent. However, many NGOs are themselves arguably large global organisations driven by Western agendas and funding sources (see Chapter 7). Indeed, many NGOs have been criticised for assisting in the privatisation of resource provision and the retreat of the state. In this context the underprivileged have little option but to engage in their own protests and civil action for improved access to urban resources.

For some analysts, such as Escobar (1995; see also Chapter 1), these movements could form the basis of new development strategies, but often they are deliberately limited in their objectives and they are consciously non-political. If and when they achieve some of their aims, such social movements tend to fade away.

There is no doubt that the appropriate level at which to tackle problems related to urban sustainability is the local state, the city itself. At present, however, most, but not all, urban management is poorly informed, poorly motivated and poorly organised. A decentralisation of power, funding and responsibilities from the national to the local state would be a start, but it must also be accompanied by greater democratisation at the level of the city itself. While many countries have notionally pursued decentralisation policies, this is seldom accompanied by the devolution of adequate legal mechanisms and financial resources to effect meaningful local change and empowerment.

Those most affected by the inadequacies and inequalities of unsustainable urban development – in short, those whose coping mechanisms sustain the unsustainable – must become part of the process of policy formulation and enactment.

At present, there is little sign of this occurring on a wide scale, and with urban populations and poverty continuing to grow, the problems of urban sustainability for a whole range of different cities within the South are likely to get worse, rather than better.

Key points

> The chapter has illustrated the key importance of the contemporary processes of urbanisation and urban growth in the poorer nations of the world.

> It is these nations that are now showing some of the highest rates of urbanisation ever recorded. Further, they now account for some of the largest cities in the world.

> Rapid urban growth and migration to the cities of the South has exacerbated the challenge posed by the growth of large-scale slums and burgeoning poverty.

> Levels of regional inequality and regional urban primacy are frequently higher in countries in the South than in the North.

> Urban and regional planning, which is appropriate to local and national requirements and realities, is needed to ameliorate some of the worst effects of spatially polarised and unequal development. There is a range of national urban development strategies that can be employed by the state machinery.

> The linkages existing between urban and rural components of the national space are frequently appreciably stronger and more complex than has previously been conceptualised. This is witnessed in the recognition of extended metropolitan regions (EMRs) and 'compound urban regions'.

> Cities in the Global South are showing a variety of forms as they grow and develop. They are not universally converging on the norms associated with 'Western' cities.

> The informal sector has played a vital role in the provision of both homes and jobs and particularly for the poor in the cities of the Global South.

> Service supplies in cities are frequently inadequate and pose major health risks, while city environments are often compromised by lack of resources and poor planning.

> The green and brown agendas serve to stress the environmental impacts of urbanisation, with emphasis on the need for sustainable principles of urbanisation.

Further reading

Chant, S. and McIlwaine, C. (2009) *Geographies of Development in the 21st Century.* Cheltenham: Edward Elgar.
This book contains useful sections which reflect on urban processes and developments in the South.

Cities Alliance (2006) *Poverty in the Urban Environment.* Washington: Cities Alliance.
This source provides a detailed overview of the nature and scale of urban poverty.

Davies, M. (2006) *Planet of Slums.* London: Verso.
This book critiques current urban policy and discusses the nature, causes and the seriousness of the rapid growth of slums.

Desai, V. and Potter, R.B. (eds) (2014) *The Companion to Development Studies*, 3rd edn. London: Arnold, Part 5: Urbanization, 275–328.

An accessible source book that brings together over 100 key essays dealing with all aspects of the field of development studies, and Part 5 deals with urban processes.

Drakakis-Smith, D. (2000) *The Third World City*, 2nd edn. London: Routledge.
A good introductory account on cities in the developing world.

Hardoy, J.E., Mitlin, D. and Satterthwaite, D. (2001) *Environmental Problems in an Urbanizing World.* London: Earthscan Publications.
The environmental aspects of rapid urban growth and urbanisation are the focus of this detailed text.

Mitlin, D. and Satterthwaite, D. (2013) *Urban Poverty in the Global South.* Abingdon: Routledge.
This book provides a detailed insight into the nature and scale of poverty in urban areas in the South

Pacione, M. (2009) *Urban Geography*, London: Routledge.
The chief merit of this general introduction to urban geography is that it covers cities both in the North and the South.

Potter, R.B. and Lloyd-Evans, S. (1998) *The City in the Developing World*. London: Pearson.
A detailed overview of the role of cities and urbanisation in the development process.

Satterthwaite, D. and Mitlin, D. (2014) *Reducing Urban Poverty in the Global South*. Abingdon: Routledge.
This provides a useful overview of the focus and effectiveness of current urban interventions, with a focus on those designed to address poverty.

UN-Habitat (2015) *World Atlas of Slum Evolution*. Nairobi: UN-Habitat.
A useful source on the nature and scale of slum development.

United Nations (2014) *World Urbanization Prospects Report, 2014*. New York: United Nations. http://esa.un.org/unpd/wup/Publications/Files/WUP2014-Report.pdf
A good source of basic statistics concerning urbanisation in the current global context.

Websites

www.citiesalliance.org
The Cities Alliance website provides details of key urban policies and intervention.

https://www.un.org/development/desa/en/
Website of the United Nations Department of Economic and Social Affairs, which includes access to urban-oriented reports such as the United Nations World Urbanisation Prospects 2014 revised report cited here.

www.unchs.org
This is the website for UN-HABITAT, the United Nations Human Settlement Programme, the mission of which is to promote sustainable development. The accent is very much on issues of shelter and the provision of legal titles to land, and on urban governance.

www.iied.org
IIED is the International Institute for Environment and Development. The Human Settlements section contains features on urban poverty, urban environmental issues, and rural–urban linkages.

Discussion topics

➤ 'Rapid urbanisation, slow everything else.' Examine this statement in relation to urbanisation in the South and the challenges.

➤ Examine the contention that sustainably managing the rapid growth of cities is one of the world's major development challenges.

➤ Examine the evidence suggesting that cities in the South are not converging on a global norm, i.e. the Northern model in respect of their urban functions and management.

➤ Assess the extent to which the term 'self-help' aids our understanding of both housing and employment in societies of the Global South.

➤ 'Environmental problems in cities of the Global South require good governance.' Discuss.

Chapter 10
Rural spaces

This chapter examines the ways in which the strategies, policies and processes of development examined in earlier chapters impact on rural spaces of the Global South. Whilst the world officially became predominantly urban in 2007, this chapter details the continued challenges for some of the poorest groups of people worldwide and for securing the conservation of globally valued natural resources and resource functions.

This chapter:

➤ Reviews how agriculture and rural development have featured within development thinking over time and identifies why they are currently 'back on' international policy agendas;
➤ Critically investigates the 'livelihoods framework' as a tool for understanding the diversity and flexibility of rural livelihoods and its influence in shaping rural development practice;
➤ Examines the persistence of poverty and hunger in rural spaces;
➤ Examines how questions of security over rights to land and resources and women's empowerment remain central to rural development and how these are being addressed through policies of land reform and gender mainstreaming;

➤ Identifies the challenges for large- and small-scale agriculture in the context of globalisation of agriculture and the internationalisation of land markets. The equity and livelihood impacts of 'land' and 'green' grabs are investigated;
➤ Examines the challenges of reconciling global environmental with local livelihood objectives in rural spaces through the case of forestry resources.

Introduction

Currently 54% of the world's population lives in cities and towns and the trend for increasing urbanisation are expected to continue (World Bank, 2016). However, in many parts of the Global South it is rural areas which will continue to accommodate the majority of people for the foreseeable future. Not only will these rural areas have to deliver food and incomes to expanding populations in the next decades, but they will also be expected to safeguard many aspects of the 'global commons', including in climate regulation and the conservation of biodiversity. However, these areas are the locus for some of the most insecure livelihoods globally and poverty is 'disproportionately concentrated' in rural areas (FAO, 2015). For example, of the 1.4 billion people in extreme poverty (defined as living on less than $1.25 a day), 70% of these people live in rural areas of the Global South. In sub-Saharan Africa, almost half of the rural population is extremely poor (FAO, 2015).

As seen in Chapter 6, livelihoods and wellbeing in rural areas of the Global South are closely related to environmental resources, including land for agricultural production and access to forests and fisheries, and the health of ecological systems (for safe water and disease regulation and for security from floods and other hazards for example). The Millennium Ecosystem Assessment (2005) confirmed how the rural poor are highly vulnerable to processes of environmental change, most obviously when the 'provisioning services' supporting food production, in agriculture, livestock, fishing and hunting, or in protecting and providing fuels and water resources are threatened. Ecosystem change also undermines wider aspects of wellbeing such as freedom of choice and action. Furthermore, dependence on such ecosystem

services was found to increase with diminished human well-being. Hence, trajectories of environmental change, such as discussed in Chapter 6, have huge implications for rural development, particularly for the way that they affect agricultural futures and access to fundamental resources such as land.

However, livelihoods and occupations in rural areas of the Global South are also diversifying, including moving away from agriculture as highlighted in Table 10.1. Box 10.1 defines the key concepts being used to understand these processes. A variety of 'off-farm' and 'non-farm' activities and enterprises, for example, increasingly feature in household livelihood strategies (Plate 10.1), although there are substantial differences between and within countries and by gender and the vast majority of rural households still maintain on-farm production (Davis et al., 2010). When considered at the scale of the rural economy as a whole, these patterns support debates concerning the longer term processes of 'de-agrarianisation' of countries of the Global South.

Plate 10.1 Diversifying rural livelihoods
a: 'Non-farm' self-employment in mountain tourism, Imlil, Morocco
(*photo*: Jennifer Elliott)

b: 'Off-farm' wage employment, brick making, India
(*photo*: Jennifer Elliott)

c 'Off-farm' wage employment, forest clearance for oil palm production, Indonesia
(*photo*: Rebecca Elmhirst)

Table 10.1 Broad processes and trends in the rural South

➤ Increased diversification of occupations and livelihoods
➤ More common and pronounced occupational multiplicity
➤ A shift in the balance of household income from farm to non-farm
➤ A de-linking of livelihoods and poverty from land (and from farming)
➤ Livelihoods are increasingly delocalised as lives become more mobile
➤ A growing role of remittances within rural household incomes
➤ Rising average age of farmers
➤ Cultural and social changes are operating in new ways to modify livelihoods

Source: compiled from Rigg, 2006.

There is also evidence, particularly from Asia and Latin America, that migration, remittances and 'multi-local' livelihoods increasingly characterise how people secure a means for living. The opportunities of rapid urbanisation, combined with enhanced mobility through communications and transport technologies, has enabled some people to engage in both rural and urban life, whereby 'considerable numbers of rural poor are no longer rooted in one place; although they maintain relations with their home communities, they are also attached to other places and function in larger networks' (Zoomers, 2014: 234).

It is clear that, as Rigg (1997: 197) asserts (and highlighted further in the Key idea box), 'there is more to rural life than agriculture'. This has challenged rural development planning and practice to go beyond invigorating agricultural production or the redistribution of land resources. However, agricultural sources of income (in crop and livestock activities and in agricultural wage labour) continue to form a higher share of total income for poor households amongst all countries in the Global South (Davis et al., 2010), making these 'fundamentally rural' issues of agriculture and access to productive resources persistent challenges for rural development. Furthermore, beyond these 'private' functions of agriculture in providing food, fodder, medicines etc., agriculture is now expected also to deliver a range of public functions such as climate regulation and the conservation of biodiversity and cultural heritages, ensuring the continued centrality of questions of agriculture in rural development. It also clear that the distinction between rural and urban livelihoods may be 'increasingly difficult to make' (Zoomers, 2014: 233), such that these challenges are also shaped by changes in the urban sphere.

Box 10.1

Key concepts in understanding rural change

A livelihood comprises: the capabilities, assets (stores, resources, claims and access) and activities required for a means of living; a livelihood is sustainable when it can cope with and recover from stress and shocks, maintain or enhance its capabilities and assets, and provide sustainable livelihood opportunities for the next generation; and which contributes net benefits to other livelihoods at the local and global levels in the long and short term (Chambers and Conway, 1992: 7/8).

Rural livelihood diversification: the process by which rural households construct an increasingly diverse portfolio of activities and assets in order to survive and to improve their standard of living (Ellis, 2000: 15).

De-agrarianisation: the long-term process of occupational adjustment, income-earning reorientation, social identification and spatial relocation of rural dwellers away from strictly agricultural-based modes of livelihood (Bryceson, 2002: 726)

Key idea

There is more to rural life than agriculture

It is increasingly appreciated that there is more to rural life than agriculture and rural people are not just farmers (Scoones, 1996). Table 10.2 identifies a range of ways in which people may compile the stocks and flows of food and cash to meet their needs in rural areas. Evidently, many go beyond the direct production of agricultural goods, or what Ellis (2000) refers to as 'own-account agriculture'.

The idea of a 'livelihood portfolio' is used to encompass the varied ways in which people secure an income (as the most visible outcomes of the processes by which a livelihood is constructed) within rural areas. Livelihood diversity in which different activities are often combined, to varying degrees at different times, has been identified as an essential way in which people respond to economic, social and environmental changes for example.

Figure 10.1 represents a portfolio for an 'average' rural livelihood within sub-Saharan Africa (Ellis, 2000). While own-account agricultural activities are evidently significant, delivering 40 per cent of the total income portfolio, 18 per cent is secured through 'off-farm' activities (that may include income gained through working for other people on neighbouring farms as well as gathering activities). A further 42 per cent of income of typical households comes through 'non-farm' activities, including remittances from outside the rural area, but also self-employment locally in services and manufacturing activities.

Whilst there are some problems of comparability of data over time, this is now some evidence that non-farm income in overall livelihood portfolios is increasing (Davis et al., 2010). Own-account

Table 10.2 Sources of rural livelihood

➤ Home gardening – the exploitation of small, local micro-environments
➤ Common property resources – access to fuel, fodders, fauna, medicines, etc. through fishing, hunting, gathering, grazing and mining
➤ Processing, hawking, vending and marketing
➤ Share-rearing of livestock – the lending of livestock for herding in exchange for rights to some products including offspring
➤ Transporting goods
➤ Mutual help – small loans from saving groups or borrowing from relatives and neighbours
➤ Contract outwork
➤ Casual labour or piecework
➤ Specialised occupations such as tailors, blacksmiths, carpenters, sex workers
➤ Domestic service
➤ Child labour – domestic work at home in collecting fuel and fodder, herding, etc. and working away in factories, shops or other people's houses
➤ Craft work – basket making, carving, etc.
➤ Selling assets – labour, children
➤ Family splitting – putting children out to other families or family members
➤ Migration for seasonal work
➤ Remittances from family members employed away
➤ Food for work and public works relief projects
➤ Begging
➤ Theft

Source: compiled from Chambers, 1997

▶

Key idea (continued)

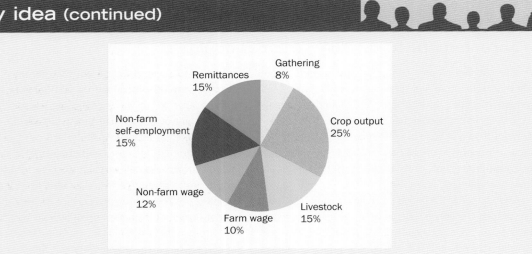

Figure 10.1 The average rural livelihood in sub-Saharan Africa
Source: Ellis, 2000

agriculture remains more widespread in sub-Saharan Africa than it does in South Asia and Latin America, where wage labour on other farms tends to be more important. Important work is also considering whether livelihood diversification operates as a 'coping mechanism', such as in response to drought, and thereby could be a sign of mounting vulnerability, or whether diversification can provide longer term sustainability and 'resilience' in the face of climate change, for example.

Rural spaces in development thinking

Eurocentric models of modernisation

Early models of development (as explored in Chapter 3) emphasised the importance of agricultural innovation and improved rural productivity for the release of capital and surplus labour, which could then be used in emerging urban and industrial activities that formed the basis for a modern society. Based largely on the historical experience of Western Europe, the interdependence of the rural-agricultural and urban-industrial sectors and the transformation of a country's economy from 'one that is dominantly rural and agricultural to one that is dominantly urban, industrial, and service-oriented in composition' (Mellor, 1990: 70) were central to the concept of development itself. For example, in his classic text *The Theory of Economic Growth*, Arthur Lewis (1955: 433) argues that:

industrialisation is dependent upon agricultural improvement: it is not profitable to produce a growing volume of manufactures unless agricultural production is growing simultaneously. This is also why industrial and agricultural revolutions always go together, and why economies in which agriculture is stagnant do not show industrial development.

Rigg (2001: 19) suggests that 'on the face of it' this 'classical agrarian question' remains 'highly pertinent' in the Global South where:

the transition to capitalism is an ongoing project and, notwithstanding far-reaching structural change in some countries, agriculture remains an important economic sector employing the largest proportion of the workforce. Thus we have, on the one hand, a completed historical process in the developed North, while in the South the process is contemporary and continuing. In the North, obstacles to accumulation were overcome and capitalist transformation and industrialisation ensured. In the South, significant obstacles remain.

Table 10.3 Dominant concepts in rural development

Period	Dominant Concepts	Dominant Actor
1950s	Green Revolution	Governments, private sector
1960s–1970s	Land Reforms	Governments, international donors
1970s–1980s	Integrated Rural Development	Governments, NGOs, donors
1980s–today	Sustainable Development	Local governments, NGOs, donors
1990s–today	Pro-poor growth / MDGs	Market forces, local governments, donors, private sector, NGOs
2007/8–today	Land governance / Titling / Responsible investment	Market forces, national governments, donors, private sector, NGOs

Source: adapted from Zoomers, 2014.

However, more recently, Rigg (2007) and others (see Woodhouse, 2009) caution how such models oversimplify the diversity of agrarian transitions occurring in the Global South and the complexity of rural living, including the many connections between agriculture and urban parts of the economy. On independence, national development plans regularly attached great importance to rural and agricultural development, often depending on substantial domestic and foreign resources. As seen in Table 10.3, in the early decades of planned rural development interventions, approaches such as the Green Revolution and programmes of land reforms (the characteristics of these are discussed further below) both rested on a dominant modernisation model of development and a strong role for the state in developing the agricultural sector.

In 2008, the World Bank made 'Agriculture for Development' the focus of its World Development Report, for the first time in 25 years. Central to the report was a model of three 'rural worlds' across the Global South according to the share of agriculture in economic growth and the share of total poverty in rural areas. On this basis, three 'types of country' were identified: agriculture-based, transforming and urbanised. Whilst the report has been welcomed in terms of helping to put agriculture back on the international development agenda, after several decades of relative absence as considered below, it has been criticised for the strongly linear model of agrarian transition and economic development implied 'where economic development occurs in a series of clearly defined steps and the challenge is to find the technology and market incentives to push agriculture and rural society from one stage to the next' (Elliott, 2013: 194).

Urban bias

A persistent concern in the development literature has been the suggested state and processes of 'urban bias'. This thesis was first put forward in 1997 by Michael Lipton. He argued that the key explanation for persistent poverty in the Global South was the 'anti-rural' development strategies that have been followed, whereby the urban sector and residents benefit disproportionately from public spending, for example (see Chapters 1 and 9). The suggestion is that national politicians, keen to maintain a hold on power, have generally been much more concerned to keep their urban populations contented, since these communities are invariably better educated, more articulate, organised in trade unions and other groupings, and therefore likely to be a much greater potential threat to economic and political stability than the less educated and less well-organised rural poor.

Whilst rural-based strategies for development became more prominent in development in the 1970s/80s particularly through integrated, area-based investments focusing on 'development from below' (see Table 10.3), the Key idea box discusses a number of biases that have also operated *within* rural development practice that have served to limit understanding of the needs of rural communities.

More than 30 years on, it is considered that these biases still hold relevance (Jones and Corbridge, 2010). As Bebbington (1999: 2021) suggests, misperceptions concerning the 'way people get by and get things done' in rural areas continue to compromise rural development approaches and practice. However, as seen in Chapter 7, the capacity of governments in all arenas of development, including in agriculture and rural development, was reduced substantially through the 1980s and 1990s under the pressures of mounting debt and requirements to meet the demands of the international financial institutions (IFIs) in economic restructuring. Under the predominant neo-liberal thinking and approach to development that characterised this period, agriculture was not a priority for the IFIs and many other donors. For example, World Bank lending for agriculture declined from 32% of the total portfolio in 1976–78 to 6.5% in 2000–05, and the number of technical experts employed by the Bank in agriculture and rural development fell from 40 to 17 over a similar period (World Bank, 2008). Whilst many governments of the Global South were expected to raise agricultural exports as the basis for generating the income to repay debts, agricultural reforms did not feature heavily in the structural adjustment programmes required by the IFIs.

Key idea

The bias of rural development planning and practice

In 1983, Robert Chambers put forward a number of reasons why rural development interventions were failing to have the impacts that they were planned to have. He suggested that key national decision makers, and development institutions more widely, had inadequate knowledge about rural dwellers and their needs due to a number of 'biases' in research and practice. Fundamentally, rural communities and their people are often regarded as being 'out of the way' and 'off the beaten track' as far as development planners are concerned:

> In Third World countries as elsewhere, academics, bureaucrats, foreigners and journalists are all drawn to towns or based in them. All are victims, though usually willing victims, of the urban trap.
>
> (Chambers, 1983: 7)

Further biases in the investigation process may also contribute to an incomplete and inaccurate understanding of rural needs, such as 'dry season bias', that results from only visiting rural areas during the dry season when travel is usually easier. This is despite the fact that in tropical countries with well-defined wet and dry seasons, it is during the rainy season that most crops are grown, people have to work for long hours in the fields, and disease and malnutrition are more common. 'Tarmac bias', refers to the reality that many visitors to rural areas travel only on good roads and rarely venture into remote areas, thus failing to make contact with what are often the poorest communities. A further factor in generating inaccurate perceptions is 'person bias', where visitors only speak to influential community leaders, who are invariably men. The views of women and 'ordinary' community members are therefore rarely heard (Chambers, 1983).

Chambers' subsequent work (1993, 1997, 2008), has been important in continuing to foster the 'Farmer First' approach in rural development. This is broadly defined to include not just sedentary, small holder farmers, but also pastoralists, forest dwellers, fisherfolk and other small scale producers of food and feedstuff. It includes understanding how the priorities and realities of such 'farmers' may be quite contrasting to those of 'outsiders', such as scientists and development practitioners as illustrated in Table 10.4

Adopting a Farmer First approach in rural development has widespread implications, including for how research is undertaken, how projects are designed and the role of different kinds of expertise in shaping more sustainable outcomes. There are powerful forces which continue to perpetuate outsider priorities, that focus on 'economies not people' and the 'view from the office not the field' and tend to generate standard prescriptions for change, rather than the flexible, evolving, collaborative technologies rooted in farmer realities. Furthermore, there are now many stakeholders in rural development, including businesses and entrepreneurs in the private sector and varied organisations working to support communities. As such innovation and co-learning needs to be undertaken in this rapidly changing context.

Key idea (continued)

Table 10.4 How scientists' and farmers' priorities may diverge

	Priorities	
	Scientists	**Resource-poor farmers**
Crops	Yield	Flavour
	Compatible with machine harvesting	Local marketability
	Single variety	Multiple variety cropping
Cropping systems	Mono-cropping	Diverse cropping
	High external input	Low external input
	High yield	Yield less important
Management	Maximise production	Minimise risk
	Maximise growth	Livelihood security
Use of labour	Minimise labour input	Use all family labour
Constraints	Meeting demands of scientific community	Meeting traditional obligations
	Project cycles	Maintaining good community relations
	Meeting demands of donors	

Source: compiled from Chambers, 1997.

The return of rural development to policy agendas

After a substantial period of 'non-intervention' (Zoomers, 2014: 230), it is considered that rural development is now back on the policy agenda of the international organisations and amongst governments of the Global South, including for the 'newer' integrated challenges of global food, energy and climate change. Civil society organisations have also been important in putting fundamental rural concerns, such as over land and control over local resource use decisions, to the fore of contemporary rural development planning and practice. This has been part of the wider challenge to the injustices of neo-liberalism and globalisation, as seen in Chapters 4 and 7.

An important factor in prompting a re-evaluation of rural areas in development thinking and practice has been the search for patterns and processes of 'sustainable development', as identified in Table 10.3 and discussed more fully in Chapter 6. As Potter et al. (2012: 115) state; 'it is difficult to talk about rural livelihoods and poverty without thinking about the concept of sustainable development, which has framed environmental and development discourse since the 1980s'. In short, if

globally valued environmental resources, landscapes and resource functions are to be conserved, it will depend on meeting the development needs of some of the poorest groups worldwide, often based in rural areas of the Global South. Central to progressing more sustainable rural development has been the substantial rethinking of the value of indigenous skills and capacities in understanding rural resource outcomes and environmental transformations (see Batterbury and Warren, 2001; Leach and Mearns, 1996). In addition, understanding the diversity and flexibility of rural livelihoods are features that have been regularly neglected within past rural development policies and projects, but form the basis for many of the more successful and sustainable rural development initiatives (see Elliott, 2013).

Understanding livelihoods in rural areas

As established, there are diverse ways in which people secure the means to a living in rural areas that may include various forms of agricultural production and, to a greater or lesser extent, overall livelihood portfolios. A close association with, and often intricate

Plate 10.2 Ecosystem services in rural livelihoods
(a) Fishing, Kisumu, Kenya
(*photo*: Tony Binns)

(b) Date harvesting, Tunisia
(*photo*: Jennifer Elliott)

(c) Timber production, Guyana
(*photo*: Jennifer Elliott)

(d) Rain fed crop production, Zimbabwe
(*photo*: Jennifer Elliott)

knowledge of, natural resources, ecosystem functioning and services provided by ecosystems are often of key importance (MEA, 2005; Plate 10.2). As well as being diverse, livelihoods systems are dynamic as people make decisions in the context of changing economic, political, social and environmental circumstances. Substantial insights into and understanding of the way that complex livelihoods of the rural poor interact with a range of political economic and environmental processes emerged through the 1990s with the development of the 'livelihoods approach' or perspective, that in short, 'starts with how different people in different places live' (Scoones, 2009: 172).

Whilst the roots of the approach are varied and quite long-standing, elements can be identified in farming systems research, in sustainability science and political

ecology, for example, the landmark paper is regularly cited as that by Robert Chambers and Gordon Conway from the Institute of Development Studies at the University of Sussex (UK) in 1992. The influence of Robert Chambers in development studies more widely is considered in the Key thinker box. Chambers and Conway proposed that livelihoods comprise the capabilities, assets and activities needed to make a living, which substantially broadened understanding of the non-material dimensions of poverty and wellbeing. The idea is that people's livelihoods depend on their ability to access a range of assets or 'capitals' which are combined (and traded-off) in different ways to secure particular livelihood objectives. The livelihood perspective puts people, what they have and their agency central to development processes. This is a substantial 'reversal' of the bias of previous approaches that emphasised the priorities of the 'first', those of researchers and practitioners as seen in the Key idea above. In short, it was a response to the overly technocratic and single-sector approaches to rural development in the past and, in particular, to those centered on agricultural efficiency, with little insight into how people make decision or factors that may constrain their ability to implement the 'solutions'. As Potter et al. (2012: 118/119) assert:

'livelihood approaches symbolised an elemental shift in development thinking from top-down, macro-development policies that viewed the rural poor as victims of structural constraints, to a more grass-roots and empowering approach that emphasised the agency of households over their lives'.

The central elements of the livelihoods framework developed to deliver the approach are identified in Box 10.2. Whilst the capitals and agency are central, it is also recognised that people's choices and opportunities are shaped by the broader political, institutional, cultural and environmental context in which they live. Hence, the framework embraces how people's asset status is shaped by a dynamic 'vulnerability context'. This refers to the wider external environment that shapes the availability of assets, including trends in population and economy, shorter term shocks such as in human and livestock health and seasonality, that is in turn shaped by transforming structures and processes through government and private sector actions, for example.

Key thinker

Robert Chambers

Robert Chambers (1932–) has worked as both a practitioner in development (including as a District Officer in Kenya, 1958–1962) and as an academic (particularly at the Institute of Development Studies at the University of Sussex from 1972) and is widely recognised to have had a profound impact on the ideologies, strategies and practice of development. As Parnwell (2006: 77) suggests,

> his thumbprint is everywhere one looks in the modern development field: bottom-up development, participatory development, sustainable livelihoods, the redefinition of poverty, the strengthening of civil society, and the entire ethos of appropriate development.

Since the early 1980s, his burgeoning writings in articles and books have detailed why and how the most marginalised, historically excluded and most powerless groups in society should and could be put at the heart of the processes of research, policy formulation, decision making and project implementation in development. He identified and popularised notions of 'Farmer First', for example, and 'challenged' the professions (of academia and within state and donor structures) to change their values, and the ways and with whom, they work to deliver the 'reversals' required.

BOX 10.2

The sustainable livelihoods framework (SLF)

The 'sustainable livelihoods framework' is an analytical framework that was developed in the 1990s. It has been most well developed in relation to rural livelihoods, but is also increasingly applied in wider contexts and to cross-cutting themes.

A livelihood comprises:

> the capabilities, assets (stores, resources, claims and access) and activities required for a means of living: a livelihood is sustainable which can cope with and recover from stress and shocks, maintain or enhance its capabilities and assets, and provide sustainable livelihood opportunities for the next generation; and which contributes net benefits to other livelihoods at the local and global levels in the long and short term.
>
> (Chambers and Conway, 1992: 7–8)

The framework aims to help in the understanding and analysis of the livelihoods of poor people, and to assist in the identification of appropriate entry points

and sequencing of, more effective development policy and interventions. It is a simplification of real life and does not attempt to represent that complex reality directly, but rather to ease the identification of the main factors affecting people's livelihoods and the typical relationships between them. It is

> essentially people-centred and aims to explain, in a necessarily abstract and simplified way, the relationships between people, their livelihoods, and their environments, (macro) policies, and all kinds of institutions.
>
> (Neefjes, 2000: 82)

Substantial development and application of the framework has been funded by the UK Department for International Development (DfID) and evolved through the research and practical activities of DfID, UNDP, CARE and Oxfam during the 1990s (Carney et al., 1999). It is used as a tool in raising the understanding of local livelihoods, for planning new development

BOX 10.2 (continued)

activities and in the monitoring and evaluation of development interventions.

The 'asset pentagon' is at the core of the SLF, as shown in Figure 10.2. Five asset categories, or types of capital that people may or may not have as a basis for pursuing their livelihoods, are identified. More fully, these capitals are:

1 Human capital: the skills, knowledge, ability to work and good health. It is both a means of achieving livelihood outcomes and an end in itself; overcoming a lack of education, for example, can be a primary livelihood objective.
2 Social capital: in the context of the SLF is taken to mean the social resources (networks, membership of groups, relationships of trust, access to wider institutions of society) upon which people draw in pursuit of their livelihood objectives. Social resources may be enhanced through networks that increase people's ability to work together and to access wider institutions, such as political or civic bodies. Relationships of trust and exchange also provide the basis for many informal safety nets among the poor.
3 Natural capital: the natural resource stocks from which resource flows and services useful for livelihoods are derived. These may include assets

used directly in production, such as land or trees, and less tangible public goods such as biodiversity or the atmosphere.

4 Physical capital: the basic infrastructure and producer goods needed to enable people to meet their basic needs and function more productively. These typically include secure shelter, affordable energy, adequate water and sanitation and access to transport and information.
5 Financial capital: the financial resources which are available to people such as savings, credit, remittances or pensions, that provide different livelihood options.

A large part of people's asset status, however, is the external environment in which people operate, termed the 'vulnerability context' in the SLF. Fire or flood can (and do) devastate the livelihoods of the poor. The term vulnerability is used to draw attention to how the poorest groups often have very little control over many of the factors that are responsible, directly or indirectly, for their poverty. Fire and flood would be considered natural 'shocks' within the framework, in that they are largely unpredictable. Other shocks may be economic, conflict scenarios and shocks relating to human, livestock or crop health.

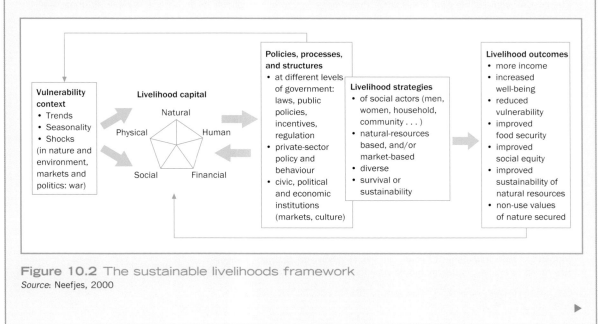

Figure 10.2 The sustainable livelihoods framework
Source: Neefjes, 2000

BOX 10.2 (continued)

Changes to the vulnerability context can also occur through 'trends', the source of which may similarly lie in the economy, natural resources, in governance or population issues, but are generally more predictable than shocks. 'Seasonality' in terms of prices, production, health and employment opportunities, is certainly one of the biggest and most enduring sources of hardship and a strong determinant of vulnerability among the poor, whose margins may be very small.

The arrows within the framework, as shown in Figure 10.2, are used to suggest that policies, processes and structures, at various levels and spheres, can influence this vulnerability context. Government fiscal or health policy, for example, can shape particularly the non-natural trends and shocks.

Furthermore, the arrows are used to confirm that there is a need to think beyond people's assets per se in any context, to consider how these are transformed into 'livelihood outcomes', via varied processes and structures.

'Livelihood strategy' refers to the range and combination of activities and choices people undertake to achieve their livelihood goals. The outcomes of those strategies are diverse. A number of categories of outcome are listed in the diagram, and give a sense of what motivates people to behave as they do. These can assist agencies in considering how likely people are to respond to new initiatives, and can also be used to identify performance indicators in project monitoring.

Table 10.5 Strengths and weaknesses of the livelihood approach in development

Strengths

➤ Highlights the flexibility and dynamism of livelihood systems
➤ Takes a people-centred approach to understanding the struggles of the poor in diverse rural contexts
➤ Recognises the multi-dimensional nature of poverty embracing economic, social, cultural, ecological and political aspects
➤ Emphasises what people have rather than what they lack, and in turn people as active agents rather than passive victims in development
➤ Exposes the difference between the aspirations and priorities of rural people and those of policy makers and helps explain the often disappointing outcomes of rural development initiatives
➤ Encourages holistic, multi-disciplinary research and participatory ways of learning between local people and outsiders
➤ Embraces the diversity that comprises the realities of rural living and counteracts the limitations of single sector approaches to complex rural development problems
➤ Is a framework that sets out many possible areas which influence livelihoods and different ways of approaching particular research questions
➤ Is sufficiently flexible and has evolved and adapted to address new issues whilst retaining the core of the perspective

Weaknesses

➤ Is too complicated to be useful in practice
➤ Has the potential to romanticise poverty and diverts attention from the fact that poverty is 'bad'
➤ Emphasis can be on coping and keeping a position rather than finding ways out of poverty
➤ The focus on assets and capabilities has been to the relative neglect of the broader structures of society that shape peoples' choices and actions
➤ Gives insufficient attention to power and politics at a local level and with wider structures of inequality
➤ Has been dominated by practitioners and researchers engaged in local level development with lack of engagement with longer term trajectories of economic globalisation and agrarian changes
➤ Has failed to address issues including violence and conflict, gender and climate change

Source: compiled from Scoones, 2009; Zoomers, 2014; Levine, 2014, Carr, 2014.

The livelihood approach was taken up enthusiastically in the late 1990s by many institutions. The newly formed Department for International Development in the UK promoted the approach extensively, including through financing further research, and in practice, through making it central to their institutional goal for poverty elimination. Oxfam and CARE International, as two large NGOs with established programmes to address global inequality and basic needs for the poorest respectively, also introduced the approach into their activities. It became part of the mandate of UNDP as an approach for achieving sustainable human development. Scoones (2009: 179) refers to a 'snowballing of interest' and 'a veritable avalanche of papers' emerging around the end of the 1990s/early 2000s, as the approach became more central to development planning and was applied including across forestry, livestock, health and urban development. It has also been used to open up themes including migration, HIV/AIDS discussions and disaster responses. With this emerging research and practice, the approach has had its strong advocates and critics. Table 10.5 summarises some of the considered advantages and weaknesses of the livelihood approach.

It is acknowledged that the approach rather 'fell out of favor' by the mid-2000s as development debates became dominated by neo-liberal thinking and economists 'who favored an emphasis on national scale transformation rather than the use of approaches suited to local-level analysis' (Thulstrup, 2015: 353). However, it is again being argued to be a very valuable approach in the context of resource management and rural development, particularly as a number of international organisations and donors have recently begun to focus on small-scale agriculture and family farming (see FAO, 2014). The concept of 'resilience' is also increasingly applied in understanding climate change adaptation, as seen in Chapter 6, and draws directly on the ability of livelihoods to cope with, and recover from, stresses and shocks through both temporary adjustments and longer-term shifts in livelihood strategies. Box 10.3 considers the characteristics of pastoral-based livelihoods in drylands and how diversity and flexibility have enabled survival in the unpredictable physical environments of dryland regions. The Box also identifies current concerns for the increased vulnerability of pastoral systems to environmental change and how these may be underpinned by weaknesses in past approaches to rangeland management.

Box 10.3

Adapting to environmental change: the case of pastoral livelihoods

Pastoralists are people who 'derive most of their income or sustenance from keeping domestic livestock in conditions where most of the feed that their livestock eat is natural forage rather than cultivated fodders and pastures' (Sandford, 1983: 1). As such, mobility is central to pastoral livelihoods, in moving livestock to exploit new growth of flora in response to local rainfall patterns and ecological niches, for example (Plate 10.3).

Pastoral based livelihoods are found most commonly in arid and semi-arid dryland regions, such as the Sahel and the Horn of Africa, in the Middle East and Central Asia. These dryland ecosystems are characterised by high temperatures and high rainfall variability and recurrent and unpredictable droughts (MEA, 2005). They also provide important global environmental services, including the storing of an estimated 34% of the global stock of carbon dioxide (IFAD, 2011).

Pastoralism based livelihoods have evolved over centuries and the adaptation strategies of pastoral communities to changing environmental conditions, as well as the longer-term shifts in livelihoods strategies in response to actual or anticipated climatic stimuli, are long-studied. Interest in these adaptations and shorter term, 'coping strategies', whereby adjustments are in response to change or to mitigate shocks and stresses on livelihood, has also been re-invigorated

▶

BOX 10.3 (continued)

Plate 10.3 Cattle being taken to Ballyera market, Niger
(*photo*: Mark Edwards, Still Pictures)

recently as climate changes are expected to increase climatic extremes in the drylands and increase water stress (see Opiyo et al., 2015; Headey et al., 2014).

However, pastoralism has frequently been misunderstood in development literatures, with persistent narratives of pastoralists overgrazing rangelands, keeping herds in excess of 'carrying capacities' and being key actors in the degradation and desertification of dryland ecosystems (see Leach and Mearns, 1996). Furthermore, 'there are wide gaps between pastoral policy prescriptions and the ways pastoralists actually manage their herd and rangelands' (Adams, 2009: 228).

For example, pastoral development policies have focused on the production of slaughtered cattle products, such as meat and hides, whereas it is products from (live) stock, such as milk or blood and from a mix of species, that are more typically valued in indigenous systems (Adams, 2009). Another common misunderstanding has been that pastoralists do not engage in cultivation or wage employment. Table 10.6 confirms the range of economic activities beyond livestock, amongst pastoralist groups in the Somali region of Ethiopia. Natural resource based activities are

evidently of key importance, but include also some services and employment that depend on local markets.

Whilst a completely nomadic lifestyle is now quite rare across the drylands, with many pastoralists relying on a combination of seasonal movements and engaging in cultivation to a greater or lesser extent (and/or members of the household and part of the livestock herd engaging in migratory elements), mobility remains essential – for production, trade and survival. However, too often, policies have also served to restrict the mobility of pastoralists. This is seen very overtly in policies of sedentarisation, such as under the Tribal Grazing Lands Policy implemented in Botswana from 1975, that centered on fenced, bore-hole based ranches and sedentarised livestock production, with the aims to reduce environmental pressure and foster social and economic development in the Kalahari. However, it has been much criticised, including for its suggested role in aggravating desertification, and for enhancing rural poverty and social inequality. Thomas et al. (2000) suggest that the impacts of the policy have not been entirely negative, nor has it specifically caused severe degradation of the resource base. What they do assert, however, is that

BOX 10.3 (continued)

1. Livestock: rearing animals (cattle, camels, sheep, goats)
2. Farming: cereal crops (sorghum, maize, wheat)
3. Natural products: firewood
4. Natural products: charcoal
5. Livestock: dairy products (milk, butter, ghee, cheese)
6. Craftwork: basket-making, mat-making
7. Farming: pulses (beans, cow-pea, chick-pea)
8. Services: selling tea, coffee, cake, bread
9. Farming: oil crops (sesame, sunflower)
10. Trading: livestock (cattle, sheep, goats, camels)
11. Farming: vegetables (onion, tomato, pumpkin)
12. Natural products: construction materials (grass, poles)
13. Employment: salaried job
14. Services: religious teacher (Koranic)
15. Services: traditional healer
16. Employment: daily labourer
17. Farming: root crops (Irish potato, sweet potato)
18. Farming: fruits (mango, papaya, banana, orange)
19. Farming: khat
20. Livestock: rearing chickens (selling eggs)

Source: compiled from Devereux, 2006.

future policies that impact on livestock production and residents in rural areas need to be underpinned with a clearer knowledge of resource-use practices prior to policy implementation, a stronger and better implemented social component, and a clear understanding of the nature of likely environmental impacts, including their relationship to natural environmental variability.

(Thomas et al., 2000: 340)

Restrictions on mobility have also come more indirectly through a range of processes including conflict over national borders and with settled cultivators, through bush encroachment and changing disease ecologies, with water scarcity, through urban developments and large infrastructures including dams and through private enclosures of land for commercial crop production (see Headey et al., 2014; de Jode,

2009). It is increasingly understood that the loss of lands and pasture, and policies that have restricted mobility on behalf of pastoral communities, are key underlying drivers of their enhanced vulnerability, particularly in breaking down traditional methods of coping with drought.

Substantial re-thinking of pastoral-based systems of livelihood and previous policy approaches has occurred with what's termed, 'new ecological thinking', and the revision of the 'equilibrium view' of range management (see Scoones, 1995). New ecological thinking centres on understanding the 'unpredictable variability' of arid and semi-arid ecosystems where,

ecosystem state and productivity are largely driven by rainfall and pastoral strategies are designed to track environmental variation (taking advantage of wet years and coping with dry ones), rather than being conservative (seeking a steady-state equilibrial output). . . . Once this is appreciated, much of what appeared to be perversity or conservatism on the part of pastoralists is revealed to be highly adaptive.

(Adams, 2009: 231)

In turn, notions of a single 'carrying capacity' of the ecosystem, used to determine the number of people and livestock that can be supported without setting in motion processes of land degradation, are challenged. As Homewood and Rogers (1987) suggest:

The unpredictable nature of the environment is the central factor affecting not only attempts to measure productivity and population density in semiarid rangelands, but also the applicability of the concept of carrying capacity that is used to link the two. Irregular rainfall falling at unpredictable places and times results in unpredictable primary production. Measures of grassland productivity may be accurate but are only valid for a particular place and time and do not support extrapolation to a wider or longer term.

(Quoted in Mortimore, 1998: 73)

Similarly, Scoones (1995: 26) reflects on the contrasting approaches of conventional range management and indigenous strategies:

▶

BOX 10.3 (continued)

Stocking rate [numbers/area/time] adjustments have always concentrated on the changing of animal numbers, rather than seeking management options that manipulated area or time. Pastoralists operating in the non-equilibrium environments of the drylands use the range of strategies, but flexible movement and spatial and temporal adjustments are the key to success.

The insights of new ecological thinking continue to present substantial challenges to conventional approaches to range management and the development of pastoralism in dryland areas. It is recognised that there is need for more support for herders, who are operating under an increasingly difficult policy environment and which is undermining traditional adaptive strategies (Devereux, 2006; Adams, 2009). But, rather than mass resettlement, for

example, it is understood that a diversity of livelihood possibilities need to be supported and an expansion in people's options to spread risks and retain flexibility. Mobility remains important, but options for herders to move in and out of stock-keeping also need to be ensured. Supporting tenure of key dry-season grazing sites, promoting better services in animal health and education and promoting human rights are all considered key in future pastoral development policies. As Devereux (2006: 171) summarises:

Flexibility is the key to pastoralist survival in an unpredictable environment, and policy-makers need to learn from the pastoralists and to plan for unpredictability – to allow for alternative scenarios that might or might not occur, or that might occur for some people but not for others.

'Older' challenges in rural development

The persistence of rural poverty and hunger

In 2000, Amartya Sen in his groundbreaking work on *Development as Freedom* (see Key thinker box in Chapter 1) identified a range of new challenges for development into the coming century. However, he also identified how the rural areas of the Global South continue to host the major and persistent 'old' problems in development – of hunger and poverty. In 2000, some 785 million people were chronically undernourished, currently that figure is 793 million (FAO, 2015). Whilst 72 of 129 countries have achieved the Millennium Development Goal 1 target to halve the proportion of chronically undernourished people, regional progress has been varied. It was largely unachieved across Southern and Eastern Africa, for example, and worldwide, 'rural people make up a high percentage of the hungry and malnourished' (FAO, 2015: 42).

The effects of undernourishment impact throughout the lifecycle and start at birth, as seen in Figure 10.3. Undernourished women are more likely to give birth to

underweight children, and underweight children are more likely to die during their early months. Childhood malnourishment is also associated with growth stunting and slower development, including in entering and progressing through school, and higher susceptibility to chronic illness later in life. Adequate nutrition is essential for good health and physical and cognitive development, as well as for economic prosperity. Food availability and access is key to adequate nutrition, but so too are factors such as access to safe water and sanitation that substantially influence health. In short, there are close links between undernutrition and poverty.

Table 10.7 confirms that poverty rates are higher in rural areas than urban areas across the world. Whilst rates are falling, this is occurring more quickly in urban than rural areas. Figure 10.4 shows the continued importance of agriculture in rural areas, particularly in regions such as South Asia and sub-Saharan Africa where levels of urbanisation are lower than in other major world regions. Globally, agriculture remains overwhelmingly based on 'family farms', owner operated and largely reliant on household labour (Lowder, 2016: FAO, 2014) as discussed further below. Family farming often provides a fallback position for people where job opportunities outside agriculture are limited and/or unstable

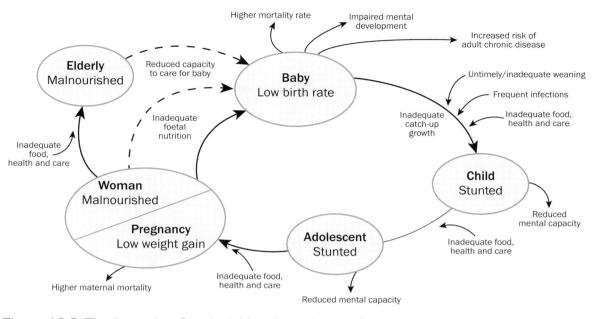

Figure 10.3 The impacts of malnutrition through the life cycle
Source: adapted from FAO (n.d.).

such that labour is often underemployed and labour productivity is less (World Bank, 2013a). The close association between smallholder farming, poverty and food insecurity is recognised as a persistent challenge and a required contemporary policy focus (FAO, 2014). Those countries making most progress on the hunger targets within MDG1, for example, were those countries investing most in the agricultural sector and particularly in the development of family farming (FAO, 2015).

Rural areas also continue to be poorly served in relation to urban centres in terms of a range of services that are key to supporting good nutrition, good health and opportunities for development. Figure 10.5 shows that whilst there has been some progression towards closing the urban–rural gaps in access to safe water, from a 49% difference in coverage in 1990 to 32% in 2010, levels of urban service delivery continue to be significantly higher than in rural areas. Such disparities have a major bearing on the development opportunities in rural areas, most overtly through impacting on health, but also more widely in terms of people's ability to engage socially and economically, as discussed in Chapter 6. Table 10.8 shows the urban-rural gaps in access to electricity and the often very low levels of rural electrification in a number of countries. Lack of access to electricity in

rural areas has widespread implications including for people's health, as indoor air pollution through the burning of biomass sources is a key cause of ill-health and premature death. Lack of safe and reliable energy supplies also impact on educational opportunities and children's ability to study after dark, as well as on income-earning opportunities, particularly those based within the home (IEA, 2009; Plates 10.4, 10.5). Lack of access to electricity has been identified as a key constraint on the development of non-farm activities in rural areas (World Bank, 2013a).

Mainstreaming gender in rural development

A further 'enduring obstacle' (Potter, 2008a: 121) for rural development, is the persistent lack of recognition of the key role of women in livelihoods and resource management. Despite longstanding work to understand women's 'substantial interest' in environmental resources and their management, gender discrimination in many rural communities continues to be an obstacle to poverty alleviation, to raising agricultural production and to the sustainable management of resources (Potter, 2008a; FAO, 2011). Gender bias has also characterised much previous

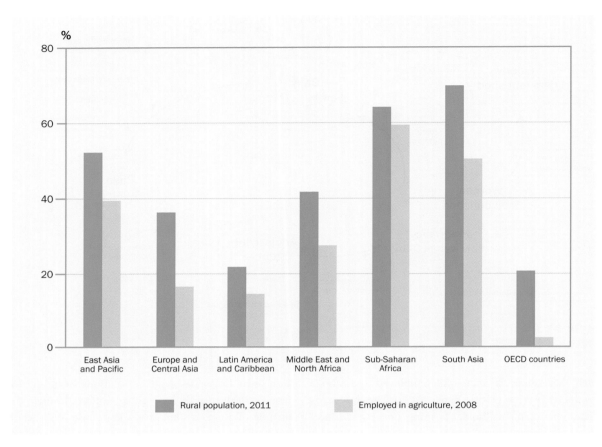

Figure 10.4 Population in rural areas and employment in agriculture
Source: adapted from World Bank (2013) *Global Monitoring Report*.

Table 10.7 Poverty rates in urban and rural areas by world region (1990–2008). Share of the population below $1.25/day

	1990		1996		2002		2008	
	Rural	**Urban**	**Rural**	**Urban**	**Rural**	**Urban**	**Rural**	**Urban**
East Asia and Pacific	67.5	24.4	45.9	13.0	39.2	6.9	20.4	4.3
Europe and Central Asia	2.2	0.9	6.3	2.8	4.4	1.1	1.2	0.2
Latin America and the Caribbean	21.0	7.4	20.3	6.3	20.3	8.3	13.2	3.1
Middle East and North Africa	9.1	1.9	5.6	0.9	7.5	1.2	4.1	0.8
South Asia	50.5	40.1	46.1	35.2	45.1	35.2	38.0	29.7
Sub-Saharan Africa	55.0	41.5	56.8	40.6	52.3	41.4	47.1	33.6
TOTAL	52.5	20.5	43.0	17.0	39.5	15.1	29.4	11.6

Source: World Bank (2013) *Global Monitoring Report 2013: Rural-Urban Dynamics and the MDGs.*

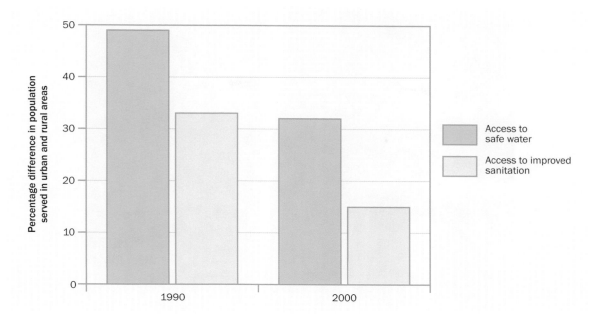

Figure 10.5 Persistent urban–rural gaps in access to water and sanitation
Source: adapted from World Bank, 2013a.

Plate 10.4 Drying cow-dung for use as fuel, India
(*photo*: Jennifer Elliott)

Plate 10.5 Solar energy, Botswana
(*photo*: Jennifer Elliott)

Table 10.8 Access to electricity in rural and urban areas (percentage of population served) in selected countries

Country	Rural	Urban
Bangladesh	49.3	90.2
Bolivia	72.5	99.3
Botswana	23.9	71.0
Cambodia	18.8	91.3
Ethiopia	7.6	100
India	69.7	98.2
Indonesia	92.9	99.1
Malawi	2.0	37.1
Nigeria	34.4	83.6
Peru	72.9	98.3
South Africa	66.9	96.6

Source: World Bank, 2015c

development policy in key sectors of rural development. In fisheries, for example, the bulk of attention has been focused on production goals that have favoured the male-dominated catching sector, where men are more regularly engaged in off-shore and higher value fishing activities, and women are more heavily involved in intertidal fishing of invertebrates and fish processing. Similarly, forest policies have supported timber-related production and higher value non-timber product development, principally men's engagements with forests, rather than being focused on how women use forests, that are more often associated with fuel and animal fodder collection and the collection of products for home consumption (Leisher et al., 2015; Plate 10.6). Many policies for the commercialisation of agriculture have effectively excluded women, who generally own smaller plots of land and tend to concentrate to a greater extent on subsistence crops and sales for local markets (Momsen, 2010).

Yet women have a key role in agriculture, representing 43% of the agricultural labour force worldwide, ranging from approximately 20% in Latin America to 50% in parts of Africa and Asia (FAO, 2011). Women are estimated to provide between 60 and 80 per cent of all food in most parts of the Global South (WB/FAO/IDAD, 2009). 5.4 million women work as fishers and fish-farmers in the primary capture fisheries and aquaculture sectors (FAO, 2012). Many more women are also working in the post-harvest sectors, particularly in fish processing, where women's labour dominates. More than 600 million women depend on agro-forestry farming and forests for their livelihood (Pierce-Colfer et al., 2016). As stated by the Food and Agriculture Organization, 'Women are farmers, workers and entrepreneurs, but almost everywhere they

Plate 10.6 Collecting firewood, Eastern Cape, South Africa
(*photo*: Tony Binns)

face more constraints than men in accessing productive resources, markets and services (2010: 3). This 'gender gap' is understood by the FAO to hinder productivity and compromises the achievement of broader economic and social development goals. The FAO estimates that if women had the same resources as men, agricultural productivity in the Global South could rise from 2.5 to 4% and reduce world hunger by 12–17%. More profoundly, Sweetman (2015: 32) asserts, 'development requires the perspectives and solutions of women, and women require equality, human rights and justice'.

The Key idea box introduces the concept of gender mainstreaming that now informs the approach to gender issues and women's rights across many arenas and most organisations in development. It confirms the substantial range of initiatives that have been taken to raise understanding of how women and men's interest in development, including in resource use, can be very different, to changes within organisations and institutions to get them 'right for women', and to addressing gender issues in practice. However, too often project initiatives have worked within existing household divisions of labour, addressing women's immediate 'practical gender needs' (Pearson, 2000) and 'lumping women's varied interests together' (Middleton et al., 1993), rather than substantially addressing more fundamental, underlying issues of power and gender relations.

Key idea

Gender mainstreaming

Gender mainstreaming is an approach to women's rights and gender issues that emerged substantially from the UN world Conference on Women, held in Beijing in 1995. The UN commited to working to mainstream gender across the entire UN system as the basis for the advancement of its women and gender equality goals. The UN defines gender mainstreaming as follows:

▶

Key idea (continued)

Mainstreaming a gender perspective is the process of assessing the implications for women and men of any planned action, including legislation, policies or programmes, in all areas and at all levels. It is a strategy for making women's as well as men's concerns and experiences an integral dimension for the design, implementation, monitoring and evaluation of policies and programmes in all political, economic and societal spheres so that women and men benefit equally and inequality is not perpetuated. The ultimate goal of mainstreaming is to achieve gender equality.

(United, Nations, 1997:1)

It has been widely adopted across the spectrum of development organisations, with some form of gender mainsreaming now part of the work of international organisations, governments and civil soceity organisations across many sectors. In many cases, work has been focused on institutionalising gender mainstreaming, that is looking within the organisations and 'getting them right for women' (Goetz, 1995, cited in Sweetman 2015: 26). This includes the development of gender policies, management procedures, recruitment and tools used in planning and implementation, to ensure they support gender equality and womens rights. This is seen as essential to eliminating bias informed by race and class, as well as gender, within the structures and activities of all development organisations. It also fitted well with development and feminist thinking of the 1990s, when debates were dominated by discussions of the role of different social institutions (state, market and civil society) in all areas, and in perpetuating or challenging gender inequality.

However, there has been less work regarding the impact of gender mainstreaming on the beneficiaries involved, those women and men, girls and boys. Many initiatives in practice have involved transfering small amounts of financial resources for women's projects, such as in education, fertility reduction, natural

Plate 10.7 Women's handicraft project, Kathmandu, Nepal
(*photo*: Lola Odessey Waters)

Key idea (continued)

resources management and micro-credit, with anticapted economic and social impacts for women and in turn, their families and wider society (Plate 10.7). This approach rests on ideas that better income for women was essential for gender equality and women's empowerment. However, many programmes and projects, whilst addressing women's immediate needs, often did not challenge existing divisions of labour or improve the status of women. In failing to address the complex structural inequalities that shape the realities of women's lives (the transformative aims of gender mainstreaming as forwarded by the international women's movements), existing power relations remain unchallenged.

Source: compiled using Sweetman, 2015. See *The Routledge Handbook of Gender and Development* for ways in which academics, gender specliasts and feminist organisations and networks are now working 'beyond' gender mainstreaming.

Through the 1990s, many 'Women, Environment and Development' projects sought to work with women on the basis that they were key 'users' and 'managers' of environmental resources (Braidotti et al., 1994). Such projects were built on existing household divisions of labour, whereby women take primary responsibility for the household needs for water and energy, and integrated women into initiatives to develop community wells and woodlots. Whilst their practical needs (access to safe water and reduced time spent in foraging for wood fuel) were met, the more challenging (and transformative in terms of women's empowerment) aspects of changing relations between women and men at household and village levels, often went unaddressed. It is recognised that it is not sufficient to work only with women or to assume that women are a homogenous group. Gender relations are complex and dynamic and issues of class and race, for example, may be as important as gender in shaping outcomes in development (see Coles et al., 2015).

Box 10.4 considers the impacts of a well-known micro-finance programme on women's empowerment in Bangladesh. Micro-finance programmes generated significant interest through the 1990s on behalf of donors and NGOs, including DFID and Oxfam, as a means for addressing poverty, particular amongst the rural poor. These built on the dominant development thinking of the time, which was rooted in market-led growth as seen in Chapter 3. The basis of these micro-finance initiatives was to provide access to credit by poorer groups, that was substantially unavailable through formal banking institution, and to avoid exploitative relationships that poor people had with local business people and moneylenders. At the time of the first International Micro-Credit Summit in 1997, over 1,000 different micro-finance initiatives were in operation, reaching over 13 million people (75% of whom were women) in over 100 countries of the Global South (Wheat, 2000). Typically, these initiatives made small loans to poor borrowers organised into groups, which used joint-liability structures and peer mentoring for the repayment of loans. Whilst often not explicitly targeted at women, women were regularly found to be the most reliable borrowers. Furthermore, their increased income was most likely to be spent on improvements to family welfare and on children in particular (Pearson, 2000).

However, there remains some dispute, including in the case of the Grameen Bank discussed in Box 10.4, as to the impact of micro-credit on women's empowerment. It is recognised that the outcomes can be highly varied according to the complexities and specificities of gender relations within the household, the community and wider society. It is apparent that in some contexts, women's access to credit does not increase their control over economic activities as the credit in fact facilitates activities controlled by men, and women may just have the responsibility of repayment. As in relation to work on gender and environmental management, it is recognised that there are divergent experiences for particular women in different contexts, and it is a more complex task to substantially change women's status as well as their poverty.

BOX 10.4

The Grameen Bank: poverty alleviation and women's empowerment in rural Bangladesh

The Grameen Bank originated in 1976 as an experimental research project led by economist Professor Muhammad Yunus at Chittagong University. The initial aim of the project was to tackle the serious problem of indebtedness (and the dependence on money lenders) among the rural poor in Bangladesh, through providing loans to households which owned less than 0.5 acres of land.

The word Grameen means 'village' and the project was concerned with assessing whether if the poor received financial help at reasonable terms and conditions, they could then generate productive self-employment without external assistance. Professor Yunus persuaded a local branch of a commercial bank to provide credit at an interest rate of 13 per cent a year, provided he could guarantee recovery of the loans.

The pilot project was successful. In June 1979, the Grameen Bank Project was launched in five districts of Bangladesh, with support from rural branches of commercial banks and the agricultural development bank, and with financial assistance from the state bank of Bangladesh and the International Fund for Agricultural Development. Within a year, 24 branches had been set up, though expansion was constrained by some reluctance from participating banks. A government ordinance in September 1983 transformed the project into the Grameen Bank, a specialised financial institution for the rural poor, in which government has a 60 per cent share and the borrowers 40 per cent.

As Todd (1996: 7) summaries:

> The 'essential Grameen' . . . is an exclusive focus on the poor, with preference to poor women, simple loan procedures administered in the village, small loans repaid weekly and used for any income-generating activity chosen by the woman herself, collective responsibility through groups, bolstered by compulsory group savings, strict credit discipline and close supervision through weekly meetings and home visits.

Each branch of the Grameen Bank covers between 15 and 20 villages, and members of households owning less than 0.5 acres of cultivated land, or with assets with a value equivalent to less than 1.0 acres of medium-quality land, are eligible to receive a loan. In order to receive loans, the poor have to organise themselves into groups and associations and must be prepared to interact with each other. A group should comprise at least five members and several groups from each village constitute a 'centre'. Loans have to be paid back within a year in weekly installments.

The system is based on principles of trust and solidarity, with members operating all the necessary transactions themselves (Huq-Hussain, 2015). The guiding motto of the Bank is 'Take the bank to the people, not the people to the bank', with bank workers often visiting people in their homes to assist with loan arrangements and attending centre meetings. All business is conducted in a transparent manner in front of the members, and an important incentive for regular repayment is the assurance of a new and bigger loan at the end of the repayment cycle.

In 1984, sixteen rules, known as 'decisions' shown in Table 10.9, were introduced that all groups had to adhere to. This 'Social Development Constitution' (Hossain, 1988) for the Bank, moved it from being merely an agency for disbursing loans, into a much wider involvement in the life of the rural poor. As seen, the rules encompass aspects of family well-being, empowerment and social and cultural change.

The Grameen model has been replicated widely within Bangladesh and similar microfinance initiatives are operating in more than fifty countries (Huq-Hussain, 2015). In particular, it has been promoted as a key strategy for empowering women, through providing access to material resources to generate income, expand choices and increase their participation and voice in household decision making and wider social networks. The impacts of micro-credit on women's empowerment are now widely studied. In addition to positive impacts on income, health and labour force

BOX 10.4 (continued)

Table 10.9 The sixteen decisions of the Grameen Bank

1. The four principles of Grameen Bank – discipline, unity, courage and hard work – we shall follow and advance in all walks of our lives
2. We shall bring prosperity to our families
3. We shall not live in dilapidated houses. We shall repair our houses and work towards constructing new houses as soon as possible
4. We shall grow vegetables all the year round. We shall eat plenty of them and sell the surplus
5. During the planting seasons, we shall plant as many seedlings as possible
6. We shall plan to keep our families small. We shall minimise our expenditures. We shall look after our health
7. We shall educate our children and ensure that they can earn enough to pay for their education
8. We shall always keep our children and the environment clean
9. We shall build and use pit latrines
10. We shall drink tube well water. If it is not available, we shall boil water or use alum
11. We shall not take any dowry in our sons' weddings, neither shall we give any dowry in our daughters' weddings. We shall keep the centre free from the curse of dowry. We shall not practice child marriage
12. We shall not inflict any injustice on anyone, neither shall we allow anyone to do so
13. For higher income we shall collectively undertake bigger investments
14. We shall always be ready to help each other. If anyone is in difficulty, we shall all help
15. If we come to know of any breach of discipline in any centre, we shall all go there and help restore discipline
16. We shall introduce physical exercise in all our centres. We shall take part in all social activities collectively

participation, findings include that women experience less spousal violence, are more likely to vote in local and national elections, are more mobile and are more involved in family planning and decisions regarding children's education (see Huq-Hussain, 2015).

However, there remain concerns, including the potential to transfer the burden of household debt onto women (Momsen, 2010). Debate continues over the capacity to address women's strategic, rather than immediate practical, needs through such initiatives. Some studies have shown that male family members may control the loans women received and there are cases of women entering more serious levels of debt. Further research is needed into the processes of repaying loans and regarding the levels of interest involved for particular groups.

The future of the Grameen Bank specifically has come under recent attention. In 2011, Prof. Yunus was removed from his post as managing director of the Bank by the government (that has the power to monitor and regulate the Bank). The official statement was that he had reached retirement age of 60. In 2013, the government changed the ordinance of the Bank, to give them more seats on the Board of Directors and more power to the Chairman, who is a government nominee. Further control over the bank was transferred away from members in 2014, when the government gave the Central Bank of Bangladesh power to appoint the Board. All these moves have created significant resentment on behalf of Bank members, women's activists and Bangladeshi intellectuals (Huq-Hussain, 2015).

The significance of land: agrarian structures and landholding in rural areas

A further ongoing and persistent challenge in rural development concerns land ownership and rights over land and linked resources such as forestry. Indeed,

Middleton et al. (1993: 124) refer to 'two inseparable starting points' in rural development, as the rights of women and questions of land. Agriculture remains fundamental to the economy and society in the rural areas of the Global South, as was seen in Figure 10.4. In turn, patterns of landholding in agrarian economies are key determinants of 'agrarian structure', which concerns the different ways in which land and labour are combined in varying forms of production, as well as the social rela-tions, such as class, which 'structure' the processes of production and reproduction.

Fundamentally, an analysis of agrarian structure attempts to answer the questions: 'Who owns what, does what, gets what and what do they do with it?' (Bernstein, 1992c: 24). Not only do patterns of landownership pro-vide a context in which land and labour are combined in the production process, but land is also often the pri-mary means through which people define their personal, social and political identities. As such, land ownership is a major correlate of political and social prestige in rural areas. Furthermore, since food is the major product of the land, such patterns have clear implications for the relative and absolute well-being of the population (Ghose, 1983). Programmes to actively change patterns of land ownership and/or the tenancy systems con-trolling land use (policies of 'land reform') have featured strongly in both colonial and more recent approaches to regional and national development and are considered in the next section.

Agrarian structures are neither static nor uniform across space. They reflect varied historical experience in rural areas, encompassing factors such as environment, culture and political economy. In many parts of the Global South, colonialism had a significant impact on agrarian structures and processes and the legacy is still seen in terms of patterns of landholding. It needs to be acknowledged that colonialism took diverse forms, was variously imposed, taken up or rejected over time and space, and thereby the legacies have complex geogra-phies (see Williams et al., 2014; Lipton, 2009). However, core regional patterns can be identified and indeed, have been persistent over time. Lipton (2009) for example, in an authoritative review finds relatively little evidence of recent change in the agrarian structures in land scarce countries. Although there are some problems of assess-ing land scarcity and abundance, the majority of farms and farmland areas in the Global South, with the excep-tion of Latin America and the Caribbean, are very small (Lowder et al., 2016) and have been declining as seen in Figure 10.6.

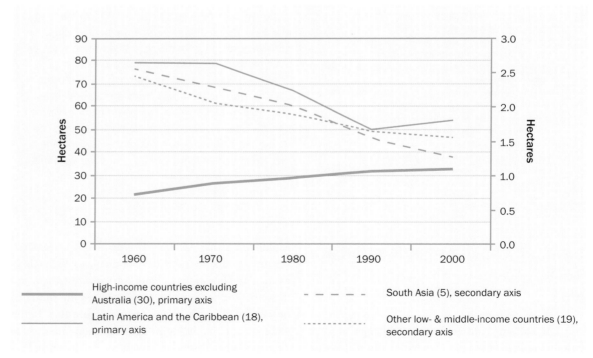

Figure 10.6 Average farm sizes worldwide, 1960–2000
Source: adapted from Lowder et al., 2016.

Latin America

While land is relatively abundant in Latin America, inequality in landownership is marked. Brazil, for example, has one of the most unequal distributions of landholding in the world, where 3% of population owns two-thirds of all arable land (Zobel, 2009). Figure 10.7 identifies that almost half of the total agricultural area in Latin America is operated by a very small number of very large farms, with the vast majority of farms comprising very small landholdings.

The polarisation of landholding in contemporary Latin America is deeply rooted in the colonial history of the region, despite widespread programmes of land reform since independence. In the seventeenth century, Spanish colonists were given rights to expropriate land, originally in return for military service, and were able to levy tribute from indigenous communities in the form of labour or goods (Bernstein, 1992b). With the capital acquired, large landed estates, *latifundia* or *haciendas,* were established, on which peasants typically cultivated land allocated to them, in return for paying rent to the landlord in cash or a share of their crops, or alternatively worked on the landlord's farm in return for a small subsistence plot.

The expansion of this system depended on acquiring further labour and appropriating land from Indians,

a process which was often unpopular and resisted by indigenous communities. For those people who resisted such incorporation, the alternative 'mini fundio' system often proved inadequate for subsistence production, since plots were often too small or located in areas which were marginal for agricultural production. Many small farmers had no alternative but to seek out other sources of income, often through wage employment. Lack of access to land is understood as a key factor in contemporary rural poverty (Inter-American Development Bank, 1998).

Evidently, large-scale agribusiness has been a long-standing feature of agricultural production in Latin America. Following the liberalisation of markets and trade from the 1980s onwards, subsequent policy in the agricultural sector of many Latin American countries has reinforced aspects of the *latifundio* system. It was seen in Chapter 6, for example, that extensive livestock ranching and the establishment of land rights in the Amazon basin led to a rapid expansion of agricultural area (and deforestation) as countries, including Argentina, Brazil, Paraguay and Uruguay sought to increase their position in world markets for products including meat, soy beans and sugar. Whilst small farmers were able to expand into these frontiers, land was often of poor quality and farm sizes quickly became more concentrated (Deininger and Byerlee, 2012). In Brazil, the expansion of soybeans, and

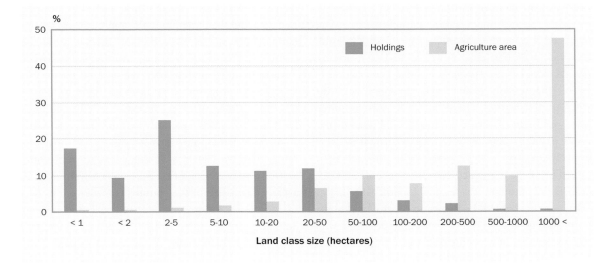

Figure 10.7 Average distribution of farms and farmland areas by land size class in Latin America and the Caribbean
Source: adapted from Lowder et al., 2016.

other crops, has been largely in the *Cerrado* region. Agricultural production rests substantially on highly mechanised cultivation on large farms, with many companies operating more than 100,000 hectares of cropland in the region (Deininger and Byerlee, 2012). As such, employment and poverty impacts have been low (Deininger and Byerlee, 2012).

Asia

Landholding in Asia is heavily concentrated, as in Latin America. But due to land scarcity, the size of farms in Asia is much smaller and the cultivation of land tends to be more decentralised through systems of tenancy and sharecropping. 74% of all farms globally are located in Asia (35% of all farms are in China which also has the largest share of the world's agricultural area). Across Asia as a whole, 75–80% of all farms are under 2 hectares in size (Lowder et al., 2016).

Much of Asia has a relatively recent colonial history, and the legacy of that period is evident in present agrarian structures, particularly with respect to the introduction and reinforcement of private property ownership. Before British rule in India, for example, property rights had rested with the community, with village heads allocating individual rights to land, supervising the management of common resources, such as meadows and rangelands, and collecting taxes in kind. Under Crown rule from 1868, a system of private property rights in land and taxation payable in cash was introduced. Under the *zamindari* system of landholding, which was particularly widespread in northern India, de facto landlords were created as intermediaries between the tenants (the real landowners) and the British Administration. These 'landlords' were required to pass on to the government treasury an agreed percentage of land rents collected. In return, they were effectively given private property rights through their assigned privilege to extract rents from tenants at whatever level they thought was feasible (Shariff, 1987).

This system enabled the British to control land in the colony and to extract rents from the peasants who worked it without intervening directly in the production process. Rents were not reinvested to enhance the productivity of farming and, unlike the communal land system, landlords had no duties to the tenant, such as

providing assistance in times of hardship. Although peasant cash crop production grew, indebtedness and landlessness also rose and peasants found themselves subordinated to a newly created class of overlords – the landlords and moneylenders (Bernstein, 1992a).

At India's independence in 1947, 50 per cent of the land area was held by approximately 4 per cent of the rural population. Some 27 per cent of the population were landless, and a further 53 per cent had farms of less than 5 acres (Ghose, 1983). In the 1950s, India abolished the *zamindari* system of rent collecting intermediaries, but the process of redistributing land rights and improving the terms of tenancy 'remains very incomplete' (Lipton, 2009: 284). In 1996, the median farm size in India remained less than one hectare (Hazell et al., 2010).

Programmes of tenancy reform as part of strategies for rural development are a widespread feature of many countries in Asia post-independence, as discussed further in the next section. In East Asia prior to 1945, many countries featured middle-to-large owner farms with employees, many small owner farmers and many small farms sharecropped on substantially 'harsh terms' (Lipton, 2009: 162). Responses to tenancy reform included 'revolutionary collectivism', that is the reduction or removal or private ownership and collectivisation of tenure, such as in China, Vietnam, Laos and Cambodia. Another response was to impose a ceiling on the amount of land that could be held privately, the approach in Japan, South Korea and Taiwan. In countries including Indonesia, Malaysia and the Philippines, the approach was a combination of tenancy reform and resettlement of households.

In some cases, these programmes of land reform have been subsequently reversed. China, for example, moved to a programme of de-collectivisation between 1977 and 1984, returning farms to small-scale household tenure. Most recently, China has introduced changes in land policy facilitating private ownership, rather than use rights, which may lead to some consolidation and reversing of recent trends toward declining average farm size in the country (Lowder et al., 2016). In Indonesia, the government redistributed 0.85 million hectares of lands to 1.29 million families in the early 1960s, principally in Java which is the most land-hungry region of the country (Lipton, 2009). However, the average lands received were small, land reform has substantially stalled since then and land remains short in the country. In 2008, 14 million farmers depended on agricultural plots of less than one hectare (FAO cited in Lipton, 2009: 292).

Africa

In broad terms, African agrarian structures are more widely characterised by communal systems of landownership, a lower concentration of landholding, and less widespread tenancy and leasing arrangements than in Asia or Latin America. At a continental scale, and in comparison with other major world regions, land is relatively abundant in Africa. This 'comparative advantage' of Africa continues to frame discussions of addressing future global food requirements and for poverty alleviation within the continent. However, over 60% of landholdings in sub-Saharan Africa are of less than one hectare in size (Lowder et al., 2016).

Colonialism occurred much later in Africa than elsewhere and, generally speaking, in many countries, peasant farmers were neither incorporated into a system of private property rights, nor had their land expropriated. However, there are some exceptions to this rule, particularly in French colonial countries such as Cameroon, Madagascar, Guinea and Ivory Coast, where large-scale European settlement occurred. The so-called White Highlands in British-ruled Kenya are another example of this.

In southern Africa, the expropriation of land for European agriculture forced African farmers into 'reserve' areas. These reserves were often more marginal for cultivation, and together with policies such as compulsory labour recruitment, the active blocking of opportunities for cash cropping by African farmers and many more indirect means such as policies on soil conservation, African labour was released into European agriculture, mining and infrastructural development projects.

Colonial interests in increasing cash crop production in Africa were generally undertaken without fundamental change to the system of landholding. However, whilst peasant producers remained in control of their lands, the 'colonial triad' (Watts, 1984) of taxation, export commodity production and monetisation impacted significantly on the relations of production throughout the continent. In short, land and labour became goods to be bought and sold, and there was a decline, for example, in the 'moral economy' in rural areas – the reciprocal sharing of tasks and goods

within communities – that exacerbated vulnerability to drought and food insecurity for many (Watts, 1984).

The legacy of colonial policies on agrarian structures in Africa is therefore extremely varied. Rarely in Africa today is there a neat distinction between imposed systems of individual freehold ownership and customary African tenure, as has often been suggested. Rather, as Siddle and Swindell (1990: 72) proposed,

> diverse and parallel systems of tenure and rights to farm, which include communal usufructary systems, loaning, pledging, different forms of labour renting associated with squatters and share contractors, fixed rents, leasing freehold purchase and land nationalisation. These different forms of landholding and farming are rooted in different relations of production underwritten by religion, kinship and political authority, as well as varying with ecological circumstance.

As seen above, there is currently much debate concerning the rapid expansion of large-scale corporate (transnational and domestic) acquisitions of contested lands and common lands in the Global South that are particularly pertinent in sub-Saharan Africa, where at least 60% of these transactions to date have been (Hall et al., 2014). There is widespread concern regarding the negative impacts on land and resource rights for local farmers, pastoralists and forest users, and for the deepening of the dualism between small- and large-scale farming on the continent, whereby,

> large-scale farms engaged in capitalist production mainly for export, while smallholder farms gradually disappear or are incorporated as part of contract-farming arrangements, with the former peasanty proletarianised, providing low paid labour to the new estates and plantations.
>
> (Hall et al. 2014: 263)

Land reform as a strategy for rural development

> At one time or another, but especially since 1960, virtually every country in the world has passed land reform laws . . . Yet in spite of decades of land reform activities, land ownership remains

extremely skewed, concentration of land owner-ship is almost universally increasing, the mass of landless is growing rapidly, and the extent of rural poverty and malnutrition has reached horrendous proportions.

(de Janvry, 1984: 263)

This quotation alludes to the widespread and long-standing recognition of the linkages between access to land and the prospects for human development. It also points to how the outcomes of land reform activities may not live up to their anticipated benefits. Whilst there are multiple definitions and objectives for land reform, Lipton (2009) summarises that land reform 'matters' mainly for its effect on poor people, and that:

At least 1.5 billion people today have some farm-land as a result of land reform, and are less poor, or not poor, as a result. But huge, inefficient land ine-qualities remain, or have re-emerged, in many low income countries. Land reform remains both 'unfinished business' and 'alive and well'.

(p. 8)

Land reform programmes may take many different forms, but generally involve tenancy reforms and/or changes in the distribution and scale of land owner-ship. 'Land reform' is commonly distinguished from wider 'agrarian reforms' that promote landholders' access to credit, markets and extension support, for example, the inputs required to enhance productivity and sustainability. However, as Hall et al. (2014: 261) point out, 'any successful "land reform" is necessarily accompanied by such supporting measures, rendering the distinction redundant'.

In practice, land reform may involve such measures as the elimination of certain kinds of rent or cropping arrangements, the creation of new kinds of farm, such as cooperatives or state farms, or the expropriation and redistribution of lands, including through the imple-mentation of ceilings on ownership and resettlement programmes. The objectives of land reform may com-bine social, political and economic intentions, including enhancing social stability, increasing political participa-tion and patronage, widening economic opportunity and promoting more efficient use of land and labour. As was considered in the previous section, any intervention

in the prevailing agrarian structures has implications not only for the material conditions of rural life, but also for personal and social identity, for power relations within and between households and for traditions and customs associated with land, its use and its significance within society.

The political significance of land reform is con-firmed by the number of countries which initiated programmes following their gaining independence or other major political events. In cases such as post-revolutionary Ethiopia in 1974, China in 1958, Cuba in 1959 and Tanzania in 1964, the radical nature of land reform is confirmed by the new forms of societal organisation created. In Africa, radical land reform programmes following independence were most likely in settler-dominated regimes, such as Zimbabwe (see Case study).

Programmes of land reform have also been under-taken with more reformist intentions, such as to prevent the accumulation of large landholdings, or to enhance security of tenure. In South Korea, a major programme of land reform initiated after the Japanese colonial period in 1949, required those landlords holding more than 3 hectares to turn over lands to tenants, in return for compensation from the state. In Taiwan, during a programme of land reform in the 1950s, rents were cut to a maximum of 37.5 per cent of crop value from a figure in excess of 70 per cent (Barke and O'Hare, 1991). Land reform in the Philippines involved the conversion of share tenancies to fixed rents in the 1970s. In India, the exploitative tenancy arrangements inherited from the British colonial period were identified within the first five-year plan of 1950 as fundamental barriers to raising agricultural production and as the source of much social injustice in the rural sector. A four-fold programme of land reform was subsequently intro-duced in 1951.

The specific impacts of land reform are hard to iden-tify in many cases, since they often arise from diverse programmes and are frequently implemented in phases and in conjunction with wider agrarian reform mea-sures. As Lipton (2009) identifies, the outcomes of land reform for the poor depends as much on how it affects employment, non-farm activity, GDP growth and distri-bution and the village status and power of the poor as it does on land transfers. Many programmes remain incomplete or evolve and there is frequently a lack of data monitoring their performance. They often demand considerable financial investment such as in infrastructures, in compensation and in wider support and extension activities. Large amounts of aid from the USA are generally considered to have been a critical factor in the relative success of South Korea's land reform programme, for example, whereas underfunding is deemed a principal reason for the failure of land redistribution efforts in the Philippines (Dixon, 1990).

International support for programmes of land reform were prominent in the 1960s and 1970s as seen in Table 10.3. At that time, the prevailing development ideologies stressed active, 'top-down' intervention in rural areas and agriculture to both enhance economic growth and spread the benefits of growth. In addition, the decolonisation era of that time saw extensive reforms, particularly in sub-Saharan Africa and Asia (Hall et al., 2014). Cold War politics were also important in cases of international support for programmes of land reform, the USSR supporting, and at times imposing, collective agriculture and the breakup of private property in Eastern Europe, and the USA through its 'Alliance for Progress' (1962–4) providing aid to land reform in Latin America to counter the spread of communist approaches. However, Lipton (2009) cautions that this is an over-simplification of support for land reform from Cold War leaders and argues that the end of the Cold War is not a good argument for suggesting that land reform is no longer a necessary component of rural development as some suggest.

However, international commitment to land reform waned substantially during the 1980s (FAO, 1991; Hall et al., 2014), although the end of the Cold War led to a resurgence of programmes of decollectivisation and privatising land reforms in many post-socialist countries. Since 2000, and particularly through the influence of the World Bank and IMF, there has been enhanced interest in market-assisted (rather than state-led) land reform programmes. Many of these centre on improving the legal, technical and institutional framework to enhance tenure security amongst small-scale land holders (Hall et al., 2013), i.e. on land titling rather than redistribution of land. This is part of the recent 'return to agriculture' within World Bank policy, supporting the promotion of owner-operated farms on both efficiency and equity grounds. Secure land rights are considered the basis for facilitating land transactions and the move to more efficient land uses. Security of rights to resources, including land, is recognised as essential for more sustainable rural development (Elliott, 2013). The World Bank also recognises a continued role for redistributive land reforms, such as in South Africa, where agrarian structures continue to be highly dualistic and inequitable.

Increasingly, the drivers of, and support for, land reform is coming through internal dynamics within countries of the Global South, including through spreading democracy, strengthening political organisation and civil society activism (Lipton, 2009). In recent years, concerns around food prices and food security, and the threats to small farmers and indigenous people through recent large-scale land transfers, have also focused attention back on land reform and redistribution (Jacobs, 2009).

An outstanding challenge is the gender discrimination that persists in land policy and practice (Hall et al., 2013) and the need to address the often detrimental impacts that land reform has had on women. Gender has been a neglected topic within the study of land reform, despite the strong case for the potential of legal land rights to transform women's lives (Jacobs, 2014). Whilst many land reform programmes have allowed widows or divorcees to hold land or land permits, land titles within state sponsored redistribution programmes are almost universally allocated to the 'household head' (assumed to be male) on behalf of the family unit (Jacobs, 2014). Negative outcomes include loss of women's existing customary land rights, loss of income sources or loss of control over the proceeds of their labour. Mainstreaming gender into land and agrarian reform programmes so that they do not marginalise women is recognised as a justice issue. Women are often the main 'tillers' of the land and therefore should be able to control land and the proceeds from agriculture. It is also identified as an efficiency issue – improving women's access to land and secure tenure can have direct impacts on farm productivity (FAO, 2013) and in the longer term improve family welfare.

Case study

Experiences of land reform in Zimbabwe

On independence in 1980, the new majority government in Zimbabwe quickly committed itself to a programme of land reform. The objectives included overcoming the dualist agricultural history of the country, satisfying the political demands of the peasantry and fostering the proposed socialist transformation of society. The resettlement programme aimed to provide 162,000 landless families and persons displaced by the war, with land in newly serviced resettlement villages on former European farms. Several 'models' for resettlement were implemented, including cooperative farms run on a collective basis, and the more widespread, individual family farms with common grazing resources (Elliott, 1995).

However, the Lancaster House Agreement between Britain and Zimbabwe served to protect private property interests in the country for a further ten years and was an important factor in limiting the pace of land reform. By the beginning of the 1990s, only 52,000 families had been moved to 3.3 million hectares of land, and since the government had no control as to where lands became available for purchase, scheme areas tended to be in fragmented rather than contiguous blocks, and they were often located in more marginal areas. The cooperative model for resettlement proved particularly limited, with uptake on those schemes only 42 per cent of planned capacity by 1991 (Elliott, 1995). There were also wider problems of management, infrastructural developments and finance, with the British government refusing to provide aid to this model, for example.

In 1992 legislation was passed to enable the compulsory purchase of lands for the resettlement programme and in 1997 a large number of privately owned 'commercial' farms were designated for acquisition, 'in an attempt to answer the clamour for land reform and shore up the waning popularity of ZANU (PF) – the former liberation movement party' (Wolmer et al., 2004: 91). Many of these designations were successfully challenged in court, but in 2000 a wave of land invasions occurred, led by members of the War Veterans Association and with the tacit support of Mugabe's government. Violence was often used to expel famers sometimes 'replacing them by people neither poor nor intending to farm' (Lipton, 2009: 266). While these farm occupations are the basis for the 'Fast Track' land reform programme that continues currently in Zimbabwe, they also heralded a new era of political violence, economic decline and collapse of the rule of law in the country.

Escalating costs, population increase, changing class interests and mounting political unrest are among a variety of factors that restrict the impact of land reform on Zimbabwe's economy and society.

Newer challenges for rural development

The globalisation of agriculture and the future of farming

Processes of globalisation have had profound impacts on local development and environmental outcomes that shape current challenges in rural development. In particular, food and farming have become increasingly globalised and dominated by large-scale commercial agri-business. 'The farm' which had been the core of agricultural production in many places has in some cases and to varying degrees become just one part of a multi-level, integrated system of production, processing, marketing and distribution of food and fibre products (Redclift, 1987). In this context, there are new risks and relationships for farmers engaged in agricultural production, including entering into advanced contracts with these MNCs and through the decline in government support for training, extension or prices for inputs. The prospects for local small-scale producers, or indeed Southern-based commercial agricultural enterprises, to thrive under current World Trade Organization rulings has been the focus of challenges to globalisation, such as by international non-governmental organisations as considered in Chapter 7. The continued use of subsidies in agriculture across the European Union and many OECD countries adds further pressure on farmers and the agricultural sector in countries of the Global South and reduces their potential competitiveness (Hazell et al., 2010).

There are longstanding debates regarding the role of agriculture in development as summarised in Table 10.10. Discussions over the relative merits of large- versus small-scale farming have been re-invigorated in recent years. There are concerns as to how and where future world food supplies can be met and the outlook for small-scale farming in a globalised food system and the liberalisation of land markets (see Deininger and Byerlee, 2012; Hazzell et al., 2010). Of particular interest has been the expansion of very large scale agriculture schemes in the Brazilian *Cerrado* (savannah) region, Brazil's second largest biome after the Amazon. Substantial public investment in research and development, including in infrastructure, has enabled the extension of cultivation onto very weathered and acidic soils previously unsuited to agriculture. This has suggested a potential for enhancing global agricultural output in the context of rising pressures on limited land resources. The technological success of this initiative and its impact on raising Brazil as a major global agricultural producer has been referred to as the 'Miracle of the Cerrado' (*The Economist*, 2010; Rada, 2013). Proponents of this kind of future for global food supplies include the World Bank. Its recent report titled 'Awakening Africa's Sleeping Giant'

(World Bank, 2009a) considers the potential transfer of this model to the savanna areas of West Africa. On the other side of the debate are those that argue that small-scale farming has the potential to be more productive and more sustainable. As seen in Chapter 6, there are substantial concerns regarding the global scale impacts of the dominant industrial model of agriculture, depending as it does on fossil fuels, synthetic fertilisers and chemical insecticides. These include the disruption of global nitrogen and phosphorus cycles, possibly beyond 'planetary boundaries', with impacts on hydrological and atmospheric systems and in turn, far-reaching implications for human well-being and ecosystem functioning. The recent food price crisis and rising hunger levels have also signaled a 'crisis of industrial agriculture' that is argued to provide 'an opportunity to refocus agriculture around questions of social and ecological sustainability' (McMichael and Schneider, 2011: 120).

Interest in lower external input, ecology-based alternatives to industrial agriculture, including 'organic' and 'biodynamic' farming, are now being developed worldwide. All center on the integration of ecological processes and principles into the way that food is produced to deliver multi-functional benefits, such as habitat conservation or flood control in addition to food products (Pretty, 2014). They are also closely adapted to local contexts, using local skills, knowledge and human capital rather than costly external inputs, and aim to reduce environmental impacts including via locally adapted resource conserving technologies. The technologies showing high potential sustainability include practices such as inter-cropping

Table 10.10 Summary of the debate about the role of agriculture in development

Type of Argument	Case for Agriculture	Case against Agriculture
Engine of Growth	It is large enough to impact on rural living standards. Powerful links to the rest of the economy.	Often a small sector of growing economies. Poor countries often have low productivity.
Alternatives to Agriculture	Few alternatives in poor countries.	New trade opportunities exist in manufacturing and services.
Technical Feasibility	Science is increasing productivity.	Diminishing returns from investment and risk of environmental degradation.
Poverty Impact	Agricultural growth can be pro-poor.	Limited opportunities for small farmers.
Policy Environment	Structural adjustment has removed biases against agriculture.	Public intolerance of public spending and subsidies.

Source: adapted from Hazell et al., 2010.

(the growing of two or more crops simultaneously on the same piece of land) and agro-forestry farming (a form of intercropping in which annual herbaceous crops are grown interspersed with perennial trees or shrubs). Many of these have been used widely by farmers in the Global South over very long periods of time, yet these indigenous technologies were often criticised by outsiders, or even banned under colonial policies, on the basis of being environmentally destructive and detrimental to modern farming approaches (Conway, 1997: Hill, 1972).

Support for the future of small-scale farming has also come from rural social movements within the Global South such as the *Movimento do Trabalhadores Sem Terra* (MST), a Brazilian landless workers movement that works to support wider access to land and the development of cooperative farming. *Via Campesina* is a global network of peasant movements supporting small-scale farmers as the basis for more sustainable and equitable development of agriculture and has been significant in promoting the productivity benefits of small-scale farming. Indeed, social movements have been increasingly important in contemporary debates about rural development more widely and particularly in Latin America (Bebbington et al., 2008), as seen in Chapter 1.

Programmes of agricultural intensification: 'green' and 'gene' revolutions in the Global South

In contrast to programmes of land reform that have looked to intervene directly in the agrarian structure within a country, many more rural development strategies have focused on transforming the way in which agricultural production occurs, typically through various packages of introduced technology and assisting the move from labour-intensive farming to more capital-intensive production. In the 1960s, a number of breakthroughs in the development of high-yielding varieties (HYVs) of grains such as rice and wheat were made in research institutes in the Philippines and in Mexico, largely with overseas public finance such as from the Rockefeller Foundation. The extensive transfer of these technologies, along with the fertilisers, pesticides, irrigation and machinery required, to many countries of the Global South is widely referred to as the 'Green Revolution' as discussed in the Key idea box. The largest impacts of these developments were in Asia, where more than 75 per cent of the wheat plantings and 30 per cent of the rice plantings by the early 1980s were HYVs (Barke and O'Hare, 1991: 107).

Key idea

The future source of world food supply

Increased food production can be achieved in one of two ways: by extending the area under production or through raising the intensity of production. Since the area of land available for cultivation globally is fundamentally limited, and world population numbers are increasing, further increases in global food production will have to come through increasing the intensity of production. In recent years, the debate concerning how this will be achieved has shifted from a 'Green' to a 'Gene' revolution (Atkins and Bowler, 2001).

> Green revolution – a series of phases of the development of high-yielding varieties of crops, via breakthroughs in plant breeding and the crossbreeding

of one crop with another, the development of associated technologies allied to the cultivation of these, and the transfer of these packages to further and further areas of the world.

Gene revolution – the development of new organisms, through the artificial introduction of alien genetic material into existing plants and crops. Genetically modified crops are produced that can fix their own nitrogen, require less pesticide and will yield in very dry conditions, for example. It encompasses the research and development financed by global biotechnology companies.

Part of the attraction for planners of the Green Revolution lay in the assumed scale-neutrality of the technologies and the power of the market to encourage and disseminate improvements in well-being. It was assumed that the biochemical technologies of seeds and fertilisers would be equally viable at all scales of operation, whether on small or large farms. It was therefore thought that the yields and incomes of all farmers could be enhanced without raising rural inequalities. In practice, however, the Green Revolution had very uneven regional and social impacts.

In India the Green Revolution is considered to have been responsible for delivering national self-sufficiency in food grains by the late 1970s, but as Bernstein (1992a) pointed out, per capita grain production actually fell in 11 of the 15 major states of India between 1960 and 1985, with success being correlated strongly with the distribution of irrigation to secure multiple cropping. Social inequality was also aggravated in circumstances where rising landlessness forced increasing numbers of women into wage employment to ensure household survival. Some employment opportunities for women in the traditional areas of harvesting and grain processing also declined. For women in households which owned land, their burden in agriculture was often increased with double cropping. Research has shown that investment in technology at this income level tends to be in areas which save male labour time, such as tractors for land clearance, rather than women's time taken up in tasks such as weeding (Pearson, 1992). Table 10.11 summarises a number of gendered impacts of rural development strategies based on such technocratic packages of agricultural development.

This era of the Green Revolution also had limited impacts in South America and Africa. As noted by Dixon (1990: 92), 'the crops that have formed the mainstay of the green revolution, rice and wheat, are simply not grown by large numbers of Third World farmers'. In much of Africa, agricultural production is dominated by rainfed cultivation of coarse grains such as maize, millet and sorghum, often for subsistence requirements. Research into improved varieties of these crops has generally been more limited, with 'large swathes of farmers in Africa' being substantially 'by-passed by the Green Revolution' (Robinson, 2004: 195).

There have been efforts to develop a second Green Revolution, more suited to the dry lands of the Global South and to the resource-poor conditions of the majority of farmers. For example, plant breeding schemes in the 1980s developed high-yielding strains of millet, sorghum, cowpeas and cassava, which achieved some success in raising production in parts of India and Africa, without requiring increased farm inputs (Barke and O'Hare, 1991). However, many consider that further increases in yields through conventional plant breeding methods are now limited and it is through biotechnology, including genetic engineering of crops, that the most profound changes are predicted.

Proponents of a 'gene' revolution for agriculture argue that biotechnology can deliver further increases in food supply, from a restricted land base with fewer environmental costs than can be achieved through conventional crop breeding technologies. Through the artificial introduction of genetic material, rather than the traditional breeding or cross-breeding from one organism to another, crop varieties are being created to require less pesticides, be herbicide tolerant and to fix their own nitrogen and be more drought resistant, for example. All such developments may have benefits in terms of reducing overall energy requirements. They also rest, however, on the premise that the problems of world hunger are due to a food shortage.

Cultivation of GM (genetically modified) crops has expanded rapidly since the first commercial planting in 1996. Figure 10.8 shows this expansion from approximately 1.7 million hectares in 1996, to over 1.8 billion hectares in 2014. Whilst 68% of total GM production in 2000 was in the US, production now takes place in 28 countries by an estimated 18 million farmers (although the US remains the largest producer). Over 90% of producers are 'small and poor' (James, 2014: v). Maize, soybean and cotton are the principle GM crops currently grown, although some of the newer biotech crops include food staples such as potatoes (recently approved for planting in the USA) and eggplant (brinjal) in Bangladesh (James, 2014).

The opportunities provided by, and the risks associated with, GM crops and foodstuffs are an arena for substantial debate, as with wider biotechnology and genetic engineering in the health and human reproduction fields. Whilst James (2014) reports a review of 147 studies over 20 years to suggest overall benefits of GM crops to include 37% reduction in pesticide use, 22% increase in yields and 68% improvements in farmers' profits, substantial scientific

Table 10.11 Rural development: technology and its impacts on women

Property ownership	Employment	Decision making	Status	Level of living and nutrition	Education
NEW SEEDS, BREEDS AND AGROCHEMICALS					
May lose usufruct rights as land is used more intensively. Land owned by women is often physically marginal and not suitable for optimum applications of new inputs	Women exclude themselves from use of chemicals because of threat to their reproductive role. New crops may not need traditional labour inputs of women. Women generally displaced from the better paid, permanent jobs	Decline. Training in new methods in agriculture limited to men. Use of new technology and crops generally subsumed by men. Women farmers equally innovative when given opportunity	Increase in family income may allow women to concentrate on reproductive activities. In patriarchal society this increases status of male head of household	New crops may be less acceptable in family diet and nutritionally inferior because of chemicals	Increase in additional disposable income of family may be used for children's education
MECHANISATION					
Women operate smaller farms in general and so may not find it economical to invest in new implements	Women usually excluded from use of mechanical equipment. Women farmers have difficulty obtaining male labourers	Decline	Decline because of reduced role on farm and downgrading of female skills	New implements not used for subsistence production	Growth of interest in mechanical training but limited to males
COMMERCIALISATION OF AGRICULTURE AND CHANGES IN CROP PATTERNS					
Female-operated farms tend to concentrate on subsistence crops and crops for local market. Tend to remain at small scale	Decline because technical inputs substituted for female labour	Decline because less involved in major crop production activity	Decline	Decline because cash crops take over land traditionally used for subsistence production by women. Males allocate more income to developing enterprise and for personal gratification than to family maintenance	Increased time available for education
POST-HARVEST TECHNOLOGY					
New equipment owned by men	Women's traditional food processing skills no longer in demand. May employ young women in unskilled jobs in agro-industries	Decline because ownership of equipment and skills passed to men	Decline because female skill downgraded	Decline because loss of women's independent income from food processing activities. New product may be nutritionally inferior. Women deprived of use of waste products for animal feed and so lose important part of traditional family diet	

Source: compiled from Momsen (2010)

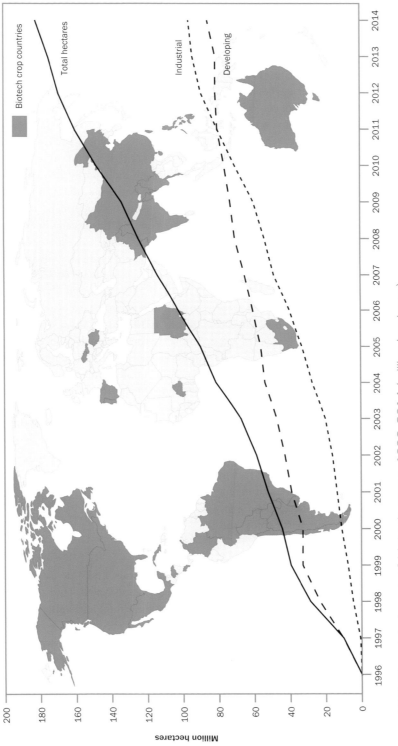

Figure 10.8 The global area of biotech crops, 1996–2014 (million hectares)
Source: adapted from James, 2014.

uncertainty is acknowledged by many others regarding the ecological and human health implications of GM foods. For example, these concerns continue to underpin public opposition in the UK, where both the trialing and production of GM crops remains illegal.

Critics of the expansion of GM crops also fear the rising corporate control of the overall food chain encompassed in these developments. Through the 1990s, major corporations such as Monsanto, increasingly bought up biotechnology, plant breeding and seed interests worldwide. Whereas previously, seeds, for example, were in the hands of farmers and public sector plant breeders, by 2000, ten corporations supplied 30% of the global seed market (Actionaid, 2004). Currently, just three companies, namely Monsanto (US), DuPont (US) and Syngenta (Switzerland), control more than 50% of that market (www.gmwatch.org). In May 2016, Monsanto was looking to take-over Syngenta and itself was battling an unsolicited take-over by Bayer, a German chemicals company (Neate, 2016). At the same time, a UN investigation into one of Monsanto's major weed-killer products, 'Roundup', was threatening its withdrawal due to carcinogenic properties of its components.

There is substantial concern as to how this rising concentration of corporate power impacts on small farmers. The production of many agricultural commodities in a globalised world now involves entering into some kind of advanced contract, including with these companies but also in terms of product price and quality, with other global actors in the food industries. As such, farmers are now exposed to market forces in quite different ways than in the past, when they could deal with several different and smaller firms and with government controlled marketing boards, for example, to purchase seeds and fertlisers or to sell products (Thompson et al., 2007). Fears include the greater economic uncertainty and vulnerability of poorer farmers. A study of farmer suicides in India, where there were over 17,000 such suicides in 2009 alone, found that indebtedness was a major factor in farmers' decisions to take their own lives and that the majority of these farmers were growing GM cotton (Center for Human Rights and Global Justice, 2011). India opened its doors to GM crops in 2002 after many years of resistance by local NGOs. By that point, Monsanto had already bought up several of India's largest seed companies in order that it would be in a position to promote GM varieties across the sub-continent once government approval was forthcoming (Vidal, 2002). Between 1995

and 1998, Monsanto spent over US$8 billion buying seed companies in India (Shiva, 2000). This was part of the Indian Government's policies of economic liberalisation and encouragement of foreign direct investment to fuel national economic development. It was also the period when they were cutting subsidies formerly available to farmers, such as in accessing credit and fertilisers (Center for Human Rights and Global Justice, 2011).

One of the more recent GM developments, dubbed 'terminator technology', perhaps most clearly illustrates the fears of critics. It is now possible to create plant varieties that are biologically sterile, ensuring that farmers will have to buy new seeds each year. Vandana Shiva has been a vociferous opponent of such developments, pointing out that historically, 'the seed, for the farmer, is not merely the source of future plants and food; it is the storage place of culture and history' (Shiva, 2000: 8). For centuries, farmers have evolved crops, experimented, innovated and exchanged knowledge as well as seeds, and these processes have been an essential part of local culture and heritage. Shiva refers to a 'growth illusion' and a 'corporate myth' concerning the extension of industrial agriculture, that 'hides theft from nature and the poor, masking the creation of scarcity as growth' (2000: 1). In short, this commodification of nature and culture provides further confirmation of what Robinson (2004: 196) has suggested: 'the application of GM "solutions" is regarded by many as the antithesis of a sustainable option for further agricultural development'.

The liberalisation of land markets and rise of international land deals

The rising scale and intensity of international land transfers (the so-called 'land grab' or 'land rush') has also been important in shaping debates about the future role of small- versus large-scale farming. As seen in Chapter 6, a combination of drivers, including the world food price spikes of 2007–08 and the search for lower carbon energy sources, has led to the wide-scale purchasing or leasing of land by governments and corporations in countries of the Global South. In large measure, the pattern of production in these newly opened sites is dominated by large-scale, industrial monoculture (UNEP, 2012) and is seen in the Brazilian case mentioned above, where much of the soybean is grown in the *Cerrado* region through heavy investments in technology and mechanisation. Even when small-holder farming is promoted through contract growing, such as in the case of oil palm in Indonesia, monoculture and industrial methods are adopted (UNEP, 2012).

Whilst ownership of large areas of land by foreigners is not a new phenomenon in the Global South, the scale and intensity of land transfers is. Acquisitions in Africa in 2009 alone amounted to 39.7 million hectares, an area larger than the combined agricultural areas of Belgium, Denmark, France, Germany, the Netherlands and Switzerland (Deininger and Byerlee, 2012). There is also some indication that the rate of land acquisitions has slowed in recent years and some acquisitions remain unused and/or are speculative investments (Deininger and Byerlee, 2012). However, Table 10.12 identifies a range of interacting drivers, including infrastructures for economic development and tourism ventures and the creation of protected areas for conservation objectives, that continue to drive international land markets.

The range of actors involved in land transactions, for diverse purposes and in different policy settings, all mean that the impacts in practice are likely to be context specific. There has been a tendency for debates to be polarised and the livelihood impacts in particular remain under-researched (Hunsberger et al., 2014; McCarthy, 2010). However, international land deals are acknowledged to have led to radical changes in the use and ownership of land resources in the Global South (Zoomers, 2010) and have put concepts of land governance and titling central to contemporary challenges of rural development, as seen in Table 10.3. There are indications that land deals have in fact encroached on existing prime agricultural lands (with good access to water and infrastructure, for example) rather than taking place in under-used or available lands (UNEP, 2012). They have also led to dispossession and displacement of local and indigenous people. Poorer groups are often the first to lose land, particularly where formal title is lacking or where customary rights have little protection from the law (Zoomers, 2010). They may lack the financial resources to buy land elsewhere and also not possess the necessary skills to take advantage of any newly created job opportunities. Local communities also see their home territories and cultures significantly changed by the influx of agro-industrial firms, tourists and the inflow of migrants for work.

Table 10.12 Interacting drivers of the global land grab

➤ 'Offshore' farming for food security – the outsourcing of domestic food production through buying or leasing land abroad. China and the Gulf States are large players.

➤ Rising global demand for biofuels and non-food agricultural commodities – rising land values and financial incentives in biofuels make investment in land a new source of profit for private investors in the context of financial crisis.

➤ Development of protected areas, nature reserves and ecotourism – international organisations and private investors make land purchases for environmental ends such as biodiversity protection, reforestation, and wildlife production and commercial conservation.

➤ The creation of Special Economic Zones and large scale infrastructure works and urban extensions – all require land for roads, air fields, ICT parks, dams and reservoirs etc. leading to rising land prices and the 'development-induced displacement' of agriculture and people.

➤ Large scale tourist complexes – large international hotel chains actively seeking attractive new locations for all-inclusive resorts, including places associated with world heritage sites and coastlines. Many countries of the Global South are seeing tourism investment as basis for rapid economic growth.

➤ Retirement migration – rising costs of living in USA and Europe, for example, driving migration to cheaper regions including Mexico and Central America, the Maghreb countries and South Africa. Rising demand for land for retirement complexes and gated communities.

➤ Land purchases by migrants in their countries of origin – the last decade has seen rapid growth in long-distance migrations, 'diaspora', where people from many different countries live temporarily or permanently in other regions (including South-South migration but also to Europe, the USA and the Gulf States). Rise of remittances begin used to buy houses and land in home countries.

Source: compiled from Zoomers, 2010.

The substantial abuses often involved in recent land deals are well recognised by major development organisation and donor agencies, but there are competing views on how to respond (Hall et al., 2014). For example, the World Bank (2010b) has proposed a voluntary corporate code of conduct embracing seven 'Principles for Responsible Agro-Investment': respecting land and resource rights; ensuring food security; ensuring transparency, good governance, and a proper enabling environment; consultation and participation; responsible agro-enterprise investing; social sustainability and environmental sustainability. The FAO promotes similar voluntary guidelines, although their emphasis is on binding member states to mandatory reporting. However, others argue, particularly from civil society groups and human rights perspectives, that voluntary codes will be insufficient to ensure benefits to the poor in the South. The UN Special Rapporteur on the 'Right to Food' argues that any land investments leading to changes to local peoples' land rights should be the last and least desirable option and urges the development of alternative investment models in agricultural and rural development.

The expansion of biofuels production has been associated with both 'land grabs' and 'green grabs', intensifying competition for agricultural land and altering patterns of land use and property relations (Hunsberger et al., 2014). Whilst countries such as Indonesia have introduced new conditions for where biofuel production can take place, and some countries (including the US, EU and UK) now have sustainability requirements within their biofuel use targets, the social and equity elements of these new governance arrangements are considered to remain weak, in that there remains insufficient attention to how biofuel governance initiatives 'seek to protect and enhance livelihoods at sites of production and along the value chain' (Hunsberger et al., 2014: 249).

If linking with agri-business is to provide a route for integrating small-scale farmers and remote rural areas into new markets with positive impacts on poverty (as modeled by the World Bank), further research is evidently required into the complex ways in which smallholders can be excluded or included into the oil palm sector, for example, but also 'adversely incorporated', whereby poverty and disadvantage can also flow from inclusion on disadvantageous terms (McCarthy, 2010).

Protecting the global commons whilst ensuring livelihoods: the case of forestry

Trees, woodlands and forests are multipurpose resources that provide varied ecosystem functions and services at a global level, including for biodiversity protection and in regulating atmospheric processes, as discussed in Chapter 6

Table 10.13 Types of forest ecosystem services

Environmental goods	Food
	Freshwater
	Fuel
	Fibre
Regulating services	Climate regulation
	Flood regulation
	Disease regulation
	Water purification
Supporting services	Nutrient cycling
	Soil formation
Cultural services	Aesthetic
	Spiritual
	Educational
	Recreational

Source: compiled from MEA, 2005.

and summarised in Table 10.13. Fifty-two per cent of the world's remaining forests are in the tropics, which ensures that international attention to the management and development of forest resources is high. However, trees, woodlands and forests are also often central to rural livelihoods, with an estimated 1.2 billion people worldwide depending to some degree on agroforestry farming and forest resources for livelihood. This pattern is the basis for the further attention given in the following section to these resources within livelihoods below. Forest-based activities also provide approximately 30 million jobs in the informal sector in the Global South and provide up to one-third of all rural non-farm employment (Center for International Forestry Research cifor.org/forest-livelihoods). At all scales, patterns of forest resource use and management reflect the diverse ecologies of forests over space, the numerous different combinations of forest type, the changing value placed on particular forest products and services, and the many different interventions over time which have aimed to secure those resources for human development.

Forests and woodlands within livelihoods

Forests have been the locus of indigenous livelihoods built upon a close association with the forest ecologies and dynamics dating back thousands of years. It is estimated that as many as 15–20 million people dependent on hunting, gathering and shifting cultivation techniques lived in the Amazon Basin in the sixteenth century, for example (Mather and Chapman, 1995).

Shifting cultivation systems, by definition, depend on the manipulation of the dynamics of forest ecologies:

> All tropical regions provide examples of the way in which farmers, as part of their traditional systems of shifting cultivation, incorporate trees from the original forest stand into their fields, for ground protection or for useful products.
>
> (Weidelt, 1993: 39)

For many more rural people, it is the resources of open woodlands and scrub vegetation which play a particularly significant role in farming systems and livelihoods. The generally high dependence of communities on biomass sources of energy, as noted in Chapter 6, in itself demands a close association with local woodland ecologies to secure fuelwood for cooking, heating and lighting. In addition to firewood, woodlands may also provide a whole host of timber-related and 'non-timber' forestry products (NTFPs), including:

> building timber; wood for kraal fences, tools, transport and construction (boats, scotchcarts, sledges, etc.); edible leaves, pods, nuts and fruits; honey; natural fibres; fodder; medicines; utensils; and a whole range of other items.
>
> (Munslow et al., 1988: 45)

Table 10.14 illustrates the varied uses of wood in rural livelihoods in Zimbabwe. The table highlights the different values that such uses have within the overall livelihood system, such as in providing inputs into productive activities or raising cash income through sales.

Securing such woodland products often requires extensive local environmental knowledge and active management of those resources. For example, in arid zones of sub-Saharan Africa, knowledge of local ecologies and the regenerative capacity of the natural vegetation is used by livestock herders to secure fodder for livestock and to provide shade and rubbing poles for pest control (Stock, 1995). At the other end of a continuum of management, in areas of high population density and plentiful rainfall, trees of various indigenous and exotic species are planted and managed carefully and intensively for their varied products. In many parts of Southeast Asia, multi-storey home or kitchen gardens are host to varied tree and plant species, often with distinct horizontal levels, with food crops at ground level, coffee bushes and medicinal plants in the next zone, through fruit, fuel and fodder species at higher levels (Christanty, 1986).

Table 10.14 The multiple economic uses of wood in Zimbabwe

The multiple use of wood	Consumption	Durable	Production input	ASSET FORMATION	SALE
Timber (for commercial use, carvings)		*	*	*	
Firewood (cooking, heat, light, beer brewing, brick burning)	*		*		*
Construction wood (huts, granaries, livestock pens, field fencing)		*	*	*	*
Agricultural implements (carts, yokes, hoes, axe handles, ploughs)		*	*		*
Furniture (wardrobes, beds, tables, chairs, stools, shelving, etc.)		*		*	*
Household utensils (cook sticks, mortars, pestles, plates, etc.)		*	*		*
Musical instruments (*mbiras, marimba, drums*, guitars)		*			*
Hunting implements (knobkerries, bows, arrows, fishing rods, etc.)		*	*		
Rope from bark (roofing, binding, whips, baskets, mats, nets)			*		*

Source: Cavendish (2000)

Approaches to forestry development

Much of the history of conservation in the Third World is not one of happily shared interests between rural people and state conservation bodies, but one of exclusion and latent or actual conflict.

(Adams, 2009: 277).

Many approaches to forest management in the Global South, as with the history of conservation more generally, have involved the separation of people from forests and excluding people from accessing forest resources. The creation of protected areas, whereby land was set aside for 'nature' or 'wildlife' and where human use was prevented or severely constrained, formed the basis of what has been termed 'fortress conservation'. This approach became mainstream in conservation practices in the North and was transferred widely in the Global South and particularly to the African continent under colonialism (sees Adams, 2009). In recent years, similar approaches to forest management have involved conflict for local communities not just with state authorities, but increasingly with private sector interests. As seen in Table 10.3, attracting new sources of private investment into national economies to finance public development objectives in conservation and development is very much part of the current approach to rural development. It was seen in Chapter 6, that the area of forest plantations globally rose by over 48% between 1990 and 2010. A significant factor has been the attraction of foreign investors into plantation forestry, as markets for forestry related ecosystem services, particularly the market in carbon, have expanded. This is happening

particularly widely in Africa, where it is suggested that plantation forestry governance will soon be dominated by private sector interests and 'in this context, local and indigenous knowledge of and approaches to forest management has been largely replaced by scientific logic and management regimes' (Lyons and Westoby, 2014: 14).

In 1996, Cline-Cole contrasted the mainstream approach to forest management with how local people undertook the management of forest and woodland resources. Table 10.15 identifies the key features of what he termed 'outsider' forestry, with indigenous or 'insider' forestry. Whereas outsider forestry prioritises particular functions of forests (and 'neat management' of these), insider forestry is charactersied by diversity, multiple values and services of forestry within livelihood systems and the integrated management of forests and woodlands in combination with farmland.

An 'outsider' perspective towards forestry management was seen in the 1980s in response to the so-called 'woodfuel crisis', where deforestation was considered to be the outcome of demand for energy exceeding supply. The solution was technology-based – through the large-scale planting of fast growing tree species, such as eucalyptus, across large parts of India and in many African countries, for example. However, many of these programmes had limited success both in terms of restoring forests and in meeting people's needs (Agarwal, 1986, 2001). Many were implemented in a top-down, nonparticipatory way, did not address the underlying drivers of deforestation and failed to consider how insecurities of land and tree tenure could constrain more effective management. Powerful narratives of misuse of forests by local land and resource users often underpinned such policies and were sustained by factors

Table 10.15 Characteristics of outsider and insider forestry compared

Outsider forestry	Insider forestry
Introduced	Indigenous
Focused on production and protection functions of forestry	Integrated social, cultural, health and economic values of forestry and woodlands
Uses powerful environmental conservation imperatives to enforce legislation and management	Multipurpose species prioritised
Forestry and agriculture as separate endeavours	Forest management integral to agricultural activities and vice versa
Nature and culture conceived as separate and shapes interventions in forestry	Environmental change not separate from human history

Source: compiled from Cline-Cole, 1996.

including the training of forest professionals and the imperatives of the aid industry (see the Critical reflection box in Chapter 6).

However, an improved understanding of the role of trees in farming systems of the Global South and the value of indigenous knowledge, skills and institutions, has challenged some of these mainstream forest management policies and practices. For example, through the 1980s, 'agroforestry' was a focus of interest amongst development practitioners, as the relative failure of many large agriculture and forestry initiatives started to become evident. *Agroforestry* refers to the deliberate growing and management of woody perennials in conjunction with annual crops and/or animals. Although the concept was not new (certainly not to local people), agroforestry initiatives were developed widely in the Global South towards enhancing the integrated production of food products, browse and fodder, fruit and plantation crops and even aquaforestry (Gholz, 1987).

Through the 1990s, the reconceptualisation of the role of public, private and civic organisations in development generally and the increased emphasis on community participation (see Chapters 3 and 7), was also evidenced within forestry interventions. Programmes of 'community forestry', rooted in the ideas that there were better outcomes for both conservation and human development when local communities and institutions were empowered to manage local resources, were widely implemented. In India, for example, programmes of Joint Forest Management (JFM) were initiated in 1990 and had extended to 22 states by the end of the decade, with an estimated 36,000 JFM groups embracing 10.2 million hectares of forest (Agarwal, 2001). JFM is based on a model where villagers (within newly formed local community organisations) and the government, share the responsibility for, and benefits of, the regeneration of degraded local forests. Nepal launched a similar large-scale, state-initiated programme based on the formation of identified Forest User Groups who have the responsibility for all management and benefits. In both cases, NGOs often acted as intermediaries between villagers and the state, such as in catalysing group formation and functioning. The role played by NGOs in development is discussed further in Chapters 1 and 7.

In other cases of community forestry, the emphasis has been on working to strengthen existing, 'traditional' local institutions, that have historically been responsible for the management of what are often 'common property resources', but which are under stress, including with increased resource scarcities and economic change. In many African countries, although with substantial local variation according to different cultures and ecologies, these were often underpinned by communal tenures and the role of chiefs in exerting local authority (Blaikie, 2006). However, the substantial optimism in the literature surrounding the potential of local institutions to serve as the building blocks for community management of forest resources was often not forthcoming in practice. Campbell et al. (2001), working in Zimbabwe, report the breakdown of traditional leadership, low observance and enforcement of local controls, a rise in illegal practice related to woodland use and a decline in community values and cooperation.

Experiences of decentralising control for forest management have been the basis for the development of many subsequent 'community based natural resource management' (CBNRM) models that have significantly influenced rural development thinking and practice across sectors, including the management of wildlife, water and grazing lands (see Adams and Hulme, 2001; Blaikie, 2006) and most recently in relation to climate change adaptation, as seen in Chapter 6. However, programmes of community forestry, and CBNRM more widely, have been criticised for the undifferentiated view of 'community' embraced within them. In short, they have assumed 'distinct' communities with shared characteristics and common environmental interests, when in fact, communities are extremely diverse and dynamic with many dimensions of inequality, varied interests and differences in power to shape change. Of particular concern has been the 'striking neglect' of a gender perspective in community participation (Agarwal, 2001).

There have been substantial efforts made by governments, donors and civil society organisations towards mainstreaming gender into forest progammes, although Basnett (2016) identifies a persistent tendency to consider women as a uniformly marginalised group and individuals and communities in rural areas as spatially bounded, even as migration plays an increasing role in many such livelihoods. In 2012, Nepal introduced a new forest strategy with a mandate that requires Forest User Group committees to have at least 30% women (Basnett, 2016). Whilst some consider that this may help in ensuring women's interests in forests are heard, there is also evidence that merely increasing the number of women in forest governance systems is no guarantee of equitable gender outcomes.

Box 10.5 highlights why the effective participation of women is considered essential in the future governance of forest resources. It is based on research into the pilot projects of the REDD+ programme. This programme was seen in Chapter 6 to be receiving substantial international interest and donor investment for its potential to avoid further degradation of forests in the Global South and support their role as a carbon sink with global benefits through the mitigation of climate change. Whilst these projects are in the pilot stage, aiming to prepare countries to implement full projects and to

determine the final details of the programme, there is concern regarding the potential negative impacts for forest-dependent communities and indigenous peoples who livelihoods, and cultures, are closely inter-linked to forests and forest resources. These include the violation of customary and territorial rights, unequal contracts and the potential for increasing conflict and inequality within communities (Griffiths, 2007). Clear and secure tenure rights are understood as key factors in shaping the outcomes of such programmes for local people and for conservation success. However, the sustainability and equity implications are also considered to be dependent on the recognition of women's interests in forest resources and their effective participation in the future governance of forest resources.

BOX 10.5

The importance of women's participation in forest governance

The prospects of detrimental impacts of programmes such as REDD+, on poor people living in and near forests, is widely recognised including by the international institutions and donors currently piloting projects. There is particular concern regarding the potential loss of land and use rights and how these may impact on women.

Mounting research evidence has confirmed that women tend to have less voice than men in forest communities and participate less in structures of forest governance. Women also tend to use forests differently to men, although this is often unacknowledged in projects. Whilst the specific roles and responsibilities of men and women do differ across cultures and regions, there are often broadly similar divisions of labour. For example, men typically use and manage forests for cash-related agriculture, hunting, forest products including logging and higher value activities, whilst women use and manage resources more for subsistence agriculture, the collection of wild resources for household use and for food security.

Women's land rights are typically not as secure as men's; women under collective and individual tenure systems often may not be included on land titles or be allowed to control their own plots. In practice, their rights are shaped by a complex mix of factors,

including their social position, whether they are married or widowed, for example, and their relationships to husbands, fathers and brothers. Often such complexities have not been recognised in past projects and policies and have led to increased hardship for women.

Researchers from the Centre for International Forestry Research (CIFOR) are monitoring 20 pilot REDD+ projects in six countries. Qualitative research combining key informant interviews, focus group discussions and surveys, have been conducted in 77 villages within these pilot projects. Part of this research has considered the ways in which women are participating within meetings surrounding the project, their levels of knowledge relative to men and how women perceive the efficacy of their involvement.

Key findings have included that:

Women's knowledge about the REDD+ initiative is lower than men's.

Whilst women are often 'satisfied' with their level of representation within village decision making bodies, there was often a mismatch with how influential they perceived their role to be and how they engaged (see Table 10.16).

BOX 10.5 (continued)

Overall women were more involved in forestry related decisions at the household level than at the village level.

Women's perceptions of their role in forest decisions was lower than their perceived influence in community decision making in general.

There were differences across the sites in terms of levels of use of the forest by men and women. In 56% of cases, men went more often to the forest; in 33% there was no difference by gender; and in 11% of cases, women went more often than men.

There was no relationship between the number of visits made by women and their understanding of REDD+ projects and policies.

Where women were more involved in forest-use decisions and monitoring, they were more likely to have an understanding of REDD+ processes and projects.

The research shows that, even when considering women's participation in the rather limited way of their inclusion in meetings, understanding women's participation, representation and influence is a complex task. The variation across countries, sites and villages confirms that there are no single models for improving women's participation. However, the disconnect found between the presence of women on village committees and their perception of their participation and influence in the village, confirms that current arrangements are failing to result in effective representation for women. The finding that women are not equally informed of REDD+ projects, and do not participate in rule making on forests (despite using forests as much or more than men in some cases), is a concern given that full REDD+ projects will involve changes in the rules regarding forest use.

Table 10.16 Perception of women's participation in village-level decision making (share of women agreeing and disagreeing within focus groups averaged across villages and sites)

Country	Sufficiently represented		Usually able to influence		Participate actively in	
	Agree	Disagree	Agree	Disagree	Agree	Disagree
Brazil	31	66	65	31	67	27
Peru	88	12	78	22	83	17
Cameroon	67	33	83	17	83	17
Tanzania	79	08	55	33	93	01
Indonesia	60	40	65	30	70	24
Vietnam	73	28	75	25	100	0
Total	**64**	**32**	**65**	**29**	**79**	**15**

Source: compiled from Larson et al., 2016

Conclusion

It is evident that there has been much progress in understanding the realities of rural living and the nature of rural livelihoods. This includes the often close association with environmental resources, but also how use differs including by gender. It also embraces the diverse and flexible ways in which people combine and use assets to achieve livelihood objectives, which may differ substantially from outsider perspectives and goals. Furthermore, the significance of secure rights over resources, particularly land, for people's well-being (itself embracing multiple dimensions beyond income, including social status and the power to shape decisions) is now more fully understood.

But, as Scoones (1996: 3) identified, 'the social and economic worlds that influence local-level decisions go well beyond the farm gate' and this has become more pertinent in recent years. As seen through this chapter, the rapid and widespread processes associated with the globalisation of agriculture and the rising significance of international private investment in response to the crisis in food, energy and climate, have substantially changed the context for local decision making across the Global South. However, it was also seen that the livelihood outcomes of these newer approaches to the development of agriculture, or to secure forest protection, for example, remain under-researched. Furthermore, it seems that the lessons from rural development in the past, such as regarding the central importance of secure rights to resources and the benefits from investments, of participation and shared learning in the development of pro-grammes, and the significance of the empowerment of the poorest groups, continue to be overlooked. The key challenges for rural development going forward may be more political than technical.

Key points

> Whilst the world's population is increasingly an urban one, rural development remains key to understanding and resolving global challenges of poverty, food, energy and climate;

> Rural livelihoods are diverse and dynamic and are increasingly shaped by processes of global change, including the dominance of globalised agri-business and an international land market;

> Programmes for rural development have included interventions to radically change access to productive assets such as land and those that have focused on technological solutions to raising agricultural production;

> Issues of gender discrimination and security of rights to resources remain persistent challenges in rural development.

Further reading

Chambers, R. (1997) *Whose Reality Counts? Putting the First Last*. London: IT Publications
A classic text putting forward how and why the rural poor are so often 'left out' of rural development.

Leach, M. and Mearns R. (eds) (1996) *The Lie of the Land: Challenging Received Wisdom on the African Environment*. Oxford: James Currey
Another classic text that explains how and why society-environment relationships were often misunderstood. Individual chapters provide country examples of colonial and post-colonial approaches to particular resource development issues

Lipton, M. (2009) *Land Reform in Developing Countries: Property Rights and Property Wrongs*. New York: Routledge
The well-cited review of the practice and debates surrounding land reform across the world.

Pierce Colfer, C.J., Basnett, B.S. and Elias, M. (eds) (2016) *Gender and Forests: Climate Change, Tenure, Value Chains and Emerging Issues*. London: Routledge.
Lots of case studies illustrating the challenges of gender and land rights within contemporary processes of change.

Scoones, I. (2009) Livelihoods perspectives and rural development. *The Journal of Peasant Studies,* 36(1), 171–96
A thorough review of the development and impact of the livelihoods approach in rural development.

World Bank (2008) *World Development Report 2008: Agriculture for Development*. Washington: World Bank
The first report on agriculture after a 25-year gap – important in arguing the case for further integration of smallholder agriculture into globalising economy as route to development.

Websites

www.cifor.org
The Center for International Forestry Research based in Bogor, Indonesia provides research to support policy makers, practitioners and communities in developing more sustainable approaches to forestry management worldwide.

www.ids.org
The Institute of Development Studies at the University of Sussex, UK is a longstanding and leading institution for development research, particularly for work on addressing the persistence of global poverty.

www.iied.org

Site for the International Institute for Environment and Development which is an independent non-profit organisation. A good source for research on pastoral development, fisheries and biodiversity.

www.fao.org

Website of the Food and Agriculture Organisation, a UN body with responsibilities in collating and disseminating information and sharing policy experience across agriculture and food sectors globally. As such, a good source of statistical data and insight to policy developments at an international scale.

Discussion topics

➤ Review the evidence given in the chapter to suggest that there are no 'blueprints' or 'standard packages' for rural development.

➤ Illustrate the suggestion that there is nothing simple about survival in the drylands.

➤ Why is it hard for 'outsiders' to understand the realities of rural living in the Global South?

➤ Why has gender mainstreaming been so hard to achieve in rural development policies?

➤ Select a particular country in the Global South. What are the prospects for smallholder agriculture in this country? Find out as much as you can concerning its economy, its environmental conditions and its policies on agriculture. Sources from the Food and Agriculture Organisation and the World Bank are useful starting points. Recent academic research can also be sourced through the web-links above.

Conclusion

Development is undoubtedly a complex topic, but we hope that *Geographies of Development* has illuminated some of the key concepts, patterns and processes involved, as well as presenting case studies which illustrate and clarify particular issues. We have endeavoured to 'demystify' development, although in reaching this section of the book readers will be all too aware that development remains a highly contested topic, and we encourage you to engage in the critical reflections and suggestions for further reading and discussion concerning the different perspectives and questions raised in this text.

As we stand back from the material presented in *Geographies of Development*, we could perhaps ask ourselves once again, 'what is development all about?' You will be aware by now that there are many possible answers to this question, but essentially, development embraces processes of change leading hopefully to an improvement in the quality of life among individuals and groups living on this planet (see particularly Chapters 1 and 3). Furthermore, we have seen that processes of development and human well-being, both now, and in the future, are intricately related to how human society impacts on the natural resources, ecosystem functioning and health of non-human species on Earth

(see particularly Chapter 6). We have seen also how the processes of development can be examined at many different scales from the local to the regional, national, international and global.

This book has focused mainly on the world's poorest countries and peoples, those of the Global South, but development can also be examined in the context of our own communities. Dudley Seers (1969, 1972), a pioneer in development studies, saw development as primarily about reducing poverty, inequality and unemployment, and fulfilling individual and community ambitions. Such key diagnostic features can be identified and evaluated in all communities since, as we can all too easily observe for ourselves, even the world's wealthiest countries, such as those in Western Europe and North America, have their share of poor and marginalised people, and in recent years, inequalities within countries, both between and among different groups and different regions, have been rising rather than falling, with 'development'. Indeed, as discussed in Chapter 1, the Sustainable Development Goals (SDGs) are global in their focus and do not just seek to address the challenges of the Global South. As Chapter 4 showed all too clearly, inequalities at the global scale have been rising progressively since the 1970s, and this global reality has increasingly been etched out at the national and regional scales, including under the influence of neo-liberalism and through the recent Global Financial Crisis. Development should, ideally, begin at home, but, as we have argued in this book, it is also essential that we understand more distant places where peoples and environments are often very different from our own, notwithstanding that processes of globalisation may be bringing us ever closer, certainly in terms of information and communication technologies and social media. In the context of the Global Financial Crisis, we have seen how aspirations in one part of the world are inextricably linked to processes taking place elsewhere. In trying to understand the pace and ramifications of climate change, we also see how much of the development in countries of the North has been based on large-scale fossil fuel burning, whilst it is the poorer countries of the South which are experiencing now, and most directly, some of the key impacts, such as associated with rising sea levels and severe weather events which threaten many small Pacific island countries. The challenges of climate change have raised deep questions regarding what we mean by 'development' and 'progress', given that its impacts will be felt far into the future, even if carbon emissions were to be halted immediately.

Throughout *Geographies of Development* we have repeatedly alluded to the 'plural' nature of development, with different disciplines having their own distinctive focus and methodologies for interpreting issues concerning development. Politics, international relations, economics, anthropology, sociology and history, among others, have particular contributions to make in understanding development patterns and processes. Within geography, there is a longstanding interest in how people interact with environments, as well as a concern for appreciating development issues at different scales. However, perhaps geography, more than any other social science discipline, is concerned with adopting a holistic approach to the study of development.

But the links between practitioners in these various disciplines are themselves complex, and development studies draws upon the different perspectives and methodologies offered by a wide range of social sciences, as well as other disciplines such as agricultural science, ecology and health science. It is important to strive for a holistic approach, in both research and practice, when planning possible development interventions, but bringing together perspectives and initiatives from the physical sciences with those from the social sciences is not always straightforward, as dealing with a complex issue such as climate change reveals. Many of the issues considered in development studies are truly global and transnational in reach, ranging from climate change to poverty, to global trade and aid and migration, to the transmission and impact of diseases such as malaria and HIV/AIDS (Chapters 5 and 8). But at the local level we may be just as interested in issues such as community-based development and the reduction of social and personal inequality within particular communities, which also require an inter-disciplinary approach. All these issues can be considered in terms of the challenges and opportunities for more sustainable patterns and processes of development in the future (see particularly Chapters 6 and 7).

In studying development at different scales and in different locations, we need to ask ourselves whether development, in the sense of 'planned interventions', is actually occurring – is development working? This question was raised directly in Chapter 1, specifically in relation to the arguments of the 'anti-development' writers. Further, in Part II of this book we considered 'development in practice' through a number of different perspectives including people, environments, institutions and communities, revealing multiple and often competing interests in the outcomes of development.

In Chapter 1, the MDGs were identified, as illustrating an important international consensus on 'what development is about', and detailing a set of measurable targets for 2015 against which progress in development and the effectiveness of international development assistance (Chapter 8) could be monitored. Whilst the MDGs are considered to have provided an important focal point for domestic and international policies and galvanised action around poverty reduction with some evident successes (Chapters 1 and 3), there are also concerns that targets can oversimplify complex challenges and the holistic nature of development (Chapter 7). The Sustainable Development Goals that now succeed the MDGs have drawn on more participatory processes in their development; they seek to focus action within all countries through their adaptability to diverse contexts and capacities, and aim to recognise more fully the mutually dependent nature of economic, social and environmental outcomes. There have also been recent moves towards identifying measurable targets for progress in development, and for monitoring the effectiveness of international aid (Chapter 8).

In some parts of the world, the development record is very evidently lamentable. Many countries in sub-Saharan Africa in particular, are now worse off in terms of a range of economic, social and environmental dimensions than they were over 50 years ago. One of the world's poorest countries, Sierra Leone, had an average life expectancy of 44 years in 1974, yet 40 years later it was still only 51 years. In Zimbabwe, male life expectancy in 1980 was 56 years, but in 2014 was only slightly better at 57 years. Some countries, like Sierra Leone, have suffered from civil war, whereas in some southern African countries HIV/AIDS has had a devastating impact on a range of development indicators including life expectancy. The reasons behind these seemingly 'no development' or 'regressive' scenarios are both complex and variable, through space and time. By contrast, in many Asian and Latin American countries life expectancy levels have increased and there have been significant improvements in the indicators which the MDGs assessed.

The Western media (as well as some academic writing) seem to quite relentlessly portray people in the Global South as victims of the environment and, in turn, that the environment is a victim of human malpractice (Binns, 1997; Milner-Smith and Potter, 1995). This is a heavily distorted and oversimplified view of things, which fails to appreciate that people within these countries who are actually experiencing such environmental change frequently have a detailed understanding of the characteristics and capabilities of their environments, as seen in Chapter 10. Some of the biases, constraints and inherently political factors that serve to sustain such images of environments and people were considered explicitly in Chapters 7 and 10. Chapter 7, for example, revealed that, despite substantial change in the way that the key institutions in development are working, external factors such as global economic management, trade and international finance are often regarded as being fundamental to overcoming poverty, rather than being considered as part of the dynamic of creating poverty, thereby enabling 'blame' and 'responsibility' to be placed on governments and society in the South.

It is essential that all of us who engage in development theory and practice try to understand why specific development initiatives succeed and why others fail. It is certainly possible to identify common characteristics and patterns that underpin both successes and failures and it is important to learn from these. A number of principles for projects exhibiting greater sustainability were considered in Chapter 7, including engaging with and empowering local community organisations. Projects regularly fail for similar reasons, such as through inadequate inputs, persistent insecurities in access to basic resources, such as land, a lack of human capacity or through market bias which excluded the poor and the marginalised.

Good practice must be understood, but so too the context in which that success is achieved. For example, the often cited case of the Grameen Bank in Bangladesh, in providing much-needed credit for community-based development projects, was highlighted in Chapter 10. That 'Grameen model' has been extended and developed widely in other countries. However, it has also been shown that simply because something succeeds in one particular social and environmental context, it does not necessarily mean that it will succeed in a very different context. A 'blueprint approach' to development often fails because development initiatives are not carefully attuned to local environments, local cultures and the diverse needs and aspirations within local communities. Whilst it is important to understand the common factors and features that shape the nature of development in particular contexts, it is also essential to learn and change through the very processes of development research, planning and implementation – quite different challenges to a blueprint approach.

There is also a need to be aware of the structural–political argument that world patterns of development have been so unequal for so many centuries, that all 'development projects' and 'schemes' can be considered as attempts merely to 'paper over' the geo-political realities of structural poverty and inequality. For those of a radical orientation, it is the global system that is wrong – or rather the lack of a global set of solutions to what are global problems that is needed (see Chapters 1 and 4). It can be argued that the MDGs / SDGs did not and do not address the root causes of global economic inequality, such as unfair trading relations between the North and the South and the subservient economic position which much of the South appears to be locked into. As such, a radical rethink of how to achieve development may be imperative, which does not just address basic needs, but which truly empowers and benefits all peoples and countries. Steps such as the 'Tobin tax' (see Chapter 4) may well be a logical approach to addressing structural inequality and could possibly fund key outcomes such as universal education.

In almost two decades since publication of the first edition of *Geographies of Development*, some clear and measurable targets for development have emerged, such as those embodied in the Millennium Development Goals (MDGs) and the Sustainable Development Goals (SDGs) (see Chapters 1 and 7). While the MDGs did not achieve all their objectives, nor did they adequately address basic global inequality, their pursuit did make a qualitative difference in the lives of hundreds of millions of people, particularly in Asia and Latin America. One can only hope that the SDGs are able to further improve on the situation. The MDGs and SDGs have received much publicity and considerable political support internationally. Critically, they identify the significance of global responsibilities and partnerships, but they do not seek to alter the fundamental operation of the world economy, which will continue to disadvantage much of the South. They offer the potential to move beyond a view that countries in the South need to be responsible for getting their 'own house in order', and that the role of the wealthier countries in the North is to support such efforts. Chapter 7 highlighted the ongoing challenges for some of the key global institutions, as well as governments in the North, to further change the ways in which they operate and how they work with other organisations towards achieving these goals.

There is a consensus that achieving success in the SDGs will depend on improvements in governance locally within the Global South, as well as embarking on development as a 'global' project which involves all nations and peoples. As we have seen, the challenges of 'good governance' are multifaceted (Chapter 7) and encompass much more than overcoming corruption within government. In terms of financing development, there remains also a long way to go before many bilateral donors achieve the 0.7 per cent of GNP target for Official Development Assistance that was set back in 1960 (Chapter 8). The context for development has changed a great deal in the last two decades. For example, the pace of globalisation has quickened, with the progressive sophistication of information technology and the enhanced mobility of international capital (Chapter 4), while the GFC has enhanced vulnerability and susceptibility of all countries to change. Powerful North American and European-based transnational companies, and increasingly companies from the BRICS (Brazil, Russia, India, China and South Africa) countries, continue to locate more of their activity in certain countries in the South and very rapid processes of economic development have been seen in countries such as China and India (Chapters 6 and 7). But the essential challenge remains the same: to continue to question critically the benefits and costs to particular groups of people and to places both distant and less further afield.

At a more personal level, commitment to the geographies of development includes pursuing an understanding of what are the economic benefits and costs of our own consumption choices. Who we buy from, how we choose to act as global citizens, and how we consider our actions which might impact on climate change, individually and collectively, can have a profound impact on the world and its future. It is salutary to remember that despite the extension of more sophisticated communications technologies and the increasing connectivity between the Global North and South, there are still millions of people in the world's poorest regions who are without a reliable supply of fresh drinking water, let alone the electricity to power a computer (Chapters 4, 7 and 9). Another important change in the context of development seen over the last two decades has been the emergence of the so-called BRICS countries, including their rapid economic successes and power to shape resource use and new trade linkages. As we saw in Chapters 6 and 8, China's trade with Africa and Latin America has burgeoned in the last two decades and very considerable amounts of Chinese investment are now going into resource extraction and construction projects in many countries within Africa and Latin America. Such trade and investment networks are raising new questions regarding the prospects for economic stability, sovereign control, sustainability and democracy.

We firmly believe that geography and geographers have an important and distinctive role to play in understanding development, and we trust that this fourth edition of *Geographies of Development* provides good evidence of this. There has been no shortage of academic debate concerning the commitment to understanding development issues, and Potter (1993, 2001), Gilbert (1987) and others, for example, have criticised their fellow geographers for a lack of attention towards countries of the Global South (Binns, 2007). We strongly suspect that there are similar ongoing debates in other social science disciplines, where, as in geography, there is significantly more research and publishing that focuses on the Global North rather than South. But we would strongly agree with Smith (1994: 366) that there is a genuine moral and professional motivation for being concerned about improving the quality of life for the world's poorest and most marginalised people, that 'We owe distant others far more than we give them'.

We also believe that a greater understanding of the world and its peoples is an essential endeavour and one which remains important. As Johnston succinctly puts it:

> World understanding is fundamental to world peace and ultimately to world survival. Ignorance leads to the development of stereotypes, negative reactions to other peoples and cultures which breed hostility. Geography must be used to break down those barriers of ignorance.
>
> (Johnston, 1984: 458)

Above all, we hope that *Geographies of Development* can assist in this evidently necessary reduction in stereotypical, negative and pejorative thinking about other peoples, cultures and lands.

Bibliography

Actionaid (1994) *Kyuso Rural Development Area Plan and Budget*. Nairobi: Actionaid.

Actionaid (1995) *Listening to Smaller Voices: Children in an Environment of Change*. Chard: Actionaid.

Actionaid International (2004) *Money Talks: How Aid Conditions Continue to Drive Utility Privatisation in Poor Countries*. London: Actionaid International.

Actionaid International (2006) *Under the Influence: Exposing under Corporate Influence over Policy-making at the World Trade Organisation*. Johannesburg: Actionaid.

Adams, R.H. and Page, J. (2005) Do international migration and remittances reduce poverty in developing countries? *World Development*, 33(10), 1645–69.

Adams, W.M. (1990) *Green Development: Environment and Sustainability in the Third World*. London: Routledge.

Adams, W.M. (1996) Irrigation, erosion and famine: visions of environmental change in Marakwet, Kenya, in Leach, M. and Mearns, R. (eds) *The Lie of the Land: Challenging Received Wisdom on the African Environment*. Oxford: International African Institute.

Adams, W.M. (2009) *Green Development,* 3rd edn. London: Routledge.

Adams, W.M. and Anderson, D.M. (1988) Irrigation before development: indigenous and induced change in agricultural water management in East Africa. *African Affairs*, 87, 519–35.

Adams, W.M. and Hulme, D. (2001) Conservation and community: changing narratives, policies and practices in African conservation, in Hulme, D. and Murphree, M. (eds) *African Wildlife and Livelihoods: The Promise and Performance of Community Conservation*. Oxford: James Currey, 9–23.

Adger, W.N., Huq, S., Brown, K., Conway, D. and Hulme, M. (2003) Adaptation to climate change in the developing world. *Progress in Development Studies*, 3(3), 179–95.

Aeroe, A. (1992) The role of small towns in regional development in Southeast Africa, in Baker, J. and Pedersen, P.O. (eds) *The Rural–Urban Interface in Africa*. Uppsala: Nordic Institute for African Studies, 51–65.

Africa, in Leach, M. and Mearns, R. (eds) *The Lie of the Land: Challenging Received Wisdom on the African Environment*. Oxford: International African Institute/James Currey, 34–53.

African Union (2002) Transition from the OAU to the African Union. www.au2002.gov.za/docs/background/oau_to_au.htm.

Agarwal, B. (1986) *Cold Hearths and Barren Slopes: The Woodfuel Crisis in the Third World*. London: Earthscan.

Agarwal, B. (2001) Participatory exclusion, community forestry, and gender: an analysis for South Asia and a conceptual framework. *World Development*, 29(10), 1623–48.

Ageing and Development (2002) News and analysis of issues affecting the lives of older people. www.helpage.org/publications.

Agrawal, A. and Gibson, C.C. (1999) Enchantment and disenchantment: the role of community in natural resource conservation. *World Development*, 27(4), 629–49.

Aguilar, A.G., Ward, P.M. and Smith, C.B. (2003) Globalization, regional development, and mega-city expansion in Latin America: analyzing Mexico City's peri-urban hinterland. *Cities,* 20(1), 3–21.

Ahmend, K. (2002) British arms sales to Africa soar. *The Observer*, 3 February.

Aikman, D. (1986) *Pacific Rim: Area of Change, Area of Opportunity*. Boston, MA: Little Brown.

Aker, J.C. and Mbiti, I.M. (2010) *Mobile Phones and Economic Development in Africa*. CGD Working Paper 211. Washington, DC: Centre for Global Development.

Alden, C. (2012) China and Africa: the relationship matures. *Strategic Analysis*, 36(5), 701–7.

Allen, A. (2003) Environmental planning and management of the peri-urban interface: perspectives on an emerging field, *Environment and Urbanization*, 15(1), 135–47.

Allen, C. (1979) *Tales from the Dark Continent*. London: BBC/Andre Deutsch.

Allen, C. (1999) Warfare, endemic violence and state collapse in Africa. *Review of African Political Economy*, 81, 367–84.

Allen, J. (1995) Global worlds, in Allen, J. and Massey, D. (eds) *Geographical Worlds*. Oxford: Oxford University Press and Open University, 105–44.

Allen, J. and Hamnett, C. (1995) Uneven worlds, in Allen, J. and Hamnett, C. (eds) *A Shrinking World*. Oxford: Oxford University Press, 233–54.

Allen, T. and Thomas, A. (eds) (2000) *Poverty and Development into the 21st Century*. Oxford: Oxford University Press.

Alonso, W. (1968) Urban and regional imbalances in economic development. *Economic Development and Cultural Change*, 17, 1–14.

Alonso, W. (1971) The economics of urban size. *Papers of the Regional Science Association*, 26, 67–83.

Amnesty International (2002a) Children devastated by war: Afghanistan's lost generations. www.amnesty.org.

Amnesty International (2002b) Sierra Leone: childhood – a casualty of conflict. www.amnesty.org.

AND Cartographic Publishers (1997, 1999) *Political Atlas of the World*. Abingdon, Oxfordshire: Helicon Publishing.

Anderson, A. (ed) (1990) *Alternatives to Deforestation: Steps Towards Sustainable Use of the Amazon Rainforest*. New York: Columbia University Press.

Anderson, M. (2014) Aid to Africa: donations from West mask '$60bn looting' of continent. *The Guardian*, 15 July. http://www.guardian.com/global-development/2014/jul/15/aid-afri sourced (accessed 12 Feb 2015).

Andrews, N. and Bawa, S. (2014) A post-development hoax? (Re)-examining the past, present and future of development studies. *Third World Quarterly*, 35, 6, 922–938.

Annan, K. (2000) *We the Peoples: The Role of the United Nations in the Twenty-First Century*. New York: UN Department of Public Information.

Ansell, N. (2005) *Children, Youth and Development*. London: Routledge.

Apter, D. (1987) *Rethinking Development: Modernization, Dependency and Postmodern Politics*. Newbury Park, CA: Sage.

Armon, J. (2007) Aid, politics and development: a donor perspective. *Development Policy Review*, 25(5), 653–6.

Armstrong, W. and McGee, T.G. (1985) *Theatres of Accumulation: Studies in Asian and Latin American Urbanization*. London: Methuen.

Arndt, C. and Lewis, J.D. (2000) *The Macro Implications of HIV/AIDS in South Africa: A Preliminary Assessment*. Muldersdrift: Trade and Industrial Policy Secretariat.

Arnell, N.W., Livermore, M.J.L., Kovats, S., Levy, P.E., Nicholls, R., Parry, M.L. and Gaffin, S.R. (2004) Climate and socio-economic scenarios for global-scale climate change impacts assessments: characterising the SRES storylines. *Global Environmental Change*, 14, 3–20.

Ashcroft, B., Griffiths, G. and Tiffin, H. (1998) *Key Concepts in Post-Colonial Studies*. London: Routledge.

Ashley, C. and Roe, D. (2002) Making tourism work for the poor: strategies and challenges in southern Africa. *Development Southern Africa*, 19, 61–82.

Atkins, P.J. and Bowler, I.R. (2001) *Food and Society: Economy, Culture, Geography*. London: Arnold.

Augelli, J.P. and West, R.C. (1976) *Middle America: Its Land and Peoples*. Englewood Cliffs, NJ: Prentice Hall.

Auret, D. (1995) *Urban Housing: A National Crisis*. Gweru: Mambo Press.

Austin-Broos, D.J. (1995) Gay nights and Kingston Town: representations of Kingston, Jamaica, in Watson, S. and Gibson, K. (eds) *Postmodern Cities and Spaces*. Oxford: Blackwell, 149–64.

Auty, R. (1979) World within worlds. *Area*, 11, 232–35.

Auty, R. (1993) *Sustaining Development in Mineral Economies: The Resource-Curse Thesis*. London: Routledge.

Auty, R. (1994) *Patterns of Development*. London: Methuen.

Avert (2015) *Sources for HIV and AIDS Funding*. http://www.avert.org/funding-hiv-and-aids.htm (accessed 16 Mar 2015).

Azam, J.P. and Gubert, F. (2006) Migrants' remittances and the household in Africa: a review of evidence. *Journal of African Economies*, 15(AERC Supplement 2), 426–62.

Baez, A.L. (1996) Learning from experience in the Monteverde Cloud Forest, Costa Rica, in Price, M.F. (ed) *People and Tourism in Fragile Environments*. Chichester: John Wiley, 109–22.

Bairoch, P. (1975) *The Economic Development of the Third World Since 1900*. London: Methuen.

Baker, J. and Pedersen, P.O. (eds) (1992) *The Rural–Urban Interface in Africa*. Uppsala: Nordic Institute for African Studies.

Balagangadhara, S.N. and Keppens, M. (2009) Reconceptualizing the postcolonial project. *International Journal of Postcolonial Studies*, 11(1), 50–68.

Banks, N. and Hulme, D. (2014) New development alternatives or business as usual with a new face? The transformative potential of new actors and alliances in development. *Third World Quarterly*, 35(1), 181–95.

Banks, N., Hulme, D. and Edwards, M. (2015) NGOs, states, and donors revisited: still too close for comfort? *World Development*, 66, 707–18.

Baran, P. (1957) *Political Economy of Growth*. Monthly Review Press: New York.

Baran, P. (1973) *The Political Economy of Growth*. Harmondsworth: Penguin.

Baran, P. and Sweezy, P. (1968) *Monopoly Capitalism*. Harmondsworth: Penguin.

Baran, P. and Sweezy, P. (1998) *Monopoly Capital*. Harmondsworth: Penguin.

Barbier, E. (2011) The policy challenges for green economy and sustainable development. *Natural Resources Forum*, 35, 233–45.

Barff, R. and Austen, J. (1993) 'It's gotta be da shoes': domestic manufacturing, international subcontracting, and the production of athletic footwear. *Environment and Planning A*, 25, 1103–14.

Barke, M. and O'Hare, G. (1991) *The Third World*, 2nd edn. Harlow: Oliver & Boyd.

Barnett, T. (2002a) HIV/AIDS impact studies II: some progress evident. *Progress in Development Studies*, 2, 219–25.

Barnett, T. (2002b) The social and economic impacts of HIV/AIDS on development, ch. 8.3 in Desai, V. and Potter, R.B. (eds) *The Companion to Development Studies*. London: Arnold, 391–5.

Barnett, T., Whiteside, A. and Desmond, D. (2001) The social impact of HIV/AIDS in poor countries: a review of studies and lessons. *Progress in Development Studies*, 1, 151–70.

Barratt-Brown, M. (1974) *The Economics of Imperialism*. Harmondsworth: Penguin.

Barrett, H. and Browne, A. (1995) Gender, environment and development in Sub-Saharan Africa, in Binns, T. (ed) *People and Environment in Africa*. Chichester: John Wiley, 31–8.

Barrett, H.R., Binns, T., Browne, A.W., Ilbery, B.W. and Jackson, G.H. (1997) Prospects for horticultural exports under trade liberalisation in adjusting African economies. Unpublished report to the Overseas Development Administration, London.

Barrett, H.R., Browne, A.W., Ilbery, B.W. and Binns, T. (1999) Globalisation and the changing networks of food supply: the importation of fresh horticultural produce from Kenya into the UK. *Transactions of the Institute of British Geographers*, NS 24(2), 159–74.

Barrow, C. (1987) *Water Resources and Agricultural Development in the Tropics*. London: Longman.

Barrow, C.J. (1995) *Developing the Environment: Problems and Management*. London: Longman.

Bartone, C. et al. (1994) *Towards Environmental Strategies for Cities*. Urban Management Policy Paper 18, 'Strategic Options for Managing the Urban Environment'. Washington, DC: World Bank.

Basnett, B.S. (2016) Gender, migration and forest governance: rethinking community forestry policies in Nepal, in Pierce-Colfer, C.J., Basnett, B.S. and Elias, M. (eds) *Gender and Forests: Climate Change, Tenure, Value Chains and Emerging Issues*. London: Routledge, 283–98.

Bassett, T.J. (1993) The land question and agricultural transformation in sub-Saharan Africa, in Bassett, T.J. and Crummey, D.E. (eds) *Land in African Agrarian Systems*. Madison, WI: University of Wisconsin Press, 3–34.

Batley, R. (2002) The changing role of the state in development, ch. 2.16 in Desai, V. and Potter, R.B. (eds) *The Companion to Development Studies*. London: Arnold, 135–9.

Batterbury, S. and Warren, A. (2001) The African Sahel 25 years after the great drought: assessing progress and moving towards new agendas and approaches. *Global Environmental Change*, 11, 1–8.

Bauer, P.T. (1975) Western guilt and Third World poverty. *Quadrant*, 20(4), 13–22.

Bauer, P.T. (1976) *Dissent on Development*. London: Weidenfeld & Nicolson.

BBC (2016) *Are Young South Africans Ignoring the AIDS Message?* http://www.bbc.co.uk/news/world-africa-36795484 (accessed 19 July 2016).

Bebbington, A. (1999) Capitals and capabilities: a framework for analysing peasant viability, rural livelihoods and poverty. *World Development*, 27(12), 2021–44.

Bebbington, A., Bebbington, D.H., Bury, J., and Munoz, J.P. (2008) Mining and social movements: struggles over livelihood and rural territorial development in the Andes. *World Development,* 36(12), 2888–905.

Becker, C.M. and Morrison, A.R. (1997) Public policy and rural–urban migration, in Gugler, J. (ed) *Cities in the Developing World*. Oxford: Oxford University Press, 88–105.

Beckford, G. (1972) *Persistent Poverty: Underdevelopment in Plantation Economies of the Third World*. New York: Oxford University Press.

Behnke, R. and Mortimore, M. (eds) (2016) *The End of Desertification?: Disputing Environmental Change in the Drylands*. Heidelberg: Springer.

Beijing Review (1987) Tibet is an inalienable part of Chinese territory. *Beijing Review*, 19 October, 14.

Bek, D., Binns, T. and Nel, E. (2013) Wild flower harvesting on South Africa's Agulhas Plain: a mechanism for achieving sustainable local economic development? *Sustainable Development*, 21(5), 281–93.

Bek, D., Binns, T., Nel, E. and Ellison, B. (2006) Achieving grassroots transformation in post-apartheid South Africa. *International Journal of Development Issues*, 5(2), 65–94.

Bell, M. (1980) Imperialism: an introduction, in Peet, R. (ed) *An Introduction to Marxist Theories of Underdevelopment*, Monograph HG14, RSPACS. Canberra: Australian National University, 39–50.

Benjaminsen, T.A. and Bryceson, I. (2012) Conservation, green/blue grabbing and accumulation by dispossession in Tanzania. *Journal of Peasant Studies*, 39(2), 335–55.

Bernstein, H. (1992a) Agrarian structures and change: India, in Bernstein, H., Crow, B. and Johnson, H. (eds) *Rural Livelihoods: Crises and Responses*. Oxford: Oxford University Press, 51–64.

Bernstein, H. (1992b) Agrarian structures and change: Latin America, in Bernstein, H., Crow, B. and Johnson, H. (eds) *Rural Livelihoods: Crises and Responses*. Oxford: Oxford University Press, 27–50.

Bernstein, H. (1992c) Poverty and the poor, in Bernstein, H., Crow, B. and Johnson, H. (eds) *Rural Livelihoods: Crises and Responses*. Oxford: Oxford University Press, 13–26.

Bernstein, H., Crow, B. and Johnson, H. (eds) (1992) *Rural Livelihoods: Crises and Responses*. Oxford: Oxford University Press.

Berry, B.J.L. (1961) City size distributions and economic development. *Economic Development and Cultural Change*, 9, 573–87.

Berry, B.J.L. (1972) Hierarchical diffusion: the basis of development filtering and spread in a system of growth centres, in Hansen, N.M. (ed) *Growth Centres in Regional Economic Development*. New York: Free Press.

Bhabha, H. (1994) *The Location of Culture*. London: Routledge.

Bicknell, J., Dodman, D. and Satterthwaite, D. (2009) *Adapting Cities to Climate Change*. London: Earthscan.

Biermann, F. (2013) Curtain down and nothing settled: global sustainability governance after the 'Rio+20' Earth Summit. *Environment and Planning C,* 31, 1099–1114.

Bigg, T. (ed) (2004) *Survival for a Small Planet: The Sustainable Development Agenda*. London: Earthscan/IIED.

Binns, T. (1992) Traditional agriculture, pastoralism and fishing, in Gleave, M.B. (ed) *Tropical African Development*. London: Longman, 153–91.

Binns, T. (1994a) *Tropical Africa*. London: Routledge.

Binns, T. (1994b) Ghana: West Africa's latest success story? *Teaching Geography*, 19(4), 147–53.

Binns, T. (1995a) Geography in development: development in geography. *Geography*, 80(4), 303–22.

Binns, T. (ed) (1995b) *People and Environment in Africa*. Chichester: John Wiley.

Binns, T. (1997) People, environment and development in Africa. *South African Geographical Journal*, 79(1), 13–18.

Binns, T. (2007) Marginal lands, marginal geographies. *Progress in Human Geography*, 31(5), 587–91.

Binns, T. and Fereday, N. (1996) Feeding Africa's urban poor: urban and peri-urban horticulture in Kano, Nigeria. *Geography*, 81, 380–4.

Binns, T. and Funnell, D.C. (1983) Geography and integrated rural development. *Geografiska Annaler B*, 65(1), 57–63.

Binns, T. and Funnell, D.C. (1989) Irrigation and rural development in Morocco. *Land Use Policy*, 6(1), 43–52.

Binns, T. and Lynch, K. (1998) Feeding Africa's growing cities into the 21st century: the potential of urban agriculture. *Journal of International Development*, 10, 777–93.

Binns, T. and Maconachie, R. (2006) Post-conflict reconstruction and sustainable development: diamonds, agriculture and rural livelihoods in Sierra Leone. *International Journal of Cultural, Economic and Social Sustainability*, 2, 205–16.

Binns, T. and Mortimore, M. (1989) Ecology, time and development in Kano State, Nigeria, in Swindell, K., Baba, J.M. and Mortimore, M.J. (eds) *Inequality and Development: Case Studies from the Third World*. London: Macmillan, 359–80.

Binns, T. and Nel, E.L. (2002) Tourism as a local development strategy in South Africa. *Geographical Journal*, 168(3), 235–47.

Binns, T. and Robinson, R. (2002) Sustaining democracy in the 'new' South Africa. *Geography*, 87(1), 25–37.

Birner, R., Cohen, M.J. and Ilukor, J. (2011) *Rebuilding Agricultural Livelihoods in Post-Conflict Situations: What are the Governance Challenges?* The Case of Northern Uganda, USSP Working Paper 07. Washington: IFPRI. http://www.ifpri.org/sites/default/files/publications/usspwp07.pdf (accessed 20 Mar 2015).

Biswas, A.K. (1992) Water for Third World development. *Water Resources Development*, 8(1), 3–9.

Biswas, A.K. (1993) Management of international waters. *International Journal of Water Resources Development*, 9(2), 167–89.

Biswas, A.K. (2004) From Mar del Plata to Kyoto: an analysis of global water policy dialogue. *Global Environmental Change*, 14, 81–8.

Biswas, A.K. and Biswas, A. (1985) The global environment. *Resources Policy*, 11(1), 25–42.

Black, R. (1996) Refugees and environmental change: the case of the forest region of Guinea. Unpublished Project CFCE Report No. 2, University of Sussex, Brighton.

Black, R. (1997) Refugees, land cover, and environmental change in the Senegal River Valley. *Geojournal*, 41(1), 55–67.

Black, R., Bennett, S.R.G., Thomas, S.M. and Beddington, J.R. (2011) Climate change: migration as adaptation. *Nature*, 478, 477–9.

Black, R. and White, H. (eds) (2004) *Targeting Development: Critical Perspectives on the Millennium Development Goals*. Abingdon, London and New York: Routledge.

Blaikie, P. (1985) *The Political Economy of Soil Erosion in Developing Countries*. London: Longman.

Blaikie, P. (2000) Development, post-, anti-, and populist: a critical review. *Environment and Planning A*, 32, 1033–50.

Blaikie, P. (2002) Vulnerability and disasters, in Desai, V. and Potter, R.B. (eds) *The Companion to Development Studies*. London: Arnold, 298–305.

Blaikie, P. (2006) Is small really beautiful? Community based natural resource management in Malawi and Botswana. *World Development*, 34(11), 1942–57.

Blaikie, P. and Brookfield, H. (eds) (1987) *Land Degradation and Society*. London: Methuen.

Blanton, R., Mason, T.D. and Athow, B. (2001) Colonial style and post-colonial ethnic conflict in Africa. *Journal of Peace Research*, 38(4), 473–491.

Blaut, J. (1993) *The Colonizers' Model of the World*. London: Guildford.

Blouet, B.W. and Blouet, O.M. (2002) *Latin America and the Caribbean: A Systematic and Regional Survey*. New York: John Wiley.

Blunt, A. (1994) *Travel, Gender and Imperialism: Mary Kingsley and West Africa*. New York: Guilford.

Blunt, A. and McEwan, C. (eds) (2002) *Postcolonial Geographies*. London: Continuum.

Blunt, A. and Wills, J. (2000) *Dissident Geographies*. London: Prentice Hall.

Boas, M. (2014) Multilateral institutions, in Desai, V. and Potter, R.B. (2014) (eds) *The Companion to Development Studies*, 3rd edn. London: Routledge, 578–83.

Bojo, J., Green, K., Kishore, S., Pilapitiya, S. and Chandra Reddy, R. (2004) *Environment in Poverty Reduction Strategies and Poverty Reduction Support Credits*. Washington: World Bank Environment Department, IBRD.

Bond, P. (2006) *Looting Africa*. London: Zed Books.

Bongaarts, J. (1994) Demographic transition, in Eblen, R.A. and Eblen, W.R. (eds) *Encyclopedia of the Environment*. Boston, MA: Houghton-Mifflin, 132.

Bongaarts, J. (1995) Global and regional population projections to 2025, in Islam, N. (ed) *Population and Food in the Early Twenty-First Century: Meeting Future Food Demand of an Increasing Population*. Washington, DC: International Food Policy Research Institute, 7–16.

Booth, D. (1985) Marxism and development sociology: interpreting the impasse. *World Development*, 13, 761–87.

Booth, D. (1993) Development research: from impasse to new agenda, in Schurmann, F. (ed) *Beyond the Impasse: New Directions in Development Theory*. London: Zed Books.

Booth, K. (1997) Exporting ethics in place of arms. *The Times Higher Education Supplement*, 7 November, 118.

Borchert, J.R. (1967) American metropolitan evolution. *Geographical Review*, 57, 301–23.

Boserup, E. (1965) *The Conditions of Agricultural Growth: The Economics of Agricultural Change Under Population Pressure*. London: Allen & Unwin.

Boserup, E. (1993) *The Conditions of Agricultural Growth*. London: Earthscan (first published in 1965).

Botes, L.J. (1996) *Promoting Community Participation in Development Initiatives*. Paper presented to the Development Studies Association Annual Conference, University of Reading.

Bourdieu, F. (1998) The essence of neoliberalism. *Le Monde Diplomatique*, December 1998.

Boyd, E. (2014) Climate change and development, in Desai, V. and Potter, R.B. (eds) (2014) *The Companion to Development Studies*, 3rd edn. London: Arnold, 341–6.

Boyden, J. and Holden, P. (1991) *Children of the Cities*. London: Zed Books.

Braidotti, R., Charkiewicz, E., Hausler, S. and Wieringa, S. (1994) *Women, the Environment and Sustainable Development: Towards a Theoretical Synthesis*. London: Zed Books.

Brandt, W. (1980) *North–South: A Programme For Survival*. London: Pan.

Brandt, W. (1983) *Common Crisis. North–South: Co-operation for World Recovery*. London: Pan.

Brazier, C. (1994) Winds of change. *New Internationalist*, 262, 4–7.

Brierley, J. (1989) A review of development strategies and programmes of the People's Revolutionary Government in Grenada, 1979–83. *Geographical Journal*, 151, 40–52.

Brierley, J.S. (1985a) Idle land in Grenada: a review of its causes and the PRG's approach to reducing the problem. *Canadian Geographer*, 29, 298–309.

Brierley, J.S. (1985b) The agricultural strategies and programmes of the People's Revolutionary Government in Grenada, 1979–1983, in *Conference of Latin American Geographers Yearbook*, 55–61.

Brimblecombe, P. (2000) Urban air pollution and public health, in O'Riordan, T. (ed) *Environmental Science for Environmental Management*. Harlow: Pearson Education, 399–416.

Brohman, J. (1996) *Popular Development: Rethinking the Theory and Practice of Development*. Oxford: Blackwell.

Brookfield, H. (1975) *Interdependent Development*. London: Methuen.

Brookfield, H. (1978) Third World Development. *Progress in Human Geography*, 2(1), 121–32.

Brookfield, H. and Stocking, M. (1999) Agrodiversity: definition, description and design. *Global Environmental Change*, 9, 77–80.

Brown, D.L. and Fox, J. (2001) Transnational civil society coalitions and the World Bank: lessons from project and policy influence campaigns, in Edwards, M. and Gaventa, J. (eds) *Global Citizen Action*. London: Earthscan, 43–58.

Brown, I. (2014) The company they keep. *New Internationalist*, 478, 16–7.

Brown, L.R. (1996a) *The Potential Impact of AIDS on Population and Economic Growth Rates*. Food,

Agriculture and the Environment, Discussion Paper 15. Washington, DC: International Food Policy Research Institute.

Brown, L.R. (ed) (1996b) *Vital Signs, 1996/1997: The Trends That are Shaping our Future*. London: Earthscan.

Browne, A.W. and Barrett, H.R. (1995) *Children and AIDS in Africa*. African Studies Centre Paper 2. Coventry: Coventry University.

Browne, S. (2011) *The UN Development Programme and System*. London: Routledge.

Browne, S. (2014) A changing world: is the UN development system ready? *Third World Quarterly*, 35(10), 1845–59.

Bruce, J.W. (1998) *Country Profiles of Tenure: Africa, 1996*. Land Tenure Center, University of Wisconsin-Madison.

Brundtland Commission (1987) *Our Common Future*. Oxford: Oxford University Press.

Bryant, R.L. and Bailey, S. (1997) *Third World Political Ecology*. London: Routledge.

Bryceson, D.F. (2002) The scramble in Africa: reorienting rural livelihoods. *World Development*, 30(5), 725–39.

Buchanan, K. (1964) Profiles of the Third World. *Pacific Viewpoint*, 5(2), 97–126.

Buckley, R. (1994) *NAFTA and GATT: The Impact of Free Trade*, Understanding global issues series, 94(2). Cheltenham: Understanding Global Issues Ltd.

Buckley, R. (1995) *The United Nations: Overseeing the New World Order*, Understanding global issues series 93(6). Cheltenham: Understanding Global Issues Ltd.

Buckley, R. (ed) (1996) *Fairer Global Trade: The Challenge for the WTO*, Understanding global issues series 96(6). Cheltenham: Understanding Global Issues Ltd.

Budds, J. and Loftus, A. (2014) Water and hydropolitics, in Desai, V. and Potter, R.B. (2014) (eds) *The Companion to Development Studies,* 3rd edn. London: Routledge, 365–9.

Budds, J. and McGranahan, G. (2003) Are the debates on water privatisation missing the point? *Environment and Urbanisation*, 15(2), 87–113.

Bugalski, N. and Pred, D. (eds) (2013) *Reforming the World Bank Policy on Involuntary Resettlement*. Calabasas, USA: Inclusive Development International.

Bulkeley, H. et al. (2013) Governing sustainability: Rio+20 and the road beyond. *Environment & Planning C*, 31, 958–70.

Bunsha, D. (2014) Contested territory. *New Internationalist,* 478, 22–4.

Burgess, R. (1990) The state and self-help building in Pereira, Colombia. Unpublished PhD thesis, University of London.

Burgess, R. (1992) Helping some to help themselves: Third World housing policies and development strategies, in Mathéy, K. (ed) *Beyond Self-Help Housing*. London: Mansell, 75–91.

Burgess, R., Carmona, K. and Kolstree, T.C. (1997) *The Challenge of Sustainable Cities*. London: Zed Books.

Burns, J.P. (1999) The Hong Kong civil service in transition. *Journal of Contemporary China*, 8(20), 67–87.

Bury, J. (2001) Corporations and capitals: a framework for evaluating the impacts of transnational corporations in developing countries. *Journal of Corporate Citizenship*, 1(1), 75–91.

Buvinic, M. (1993) *The Feminisation of Poverty? Research and Policy Needs*. Paper presented at ILS Symposium on Poverty: New Approaches to Analysis and Policy, Geneva, 22–24 November.

Campbell, B., Mandondo, A., Nemarundwe, N., Sithole, B., de Jong, W. and Matose, F. (2001) Challenges to proponents of common property resource systems: despairing voices from the social forests of Zimbabwe. *World Development* 29(4), 589–600.

Carbon Trust (2006) *The Carbon Trust Three Stage Approach to Developing a Robust Offsetting Strategy*. London: Carbon Trust, www.carbontrust.co.uk/publications.

Cardoso, F.H. (1969) *Dependency and Development in Latin America*. Los Angeles: University of California Press.

Cardoso, F.H. (1976) The consumption of dependency theory in the United States. *Proceedings of the Third Scandinavian Research Conference on Latin America*, Bergen.

Carney, D., Drinkwater, M., Rusinow, T., Neefjes, K., Wanmali, S. and Singh, N. (1999) *Livelihood Approaches Compared*. London: Department for International Development.

Carr, D.L., Suter, L. and Barbieri, A. (2005) Population dynamics and tropical deforestation: state of the debate and conceptual challenges. *Population and Environment*, 27(1), 89–113.

Carr, E.R. (2014) From description to explanation: using the Livelihoods as Intimate Government (LIG) approach. *Applied Geography*, 52, 110–22.

Cashin, P.C., Liang, H. and McDermott, C.J. (1999) Do commodity price shocks last too long for stabilization schemes to work? *Finance and Development*, 36(3), 40–3.

Castells, M. (1977) *The Urban Question: A Marxist Approach*. London: Edward Arnold.

Castells, M. (1978) Urban social movements and the struggle for democracy. *International Journal of Urban and Regional Research*, 1, 133–46.

Castells, M. (1983) *The City and the Grassroots*. London: Edward Arnold.

Castells, M. (1996) *The Rise of the Network Society*. Oxford: Blackwell.

Cater, E. (1992) Must tourism destroy its resource base? in Mannion, A.M. and Bowlby, S.R. (eds) *Environmental Issues in the 1990s*. London: John Wiley, 309–24.

Cavendish, W. (2000) Empirical regularities in the poverty–environment relationship of rural households: evidence from Zimbabwe. *World Development*, 28(11), 1979–2000.

Center for Human Rights and Global Justice (2011) *Every Thirty Minutes: Farmer Suicides, Human Rights and the Agrarian Crisis in India*. New York: NYU School of Law.

Chambers, R. (1983) *Rural Development: Putting the Last First*. London: Longman.

Chambers, R. (1993) *Challenging the Professions: Frontiers for Rural Development*. London: Intermediate Technology Publications.

Chambers, R. (1997) *Whose Reality Counts?* London: Intermediate Technology Publications.

Chambers, R. (2005) *Ideas for Development*. London: Earthscan.

Chambers, R. (2008) *Revolutions in Development Inquiry*. London: Earthscan.

Chambers, R. and Conway, G. (1992) *Sustainable Rural Livelihoods: Practical Concepts for the Twenty-first Century*. IDS discussion paper 296. Brighton: IDS.

Chambers, R., Pacey, A. and Thrupp, L.A. (1989) *Farmer First*. London: Intermediate Technology Publications.

Chandra, R. (1992) *Industrialization and Development in the Third World*. London and New York: Routledge.

Chant, S. (1996) *Gender, Uneven Development and Housing*. New York: UNDP.

Chant, S. and McIlwaine, C. (2009) *Geographies of Development in the 21st Century*. Cheltenham: Edward Elgar.

Chatterjee, P. (1994) Riders of the apocalypse. *New Internationalist*, 262, 10–11.

Chen, Y. (2014) Five fingers or one hand? The BRICS in development cooperation. *IDS Policy Briefing*, 69(June). Brighton: Institute for Development Studies.

Chin, G.T. (2014) The BRICS-led development bank: purpose and politics beyond the G20. *Global Policy*, 5(3/Sept).

Choguill, C. (1994) Crisis, chaos, crunch: planning for urban growth in the developing world. *Urban Studies*, 31, 935–45.

Chonghaile, C.N. (2014) Poor countries must undergo economic transformation to beat poverty, says UN. *The Guardian*. http://www.theguardian.com/global-development/2014/nov/27/poor-c (accessed 12 Jan 2015).

Christaller, W. (1933) Die zentralen Onte in Suddeutschland. Doctoral thesis translated by Baskin, C.W. (1966) *Central Places in Southern Germany*. Englewood Cliffs, NJ: Prentice Hall.

Christanty, L. (1986) Traditional agroforestry in West Java: the *pekarangan* (home garden) and *kebuntalun* (annual perennial rotation) cropping systems, in Marten, G.G. (ed) *Traditional Agroforestry in Southeast Asia: A Human Ecology Perspective*. Boulder, CO: Westview, 132–58.

Christian Aid (1996) *The Global Supermarket*. London: Christian Aid.

Christian Aid (2004) *Fuelling Poverty*. London: Christian Aid.

Chuta, E. and Liedholm, C. (1990) Rural small-scale industry: empirical evidence and policy issues, in

Eicher, C.K. and Staatz, J.M. (eds) *Agricultural Development in the Third World*, 2nd edn. Baltimore, MD: Johns Hopkins University Press, 327–41.

Cities Alliance (1999) *Cities Without Slums: Global Action Plan for Moving Slum Upgrading to Scale*. Washington: Cities Alliance.

Cities Alliance (2006) *Poverty in the Urban Environment*. Washington: Cities Alliance.

Cities Alliance (2013) *Cities Alliance for Cities Without Slums: Action Plan for Moving Slum Upgrading to Scale*. Washington: Cities Alliance and World Bank.

Cities Alliance (2015) *National Urban Policies: A Global Overview*. Washington: Cities Alliance and UN-HABITAT.

Clapham, C. (1985) *Third World Politics*. London: Croom Helm.

Clark, D. (1996) *Urban World–Global City*. London: Routledge.

Clark, D. (2006) *The Elgar Companion to Development Studies*. Cheltenham: Edward Elgar.

Clarke, C. (2002) The Latin American structuralists, ch. 2.7 in Desai, V. and Potter, R.B. (eds) *The Companion to Development Studies*. London: Arnold, 92–6.

Clarke, K. (2001) ICT: What does it all mean? *Developments (DfID)*, 16, 5–9.

Clayton, A. and Potter, R.B. (1996) Industrial development and foreign direct investment in Barbados. *Geography*, 81, 176–80.

Clayton, K. (1995) The threat of global warming, in O'Riordan, T. (ed) *Environmental Science for Environmental Management*. London: Longman, 110–31.

Cliff, A.D. and Smallman-Raynor, M.R. (1992) The AIDS pandemic: global geographical patterns and local spatial processes. *Geographical Journal*, 158(2), 182–98.

Clifford, M. (1994) Social engineers. *Far Eastern Economic Review*, 14 April, 56–58.

Cline-Cole, R. (1996) Dryland forestry: manufacturing forests and farming trees in Nigeria, in Leach, M. and Mearns, R. (eds) *The Lie of the Land*. Oxford: James Currey.

Clinton, B. (2001) The struggle for the soul of the 21st century. The Richard Dimbleby Lecture 2001. www.bbc.co.uk/arts/news-comment/dimbleby.

Cochrane, A. (1995) Global worlds and worlds of difference, in Anderson, J., Brook, C. and Cochrane, A. (eds) *A Global World?* Oxford: Oxford University Press and Open University, 249–80.

Coe, N.M. and Yeung, H.W-C. (2015) Global Production Networks: Theorizing Economic Development in an Interconnected World. Oxford: Oxford University Press.

Cohen, B. (2004) Urban growth in developing countries: a review of current trends and a caution regarding existing forecasts. *World Bank*, 32(1), 23–51.

Colchester, M. (1991) Guatemala: the clamour for land and the fate of the forests. *The Ecologist*, 21(4), 177–85.

Colchester, M. and Lohmann, L. (eds) (1993) *The Struggle for Land and the Fate of the Forests*. London: Zed Books.

Coles, A., Gray, L. and Momsen, J. (eds) *The Routledge Handbook of Gender and Development,* London: Routledge.

Collier, P. (2008) *The Bottom Billion*. Oxford: Oxford University Press.

Commodityexpert (1999) World coffee production estimates detailed. 5 August 1999. www.commodityexpert.com/Archive/Analysis/990805wrdprod2.htm.

Commission for Africa (2005) *Final Report*. 11 March. http://www.commissionforafrica.info/2005-report (accessed 15 July 2017).

Concise Oxford Dictionary (1999) Oxford: Oxford University Press.

Conroy, C. and Litvinoff, M. (1988) *The Greening of Aid: Sustainable Livelihoods in Practice*. London: Earthscan.

Conway, D. and Heynen, N. (2002) Classical dependency theories: from ECLA to Andre Gunder Frank, ch. 2.8 in Desai, V. and Potter, R.B. (2002) *The Companion to Development Studies*. London: Arnold.

Conway, D. and Heynen, N. (2006) *Globalization's Contradictions: Geographies of Discipline, Destruction and Transformation*. London and New York: Routledge.

Conway, D. and Potter, R.B. (2007) Caribbean transnational return migrants as agents of change. *Geography Compass*, I, 25–45.

Conway, G. (1997) *The Doubly Green Revolution: Food for All in the 21st Century*. London: Penguin.

Conway, G. and Barbier, E. (1995) Pricing policy and sustainability in Indonesia, in Kirkby, J., O'Keefe, P. and Timberlake, L. (eds) The *Earthscan Reader in Sustainable Development*. London: Earthscan, 151–7.

Conyers, D. (1982) *An Introduction to Social Planning in the Third World*. Chichester: Wiley.

Cooke, B. and Kothari, U. (eds) (2001) *Participation: The New Tyranny?* London: Zed Books.

Cooke, P. (1990) Modern urban theory in question. *Transactions of the Institute of British Geographers*, New Series, 15, 331–43.

Corbridge, S. (1986) *Capitalist World Development*. London: Macmillan.

Corbridge, S. (1992) Third World development. *Progress in Human Geography*, 16(54), 584–95.

Corbridge, S. (1993a) Colonialism, post-colonialism and the Third World, in Taylor, P. (ed) *Political Geography of the Twentieth Century*. London: Belhaven, 173–205.

Corbridge, S. (1993b) Marxisms, modernities and moralities: development praxis and the claims of distant strangers. *Environment and Planning D*, 11, 449–72.

Corbridge, S. (1997) Beneath the pavement only soil: the poverty of post-development. *Journal of Development Studies*, 33, 138–48.

Corbridge, S. (2002a) Development as freedom: the spaces of Amartya Sen. *Progress in Development Studies*, 2, 183–217.

Corbridge, S. (2002b) Third World debt, in Desai, V. and Potter, R.B. (eds) *The Companion to Development Studies*. London: Arnold, 477–80.

Corbridge, S. (ed) (1995) *Development Studies: A Reader*. London: Edward Arnold.

Cornia, G.A., Jolly, R. and Stewart, F. (eds) (1987) *Adjustment with a Human Face: Vol. 1, Protecting the Vulnerable and Promoting Growth*. Oxford: Clarendon.

Council of Europe (1998) *Conceptual Framework, Methodologies and Presentation of Good Practices*. Final Report of Activities of the Group of Specialists on Mainstreaming (EG-S-MS), Strasbourg, May 1998.

The Courier (1996) Country report – Kenya. *The Courier*, 157, 19–36.

Courtenay, P.P. (ed) (1994) *Geography and Development*. Melbourne: Longman Cheshire.

Cowen, M.P. and Shenton, R. (1995) The invention of development, in Crush, J. (ed) *Power of Development*. London: Routledge, 27–43.

Cowen, M.P. and Shenton, R.W. (1996) *Doctrines of Development*. London: Routledge.

Craig, D. and Porter, D. (2006) *Development beyond Neo-liberalism? Governance, Poverty Reduction and Political Economy*. London: Routledge.

Craig, G. and Mayo, M. (eds) (1995) *Community Empowerment: A Reader in Participation and Development*. London: Zed Books.

Crang, P. (2000) Worlds of consumption, ch. 4 in Daniels, P., Bradshaw, M., Shaw, D. and Sidaway, J. (eds) *Human Geography: Issues for the Twenty-First Century*. London and New York: Prentice Hall, 399–426.

Crehan, K. (1992) Rural households: making a living, in Bernstein, H., Crow, B. and Johnson, H. (eds) *Rural Livelihoods: Crises and Responses*. Oxford: Oxford University Press, 87–112.

Crook, C. (1991) Two pillars of wisdom. *The Economist*, 12 October, 3–4.

Crook, N. (1997) *Principles of Population and Development*. Oxford: Oxford University Press.

Crow, B. (1992) Rural livelihoods: action from above, in Bernstein, H., Crow, B. and Johnson, H. (eds) *Rural Livelihoods: Crises and Responses*. Oxford: Oxford University Press, 251–74.

Crush, J. (1995a) Imagining development, in Crush, J. (ed) *Power of Development*. London: Routledge, 1–26.

Crush, J. (ed) (1995b) *Power of Development*. London: Routledge.

Curtis, M. (2001a) What's wrong with international trade rules? *Christian Aid News*, 14(Autumn), 12–13.

Curtis, M. (2001b) *Trade for Life: Making Trade Work for Poor People*. London: Christian Aid.

Cuthbert, A. (1995) Under the volcano: postmodern space in Hong Kong, in Watson, S. and Gibson, K. (eds) *Postmodern Cities and Space*. Oxford: Blackwell, 138–48.

Dandekar, H.C. (1997) Changing migration strategies in Deccan Maharashtra, India, 1885–1990, in Gugler, J. (ed) *Cities in the Developing World*. Oxford: Oxford University Press, 48–61.

Daniel, M.L. (2000) The demographic impact of HIV/ AIDS in sub-Saharan Africa. *Geography*, 85(1), 46–55.

Dankelman, I. and Davidson, J. (1988) *Women and Environment in the Third World: Alliance for the Future*. London: Earthscan.

Dann, G. and Potter, R.B. (2001) Supplanting the planters: new plantations for old in Barbados. *International Journal of Tourism and Hospitality Research,* 2, 51–84.

Dann, G.M.S. and Potter, R.B. (1994) Tourism and postmodernity in a Caribbean setting. *Cahiers du Tourisme, Series C*, 185, 1–45.

Dann, G.M.S. and Potter, R.B. (1997) Tourism in Barbados: rejuvenation or decline? in Lockhart, D.G. and Drakakis-Smith, D. (eds) *Island Tourism: Trends and Prospects*. London: Mansell, 205–28.

Daskon, C. and Binns, T. (2010) Culture, tradition and sustainable rural livelihoods: exploring the culture-development interface in Kandy, Sri Lanka. *Community Development Journal,* 45(4), 494–517.

Daskon, C. and Binns, T. (2012) Practising Buddhism in a development context: Sri Lanka's Sarvodaya movement. *Development in Practice*, 22(5/6), 867–74.

Daskon, C. and McGregor, A. (2012) Cultural capital and sustainable livelihoods in Sri Lanka's rural villages: Towards culturally aware development. *Journal of Development Studies*, 48(4), 549–63.

Datta, G. and Meerman, J. (1980) *Household Income and Household Income Per Capita in Welfare Comparisons*. World Bank Staff Working Paper 378. Washington, DC: World Bank.

Davies, M. (2006) *Planet of Slums*. London: Verso.

Davin, D. (1996) Migration and rural women in China: a look at the gendered impact of large-scale migration. *Journal of International Development*, 8(5), 655–65.

Davis, B., Winters, P. and Carletto, G. (2010) A cross-country comparison of rural income generating activities. *World Development*, 38(1), 48–63.

de Albuquerque, K. (1996) Computer technologies and the Caribbean. *Caribbean Week*, 8, 32–3.

de Janvry, A. (1984) The role of land reform in economic development, in Eicher, C. and Staatz, J.M. (eds) *Agricultural Development in the Third World*. Baltimore, MD: Johns Hopkins University Press, 262–77.

de Jode, J. (ed) (2009) *Modern and Mobile: The Future of Livestock Production in Africa's Drylands*. London: IIED.

De Stefano, L., Edwards, P., de Silva, L. and Wold, A.T. (2010) Tracking cooperation and conflict in international basins: historic and recent trends. *Water Policy* 12(2010), 871–84.

Debray, R. (1974) *A Critique of Arms*. Paris: Seuil.

DEFRA (UK Government) (2005) The validity of food miles as an indicator of sustainable development. statistics.defra.gov.uk/esg/reports/foodmiles/ execsumm.pdf.

Deininger, K. and Byerle, D. (2012) The rise of large farms in land abundant countries: do they have a future? *World Development*, 40(4), 701–14.

Deneulin, S. and Rakodi, C. (2011) Revisiting religion: development studies thirty years on. *World Development*, 39(1), 45–54.

Denny, C. (2001) For richer – and for poorer. *The Guardian*, 23 January.

Department for International Development (DFID) (1997) *White Paper on Eliminating World Poverty: A Challenge for the Twenty First Century*. London: Government Stationery Office.

Department for International Development (DFID) (2000a) *Eliminating World Poverty: Making Globalisation Work for the Poor*. White Paper on International Development. London: DfID.

Department for International Development (DFID) (2000b) *Debt Relief for Poverty Reduction*, background briefing, September. London: DfID.

Department for International Development (DFID) (2000c) *The Crisis in Ethiopia*, background briefing, April. London: DfID.

Department for International Development (DFID) (2001a) *Addressing the Water Crisis, Strategies for Achieving the International Development Targets*. London: DfID.

Department for International Development (DFID) (2001b) *Untying Aid*, background briefing, September. London: DfID.

Department for International Development (DFID) (2013) *Multilateral Aid Review Update: Driving Reform to Achieve Multilateral Effectiveness*. London: DFID.

Department for International Development (DFID) (2015) *Summary of DfID's Work in Zambia, 2011–2015*. London: DfID.

Desai, R.M. and Kharas, H. (2009) Democratizing foreign aid: online philanthropy and international development assistance. *International Law and Politics*, 22, 1111–42.

Desai, V. (2014) The role of non-governmental organisations, in Desai, V. and Potter, R.B. (2014) (eds) *The Companion to Development Studies*, 3rd edn. London: Routledge, 568–73.

Desai, V. and Potter, R.B. (eds) (2006) *Doing Development Research*. London, Thousand Oaks and New Delhi: Sage Publications.

Desai, V. and Potter, R.B. (eds) (2008) *The Companion to Development Studies*, 2nd edn. London: Hodder-Arnold and New York: Oxford University Press.

Desai, V. and Potter, R.B. (eds) (2014) *The Companion to Development Studies*, 3rd edn. London: Arnold.

Devas, N. and Rakodi, C. (eds) (1993) *Managing Fast Growing Cities: New Approaches to Urban Planning and Management in the Developing World*. Harlow: Longman.

Devereux, S. (2006) *Vulnerable Livelihoods in Somali Region, Ethiopia*, IDS Research Report, no. 57. Brighton: Institute of Development Studies.

Devereux, S. and Maxwell, S. (2001) *Food Security in Sub-Saharan Africa*. London: ITDG Publishing.

Dey, J. (1981) Gambian women: unequal partners in rice development projects? *Journal of Development Studies*, 17(3), 109–22.

Dicken, P. (1993) The growth economies of Pacific Asia in their changing global context, in Dixon, C. and Drakakis-Smith, D. (eds) *Economic and Social Development in Pacific Asia*. London: Routledge, 22–42.

Dicken, P. (1998) *Global Shift: Transforming the World Economy*, 3rd edn. London: Paul Chapman.

Dicken, P. (2011) *Global Shift: Mapping the Changing Contours of the World Economy*, 6th edn. London: Sage.

Dicken, P. (2015) *Global Shift: Mapping the Changing Contours of the World Economy*, 7th edn. London: Sage.

Dickenson, J., Gould, B., Clarke, C., Mather, C., Prothero, M., Siddle, D., Smith, C. and Thomas-Hope, E. (1996) *A Geography of the Third World*, 2nd edn. London: Routledge.

Dickenson, J.P. (1994) Manufacturing industry in Latin America and the case of Brazil, in Courtenay, P.P. (ed) *Geography and Development*. Melbourne: Longman Cheshire, 165–91.

Diplomatic Courier (2013) Zambia: standing up to Chinese businesses. 22 July 2013. http://www.diplomaticcourier.com/news/regions/africa/1608-zambia-standing-up-to-chinese-businesses (accessed 1 May 2015).

Dirlik, A. (2002) Rethinking colonialism: globalization, postcolonialism and the nation. *Interventions*, 4(3), 428–48.

Dixon, C. (ed) (1987) *Rural–Urban Interaction in the Third World*. London: Developing Areas Research Group.

Dixon, C. (1990) *Rural Development in the Third World*. London: Routledge.

Dixon, C. (1998) *Thailand*. London: Routledge.

Dixon, C. and Drakakis-Smith, D. (eds) (1997) *Uneven Development in Southeast Asia*. Aldershot: Ashgate.

Dixon, C. and Heffernan, M. (eds) (1991) *Colonialism and Development in the Contemporary World*. London: Mansell.

Dobbs, R., Oppenheim, J., Thompson, F., Brinkman, M. and Zornes, M. (2011) *Resource Revolution: Meeting the World's Energy, Materials, Food, and Water Needs*. McKinsey Global Institute: McKinsey Sustainability & Resource Productivity Practice.

Doctors Without Borders (MSF) (1999) *Psychosocial Survey, Freetown*. http://www.doctorswithoutborders.org/news-stories/special-report/assessing-trauma-sierra-leone (accessed 20 Mar 2015).

Doctors Without Borders (MSF) (2015) *Ebola emergency*. http://www.msf.org.uk/ebola?gclid=CLS47-fkxcQCFWEOwwod7msASQ (accessed 26 Mar 2015).

Dodds, F. and Strauss, M. with Strong, M. (2012) *Only One Earth*. London: Routledge.

Dodds, F. (2002) Reforming the international institutions, in Dodds, F. (ed) *Earth Summit 2002: A New Deal*. London: Earthscan, 291–314.

Dodds, K. (2008) The Third World, Developing Countries, the South, Poor Countries, ch. 1.1 in Desai, V. and Potter, R.B. (eds) *The Companion to Development Studies*, 2nd edn. London: Hodder-Arnold and New York: Oxford University Press, 3–7.

Dolan, C. and Humphrey, J. (2000) Governance and trade in fresh vegetables: the impact of UK supermarkets on the African horticulture industry. *Journal of Development Studies*, 37(2), 147–76.

Dolman, P. (2000) Biodiversity and ethics, in O'Riordan, T. (ed) (2000) *Environmental Science for Environmental Management*. Harlow: Pearson Education, 119–48.

Donaghue, M.T. and Barff, R. (1990) Nike just did it: international subcontracting, flexibility and athletic footwear production. *Regional Studies*, 24, 537–52.

Dooge, J.C.I. (1992) *An Agenda for Science for Environment and Development in a Changing World*. Cambridge: Cambridge University Press.

Dorian, J.P., Franssen, H.T. and Simbeck, D.R. (2006) Global challenges in energy. *Energy Policy*, 34, 1984–91.

Dos Santos, T. (1970) The structure of dependency. *American Economic Review*, 60, 125–58.

Dos Santos, T. (1977) Dependence relations and political development in Latin America: some considerations. *Ibero-Americana*, 7, 245–59.

Dowdeswell, E. (n.d.) Editorial. *Our Planet*, 6(5), 2.

Doxiadis, C.A. (1967) Developments toward ecumenopolis: the Great Lakes megalopolis. *Ekistics*, 22, 14–31.

Doxiadis, C.A. and Papaioannou, J.G. (1974) *Ecumenopolis: The Inevitable City of the Future*. New York: Norton.

Drakakis-Smith, D. (1981) *Urbanization, Housing and the Development Process*. London: Croom Helm.

Drakakis-Smith, D. (1983) Advance Australia fair: internal colonialism in the Antipodes, in Drakakis-Smith, D. and Wyn Williams, S. (eds) *Internal Colonialism: Essays Around a Theme*, Developing Areas Research Group, Monograph 3. London: Institute of British Geographers, 81–103.

Drakakis-Smith, D. (1987) *The Third World City*. London: Methuen.

Drakakis-Smith, D. (1989) Urban social movements and the built environment. *Antipode*, 21(3), 207–31.

Drakakis-Smith, D. (1990) Food for thought or thought about food: urban food distribution systems in the Third World, in Potter, R.B. and Salau, A.T. (eds) *Cities and Development*. London: Mansell, 100–20.

Drakakis-Smith, D. (1991) Colonial urbanization in Africa and Asia: a structural review. *Cambria*, 16, 123–50.

Drakakis-Smith, D. (1992) *Pacific Asia*. London: Routledge.

Drakakis-Smith, D. (1995) Third World cities: sustainable urban development I. *Urban Studies*, 32, 659–77.

Drakakis-Smith, D. (1996) Third World cities: sustainable urban development II. *Urban Studies*, 33, 673–701.

Drakakis-Smith, D. (1997) Third World cities: sustainable urban development III. *Urban Studies*, 34(5/6), 797–823.

Drakakis-Smith, D. (2000) *Third World Cities*, 2nd edn. London: Routledge.

Drakakis-Smith, D. and Dixon, C. (1997) Sustainable urbanisation in Vietnam. *Geoforum*, 28(1), 21–38.

Drakakis-Smith, D., Doherty, J. and Thrift, N. (1987) What is a socialist developing country? *Geography*, 72(4), 333–5.

Drakakis-Smith, D., Graham, E., Teo, P. and Ling, O.G. (1993) Singapore: reversing the demographic transition to meet labour needs. *Scottish Geographical Magazine*, 109, 152–63.

Dreher, A., Sturm, J.E. and Vreeland, J.R. (2009) Development aid and international politics: Does membership on the UN Security Council influence World Bank decisions? *Journal of Development Economics*, 88(1), 1–18.

Driscoll, R. and Evans, A. (2005) Second-generation poverty reduction strategies: new opportunities and emerging issues. *Development Policy Review*, 23(1), 5–25.

Driver, F. (1992) Geography's empire: histories of geographical knowledge. *Environment and Planning D: Society and Space*, 10, 23–40.

Duncan, J.S., Johnson, N.C. and Schein, R.H. (eds) (2004) *A Companion to Cultural Geography*. Oxford: Blackwell.

Dwyer, D.J. (1975) *People and Housing in Third World Cities*. London: Longman.

Dwyer, D.J. (1977) Economic development: development for whom? *Geography*, 62(4), 325–34.

Earth Summit (2002) *Earth Summit 2002*. Briefing paper. www.earthsummit2002.org.

Eade, D. (2002) Preface, in Eade, D. (ed) *Development and Culture*. Oxford: Oxfam GB, ix–xiv.

Economist Intelligence Unit (1996a) *Country Profile: Côte d'Ivoire*. London: EIU.

Economist Intelligence Unit (1996b) *Country Profile: Kenya*. London: EIU.

Economist Intelligence Unit (2001) *Kenya: Country Profile, 2001*. London: EIU.

Economist Intelligence Unit (2002a) *Côte d'Ivoire and Mali: Country Profile, 2002*. London: EIU.

Economist Intelligence Unit (2002b) *South Korea, North Korea: Country Profile, 2002*. London: EIU.

The Economist (2006) Voting with your trolley. *The Economist*, 7 Dec. www.economist.com/business/displaystory.cfm?story_id=8380592.

The Economist (2010) The miracle of the Cerrado. *The Economist*, 28 Aug.

The Economist (2013) Africa and China: more than minerals. *The Economist*, 23 Mar 2013, http://www.economist.com/news/middle-east-and-africa/21574012-chinese-trade-africa-keeps-growing-fears-neocolonialism-are-overdone-more (accessed 1 Apr 2015).

The Economist (2015) The 169 commandments. *The Economist*, 28 Mar, 12.

Eden, M.J. and Parry, J. (eds) (1996) *Land Degradation in the Tropics: Environment and Policy Issues*. London: Mansell.

Edge, G. and Tovey, K. (1995) Energy: hard choices ahead, in O'Riordan, T. (ed) *Environmental Science for Environmental Management*. London: Longman, 317–34.

Edwards, M. (2001a) The rise and rise of civil society. *Developments: The International Development Magazine*, 14(2nd quarter), 5–7.

Edwards, M. (2001b) Introduction, in Edwards, M. and Gaventa, J. (eds) *Global Citizen Action*. London: Earthscan, 1–14.

Edwards, M. (2011) *The Role and Limitations of Philanthropy*. commissioned paper, The Bellagio Initiative, Institute of development Studies, The Resource Alliance and the Rockefeller Foundation.

Edwards, M. and Gaventa, J. (eds) (2001) *Global Citizen Action*. London: Earthscan.

Edwards, M. and Hulme, D. (eds) (1992) *Making A Difference: NGOs and Development in a Changing World*. London: Earthscan.

Edwards, M. and Hulme, D. (eds) (1995) *Nongovernmental Organisations – Performance and Accountability: Beyond the Magic Bullet*. London: Earthscan.

Ehrlich, P.R. (1968) *The Population Bomb*. New York: Ballantine Books.

Eicher, C.K. and Staatz, J.M. (eds) (1990) *Agricultural Development in the Third World*, 2nd edn. Baltimore, MD: Johns Hopkins University Press.

El-Hinnawi, E. (1985) *Environmental Refugees*. Nairobi: UNEP.

Elliott, J. (2014) Development and social welfare/human rights, in Desai, V. and Potter, R.B. (eds) *The Companion to Development Studies*, 3rd edn. London: Routledge, 28–33.

Elliott, J.A. (1990) The mechanical conservation of soil in Zimbabwe, in Cosgrove, D. and Petts, G. (eds) *Water, Engineering and Landscape*. London: Belhaven, 115–28.

Elliott, J.A. (1995) Government policies and the population–environment interface: land reform and distribution in Zimbabwe, in Binns, T. (ed) *People and Environment in Africa*. Chichester: John Wiley, 225–30.

Elliott, J.A. (2013) *An Introduction to Sustainable Development*, 4th edn. London: Routledge.

Elliott, L. (2000) A setback for Global Megabucks PLC. *The Guardian*, 11 December, 27.

Elliott, L. (2001) Brown must push harder for G7 change. *The Guardian*, 19 Nov, 23.

Ellis, F. (2000) *Rural Livelihoods and Diversity in Developing Countries*. Oxford: Oxford University Press.

Elsom, D. (1996) *Smog Alert: Managing Urban Air Quality*. London: Earthscan.

Elson, D. (1995) *Male Bias in the Development Process*. Manchester: Manchester University Press.

Elson, D. (1995) *Male Bias in the Development Process*, 2nd edn. Manchester: Manchester University Press.

Emel, J., Bridge, G. and Krueger, R. (2002) The earth as input: resources, in Johnston, R.J., Taylor, P.J. and Watts, M. (eds) *Geographies of Global Change: Remapping the World*, 2nd edn. London: Blackwell, 377–90.

Endicott, S. (1988) *Red Earth: Revolution in a Sichuan Village*. London: I.B. Tauris.

Engler, M. (2005) Human development. *New Internationalist*, 375, 30–31.

Escobar, A. (1995) *Encountering Development*. Princeton, NJ: Princeton University Press.

Estes, R. (1984) World social progress, 1969–1979. *Social Development Issues*, 8, 8–28.

Esteva, G. (1992) Development, in Sachs, W. (ed) *The Development Dictionary*. London: Zed Books, 6–25.

European Commission (2015) Corporate Social Responsibility (CSR). http://ec.europa.eu/enterprise/policies/sustainable-business/corporate-social-responsibility/index_en.htm (accessed 1 May 2015).

Evans, J.P. (2012) *Environmental Governance*. London: Routledge.

Evans, R. (1993) Reforming the union. *Geographical Magazine*, February, 24–27.

Evans, R. (2001) Uganda: winning one battle in the long war against AIDS. *The Courier*, 188(September–October), 27–30.

Evers, D. and de Vries, J. (2013) Explaining governance in five megacity regions. *European Planning Studies,* 21(4), 536–55.

Eyre, J. and Dwyer, D.J. (1996) Ethnicity and uneven development in Malaysia, in Dwyer, D.J. and Drakakis-Smith, D. (eds) *Ethnicity and Development*. London: John Wiley, 181–94.

Fadl, O.A.A. (1990) Gezira: the largest irrigation scheme in Africa. *The Courier*, November/December, 91–95.

Fage, J.D. (1995) *A History of Africa*, 3rd edn. London: Routledge.

Fairhead, J. (2004) Achieving sustainability in Africa, in Black, R. and White, H. (eds) *Targeting Development: Critical Perspectives on the Millennium Development Goals*. Abingdon: Routledge, 292–306.

Fairhead, J. and Leach, M. (1995) Local agroecological management and forest–savanna transitions: the case of Kissidougou, Guinea, in Binns, T. (ed) *People and Environment in Africa*. Chichester: John Wiley, 163–70.

Fairhead, J. and Leach, M. (eds) (1998) *Reframing Deforestation: Global Analysis and Local Realities: Studies in West Africa*. London: Routledge.

Fairhead, J., Leach, M. and Scoones, I. (2012) Green grabbing: a new appropriation of nature. *The Journal of Peasant Studies*, 39(2), 237–61.

Fairtrade Foundation (2002) Guide to the fairtrade mark. www.fairtrade.org.uk/guide.htm.

Fairtrade International (2014) Monitoring the scope and benefits of fair trade. http://www.fairtrade.net/fileadmin/user_upload/content/2009/resources/2014-Fairtrade-Monitoring-Scope-Benefits-final-web.pdf (accessed 22 July 2016).

Fairtrade Foundation (2016) What Fairtrade does. http://www.fairtrade.org.uk/en/what-is-fairtrade/what-fairtrade-does (accessed 25 July 2016).

FAO/ITPS (2015) *Status of the World's Soil Resources – Main Report*. Rome, Italy: Food and Agriculture Organisation of the United Nations and Intergovernmenal Technical Panel on Soils.

Farole, M. (2011) *Special Economic Zones in Africa*. Washington: World Bank.

Feeney, G. and Wang, F. (1993) Parity progression and birth intervals in China: the influence of policy in hastening fertility decline. *Population and Development Review*, 19(1), 61–100.

Feliciano, D. and Berkhout, F. (2013) The consequences of global environmental change, in ISSC/UNESCO *World Social Science Report 2013: Changing Global Environments*. Paris: OECD Publishing and UNESCO Publishing, 225–29.

Felix, M. (2012) Neo-developmentalism: beyond neoliberalism? *Historical Materialism*, 20(2), 1–19.

Ferguson, J. (1990) *Grenada: Revolution in Reverse*. London: Latin American Bureau.

Fik, T.J. (2000) *The Geography of Economic Development: Regional Changes, Global Challenges*, 2nd edn. Boston, MA: McGraw Hill.

Financial Times (2001) Leaders in denial as graves fill up, South Africa survey. *Financial Times*, 26 November.

Finger, M. (2008) Which governance for sustainable development? An organisational and institutional perspective, in Park, J., Conca, K. and Finger, M. (eds) *The Crisis of Global Environmental Governance, towards a New Political Economy of Sustainability*, London: Routledge, 34–57.

Foley, J.A., Ramankutty, N., Brauman, K.A., Cassidy, M.S., Gerber, J.S., Johnston, M., Mueller, N.D., O'Connell, C., Ray, D.K., West, P.C., Balzer, C., Bennett, E.M.M., Carpenter, S.R., Hill, J., Monfreda, C., Polasky, C., Rockström, J., Sheehan, J., Siebert, S., Tilman, D. and Zaks, D.P.M (2011) Solutions for a cultivated planet. *Nature,* 478(October 20), 337–42.

Food and Agriculture Organisation (FAO) (1987) *Consultation on Irrigation in Africa*. Irrigation and Drainage Paper 42. Rome: FAO.

Food and Agriculture Organisation (FAO) (1991) *Third Progress Report on Action Programme of World Conference on Agrarian Reform and Rural Development*. Rome: FAO.

Food and Agriculture Organisation (FAO) (2001) *Global Forest Resources Assessment 2000*. FAO Forestry Paper 140. Rome: FAO.

Food and Agriculture Organisation (FAO) (2005) *Global Forest Resources Assessment 2005*. Rome: FAO (UN).

Food and Agriculture Organisation (FAO) (2005–06) *Statistical Yearbook*. www.fao.org/statistics/yearbook/vol1_1_1/pdf.

Food and Agriculture Organisation (FAO) (2011) *The State of Food and Agriculture, 2010–2011: Women in Agriculture – Closing the Gender Gap for Development*. Rome: FAO.

Food and Agriculture Organisation (FAO) (2012) *The State of World Fisheries and Aquaculture*. Rome: UN Food and Agriculture Organisation.

Food and Agriculture Organisation (FAO) (2013) *FAO Policy on Gender Equality: Attaining Food Security Goals in Agriculture and Rural Development*. FAO.

Food and Agriculture Organisation (FAO) (2014) *Family Farmers: Feeding the World, Caring for the Earth*. Rome: FAO.

Food and Agriculture Organisation (FAO) (2015a) *Global Forest Resources Assessment 2015*. Rome: UN Food and Agriculture Organisation.

Food and Agriculture Organisation (FAO) (2015b) *State of Food Insecurity in the World 2015*. Rome: FAO.

Food and Agriculture Organization (FAO) (n.d.) *The Spectrum of Malnutrition FAO Factsheet*. Rome: FAO.

Ford, L.H. (1999) Social movements and the globalisation of environmental governance. *IDS Bulletin*, 30(3), 68–74.

Foroohar, R. (2015) Why the mighty BRIC nations have finally broken. *Time*, 10 November 2015, 1–5.

Forum on China-Africa Cooperation (2000) *Beijing Declaration*. http://www.focac.org/eng/wjjh/hywj/t157833.htm (accessed 28 Apr 2015).

Forum on China-Africa Cooperation (2011) *Africa Hails China's Tariff Policy*. 28 Nov. http://www.focac.org/eng/zfgx/dfzc/t881868.htm (accessed 1 April 2015).

Frank, A.G. (1966) The development of underdevelopment. *Monthly Review*, September, 17–30.

Frank, A.G. (1967) *Capitalism and Underdevelopment in Latin America*. New York: Monthly Review Press.

Frank, A.G. (1980) North–South and East–West paradoxes in the Brandt Report. *Third World Quarterly*, 2(4), 669–80.

French, H. (2002) Reshaping global governance, in Worldwatch Institute *State of the World 2002*, 174–98.

Friedland, W.H. (1994) The global fresh fruit and vegetable system: an industrial organization analysis, in McMichael, P. (ed) *The Global Restructuring of Agro-food Systems*. Ithaca, NY: Cornell University Press, 173–89.

Friedman, M. (1962) *Capitalism and Freedom*. Chicago, IL: University of Chicago Press.

Friedmann, M. (1992) *Empowerment: The Politics of Alternative Development*. Cambridge MA: Blackwell.

Friedmann, J. (1966) *Regional Development Policy: A Case Study of Venezuela*. Cambridge, MA: MIT Press.

Friedmann, J. (1986) The world city hypothesis. *Development and Change*, 17, 69–83.

Friedmann, J. (1995) Where we stand: a decade of world city research, in Knox, P.L. and Taylor, P.J. (eds) *World Cities in a World-System*. Cambridge: Cambridge University Press, 21–37.

Friedmann, J. and Weaver, C. (1979) *Territory and Function: The Evolution of Regional Planning*. London: Edward Arnold.

Friedmann, J. and Wulff, G. (1982) World city formation: an agenda for research and action. *International Journal of Urban and Regional Research*, 6, 309–43.

Fukuda-Parr, S. (2010) Reducing inequality – the missing MDG: A content review of PRSPs and bilateral donor policy statements. *IDS Bulletin*, 41(1), 26–35.

Fukuda-Parr, S. (2012) *Recapturing the Narrative of International Development*. United Nations Research Institute for Social Development (UNRISD) Research Paper 2012-5. New York: United Nations.

Fukuyama, F. (2001) Social capital, civil society and development. *Third World Quarterly*, 22, 7–20.

Furniss, C. (2006) The hungry dragon and the dark continent. *Geographical Magazine*, 78(12), 53–61.

Furtado, C. (1964) *Development and Underdevelopment*. Berkeley, CA: University of California Press.

Furtado, C. (1965) *Diagnosis of the Brazilian Crisis*. Berkeley, CA: University of California Press.

Furtado, C. (1969) *Economic Development in Latin America*. Cambridge: Cambridge University Press.

Future of Development Studies. (2014) *Third World Quarterly,* 35(6), 922–38.

Galaty, J.G. and Johnson, D.L. (1990) Introduction: pastoral systems in global perspective, in Galaty, J.G. and Johnson, D.L. (eds) *The World of Pastoralism*. London: Belhaven, 1–31.

Gale, D.J. and Goodrich, J.N. (eds) (1993) *Tourism Marketing and Management in the Caribbean*. London: Routledge.

Gandhi, L. (1998) *Postcolonial Theory: A Critical Introduction*. Edinburgh: Edinburgh University Press.

Gasper, D. (2004) *The Ethics of Development: From Economism to Human Development*. Edinburgh: Edinburgh University Press.

Geheb, K. (1995) Exploring people–environment relationships: the changing nature of the small-scale fishery in the Kenyan sector of Lake Victoria, in Binns, T. (ed) *People and Environment in Africa*. Chichester: John Wiley, 91–101.

Geheb, K. and Binns, T. (1997) 'Fishing farmers' or 'farming fishermen'? The quest for household income and nutritional security on the Kenyan shores of Lake Victoria. *African Affairs*, 96, 73–93.

Geist, H.J. and Lambin, E.F. (2002). Proximate causes and underlying driving forces of tropical deforestation. *BioScience,* 52(2), 143–50.

George, S. (2002) Global citizens movement. *New Internationalist*, 343, 7.

George, S. (2013) Debt, austerity, devastation: it's Europe's turn. *New Internationalist,* 464, 20–3.

German, T. and Randel, J. (eds) (1993) *The Reality of Aid*. London: Actionaid.

Getis, A., Getis, J. and Fellman, J. (1994) *Introduction to Geography*, 4th edn. Dubuque, IA: William C. Brown.

Ghee, L.T. (1989) Reconstituting the peasantry: changes in landholding structure in the Muda irrigation scheme, in Hart, G., Turton, A. and White, B. (eds) *Agrarian Transformations: Local Processes and the State in Southeast Asia*. Berkeley, CA: University of California Press, 193–212.

Gholz, H.L. (ed) (1987) *Agroforestry: Realities, Possibilities and Potentials*. Dordrecht: Martinus Nijhoff.

Ghose, A.K. (ed) (1983) *Agrarian Reform in Contemporary Developing Countries*. London: Croom Helm.

Gibbon, D. (ed) (1995) *Structural Adjustment and the Working Poor in Zimbabwe*. Uppsala: Nordic Institute for African Studies.

Gibbs, C., Fumo, C. and Kuby, T. (1999) *Nongovernmental Organisations in World Bank-Supported Projects: A Review*, Operations Evaluation Department. Washington, DC: World Bank.

Gibson, R.B. (2005) *Sustainability Assessment*. Earthscan: London.

Gibson-Graham, J.K. (2006) *A Postcapitalist Politics*. Minneapolis: University of Minnesota Press.

Gibson-Graham, J.K. (2008) Diverse economies: performative practices for 'other worlds'. *Progress in Human Geography*, 32(5), 613–32.

Gibson-Graham, J.K. (2014) Rethinking the economy with thick description and weak theory. *Current Anthropology*, 55(9), S147–53.

Gilbert, A. (1987) Research policy and review, No.15. From little Englanders to big Englanders: thoughts on the relevance of relevant research. *Environment and Planning A*, 19, 143–51.

Gilbert, A. (2002) The new international division of labour, ch. 4.2 in Desai, V. and Potter, R.B. (eds) *The Companion to Development Studies*. London: Arnold, 186–91.

Gilbert, A.G. (1976) The arguments for very large cities reconsidered. *Urban Studies*, 13, 27–34.

Gilbert, A.G. (1977) The argument for very large cities reconsidered: a reply. *Urban Studies*, 14, 225–7.

Gilbert, A.G. (1992) Third World cities: housing, infrastructure and servicing. *Urban Studies*, 29, 435–60.

Gilbert, A.G. (1993) Third World cities: the changing national settlement system. *Urban Studies*, 30, 721–40.

Gilbert, A.G. (1994) Third World cities: poverty, employment, gender roles and the environment during a time of restructuring. *Urban Studies*, 31, 605–33.

Gilbert, A.G. (1996) *The Mega-City in Latin America*. Tokyo: United Nations University Press.

Gilbert, A.G. and Goodman, D.E. (1976) Regional income disparities and economic development, in Gilbert, A.G. (ed) *Development Planning and Spatial Structure*. Chichester: John Wiley.

Gilbert, A.G. and Gugler, J. (1982) *Cities, Poverty and Development: Urbanization in the Third World*. Oxford: Oxford University Press.

Gilbert, A.G. and Gugler, J. (1992) *Cities, Poverty and Development: Urbanization in the Third World*, 2nd edn. Oxford: Oxford University Press.

Girvan, N. (1973) The development of dependency economics in the Caribbean and Latin America: review and comparison. *Social and Economic Studies*, 22, 1–33.

Global Eye (2002) Focus on population: Kerala, South India. www.globaleye.org.uk.

Godrej, D. (2014) NGOs – do they help. *New Internationalist*, 478, 12–5.

Good, D. (2015) Aid can help to eliminate inequity by 2030 – if five key lessons are heeded. *The Guardian*. http://www.theguardian.com/global-development/2015/sept/14/aid-help-eliminate-inequality (accessed 21 Sept 2015).

Goodrich, R. (2001) *Sustainable Rural Livelihoods: A Summary of Research in Mali and Ethiopia*. Brighton: IDS.

Gottmann, J. (1957) Megalopolis, or the urbanization of the north-eastern seaboard. *Economic Geography*, 33, 189–200.

Gottmann, J. (1961) Megalopolis: the urbanization of the north-east seaboard of the United States. Oxford: Oxford University Press.

Gottmann, J. (1978) Megalopolitan systems around the world, in Bourne, L.S. and Symmons, J.W. (eds) *Systems of Cities*. Oxford: Oxford University Press, 53–60.

Gould, P. (1969) The structure of space preferences in Tanzania. *Area*, 1, 29–35.

Gould, P. (1970) Tanzania, 1920–63: the spatial impress of the modernisation process. *World Politics*, 22, 149–70.

Gould, P. and White, R. (1974) *Mental Maps*. Harmondsworth: Penguin.

Gould, W.T.S. (1992) Urban development and the World Bank. *Third World Planning Review*, 14, iii–vi.

Gould, W.T.S. (1993) *People and Education in the Third World*. Harlow: Longman.

Gould, W.T.S. (2009) *Population and Development*. London: Routledge.

Government of India (2009) *India Urban Poverty Report 2009*. Oxford University Press: Oxford.

Graham, E. (1995) Singapore in the 1990s: can population policies reverse the demographic transition? *Applied Geography*, 15, 219–32.

Grainger, A. (1993) *Controlling Tropical Deforestation*. London: Earthscan.

Grant, M.C. (1995) Movement patterns and the intermediate sized city. *Habitat International*, 19, 357–70.

Gregson, S., Garnett, G.P. and Anderson, R.M. (1994) Assessing the potential impact of the HIV-1 epidemic on orphanhood and the demographic structures of populations in sub-Saharan Africa. *Population Studies*, 48, 435–58.

Greig, A., Hulme, D. and Turner, M. (2007) *Challenging Global Inequality: Development Theory and Practice in the 21st Century*. Basingstoke: Palgrave Macmillan.

Grier, R.M. (1999) Colonial legacies and economic growth. *Public Choice*, 98, 317–35.

Griffin, K. (1980) Economic development in a changing world. Annual Lecture of the Development Studies Association, University of Swansea.

Griffiths, I.L. (1995) *The African Inheritance*. London: Routledge.

Griffiths, I.L.L. (1993) *The Atlas of African Affairs*, 2nd edn. London: Routledge.

Griffiths, T. (2007) *Seeing 'Red'? 'Avoided Deforestation and the Rights of Indigenous Peoples and Local Communities*. Moreton-in-the March, UK: Forest Peoples Programme.

Grugel, J. and Riggirozzi, P. (2012) Post-neoliberalism in Latin America: rebuilding and reclaiming the state after crisis. *Development and Change*, 43(1), 1–21.

Grummer-Strawn, L., Hughes, M., Khan, L.K. and Martorell, R. (2000a) Obesity in women from developing countries. *European Journal of Clinical Nutrition*, 54, 247–52.

Grummer-Strawn, L., Hughes, M., Khan, L.K. and Martorell, R. (2000b) Overweight and obesity in preschool children from developing countries. *International Journal of Obesity*, 24, 959–67.

The Guardian (2001) G8 leaders survive the siege of Genoa. *The Guardian*, 28 July 2, 9.

The Guardian (2014) Primark to pay £6m more to victims of Rana Plaza factory in Bangladesh. http://www.theguardian.com/world/2014/mar/16/primark-payout-victims-rana-plaza-bangladesh (accessed 1 May 2015).

The Guardian (2015a) What have the Millennium Development Goals achieved. 7 Sept. www.theguardian.com/global-develppment/datablog/2015 (accessed 10 Sept 2015).

The Guardian (2015b) UK passes bill to honour pledge of 0.7% foreign aid target. http://www.theguardian.com/global-development/2015/mar/09/uk-passes-bill-law-aid-target-percentage-income (accessed 6 May 2015).

Gugler, J. (ed) (1996) *The Urban Transformation of the Developing World*. Oxford: Oxford University Press.

Gugler, J. (1997) Over-urbanization reconsidered, in Gugler, J. (ed) *Cities in the Developing World*. Oxford: Oxford University Press, 114–23.

Guha, R. (ed) (1982) *Subaltern Studies I: Writings on South Asian History and Society*. Delhi: Oxford University Press.

Guha, R. (1983) *Elementary Aspects of Peasant Insurgency in Colonial India*. Delhi: Oxford University Press.

Guijt, I. and Shah, M. (eds) (1998) *The Myth of the Community: Gender Issues in Participatory Development*. London: IT Publications.

Gupta, A. (1988) *Ecology and Development in the Third World*. London: Methuen.

Gutkind, P.C.W. (1969) Tradition, migration, urbanization, modernity and unemployment in Africa: the roots of instability. *Canadian Journal of African Studies*, 3, 343–65.

Gwin, C. (1995) A comparative assessment, in Ul-Haq, M., Jolly, R., Streeten, P. and Haq, K. (1995) *The UN and the Bretton Woods Institutions: New Challenges for the Twenty-First Century*. Basingstoke: Macmillan, 95–116.

Gwynne, R.N. (2002) Export processing and free trade zones, in Desai, V. and Potter, R.B. (eds) *The Companion to Development Studies*. London: Arnold, 201–6.

Habitat (1996) *An Urbanising World: Global Report on Human Settlements, UN Centre for Human Settlements*. Oxford: Oxford University Press.

Haddad, L. (1992) Introduction, in *Understanding How Resources are Allocated Within Households*. Washington, DC: International Food Policy Research Institute.

Haffajee, F. (2001) AIDS in South Africa – bold steps in a discouraging climate. *The Courier*, 188(September–October), 46–7.

Hagerstrand, T. (1953) *Innovationsforloppet ur Korologisk Synpunkt*. Lund: University of Lund.

Haggett, P. (1990a) *Geography: A Modern Synthesis*. London: Harper & Row.

Haggett, P. (1990b) *The Geographer's Art*. Oxford: Blackwell.

Hall, P. (1982) *Urban and Regional Planning*, 3rd edn. London: George Allen & Unwin.

Hall, R., Borrass, S.M. and White, B. (2014) Land reform, in Desai, V. and Potter, R.B. (eds) *The Companion to Development Studies*, 3rd edn. London: Routledge, 260–5.

Hall, R., Scoones, I. and Tsikata, D. (eds) (2015) *Africa's Land Rush: Rural Livelihoods and Agrarian Change*. Melton, UK: James Currey.

Hall, S. (1995) New cultures for old, in Massey, D. and Jess, P. (eds) *A Place in the World?* Oxford: Oxford University Press and Open University, 175–213.

Hall, S. and Gieben, B. (1992) *Foundations of Modernity*. Cambridge: Polity.

Hancock, G. (1997) Transmigration in Indonesia: how millions are uprooted, in Rahnema, M. and Bawtree, V. (eds) *The Post-Development Reader*. London: Zed Books, 234–43 (Reprinted from Hancock, G. (1989) *Lords of Poverty*. London: Macmillan).

Hansen, N.M. (1981) Development from above: the centre-down development paradigm, in Stöhr, W.B. and Taylor, D.R.F. (eds) *Development from Above or Below? The Dialectics of Regional Development in Developing Countries*. Chichester: John Wiley.

Harden, B. (1993) *Africa: Dispatches from a Fragile Continent*. London: HarperCollins.

Hardin, G. (1968) The tragedy of the commons. *Science*, 162, 1243–8.

Hardoy, J.E., Cairncross, S. and Satterthwaite, D. (eds) (1990) *The Poor Die Young: Housing and Health in Third World Cities*. London: Earthscan.

Harmsen, R. (1995) The Uruguay Round: a boon for the world economy. *Finance and Development*, March, 24–26.

Harris, J. (2001) The second 'Great Transformation'? Capitalism at the end of the twentieth century, in Allen, T. and Thomas, A. (eds) *Poverty and Development into the 21st Century*. Oxford: Oxford University Press, 325–42.

Harris, L.M. and Roa-Garcia, M.C. (2013) Recent waves of water governance: constitutional reform and resistance to neo-liberalisation in Latin America (1990–2012). *Geoforum*, 50, 20–30.

Harris, N. (1989) Aid and urbanization. *Cities*, 6, 174–85.

Harris, N. (1992) Cities in the 1990s: The Challenge for Developing Countries. London: UCL Press.

Harrison, P. and Palmer, R. (1986) *News Out of Africa: Biafra to Band Aid*. London: Hilary Shipman.

Harriss, B. and Crow, B. (1992) Twentieth century free trade reform: food market deregulation in sub-Saharan Africa and south Asia, in Wuyts, M., Mackintosh, M. and Hewitt, T. (eds) *Development Policy and Public Action*. Oxford: Oxford University Press, 199–227.

Harriss, J. (2006) Michael Lipton, in Simon, D. (ed) *Fifty Key Thinkers on Development*. London and New York: Routledge, 149–54.

Harriss, J. and Harriss, B. (1979) Development studies. *Progress in Human Geography*, 3(4), 577–82.

Harvey, D. (1973) *Social Justice and the City*. London: Edward Arnold.

Harvey, D. (1989) *The Condition of Postmodernity*. Oxford: Blackwell.

Harvey, D. (2006) *Spaces of Global Capitalism: Towards a Theory of Uneven Geographical Development*. London: Verso.

Harvey, D. (2011) *The Enigma of Capital and Crises of Capitalism*. London: Profile Books.

Harvey, D. (2015) *Seventeen Contradictions and the End of Capitalism*. London: Profile Books.

Hazell, P., Poulton, C., Wiggins, S. and Dorward, A. (2010) The future of small farms: trajectories and policy priorities. *World Development*, 38(10), 1349–61.

Headey, D., Taffesse, A.S. and You, L. (2014) Diversification and development in pastoralist Ethiopia. *World Development*, 56, 200–13.

Healey, P. (1997) *Collaborative Planning: Shaping Places in Fragmented Societies*. London: Macmillan.

Healey, P. (1998) Building institutional capacity through collaborative approaches to urban planning. *Environment and Planning A*, 30, 1531–46.

Healey, P. (1999) Deconstructing communicative planning theory: a reply to Tewdwr-Jones and Allmendinger. *Environment and Planning A*, 31, 1129–35.

Heathcote, R.L. (1983) *The Arid Lands: Their Use and Abuse*. London: Longman.

Henning, R.O. (1941) The furrow makers of Kenya. *Geographical Magazine*, 12, 268–79.

Hentati, A. (n.d.) Taking effective action. *Our Planet*, 6(5), 5–7.

Hettne, B. (1995) *Development Theory and the Three Worlds*, 2nd edn. Harlow: Longman.

Hettne, B. (1995) *Development Theory and the Three Worlds*. New York: Wiley.

Hewitt, T., Johnson, H. and Wield, D. (eds) (1992) *Industrialization and Development*. Oxford: Oxford University Press and Open University.

Hezri, A.A. (2013) Broadening the environmental dimension in the post-2015 development agenda. *IDS Bulletin*, 44(5–6), 81–8.

Hickel J. (2014) The death of international development. *Al Jazeera*, 20 Nov 2014.

Hickel J. (2015) A short history of neoliberalism (and how we can fix it). *New Left Project*, 22 Feb 2015. www.newleftproject.org/index.phs/site/article_comments/a_short_history_of_neoliberalism (accessed 12 Dec 2015).

Hickel, J. (2016) The true extent of global poverty and hunger. *Third World Quarterly*, 37(5), 749–67.

Hiebert, M. (1993) Long shot? *Far Eastern Economic Review*, 14 October, 58.

Hildyard, N. (1994) The big brother bank. *Geographical*, June, 26–8.

Hill, P. (1963) *The Migrant Cocoa-Farmers of Southern Ghana: A Study in Rural Capitalism*. Cambridge: Cambridge University Press.

Hill, P. (1970) *Studies in Rural Capitalism in West Africa*. Cambridge: Cambridge University Press.

Hill, P. (1972) *Rural Hausa: A Village and a Setting*. Cambridge: Cambridge University Press.

Hill, P. (1986) *Development Economics on Trial: The Anthropological Case for a Prosecution*. Cambridge: Cambridge University Press.

Hirschman, A.O. (1958) *The Strategy of Economic Development*. New Haven, CT: Yale University Press.

Hoch, I. (1972) Income and city size. *Urban Studies*, 9, 299–328.

Hochstetler, K. and Montero, A.P. (2013) The renewed developmental state: the National Development Bank and the Brazil Model. *The Journal of Development Studies*, 49(11), 1484–99.

Hodder, R. (1992) *The West Pacific Rim*. London: Belhaven.

Hoekstra, A.Y. and Mekonnen, M.M (2011) *Global Water Scarcity*, Value of Water Research Report Series no. 53. Delft: UNESCO-IHE.

Holdern, J. and Pachauri, R.K. (1992) Energy, in Dooge, J.C.I. (ed) *An Agenda of Science for Environment and Development into the 21st Century*. Cambridge: Cambridge University Press, 111.

Homewood, K. and Rogers, W.A. (1987) Pastoralism, conservation and the overgrazing controversy, in Anderson, D. and Grove, R. (eds) *Conservation in Africa: People, Policies and Practice*. Cambridge: Cambridge University Press, 111–28.

Hoogvelt, A. (2001) *Globalization and the Postcolonial World: The New Political Economy of Development*, 2nd edn. Basingstoke: Palgrave.

Hopkins, A.G. (1973) *An Economic History of West Africa*. London: Longman.

Hopper, P. (2012) *Understanding Development; Issues and Debates*. Cambridge: Polity Press.

Horvath, R. (1988) *National Development Paths 1965–1987: Measuring a Metaphor*. Paper presented to the International Geographic Congress, Sydney University.

Hossain, M. (1988) *Credit for Alleviation of Rural Poverty: The Grameen Bank in Bangladesh*, Research Report 65. Washington, DC: International Food Policy Research Institute.

Houghton, J.T. (2015) *Global Warming: The Complete Briefing*, 5th edn. Cambridge: Cambridge University press.

Hoyle, B.S. (1979) African socialism and urban development: the relocation of the Tanzanian capital. *Tijdschrift voor Economische en Sociale Geografie*, 70, 207–16.

Hoyle, B.S. (1993) The 'tyranny' of distance – transport and the development process, in Courtney, P.P. (ed) *Geography and Development*. Melbourne: Longman Cheshire, 117–43.

Hudson, B. (1989) The Commonwealth Eastern Caribbean, in Potter, R.B. (ed) *Urbanization, Planning and Development in the Caribbean*. London and New York: Mansell.

Hudson, B. (1991) Physical planning in the Grenada Revolution: achievement and legacy. *Third World Planning Review*, 13, 179–90.

Hudson, J.C. (1969) Diffusion in a central place system. *Geographical Analysis*, 1, 45–58.

Huggler, J. (2006) The banker who changed the world. *The Independent*, 14 October, 38–9.

Hughes, A. (2001) Global commodity networks, ethical trade and governmentality: organizing business responsibility in the Kenyan cut flower industry. *Transactions of the Institute of British Geographers*, NS 26, 390–406.

Hughes, J.M.R. (1992) Use and abuse of wetlands, in Mannion, A.M. and Bowlby, S.R. (eds) *Environmental Issues in the 1990s*. London: John Wiley, 211–26.

Hulme, D. and Edwards, M. (eds) (1977) *NGOs, States and Donors: Too Close for Comfort?* London: Macmillan.

Hulme, D. (2010) Lessons from the making of the MDGs: human development meetings results-based management in an unfair world. *IDS Bulletin*, 41(1), 15–25.

Hunsberger, C., Bolwig, S. Corbera, E. and Creutzig, F. (2014) Livelihood impacts of biofuel crop production: implications for governance. *Geoforum*, 54, 248–60.

Hunt, D. (1984) *The Impending Crisis in Kenya: The Case for Land Reform*. London: Gower.

Huntington, E. (1945) *Mainsprings of Civilisation*. New York: John Wiley.

Huq-Hussain, S. (2015) Gender empowerment and microcredit in Bangladesh, in Coles, A., Gray, L. and Momsen, J. (eds) *The Routledge Handbook of Gender and Development*. London: Routledge, 490–7.

Hutton, W. (1993) Gatt's principles have been corrupted by free market nihilism. *The Guardian*, 16 November.

Hyden, G. (2008) After the Paris Declaration: taking on the issue of power. *Development Policy Review*, 26(3), 259–74.

ICO (International Coffee Organization) (2015) World coffee production. http://www.ico.org/prices/po.htm (accessed 22 Mar 2015).

ICPQL (Independent Commission on Population and Quality of Life) (1996) *Caring for the Future.* Oxford: Oxford University Press.

IFAD (2011) *Rural Poverty Report: New Realities, New Challenges, New Opportunities for Tomorrow's Generation.* Rome: IFAD.

Ignatieff, M. (1995) Fall of a blue empire. *The Guardian,* 17 October.

Iliffe, J. (1995) *Africans: The History of a Continent.* Cambridge: Cambridge University Press.

The Independent (1998) The population bomb defused. *The Independent,* 12 Jan.

The Independent (1999) Shirts for the fashionable, at a price paid in human misery. *The Independent,* 24 Sept, 3.

The Independent (2002) Mr Blair's visit will not heal Africa's scars, but it is better than ignoring them. *The Independent,* 6 Feb, 11.

Independent Evaluation Group (IEG) (2013*) The World Bank Group's Partnership with the Global Environment Facility,* volume 1 main report, Global Program Review.

ING Barings (2000) *Economic Impact of AIDS in South Africa: A Dark Cloud on the Horizon.* Johannesburg: ING Barings.

Inter-American Development Bank (1998) *The Path Out of Poverty: The Inter-America Development Bank's Approach to Reducing Poverty.* Washington, DC: IADB.

International Development Research Centre (IDRC) (n.d.) Facts and figures on food and biodiversity. http://www.idrc.ca/EN/Resources/Publications/Pages/ArticleDetails.aspx?PublicationID=565 (accessed 28 Mar 2016).

International Energy Agency (IEA) (2009) *World Energy Outlook.* Paris: International Energy Agency.

International Energy Agency (IEA) (2013) *World Energy Outlook 2013.* Paris: IEA.

International Energy Agency (IEA) (2015) *World Energy Outlook 2015.* Paris: IEA.

International Food Policy Research Institute (1995a) *A 2020 Vision for Food, Agriculture, and the Environment in Latin America: A Synthesis.* Washington, DC: IFPRI.

International Food Policy Research Institute (1995b) *A 2020 Vision for Food, Agriculture, and the Environment in South Asia: A Synthesis.* Washington, DC: IFPRI.

International Fund for Agricultural Development (2001) *Rural Poverty Report: The Challenge of Ending Rural Poverty.* Oxford: Oxford University Press.

International Monetary Fund (IMF) (1998) Cameroon statistical appendix. *IMF Staff Country Report,* no. 98/17. Washington, DC: IMF.

International Monetary Fund (IMF) (2015) *Debt Relief under the Heavily Indebted Poor Countries (HIPC) Initiative,* Factsheet. 15 Apr 2015. http://www.imf.org/external/np/exr/facts/hipc.htm (accessed 7 May 2015).

International Monetary Fund (IMF) (2015) *Causes and Consequences of Income Inequality: A Global Perspective.* IMF Staff Discussion Note SDN/15/13. Washington: IMF.

Internet and Mobile Association of India (2015) http://www.oneindia.com/india/india-to-cross-400-million-internet-users-by-dec-2015-iamai-report-1929570.html (accessed 20 Jan 2016).

IPCC (Intergovernmental Panel on Climatic Change) (1990) *Climate Change: The IPCC Assessment.* Cambridge: Cambridge University Press.

IPCC (Intergovernmental Panel on Climatic Change) (2001) *Climate Change 2001: Synthesis Report.* Robert T. Watson and the Core Writing Team (eds). Cambridge: Cambridge University Press.

IPCC (Intergovernmental Panel on Climatic Change) (2007) *Climate Change 2007: The Physical Science Basis.* Summary for Policymakers. Geneva: IPCC.

IPCC (Intergovernmental Panel on Climatic Change) (2014) *Climate Change 2014: Impacts, Adaptation and Vulnerability.* IPCC Working Group II. Geneva: IPCC.

IPCC (Intergovernmental Panel on Climatic Change) (2015) *Climate Change 2014: Synthesis Report. Summary for Policy Makers.* Geneva: IPCC.

IPEC (International Programme on the Elimination of Child Labour) (2015) *Child Labour.* http://www.ilo.org/global/topics/child-labour/lang—en/index.htm (accessed 11 Mar 2015).

ISSC/UNESCO (2013) *World Social Science Report 2013: Changing Global Environments.* Paris: OECD Publishing and UNESCO Publishing.

Jacobs, S. (2009) Gender and land reforms. *Geography Compass*, 3(5), 1675–87.

Jacobs, S. (2014) Gender, agriculture and land rights, in Desai, V. and Potter, R.B. (eds) *The Companion to Development Studies*, 3rd edn. London: Routledge, 265–9.

Jaffee, S. (1994) *Exporting High Value Food Commodities*. Washington, DC: World Bank.

Jain, P.S. (1996) Managing credit for the rural poor: lessons from the Grameen Bank. *World Development*, 24(1), 79–89.

Jägerskog, A. (2013) Glass half full or half empty? Transboundary water co-operation in the Jordan River Basin. *World Social Science Report*, 464–6.

Jamal, V. and Weeks, J. (1994) *Africa Misunderstood: Or Whatever Happened to the Rural–Urban Gap?* Basingstoke: Macmillan.

James, C. (2014) Global status of commercialised biotech/GM crops 2014, ISAAA Brief no 49. Ithaca, NY: International Service for the Aqcusition of Agri-biotech Applications.

Jameson, F. (1984) Postmodernism, or the cultural logic of late capitalism. *New Left Review*, 146, 53–92.

Janelle, D.G. (1969) Spatial reorganization: a model and a concept. *Annals of the Association of American Geographers*, 59, 348–64.

Janelle, D.G. (1973) Measuring human extensibility in a shrinking world. *Journals of Geography*, 72, 8–15.

Jenkins, R. (1987) *Transnational Corporations and Uneven Development*. London: Methuen.

Jenkins, R. (1992) Industrialization and the global economy, in Hewitt, T., Johnson, H. and Wield, D. (eds) *Industrialization and Development*. Oxford: Oxford University Press in association with the Open University.

Jimenez-Diaz, V. (1994) The incidence and causes of slope failures in the barrios of Caracas, Venezuela, in Main, H. and Williams, S.W. (eds) *Environment and Housing in Third World Cities*. Chichester: Wiley.

Johnson, B.L.C. (1983) *India: Resources and Development*, 2nd edn. London: Heinemann.

Johnston, R. (1984) The world is our oyster. *Transactions of the Institute of British Geographers*, NS 9(4), 443–59.

Johnston, R.J. (1996) *Nature, State and Economy: A Political Economy of the Environment*, 2nd edn. Chichester: John Wiley.

Jones, E. and Eyles, J. (1977) *An Introduction to Social Geography*. Oxford: Oxford University Press.

Jones, G. and Corbridge, S. (2008) Urban bias, in Desai, V. and Potter, R.B. (eds) *The Companion to Development Studies*, 2nd edn. London: Hodder-Arnold and New York: Oxford University Press, 243–7.

Jones, G. and Hollier, G. (1997) *Resources, Society and Environmental Management*. London: Paul Chapman.

Jones, G.A. and Corbridge, S. (2010) The continuing debate about urban bias: the thesis, its critics, its influence and its implications for poverty-reduction strategies. *Progress in Development Studies*, 10(1), 1–18.

Jones, I., Pollit, M. and Bek, D. (2007) *Multinationals in their Communities: A Social Capital Approach to Corporate Citizenship Projects*. London: Palgrave.

Jones, J.P., Natter, W. and Schatzki, T.R. (1993) *Postmodern Contentions: Epochs, Politics, Space*. London: Guildford Press.

Jordan, A. and Brown, K. (1997) The international dimensions of sustainable development: Rio reconsidered, in Auty, R.M. and Brown, K. (eds) *Approaches to Sustainable Development*. London: Pinter, 270–95.

Jowett, J. (1990) People: demographic patterns and policies, in Cannon, T. and Jenkins, A. (eds) *The Geography of Contemporary China: The Impact of Deng Xiaoping's Decade*. London: Routledge, 102–32.

Jubilee 2000 (2002) About 'Jubilee Research', successor to Jubilee 2000. UK, www.jubilee2000uk.org.

Kaarsholm, P. (ed) (1995) *From Post-Traditional to Post-Modern? Interpreting the Meaning of Modernity in Third World Urban Societies*. Occasional Paper 14. International Development Studies, Roskilde University.

Kabbani, R. (1986) *Imperial Fictions*. London: Pandora.

Kabeer, N. (1992) Beyond the threshold: intrahousehold relations and policy perspectives, in *Understanding How Resources are Allocated Within Households*. Washington, DC: International Food Policy Research Institute, 51–52.

Kabeer, N. (2001) Conflicts over credit: re-evaluating the empowerment potential of loans to women in rural Bangladesh. *World Development*, 29(1), 63–84.

Kalisch, A. (2002) *Corporate Futures, Consultation on Good Practices: Social Responsibility in the Tourism Industry*. London: Tourism Concern.

Kats, G. (1992) Achieving sustainability in energy use in developing countries, in Holmberg, J. (ed) *Policies for a Small Planet*. London: Earthscan, 258–89.

Kayser, D. and Shepardson, K. (2012) Two decades of GEF partnership. *Environment Matters at the World Bank*, 45–7.

Keeling, D.J. (1995) Transport and the world city paradigm, in Knox, P.L. and Taylor, P.J. (eds) *World Cities in a World-System*. Cambridge: Cambridge University Press, 115–31.

Keenan, R.J., Reams, G.A., Achard, F., de Freitas, J.V., Grainger, A. and Lindquist, E. (2015) Dynamics of global forest area: results from the FAO Global Forest Resources Assessment 2015. *Forest Ecology & Management*, 352, 9–20.

Kelly, M. and Granich, S. (1995) Global warming and development, in Morse, S. and Stocking, M. (eds) *People and Environment*. London: UCL Press, 69–107.

Kennedy, E. and Bouis, H.E. (1993) *Linkages Between Agriculture and Nutrition: Implications for Policy and Research*. Washington, DC: International Food Policy Research Institute.

Kennes, W. (1990) The European community and food security. *IDS Bulletin*, 21(3), 67–71.

Khan, H. and Bashar, O.K.M.R. (2008) *Religion and Development: Are They Complementary?* U21 Global Working Paper, 006/2008.

Kiely, R. (1999a) Globalisation, (post)-modernity and the Third World, in Kiely, R. and Marfleet, P. (eds) *Globalisation and the Third World*. London: Routledge, 1–22.

Kiely, R. (1999b) Transnational companies, global capital and the Third World, ch. 2 in Kiely, R. and Marfleet, P. (eds) *Globalisation and the Third World*. London: Routledge, 45–66.

Kiely, R. (1999c) The last refuge of the noble savage? A critical assessment of post-development theory. *The European Journal of Development Research*, 11, 30–55.

Kiely, R. (2002) Global shift: industrialization and development, ch. 4.1 in Desai, V. and Potter, R.B. (eds) *The Companion to Development Studies*. London: Arnold, 183–6.

Killick, A. (1990) Whither development economics? *Economics*, 26(2), 62–69.

Killick, T. (1995) Structural adjustment and poverty alleviation: an interpretative survey. *Development and Change*, 26, 305–31.

King, A. (1976) *Colonial Urban Development*. London: Routledge and Kegan Paul.

King, A. (1990) *Urbanism, Colonialism and the World Economy*. London: Routledge.

Kirton, C.D. (1988) Public policy and private capital in the transition to socialism: Grenada 1979–85. *Social and Economic Studies*, 37, 125–50.

Klak, T. (2008) World-systems theory: cores, peripheries and semi-peripheries, ch. 2.8 in Desai, V. and Potter, R.B. (eds) *The Companion to Development Studies*, 2nd edn. London: Hodder-Arnold and New York: Oxford University Press, 101–7.

Klein, N. (2001) Between McWorld and jihad. *The Guardian Weekend*, 27 October, 30–2.

Kleine, D. (2014) Corporate social responsibility and development, in Desai, V. and Potter, R.B. (eds) *The Companion to Development Studies*, 3rd edn. 195–9.

Knight, J.B. (1972) Rural–urban income comparisons and migration in Ghana. *Bulletin of the Oxford University Institute of Economics and Statistics*, 34(2), 199–229.

Knox, P. and Marston, S. (2001) *Places and Regions in Global Context: Human Geography*. Englewood Cliffs, NJ: Prentice Hall.

Knox, P., Agnew, J. and McCarthy, L. (2014) *The Geography of the World Economy*, 6th edn. London: Routledge.

Knox, P.L and McCarthy, L. (2012) *Urbanization: An Introduction to Urban Geography*. Boston, MA: Pearson.

Knox, P.L. and Taylor, P.J. (eds) (1995) *World Cities in a World-System*. Cambridge: Cambridge University Press.

Komin, S. (1991) Social dimensions of industrialization in Thailand. *Regional Development Dialogue*, 12, 115–37.

Korf, B. (2004) War, livelihoods and vulnerability in Sri Lanka. *Development and Change*, 35(2), 275–95.

Korten, D. (1990a) *Voluntary Organisations and the Challenge of Sustainable Development*. Briefing Paper 15. Australia Development Studies Network, Australian National University, Canberra.

Korten, D.C. (1990b) *Getting to the Twenty-First Century: Voluntary Action and the Global Agenda.* Connecticut: Kumarian Press.

Kothari, U. (ed) (2005) *A Radical History of Development Studies: Individuals, Institutions and Ideologies.* London and New York: Zed Books and Cape Town: David Philip.

Kuhn, T. (1962) *The Structure of Scientific Revolutions.* Chicago, IL: University of Chicago Press.

La Chard, L.W. (1906) Some recent impressions of northern Nigeria. *The Geographical Teacher*, 3, 191–201.

Lange, M.K. (2004) British colonial legacies and political development. *World Development*, 32(6), 905–22.

Larner, W. and Laurie, N. (2010) Travelling technocrats, embodied knowledges: globalising privatisation in telecoms and water. *Geoforum*, 41, 218–26.

Larson, A.M., Brockhaus, M., Sunderlin, W.D., Duchelle, A., Babon, A., Dokken, T., Pham, T.T., Resosudarmo, I.A.P, Selaya, G., Awono, A. and Huynh, T.-B. (2013) Land tenure and REDD+: The good, the bad and the ugly. *Global Environmental Change,* 23, 678–89.

Larson, A.M., Dokken, T., Duchelle, A.E., Atrmadja, S., Resosudarmo, I. A. P., Cronkleton, P., Crombery, M., Sunderlin, W., Awono, A. and Selaya, G. (2016) Gender Gaps in Redd+: women's participation is not enough, in Pierce-Colfer, C.J., Basnett, B.S. and Elias, M. (eds) *Gender and Forests: Climate Change, Tenure, Value Chains and Emerging Issues.* London: Routledge, 68–88.

Lasuen, J.R. (1973) Urbanisation and development – the temporal interaction between geographical and sectoral clusters. *Urban Studies*, 10, 163–88.

Lea, J.P. (2006) Terence Gary McGee, in Simon, D. (ed) *Fifty Key Thinkers on Development.* London and New York: Routledge, 176–80.

Leach, M. (1991) Locating gendered experience: an anthropologist's view from a Sierra Leonean village. *IDS Bulletin*, 22(1), 44–50.

Leach, M. and Mearns, R. (eds) (1996) *The Lie of the Land: Challenging Received Wisdom on the African Environment.* Oxford: James Currey.

Leach, M., Raworth, K. and Rocktröm, J. (2013) Between social and planetary boundaries: navigating pathways in the safe and just space for humanity, in

ISSC/UNESCO (2013). *World Social Science Report 2013: Changing Global Environments.* Paris: OECD Publishing and UNESCO Publishing, 84–9.

Lean, G. (2002) World will ratify protocol that Bush wants to destroy. *The Independent*, 4 Sept.

Lee, J. and Bulloch, J. (1990) Spirit of war moves on Mid-East waters. *The Independent on Sunday*, 13 May, 13.

Leeming, F. (1993) *The Changing Geography of China.* Oxford: Blackwell.

Lefevre, A. (1995) *Islam, Human Rights and Child Labour.* Copenhagen: Nordic Institute of Asian Studies.

Leftwich, A. (1993) Governance, democracy and development in the Third World. *Third World Quarterly*, 14(3), 605–24.

Leinbach, T.R. (1972) The spread of modernization in Malaya: 1895–1969. *Tijdschrift voor Economische en Sociale Geografie*, 63, 262–77.

Leisher, C., Temsah, G., Booker, F., Day, M., Agarwal, B., Matthews, E., Roe, D., Smaberg, L., Sunderland, T. and Wilkie, D. (2015) Does the gender composition of forest and fishery management groups affect resource governance and conservation outcomes? *Environmental Evidence*, 4(13).

Lester, A., Nel, E. and Binns, T. (2000) *South Africa Past, Present and Future.* Harlow: Longman.

Levine, S. (2014) *How to Study Livelihoods: Bringing a Sustainable Livelihoods Framework to Life.* Overseas Development Institute Working Paper no. 22.

Lewcock, C. (1995) Farmer use of urban waste in Kano. *Habitat International*, 19, 225–34.

Lewis, W.A. (1950) The industrialisation of the British West Indies. *Caribbean Economic Review*, 2, 1–61.

Lewis, W.A. (1955) *The Theory of Economic Growth.* London: George Allen & Unwin.

Leys, C. (1996) *The Rise and Fall of Development Theory.* London: James Currey.

Leyshon, A. (1995) Annihilating space? The speed-up of communications, in Allen, J. and Hamnett, C. (eds) *A Shrinking World?* Oxford: Oxford University Press and the Open University, 11–54.

Lin, G.C.S. (1997) *Red Capitalism in South China: Growth and Development of the Pearl River Delta.* Vancouver: University of British Columbia Press.

Linsky, A.S. (1965) Some generalizations concerning primate cities. *Annals of the Association of American Geographers*, 55, 506–13.

Lipton, M. (1977) *Why Poor People Stay Poor: Urban Bias in World Development*. London: Temple Smith.

Lipton, M. (2009). *Land Reform in Developing Countries: Property Rights and Property Wrong*. New York: Routledge.

Little, P.D., Smith, K., Cellarius, B.A., Coppock, D.L. and Barrett, C.B. (2001) Diversification and risk management amongst East African Herders. *Development and Change*, 32, 401–33.

Livingstone, D. (1993) *The Geographical Tradition: Episodes in the History of a Contested Enterprise*. Oxford: Blackwell.

Lloyd, P. (1979) *Slums of Hope?* Harmondsworth: Penguin.

Lloyd-Evans, S. and Potter, R.B. (1996) Environmental impacts of urban development and the urban informal sector in the Caribbean, in Eden, M.J. and Parry, J. (eds) *Land Degradation in the Tropics*. London: Mansell, 245–60.

Lloyd-Evans, S. and Potter, R.B. (2008) Third World cities, in Kitchen, R. and Thrift, N. (eds) *International Encyclopedia of Human Geography*. Oxford: Elsevier.

Lockhart, D. (1993) Tourism to Fiji: crumbs off a rich man's table? *Geography*, 78(3), 318–23.

Longhurst, R. (1988) Cash crops and food security. *IDS Bulletin*, 19(2), 28–36.

Lonsdale, J. and Berman, B. (1979) Coping with the contradictions: the development of the colonial state in Kenya, 1895–1914. *Journal of African History*, 20(4), 487–505.

Lösch, A. (1940) *Die räumliche Ordnung der Wirtschaft*, Jena, translated by Woglom, W.H. and Stolpen, W.F. (1954) *The Economics of Location*. New Haven, CT: Yale University Press.

loveLife/Henry J. Kaiser Family Foundation (2001) Impending catastrophe revisited: an update on the HIV/AIDS epidemic in South Africa, Parklands. loveLife, www.lovelife.org.za.

Lowder, S. (1986) *Inside Third World Cities*. Beckenham: Croom Helm.

Lowder, S. K, Skoet, S. and Raney, T. (2016) The number, size, and distribution of farms, smallholder farms, and family farms worldwide. *World Development*, 87, 16–29.

Lowenthal, D. (1960) *West Indian Societies*. Oxford: Oxford University Press.

Lucas, C. (2001a) *Stopping the Great Food Swap – Relocalising Europe's Food Supply*. London: The Green Party.

Lucas, C. (2001b) The crazy logic of the continental food swap. *The Independent*, 25 March, 15.

Lugard, F.J.D. (1965) *The Dual Mandate in British Tropical Africa*. London: Frank Cass.

Lundqvist, J. (1981) Tanzania: socialist ideology, bureaucratic reality, and development from below, in Stöhr, W.B. and Taylor, D.R. (eds) *Development from Above or Below*? Chichester: John Wiley, 329–49.

Lynch, K. (2005) *Rural-Urban Interactions in the Developing World*. London: Routledge.

Lynch, K., Binns, T. and Olofin, E.A. (2001) Urban agriculture under threat; the land security question in Kano, Nigeria. *Cities*, 18, 159–71.

Lyons, K. and Westoby, P. (2014) Carbon colonialism and the new land grab; plantation forestry in Uganda and its livelihood impacts. *Journal of Rural Studies*, 36, 13–21.

MacAskill, E. (2000) Britain's ethical foreign policy: keeping the Hawk jets in action. *The Guardian*, 20 January.

MacCannell, D. (1976) *The Tourist: A New Theory of the Leisure Class*. New York: Schocken.

MacGinty, R. and Williams, A. (2009) *Conflict and Development*. London: Routledge.

Mackenzie, F. (1992) Development from within? The struggle to survive, in Taylor, D.R. and Mackenzie, F. (eds) *Development from Within: Survival in Rural Africa*. London: Routledge, 1–33.

Mackintosh, M. (1992) Questioning the state, in Wuyts, M., Mackintosh, M. and Hewitt, T. (eds) *Development Policy and Public Action*. Oxford: Oxford University Press, 61–89.

MacLeod, S. and McGee, T. (1990) The last frontier: the emergence of the industrial palate in Hong Kong, in Drakakis-Smith, D. (ed) *Economic Growth and Urbanization in Developing Areas*. London: Routledge.

Maconachie, R., Binns, T. and Tengbe, P. (2012) Urban farming associations, youth and food security in post-war Freetown, Sierra Leone. *Cities*, 29, 192–200.

Madeley, J. (1999) *Big Business, Poor Peoples: The Impact of Trans-National Corporations on the World's Poor*. London: Zed Books.

Madeley, J. (2000) An astonishing week in Seattle. *Developments*, 9, 6–9.

Madeley, J. (2001) WTO members agree new trade round. *Developments*, Fourth Quarter, 26/27.

Mail and Guardian (2001a) Drug giants back down. *Mail and Guardian*. Johannesburg, 20–25 Apr.

Mail and Guardian (2001b) A disastrous reign. *Mail and Guardian*. Johannesburg, 26 Apr–3 May.

Main, H. and Williams, S.W. (eds) (1994) *Environment and Housing in Third World Cities*. London: John Wiley.

Makuch, Z. (1996) The World Trade Organisation and the General Agreement on Tariffs and Trade, in Werksman, J. (ed) *Greening International Institutions*. London: Earthscan, 94–116.

Maldives Government (2009) *National Adaptation to Climate Change*. Male, Ministry of Housing, Transport and the Environment. http://www.ifrc.org/docs/IDRL/National%20Adaptation%20Programme%20%28Climate%20change%29%29/MALDIVES%20Adaptation%20to%20Climate%20Change.pdf (accessed 25 Mar 2015).

Malena, C. (2000) Beneficiaries, mercenaries, missionaries and revolutionaries: unpacking NGO involvement in World Bank financed project. *IDS Bulletin*, 31(3), 19–34.

Mallett, R. and Slater, R. (2012) *Growth and Livelihoods in Fragile and Conflict-Affected Situations*. Working Paper 9. London: Overseas Development Institute.

Maltby, E. (1986) *Waterlogged Wealth: Why Waste the World's Wet Places?* London: Earthscan.

Mangin, W. (1967) Latin American squatter settlements: a problem and a solution. *Latin American Research Reviews*, 2, 65–98.

Mannion, A.M. and Bowlby, S.R. (eds) (1992) *Environmental Issues in the 1990s*. London: John Wiley.

Manzo, K. (1995) Black consciousness and the quest for counter-modernist development, in Crush, J. (ed) *Power of Development*. London: Routledge, 228–52.

Marshall, D. (2002) The New World group of dependency scholars: reflections on a Caribbean Avant-garde movement, ch. 2.9 in Desai, V. and Potter, R.B. (eds) *The Companion to Development Studies*. London: Arnold, 102–7.

Martinez-Alier, J. (2002) *The Environmentalism of the Poor: A Study of Ecological Conflicts and Valuation*. Cheltenham: Edward Elgar.

Martorell, R. (2001) Obesity – an emerging health and nutrition issue in developing countries, in Pinstrup-Andersen, P. and Pandya-Lorch, R. (eds) *The Unfinished Agenda: Perspectives on Overcoming Hunger, Poverty and Environmental Degradation*. Washington, DC: International Food Policy Research Institute, 49–53.

Massa, I. and Brambila-Macia, J. (2014) Global governance issues and the current crisis, in Desai, V. and Potter, R.B. (eds) *The Companion to Development Studies*, 3rd edn, 555–9.

Masselos, J. (1995) Postmodern Bombay: fractured discourses, in Watson, S. and Gibson, K. (eds) *Postmodern Cities and Spaces*. Oxford: Blackwell, 200–15.

Massey, D. (1991) A global sense of place. *Marxism Today*, June, 24–29.

Massey, D. (1995) Imaging the world, in Allen, J. and Massey, D. (eds) *Geographical Worlds*. London: Oxford University Press, 5–52.

Massey, D. and Jess, P. (1995) *A Place in the World? Places, Cultures and Globalization*. Oxford: Oxford University Press and the Open University.

Mather, A.S. and Chapman, K. (1995) *Environmental Resources*. London: Longman.

Matsumoto, D. (1996) *Culture and Psychology*. Pacific Grove, CA: Brooks/Cole.

Matthews, E. (2001) Understanding the Forest Resources Assessment 2000. *World Resources Briefing No. 1*, www.pdf.wri.org/fra2000.pdf.

Mawdsley, E., Savage, L. and Kim, S. (2014) A 'post-aid world'? Paradigm shift in foreign aid and development cooperation at the 2011 Busan High Level Forum. *The Geographical Journal*, 180(1), 27–38.

Maxwell, S. (1988) *National Food Security Planning: First Thoughts from Sudan*. Unpublished paper presented to Workshop on Food Security in the Sudan, Institute of Development Studies, Sussex, 3–5 October.

Maxwell, S. (1996) Food security: a post-modern perspective. *Food Policy*, 21(2), 155–70.

Maxwell, S. (2004) Heaven or hubris: reflections on the 'New Poverty Agenda', in Black, R. and White, H. (eds) *Targeting Development: Critical Perspectives on the Millennium Development Goals*. Abingdon: Routledge, 25–46.

Mayhew, S. (1997) *A Dictionary of Geography*, 2nd edn. Oxford: Oxford University Press, 122.

Mayoux, L. (2001) Tackling the down side: social capital, women's empowerment and micro-finance in Cameroon. *Development and Change*, 32, 435–64.

McAslan, E. (2002) Social capital and development, ch. 2.17 in Desai, V. and Potter, R.B. (eds) *The Companion to Development Studies*. London: Arnold, 139–43.

McCarthy, J.F. (2010) Processes of inclusion and adverse incorporation: oil palm and agrarian change in Sumatra, Indonesia. *The Journal of Peasant Studies*, 37(4), 821–50.

McCormick, J. (1995) *The Global Environment Movement*, 2nd edn. Chichester: John Wiley.

McElroy, J.L. and Albuquerque, K. (1986) The tourism demonstration effect on the Caribbean. *Journal of Travel Research*, 25, 31–4.

McEwan, C. (2002) Postcolonialism, in Desai, V. and Potter, R.B. (eds) *The Companion to Development Studies*. London: Arnold, 127–31.

McEwan, C. (2009) *Postcolonialism and Development*. London: Routledge.

McGee, T. (1979) Conservation and dissolution in the Third World city: the 'shanty town' as an element of conservation. *Development and Change*, 10, 1–22.

McGee, T. (1994) The future of urbanisation in developing countries: the case of Indonesia. *Third World Planning Review*, 16, iii–xii.

McGee, T.G. (1967) The Southeast Asian City: A Social Geography of the Primate Cities of Southeast Asia. London: Bell.

McGee, T.G. (1989) 'Urbanisasi' or Kotadesasi: evolving patterns of urbanisation in Asia, in Costa, F.J. (ed) *Urbanization in Asia*. Honolulu, HI: University of Hawaii Press.

McGee, T.G. (1991) The emergence of desakota regions in Asia: expanding a hypothesis, ch. 1 in Ginsburg, N., Koppell, B. and McGee, T.G. (eds) *The Extended Metropolis: Settlement Transition in Asia*. Honolulu, HI: University of Hawaii Press, 3–25.

McGee, T.G. (1995) Eurocentralism and geography, in Crush, J. (ed) *Power of Development*. London: Routledge, 192–207.

McGee, T.G. (1997) *The Problem of Identifying Elephants: Globalization and the Multiplicities of Development*. Paper presented at the Lectures in Human Geography Series, University of St Andrews.

McGee, T.G. and Greenberg, L. (1992) The emergence of extended metropolitan regions in ASEAN. *ASEAN Economic Bulletin*, 1(6), 5–12.

McGee, T.G. and Robinson, I. (eds) (1995) *The Mega-Urban Regions of Southeast Asia*. Vancouver: UBC Press.

McGeoy, L. (2014) The philanthropic state: market-state hybrids in the philanthrocapitalist turn. *Third World Quarterly*, 35(1), 109–25.

McGinn, A.P. (2002) Reducing our toxic burden, in Worldwatch Institute. *State of the World 2002: Progress Towards a Sustainable Society*. London: Earthscan, 75–100.

McGranahan, G. and Satterthwaite, D. (2000) Environmental Health and Ecological Sustainability, in Pugh, C. (ed) *Sustainable Cities in Developing Countries*, New York: Earthscan, 73–90.

McIlwaine, C. (1997) Fringes or frontiers? Gender and export-oriented development in the Philippines, in Dixon, C. and Drakakis-Smith, D. (eds) *Uneven Development in Southeast Asia*. Aldershot: Ashgate, 100–23.

McLachlan, S. and Binns, T. (2014) Tourism, development and corporate social responsibility in Livingstone, Zambia. *Local Economy*, 29(1/2), 98–112.

McLennan, A. and Ngomas, W.Y. (2004) Quality governance for sustainable development? *Progress in Development Studies*, 4(4), 279–93.

McLeod, J. (2000) *Beginning Postcolonialism*. Manchester: Manchester University Press.

McLuhan, M. (1962) *The Gutenburg Galaxy: The Making of Typographic Man*. London: Routledge and Kegan Paul.

McMichael, P. (2000) *Development and Social Change: A Global Perspective*, 2nd edn. London: Sage Publications.

McMichael, P. and Schneider, M. (2011) Food security politics and the Millennium Development Goals. *Third World Quarterly*, 32(1), 119–39.

Millennium Ecosystem Assessment (MEA) (2005) *Ecosystems and Human Well-Being: Synthesis*. Washington: Island Press.

Meadows, D.H., Meadows, D.L., Randers, J. and Behrens, W.W. (1972) *The Limits to Growth*. London: Pan.

Mehmet, O. (1995) *Westernising the Third World*. London: Routledge.

Mehmet, O. (1999) *Westernizing the Third World*, 2nd edn. London: Routledge.

Mehta, S.K. (1964) Some demographic and economic correlates of primate cities: a case for revaluation. *Demography*, 1, 136–47.

Meier, G.M. and Baldwin, R.E. (1957) *Economic Development: Theory, History, Policy*. New York: John Wiley.

Meillassoux, C. (1972) From reproduction to production. *Economy and Society*, 1, 93–105.

Meillassoux, C. (1978) The social organization of the peasantry: the economic basis of kinship, in Seddon, D. (ed) *Relations of Production: Marxist Approaches to Economic Anthropology*. London: Frank Cass, 159–70.

Mellor, J.W. (1990) Agriculture on the road to industrialization, in Eicher, C.K. and Staatz, J.M. (eds) *Agricultural Development in the Third World*, 2nd edn. Baltimore, MD: Johns Hopkins University Press, 70–88.

Menzel, M. (2006) Walt William Rostow, in Simon, D. (ed) *Fifty Key Thinkers on Development*. London and New York: Routledge, 211–17.

Mera, K. (1973) On the urban agglomeration and economic efficiency. *Economic Development and Cultural Change*, 21, 309–24.

Mera, K. (1975) *Income Distribution and Regional Development*. Tokyo: University of Tokyo Press.

Mera, K. (1978) The changing pattern of population distribution in Japan and its implications for developing countries, in Lo, F.C. and Salih, K. (eds) *Growth Pole Strategies and Regional Development Policy*. Oxford: Pergamon.

Mercer, C. (2002) NGOs, civil society and democratisation: a critical review of the literature. *Progress in Development Studies*, 2(1), 5–22.

Merriam, A. (1988) What does 'Third World' mean? in Norwine, J. and Gonzalez, A. (eds) *The Third World: States of Mind and Being*. London: Unwin-Hyman.

Merrick, T. (1986) World population in transition. *Population Bulletin*, 41(2), 1–51.

Messkoub, M. (1992) Deprivation and structural adjustment, in Wuyts, M., Mackintosh, M. and Hewitt, T. (eds) *Development Policy and Public Action*. Oxford: Oxford University Press, 175–98.

Middleton, N. (2013) *Global Casino: An Introduction to Environmental Issues*, 5th edn. London: Routledge.

Middleton, N., O'Keefe, P. and Moyo, S. (1993) *Tears of the Crocodile: From Rio to Reality in the Developing World*. London: Pluto Press.

Mijere, N. and Chilivumbo, A. (1987) Rural urban migration and urbanization in Zambia during the colonial and post-colonial periods, in Kaliperi, E. (ed) *Population, Growth and Environmental Degradation in Southern Africa*. New York: Reinner.

Millennium Ecosystem Assessment (2005) *Ecosystems and Well-being: Biodiversity Synthesis*. Washington, DC: World Resources Institute.

Miller, D. (1992) The young and the restless in Trinidad: a case of the local and the global in mass consumption, in Silverstone, R. and Hirsch, E. (eds) *Consuming Technology*. London: Routledge, 163–82.

Miller, D. (1994) *Modernity: An Ethnographic Approach: Dualism and Mass Consumption in Trinidad*. Oxford: Berg.

Milner-Smith, R. and Potter, R.B. (1995) *Public Knowledge of Attitudes Towards the Third World*. CEDAR Research Paper 13. Royal Holloway College, University of London.

Mingst, K.A. and Karns, M.P. (2012) *The United Nations in the 21st Century*, 4th edn. Boulder: Westview Press.

Mitchell, R.E. and Reid, D.G. (2001) Community integration: island tourism in Peru. *Annals of Tourism Research*, 28, 113–39.

Mitlin, D. and Satterthwaite, D. (2013) *Urban Poverty in the Global South*. Abingdon: Routledge.

MoBbrucker, H. (1997) Amerindian migration in Peru and Mexico, in Gugler, J. (ed) *Cities in the Developing World*. Oxford: Oxford University Press, 74–87.

Mohan, G. (1996) SAPs and Development in West Africa. *Geography*, 81(4), 364–8.

Mohan, G. (2002) Participatory development, in Desai, V. and Potter, R.B. (eds) *The Companion to Development Studies*. London: Arnold, 49–54.

Mohan, G. and Stokke, K. (2000) Participatory development and empowerment: the dangers of localism. *Third World Quarterly*, 21, 247–68.

Mohan, G., Brown, E., Milward, B. and Zack-Williams, A.B. (2000) *Structural Adjustment: Theory, Practice and Impacts*. London: Routledge.

Momsen, J. (2010) *Gender and Development*, 2nd edn. Routledge: London.

Momsen, J.H. (1991) *Women and Development in the Third World*. London: Routledge.

Momsen, J.H. (2004) *Gender and Development*. London: Routledge.

Monastersky, R. (2015) Anthropocene: the human age. *Nature*, 11 March.

Moon. B.-K. (2012) Secretary-General's remarks to High Level Delegation of Mayors and Regional Authorities. http://www.un.org/sg/STATEMENTS/index.asp?nid=6014.

Moradi, A. (2008) Confronting colonial legacies – lessons from human development in Ghana and Kenya, 1880–2000. *Journal of International Development*, 20, 1107–21.

Morrissey, D. (1999) An ageing world. *The Courier*, 176, 38–9.

Morrissey, O. (2001) Does aid increase growth? *Progress in Development Studies*, 1, 37–50.

Morse, S. (1995) Biotechnology: a servant of development? in Morse, S. and Stocking, M. (eds) *People and Environment*. London: UCL Press, 131–55.

Morse, S. and Stocking, M. (eds) (1995) *People and Environment*. London: UCL Press.

Mortimore, M. (1998) *Roots in the African Dust: Sustaining the Drylands*. Cambridge: Cambridge University Press.

Mortimore, M.J. (1989) *Adapting to Drought: Farmers, Famines and Desertification in West Africa*. Cambridge: Cambridge University Press.

Mountjoy, A.B. (1976) Urbanization, the squatter and development in the Third World. *Tijdschrift voor Economische en Sociale Geografie*, 67, 130–7.

Mountjoy, A.B. (1980) Worlds without end. *Third World Quarterly*, 2(4), 753–57.

Moyo, S. (1995) *The Land Question in Zimbabwe*. Harare: Sapes Books.

Muggah, R. (2005) No magic bullet: A critical perspective on disarmament, demobilisation and reintegration (DDR) and weapons reduction in post-conflict contexts. *The Round Table*, 94 (379), 239–52.

Munslow, B. and Ekoko, F. (1995) Is democracy necessary for sustainable development? *Democratisation*, 2, 158–78.

Munslow, B., Katerere, Y., Ferf, A. and O'Keefe, P. (1988) *The Fuelwood Trap: A Study of the SADCC Region*. London: Earthscan.

Muradian, R., Walker, M. and Martinez-Alier, J. (2012) Hegemonic transitions and global shifts in social metabolism: implications for resource-rich countries. Introduction to the Special section, *Global Environmental Change*, 22, 559–67.

Murphy, D.F. and Mathew, D. (2001) Nike and global labour practices: a case study prepared for the New Academy of Business Innovation Network for Socially Responsible Business. www.new-academy.ac.uk/nike/nike-report.pdf.

Murray, M. (1995) The value of biodiversity, in Kirkby, J., O'Keefe, P. and Timberlake, L. (eds) *The Earthscan Reader in Sustainable Development*. London: Earthscan, 17–29.

Murray, W.E. (2006) *Geographies of Globalization*. London and New York: Routledge.

Myint, H. (1964) *The Economics of Developing Countries*. London: Hutchinson.

Myrdal, G. (1957) *Economic Theory and Underdeveloped Areas*. London: Duckworth.

Nachtergaele, F., Petri, M., Biancalani, R., Van Lynden, G. and Van Velthuizen, H. (2010) *Global Land Degradation Information System (GLADIS): Beta Version*. An Information Database for Land Degradation Assessment at Global Level. Land Degradation Assessment in Drylands Technical Report No. 17. Rome: FAO.

Naim, M. (2000) Fads and fashion in economic reforms: Washington consensus or Washington confusion? *Third World Quarterly*, 21(3), 505–28.

Narayan, D., Patel, R., Schafft, K., Rademacher, A. and Koche-Schulte, S. (2000) *Voices of the Poor: Can Anyone Hear Us?* New York: Oxford University Press.

Narlikar, A. (2011) New powers in the club: the challenges of global trade governance. *International Affairs*, 86(3), 717–28.

Neate, R. (2016) The other Hugh Grant – boss of Monsanto who plays the bad guy. *The Guardian*, 21 May.

Nederveen Pieterse, J. (2000) After post-development. *Third World Quarterly*, 21, 175–91.

Neefjes, K. (2000) Environments and Livelihoods: Strategies for Sustainability. Oxford: Oxfam.

Nelson, N. and Wright, S. (eds) (1995) *Power and Participatory Development: Theory and Practice*. London: IT Publications.

Nelson, P. (2000) Whose civil society? Whose governance? Decision making and practice in the new agenda at the Inter-American Development Bank and the World Bank. *Global Governance*, 6, 405–31.

Nelson, P. (2006) The varied and conditional integration of NGOs in the aid system: NGOs and the World Bank. *Journal of International Development,* 18, 701–13.

Nelson, P.J. (2002) The World Bank and NGOs, in Desai, V. and Potter, R.B. (eds) *The Companion to Development Studies.* London: Arnold, 499–504.

NEPAD (2001) New Partnership for Africa's Development. October, www.nepad.org.

NEPAD (2002) Declaration on democracy, political, economic and corporate governance. 18 June, *New Partnership for Africa's Development.* www.nepad.org.

Neumayer, E. (2001) *Greening Trade and Investment: Environmental Protection Without Protectionism.* London: Earthscan.

New Internationalist (2001a) World Trade Organization: shrink it or sink it. *New Internationalist*, 334.

New Internationalist (2001b) Faces of global resistance: we are everywhere. *New Internationalist*, 338.

New Internationalist (2006) CO2nned: carbon offsets stripped bare. *New Internationalist*, 391(July).

News 24 (2015) UN goals helped lift 1 billion from extreme poverty. www.news24.cm/World/News/UN-goals-helped-lift-1-billion-out-of-poverty (accessed 7 Aug 2015).

Newsweek (1995) The UN turns. *Newsweek*, 30 Oct.

Nike (2007) Financial statement. www.nike.com/nikebiz/nikebiz.jhtml?page=16.

Nike (2015) Net income worldwide, 2014. http://www.statista.com/statistics/241685/net-profit-of-nike-since-2005/ (accessed 1 May 2015).

NOAA (2016) Trends in atmospheric carbon dioxide. *National Oceanic and Atmospheric Administration.* http://www.esrl.noaa.gov/gmd/ccgg/trends/weekly.html (accessed 26 May 2016).

Noonan, T. (1996) In the rough. *Far Eastern Economic Review*, 25 January, 38–9.

Norwine, J. and Gonzalez, A. (1988) Introduction, in Norwine, J. and Gonzalez, A. (eds) *The Third World: States of Mind and Being.* London: Unwin-Hyman, 1–6.

NZMFAT (New Zealand, Ministry of Foreign Affairs and Trade) (2015) *New Zealand's immigration relationship with Tuvalu.* http://www.mfat.govt.nz/Foreign-Relations/Pacific/NZ-Tuvalu-immigration.php (accessed 25 Mar 2015).

O'Brien, R. (1991) *Global Financial Integration: The End of Geography.* London: Pinter.

O'Connor, A. (1976) Third World or one world. *Area*, 8, 269–71.

O'Connor, A. (1983) *The African City.* London: Hutchinson.

O'Connor, A. (1991) *Poverty in Africa: A Geographical Approach.* London: Belhaven.

O'Hare, G. (2002a) Climate change and the temple of sustainable development. *Geography*, 87(3), 234–46.

O'Hare, G. (2000b) Reviewing the uncertainties in climate change science. *Area*, 32(4), 357–68.

O'Riordan, T. (ed) (1995) *Environmental Science for Environmental Management.* London: Longman.

O'Riordan, T. (2000a) Climate change, in O'Riordan, T. (ed) *Environmental Science for Environmental Management.* Harlow: Pearson Education, 171–211.

O'Riordan, T. (ed) (2000b) *Environmental Science for Environmental Management.* Harlow: Pearson Education.

O'Riordan, T. (2001) *Globalism, Localism and Identity.* London: Earthscan.

O'Riordan, T. (2013) Sustainability for wellbeing. *Environmental Innovation and Societal Transitions,* 6, 24–34.

O'Riordan, T. and Jordan, A. (2000) Managing the global commons, in O'Riordan, T. (ed) (2000) *Environmental Science for Environmental Management.* Harlow: Pearson Education, 485–511.

O'Tuathail, G. (1994) Critical geopolitics and development theory: intensifying the dialogue. *Transactions of the Institute of British Geographers, New Series*, 19, 228–38.

Oberai, A.S. (1993) *Population Growth, Employment and Poverty in Third World Mega-Cities: Analytical and Policy Issues.* Basingstoke: Macmillan and New York: St Martin's Press.

Ochieng, J., Ouma, E. and Birachi, E. (2014) Gender participation and decision making in crop management in Great Lakes Region of Central Africa. *Gender, Technology and Development*, 18(3), 341–62.

OECD (Organisation for Economic Cooperation and Development) (2006) *Development Cooperation Report, 2005*. Paris: OECD.

OECD (Organisation for Economic Cooperation and Development) (2008) *The Paris Declaration on Aid Effectiveness and the Accra Agenda for Action*. http://www.oecd.org/dac/effectiveness/34428351.pdf (accessed 19 May 2015).

OECD (Organisation for Economic Cooperation and Development) (2012) *Aid Effectiveness 2011: Progress in Implementing the Paris Declaration*. Better Aid, OECD Publishing.

OECD (Organisation for Economic Cooperation and Development) (2014) Focus on Inequality and Growth. Paris: OECD.

OECD (Organisation for Economic Cooperation and Development) (2015a) *Multilateral Aid 2015: Better Partnerships for a Post-2015 World*. Paris: OECD.

OECD (Organisation for Economic Cooperation and Development) (2015b) *States of Fragility 2015: Meeting the Post-2015 Ambitions*. Paris: OECD.

OECD/IEA (2015) *Key World Energy Statistics 2015*. Paris: International Energy Agency.

Oliver, R. and Fage, J.D. (1966) *A Short History of Africa*. Harmondsworth: Penguin.

Olthof, W. (1995) Wildlife resources and local development: experiences from Zimbabwe's Campfire programme, in van de Breemer, J.P.M., Drijver, C.A. and Venema, L.B. (eds) *Local Resource Management in Africa*. Chichester: John Wiley, 111–28.

Opiyo, F., Wasonga, O., Nyangito, M., Schilling, J. and Munang, R. (2015) Drought adaptation and coping strategies among the Turkana pastoralists of northern Kenya. *International Journal of Disaster Risk Science*, 6(3), 295–309.

Oxfam (1984) *Behind the Weather: Lessons to be Learned. Drought and Famine in Ethiopia*. Oxford: Oxfam.

Oxfam (1993) *Africa: Make or Break. Action for Recovery*. Oxford: Oxfam.

Oxfam (1994) *The Coffee Chain Game*. Oxford: Oxfam.

Oxfam (2002) Rigged rules and double standards: trade, globalisation and the fight against poverty. www.maketradefair.com.

Oxfam (2013) Oxfam's reaction to the 9th WTO Ministerial Conference in Bali. https://www.oxfam.org/en/pressroom/reactions/oxfams-reaction-9th-wto-ministerial-conference-bali (accessed 27 March 2015).

Pachai, B. (ed) (1973) *Livingstone: Man of Africa. Memorial Essays 1873–1973*. Harlow: Longman.

Pacione, M. (2005) *Urban Geography: A Global Perspective*, 2nd edn. London and New York: Routledge.

Pacione, M. (2009) *Urban Geography*, 3rd edn. London: Routledge.

Page, J. and Plaza, S. (2006) Migration remittances and development: a review of global evidence. *Journal of African Economies*, 15(AERC Supplement 2), 245–336.

Panayiotopoulos, P. and Capps, G. (2001) *World Development: An Introduction*. London: Pluto Press.

Parfitt, T. (2002) *The End of Development: Modernity, Post-Modernity and Development*. London: Pluto Press.

Parnwell, M. (1994) Rural industrialisation and sustainable development in Thailand. *Quarterly Environment Journal*, 2, 24–29.

Parnwell, M. (2006) Robert Chambers, in Simon, D. (ed) *50 Key Thinkers on Development*. London: Routledge, 73–7.

Parnwell, M. and Turner, S. (1998) Sustaining the unsustainable: city and society in Southeast Asia. *Third World Planning Review*, 20, 147–164.

Parry, M. (1990) *Climate Change and World Agriculture*. London: Earthscan.

Patullo, P. (1996) *Last Resort? Tourism in the Caribbean*. London: Mansell and the Latin American Bureau.

Payn, T., Carnus, J.M., Freer-Smith, P., Kimberley, M., Kollert, M., Liu, S., Orazio, C., Rodriguez, L., Silva, L.N. and Wingfield, M.J. (2015) Changes in planted forests and future global implications. *Forest Ecology and Management*, 352, 57–67.

Peake, S. and Smith, J. (2009) *Climate Change: From Science to Sustainability*, 2nd edn. OUP: Oxford.

Pearce, D. (1995) *Blueprint 4: Capturing Global Environmental Value*. London: Earthscan.

Pearce, F. (1993) How green is your golf? *New Scientist*, 25 September, 30–5.

Pearce, F. (1997) The biggest dam in the world, in Owen, L. and Unwin, T. (eds) *Environmental Management: Readings and Case Studies*. Oxford: Blackwell, 349–54.

Pearson, R. (1992) Gender matters in development, in Allen, T. and Thomas, A. (eds) *Poverty and Development in the 1990s*. Oxford: Oxford University Press, 291–313.

Pearson, R. (2000) Rethinking gender matters in development, in Allen, T. and Thomas, A. (eds) *Poverty and Development into the Twenty First Century*. Oxford: Oxford University Press, 383–402.

Pedersen, P.O. (1970) Innovation diffusion within and between national urban systems. *Geographical Analysis*, 2, 203–54.

Peet, R. and Watts, M. (eds) (1996) *Liberation Ecologies: Environment, Development, Social Movements*. London: Routledge.

Pelling, M. (2002) The Rio Earth Summit, ch. 6.3 in Desai, V. and Potter, R.B. (eds) *The Companion to Development Studies*. London: Arnold, 284–9.

Peluso, N. and Watts, M (eds) (2001) *Violent Environments*. Ithaca: Cornell Univ. Press.

Perloff, H.S. and Wingo, L. (1961) Natural resource endowment and regional economic growth, in Spengler, J.J. (ed) *Natural Resources and Economic Growth*. Washington, DC: Resources for the Future.

Pernia, E. (1992) Southeast Asia, in Stren, R. (ed) *Sustainable Cities: Urbanization and the Environment in International Perspective*. Oxford: Westview Press, 233–58.

Perroux, F. (1950) Economic space: theory and applications. *Quarterly Journal of Economics*, 64, 89–104.

Perroux, F. (1955) Note sur la notion de 'pôle de croissance'. *Économie Appliquée*, 1(2), 307–20.

Phillips, D.R. (1990) *Health and Health Care in the Third World*. Harlow: Longman.

Phillips, D.R. and Yeh, G.O. (1990) Foreign investment and trade: impact on spatial structure of the economy, in Cannon, T. and Jenkins, A. (eds) *The Geography of Contemporary China*. London: Routledge, 224–48.

Pierce-Colfer, C.J., Basnett, B.S. and Elias, M. (eds) (2016) *Gender and Forests: Climate Change, Tenure, Value Chains and Emerging Issues*. London: Routledge.

Pillai, P (2008) *Strengthening Policy Dialogue on the Environment: Learning from Five Years of Country Environmental Analysis*. Paper number 114. Washington: Environment Department, World Bank.

Pillay, C. (2013) Winning environmental justice for the lower Mekong Basin. *World Social Science Report 2013: Changing Global Environments*. Paris: OECD Publishing and UNESCO Publishing, 376–7.

Pinches, M. (1994) Urbanisation in Asia: development, contradiction and conflict, in Jayasuriya, L. and Lee, M. (eds) *Social Dimensions of Development*. Sydney: Paradigm Press.

Pinstrup-Andersen, P. (1994) *World Food Trends and Future Food Security*. Washington, DC: International Food Policy Research Institute.

Pletsch, C. (1981) The three worlds or the division of social scientific labour 1950–1975. *Comparative Studies in Society and History*, 23, 565–90.

Pleumarom, A. (1992) Course and effect: golf tourism in Thailand. *The Ecologist*, 22(3), 104–10.

Pogge, T. (n.d.) Poverty, human rights and global order: framing the post-2015 agenda. http://www.beyond2015.org/sites/default/files/SSRN-id2046985.pdf (accessed 12 Dec 2015).

Pogge T. and Sengupta M (2014) Rethinking the post-2015 development agenda: eight ways to end poverty now. *Global Justice: Theory Practice Rhetoric*, 7, 3–11.

Pogge, T. and Sengupta, M. (2015) The sustainable development goals (SDGs) as drafted: nice idea, poor execution. *Washington International Law Journal*, 24(3), 571–87.

Porteous, D. (1995) in Crush, J. (ed) *Power of Development*. London: Routledge.

Porter, D.J. (1995) Scenes from childhood, in Crush, J. (ed) *Power of Development*. London: Routledge, 63–86.

Porter, G. (1996) SAPs and road transport deterioration in West Africa. *Geography*, 81(4), 368–71.

Porter, G. and Phillips-Howard, K. (1997) Contract farming in South Africa: a case study from Kwazulu-Natal. *Geography*, 82(3/4), 1–38.

Porter, P.W. and Sheppard, E.S. (1998) *A World of Difference: Society, Nature, Development*. London: The Guilford Press.

Portes, A., Castells, M. and Benton, L. (eds) (1991) *The Informal Economy: Studies in Advanced and Less Developed Countries*. Baltimore, MD: Johns Hopkins University Press.

Portes, A., Dore-Cabral, C. and Landolt, P. (1997) *The Urban Caribbean: Transition of the New Global Economy*. Baltimore, MD: Johns Hopkins University Press.

Potter, D. (2000) Democratisation, 'good governance' and development, in Allen, T. and Thomas, A. (eds) *Poverty and Development into the 21st Century*. Oxford: Oxford University Press, 365–82.

Potter, R.B. (1981) Industrial development and urban planning in Barbados. *Geography*, 66, 225–8.

Potter, R.B. (1983) Tourism and development: the case of Barbados, West Indies. *Geography*, 68, 46–50.

Potter, R.B. (1985) Urbanisation and Planning in the Third World: Spatial Perceptions and Public Participation. London: Croom Helm and New York: St Martin's Press.

Potter, R.B. (1989) Rural–urban interaction in Barbados and the southern Caribbean, in Potter, R.B. and Unwin, T. (eds) *Urban–Rural Interaction in Developing Countries*. London and New York: Routledge, 257–93.

Potter, R.B. (1990) Cities, convergence, divergence and Third World development, in Potter, R.B. and Salau, A.T. (eds) *Cities and Development in the Third World*. London: Mansell.

Potter, R.B. (1992a) *Urbanisation in the Third World*. Oxford: Oxford University Press.

Potter, R.B. (1992b) *Housing Conditions in Barbados: A Geographical Analysis*. Mona, Kingston, Jamaica: Institute of Social and Economic Research, University of the West Indies.

Potter, R.B. (1993a) Little England and little geography: reflections on Third World teaching and research. *Area*, 25, 291–4.

Potter, R.B. (1993b) Basic needs and development in the small island states of the Eastern Caribbean, in Lockhart, D. and Drakakis-Smith, D. (eds) *Small Island Development*. London: Routledge.

Potter, R.B. (1993c) Urbanization in the Caribbean and trends of global convergence–divergence. *Geographical Journal*, 159, 1–21.

Potter, R.B. (1994) *Low-Income Housing and the State in the Eastern Caribbean*. Barbados: University of the West Indies Press.

Potter, R.B. (1995a) Urbanisation and development in the Caribbean. *Geography*, 80, 334–41.

Potter, R.B. (1995b) Whither the real Barbados? *Caribbean Week*, 7(4), 64–7.

Potter, R.B. (1996) Environmental impacts of urban-industrial development in the tropics: an overview, in Eden, M. and Parry, J.T. (eds) *Land Degradation in the Tropics*. London: Pinter.

Potter, R.B. (1997) Third World urbanisation in a global context. *Geography Review*, 10, 2–6.

Potter, R.B. (1998) From plantopolis to mini-metropolis in the eastern Caribbean, ch. 3 in McGregor, D., Barker, D. and Lloyd-Evans, S. (eds) *Resource Sustainability and Caribbean Development*. Barbados: University of the West Indies Press, 51–68.

Potter, R.B. (2000) *The Urban Caribbean in an Era of Global Change*. Aldershot: Ashgate.

Potter, R.B. (2001a) Geography and development: core and periphery? *Area*, 33, 422–7.

Potter, R.B. (2001b) Progress, development and change. *Progress in Development Studies*, 1, 1–4.

Potter, R.B. (2002a) Geography and development: core and periphery? A reply. *Area*, 34, 213–14.

Potter, R.B. (2002b) Making progress in development studies. *Progress in Development Studies*, 2, 1–3.

Potter, R.B. (2003) The environment of development. *Progress in Development Studies*, 3, 1–4.

Potter, R.B. (2008a) Global convergence, divergence and development, ch. 4.3 in Desai, V. and Potter, R.B. (eds) *The Companion to Development Studies*, 2nd edn. London: Hodder-Arnold and New York: Oxford University Press, 192–6.

Potter, R.B. (2008b) World cities and development, ch. 5.3 in Desai, V. and Potter, R.B. (eds) *The Companion to Development Studies*, 2nd edn. London: Hodder-Arnold and New York: Oxford University Press, 247–52.

Potter, R.B. and Conway, D. (eds) (1997) *Self-Help Housing, the Poor and the State in the Caribbean*. Knoxville, TN: Tennessee University Press and Barbados: University of the West Indies Press.

Potter, R.B. and Dann, G. (1996) Globalization, postmodernity and development in the Commonwealth Caribbean, in Yeung, Y. (ed) *Global Change and the Commonwealth*. Hong Kong: Hong Kong Institute of Asia-Pacific Studies, Chinese University of Hong Kong, 103–29.

Potter, R.B. and Dann, G.M.S. (1994) Some observations concerning postmodernity and sustainable development in the Caribbean. *Caribbean Geography*, 5, 92–107.

Potter, R.B. and Lloyd-Evans, S. (1998) *The City in the Developing World*. London: Pearson.

Potter, R.B. and Lloyd-Evans, S. (2008) Development: the Brandt Commission, in Kitchen, R. and Thrift, N. (eds) *International Encyclopedia of Human Geography*. Oxford: Elsevier.

Potter, R.B. and Philips, J. (2004) The rejuvenation of tourism in Barbados, 1993–2003: reflections on the Butler model. *Geography*, 89, 240–47.

Potter, R.B. and Phillips, J. (2006a) 'Mad dogs and transnational migrants?' Bajan-Brit second-generation migrants and accusations of madness. *Annals of the Association of American Geographers*, 96, 586–600.

Potter, R.B. and Phillips, J. (2006b) Both black and symbolically white: the Bajan-Brit return migrants as post-colonial hybrid. *Ethnic and Racial Studies*, 29, 901–27.

Potter, R.B. and Phillips, J. (2008) 'The past is still right here in the present': second-generation Bajan-Brit transnational migrants' views on issues relating to race and colour class. *Environment and Planning D: Society and Space*.

Potter, R.B. and Pugh, J. (2001) Planning without plans and the neo-liberal state: the case of St Lucia, West Indies. *Third World Planning Review*, 23, 323–40.

Potter, R.B. and Unwin, T. (1987) Urban–Rural Interaction in Developing Countries: Essays in Honor of Alan B Mountjoy. London and New York: Routledge.

Potter, R.B. and Unwin, T. (1988) Developing areas research in British geography. *Area*, 20, 121–6.

Potter, R.B. and Unwin, T. (eds) (1992) *Teaching the Geography of Developing Areas*. Monograph 7, Developing Areas Research Group. London: Institute of British Geographers.

Potter, R.B. and Unwin, T. (1995) Urban–rural interaction: physical form and political process in the Third World. *Cities*, 12, 67–73.

Potter, R.B. and Welch, B. (1996) Indigenization and development in the Caribbean. *Caribbean Week*, 8, 13–4.

Potter, R.B., Barham, N. and Darmame, K. (2007) The polarised social and residential structure of the city of Amman: a contemporary view using GIS data.

Bulletin of the Council for British Research in the Levant, 2, 48–52.

Potter, R.B., Barham, N., Darmame, K. and Nortcliff, S. (2007) An introduction to the urban geography of Amman, Jordan. *Reading Geographical Paper*, 182.

Potter, R.B., Conway, D., Evans, R. and Lloyd-Evans, S. (2012) *Key Concepts in Development Geography*. London: SAGE Publications Ltd.

Potter, R.B., Darmame, K. and Nortcliff, S. (2007) The provision of water under conditions of 'water stress', privatisation and de-privatisation in Amman. *Bulletin of the Council for British Research in the Levant*, 2, 52–4.

Potts, D. (1995) Shall we go home? Increasing urban poverty in African cities and migration processes. *Geographical Journal*, 161(3), 245–64.

Power, M. (2002) Enlightenment and the era of modernity, ch. 2.2 in Desai, V. and Potter, R.B. (eds) *The Companion to Development Studies*. London: Arnold, 65–70.

Power, M. (2003) *Rethinking Development Geographies*. London and New York: Routledge.

Prebisch, R. (1950) *The Economic Development of Latin America*. New York: United Nations.

Pred, A. (1977) *City-Systems in Advanced Economies*. London: Hutchinson.

Pred, A.R. (1973) The growth and development of systems of cities in advanced economies, in Pred, A. and Törnqvist, G. (eds) *Systems of Cities and Information Flows: Two Essays*. Lund: University of Lund, 9–82.

Preston, D. (1987) Population mobility and the creation of new landscapes, in Preston, D. (ed) *Latin American Development: Geographical Perspectives*. London: Longman, 229–59.

Preston, P.W. (1985) *New Trends in Development Theory*. London: Routledge.

Preston, P.W. (1987) *Making Sense of Development: An Introduction to Classical and Contemporary Theories of Development and their Application to Southeast Asia*. London: Routledge.

Preston, P.W. (1996) *Development Theory: An Introduction*. Oxford: Blackwell.

Pretty, J. (2014) The sustainable intensification of agriculture, in Desai, V. and Potter, R.B. (eds) *The Companion to Development Studies*, 3rd edn. London: Routledge, 270–4.

Prior, T., Giurco, D., Mudd, G., Mason, L. and Behrisch, J. (2012) Resource depletion, peak minerals and the implications for sustainable resource management. *Global Environmental Change*, 22, 577–87.

Pritchard, S. (2014) Evicted by charity. *New Internationalist*, 478, 20–1.

Pro-Poor Tourism (2002) How is PPT different from other forms of 'alternative' tourism? www.propoortourism.org.uk/ppt_vs_alternative.html.

Prothero, R.M. (1959) *Migrant Labour from Sokoto Province, Northern Nigeria*. Kaduna: Government Printer, 46.

Prothero, R.M. (1994) Forced movements of population and health hazards in tropical Africa. *International Journal of Epidemiology*, 23(4), 657–64.

Prothero, R.M. (1996) Migration and AIDS in West Africa. *Geography*, 81(4), 374–7.

Pryer, J. (1987) Production and reproduction of malnutrition in an urban slum in Khulna, Bangladesh, in Momsen, J.H. and Townsend, J. (eds) *Geography of Gender in the Third World*. London: Hutchinson, 131–49.

Pugh, C. (ed) (1996) *Sustainability, the Environment and Urbanization*. London: Earthscan.

Pugh, J. (2002) Local Agenda 21 and the Third World, ch. 6.4 in Desai, V. and Potter, R.B. (eds) *The Companion to Development Studies*. London: Arnold, 289–93.

Pugh, J. and Potter, R.B. (2000) Rolling back the state and physical development planning: the case of Barbados. *Singapore Journal of Tropical Geography*, 21, 175–91.

Pugh, J. and Potter, R.B. (eds) (2003) *Participatory Planning in the Caribbean: Lessons from Practice*. Aldershot, UK and Burlington, VT: Ashgate.

Purcell, M. and Brown, J.C. (2005) Against the local trap: scale and study of environment and development. *Progress in Development Studies*, 5, 279–97.

Putnam, R. (1993) The prosperous community: social capital and public life. *American Prospect*, 13, 35–42.

Pye-Smith, C. and Feyerarbend, G.B. (1995) What next? in Kirkby, J., O'Keefe, P. and Timberlake, L. (eds) *The Earthscan Reader in Sustainable Development*. London: Earthscan, 303–9.

Quader, M.A. (2000) Ruralopolis: the spatial organization and residential land economy of high-density rural regions in South Asia. *Urban Studies*, 37, 1583–600.

Raath, J. (1997) Mugabe wants aid to seize white land. *The Times*, 20 October.

Rada, N. (2013) Assessing Brazil's Cerrado agricultural miracle. *Food Policy,* 38, 146–55.

Radcliffe, S.A. (2015) Development alternatives. *Development and Change*, 46(4), 855–74.

Rakodi, C. (1995) Poverty lines or household strategies? *Habitat International*, 19(4), 407–26.

Rakodi, C. (2002) A livelihood approach – conceptual issues and definitions, in Rakodi, C. and Lloyd-Jones, T. (eds) *Urban Livelihoods: A People-Centred Approach to Reducing Poverty*. London: Earthscan.

Rakodi, C. and Lloyd-Jones, T. (eds) (2002) *Urban Livelihoods: A People-Centred Approach to Reducing Poverty*. London: Earthscan.

Ransom, D. (2001) A world turned upside down. *New Internationalist*, 334(May), 26–8.

Ransom, D. (2005) Upside down: the United Nations at 60. *New Internationalist*, 375, 9–12.

Rapley, J. (1996) *Understanding Development: Theory and Practice in the Third World*. London: University College of London Press.

Rapley, J. (2001) Convergence: myths and realities. *Progress in Development Studies*, 1, 295–308.

Raworth, K. (2012) *A Safe and Just Space for Humanity: Can We Live Within the Doughnut. Oxfam Discussion Paper*. February.

Reading, A.J., Thompson, R.D. and Millington, A.C. (1995) *Humid Tropical Environments*. Oxford: Blackwell.

Reality of Aid (2002) An independent review of poverty reduction and development assistance. www.devint.org/realityofaid.

Reardon, T. (1997) Using evidence of household income diversification to inform study of the rural nonfarm labor market in Africa. *World Development*, 25(5), 735–47.

Redclift, M. (1987) *Sustainable Development: Exploring the Contradictions*. London: Methuen.

Redclift, M. (1997) Sustainable development: needs, values and rights, in Owen, L. and Unwin, T. (eds) *Environmental Management: Readings and Case Studies*. Oxford: Blackwell, 438–50.

Redclift, M. (2005) Sustainable development (1987–2005): an oxymoron comes of age. *Sustainable Development*, 13, 212–27.

Redclift, M. (2014) Sustainable development, in Desai, V. and Potter, R.B. (2014) (eds) *The Companion to Development Studies*, 3rd edn. London: Routledge, 333–6.

Reed, D. (ed) (1996) *Structural Adjustment: The Environment and Sustainable Development*. London: Earthscan.

Rees, J. (1990) *Natural Resources: Allocation, Economics and Policy*, 2nd edn. London: Methuen.

Reiterer, M. (2009) The Doha development agenda of the WTO: possible institutional implications. *Progress in Development Studies*, 9(4), 359–75.

Renaud, B. (1981) *National Urbanization Policy in Developing Countries*. Oxford: Oxford University Press for the World Bank.

Renaud, F., Bogardi, J.J., Dun, O. and Warner, K. (2007) Control, adapt or flee: How to face environmental migration? *Intersections*, 5/2007. Bonn: UNU Institute for Environment and Human Security.

Renner, M. (2002) Breaking the link between resources and repression, in Worldwatch Institute, *State of the World 2002: Progress Towards a Sustainable Society*. London: Earthscan, 149–72.

Rich, B. (1994) *Mortgaging the Earth: The World Bank, Environmental Impoverishment and the Crisis of Development*. London: Earthscan.

Richards, P. and Thomson, A. (1984) *Basic Needs and the Urban Poor*. London: Croom Helm.

Richardson, H.W. (1973) *The Economics of Urban Size*. Farnborough: Saxon House.

Richardson, H.W. (1976) The argument for very large cities reconsidered: a comment. *Urban Studies*, 13, 307–10.

Richardson, H.W. (1977) *City size and National Spatial Strategies in Developing Countries*, World Bank Staff Working Paper 252.

Richardson, H.W. (1980) Polarization reversal in developing countries. *Papers of the Regional Science Association*, 45, 67–85.

Richardson, H.W. (1981) National urban development strategies in developing countries. *Urban Studies*, 18, 267–83.

Richey, L.A. and Ponte, S. (2008) Better (red) than dead? Celebrities, consumption and international aid. *Third World Quarterly*, 29(4), 711–29.

Richey, L.A. and Ponte, S. (2014) New actors and alliances in development. *Third World Quarterly*, 35(1), 1–21.

Riddell, J.B. (1970) *The Spatial Dynamics of Modernization in Sierra Leone: Structure, Diffusion and Response*. Evanston, IL: Northwestern University Press.

Riddell, J.B. (1978) The migration to the cities of West Africa: some policy considerations. *Journal of Modern African Studies*, 16(2), 241–60.

Rigg, J. (1997) *Southeast Asia*. London: Routledge.

Rigg, J. (2001) *More than the Soil: Rural Change in Southeast Asia*. Harlow: Pearson Education.

Rigg, J. (2002) The Asian crisis, ch. 1.6 in Desai, V. and Potter, R.B. (eds) *The Companion to Development Studies*. London: Arnold, 27–32.

Rigg, J. (2006) Land, farming, livelihoods, and poverty: rethinking the links in the rural South. *World Development*, 34(1), 180–202.

Rigg, J. (2007) *An Everyday Geography of the Global South*. Abingdon: Routledge.

Rigg, J. (2008) The Millennium Development Goals, ch. 1.7 in Desai, V. and Potter, R.B. (eds) *The Companion to Development Studies*, 2nd edn. London: Hodder-Arnold and New York: Oxford University Press, 37–40.

Righter, R. (1995) *Utopia Lost: The United Nations and the World Order*. New York: Twentieth Century Fund Press.

Riley, S. (1988) *Structural Adjustment and the New Urban Poor: The Case of Freetown*. Paper presented at the Workshop on the New Urban Poor in Africa, School of Oriental and African Studies, London, May 1988.

Rimmer, P.J. (1991) International transport and communications interactions between Pacific Asia's world cities, in Lo, F.-C. and Yeung, Y.-M. (eds) *Emerging World Cities in Asia*. Tokyo: United Nations University Press, 48–97.

Robb, C. (1998) PPAs: a review of the World Bank's experience, in Holland, J. and Blackburn, J. (eds) *Whose Voice: Participatory Research and Policy Change*. London: IT Publications.

Robins, K. (1989) Global times. *Marxism Today*, December 1989, 20–7.

Robins, K. (1995) The new spaces of global media, in Knox, P.C. and Taylor, P.J. (eds) *World Cities in a World-System*. Cambridge: Cambridge University Press, 248–62.

Robinson, G. (2004) *Geographies of Agriculture: Globalisation, Restructuring and Sustainability*. Harlow: Pearson Education.

Robinson, J. (2006) *Ordinary Cities*. London: Taylor & Francis.

Robson, B.T. (1973) *Urban Growth: An Approach*. London: Methuen.

Robson, E. (1996) Working girls and boys: children's contributions to household survival in West Africa. *Geography*, 81(4), 43–7.

Rockström, J. et al. (2009) A safe operating space for humanity. *Nature*, 461(7263) 472–5.

Rodney, W. (1972) *How Europe Underdeveloped Africa*. Washington, DC: Howard University Press.

Rojas, E. (1989) Human settlements of the Eastern Caribbean: development problems and policy options. *Cities*, 6, 243–58.

Rojas, E. (1995) Commentary: government–market interactions in urban development policy. *Cities*, 12, 399–400.

Roodman, D.M. (2001) *Still Waiting for the Jubilee: Pragmatic Solutions for the Third World Debt Crisis*. Worldwatch Paper 155. Washington, DC: Worldwatch Institute.

Rostow, W.W. (1960) *The Stages of Economic Growth: A Non-communist Manifesto*. Cambridge: Cambridge University Press.

Rotberg, R. (2014) Chinese trade with Africa hits record high. *China-US Focus*, 15 March. http://www.chinausfocus.com/finance-economy/chinese-trade-with-africa-hits-record-high/ (accessed 2 Mar 2015).

Routledge, P. (1995) Resisting and reshaping the modern: social movements and the development process, in Johnston, R.J. et al. (eds) *Geographies of Global Change*. London: Blackwell, 263–79.

Routledge, P. (2002) Resisting and reshaping destructive development: social movements and globalising networks, in Johnston, R.J., Taylor, P.J. and Watts, M.J. (eds) *Geographies of Global Change: Remapping the World*, 2nd edn. Oxford: Blackwell, 310–27 Routledge.

Rowley, C. (1978) *The Destruction of Aboriginal Society*. Ringwood: Penguin.

Ruggie, J.G. (2003) The UN and globalisation: patterns and limits of institutional adaptation. *Global Governance*, 9(3), 301–21.

Sachs, J. (ed) (2005) *Investing in Development: A Practical Plan to Achieve the MDGs*. Overview. New York: United Nations.

Sachs, W. (1992) *The Development Dictionary*. London: Zed Books.

Safier, M. (1969) Towards the definition of patterns in the distribution of economic development over East Africa. *East African Geographical Review*, 7, 1–13.

Sahnoun, M. (1994) Flashlights over Mogadishu. *New Internationalist*, 262, 9–11.

Sahr, W.D. (1998) Micro-metropolis in the eastern Caribbean: the example of St Lucia, in McGregor, D., Lloyd-Evans, S. and Barker, D. (eds) *Resources, Sustainability and Caribbean Development*. Barbados: University of the West Indies Press.

Saich, T. (2011) *Governance and Politics of China,* 3rd edn. Houndmills: Palgrave Macmillan.

Said, E. (1978) *Orientalism*. New York: Vintage.

Said, E. (1979) *Orientalism*, 2nd edn. New York: Village Books.

Said, E. (1993) *Culture and Imperialism*. London: Chatto.

Sanchez-Rodriguez, R. (2006) Fernando Henrique Cardoso, in Simon, D. (ed) *Fifty Key Thinkers on Development*. London and New York: Routledge, 61–6.

Sandbrook, R. (1999) Institutions for global environmental change. *Global Environmental Change*, 9, 171–4.

Sandford, S. (1983) *Management of Pastoral Development in the Third World*. Chichester: John Wiley.

Santos, M. (1979) *The Shared Space: The Two Circuits of the Urban Economy in Underdeveloped Countries*. London: Methuen.

Sapsford, D. (2008) Smith, Ricardo and the world market place, 1776–2007: back to the future, in Desai, V. and Potter, R.B. (eds) *The Companion to Development Studies*, 2nd edn. London: Hodder-Arnold and New York: Oxford University Press, 75–81.

Sapsford, D. (2014) Smith, Ricardo and the world marketplace, 1776 to 2012: back to the future and beyond, in Desai, V. and Potter, R.B. (2014) (eds) *The Companion to Development Studies*, 3rd edn. London: Routledge, 88–95.

Sardar, Z. (1998) *Postmodernism and the Other: The New Imperialism of Western Culture*. London and Chicago, IL: Pluto Press.

Sartre, J.P. (1964, 2001) *Colonialism and Neocolonialism*. English translation (2001), London: Routledge.

Sassen, S. (1991) *The Global City*. Princeton, NJ: Princeton University Press.

Sassen, S. (2002) *Global Networks, Linked Cities*. New York: Routledge.

Satterthwaite, D. (1997) Sustainable cities or cities that contribute to sustainable development. *Urban Studies*, 35.

Satterthwaite, D. (ed) (1999) *The Earthscan Reader in Sustainable Cities*. London: Earthscan.

Satterthwaite, D. (2008) Urbanization in low- and middle-income nations, ch. 5.1 in Desai, V. and Potter, R.B. (eds) *The Companion to Development Studies*, 2nd edn. London: Hodder-Arnold and New York: Oxford University Press, 237–43.

Satterthwaite, D. and Mitlin, D. (2014) *Reducing Urban Poverty in the Global South*. Abingdon: Routledge.

Satyavathi, C.T., Bharadwaj, C. and Brahmanand, P.S. (2010) Role of women in agriculture: lessons learned. *Gender, Technology and Development*, 14(3), 441–49.

Save the Children Fund (1995) *Towards a Children's Agenda: New Challenges for Social Development*. London: SCF.

Schaaf, R. (2013) *Development Organisations*. London: Routledge.

Schech, S. and Haggis, J. (2000) *Culture and Development: A Critical Introduction*. Oxford: Blackwell.

Scheidel, A. and Sorman, A.H. (2012) Energy transitions and the global land rush: ultimate drivers and persistent consequences. *Global Environmental Change*, 22, 588–95.

Scheyvens, R. (2011) *Tourism and Poverty*. London: Routledge.

Schneider, F. and Frey, B. (1985) Economic and political determinants of foreign direct investment. *World Development*, 13(2), 167–75.

Schultz, T.W. (1953) *The Economic Organization of Agriculture*. New York: McGraw-Hill.

Schumacher, E.F. (1974) *Small is Beautiful*. London: Abacus.

Schumpeter, J.A. (1912) *Die Theorie des Wirtschaftlichen Entwicklung*. Berlin: Duncker and Humblot.

Schumpeter, J.A. (1934) *The Theory of Economic Development*. Cambridge, MA: Harvard University Press.

Schuurman, F. (ed) (1993) *Beyond the Impasse: New Directions in Development Theory*. London: Zed.

Schuurman, F. (2000) Paradigms lost, paradigms regained? Development studies in the twenty-first century. *Third World Quarterly*, 21, 7–20.

Schuurman, F.J. (2001) *Globalization and Development Studies: Challenges for the 21st Century*. London, Thousand Oaks and New Delhi: Sage Publications.

Schuurman, F.J. (2008) The impasse in development studies, ch. 1.3 in Desai, V. and Potter, R.B. (eds) *The Companion to Development Studies*, 2nd edn. London: Hodder-Arnold and New York: Oxford University Press, 12–15.

Science for Environment Policy (2015) *Ecosystem Services and the Environment*. In-depth Report 11 produced for the European Commission, DG Environment by the Science Communication Unit, UWE, Bristol.

Scoones, I. (1995) Policies for pastoralists: new directions for pastoral development in Africa, in Binns, T. (ed) *People and Environment in Africa*. Chichester: John Wiley, 23–30.

Scoones, I. (1996) Range management science and policy: politics, polemics and pasture in Southern Africa, in Leach, M. and Mearns, R. (eds) *The Lie of the Land: Challenging Received Wisdom on the African Environment*. Oxford: International African Institute/James Currey, 34–53.

Scoones, I. (2009) Livelihoods perspectives and rural development. *The Journal of Peasant Studies*, 36(1), 171–96.

Scoones, I. (2015) Will the SDGs make a difference? Accessed 28 Sept 2015. http://steps-centre.org/2015/blog/sdgscoones/.

Scoones, I. and Thompson, J. (1994) *Beyond Farmer First*. London: Intermediate Technology Productions.

Scott, J.C. (1976) *The Moral Economy of the Peasant: Rebellion and Subsistence in South-East Asia*. New Haven, CT: Yale University Press.

Secrett, C. (1986) The environmental impact of transmigration. *The Ecologist*, 16(2/3), 77–89.

Seers, D. (1969) The meaning of development. *International Development Review*, 11(4), 2–6.

Seers, D. (1972) What are we trying to measure? *Journal of Development Studies*, 8(3), 21–36.

Seers, D. (1979) The new meaning of development, in Lehmann, D. (ed) *Development Theory: Four Critical Studies*. London: Frank Cass, 25–30.

Seitz, J.L. (2000, 2002) *Global Issues: An Introduction*, 2nd edn. Oxford: Blackwell.

Sen, A. (1981) *Poverty and Famines*. Oxford: Clarendon Press.

Sen, A. (2000) *Development as Freedom: Human Capability and Global Need*. New York: Anchor Books.

Sengupta, K. (2002) Atlas maps investment in a world of abuses. *The Independent*, 13 February, 11.

Seyfang, G. (ed) (2002) *Corporate Responsibility and Labour Rights: Codes of Conduct in the Global Economy*. London: Earthscan.

Shankland, A. (1991) The devil's design. *New Internationalist*, 219, 11–13.

Shariff, I. (1987) Agricultural development and land tenure in India. *Land Use Policy*, 4(3), 321–30.

Sharp, R. (1992) Organising for change: people-power and the role of institutions, in Holmberg, J. (ed) *Policies for a Small Planet*. London: Earthscan/IIED, 39–65.

Sharpley, R. (2002) Tourism management: rural tourism and the challenge of tourism diversification: the case of Cyprus. *Tourism Management*, 23, 233–44.

Shaw, J. and Clay, E. (eds) (1993) *World Food Aid: Experiences of Recipients and Donors*. London: James Currey.

Shaw, T. (2014) Peace-building and partnerships and human security, in Desai, V. and Potter, R.B. (2014) (eds) *The Companion to Development Studies*, 3rd edn. London: Routledge, 517–21.

Shen, S. and Binns, T. (2012) Pathways, motivations and challenges: contemporary Tuvaluan migration to New Zealand. *GeoJournal*, 77, 63–82.

Shibusawa, M., Ahmad, Z.H. and Bridges, B. (1992) *Pacific Asia in the 1990s*. London: Routledge.

Shipton, P. and Goteen, M. (1992) Understanding African land-holding: power, wealth and meaning. *Africa*, 62(3), 307–25.

Shiva, V. (2000) *Stolen Harvest: The Hijacking of the Global Food Supply*. London: Zed Books.

Short, C. (2000) Speech to the Seattle Assembly of the World Trade Organization. *Developments*, 9, 10–11.

Shrivastava, X. (1992) *Bhopal*. London: Paul Chapman.

Sidaway, J.D. (1990) Post-Fordism, post-modernity and the Third World. *Area*, 22, 301–3.

Sidaway, J.D. (2008) Post-development, ch. 1.4 in Desai, V. and Potter, R.B. (eds) *The Companion to Development Studies*, 2nd edn. London: Hodder-Arnold and New York: Oxford University Press, 16–20.

Sidaway, J.D. (2008) Spaces of post-development. *Progress in Human Geography*, 31(3), 345–61.

Siddle, D. and Swindell, K. (1990) *Rural Change in Tropical Africa*. Oxford: Blackwell.

Silvers, J. (1995) Death of a slave. *Sunday Times*, 10 October, 36–41.

Silvey, R. (2010) Development geography: politics and 'the state' under crisis. *Progress in Human Geography*, 34(6), 828–34.

Simon, D. (1992a) *Cities, Capital and Development: African Cities in the World Economy*. London: Belhaven.

Simon, D. (1992b) Conceptualizing small towns in African development, in Baker, J. and Pedersen, P.O. (eds) *The Rural–Urban Interface in Africa*. Uppsala: Nordic Institute for African Studies, 29–50.

Simon, D. (1993) *The World City Hypothesis: Reflections from the Periphery*. CEDAR Research Paper 7. Royal Holloway College, University of London.

Simon, D. (1998) Rethinking (post)modernism, postcolonialism, and posttraditonalism: north–south perspectives. *Environment and Planning D, Society and Space*, 16, 219–45.

Simon, D. (ed) (2006) *Fifty Key Thinkers on Development*. London and New York: Routledge.

Simon, D. (2007) Beyond antidevelopment; discourses, convergences, practices. *Singapore Journal of Tropical Geography*, 28, 205–18.

Simon, D. (2008) Neoliberalism, structural adjustment and poverty reduction strategies, ch. 2.5 in Desai, V. and Potter, R.B. (eds) *The Companion to Development Studies*, 2nd edn. London: Hodder-Arnold and New York: Oxford University Press, 86–91.

Simon, J.L. (1981) *The Ultimate Resource*. London: Martin Robertson.

Singer, H. (1980) The Brandt Report: a north-western point of view. *Third World Quarterly*, 2(4), 694–700.

Singh, R.P.B. (2006) Mohandas (Mahatma) Gandhi, in Simon, D. (ed) *Fifty Key Thinkers on Development*. London and New York: Routledge, 106–10.

Sinha, S. (1998) Introduction and overview. *IDS Bulletin*, 29(4), 1–10.

Slater, D. (1992a) On the borders of social theory: learning from other regions. *Environment and Planning D*, 10, 307–27.

Slater, D. (1992b) Theories of development and politics of the post-modern: exploring a border zone. *Development and Change*, 23, 283–319.

Slater, D. (1993) The geopolitical imagination and the enframing of development theory. *Transactions of the Institute of British Geographers, New Series*, 18, 419–37.

Smith, A. (2002) Translocals, critical area studies and geography's others, or why 'development' should not be geography's organizing framework: a response to Potter. *Area*, 34, 210–13.

Smith, D. (2000) *Moral Geographies: Ethics in a World of Difference*. Edinburgh: Edinburgh University Press.

Smith, D.M. (2008) Responsibility to distant others, ch. 2.14 in Desai, V. and Potter, R.B. (eds) *The Companion to Development Studies*, 2nd edn. London: Hodder-Arnold and New York: Oxford University Press, 129–32.

Smith, D.W. (1994) On professional responsibility to distant others. *Area*, 26, 359–67.

Smith, D.W. (1998) Urban food systems and the poor in developing countries, *Transactions of the Institute of British Geographers*, 23, 207–19.

Smith, N. (2000) Global Seattle. Environment and Planning: Society and Space, 18, 1–5.

So, C.-H. (1997) Economic development, state control and labour migration of women in China. Unpublished PhD thesis, University of Sussex, Brighton.

Soja, E.W. (1968) *The Geography of Modernization in Kenya: A Spatial Analysis of Social, Economic and Political Change*. Syracuse, NY: Syracuse University Press.

Soja, E.W. (1974) The geography of modernization: paths, patterns, and processes of spatial change in developing countries, in Bruner, R. and Brewer, G. (eds) *A Policy Approach to the Study of Political Development and Change*. New York: Free Press.

Soja, E.W. (1989) *Postmodern Geographies: The Reassertion of Space in Critical Social Theory*. London: Verso.

Soussan, J. (1988) *Primary Resources in the Third World*. London: Routledge.

Sparr, P. (1994) *Mortgaging Women's Lives: Feminist Critiques of Structural Adjustment*. London: Zed Books.

Spencer-Oatey, H. (2008) *Culturally Speaking. Culture, Communication and Politeness Theory*, 2nd edn. London: Continuum.

Spivak, G.C. (1993) Can the subaltern speak? in Williams, P. and Chrisman, L. (eds) *Colonial Discourse and Postcolonial Theory*. London: Prentice Hall.

St Lucia Tourist Board (2015) www.investstlucia.com/downloads/getdownload/275 (accessed 21 July 2016)

Stern, N. (2007) *The Economics of Climate Change: The Stern Review*. Cambridge: Cambridge University Press.

Stevens, L., Coupe, S. and Mitlin, D. (2006) *Confronting the Crisis of Urban Poverty*. Rugby: Intermediate Technology Publications.

Stewart, C. (1995) One more river to cross. *New Internationalist*, 273, 16–17.

Stock, R. (1995) Africa South of the Sahara: A Geographical Interpretation. New York: Guildford Press.

Stock, R. (2013) *Africa South of the Sahara*. New York: Guilford Press.

Stocking, M. (1987) Measuring land degradation, in Blaikie, P. and Brookfield, H. (eds) *Land Degradation and Society*. London: Methuen, 49–64.

Stocking, M. (1995) Soil erosion and land degradation, in O'Riordan, T. (ed) *Environmental Science for Environmental Management*. London: Longman, 223–43.

Stocking, M. (2000) Soil erosion and land degradation, in O'Riordan, T. (ed) *Environmental Science for*

Environmental Management. Harlow: Pearson Education, 287–321.

Stöhr, W.B. (1981) Development from below: the bottom-up and periphery-inward development paradigm, in Stöhr, W.B. and Taylor, D.R.F. (eds) *Development from Above or Below?* Chichester: John Wiley, 39–72.

Stöhr, W.B. and Taylor, D.R.F. (1981) *Development from Above or Below? The Dialectics of Regional Planning in Developing Countries*. Chichester: John Wiley.

Streeten, P. (1995) *Thinking About Development*. Cambridge: Cambridge University Press.

Stren, R., White, R. and Whitney, J. (eds) (1992) *Sustainable Cities: Urbanization and the Environment in International Perspective*. Oxford: Westview Press.

Stocking, M. (2000) Soil erosion and land degradation, in O'Riordan, T. (ed) *Environmental Science for Environmental Management*. Harlow: Pearson Education, 287–321.

Stycos, J.M. (1971) Family planning and American goals, in Chaplin, D. (ed) *Population Policies and Growth in Latin America*. Lexington, KY: Heath, 111–31.

Sunday Times (2002) The biggest show in town. *Sunday Times*, Johannesburg, 7 July, 17.

Sutton, K. and Zaimeche, S.E. (2002) The collapse of state socialism in the socialist Third World, ch. 1.5 in Desai, V. and Potter, R.B. (eds) *The Companion to Development Studies*. London: Arnold, 20–6.

Sweetman, C. (2015) Gender mainstreaming: changing the course of development? in Coles, A., Gray, L. and Momsen, J. (eds) *The Routledge Handbook of Gender and Development*. London: Routledge, 24–34.

Taaffe, E.J., Morrill, R.L. and Gould, P.R. (1963) Transport expansion in underdeveloped countries: a comparative analysis. *Geographical Review*, 53, 503–29.

Tanner, T. and Horn-Phathanothai, L. (2014) *Climate Change and Development*. London: Routledge.

Tasker, R. (1995) Tee masters. *Far Eastern Economic Review*, 5 January.

Tata, R. and Schultz, R. (1988) World variations in human welfare: a new index of development status. *Annals of the Association of American Geographers*, 78(4), 580–92.

Taylor, A. (2003) Trading with the environment, in Bingham, N., Blowers, A. and Belshaw, C. (eds) *Contested Environments*. Chichester: Wiley.

Taylor, D.R. and Mackenzie, F. (eds) (1992) *Development from Within: Survival in Rural Africa*. London: Routledge.

Taylor, P. (1985) *Political Geography*. London: Longman.

Taylor, P.J. (1986) The world-systems project, in Johnston, R.J. and Taylor, P.J. (eds) *A World in Crisis? Geographical Perspectives*. Oxford: Basil Blackwell, 333–54.

Teo, P. and Ooi, G.L. (1996) Ethnic differences and public policy in Singapore, in Dwyer, D.J. and Drakakis-Smith, D. (eds) *Ethnicity and Geography*. London: John Wiley, 249–70.

Tewdwr-Jones, M. and Allmendinger, P. (1998) Deconstructing communicative rationality: a critique of Habermasian collaborative planning. *Environment and Planning A*, 30, 1975–89.

Thirlwall, A.P. (1999) *Growth and Development: With Special Reference to Developing Economies*, 6th edn. London: Macmillan.

Thirlwall, A.P. (2002) Development as economic growth, ch. 1.9 in Desai, V. and Potter, R.B. (eds) *The Companion to Development Studies*. London: Arnold, 41–4.

Thomas, A. (1992) Non-governmental organisations and the limits to empowerment, in Wuyts, M., Mackintosh, M. and Hewitt, T. (eds) *Development Policy and Public Action*. Oxford: Oxford University Press, 117–46.

Thomas, A. (2000) Development as practice in a liberal capitalist world. *Journal of International Development*, 12, 773–87.

Thomas, A. (2001) NGOs and their influence on environmental policies in Africa, in Thomas, A. et al. (2001) *Environmental Policies and NGO Influence*. London: Routledge, 1–22.

Thomas, A. and Allen, T. (2000) Agencies of development, in Allen, T. and Thomas, A. (eds) *Poverty and Development in the 21st Century*. Oxford: Oxford University Press, 189–216.

Thomas, C.Y. (1989) *The Poor and the Powerless: Economic Policy and Change in the Caribbean*. London: Latin American Bureau.

Thomas, D.H.L. (1996) Fisheries, tenure and mobility in a West African floodplain. *Geography*, 81(4), 35–40.

Thomas, D.S.G. (1993) Storm in a teacup? Understanding desertification. *Geographical Journal*, 159(3), 318–31.

Thomas, D.S.G., Sporton, D. and Perkins, J. (2000) The environmental impact of livestock ranches in the Kalahari, Botswana: natural resource use, ecological change and human response in a dynamic dryland system. *Land Degradation and Development*, 11, 327–41.

Thomas, G.A. (1991) The gentrification of paradise: St John's, Antigua. *Urban Geography*, 12, 469–87.

Thompson, J., Millstone, E., Scoones, I., Ely, A., Marshall, F., Shah, E. and Stagl, S. (2007) *Agri-food System Dynamics: Pathways to Sustainability in an Era of Uncertainty*. STEPS working paper 4. Brighton: STEPS Centre.

Thompson, M. and Warburton, M. (1985) Uncertainty on a Himalayan scale. *Mountain Research and Development*, 5, 115–35.

Thomson Reuters (2014) Jim O'Neill: BRICs, MINTs strong despite emerging market wobbles. 25 March. http://www.reuters.com/article/2014/03/25/us-emergingmarkets-oneill-idUSBREA2O1CE20140325 (accessed 25 Apr 2014).

Thrift, N. and Forbes, D. (1986) *The Price of War: Urbanisation in Vietnam 1954–1986*. London: Allen & Unwin.

Thulstrup, A.W. (2015) Livelihood resilience and adaptive capacity: tracing changes in household access to capital in Central Vietnam. *World Development*, 74, 352–62.

Tickell, O. (2000) Carbon trading is the burning issue for pollution talks. *The Independent*, 15 December.

Tiffen, M. and Mortimore, M. (1990) *Theory and Practice in Plantation Agriculture: An Economic Review*. London: Overseas Development Institute.

Tiffen, M., Mortimore, M.J. and Gichuki, F. (1994) *More People, Less Erosion: Environmental Recovery in Kenya*. Chichester: John Wiley.

Tisdall, S. (2016) Has the BRICs bubble burst? *The Guardian*, 27 March 2016, 1–3.

Todaro, M. (1994) *Economic Development*. Harlow: Longman.

Todaro, M. (2015) *Economic Development,* 12th edn. Pearson: London.

Todaro, M. and Smith, S. (2011) *Economic Development*. Boston, MA: Addison Wesley.

Todd, H. (ed) (1996) *Cloning Grameen Bank: Replicating a Poverty Reduction Model in India, Nepal and Vietnam*. London: Intermediate Technology Publications.

Toffler, A. (1970) *Future Shock*. London: Bodley Head.

Tomalin, E. (2013) *Religions and Development*. London: Routledge.

Tordoff, W. (1992) The impact of ideology or development in the Third World. *Journal of International Development*, 4(1), 41–53.

Toulmin, C. (2001) *Lessons from the Theatre: Should This be the Final Curtain Call for the Convention to Combat Desertification?* WSSD Opinion Series. London: IIED.

Toulmin, C. and Quan, J. (eds) (2000) *Evolving Land Rights: Policy and Tenure in Africa*. London: IIED.

Tourism Concern (2002) Briefing on ecotourism. www.tourismconcern.org.uk.

Toye, J. (1987) *Dilemmas of Development*. Oxford: Blackwell.

Toyota (2015) Global newsroom. http://newsroom.toyota.co.jp/en/corporate/ccompanyinformatio/worldwide (accessed 20 Jan 2016).

Traisawasdichai, M. (1995) Chasing the little white ball. *New Internationalist*, 263, 16–17.

Trivedi, H. (2011) Revolutionary non-violence: Gandhi in postcolonial and subaltern discourse. *Interventions*, 13(4), 521–49.

Turner, J.R. (1967) Barriers and channels for housing development in modernizing countries. *Journal of the American Institute of Planners*, 33, 167–81.

Turner, J.R. (1982) Issues in self-help and self-managed housing, ch. 4 in Ward, P. (ed) *Self-Help Housing: A Critique*. London: Mansell, 99–113.

Turner, M. and Hulme, D. (1997) *Administration and Development: Making the State Work*. Basingstoke: Macmillan.

Tussie, D. and Tuozzo, M.F. (2001) Opportunities and constraints for civil society participation in multilateral lending operations: lessons from Latin America, in Edwards, M. and Gaventa, J. (eds) *Global Citizen Action*. London: Earthscan, 105–17.

Uitto, J.I. (2004) Multi-country cooperation around shared waters: role of monitoring and evaluation. *Global Environmental Change*, 14, 5–14.

ul-Haq, M. (1994) The new deal. *New Internationalist*, 262, 20–3.

ul-Haq, M., Jolly, R., Streeten, P. and Haq, K. (1995) The UN and the Bretton Woods Institutions: New Challenges for the Twenty-First Century. Basingstoke: Macmillan.

UN (1948) *Universal Declaration of Human Rights*. http://www.ohchr.org/EN/UDHR/Documents/ UDHR_Translations/eng.pdf (accessed 20 July 2016).

UN (1989) *Prospects for World Urbanization 1988*. New York: United Nations.

UN (1993) *The Global Partnership for Environment and Development: A Guide to Agenda 21*. New York: United Nations.

UN (1997) *The Report of the Economic and Social Council for 1997*. A/52/3 18 September.

UN (1998) *Kyoto Protocol to the UNFCCC*. New York: United Nations.

UN (2000) *World Population Prospects: The 1998 Revision, Volume iii: Analytical Report*. New York: United Nations.

UN (2012) *The future we want: Outcome document of the United Nations Conference on Sustainable Development*, Rio+20

UN (2013a) *World Population Prospects: The 2012 Revision*. Population division of the Department of Economic and Social Affairs of the United Nations Secretariat. New York: United Nations.

UN (2013b) *A New Global Partnership: Eradicate Poverty and Transform Economies through Sustainable Development*, The Report of the High-Level Panel of Eminent Persons on the Post-2015 Development Agenda.

UN (2014a) *Programme Budget for the Biennium 2014–15*. New York: United Nations General Assembly 68th Session.

UN (2014b) *Delivering as One on the MDGs and the Post 2015 Agenda*. Development Operations Coordination Office.

UN (2015a) *World Population Prospects: the 2015 Revision*, New York: United Nations.

UN (2015b) *The Millennium Development Goals Report, 2015*. New York: United Nations.

UN (2015c) *Transforming Our World: The 2030 Agenda for Sustainable Development*. General Assembly A/Res/70/1. United Nations: New York.

UN General Assembly (2012) Independent evaluation of lessons learned from 'Delivering as one'. A/66/859. New York.

UN General Assembly (2014) The road to dignity by 2030: ending poverty, transforming all lives and protecting the planet. New York.

UNAIDS (1998) *Joint United Nations Programme on HIV/AIDS and World Health Organization*. Geneva: UNAIDS.

UNAIDS (2001) *Joint United Nations Programme on HIV/AIDS: AIDS Epidemic Update*. Geneva: UNAIDS, www.unaids.org.

UNAIDS (2006) *AIDS Epidemic Update, December 2006*. Geneva: UNAIDS, www.unaids.org/en/HIV_ data/epi2006.

UNAIDS (2012) *UNAIDS Report on the Global AIDS Epidemic*. http://www.unaids.org/sites/ default/files/en/media/unaids/contentassets/ documents/epidemiology/2012/gr2012/2012 1120_UNAIDS_Global_Report_2012_with_ annexes_en.pdf (accessed 16 Mar 2015).

UNAIDS (2013) *Report on the Global AIDS Epidemic 2013*. New York: Joint United Nations Programme on HIV/AIDS.

UNAIDS (2016) *Global AIDS Update, 2016*. http://www.unaids.org/en/resources/documents/ 2016/Global-AIDS-update-2016 (accessed 19 July 2016).

UNCHS (1996) *An Urbanizing World: Global Report on Human Settlements, 1996*. United Nations Centre for Human Settlements (Habitat). Oxford: Oxford University Press.

UNCTAD (United Nations Conference on Trade and Development) (2014) *World Investment Report, 104: Investing in the SDGS – An Action Plan*. New York: UNCTAD.

UNCTAD (United Nations Conference on Trade and Development) (2015) *World Investment Report*. Geneva: UNCTAD.

UNCTAD (United Nations Conference on Trade and Development) (2016) *Global Investment Trends Monitor*. 22, Jan 2016. Geneva: UNCTAD.

UNDESA (United Nations Department of Economic and Social Affairs) (2014) *World Urbanization Prospects Report, 2014 Revision*. New York: United Nations.

UNDP (1991) *Cities, People and Poverty*. United Nations Development Programme. New York: UNDP.

UNDP (1994) *Human Development Report, 1994*. United Nations Development Programme. Oxford: Oxford University Press.

UNDP (1996) *Human Development Report, 1996*. United Nations Development Programme. Oxford: Oxford University Press.

UNDP (1997) *Human Development Report, 1997*. United Nations Development Programme. Oxford: Oxford University Press.

UNDP (1998) *Human Development Report, 1998*. United Nations Development Programme. New York: Oxford University Press.

UNDP (2001) *Human Development Report, 2001: Promoting Linkages*. United Nations Development Programme. Oxford: Oxford University Press.

UNDP (2006) *Human Development Report, 2006*. New York: UNDP.

UNDP (2007) *Human Development Report 2007/8: Fighting Climate Change: Human Solidarity in a Divided World*. New York: UNDP.

UNDP (2014) *Human Development Report, 2014*. New York: UNDP.

UNDP (2015) *Human Development Report, 2015*. New York: UNDP.

UNDP (2016) Ebola crisis in West Africa. http://www.undp.org/content/undp/en/home/ourwork/our-projects-and-initiatives/ebola-response-in-west-africa.html (accessed 19 July 2016).

UNDP/WHO (2009) *The Energy Access Situation in Developing Countries: A Review Focusing on the Least Developed Countries (LDCs) and Sub-Saharan Africa (SSA)*. New York: UNDP.

UNEP (2002) *Global Environment Outlook 3*, Nairobi: UNEP.

UNEP (2005) Millennium development project. www.environmenttimes.net/article.cfm?pageID=196&group.

UNEP (2012) *Global Environment Outlook 5: Environment for the Future We Want*. Nairobi: UNEP.

UNEP (2014) *UNEP Year Book: Energy issues in our Global Environment*, Nairobi: UNEP.

UNESCO (2009) *The United Nations World Water Development Report 3: Water in a Changing World*. Paris: UNESCO.

UNESCO (2012) *The United Nations World Water Development Report 4: Managing under Uncertainty*. Paris: UNESCO.

UNESCO (2013) *World Social Science Report: Changing Global Environments*. Paris: UNESCO.

UNESCO (2015) *The United Nations World Water Development Report: Water for a Sustainable World*. Paris: UNESCO.

UN-Habitat (2003) *The Challenge of Slums: Global Report on Human Settlement, 2003*. Nairobi: UN-Habitat.

UN-Habitat (2012) *State of the World's Cities 2012/2013*. Nairobi: UN-Habitat.

UN-Habitat (2015) *World Atlas of Slum Evolution*. Nairobi: UN-Habitat.

UN-Habitat (2016) *Urbanization and Development: Emerging Futures*. World Cities Report.

UNHCR (2002) Afghanistan – the long road home. www.unhcr.ch/cgi-bin/texis/ytx/afghan.

UNHCR (2015) *Global Trends: forced displacement in 2014*, www.unhcr.org/statistics

UNICEF (1997) *The State of the World's Children*. United Nations Children's Fund. Oxford: Oxford University Press.

UNICEF (1998) *The Impact of Conflict on Children in Afghanistan*. United Nations Children's Fund. Geneva: UNICEF.

UNICEF (2000) *The State of the World's Children 2000*. United Nations Children's Fund. New York/Geneva: UNICEF.

UNICEF (2001) *The State of the World's Children 2001*. United Nations Children's Fund. Geneva: UNICEF, www.unicef.org.

UNICEF (2006) *State of the World's Children 2007*. United Nations Children's Fund. New York: UNICEF, www.unicef.org/sowc07/docs/sowc07.pdf.

UNICEF (2015) Water and sanitation: current status and progress. http://data.unicef.org/water-sanitation/sanitation.html.

UNICEF/WHO (2015) *Progress on Sanitation and Drinking Water: 2015 Update and MDG Assessment*. UNICEF: Geneva.

UNIDO (United Nations Industrial Development Organization) (2010) *Annual Report*. New York: UNIDO.

UNIDO (United Nations Industrial Development Organization) (2015) *Annual Report*. New York: UNIDO.

Unilever (2002) Financial highlights. www.unilever.com, 31 August.

Unilever (2006a) Annual report and accounts 2006: financial review. http://unilever.com/ourcompany/investorcentre/annual_reports/annual_report_Form.asp.

Unilever (2006b) Financial highlights. www.unilever.com.

United Nations Development Group (2010) *Thematic Paper on MDG7 Environmental Sustainability*. New York: UNDG.

UNDP (2006) *Human Development Report, 2006, Beyond Scarcity: Power, Poverty and the Global Water Crisis*. New York.

United Nations Secretariat (2015) Assessment of member states' contributions to the United Nations regular budget for 2015. UN Secretariat.

United Nations Statistics (2014) Population density in 2014. http://unstats.un.org/unsd/demographic/products/dyb/dyb2014/maps/table03b.pdf (accessed 12 September 2016).

United States Department of Energy (1994) *Energy Use and Carbon Emissions: Some International Comparisons*. Washington, DC: Energy Information Administration.

UNPO (Unrepresented Nations and Peoples Organization) (2014) West Papua: Indonesian transmigration program further marginalizes the indigenous population. http://unpo.org/article/17676 (accessed 22 July 2016).

Unwin, T. and de Bastion, G. (2008) Information and communication technologies for development, ch. 1.12 in Desai, V. and Potter, R.B. (eds) *The Companion to Development Studies*, 2nd edn. London: Hodder-Arnold and New York: Oxford University Press, 54–8.

Unwin, T. and Potter, R.B. (1992) Undergraduate and postgraduate teaching on the geography of the Third World. *Area*, 24, 56–62.

Urbach, J. (2007) Development goes wireless. *Journal of the Institute of Economic Affairs*, 27, 20–8.

Urban Foundation (1993) *Managing Urban Poverty*. Johannesburg: Urban Foundation.

Urry, J. (1990) *The Tourist Gaze*. London: Sage.

US Census Bureau (1994) *Trends and Patterns of HIV/AIDS Infection in Selected Developing Countries*. Country Profiles, Research Note 15, Health Studies Branch. Washington, DC: Center for International Research.

US Census Bureau (2002) International data base. www.census.gov/ipc/www/idbnew.html.

Usbourne, D. (2001) Annan is honoured for bringing new life to the UN. *The Independent*, 13 October.

van der Gaag, N. (1997) Gene dream. *New Internationalist*, 293, 7–10.

Van Rooy, A. (2002) Strengthening civil society in developing countries, in Desai, V. and Potter, R.B. (eds) *The Companion to Development Studies*. London: Arnold, 489–95.

Vance, J.E. (1970) *The Merchant's World: The Geography of Wholesaling*. Englewood Cliffs, NJ: Prentice Hall.

Vapnarsky, C.A. (1969) On rank-size distributions of cities: an ecological approach. *Economic Development and Cultural Change*, 17, 584–95.

Vesiland, P.J. (1993) Water: the Middle East's critical resource. *National Geographic*, 183(5), 38–71.

Vestergaard, J. and Wade, R.H. (2013) Protecting power: how western states retain the dominant voice in the World Bank's governance. *World Development*, 46, 153–64.

Viana, M. et al. (2014) Impact of maritime transport emissions on coastal air quality in Europe. *Atmospheric Environment*, 90, 96–105.

Vidal, J. (2002) Britons grow dull on trivia as TV ignores developing world. *Guardian Weekly*, 18 July. https://www.theguardian.com/GWeekly/Letter_From/0,,757276,00.html (accessed 28 July 2016).

Vihma, A., Mulufetta, Y. and Karlsson-Vinkhuyzen, S. (2011) Negotiating solidarity? The G77 through the prism of climate change negotiations. *Global Change, Peace and Security,* 23(2), 315–34.

Vivian, J. (1995) How safe are safety nets? in Vivian, J. (ed) *Adjustment and Social Sector Restructuring*. London: Frank Cass.

von Moltke (1994) The World Trade Organisation: its implications for sustainable development. *Journal of Environment and Development*, 3(1), 43–57.

Walker, G. (2012) *Environmental Justice: Concepts, Evidence and Politics*. London: Routledge.

Wallerstein, I. (1974) *The Modern World System I*. New York: Academic Press.

Wallerstein, I. (1979) *The Capitalist World Economy*. Cambridge: Cambridge University Press.

Wallerstein, I. (1980) *The Modern World System II*. New York: Academic Press.

War Child (2015) https://www.warchild.org.uk/ (accessed July 2017).

War on Want (2004) *Profiting from Poverty: Privatisation Consultants, DFID and Public Services*. London: War on Want.

Ward, P. and Macoloo, C. (1992) Articulation theory and self-help housing practice in the 1990s. *International Journal of Urban and Regional Research*, 16, 60–80.

Watkins, K. (1995) *The Oxfam Poverty Report*. Oxford: Oxfam.

Watson, K. (ed) (1982) *Education in the Third World*. London: Croom Helm.

Watson, M. and Potter, R.B. (2001) *Low-Cost Housing in Barbados: Evolution or Social Revolution?* Barbados: University of the West Indies Press.

Watson, R.T. (ed) (2001) *Climate Change 2001, Synthesis Report*. Cambridge: Cambridge University Press.

Watters, R.F. and McGee, T.G. (eds) (1997) *Asia–Pacific: New Geographies of the Pacific Rim*. London: Hurst.

Watts, M. (1984) The demise of the moral economy: food and famine in a Sudano-Sahelian region in historical perspective, in Scott, E. (ed) *Life Before the Drought*. Boston, MA: Allen & Unwin, 124–48.

Watts, M. (1996) Development in the global agrofood system and late twentieth-century development (or Kautsky reduxe). *Progress in Human Geography*, 20, 2, 230–45.

Watts, M. (2006) Andre Gunder Frank, in Simon, D. (ed) *Fifty Key Thinkers on Development*. London and New York: Routledge, 90–5.

Watts, M. and McCarthy, J. (1997) *Nature as Artifice, Nature as Artefact: Development, Environment and Modernity in the Late Twentieth Century*. Paper presented in the Lectures in Human Geography Series, University of St Andrews.

Watts, M.J. (2004) Violent environments: petroleum conflict and the political ecology of rule in the Niger delta, Nigeria, in Peet, R. and Watts, M. (2004)

Liberation Ecologies: Environment, Development, Social Movements, 2nd edn. London: Routledge, 273–98.

WCED (1987) *Our Common Future*. World Commission on Environment and Development. Oxford: Oxford University Press.

Weaver, D.B. (1998) *Ecotourism in the Less Developed World*. Wallingford: CAB International.

Webster, B. (2016) Amazonian dams 'will wipe out fish, birds and mammals'. *The Times*, 16 Mar.

Webb, D. (1997) *HIV and AIDS in Africa*. London: Pluto Press.

Weidelt, H.J. (1993) Agroforestry systems in the tropics – recent developments and results of research. *Applied Geography and Development*, 41, 39–50.

Wellard, K. and Copestake, J. (1993) *Nongovernmental Organizations and the State in Africa*. London: Routledge.

Wen, Y.-K. and Sengupta, J. (eds) (1991) *Increasing the International Competitiveness of Exports from Caribbean Countries*. Washington, DC: World Bank.

Werksman, J. (1995) Greening Bretton Woods, in Kirkby, J., O'Keefe, P. and Timberlake, L. (eds) *The Earthscan Reader in Sustainable Development*. London: Earthscan, 274–87.

Werksman, J. (ed) (1996) *Greening International Institutions*. London: Earthscan.

Westendorp, M. (ed) (2010) *Transforming Sustainable Development*. Utrecht: Knowledge Centre Religion and Development.

Wheat, S. (1993) Playing around with nature. *Geographical Magazine*, LXV(8), 10–14.

Wheat, S. (2000) A path out of poverty? *The Courier*, 183, 60–2.

Whitaker's (1999) *Whitaker's Almanack 2000*, 132nd edn. London: The Stationery Office.

Whitman, J. (2002) The role of the United Nations in developing countries, in Desai, V. and Potter, R.B. (eds) *The Companion to Development Studies*. London: Arnold, 466–70.

WHO, UNAIDS, and UNICEF (2012) Global HIV/AIDS Response: Epidemic Update and Health Sector Progress towards Universal Access: Progress Report 2011. Geneva.

Wichelns, D. (2015) Virtual water and water footprints do not provide helpful insight regarding international trade or water scarcity. *Ecological Indicators*, 52, 277–83.

Wignaraja, P. (1993) Rethinking development and democracy, in Wignaraja, P. (ed) *New Social Movements in the South*. London: Zed Books, 4–35.

Williams, G., Meth, P. and Willis, K. (2014) *Geographies of Developing Areas*. London: Routledge.

Williams, M. (1994) Making golf greener. *Far Eastern Economic Review*, May, 40–1.

Williams, M. (1995) Role of the multilateral agencies after the Earth Summit, in ul-Haq, M., Jolly, R. Streeten, P. and Haq, K. (1995) *The UN and the Bretton Woods Institutions: New Challenges for the Twenty-First Century*. Basingstoke: Macmillan, 210–38.

Williams, M. and Ford, L. (1999) The World Trade Organization, social movements and global environmental management. *Environmental Politics*, 8(1), 268–89.

Williams, P. and Chrisman, L. (eds) (1993) *Colonial Discourse and Postcolonial Theory*. London: Prentice Hall.

Williamson, J.G. (1965) Regional inequality and the process of national development: a description of the patterns. *Economic Development and Cultural Change*, 13, 3–45.

Willis, K. (2014) Migration and transnationalism, in Desai, V. and Potter, R.B. (eds) *The Companion to Development Studies*, 3rd edn, London: Routledge, 212–7.

Wills, J. (2002) Political economy III: neoliberal chickens, Seattle and geography. *Progress in Human Geography*, 26, 90–100.

Wilson, D. and Purushothaman, R. (2003) *Dreaming with BRICs: The Path to 2050*. Global Economics Paper No. 99. Goldman Sachs.

Wilson, F. (1994) Reflections on the present predicament of the Mexican garment industry, in Pedersen, P. (ed) *Flexible Specialization*. London: IT Publications, 147–58.

Wolf, A.T., Natharius, J.A., Danielson, J.J., Ward, B.S. and Pender, J.K (1999) International river basins of the world. *Water Resources Development*, 15(4), 387–427.

Wolfe-Phillips, L. (1987) Why Third World – origins, definitions and usage. *Third World Quarterly*, 9(4), 1311–9.

Wolmer, W., Chaumba, J. and Scoones, I. (2004) Wildlife management and land reform in southeastern Zimbabwe: a compatible pairing or a contradiction in terms? *Geoforum*, 35, 87–98.

Wolpe, H. (1975) The theory of internal colonialism, in Oxaal, J., Barnett, T. and Booth, D. (eds) *Beyond the Sociology of Development*. London: Routledge & Kegan Paul, 229–52.

Women and Geography Study Group (1997) *Feminist Geographies: Explorations in Diversity and Difference*. London: Longman.

Woodhouse, P. (2009) Technology, environment and the productivity problem in African agriculture: comment on the World Development Report 2008. *Journal of Agrarian Change*, 9(2), 263–76.

Woodrow Wilson International Centre for Scholars (2007) *Global Urban Poverty: Setting the Agenda*. Washington: Woodrow Wilson International Centre for Scholars.

Woods, N. (2000) The challenge of good governance for the IMF and the World Bank themselves. *World Development*, 28(5), 823–41.

World Bank (1986) *Poverty and Hunger: Issues and Options for Food Security in Developing Countries*. Washington, DC: World Bank.

World Bank (1988) *World Development Report*. Washington, DC: World Bank.

World Bank (1989) *Sub-Saharan Africa: From Crisis to Sustainable Growth: A Long Term Perspective Study*. Washington, DC: World Bank.

World Bank (1990) *World Development Report, 1990*. Oxford: Oxford University Press.

World Bank (1991) *Urban Policy and Economic Development: An Agenda for the 1990s*. Washington, DC: World Bank.

World Bank (1992) *World Development Report*. Washington, DC: World Bank.

World Bank (1993) *East Asian Miracle*. Washington, DC: World Bank.

World Bank (1994) *World Bank and the Environment: Fiscal 1993*. Washington, DC: World Bank.

World Bank (1996) *World Development Report, 1996*. Oxford: Oxford University Press.

World Bank (1997) *World Development Report: The State in a Changing World*. Oxford: Oxford University Press.

World Bank (1997b) *The Impact of Environmental Assessment: A Review of World Bank Experience*. Environment Department. Washington, DC: World Bank.

World Bank (1999) Safe motherhood and the World Bank: lessons from 10 years of experience. www.worldbank. org/html/extdr/hnp/population/tenyears/text.pdf.

World Bank (2001a) *World Development Report 2000/2001*. Oxford: Oxford University Press.

World Bank (2001b) The HIPC debt initiative. December 2001, www.worldbank.org/hipc.

World Bank (2001c) Making sustainable commitments: an environment strategy for the World Bank, summary. December 2001. Washington, DC: World Bank.

World Bank (2002a) *World Development Report 2002*. Oxford: Oxford University Press.

World Bank (2002b) World Bank to commit $500 million more to fight HIV/AIDS in Africa. News Release No. 2002/197/HD. wbln0018.worldbank. org/news/pressrelease.nsf/673fa6c5a2d50a6 7852565e2006.

World Bank (2004) *The Millennium Development Goals for Health: Rising to the Challenges*. Washington, DC: World Bank.

World Bank (2007) *World Development Indicators*. http://ddp-ext.worldbank.org/ext/DDPQQ/ member.do?method=getMembers&userid=1& queryId=135.

World Bank (2008) *World Development Report 2008: Agriculture for Development*. Washington: IBRD.

World Bank (2009a) *Awakening Africa's Sleeping Giant: Prospects for Commercial Agricultural in the Guinea Savannah Zone and Beyond*. Washington: World Bank.

World Bank (2009b) *Systems of Cities: Harnessing Urbanization for Growth and Poverty Alleviation*. Washington, DC: World Bank.

World Bank (2010a) *Migration and Development Brief 13*. Migration and Remittances Unit. Washington, DC: World Bank.

World Bank (2010b) *Rising Global Interest in Farmland: Can It Yield Sustainable and Equitable Benefits?* Washington, DC: World Bank.

World Bank (2012a) *Toward a Green, Clean, and Resilient World for All: A World Bank Environment Strategy 2012–22*. Washington, DC: World Bank Group.

World Bank (2012b) *World Development Indicators 2012*. Washington, DC: World Bank Publications.

World Bank (2013a) *Global Monitoring Report 2013: Rural-Urban Dynamics and the MDGs*. Washington, DC: World Bank Group.

World Bank (2013b) *World Bank-Civil Society Engagement: Review of Fiscal Years 2010–2012*. Washington, DC: World Bank Group.

World Bank (2015a) Fact sheet: review and update of the World Bank's environmental and social framework status of key issue in revised (second) draft. 8 Apr 2015, accessed 6 Aug 2015. pubdocs. worldbank.org.

World Bank (2015b) What are the 6 dimensions of good governance? http://info.worldbank.org/governance/ wgi/index.aspx#faq-2 (accessed 30 May 2016).

World Bank (2015c) *World Development Indicators 2015*. Washington, DC: World Bank, http:// www.worldbank.org/en/topic/debt (accessed 21 Mar 2015).

World Bank (2015d) *World Development Report*. Washington, DC: World Bank.

World Bank (2015e) *Global Economic Prospects June 2015: The Global Economy in Transition*. Washington: World Bank Group.

World Bank (2016) *World Development Indicators 2016*. Washington, DC: World Bank.

World Bank/FAO/IFAD (2009) *Gender in Agriculture Sourcebook*. Washington, DC: World Bank.

World Bank/IMF (2004) *Poverty Reduction Strategy Papers: Progress in Implementation*. Washington, DC: World Bank.

World Bank Independent Evaluation Group (WB-IEG) (2006) *Debt Relief for the Poorest: An Evaluation Update of the HIPC Initiative*. Washington, DC: World Bank.

World Health Organization (WHO) (1994) *The Current Global Situation of the HIV/AIDS Pandemic*. Geneva: WHO.

World Health Organization (WHO) (1998) *Obesity – Preventing and Managing the Global Epidemic*. Geneva: WHO.

World Health Organization (WHO) (1999) Reduction of maternal mortality: a joint WHO/UNFPA/ UNICEF/World Bank statement. www.unfpa.org/ news/pressroom/1999/maternal.htm.

World Health Organization (WHO) (2006a) Obesity and overweight, online fact sheet. www.who.int/ mediacentre/factsheets/fs311/en/index.html.

World Health Organization (WHO) (2006b) *WHO Global InfoBase Online*. www.who.int/ncd_ surveillance/infobase/web/InfoBaseCommon.

World Health Organization (WHO) (2007) Epidemiological fact sheets on HIV/AIDS and sexually transmitted infections. www.who.int/globalatlas/default.asp.

World Health Organization (WHO) (2013) *Factsheet on the World Malaria Report, 2013.* http://www.who.int/malaria/media/world_malaria_report_2013/en/ (accessed 16 Mar 2015).

World Health Organisation (WHO) (2014a) Ambient (outdoor) air quality and health, factsheet no. 313. http://www.who.int/mediacentre/factsheets/fs313/en/ (accessed 1 Aug 2017).

World Health Organisation (WHO) (2014b) Household air quality and health, factsheet no. 292. http://www.who.int/mediacentre/factsheets/fs292/en/ (accessed 1 Aug 2017).

World Health Organisation (WHO) (2014c) Ambient Air Pollution Database – Update 2014. http://www.who.int/phe/health_topics/outdoorair/databases/cities/en/ (accessed 25 Mar 2016).

World Health Organisation (WHO) (2015) Media centre factsheets. http://www.who.int/mediacentre/factsheets/fs311/en/ (accessed 18 Mar 2015).

World Internet Usage Statistics (2007) http://www.internetworldstats.com/pr/edi028.htm (accessed 16 Jan 2016).

World Resources Institute (1996) *World Resources 1996–1997.* Oxford: Oxford University Press.

World Resources Institute (1998) *World Resources 1998–99: Environment and Health.* Oxford: Oxford University Press.

World Resources Institute (2003) *World Resources, 2002–4.* Washington, DC: World Resources Institute.

World Resources Institute (2005) *World Resources, 2005: The Wealth of the Poor.* Washington, DC: World Resources Institute.

World Resources Institute (2015) 6 *graphs explain the world's top 10 emitters,* http://www.wri.org/blog/2014/11/6-graphs-explain-world%E2%80%99s-top-10-emitters accessed 15 Sept 2017

World Tourism Organization (WTO) (2002) www.world-tourism.org/market_research/facts&figures.

World Tourism Organization (WTO) (2006) World tourism highlights: 2006 edition. www.unwto.org/facts/menu.html.

World Tourism Organization (WTO) (2014) *Tourism Highlights, 2014.* http://dtxtq4w60xqpw.cloudfront.net/sites/all/files/pdf/unwto_highlights14_en.pdf (accessed 25 Mar 2015).

World Trade Organization (2000) Seven common misunderstandings about the WTO, in Lechner, F.J. and Boli, J. (eds) *The Globalization Reader.* Oxford: Blackwell, 236–9.

World Trade Organisation (2011) *Understanding the WTO.* Geneva: World Trade Organisation.

World Trade Organization (2014) International trade statistics, 2014. https://www.wto.org/english/res_e/statis_e/its2014_e/its2014_e.pdf (accessed 25 May 2015).

World Watch Institute (2011) Energy intensity of global economy rises, reversing long term trend. http://www.worldwatch.org/energy-intensity-energy-efficiency-gross-world-product-emerging-economies-infrastructure-development (accessed 19 Mar 2016).

World Water Assessment Programme (2009) *The United Nations World Water Development Report 3: Water in a Changing World.* Paris: UNESCO, and London: Earthscan.

Worldwatch Institute (2002) *State of the World 2002: Progress Towards a Sustainable Society.* London: Earthscan.

Worsley, P. (1964) *The Third World.* London: Weidenfeld & Nicolson.

Worsley, P. (1979) How many worlds? *Third World Quarterly,* 1(2), 100–8.

Wratten, E. (1995) Conceptualizing urban poverty. *Environment and Urbanization,* 7(1), 11–37.

Wuyts, M., Mackintosh, M. and Hewitt, T. (eds) (1992) *Development Policy and Public Action.* Oxford: Oxford University Press.

Yeh, A.G.O. and Wu, F.L. (1995) Internal structure of Chinese cities in the midst of economic reform. *Urban Geography,* 16(6), 521–54.

Yeung, Y.-M. (1995) Commentary: urbanization and the NPE: an Asia-Pacific perspective. *Cities,* 12, 409–11.

Young, E.M. (1996) *World Hunger.* London: Routledge.

Zack-Williams, A.B. (2001) No democracy, no development: reflections on democracy and development in Africa. *Review of African Political Economy,* 88, 213–23.

Zimmerman, E.W. (1951) *World Resources and Industries*. New York: Harper & Row.

Zobel, G. (2009) We are millions. *New Internationalist*, December, 21–4.

Zook, M.A. (2005) *The Geography of the Internet Industry*. Oxford: Blackwell.

Zoomers, A. (2010) Globalisation and the foreignization of space: seven processes driving the current global land grab. *The Journal of Peasant Studies*, 37(2), 429–47.

Zoomers, A. (2014) Rural livelihoods in a context of new scarcities, in Desai, V. and Potter, R.B. (eds) *The Companion to Development Studies*, 3rd edn. London: Routledge, 230–5.

Zulkifli (2007) Speech by Mr Masagos Zulkifli, Senior Parliamentary Secretary, Ministry of Education, at the 2007 Trim & Fit Award Ceremony on Monday, 19 March 2007, 1500 hrs at MOE Edutorium, www.moe.gov.sg/speeches/2007/sp20070319.htm.

Index

GEOGRAPHIES OF DEVELOPMENT
AN INTRODUCTION TO
DEVELOPMENT STUDIES   FOURTH EDITION

ROBERT POTTER, TONY BINNS, JENNIFER A. ELLIOTT, ETIENNE NEL AND DAVID W. SMITH

"The fourth edition of *Geographies of Development* is an invaluable text for students in development studies and geography. I especially appreciate the mix of theory and practice, as well as illustrative case studies, prompts that promote critical reflection, and great maps and conceptual diagrams. This extensively revised and up-to-date book is essential for those exploring the ever-evolving realm of development studies."

William G. Moseley, Professor of Geography, Macalester College, Saint Paul, USA

"This fourth edition updates the coverage and takes account of shifts in thinking to ensure that *Geographies of Development* remains a leading textbook in what remains a dynamic and popular field of study across Geography and cognate disciplines around the world. The late David Smith and Rob Potter would be very proud of how their colleagues have ensured the continued relevance and topicality of this best-selling title."

Professor David Simon, Royal Holloway, University of London, UK and Chalmers University of Technology, Gothenburg, Sweden

Now in its fourth edition, *Geographies of Development: An Introduction to Development Studies* remains a core, balanced and comprehensive introductory textbook for students of development studies, development geography and related fields. This clear and concise text encourages critical engagement by integrating theory alongside practice and related key topics throughout. It demonstrates informatively that ideas concerning development have been many and varied and highly contested – varying from time to time and from place to place.

Clearly written and accessible for students who have no prior knowledge of development, the book provides the basics in terms of a geographical approach to development: what the situation is, where, when and why. Over 200 maps, charts, tables, textboxes and pictures break up the text and offer alternative ways of showing the information. The text is further enhanced by a range of pedagogical features: chapter outlines, case studies, key thinkers, critical reflections, key points and summaries, discussion topics and further reading.

Geographies of Development continues to be an invaluable introductory text not only for geography students, but also anyone in area studies, international studies and development studies.

Robert Potter was Professor of Human Geography at the University of Reading, UK.

Tony Binns is Professor of Geography at the University of Otago, New Zealand.

Jennifer A. Elliott is Visiting Researcher in Geography at the University of Brighton, UK.

Etienne Nel is a Professor of Geography at the University of Otago, New Zealand.

David W. Smith was Professor of Economic Geography at the University of Liverpool, UK.

Cover illustration by Matthew Richardson, based on an original sketch by Rob Potter.

DEVELOPMENT STUDIES/HUMAN GEOGRAPHY

Routledge
Taylor & Francis Group

www.routledge.com

Routledge titles are available as eBook editions in a range of digital formats

eRESOURCES

https://www.routledge.com/9781138794306

ISBN 978-1-138-79430-6

9 781138 794306

an informa business